EXETER MEDIEVAL ENGLISH TEXTS AND STUDIES

General Editors: Marion Glasscoe and M.J. Swanton

Wace's
ROMAN DE BRUT
A HISTORY
OF THE BRITISH

Judith Weiss is the author of *The Birth of Romance* and *The Life of King Arthur*, and joint editor of *Romance Reading on the Book*.

Wace's
ROMAN DE BRUT
A HISTORY
OF THE BRITISH

Text and Translation

Revised edition

JUDITH WEISS

UNIVERSITY
of
EXETER
PRESS

First published in 1999 by
University of Exeter Press
Reed Hall, Streatham Drive,
Exeter, Devon, EX4 4QR.
UK

www.ex.ac.uk/uep/

Revised edition 2002, reprinted 2006

British Library Cataloguing in Publication Data
A catalogue record of this book is available from the British Library

ISBN-10 0 85989 734 6
ISBN-13 978 0 85989 734 1

Published with the assistance of the Vinaver Trust

Designed and typeset in Caslon 10.5/12.5
by Mike Dobson, Quince Typesetting, Exeter.

Printed and bound in Great Britain by Antony Rowe Ltd, Chippenham

FOR NIGEL

CONTENTS

PREFACE

The text of Wace's *Roman de Brut* printed here is in essence that edited by Ivor Arnold in 1938, but I have made many small changes to it which restore readings in the manuscripts he used. The numbering of the lines has been retained, so as to facilitate cross-reference. I have dispensed with much of Arnold's apparatus: those wishing to know about the variants in other manuscripts should consult his book.

The English translation is all my own, but I gratefully acknowledge the help I have received from the notes and suggestions in Arnold and Pelan's *La Partie Arthurienne du Brut* and Baumgartner and Short's *La Geste du Roi Arthur*. I am entirely responsible for any errors in the translation. In preparing this corrected second edition, I have been greatly helped by several colleagues, especially Peter Damian-Grint, Ivana Djordjevic and Ian Short.

Many people have helped me with advice, support and finance while the book was under way. I am indebted to the British Academy for a research grant and to the Vinaver Trust and Robinson College for research loans. Ray Barron first suggested I undertake the whole of the *Brut* and has been a continual source of encouragement and help. Sandra Butler expertly and patiently typed the French text. Others whose wisdom and assistance smoothed the way include Jean Blacker, Martin Brett, Anne Darvall, Jenny Fellows, Rosalind Love, Chris Page, Lesley Read, Michael Swanton, Elisabeth van Houts and Tim Weiss. Simon Baker and his staff at the University of Exeter Press have been throughout long-suffering and kind. And as usual my family have helped in every way they could. This could never have been done without them.

Judith Weiss, Cambridge 2002

ABBREVIATIONS

ALMA *Arthurian Literature in the Middle Ages*, ed. Roger Sherman Loomis (Oxford: Clarendon Press, 1959)

AND *The Anglo-Norman Dictionary*, (London: The Modern Humanities Research Association, 1977–92)

AOW *The Arthur of the Welsh*, eds Rachel Bromwich, A.O.H. Jarman and Brynley F. Roberts (Cardiff: University of Wales Press, 1991)

Arnold Wace, *Le Roman de Brut*, ed. Ivor Arnold, 2 vols (Paris: SATF, 1938, 1940)

ASC *The Anglo-Saxon Chronicle*, ed. and trans. M.J. Swanton (London: J.M. Dent, 1996)

Bede Bede, *The Ecclesiastical History of the English People*, trans. Leo Sherley-Price, rev. R.E. Latham (Harmondsworth: Penguin Books, 1990)

CFMA Classiques Français du Moyen Age

EETS Early English Text Society

Greenway *Henry, Archdeacon of Huntingdon, 'Historia Anglorum'*, ed. and trans. Diana Greenway (Oxford: Clarendon Press, 1996)

HA Henry of Huntingdon, *Historia Anglorum*

HB *Historia Brittonum* in *Nennius, 'British History and the Welsh Annals'*, ed. and trans. John Morris (London: Phillimore with Rowan and Littlefield, 1980)

Houck, *Sources* Margaret Houck, *Sources of the 'Roman de Brut' of Wace*, (Berkeley: University of California Press, 1941)

HRB Geoffrey of Monmouth, *Historia Regum Britanniae*

SATF Société des Anciens Textes Français

Tatlock J.S.P. Tatlock, *The Legendary History of Britain*, (Berkeley, California: University of California Press, 1950)

VV The Variant Version of *HRB* (see below, Wright II)

Wright I *The 'Historia Regum Britanniae' of Geoffrey of Monmouth I: Bern, Bürgerbibliothek MS 568 (the 'Vulgate' version)*, ed. Neil Wright (Cambridge: D.S. Brewer, 1984)

Wright II *The 'Historia Regum Britanniae' of Geoffrey of Monmouth II: the First Variant Version*, ed. Neil Wright (Woodbridge, Suffolk: D.S. Brewer, 1988)

INTRODUCTION

The *Brut* of Wace is the earliest extant vernacular chronicle of British history, from the eponymous 'Brutus', supposedly descended from Aeneas, down to Cadwallader and the loss of British supremacy over the island. The climax of this history is the reign of king Arthur, and this is the first sustained account of his life in any vernacular language. The account is largely derived from Geoffrey of Monmouth and his *Historia Regum Britanniae* (*c.* 1138), in Latin prose, which Wace translated into octosyllabic French couplets twenty years later. By doing so, he instantly made British historiography in general, and the story of Arthur in particular, more memorable and more accessible to a far wider audience than they had previously enjoyed, and provided the starting-point and inspiration for the flowering of Arthurian romance.

WACE'S LIFE, WORK AND HISTORICAL BACKGROUND

Wace himself provides us with most of what we know about his life.[1] It was spent in the domains of the dukes of Normandy, most of whom were also, in the twelfth century, kings of England. This accident of history determined the subjects of the two principal works for which Wace is now remembered: the *Roman de Rou*, a chronicle of the Norman dukes, and the *Roman de Brut*, a history of the British people.

The island of Jersey was part of Normandy and here Wace was born, around 1110. At some early stage he was taken to Caen and taught Latin, preparatory to entering the Church. The city, with its two abbeys erected by William the Conqueror, had belonged since 1105 to William's son Henry I, who had ousted his elder brother Robert from the dukedom, made it his headquarters in Normandy and improved its walls.[2] It was also the birthplace of Henry's bastard son, Robert of Gloucester, who became governor of Caen. Wace tells us he moved to the Île de France to continue his studies and stayed there many years; it would seem, however, that he must have been back in Caen by around 1130, at the start of his twenties.

It was near the end of a relatively stable period, in both England and Normandy, but events in the 1120s looked forward to the anarchy to come. Henry I had lost his only legitimate male heir in the White Ship in 1120. He had prevailed on his barons to

---

[1] In his *Roman de Rou*; for a list of the relevant passages, see vol. III, pp. 15–18. *Wace* (*Gasse* in some MSS) is a personal, not a family, name and has no 'Robert' in front of it, erroneously

supplied by some modern critics. See Gaston Paris, *Romania* 9 (1880), p. 594.

[2] Houck, *Sources*, p. 163.

recognize his daughter Matilda, widow of the emperor of Germany, as his successor, in 1127, but she was not a popular figure, despite producing Henry's grandson in 1133, by her second marriage to Geoffrey Plantagenet of Anjou. Against this background Wace first began to write. His position is obscure and seems to have been lowly: he later refers to himself as a *'clerc lisant'*, which perhaps means he was a secretary or notary who had to read aloud.[3]

From his first surviving work, the *Vie de Sainte Marguerite*, to the end of his life, he seems to have addressed a lay audience. This saint's life, judging by its simple style, was the first of a trio of religious works in the vernacular.[4] *La Conception de Notre Dame* (*c.* 1130–40) and *La Vie de Saint Nicolas* (*c.* 1150), written for Robert FitzTiout, followed, and are all that remain of what seems to have been a large output in Wace's twenties and thirties. Meanwhile, from 1135–8 there appeared the first works of Geoffrey of Monmouth. The enormous success of his *Historia Regum Britanniae* (dedicated to Robert of Glouces- ter) must have made Wace realise he could redirect his talents as a 'translator' from Latin into French ('*romanz*', *Roman de Rou* III, ll. 151–3), from saints' lives towards secular chronicle. Some time after 1150 he probably started on his rendering of the *Historia* and made a visit to England.

If he arrived before 1153, it was a turbulent time to travel. Stephen of Blois had seized the English throne in 1135, over the claims of Matilda, and a period of civil war began. The South-West, where it is plausibly conjectured Wace travelled and picked up his detailed topographical knowledge,[5] had been cruelly harried by both Henry of Anjou, Matilda's son, and Stephen in 1149, and in 1152 Henry invaded again, to relieve Stephen's siege of Wallingford. Finally, however, the treaty of Wallingford at the end of 1153 recognized Henry as the legitimate heir to the throne, and in 1154 the duke of Anjou and Normandy became king of England.

It was an excellent moment to present a history of her new land to Henry's queen, as Laȝamon tells us Wace did,[6] when it was finished in 1155. Eleanor of Aquitaine, like her husband, was intelligent, well-educated and a patron of literature. When Wace complains[7] of the stinginess of his aristocratic audience, he makes it clear the king and queen are exceptions, generously giving him presents and, later, making him a canon with a prebend at Bayeux (*c.* 1165–9). He may by now have been accepted as a poet to the Plantagenet court. Certainly he was proud of his personal knowledge of the 'three king Henrys' (Henry I, Henry II and Henry the Young King), since he twice refers to it.[8]

---

[3] Wace, *Rou*, vol.I, Part III, l.180 and vol.III, p. 215. Wace also mentions the duty of *clercs* to read stories at feasts so that they are not for- gotten (*Rou*, vol.I, Part III, ll.5–10).

[4] For dates, see Wace, *La Vie de Sainte-Marguerite* ed. Francis, p. xvi and Wace, *Brut* ed. Arnold, vol.I, p. lxxv.

[5] Houck, *Sources*, pp. 220–7.

[6] Laȝamon, *Brut*, I ll. 20–3.

[7] In *Rou*, vol.I, *Chronique Ascendante*, ll.1–23, and vol.I, Part III, ll. 151–62.

[8] *Rou*, vol.I, Part III, ll. 177–80; vol.II, Part III, ll. 11430–4.

Around 1160, confident of royal support, he started on the *Roman de Rou*, another long chronicle, this time of Henry's ancestors, the dukes of Normandy. In 1162 he was present at Fécamp, attending the ceremony marking the removal of the bodies of two of those dukes, Richard I and Richard II, to new graves in the abbey church.

Work on the *Rou* did not go smoothly. Wace wrote the first Part, and then abandoned it for a new start in a new and longer metre (now called *La Chronique Ascendante des Ducs de Normandie*). A second Part was written in the same style. Then the poem was interrupted for several years[9]. By the time that Wace resumed writing in the 1170s, his royal patrons may have been getting impatient, and a rival had made his appearance. Benoît de Sainte-Maure had dedicated his *Roman de Troie* to Eleanor between 1160 and 1170, and it was to him that Henry now turned for a ducal history. Having brought his own poem up to the year 1106, Wace sadly recognised his rival's success and abandoned his labours. He is named in a charter of 1174 as '*Wascius canonicus*'; some time after 1174 he adds to the *Rou* an account of a siege of Rouen in that year; but the date of his death is unknown. It is, however, probably before 1183, since in that year the Young King Henry, always alluded to as a living person in the *Rou*, dies.

THE CONTEXT FOR WACE'S *BRUT*

Wace wrote for a Norman public which had a strong interest in the history and legends of their adopted country. Some fifty years after the Conquest, chroniclers like William of Malmesbury (in his *De Gestis Regum Anglorum*, 1125) and Henry of Huntingdon (in his *Historia Anglorum*, 1139) had begun constructing histories of Britain, though their efforts were somewhat vitiated by a lack of information on pre-Saxon, let alone pre-Roman, times.[10] These Latin works were dedicated to important and politically powerful Normans, Robert of Gloucester and Alexander, bishop of Lincoln, both also patrons of Geoffrey of Monmouth. Meanwhile Geffrei Gaimar, influenced by Geoffrey's *Historia* and using the *Anglo-Saxon Chronicle*, was writing his *Estoire des Engleis*, the first post-Conquest chronicle in Norman French, in the late 1130s, for a somewhat humbler noble household, the FitzGilberts, in Hampshire and Lincolnshire.[11] He had already written an *Estoire des Bretuns*, now lost.

The interest in national history helps to account for both the *Historia Regum Britanniae* and Wace's rendering of it, the *Brut*. But while their works belong recognisably to the same genre as those of William of Malmesbury or Henry of Huntingdon, they also differ significantly from them. Though in the Middle Ages 'history' is notoriously a mixture of fact and fiction, some medieval historiographers made more serious attempts than others to distinguish one from the other. Both William and Henry had, for example,

---

[9] For possible reasons why Wace stopped his work on the *Rou* see van Houts, 'Adaptation', p. 118, and Gouttebroze, 'Pourquoi congédier', pp. 289–310.

[10] See Henry of Huntingdon's letter to Warinus, quoted by Roberts, 'Geoffrey of Monmouth', *AOW*, p. 100.

[11] See Gaimar, *Estoire*, pp. ix–xii, xxi, li–ii.

found references to Arthur in the ninth-century *Historia Brittonum*, but did not greatly elaborate on what they found, already aware of many dubious stories in circulation: 'This is that Arthur, of whom the Britons fondly fable, even to the present day; a man worthy to be celebrated, not by idle fictions, but in authentic history.'[12] Henry of Huntingdon was thus 'stunned', when the *Historia Regum Britanniae* appeared, to discover a virtually single-handed creation of Arthur's biography, a celebration indeed, but where 'authentic history' played very little part. Where historical evidence on pre-Roman and pre-Saxon times had been scanty or non-existent, Geoffrey of Monmouth had creatively filled in the gaps. Wace, following him, filled them even more substantially.

BRITISH HISTORY AND HISTORIOGRAPHY BEFORE THE TWELFTH CENTURY

Such information on British history as was available to Geoffrey of Monmouth and his contemporaries was sparse. Latin writers before the sixth century had provided occasional geographical descriptions of Britain but alluded to its history only when it coincided with that of the Roman Empire. There was no foundation myth, no information on its pre-Roman past and very little on what happened between the Romans leaving Britain and the Anglo-Saxons taking over most of the island. Our earliest insular historian—though that is probably not how he saw himself—is a Welshman, Gildas, who wrote *De Excidio Britanniae* ('The Ruin of Britain') in *c.* 540.[13] He describes the coming of the Romans and of Christianity, the reign of the usurper Magnus Maximus, the encroachments of the barbarians and the building of two Walls to keep them out, and the departure of the Romans. He tells us that a 'proud tyrant' (a play on the Welsh title *Gwrtheyrn*, 'superior ruler') let in three ships of Saxons to help him repel invaders from the North. When their requests for more money are not granted, the Saxons plunder and burn, and in consequence many British migrate to France. Gildas never mentions Arthur, but he does describe a long period of peace after the Saxons had met successful British resistance under Ambrosius Aurelianus, a man of noble Roman family, and had been defeated at *mons Badonicus*, Badon Hill. He tells us this was forty-four years earlier, so this battle was around 496 A.D.[14]

Gildas' *De Excidio* was followed, and used, by Bede's *Historia Ecclesiastica* (731). Bede, unlike his predecessor, deliberately set out to write history, skifully co-ordinating information from many sources in his account of the progress and development of the Christian Church in England. In the process he repeats the story of the Saxon invaders and adds names: the title of the British ruler has now become his name, Vurtigern; the Saxon leaders are Hengist and Horsa; and again he mentions the battle of Badon Hill,

[12] William of Malmesbury, *De Gestis*, Book I, para. 8, p. 11. On the relation between historiography and truth, see Damian-Grint, '*Estoire* as Word and Genre', pp. 189–99.

[13] On Gildas, see Dumville, 'Sub-Roman Britain', Thompson, 'Gildas', and Wright, 'Geoffrey of Monmouth and Gildas'.

[14] Gildas, *De Excidio*, pp. 13, 26, 28 and notes pp. 150–1.

giving the credit for British victories to Ambrosius.[15] Bringing his history up to his own day, he charts the steady Christianization of the Saxons in the seventh century and their progressive defeats of the British.

The name 'Arthur' does not appear in chronicle until the 820s, when another, multi-lingual, Welshman (later called Nennius) wrote the *Historia Brittonum*, a synchronising history drawing on Bede, other narratives of English origin, and Welsh folk-tale, battle lists and genealogy. Here at last is a foundation myth: a descendant of Aeneas, Britto or Brutus 'the hateful' (supplied with two genealogies), makes the long journey with his Trojan followers, via Greece and France, to the island of Albion. It was to become common practice for European nations to claim they came from Roman, and ultimately Trojan, roots,[16] thereby acquiring reflected glory while suggesting their potential to become as great, if not greater, than Rome.

The *Historia Brittonum* used Bede and Orosius to repeat and elaborate on another foundation story, that of the Scots, supposedly Scythians travelling via Spain; the details of their journey would be re-used by Geoffrey of Monmouth for Brutus' travels. It repeats and enlarges upon the details of the Romans in Britain; at the other end of its chronicle it gives genealogies of various English kings and a description of the 'wonders' of Britain (*mirabilia*), such as Loch Lomond and the Severn Bore.[17] In between, it contributed substantially to the story of Arthur and his immediate forebears by telling us of the following:

a)   Guorthigirnus (Vortigern) with Hengist and Horsa and his marriage to Hengist's daughter; Octa and Ebissa (chaps. 31, 36–38);

b)   Emrys, called Ambrosius, and Vortigern's tower; Guorthemir (Vortimer), his four battles with the Saxons and his death (chaps. 40–44);

c)   The 'Night of the Long Knives': the treacherous killing of Britons by Saxons (chaps. 45–46);

d)   Vortigern's death by fire (chap. 47);

e)   Ambrosius as supreme king of Britain (chap. 48);

f)   The twelve campaigns of Arthur, battle-leader (*dux bellorum*) against Octa, ending in Badon Hill (chap. 56).

In this often discontinuous history (its author declared he had 'made a heap of all that I have found'), such stories are not always connected in a coherent narrative: any development from the boy-seer Emrys to Ambrosius the overlord is omitted, and Arthur appears unconnected to anyone except the Saxons he fights and the unnamed kings he

---

[15] Bede, *Historia Ecclesiastica* Book I, chaps. 15–16
[16] See Southern, 'Aspects', pp. 189–90.
[17] These seem to be incorporated bodily from an

existing written source. See Dumville, 'Historical Value', p. 22.

fights for. He has no parents, no queen, no throne, no overseas conquests and no death. This last was supplied briefly and mysteriously in the tenth century *Annales Cambriae* (Welsh Annals) which, assigning the battle of Badon to 516, also gives the year 537 to 'the battle of Camlann, in which Arthur and Medraut fell'.[18]

The authors of three out of four of these sources of material about Arthur and his times are Welsh, though writing in Latin. There exists also a large number of references to, and stories about, Arthur and his followers in Welsh literature, though how many of these were in existence before the first quarter of the twelfth century is difficult to determine; however, there is a handful of reliably early ones which have a bearing on the *Historia Regum Britanniae* (*HRB*) and Wace's *Brut*. The name Uther Pendragon, un-related to Arthur, occurs in *Pa Gur yw y Porthaur* (a source or analogue of *Culhwch and Olwen*, *c.* 1100, so probably before that date), a long speech of Arthur to a gatekeeper, celebrating, among others, the warriors Cei and Bedwyr.[19] *Culhwch* itself has a long cata-logue of Arthur's courtiers, the names of his weapons, ship and queen, and three giants slain by his men, notably Cei.[20] In a Latin life of St Gildas written by the Welsh Caradog of Llancarfan (1120s–30s), Arthur's queen, Guennuvar, is violated and abducted by Melwas to Glastonbury, which Arthur then besieges. There is here, perhaps, as in the Modena archivolt of 1099–1120, a precedent for Modred's usurpation of queen and crown in Geoffrey's *Historia*.[21]

GEOFFREY OF MONMOUTH

Geoffrey of Monmouth was probably born or brought up on the border of Wales, and his origins were possibly Breton: Monmouth had been ruled by Bretons since Wihenoc from Dôle took it over in 1075, and the Bretons play an honourable role in the *Historia*, supplying the dynasty which produces Arthur. But Geoffrey may, alternatively, have been Welsh; he was certainly in touch with Welsh legend and traditional Welsh history as preserved in genealogies and name-catalogues, whether or not all of these were con-tained in the (possibly fictitious) 'ancient British book' he claims was presented to him by Walter, Archdeacon of Oxford. Geoffrey had moved to Oxford by 1129, probably as a secular canon with teaching duties in the College of St George, and this was the period when he wrote the *Prophetiae Merlini* (before 1135), the *Historia* (*c.* 1138) and the *Vita Merlini* (1148). He is said to have died by 1155.[22]

---

[18] *HB*, p. 45.

[19] In the *Black Book of Carmarthen*. See Sims-Will-iams, 'Welsh Arthurian Poems', *AOW*, pp. 37–9 and Bromwich and Evans, *Culhwch and Olwen*, pp. xxxiv–vi.

[20] For giant-slaying in the Welsh Arthurian tradi-tion, see Roberts, 'Geoffrey of Monmouth', *AOW*, p. 108.

[21] See Sims-Williams, Arthurian Poems', pp. 59–

60 and Roberts, 'Geoffrey of Monmouth' p. 110, both in *AOW*, and Loomis, 'Oral Diffusion', *ALMA*, pp. 60–1.

[22] Wright, I, pp. ix–xix; Roberts, 'Geoffrey of Mon-mouth', *AOW*, pp. 29–40; Piggott, 'Sources', pp. 269–86. For a recent and plausible argument that Geoffrey was Welsh and promoting the Welsh, see Gillingham, 'Context and Purposes', pp. 99–118.

Geoffrey created for his Norman patrons a quite new history of their adopted country. Using the *Historia Brittonum*, he elaborated on the Britons' valiant Trojan origins; with little or no information about British history before the Romans came, he produced a long line of named kings with, from time to time, their life-stories, of which the most notable is Lear; and, again drawing on the *Historia Brittonum* and on Gildas, constructed for the British past a pattern of rise, decline and final loss tightly connected to moral strength and weakness.[23] His history was not a formless account of past events; it had to answer the question: why did British dominion over the island end? A long relationship between Britain and Rome is intrinsic to his imposed pattern, and Geoffrey adds to the Roman invasion under Julius Caesar two other, fictitious, confrontations before and after it, glorifying two British conquests of the Roman Empire. The first of these is led by Belinus and Brennius, the second by Arthur. Geoffrey of Monmouth's *tour de force* was to bring together those 'historical' accounts of Arthur as a British leader who checked the Saxon advance by his victories in the late fifth or early sixth centuries, and the snippets and allusions in Welsh story to a prince with a queen and a band of supporters, whose folkloric exploits were clearly widely known, generating a charismatic figure whose deeds, especially against the Romans, form the longest section and the climax of the chronicle. It is only domestic treachery that destroys Arthur's tremendous achievement. This is a recurrent theme in the *Historia*. Time and again it is the British themselves, not their enemies, who weaken the nation by 'civil discord' and familial strife: nephew betrays uncle, brother fights brother, and the noble Cadwallader sees his country racked by plague as punishment for its internecine wars.

Although a large part of the *Historia* would seem to have been invention, Geoffrey's chronicle often reads quite plausibly. Lear, Belin and Brenne and Arthur himself usually sound, allowing for exaggeration here and there, like credible medieval kings. There are two notable exceptions in the Arthurian section, however, which remind us we are dealing with fiction and folk-tale. The first concerns Merlin and his part in the birth of Arthur. Geoffrey appears to have amalgamated two separate figures, the boy-seer Emrys, in the *Historia Brittonum*, and Myrddin in early Welsh verse, a warrior and mad fugitive in the woods of Caledonia after the Northern battle of Arfderydd in 573,[24] and supposedly the author of prophecies. In Geoffrey's *Historia*, he is the mysterious product of a supernatural union and provides a suitably marvellous origin for Stonehenge and for the conception of Arthur. The second concerns Arthur's killing of the giant on Mont St Michel, an episode strongly reminiscent of *Culhwch and Olwen* and Welsh traditions of Arthur keeping the land free from giants and monsters. Once Geoffrey reaches the territory charted by Bede and the *Anglo-Saxon Chronicle* fabulous stories inevitably diminish: a story of princely cannibalism (chap. 193) is no substitute for giants and magicians. Interestingly, it is in this last section of the chronicle that Wace was able to insert extraordinary stories of his own.

---

[23] See Roberts, 'Geoffrey of Monmouth', *AOW*, pp. 102–3.

[24] See Jarman, 'The Merlin Legend', *AOW*, pp. 117–36. Many names and tales of the Northern Welsh and their kingdom of Strathclyde, whose headquarters was at Alclud (Dumbarton), migrated southwards to Wales between the sixth and eleventh centuries.

WACE

Geoffrey's *Historia* rapidly became popular, as we can see from its survival in over 200 manuscripts. A shortened, Variant Version, of the chronicle soon emerged: it survives in only eight MSS, so its early popularity did not last, but by 1155, when Wace was writing, it had already been revised at least twice. The recent scholarship of Neil Wright has conclusively demonstrated that it was this first Variant Version, in a more complete form than the extant MSS have it, that Wace used as the base text for his translation, while skilfully conflating it with the 'Vulgate', or standard, Version of Geoffrey's text (see later, pp. xxv–xxvi). The Variant Version reshaped and stylistically recast the 'Vulgate', giving it a more coherent narrative structure; it mostly made omissions but occasionally it added fuller speeches, a more pious tone, an interest in pagan rites and some details from legendary Roman history.[25]

'Translate' in the Middle Ages did not have the narrow meaning it does today, and Wace, in bringing Geoffrey's 'history' to a yet larger audience unversed in Latin, felt free to amplify and embellish his chronicle. Yet he stuck very closely to the outline, and often even the detail, of the events there. For the most part it is in the particularities which Wace adds to the narrative that the atmosphere and flavour of his account is captured. These details often point to Wace's own conception of the story and what was most important about it for him.[26]

In addition to the Vulgate and Variant texts, Wace had his immediate predecessors to draw upon: William of Malmesbury (both the *De Gestis Regum* and the *Gesta Pontificum*), Henry of Huntingdon and Geffrei Gaimar. He was also clearly informed by oral tradition, as we can see from his account of the strange adventures of St Augustine. Whether using particulars from others or inventing his own, it is clear he was adding to Geoffrey's pattern of the rise and fall of the British his own perceptions of both the causes and the results. Sometimes we see this in his use of pathos, as in the scene of the assembly in London before the Romans' departure. In *HRB* it is addressed by a Briton, Guithelinus, complaining of the degeneration of his countrymen; Wace gives the speech to an unnamed Roman who laments British weakness and ingratitude and is not applauded as inspiring courage (as in *HRB*) but received with tears and fears. The moment is dwelt on as the lowest point yet for Britain, 'a good and noble land' (*bone terre e gentil*), deserving a better fate—which it is about to get with the coming of the House of Constantine. The same phrase is repeated when, after the reigns of British kings distinguished by sodomy and hatred, Gurmunt's Africans, abetted by the Saxons, ravage the land (l.

---

[25] On all this see Wright II, pp. xi–cxiv. Wright believes that the Bern MS represents the Vulgate Version best: see later, p. xxv.

[26] Many scholars have discussed Wace's additions to Geoffrey's narrative, notably Arnold in his edition (vol. I, pp. lxxix–xci), and Pelan and Houck in their books, *Influence du Brut* and *Sources*. Neither of them, however, had access to a Variant Version (the first such was published by Hammer in 1951 and was in any case contaminated, drawing on a MS interpolated with the Vulgate). This meant that many details of Wace's work were attributed to his originality or at least to his having directly borrowed from such writers as Landolphus. See Wright II, pp. xxx–lxx.

13475) with awful results: it reminds us that this time history will not repeat itself. Though the reign of one powerful British king, Chadwalein, is still to come, the race as a whole is no longer worthy to rule the island and its control will pass to the Saxons.

I have already mentioned Geoffrey's theme of domestic treachery as the frequent cause of national disaster; Wace considerably improves on this. Before Caesar's invasion even gets under way, we are reminded that its success will only be possible because of disagreement between Cassibellan and his nephews (ll. 3819–26), and are then prepared for the poignant irony of the later comment: 'Cassibellan's two nephews, in whom he put complete trust' (l. 3990). Tonwenne's dramatic and affecting speech to her two warring sons, much extended by Wace, puts pressure on Brenne to yield to Belin by emphasising how his treacherous behaviour to his family puts the whole realm at risk: 'Put down the weapons you hold, you who come from a foreign land, and bring foreigners to destroy your own domains…Is this the friendship you bear us, that you come here to kill your brother?'

Above all, Wace underlines the theme by adding substance to the Arthurian triangle of the king betrayed by his queen and his nephew. He prepares us carefully for this betrayal. First he hints at a marriage which is fundamentally unsatisfactory because unfruitful: 'they could have no children.' (ll. 9653–8)[27] despite Arthur's great love for his wife. Next he inserts a highly charged passage describing Arthur's arrangements for the care of his kingdom by Modret and Guinevere in his absence abroad (ll. 11173–88). The disgust and indignation Wace feels for Modret's behaviour is conveyed through rhetorical question and exclamation. Modret betrays Arthur twice: he loves the queen—high treason—and he loves his uncle's wife—incest. Wace hammers home the shame and disgrace of this with an especially strong word, *putage* (l. 11185), and its various meanings of fornication, debauchery and whorish behaviour suggest something new about Guinevere. Does Modret's carefully concealed love (ll. 11180–1) also conceal a yielding by the queen? Is she no victim but complicit? Having planted the suggestion, Wace does not elaborate but significantly closes the subject by lamenting Arthur's transfer of power to Modret *and* to the queen.

Once Arthur has beaten the Romans, queen and nephew reappear, to ruin his victory. The corresponding moment in the *Historia* (and the Variant Version) is carefully noncommittal: Modret has married the queen 'in abominable passion, in violation of her

---

[27] Portraying Arthur and Guinevere as infertile is a new departure. In Welsh tradition before Wace, and Continental and insular texts after him, there is plenty of evidence for a fertile Arthur. His son Amr is mentioned in the *Historia Brittonum*; another son, Llacheu, is mentioned in *Pa Gur* and one of the Welsh Triads, and is Frenchified into Loholt in Chrétien's *Erec and Enide* and in *Perlesvaus*, reappearing as Lout in Ulrich von Zatzikhoven's *Lanzelet*. Both *Lanzelet* and *Perlesvaus* say Guinevere is his mother; another mother is given for him in the later Vulgate prose romances.

former vows'.[28] This suggests the queen could be a victim, and indeed her later flight to Caerleon, prompted by news of Modret's recovery from defeat and his advance to Winchester, supports this view. Wace is much less restrained; as before, he underlines the disgrace and ignominy of Arthur's position, the family bonds and the sexual disloyalty of Modret, who has 'taken the king's wife to bed, the wife of his uncle and his lord' (ll. 13028–9). A little later, the queen flees to Caerleon, but this is because of *Arthur's* advance, not Modret's[29], and her despairing lament reveals her collusion in adultery: she has wickedly disgraced herself, shamed the king and desired his nephew (ll. 13201–12). We are given glimpses into the thoughts of the treacherous nephew too, which from time to time reveal his guilt and fear (ll. 13075, 13174). The downfall of the greatest king portrayed in the *Brut* becomes both a domestic and national tragedy through this careful attention to characterisation.

It was natural for Wace to add to his chronicle particulars from his personal familiarity with England (especially the South-West) and the English. These could add immediacy, verisimilitude, or make better topographical sense, as when the Saxons are scattered by Cador, after the battle of Bath, while crossing the Teign river, instead of at Thanet (as in the *HRB*), at the opposite end of the country. As he has some knowledge of Dorset, he decides that Locrin's daughter will be called Abren (*HRB*: Habren), and the river called after her, Avren [=Avon] (rather than *HRB*'s Sabrina=Severn), which, he tells us, flows into the sea at Christchurch. He is fascinated (as in the *Rou* too) by the origin of place-names and advances many fanciful aetiologies, sometimes at inordinate length. He advertizes his knowledge of English, and his awareness of the names in various languages for famous topographical features, like Stonehenge (ll. 8175–8). But his familiarity with British topography is nonetheless not very extensive and his frequent translation of 'Britain' as 'England' suggests that he really thinks in terms of the latter. His knowledge of Continental geography and inhabitants also emerges: Langres, near the fateful battleground of Soeïse, 'lies on top of a hill surrounded by valleys' (ll. 12285–6); Kidalet, a recently ruined city, lies between Dinan and the coast (ll. 14225–7); and Bedoer commands the Herupeis, a Norman contingent in Arthur's army to whom Wace gives some prominence. He possesses some skill for vividly conveying the geographical settings for battles: Belin and Brenne's ambush of the Roman troops in the Alpine valley is precisely and chillingly located (ll. 2919–3026).

More specialist knowledge still is displayed in his fondness for describing entertainments. Corineus' wrestling-match with Gogmagog (ll. 1105–68) is a great set-piece: the description of the wrestlers' moves reveals Wace's evident familiarity with the sport. He is also interested in music, as the account of Blegabret and the list of many different musical instruments used by the entertainers after Arthur's coronation show, though the latter is perhaps less striking than the knowledgeable portrayal of the dice-play-

---

[28] *Nuntiatur ei Modredum nepotem suum...eiusdem diademate per tyrannidem et proditionem insignitum esse reginamque Ganhumeram uiolato iure priorum nuptiarum eidem nephanda uenere copulatum fuisse*, Wright I, chap. 176, p. 129. Roberts, 'Geoffrey of Monmouth', *AOW*, p. 110, like Thorpe, trans-

lates '[G.] who had broken the vows of her earlier marriage', but this suggests a more active, and reprehensible, role than Geoffrey does. See Tatlock, p. 426, note 19.

[29] A change already introduced in the First Variant Version of HRB (ed. Wright, II, chap. 177).

ers.[30] Most impressive of all is the loving description of Arthur's embarkation at South-ampton, with its plethora of technical nautical terms (ll. 11205–38). Wace has a general fondness for scenes at sea, and excels at portraying dramatic storms and shipwrecks, such as Gudlac's (ll. 2478–94) and Ursula's (6041–68). All these add richness and plau-sibility to the chronicle. He has a talent for making a scene come to life: the coronation is embellished, not just by the scenes mentioned above, but by the portrayal of the crowds around the queen, the competitive dressing of her attendant ladies, and the knights vacillating between the attractions of church music and women (ll. 10385–416). The insulting message from the Roman embassy is received with fury and hub-bub (ll. 10711–24).

Wace was, however, also exercised by what he did not know. When he introduces his single most important addition to the Arthurian section, possibly of his own invention, the Round Table,[31] he follows it with a now famous passage on the dubiety of the sto-ries around Arthur:

> *En cele grant pais ke jo di,*
> *Ne sai si vus l'avez oï,*
> *Furent les merveilles pruvees*
> *E les aventures truvees*
> *Ki d'Artur sunt tant recuntees*
> *Ke a fable sunt aturnees:*
> *Ne tut mençunge, ne tut veir,*
> *Tut folie ne tut saveir.*
> *Tant unt li cunteür cunté*
> *E li fableür tant flablé*
> *Pur lur cuntes enbeleter,*
> *Que tut unt fait fable sembler.*   (ll. 9787–98)

[In this time of great peace I speak of—I do not know if you have heard of it—the wondrous events appeared and the adventures were sought out which are so often told about Arthur that they have become the stuff of fiction: not all lies, not all truth, neither total folly nor total wisdom. The raconteurs have told so many yarns, the story-tellers so many stories, to embellish their tales that they have made it all appear fiction.]

The careful couplet connection of *pruvees* and *truvees* suggests an inextricable mix of fact (*pruver*= to appear, show, demonstrate) and fiction (*truver*= to seek, discover, invent). Referring to an apparent host of oral sources from which one must judiciously select is a common rhetorical topos in the twelfth century, used to increase a writer's esteem, and not necessarily true. It is less common, however, to make frequent sugges-

---

[30] Ll. 10543–52 and 10556–88. These passages are only in eleven of the MSS plus the Hague MS discovered in the 50s (and the Vatican MS omits most of the details of the dice-players);

Arnold thought it was possible they were inter-polations, but kept them (vol. I, pp. xlix–l).

[31] See Schmolke-Hasselmann, 'The Round Table', pp. 41–75.

tions that one's sources might be unreliable, however much one would like to believe them. There are passages both in the *Brut* and in the *Rou* where Wace evinces what has been called 'canny Norman scepticism',[32] especially in his record of a visit to Broceliande and the fountain of Barenton, hoping, in vain, to find their fabled *merveilles*.[33] In consequence, one accords a certain respect to Wace's sceptical reporting of Arthur's end and the legends of his survival; the only thing certain here is uncertainty itself.

Wace is far more interested in human emotions than either Geoffrey of Monmouth or the author of the first Variant Version of the *Historia*. He has a particular sympathy for victims, whether on the battlefield or off it, and a keen understanding of human interaction, to which he gives vent whenever the pace of the chronicle slows sufficiently to give him scope. The Lear episode is a fine demonstration of this. Throughout there is more direct speech, resulting in a characterisation of Goneril, for example, reminiscent of the person she will become in Shakespeare (ll. 1851–88). The first interchange between Cordelia and her father is described with attention to their feelings of anger, pain and humiliation; and Wace gives a touching motive to Lear when he allows Cordelia's marriage to Aganippus:

> *Leïr nen out mie oblié,*
> *Ainz out bien sovent remembré*
> *Come sa fille l'out amé.*   (ll. 1805–7)

> [Lear had not forgotten, but often remembered,
> how his daughter had loved him]

His interest in emotion is most evidently greater than Geoffrey's if we look at the way each describes battles, an important and recurrent feature in both works. The *Historia* is precise on tactics and manoeuvres; Wace is not averse to these (indeed he adds them to his account of the siege of Cirencester), but he often prefers to evoke atmosphere and feeling: in his account of the great battle in the Soeïse valley, he captures the terrifying and confusing fray, and his heavy use of anaphora catches the remorseless press of anonymous violence (ll. 12563–8). His sympathy extends to the victims on the enemy side: the fleeing Saxons, aghast at Cador's ambush (ll. 9389–92), and the starving Scots, especially their womenfolk, whose long and moving appeals elicit Arthur's mercy (ll. 9465–526). The heroic parts played by Kei, Bedoer and Walwein are all expanded so that the sadness of their deaths can be more keenly felt; what contempt, on the other hand, is displayed in Walwein's address to the Roman Emperor (using the familiar *tu*, ll. 11709–33) and in the description of the flight of Modret's soft and selfish army (ll. 13113–30)! And in Arthur's final battle, Wace again eschews the *Historia's* military and tactical details for a more powerful, general description of the horror and futility of civil war (ll. 13253–74).

---

[32] Morris, 'The *Gesta Regum Britanniae*', p. 93.

[33] Wace, *Rou*, vol. II, Part III, ll. 6373–98. See also vol. I, Part II, ll. 1366–7 and 1371–2 for Wace's care over sources. He appeals to 'those of Fé-camp' to witness his concern for veracity (*Rou*, vol. I, Part II, ll. 1354–56). See Damian-Grint, 'Truth, Trust and Evidence' p. 71.

This importation of feeling individualizes martial scenes, but in other respects they are typical of contemporary writing about war: they are infused with the epic language and concepts characteristic of the twelfth-century *chansons de geste*. The battles of Britons versus Lucius' Romans and of Arthur versus Modret are pervaded with a crusading ethos: they are seen as those of Christianity versus paganism. The kernel of this already lay in the *Historia*, and its Variant Version, but Wace takes every opportunity to remind us of Rome's heathen, especially Saracen, allies (ll. 12523, 12710–20, 12914), bent on destroying Christendom, and to stress Modret's association with pagan Northmen (ll. 13226–8). Arthur and his men engage with foes in individual combats, sometimes referred to as jousts (ll. 11954, 11959), similar to those graduated, formal encounters in the *chansons de geste*,[34] with the same jeers over the bodies of the fallen and the same touches of black humour (ll. 11832–8, 12908–11). The lament of Charlemagne over Roland, which sees him as representative of a lost generation of fine youth, *juvente bele*, (*Chanson de Roland* l. 2916) is echoed by Wace's lament over the battle of Camble: *Dunc peri la bele juvente…e de la gent Arthur la flur/E li plus fort e li meillur* ['thus perished fine youth…the flower of Arthur's men, strongest and best'] (ll. 13266, 13273–4).

In the martial portions of his chronicle (and they are considerable) Wace is, then, still firmly in the world of epic but, as has long been recognised, in other respects his work provides a bridge to the newer world of twelfth-century romance. The words *curteis*, *curteisie*, *curteisement* are attached to his characters as they were not in Geoffrey. They are undefined and seem to indicate a range of praiseworthy attributes, whose meaning we have to work out from their contexts: frequently they startle us because they seem connected more to the arts of war than of the court. As in Gaimar, *curteis*, applied to a man, may mean no more than being a skilled soldier and displaying the largesse essential to any epic leader.[35] But elsewhere it seems an adjective associated with the accomplishments valued in peacetime: education, skills in sports, music-making and conversation—as in the description of Brenne (ll. 2659–82). The women are also *curteise* if they cultivate acceptable manners and skills like these. In Wace's world one can glimpse courtesy acquiring two, perhaps ultimately contradictory, dimensions: it can virtually become a political weapon, as when Arthur uses both his own reputation and the sumptuously displayed splendours of his court to attract the best men to his retinue, to *öir ses curteisies*, and thus acquire yet more power, yet it is also a force for moral improvement. The court is marked by the civilized restraint epitomized (and deliberately encouraged) by the Round Table, and the men and women there each inspire the other to increased valour and worth.[36]

---

[34] See Rychner, *La Chanson de Geste*, chap. 5. The combat of Hyrelgas and Boccus (ll. 12655–721) is especially notable.

[35] Gaimar, *Estoire* l. 5844 (on William Rufus); *Brut* e.g. l. 2215, on Dumwallo Molmuz.

[36] For Arthur attracting the best people see ll. 9731–84; for everyone's increased worth see ll. 10493–10520. Anor, the daughter of Ebrauc, is *corteise* because she knows how to *demener richeise* (ll. 1567–8): these words, meaning how to display and make use of wealth and splendour as a political tool, are used of several 'courteous' men and women in the *Brut*. On the nexus of words defining *curteisie* in the *Brut* see the excellent remarks by Le Saux, 'Two Aspects', pp. 46–56.

Wace makes few major additions to the stories in the *Historia* and on the whole these are less noteworthy than the colouring he imparts to the whole through the details I have sketched above. What further impressions can we gain of the man behind the work, his aims in translating and his audience? He is evidently fascinated by change and especially linguistic change: the diverse names for places are constantly invoked to recall the movement from past to present and to mark the transfer of political power. But he tries to be an impartial historian of such transfers: if the Romans are villains on some occasions, they are admirable rulers on others (and Roman education is always prized); Oswald and Chadwalein are both praised and the degeneration of the British is less heavily emphasized. There are few reliable references to contemporary or recent events: the *terre desaloee* may possibly be a punning reference to the Matildine lands (see note to p. 73); the uncritical praise of Guendolien, attacking Locrin, as a 'proud and resolute woman' (l.1423) may conceivably be influenced by knowledge about Gwenlliant, wife of Gruffyd ap Rhys, who died in battle, a 'second Penthesilea', in the 1130s' anti-Norman revolt.[37] France is definitely France, not Gaul, which Arthur must emphatically hold and defend (ll. 11053, 11715–18, 12420) and sarcastic remarks are occasionally made about its inhabitants (l. 4140): probably a decidedly Norman view-point emerges here.

He is writing for a lay audience less familiar, possibly less sympathetic, with the classics than Geoffrey's one. When the Trojans find the temple of Diana on the island of Leogice, the details of pagan sacrifice are of less importance to Wace than stressing the devilish and deceptive nature of the goddess. He has to explain the Pillars of Hercules and the Sirens, and medievalize Roman terms.[38] His style is lucid and straightforward; indeed he sometimes takes it upon himself to explain more than seems warranted, and again this may have as much to do with his audience's needs as his own pedantry. He has a fondness for word-play and for reiteration of phrases, sometimes to press an ironic parallel; he is also happy to use proverbial wisdom, once again perhaps a good way of emphasizing a point to his audience.[39]

---

[37] See Gillingham, 'Context and Purposes', p. 113.

[38] Labienus, in *HRB* a tribune, becomes *sire d'une conestablie*, lord of a company headed by a constable, chief officer of a medieval household (l. 4088).

[39] Examples of word-play: the sodomite Menbriz is *desmenbrez* (l. 1491), a word meaning both 'torn limb from limb' and 'castrated', apposite both to Menbriz's vice and his name; Lucius, addressing his army before the battle of Soeïse and recalling their ancestors' achievements in creating the power of Rome, neatly expresses his apprehensions about the battle's outcome in a couplet using *adnominatio*: *Cil cunquistrent le grant empire;/ Hunte est s'en nostre tens empire.* (ll. 12483–4) [They conquered our great empire;

it's shameful if, in our lifetime, it declines]. Ironic parallel through reiterated phrase: *Fai, dist li reis, a tun plaisir,/ Tanz cum tu vuels en fai venir;/ Dune lur tant cum tu vuldras'* (ll. 6595–7; Constant in Vortigern's power) and *Fai, dist li reis, que tu vuldras./ Mande tuz cels que buens savras.* (ll. 70512; Vortigern in Hengist's power). Proverbs: I have annotated all those I was able to check with the collections of Le Roux de Lincy, Morawski and Hassell. I discovered much too late the Brosnahan collection, which confirmed my opinion that ll. 4409 (Brosnahan 24), 4533–4 (B. 321), 5882 (B. 257), 8868 (B. 257) and 10813–14 (B. 296) were proverbial, but his compendium still does not account for the surely proverbial ll. 2372 and 2374.

Wace's Text

The text of the *Brut* survives in approximately thirty-two manuscripts and fragments of manuscripts: a detailed account of these follows at the end of the Introduction. Ivor Arnold, in his 1938 edition for the Société des Anciens Textes Français, used two of them for his base manuscripts, emending them frequently, but providing most of their original readings in his apparatus at the foot of the page, which also included variants from other manuscripts. For this 're-issue' of the text—which cannot strictly be called a re-editing—I have chosen to follow Arnold in many respects, but have also diverged somewhat from his practice, and I have kept the apparatus simpler.

When Arnold began trying to establish groups of manuscripts which stayed consistent all the way through the poem, he rapidly ran into difficulties (vol. I, p. xxviii et seq.) These caused him to conclude that it was not possible to reconstruct Wace's text with certainty (p. lvi).[40] He eventually decided to use two Anglo-Norman manuscripts, sequentially: MS P (BL. Add. 45103) up to l. 11999, and MS D (Durham Cathedral C iv. 27(I), recently redated by Baumgartner and Short, *Geste*, p. 24, to the twelfth century) from l. 12000 to the end of the poem. Except for the Durham MS, there are no twelfth-century manuscripts of Wace extant. Arnold chose MSS P and D (which he believed to be thirteenth century) because their language seemed virtually identical, and closest to that which Wace would actually have used (pp. lx–lxv), and because he thought they best represented what he called *'la tradition moyenne'* of the *Brut*. This tradition he thought he could establish by closely comparing manuscripts with Geoffrey of Monmouth's *Historia Regum Britanniae*, Wace's source; where they reproduced Geoffrey most faithfully, they must be closest to the original poem. He used MS P because it was more complete than MS D, but only up to l. 11999 because after that it seemed to follow 'a very inexact model'; after that, he used MS D which appeared, from l. 12000 onwards, to stop making the regular small omissions from the text which characterized it earlier.

Some of Arnold's assumptions would today appear dubious to us; indeed he himself acknowledged that comparing the *Historia* with the manuscripts of the *Brut* to decide which were, and were not, erroneous readings was not always a helpful procedure (p. xxxiv). An early review by Ceri Fahlin (in *Romania*, 1938/39) was also doubtful whether the comparison could distinguish between Wace's text and those of copyists (p. 87). Since Arnold's death, advances in scholarship have made the procedure more dubious still. Arnold, using the work of Faral and Griscom (1929), treated Geoffrey's *Historia* as a single, monolithic text, but Neil Wright's researches (1984, 1988) have established that this is not the case. There is a 'Vulgate', or standard, version of the *Historia*, represented by a group of MSS, from which Wright prints the Bern MS (Bürgerbibliothek MS 568) as the best (Wright Vol. I). This is an advance on Griscom's text, which used a corrupt manuscript. But there is also a 'First Variant Version' of the *Historia*, which may have emerged as early as the late 1130s and which was extensively used by Wace in his *Brut* (Wright Vol. II, pp. lxx–lxxiii). It is regularly his base text, especially in the

---

[40] See also Keller, 'Wace et Geoffrey', p. 12.

first half of his poem (Wright vol. II, p. lviii; Keller, 'Wace et Geoffrey', p. 7). Arnold was unaware of the Variant Version (see fn. 26); his editorial principle is thus vitiated.

Arnold, with a low opinion of 'copyists', freely changed and 'emended' his base MSS, using this principle and also his own opinions, which as Fahlin remarked were often debatable. His reasons for small changes are sometimes inscrutable. Moreover, when he substitutes another word for a reading of the base MSS, he does not say where he takes it from; the apparatus of MSS variants at the foot of the page often throws no light on the matter, and one is left with the suspicion that sometimes the substituted word or words represent a conglomeration of variants, or, worse still, are invented by him. His system of what to include or omit was indeed 'eclectic' (Fahlin, p. 88).

In partially following Arnold, and partially deviating from his practice, I could also be charged in the same terms. I had neither the time nor the means to re-edit the *Brut* completely, so in essentially reusing his text I have stood on the shoulders of a scholar far more experienced than myself, and for whose work I have a profound respect. Nevertheless, I believe, in line with editorial practice today, that we should give the 'copyists' more credence, and let their versions of texts stand unless manifestly corrupt. I acknowledge with gratitude Fahlin's review, whose disputes with many of Arnold's emendations to the first 1000 lines of the *Brut* encouraged me to restore many original readings to MSS P and D, and likewise Baumgartner and Short's edition of MS D's version of the Arthurian section, which gave me a largely unemended parallel to Arnold's version of ll. 12000–13298 in that manuscript. I have been more conservative than Baumgartner and Short. Below are the ways in which I have mostly followed Arnold:

1. Like Arnold—and, indeed, like Baumgartner and Short—I have incorporated some major long passages from other MSS, but not in either MSS P or D, such as details of entertainments at Arthur's court (see p. 266). These have been bracketed, as have couplets added by Arnold to the base text (see p. 362).

2. I have mostly retained Arnold's corrections of grammatical faults and of rhymes.

3. I have mostly retained Arnold's corrections of scansion, but have in some cases given priority to the scribes' version.

4. I have partially followed Arnold in including in the footnotes all additions, occupying more than two lines, by other MSS to the text in MSS P and D; occasionally, interesting couplets from other MSS have also been footnoted. Very long additions have been summarized (see p. 184).

The following are the ways in which I have deviated from Arnold:

1. I have restored, without an indication in the footnotes, proper names to the form in which they appear in the base MSS, except where there is an obvious mistake (e.g. l. 8834) or the names are verging on the unrecognizable (as in the list of Ebrauc's sons and daughters, on p. 40). I have not imposed consistency in the reproduction of names.

2. I have restored lines, phrases and words original to the base MSS which seem to make perfect sense. Restored couplets, such as that on p. 296, have been bracketed and footnoted, but not included in the numbering, which follows Arnold's so as to facilitate comparison of my text with his and to avoid confusion.

3. I have restored the original order in lines if it seemed viable and sensible, as in ll. 5390–2.

4. I have not rigorously applied consistency to spelling (Arnold has done this to the manuscripts to a certain extent already: see vol. I, pp. lxvi–lxxiii).

5. I have not worried overmuch about rapid alternations of tense (see ll. 791–2).

6. I have not remarked in the footnotes on where other MSS omit lines present in MSS P or D.

As will, I hope, be clear, I have throughout preferred to retain rather than cut, which is why I have not followed all of Fahlin's suggestions. The composite text, first from MS P, then from MS D, is still not an exact reproduction of the one in the manuscripts but it is a good deal closer to them than in Arnold's edition. Those who want to check on what they might be missing are referred to that edition, in the first place, (where Arnold always noted what he was replacing), and then to the British Library and Durham Cathedral Library.

It follows that my translation here of the whole of the *Brut* differs slightly, in the Arthurian section, from what I have already published in the Everyman *Life of King Arthur*. Since there I was only translating, and not supplying a parallel French text, I based my translation entirely on Arnold's edition as it stands.

I have been inconsistent in my translation of names, sometimes keeping them as they stand in the French (Carais, rather than Carausias, Kermerdin, not Carmarthen), sometimes, if they are well known, giving them their better known modern equivalent (Guinevere, not Ganhumare). In this, I have followed the practice of Arnold and Pelan (*Partie Arthurienne*, p. 13).

In footnotes to the translation, I have throughout indicated where Wace differs in details from the Vulgate version of the *Historia*, and I have made references to the Variant Version where Wace seems to be following it, most obviously, for example, in the list of the princes attending Arthur's coronation (p. 259).

WACE'S MANUSCRIPTS

Enumeration of Wace's manuscripts varies. Arnold said he consulted twenty-two and knew of two additional fragments, but since then the number has steadily grown as more manuscripts, or parts of manuscripts, have been discovered. I append below a list of complete, or nearly complete, manuscripts and a list of fragments; the dividing line between 'substantial fragment' and 'nearly complete manuscript' is sometimes hard to draw. I am most grateful to Prof. Jean Blacker for supplying me with up-to-date information on manuscript discoveries and to Dr Christopher Page who put me on to the track of one of the fragments in the Westminster Abbey Muniments Room. The letters signifying most of the manuscripts are those used by Arnold, and the dates of the manuscripts are those supplied by him or by subsequent scholars.

Complete or nearly Complete MSS

A   Arundel xiv (London, College of Arms); Anglo-Norman, 14th c.

C   BL Cotton Vitellius A x; A.N., late 13th c.

D   Durham Cathedral Library C iv 27(I); A.N., dated to end of the 12th c.

E   BL Harley 6508; Continental, 14th c.

F   BL Addit. 32125 (ll. 10527–12772 missing); A.N., late 13th c.

G   Paris, Bibliothèque Sainte-Geniève 2447; Cont., 14th c.

                Paris Bibl. de l'Arsenal 2982 (copy of G); Cont., 18th c.

H   Paris, BN fonds fr. 1450; Cont., 13th c.

J   Paris, BN fonds fr. 1416; Cont., dated 1292.

K   Paris, BN fonds fr. 794; the 'Guiot' MS, Cont., 13th c.

L   Lincoln Cathedral Library 104; A.N., 13th c.

N   Paris, BN fonds fr. 1454; Cont., 15th c., identical to O and V.

O   Paris, BN fonds fr. 12556; Cont., 15th c.; see above.

P   BL Addit. 45103; A.N., 1275 or later (British Library, *Catalogue*, p. 88).

R   Paris, Bibl. de l'Arsenal 2981 (ll. 13944–14013 and 14064 to end are missing); Cont., 14th c.

S   Paris, BN nouv. acqu. fr.1415; A.N., 14th c.

T   Corpus Christi College, Cambridge, 50; A.N., 1250–1300.

V   Vienna, Nat. Lib. 2603; Cont., 15th c. Identical to N and O.

                Vatican Library Otto. lat. 1869 (fols. 96–183); A.N., 13th c.

Fragments of MSS

B	BL Royal 13 A xxi (begins at l. 8729); A.N., late 13th/early 14th c.
M	Montpellier, Bibl. Interuniv. Sect. Médecine 251 (stops at l. 5664); Cont., 13th c.
X	Oxford, Bodleian, Rawl. D 913; four fragments from two separate MSS, of the late 12th and the 14th c.; both A.N.
Y	Paris, BN fonds fr.12603 (ll. 67–1950); Cont., 13th–14th c.
Z	Beinecke Library, Yale, 395, item 12 (ll. 1–7141) (formerly in the Phillipps library); A.N., late 13th–early 14th c.
Hague	National Library of the Netherlands, Royale 73 J 53 (only 7348 lines remain); Cont., 13th c.
Vatican	Palatine Library MS 1971 (ll. 1219–2421 and 3613–4752); Cont., 13th c.
Cologny–Geneva	Biblio. Bodmer. 67 (ll. 13642 to end); A.N., second half 13th c.
London	Univ. Lib. 574 (ll. 6680–710 and 6782–812); A.N., late 13th or early 14th c.
Zadar, Croatia	Archepisc. Dioc. (ll. 13485–629 and 14287–443, both with lacunae); Cont., 13th c.
Berkeley	Bancroft UCB 165 (ll. 387–580 and 1769–954); Cont., late 13th c.
Westminster Abbey	Muniments Room, two fragments, one from the binding of C.5.22, the other of unknown provenance (ll. 9065–108, ll. 10523–32, 10589–600, 10623–42, 10329–80 and 10385–400, all with lacunae; 11407–12, 11447–52, 11487–92 and 11529–34); apparently both from the same MS, A.N., early 13th c.

Wace's
ROMAN DE BRUT
A HISTORY
OF THE BRITISH

Text and Translation

Ki vult oïr e vult saveir
De rei en rei e d'eir en eir
Ki cil furent e dunt il vindrent
Ki Engleterre primes tindrent,
Quels reis i ad en ordre eü,
E qui anceis e ki puis fu,[1]
Maistre Wace l'ad translaté
Ki en conte la verité.
   Si cum li livres le devise,
10 Quant Greu ourent Troie conquise
E eissillié tut le païs
Pur la venjance de Paris
Ki de Grece out ravi Eleine,
Dux Eneas a quelque peinne
De la grant ocise eschapa.
Un fiz aveit k'il en mena
Ki aveit nun Ascanius;
N'aveit ne fiz ne fille plus.
Ke de parenz, ke de maisnees,
20 Ke d'aveir out vint nés chargiees.
Par mer folead lungement;
Maint grant peril, maint grant turment
E maint travail li estut traire.
Emprés lung tens vint en Itaire:
Itaire esteit dunc apelee
La terre u Rome fu fundee.
N'ert de Rome encor nule chose,
Ne fu il puis de bien grant pose.
Eneas out mult travaillied,
30 Mult out siglé, mult out nagied,
Mainte grant mer out trespassee
E mainte tere avironee.
En Itare est venue a rive
En une terre plenteïve,
Bien pruef d'illuec u Rome siet,
La u li Teivres en mer chiet.[2]
Latins, uns reis, k'iloec maneit,
Ki tut cel regne en pais teneit,
Riches huem e mananz asez,
40 Mais velz esteit e trespassez,

Ad Eneam mult enoré.
De sa terre li ad duné
Grant partie sur la marine;
E estre le gré la reïne[3]
Li pramist sa fille a duner
E de sun regne enheriter.[4]
N'aveit fors li enfant ne eir,
[Aprés lui deveit tut aveir].[5]
La fille ert mult bele meschine,
Si ert apelee Lavine,   50
Mais prendre la deveit Turnus
Ki de Toscane ert sire e dux.
Cil Turnus, ki ert sis veisins,
Riches huem mult, sout ke Latins
Sa fille a Eneam dunout;
Dolenz en fu, envie en out,
Kar il l'aveit lunges amee
E ele lui ert graantee.
A Eneam grant guerre en fist,
Cors contre cors bataille en prist; 60
Chevaliers ert hardiz e forz,
Mais il en fu vencuz e morz.
Dunc out Eneas la meschine,
Reis fu e ele fu reïne.
Ne trova puis ki li neüst
Ne de rien li contr'esteüst.
   Puis k'Eneas Lavine out prise
E la terre tute conquise,
Vesqui il quatre anz e regna
E a un chastel k'il ferma   70
De Lavine posa le nun,
Si l'apela Laviniun.
La feme e l'onour quatre anz tint:
El quart an, quant sa fin li vint,
Aveit Lavine conceü,
Mais n'aveit pas enfant eü.
Mais li termes ne demora
Ke Lavine un fiz enfanta:
Silvius fu si propre nuns
E Postumus fu sis surnuns.[6] 80

---

[1] MS P's reading of line restored.
[2] MS P's order of ll. 35–36 restored.
[3] MS P's reading of line restored.
[4] MS P reading—*enheriter*—restored.
[5] L. 48 missing in MS P.
[6] MS P: *Porvinus*.

Aeneas travels to Italy and marries Lavinia

1 Whoever wishes to hear and to know about the successive kings and their heirs who once upon a time were the rulers of England—who they were, whence they came, what was their sequence, who came earlier and who later—Master Wace has translated it and tells it truthfully.[1]

9 As the book relates, when the Greeks had conquered Troy and laid the whole land waste to take revenge on Paris, who had stolen Helen from Greece, duke Aeneas escaped, with much difficulty, from the great slaughter. He had a son, called Ascanius, whom he took with him; he had no other sons or daughters. What with family, followers and possessions, he filled twenty ships. For a long time he drifted on the sea, forced to endure great danger, great hardship and great suffering. After a long time he came to Italy: that was then the name of the land where Rome was founded. As yet Rome did not exist, nor did it for a long while thereafter.

29 Aeneas had travelled much, rowed and sailed far, crossed many great seas and passed many lands. He arrived on the shores of Italy, a fertile country, and came very close to where Rome now stands, where the Tiber flows into the sea. Latin, a king dwelling there, who held all that realm in peace, a rich and prosperous man, but old and feeble, loaded Aeneas with honours. He gave him a large part of his land on the coast and, against the queen's wishes, promised to give him his daughter and bequeath him his kingdom. He had no heir except the child—she would have everything after his death. This daughter was a very beautiful girl, called Lavinia, but Turnus, lord and duke of Tuscany,[2] was supposed to take her to wife.

53 This Turnus, his neighbour and a very wealthy man, learnt that Latin was giving his daughter to Aeneas. He was mortified and jealous, because he had loved her for a long time and she was promised to him. He made war on Aeneas and took up arms against him in single combat. He was a bold and strong knight, but he was vanquished and killed. Then Aeneas received the girl; he became king and she queen. After that he found nothing more to resist or hinder him.

67 After Aeneas had taken Lavinia and conquered the whole land, he lived and reigned four years, and named a castle he had constructed after Lavinia, calling it Lavinium.[3] He held wife and domain for four years. In the fourth year, as his end approached, Lavinia conceived, but did not yet bear the child; but it was not long before she gave birth to a son. Silvius was his own name and Postumus his surname.

---

[1] Wace omits the geographical description of Britain with which Gildas, Bede, *HB*, Henry of Huntingdon's *HA* and *HRB* all begin.

[2] *HRB* chap. 6: king of the Rutuli; *VV*: king of the Tuscans.

[3] Not in *HRB* but in *VV* chap. 6.

En grant chierté le fist tenir
Aschanius, kil fist nurir,
Ki de Troie vint od sun pere;
Creüsa out esté sa mere
Ki fille fu Priant le rei,
Mais al tomulte e al desrei
Kant Eneas de Troie eissi,
En la grant presse la perdi.
Cil Aschanius tint l'onur
90   Puis la mort sun pere maint jor.
Une cité edifia
Ke l'on Albelunges numa,
E a sa marastre laissa
La terre, e quite li clama
Le chastel ke Eneas fist
Qu'el l'eüst tant cum el vesquist.
Mais lé Deus de Troie en ad pris
Ke Eneas i aveit mis,
En Albe les vuleit aveir,
100   Mais il n'i pourent remaneir;
Unches nes i sout tant porter
K'al main les i poüst trover;
El temple ralouent ariere,
Mais jo ne sai en quel maniere.
Trente e quatre anz maintint la terre
Ke unches guaires n'i out guerre.
    Aschanius, quant il fina,
Silvium, sun frere, herita,
Ki esteit de Lavine nez,
110   Puis ke Eneas fu finez.
Un fiz aveit Aschanius
Ki refu numez Silvius;
Le nun de sun uncle porta;
Mais poi vesqui e poi dura.
Il out amee une meschine
Celeement, niece Lavine;
Od li parla, cele conçut.
Kant Aschanius l'aperçut,
Venir fist ses sortisseors
120   E ses sages devineors;

Par els, ço dist, vuleit saveir
Kel enfant deit la dame aveir.
Cil unt sorti e deviné
E ço unt en lur sort trové
Ke un fiz ke la dame avra
Sun pere e sa mere ocirra
E en eissil chaciez sera,
Mais puis a grant honur vendra.
Issi fu veir comë il distrent
E si avint cum il pramistrent,   130
Kar al terme ke il nasqui
Murut la mere, e il vesqui:
Morte fu de l'enfantement
E li fiz fu nez sauvement,
Si li fu mis cist nun Brutus.
Quinze anz aveit e nient plus,
Kant od sun pere en bois ala,
Ki a male ure l'i mena.
A mal eür ensemble alerent,[1]
Une herde de cerfs troverent.   140
Li peres al fiz les aceinst
E li fiz a un fust s'estreinst;
A un cerf traist k'il avisa,
Mais la saiete trespassa;
Sun pere feri si l'ocist,
Mais de sun gré nient nel fist.
Tuit si parent s'en coruscerent[2]
E del regne Brutun chacerent.
    Cil passa mer, en Grece ala;
De cels de Troie iluec trova   150
Tute la lignee Eleni
Un des fiz al rei Priami,
E d'altres lignages asez
Ke l'on aveit enchaitivez;
E mult i out de sun lignage,
Mais tenu erent en servage.
Brutus trova sun parenté
Dunt en Grece aveit grant plenté:
Mult esteient multipliez
Puis ke il furent eissillez.   160

---

[1] MS P reading—eür—restored.   [2] MS P reading—si—restored.

Birth of Brutus

Ascanius, who had come from Troy with his father, brought Silvius up and held him very dear. His own mother had been Creusa, daughter of king Priam, but during the tumult and chaos of Aeneas' escape from Troy, he lost her in the huge throng.

89   This Ascanius held the domain for a long time after his father's death. He built a city, called Alba,[1] left the land to his stepmother and granted her the possession of Aeneas' castle as long as she lived. But he took from it the gods of Troy, which Aeneas had placed there, and wanted to have them in Alba. However, they would not stay there: he could never carry them away to such an extent that he would find them there in the morning. They would return to the temple, but how, I do not know.[2] For thirty-four years he ruled the land so that there was hardly ever strife.

107   When Ascanius died, the inheritance passed to his brother Silvius, born of Lavinia after Aeneas' death. Ascanius had a son also called Silvius[3]; he bore his uncle's name, but lived and lasted only a short while. He secretly loved a girl, Lavinia's niece, lay with her and she conceived. When Ascanius realised this, he summoned his soothsayers and his wise diviners: through them, he said, he wished to know what sort of child the lady would have. They predicted, and foresaw, and found in their divination that the son which the lady would have would kill his father and his mother and be sent into exile, but subsequently would achieve great honour.

129   What they said was true, and happened as they promised, for at the moment of his birth, his mother died and he lived. She died in childbirth and her son was safely delivered and given the name of Brutus. He was fifteen, no more, when he went to the forest with his father, who took him there in an evil hour. In an evil hour they went off together and found a herd of stags. The father drove them towards his son, while the son clung to a tree-trunk; he shot at a stag which he saw, but the arrow passed it by. He struck and killed his father, but not by his own will. It angered all his kin and they drove Brutus from the kingdom.

149   He crossed the sea and went to Greece. Among the Trojans he found there were all those from Helenus' lineage, one of the sons of king Priam, and many other families too, who had been taken captive. And there were many of his own family, but they were kept in servitude. Brutus found his kinsfolk, of whom there were many in Greece: since their exile they had greatly multiplied.

---

[1] *HRB* chap. 6: Alba; *VV*: Alba Longa.
[2] These mysterious habits of the pagan gods are not in *HRB* but in the *VV*, chap. 6, which has borrowed them from Landolphus Sagax's *Historia Romana* (11th c.). See Wright II, p. xliv.
[3] Wace's two Silvii are confusing. It appears he got them from a text (no longer extant) of the First Variant Version which provided two Silvii, one Silvius being the son of Ascanius (as in the Vulgate *HRB* chap. 6, and *HA* I, chap. 9, and derived from the *HB*) and the other Silvius Postumus, Aeneas' son by Lavinia, born after his father's death. See Wright II, pp. xcix–ci.

Brutus n'i out gueres esté
Kant il out grant los conquesté
De hardement e de prüesce
E de saver e de largesce.
Mult l'enorouent si parent, [1]
E tuit li chaitif ensement;
Donouent lui e prameteient
E asez sovent li diseient,
S'estre peüst e il osast,
170 Ke de servage les getast:
D'omes esteient grant compaine;
Se il eüssent chevetaine
Kis maintenist e enseinnast
E en bataille les menast,
Legerement les purreit l'on
Mettre fors de chaitivesun;
Entr'els aveit bien set milliers
De bons e de pruz chivaliers,
Estre geldë, estre servanz,
180 E estre femmes e enfanz;
E se il les vuleit guier,
A duc le fereient lever,
Kar mult suffereient grant fais
Pur vivre senz servage en pais,
N'i aveit nul ki n'en fust bel.
En Grece aveit un damoisel,
Assaracus aveit cil nun;
Fiz ert a un riche baron
Del mielz de tute la contree,
190 Mais sa mere ert de Troie nee:
Greseis esteit de par sun pere
E Troïens de par sa mere,
Mais nez esteit en soignantage,
E nekedent en eritage
Li aveit sis peres duné
Tres bons chastels de s'erité. [2]
Assaracus, ki bastarz ere,
De par sun pere aveit un frere
Sulunc lur lei, fiz de moiller.
200 Cist ne vuleit mie otrier [3]

Qu'Assaracus chastel eüst,
Ainz li tolist, si il peüst.
Assaracus s'en deffendeit [4]
E la terre a force teneit
E as Troïns se pendeit
Pur ço ke de lur gent esteit,
Ne cil n'aveient nul refui
En tute Grece fors a lui.
Par sun conseil e par sun gré
Firent Brutun lur avoé   210
E par sun los e par s'aïe
Prist Brutus d'els la seinurie.
Brutus vit ke grant gent aveient
E ke li chastel fort esteient:
Les tres chastels fist enforcier [5]
E guarnir cum a guerreier;
Puis assembla tuz les chaitis
E les chaitives del païs,
Homes e femes e enfanz
E lur bestes e lur servanz,   220
Dunt il aveient granz compaines,
Sis mist en bois e en muntaines; [6]
Dunc fist viande e robe atraire;
Puis ad sempres un breif fait faire. [7]
Le rei de Grece salua
E ces paroles li manda:
'Pur la hunte e pur le viltage
Del noble pople e del lignage
Dardani al bon ancesur,
Qui ad esté a desonur   230
En cheitivesun lungement,
Se sunt josté communement
Li chaitif, si unt fait comune
Come la gent ki deit estre une.
Lur chevetainne unt de mei fait,
Si se sunt en cel bois atrait;
Mielz vuelent vivre de racines
Come bestes e salvagines,
Pur ço ke il seient delivre,
Ke en servage a plenté vivre;   240

---

[1] MS P reading—*enorouent*—restored.
[2] MS P reading—*tres*—restored.
[3] MS P reading—*cist*—restored.
[4] MS P reading—*s'en*—restored.

[5] MS P reading—*tres*—restored.
[6] MS P reading—*en…en*—restored.
[7] MS P reading—*breif*—restored.

Brutus becomes leader of the Trojans

161 Brutus had not been there long before he won a great reputation for daring, bravery, wisdom and generosity. His kin greatly honoured him and so did all the captives. They made him gifts and promises and very often told him that, if he dared, he could be the one to release them from slavery. They were a great band of men: if they had a leader to support and teach them and lead them in battle, he could easily deliver them from captivity. Between them there were a good seven thousand fine brave knights, besides foot-soldiers, servants, women and children, and if he wished to lead them, they would raise him to a duke, for they would willingly suffer great distress in order to live in peace, free from servitude: this was pleasing to one and all.

186 There was a young man in Greece called Assaracus, son of a powerful lord over the best part of the whole land, but his mother was born in Troy: he was Greek on his father's side and Trojan on his mother's, but born from concubinage. Nevertheless, as inheritance his father had given him three fine castles from his patrimony. Assaracus, the bastard, had on his father's side a legitimate brother, son of a wife. He was unwilling to allow Assaracus to have the castles and would rather take them, if he could. Assaracus defended himself, held the land by force, and favoured the Trojans, because he belonged to their nation, nor did they have any support except him, throughout Greece. It was through his advice and will they made Brutus their lord and through his counsel and help that Brutus assumed power over them.

213 Brutus saw that there were many people and the castles were strong. He had the three castles fortified and provisioned as if for war. Then he gathered all the captives in the land, men, women and children, and their animals and servants, of which there were great bands, and placed them in the woods and the mountains. He then had food and clothes gathered in, and immediately had a letter written. He greeted the king of Greece and sent him these words: 'Because of the shame and ignominy of the noble nation and lineage of Dardanus, their great ancestor, which has for long lived in dishonour and captivity, the captives have joined together, they have formed an alliance, like a people which ought to be at one. They have made me their leader and have retired into the woods: they would rather live on roots, like beasts and wild animals, in order to be free, than live in plenty and in servitude, rather live free in poverty than captive amongst

Mielz vuelent vivre en povreté
Franc, ke chaitif en grant plenté.
Si il vuelent franchise aveir,
Ne lur en deiz mal gré saveir,
Ne tu ne t'en deiz mervailler
Se il se vuelent purchacier:
Chescuns desirre, si ad dreit,
E volenté ad ke franc seit.
Ço te prient e jo te mand
250 Ke franchement d'or en avant
Puissent vivre la u il sunt
E aler la u il vuldrunt.'
     Li reis ad le brief esculté;
Grant mervaille li ad semblé
Ke li Troïen se revelent
E que de franchise l'apelent.
Fol hardement, ço dit, unt pris,
E en fole ovre se sunt mis.
Ses ducs, ses princes, ses barons
260 E tuz ses homes ad somons,
Gent a chival e gent a piez; [1]
Vers cels de Troie ad chivalchié.
Ço dist li rois e sil pensa
Ke les chastels assegera
K'Assaracus deveit tenir
E ke Brutus feseit guarnir;
Et se Brutum poeit enz prendre,
Ja n'en fereit el que del pendre.
Brutus oï dire asez tost
270 Que li rois veneit od tel ost.
A un trespas que il saveit
Par unt li reis passer deveit
Od treis mil armez s'embuscha
Li reis vint, ki passer quida,
E Brutus i est od sun aguait; [2]
Grant ocise ad des reals fet.
Li Greu, ki furent desarmé
S'en sunt tost en fuie turné;
En Achalon, un flun bien grant,
280 En est grant masse entré fuiant.

Brutus, kis enchaucë al dos,
En ad en l'eue maint enclos;
As rives les fait tresbucher
E en l'eue parfund neier;
Neied en ad mult e ocis
E mult en ad retenu vis:
Li reis meïmes s'en fuï
E tute l'ost se departi.
     Antigonus, freres le rei,
Vit que Brutus fist tel desrei,   290
Vit les ocis, vit les neiez;
Ses compainuns ad ralïez
Par maltalent e par iror
Est turné ariere en l'estur.
Dunc veïssez aspre meslee,
Maint cop de lance e maint d'espee,
Maint home ester e maint abatre
E maint fuïr e maint combatre;
Maint cop receivent e maint rendent;
Li Troïen par mi les fendent.   300
Maint en unt mort, maint abatu,
Maint mis par fei, maint retenu.
Retenuz fu Antigonus
E de ses homes tut le plus;
Cels enmena Brutus od sei
Pris e lïez e mis par fei.
Pandrasus out grant marrement
De sun frere e de l'altre gent;
Ses genz rassembla par matin
Si mist le siege a Sparatin.   310
Ço quida que Brutus i fust
E ses prisuns mis i eüst,
Mais il fu el boscage entrez
Si out la ses prisuns menez;
El chastel out mis chivaliers
Cis cenz tut estre les archiers. [3]
Li reis le chastel asega,
Ses barons entur aloa,
A chescun dist u il serreit
E de quel part il assaudreit.   320

---

[1] MS P reading—*piez*—restored.   [3] MS P reading—*cis*—restored.
[2] MS P's reading of line restored.

Brutus ambushes the Greeks

abundance. If they wish for freedom, you should not begrudge it them, nor should you wonder if they wish to acquire it: everyone longs and desires, as is their right, to be free. They beg and I command you that henceforth they may live freely where they are and go where they like.'

252 The king[1] listened to the letter. It seemed outrageous to him that the Trojans should rebel and demand he grant them freedom. 'They have chosen foolish daring,' he said, 'and embarked upon foolish deeds.' He summoned his dukes, his princes, his barons and all his men, his knights and his foot-soldiers, and rode towards the Trojans. The king intended, and said, that he would besiege those castles which Assaracus had the right to hold and which Brutus had fortified, and if he could catch Brutus inside, there would be nothing for it but to hang him. Very soon Brutus heard that the king was approaching with such an army. He lay in ambush with three thousand armed men in a pass he knew, which the king had to traverse. The king arrived, thinking to pass, and Brutus was there with his ambush; he made a great slaughter of the king's men. The Greeks, who were unarmed, soon all turned to flee; a large number of them rushed into Achalon, a very big river. Brutus, pursuing from the rear, trapped many in the water; he made them collapse on the banks and drown in the deep water. He drowned and killed many and captured many alive. The king himself fled, and the whole army broke up.

289 Antigonus, the king's brother, saw the havoc Brutus was causing, saw the dead and the drowned. He rallied his companions: in anger and distress he returned to the fray. Then could be seen a violent battle, many a blow from lance and sword, many men standing fast and many cut down, many fleeing and many fighting, giving and receiving many a stroke. The Trojans pierced them through, killing and cutting down many; many were captured and gave their word not to flee. Antigonus was taken and most of his men; these Brutus took with him, secured, captured and bound by their word.

307 Pandrasus was in great distress for his brother and the rest of the men. In the morning he gathered his army together and put siege to Sparatin,[2] thinking Brutus was there with his prisoners. But he had entered the woods and taken his prisoners there; in the castle he had put six hundred knights, in addition to the archers. The king besieged the castle, arranging his barons round about and saying to each where he should be and from which angle he should attack. He had siege-

---

[1] *HRB* names the king here, and in the letter, as Pandrasus (chap. 8).

[2] *HRB* chap. 9: castle of Sparatinum; possibly derived from Sparta. See Tatlock p. 112.

Berfreiz fist e perreres faire
E fist suvent lancer e traire.
Le berfrai fist al mur joster
E les perreres fist geter.
Cil dedenz ki sunt as kernels
Traient saietes e quarels,
Granz pieres gettent e granz fuz
E lancent darz e pels aguz.
Engigneors ourent isnels
330 Ki tost ourent fait mangunels
As perieres contregeter;
N'i osa puis home arester.
Li autre unt feu aparailliez
Si l'unt sur le berfrei lanciez,
Tut l'unt mis en pudre e en cendre;
Mult se penouent d'els defendre.
Kant veit li reis que ne li valt,
Que nes puet prendre par assalt
Ne par nul engin ke il face,
340 Trait sei en sus e sis manace.
L'ost fist clore tut environ
De bon fossé a heriçon;
N'i laissa ke sul treis entrees
E celes furent bien gardees.
Puis jura k'il n'en turnereit
Dessi ke le chastel avreit.
Cil ki dedenz erent asis
Virent que ja ne serrunt pris [1]
Se primes ne sunt afamé.
350 La faim criement, kar poi unt blé;
Grant gent sunt e poi unt vitaille.
Pur ço k'il criement qu'ele faille,
Mandent lur duc qu'il les socure,
[Kar se li socurs lur demure,] [2]
Par la faim les estovra rendre,
De cel ne se püent defendre.
    Brutus fu forment curius
Coment li suen fussent rescus;
Purpensa sei que il fereit,
360 Par quel engin les secoreit; [3]

Engieng quere li estuveit,
Kar vers tel ost force n'aveit.
Boisdie e engin deit l'en faire
Pur destrure sun adversaire,
E pur ses amis delivrer
Deit l'en en grant peril entrer.
Brutus pensa asez briefment;
Puis est coruz mult fierement
Si ad pris al top un prisun,
Anacletus aveit cil nun,   370
Pris ert od le frere le rei.
Brutus le traist forment vers sei;
En sun poin tint tut nu sun brant,
D'ocire le fist grant semblant.
'Mal culvert, fist il, ja murras, [4]
Ja cest jor ne trespasseras,
Ne tu ne li frere le rei,
Se tu ne guariz lui e tei;
Mais tu puez tei e lui saver [5]
E de ma prisun delivrer.'   380
'Tu feras, dist il, tun pleisir,
Mais, si jo puis nus dous guarir,
Di mei coment si nus guarrai.'
Brutus dist: 'Jol t'enseinerai.
Ennuit, dist il, emprés cele ore
Que l'en apele cholcheore,
A cels ki l'ost guaitent irras;
E as eschauguaites diras
Ke par engin e a larron
T'iés eschapés de ma prisun.   390
Le frere le rei m'as emblé
Mais en cel bois l'as tresturné,
Si ne l'oses avant mener
Pur mei ki faz le bois garder;
Viengent od tei si l'en merrunt.
E quant il la venu serrunt
De mun enbuschement saldrai
E tuz ensemble les prendrai.'
Anacletus ad graanté
Ço que Brutus ad purparlé,   400

---

[1] MS P reading—*virent*—restored.
[2] Line missing in MS P.
[3] MS P reading—*secoreit*—restored.
[4] MS P reading—*fist*—restored.
[5] MS P's wording of line restored.

Brutus's stratagem

towers and catapults made, and ordered frequent throwing and shooting. He had the siege-tower brought close to the wall and the catapults shoot stones. Those on the battlements inside threw arrows and bolts, great rocks, pieces of wood, javelins and sharpened stakes. They had fast engineers who quickly constructed mangonels to combat the catapults; nobody dared be present after that. Others prepared fireballs and launched them at the siege-tower, reducing everything to ashes and powder; they made great efforts to defend themselves.

337   When the king saw it was no use and he could not capture them by attack nor through any stratagem, he retired and threatened them. He had the garrison entirely surrounded by a fine ditch with a spiked stockade. Only three openings were left and those were closely guarded. Then he swore he would never leave until he had the castle. Those within saw they would never be captured unless they were first starved out. They dreaded hunger, for their corn was scarce; they were many and their provisions few. Because they feared food would run out, they sent word to their leader to help them, for if help was delayed, hunger would make them surrender; against that, they had no defence.

357   Brutus was very anxious about the means to rescue his people. He reflected on what he should do and by what stratagem he should help them: he had to find such a stratagem, because he did not have the might to combat such an army. One must employ ruse and deception to destroy one's enemy, and to rescue one's friends one must engage in great danger. Brutus thought for a moment, then fiercely ran and seized a prisoner by the hair, Anacletus by name, who had been captured with the king's brother. Brutus pulled him vigorously towards him; in one fist he held his naked sword and made a great show of killing him. 'Wicked wretch,' he said, 'now you will die; you will never survive this day, neither you nor the king's brother, unless you save him and yourself. But you can save him and yourself and escape my prison.'

381   'You will do as you please,' Anacletus said, 'but, if I can save us both, tell me how to do it.' Brutus said: 'I will teach you. Tonight, after the hour for sleep, you will go to those guarding the army and tell the watchmen that in secret and through a trick you have escaped from my prison. You have taken the king's brother away from me but left him in this forest, not daring to lead him any further because I have the forest watched. They should come with you and take him away. And when they do come there, I shall jump out of my ambush and capture them all together.' Anacletus agreed to what Brutus had plotted, and Brutus swore and pledged to him to release him, life and limb.

E Brutus li jure e afie
A clamer quite, menbre e vie.
La nuit, quant bien fu asseri,
Ke l'en deveit estre endormi,
Ad Brutus sa gent assemblee
Si se mist en une valee
Ke il out anceis purveüe
Dedenz le bois, prés de l'eissue.
Entur la valee, es busuns,
410 En treis leus mist ses compainuns.
Kant il out tut apparaillié
Anacletus ad pris congié;
As eschaugaites vint corant
Come s'il s'en alast fuiant.
Les eschauguaites l'aperçurent,
Tels i out ki bien le conurent;
Demandé li unt cum il vait
E ke li frere le rei fait.
'De prison, dist il, l'ai jeté,
420 Mais en cel bois l'ai resconsé,
Kar sols ne s'en osë eissir
Ainz vus estuet pur lui venir.
En anels est, ne puet aler,
Ne jo nel puis par mei porter.
Venez od mei, jo vus merrai;
Assez pruef d'ici le laissai. [1]
Bien avrez le rei succuru,
Kant cestui li avrez rendu.'
Cil quiderent ke veir deïst,
430 E ki quidast ke il mentist?
De traisun n'aveient dute,
Ver le bois dreit tindrent lur rute. [2]
Anacletus en la veie entre,
Il veit avant e cil süentre;
Menez les ad al leu tut dreit
U il sout que Brutus esteit,
E Brutus, ki ert bien guarniz,
Les ad de tutes parz saisiz;
Unches un suls n'en eschapa
440 Ne home a l'ost n'en renoncia. [3]

Dunc ad Brutus tuz ses armez
En treis parties devisez.
'Baron, dist il, en l'ost ireiz
E de treis parz les assaudreiz;
E jo irrai al tref le rei,
Alquans de vus ensemble od mei.
Mais gardez bien que nuls n'i fiere,
Ne cil devant ne cil deriere,
Ne que nul mot n'i ait soné
Desi ke jo avrai corné.   450
Quant jo al tref le rei serai,
Haltement mun corn sonerai;
E des que vus soner l'orrez,
Ja mar les Greus esparnirez;
Sure lur corez en dormant
Sis ociez demeintenant.'
Li chivaler l'unt fait issi
Come Brutus lur establi;
De treis parz sunt en l'ost entré,
Enmi les trefs sunt aresté.   460
Brutus nel fist pas lentement;
Al tref lu rei vint erraument,
E quant il dut dedenz entrer,
Par aïr fist sun corn suner.
Des que li suen l'unt entendu
Par tuz les trés sunt espandu.
Li Greu esteient endormi;
Ainz que il fussent estormi,
Out par les trés maint cop doné,
Maint puin, maint braz, maint pié copé,   470
Espandue mainte cervele
E perciee mainte büele.
Li Greu n'aveient nul leisir
D'armes prendre ne de fuïr,
Kar li Troïen les detienent
Ki devant lur destriers vienent [4]
Ne d'els ocire ne se feinent
U que il unches les atteinent.
Cil que de lur mains eschapoent
La u il melz garir quidouent,   480

---

[1] MS P reading—*d'ici*—restored.
[2] MS P reading—*ver*—restored.
[3] MS P reading—*n'en*—restored.
[4] MS P reading—*lur destriers*—restored.

Brutus defeats the Greeks

403 That night, when it was quite dark, and people were bound to be asleep, Brutus gathered his men together and took up position in a valley which he had earlier spotted, within the forest, near the way out. Round the valley, in the bushes, he positioned his companions in three places. When all had been arranged, Anacletus took his leave, and came running to the watchmen as if he were in flight. The watchmen, some of whom knew him well, noticed him and asked him how he was and what he had done with the king's brother. 'I got him out of prison,' he said, 'but I've hidden him in this forest, because he dare not come out on his own: you must come for him. He's in chains, and can't walk; I can't carry him on my own. Come with me, I'll take you there; I left him very close by. You will do the king great service by restoring him to him.' They believed he spoke the truth, and who would have thought he was lying? With no suspicion of treachery they went straight to the forest. Anacletus took the path; he went before, they behind. He led them straight to the spot where he knew Brutus was, and Brutus, well reinforced, had them seized from all sides. Not a soul escaped nor anyone to inform the army.

441 Then Brutus divided all his men into three companies. 'My lords,' he said, 'you will go to the army and attack it from three sides, and I will go to the king's tent, accompanied by some of you. But take care not to strike a blow, neither those in the van nor the rear, nor to utter a word until I have blown my horn. Once I am in the king's tent, I shall blow my horn loudly, and as soon as you hear it, don't spare a single Greek. Rush upon them in their sleep and kill them immediately.'

457 The knights did as Brutus had decreed; from three sides they made their way into the army, stopping amid the tents. Brutus was not slow off the mark: he quickly reached the king's tent and when he was about to enter, he fiercely sounded his horn. As soon as his men heard it, they spread through the tents. The Greeks were asleep; before they could be called to arms, many a blow had been struck amongst the tents, many a hand, arm or foot cut off, many brains spattered and many bowels ripped open. The Greeks had no chance either to seize a weapon or to flee, because the Trojans, blocking access to their horses, held them back, and did not fail to slay them wherever they found them. Those who evaded their hands, just where they thought they could most easily escape,

As granz faleises desrochouent
U as fluives parfunz neouent;[1]
De tutes parz trovoent mal.
Brutus, ki vint al tref real,
Prist le rei tut vif e tut sain;
Quant li soleiz leva al main,
El chastel od sei le mena
E a guarder le comanda.
Puis ad le guaain assemblé
490 Tut l'ad as chevaliers duné,
E par ban comanda as vis
K'il enterrassent les ocis.
　　Le jur emprés prist de sa gent
Les plus sages priveement;
Conseil demanda k'il fereit
Del rei de Grece k'il aveit,
Si l'ocireit, u retendreit,[2]
U tut quite le clamereit;
Par lur conseil en vult errer,[3]
500 Que ne l'en puissent puis blasmer.
Cil furent de divers pensez
Si unt divers conseilz donez.
Li un li louent a requere
Une partie de sa terre
U la lur gent maner peüst
E quitance e franchise eüst;
Li un loent e mult lur pleist
Ke li reis aler les en laist;
Aler vuelent en altres regnes
510 Od lur enfanz e od lur femes.
Endementres k'il vunt dutant
Lequel conseil prengent avant,
Si s'escria Menbritius,
Uns sages hom, ki leva sus:
'Pur quei, dist il, estes en dote?
Entre vus tuz ne veez gute.
Dunt n'est ço la mieldre sentence
Ke d'aler franc querum licence?
Duinst nus li reis or e argent,
520 Duinst nus nés e duinst nus furment,

E doinst nus quanque ad mestier
As nés conduire e a mangier;
E doinst al duc, nostre seinnor,
Innorgen, sa fille, a oisur;
Puis irrum quere mansions
Par alienes regions
Kar si nus od lui remanons,
Si mal eümes, pis avroms;
Jamais as Greus nen avrom pais,
Kar il n'ublierunt jamais   530
Lur parenz, lur uncles, lur peres,
Lur cosins, lur nevuz, lur freres
Ne lur altres amis precains
Que nus avum morz a noz mains.
Sachiez que il les vengerunt
Des que tens e leu en verrunt.[4]
Mult est fols ki el en espeire,
Ja, dit l'on, cui mal faiz nel creire;
Jamais ne crerrai lur manaie;
De vieuz mesfait nuvele plaie.   540
Nus lur avum asez mesfait,
Jo ne quid ke nul en i ait
Ki n'ait par nus damage eü,
U ami u parent perdu.
Fiz i ad remis e cosins[5]
Ke nus avums fait orphenins
Ki encore en querrunt vengance,
Nel mettrunt mie en ubliance.
Nus descrestrums e il crestrunt,
Nus descharrums e il sordrunt;   550
E se il püent une feiz
Venir el desus, vus verrez,
U vus u cil ki dunc vivrunt,
Ke tut cil de Troie murrunt,
E nus l'avum bien deservi.
Pur si fait mal cum jo vus di
Vus lo jo mettrë a la veie,
Se Brutus, nostre dux, l'otreie.'
A ceste parole out grant bruit:
'Bien dit, bien dit!' ço dient tuit.   560

---

[1] MS P reading—as—restored.
[2] MS P's reading of line restored.
[3] MS P reading—errer—restored.
[4] MS P reading—verrunt—restored.
[5] MS P reading—remis—restored.

Menbritius advises the Trojans to leave Greece

fell from huge rocky cliffs or drowned in deep rivers. Misfortune met them on all sides. Brutus, coming into the royal tent, captured the king alive and well. At sunrise in the morning, he took him to the castle with him and ordered him to be guarded. Then he collected the booty and gave it all to the knights, and by proclamation ordered the living to bury the dead.

493 The day after, he took the wisest of his people aside, and privately asked them for advice on what he should do with the king of Greece. Should he kill him, keep him, or release him entirely? He wished to act according to their advice, so that they could not blame him later. They were in various minds and gave various advice. Some counselled him to demand a portion of the king's land where their people might live, formally released and exempt from dues. Others counselled what they most desired, that the king should let them go; they wanted to go to other realms with their wives and children.

511 While they were hesitating about which advice to choose, Menbritius, a wise man, got up and cried: 'Why are you uncertain? You are quite blind, the lot of you. Isn't the best decision to ask permission to freely depart? Let the king give us silver and gold, ships and wheat, and let him give us whatever we need to eat and to steer the ships. And let him give our lord the duke Innogen, his daughter, to wife. Then we will go and seek dwellings in foreign parts. For if we stay here with him, what was bad in the past will be worse in future; we shall never be at peace with the Greeks, for they will never forget their kin, their uncles, fathers, cousins, nephews, brothers or their other close friends who have died at our hands. Be sure they will avenge them as soon as they have the time and the place. Anyone who hopes for anything else is mad; an evil-doer can never be trusted. I will never believe in their mercy: fresh wounds will come from old wrongs.[1] We have wronged them, to be sure: there can't be one of them, I believe, who hasn't suffered through us, or lost a friend or relative. There remain sons and cousins whom we have orphaned, who will yet seek to avenge it and will not forget it. We will diminish and they will increase, we will decline and they will grow; and if they can once get the upper hand, then you'll see, you or those alive then, that all the Trojans will die, and we'll have well deserved it. Because of such a disaster as I describe, I advise you to set out, if Brutus, our leader, agrees.'

559 At these words there was uproar. 'Well said, well said!' cried everyone. Then they

---

[1] Probably proverbial. See Morawski, *Proverbes*, no. 2491, for a close analogy.

Dunc firent le rei amener
Si l'unt fait devant els ester.
Tuit li crient que ja murra
E sis freres ja ne garra,
Se de l'aler congied nen unt
Od l'avier que il nomerunt.
Dunc li unt tut nomé l'aveir,
Les nés, le blé, l'altre estuveir;
E sa fille li unt rovee
570 Si iert a lur duc mariee.
Li reis vit que la force ert lur
E de murir out grant poür;
A tuz ensemble ad otrié
Franchise e de l'aler congiez. [1]
'En prison, dist il, me tenez
E ma fille me demandez;
Ma fille avrez, n'en pus faire el, [2]
Mais a mun enimi mortel,
A cruel home e a felun
580 La durrai, u jo voille u nun;
Mais alques me confortera
Ke gentilz hom e pruz l'avra.
Les nés, le furment, la viande
E l'aveir ke l'en me demande
Vus durrai jo plenierement;
E si vus veneit a talent
K'en cest païs remansissiez,
Tuit franc e quite serriez,
Si vus durreie par esguard
590 De ma terre la tierce part.'
Cil ne voldrent mie remaindre
Ne de lur requeste refraindre.
Dunc tramist li reis ses messages
Par Grece as porz e as rivages;
Tutes les nés fist assembler
Ke poeient par mer sigler;
Eslites furent les meillurs,
Les plus fortes e les greinnors;
Celes furent appareillees
600 E de vitaille bien chargiees;

Les plus bels aveirs del païs
E les plus chiers unt es nés mis.
E li reis sa fille amena,
Innogen, al duc la duna;
E plus li ad assez duné
Que Brutus n'aveit demandé;
N'i out vassal, n'i out baron
Cui li reis ne donast bel don;
Sulunc ço que chescuns valeit
Plus bel dun e plus riche aveit. [3]   610
  Des que il orent buen oré
N'unt mie lunges demoré;
As porz vindrent, es nés entrerent, [4]
Lur trés e lur veilles leverent;
Seze vint nés e quatre furent
Quant des porz de Grece s'esmurent. [5]
Deus jors e une nuit siglerent,
Qu'a port n'a rive ne turnerent;
Al secund jor vindrent siglant
A Leogice a l'avesprant   620
A l'ille vindrent, sus munterent,
Home ne feme n'i troverent;
Tut unt trové le païs guast
Ke n'i aveit kil gaainnast. [6]
Utlage l'orent tut guasté
Chacied la gent, l'aveir porté.
Tute esteit la terre en guastine,
Mais mult i aveit salvagine.
Li Troïen assez en pristrent
E en lur nés assez en mistrent;   630
Lunc tens aprés, a grant fuisun,
Lur en dura la veneison.
Guaste unt trovee une cité
E un temple d'antiquité.
L'imagë ert d'une deuesse,
Diane, une divineresse:
Diables esteit, ki la gent
Deceveit par enchantement;
Semblance de feme perneit
Par quei le pople deceveit.   640

---

¹ MS P reading of line restored.   ⁴ MS P reading—*As porz*—restored.
² MS P reading—*pus*—restored.   ⁵ MS P reading—*des porz*—restored.
³ MS P reading—*riche*—restored.   ⁶ MS P reading—*kil*—restored.

Brutus and his people leave Greece

had the king brought to stand before them. They all shouted that he would certainly die, and his brother would not escape either, if they did not get leave to depart with the goods they would name. Then they described all the goods: ships, corn, the other provisions; and they asked for his daughter to be married to their leader. The king saw they had power on their side and he was very fearful of dying. He promised liberty and leave to go to everyone. 'You keep me prisoner,' he said, 'and demand my daughter. You shall have my daughter, I can't do otherwise; but I'm giving her, whether I like it or not, to my mortal enemy, a cruel and wicked man. But it is some comfort that a brave and nobly-born man will have her. The ships, the wheat, the food and goods asked of me I will give you in full; and should you wish to stay in this land, you will be quite free and at liberty, and I will give you, as is just, the third part of my land.'[1] They would neither stay nor moderate their demands.

593 Then the king sent his messengers throughout Greece, to the harbours and shores, and all the ships were gathered which could sail the seas. The best were chosen, the strongest and the largest; these were equipped and loaded full of food. They put on board ship the finest and dearest possessions in the land. And the king brought his daughter, Innogen, and gave her to the duke. And he gave him much more than Brutus had asked for: there was no knight or lord to whom the king did not give a fine gift. According to each man's worth, so he had a finer and dearer gift.

611 Once they had a good wind, they did not stay long. They arrived at the harbours, entered the ships, and raised their masts and their sails. There were three hundred and twenty-four ships when they set out from the Greek ports. They sailed for two days and a night without landing at a port or shore. On the second day, at nightfall, they came sailing towards Leogice.[2] They arrived at the island, climbed all over it, but found neither man nor woman: the land was quite deserted, with no one to cultivate it. Pirates had laid it entirely waste, driven the people away and carried off their goods. The country was a waste-land, but there was much game. The Trojans took plenty of it, and put plenty into their ships; the abundance of venison lasted them a long time afterwards.

633 They found a deserted city and an ancient temple. The idol was that of a goddess, Diana, a prophetess. She was a devil who deceived the people through sorcery, taking the appearance of a woman by which to delude them. She called

---

[1] *HRB* (chap. 15) praises Brutus at length here, and subsequently describes the grief of Innogen at leaving, and Brutus's tenderness to her, all omitted by *VV* and Wace.

[2] *HRB*: *Leogetia*, perhaps invented by Geoffrey, modelled on Leucate in the *Aeneid* (see Keller, 'Toponymical Problems' p. 694). See Tatlock p. 113 and Blenner-Hassett, *A Study of the Place-Names*, p. 44, who thinks it is probably the island of Levkas, the ancient Leucadia.

Diane se fesait numer
E deuesse del bois clamer. [1]
Kant cele terre esteit poplee,
Ert l'image bien coltivee
E tenue ert en grant enur;
La veneient li anceisur
Pur demander e pur oïr
Del tens ki esteit a venir.
Diane lur donout respuns
650 Par signes e par visiuns.
Brutus prist doze des ainz nez,
Des plus justes, des plus senez,
E un pruveire de lur lei,
Gerion, sis mena od sei;
A l'ymage vint en la crote,
Defors laissa l'altre gent tute.
En sa main destre out un vaissel
Plein de vin e de leit novel
Ki d'une blanche bisse esteit,
660 Come Diane requereit.
Par plusurs fez s'umilia [2]
E la deuesse depreia
Ke par respuns li enseinnast
U par signe li demustrast
Quel region purreit trover
Bone e paisible a converser.
Par noef feiz fist ceste preiere
Od basse voiz, od simple chiere;
E par noef feiz l'alter baisa
670 E par noef feiz l'avirona,
En sa main le hanap portant.
Puis l'espandi el fu ardant
Que il aveit fait alumer
Devant l'image, lez l'alter.
Puis ad pris le quir de la bisse
Dunt il out fait le sacrefice;
Jus a la terre l'estendi,
Desur se jut si s'endormi.
Vis li fu, la u il dormeit,
680 Que la deuesse li diseit:

'Ultre France, luinz dedenz mer
Vers Occident, purras trover
Une ille bone e abitable
E a maneir mult delitable.
Bone est la terre a cultiver,
Gaiant i soelent abiter.
Albion ad non, cele avras,
Une Troie nove i feras.
De tei vendra reial ligniede
Ki par le mund iert esalciede.'   690
Quant la vision fu finee
E Brutus l'out bien recordee,
Graces rendi a la deuesse
E si li fist vou e premesse
Ke se la terre aver poeit
Ke par sunge li prameteit,
Temple e image li fereit
E a tuz tenz l'enorereit. [3]
Puis ad sa visiun contee
Si com ele li ert mostree   700
A ses homes ki l'atendeient,
E ki el temple esté aveient.
   Dunc sunt tuit as nés repaired,
Tant unt siglé, tant unt nagied,
Tant unt eü oré e vent
Qu'en trente jors roondement
Dessi as porz d'Alfrice vindrent.
Mais par devant lur eire tindrent,
Le lac passerent de Salins
E les alteus as Philistins: 710
Rucikadam unt trespassé
E les montaines d'Azaré;
Illuec unt udlages trovez
Ki forment les unt desturbez,
Kar encontr'els se combatirent;
Mais li Troïen les venquirent,
Aveir lur tolirent mult grant,
Dunt il furent riche e manant.
Malvan cel fluvie trespasserent, [4]
E en Mauritanie ariverent.   720

---

[1] MS P reading—*del*—restored.
[2] MS P reading—*fez*—restored.
[3] MS P reading—*a tuz tenz*—restored.
[4] MS P: *Nalvant*.

Brutus leaves Leogice

herself Diana, claiming to be goddess of the forest. When the land was inhabited, the idol was worshipped and greatly revered; the men of those days came there to ask and hear about the time to come. Diana replied to them through signs and visions. Brutus took twelve of the oldest, wisest and most righteous men and a priest of their religion, Gerion, with him to the idol in the cave, leaving all the other people outside. In his right hand he had a vessel full of wine, and new milk from a white hind, as Diana required. He prostrated himself several times and begged the goddess to teach him by a reply, or show him by a sign, where he could find a good and peaceful land to dwell in. Nine times he made this prayer, with a low voice and humble face, nine times he kissed the altar and nine times he encircled it, carrying the goblet in his hand. Then he sprinkled it on the blazing fire which he had had lit before the idol, next to the altar. Then he took the skin of the hind which had been sacrificed, stretched it out on the ground, lay on it and went to sleep.

679 It seemed to him, as he lay asleep, that the goddess said: 'Beyond France, far away in the sea towards the West, you can find a fine island, fit to live in and delectable to dwell in, whose ground is good for cultivation. Giants used to live there. Its name is Albion. This you shall have, and you will make a new Troy there. From you will spring a royal lineage esteemed throughout the world.' When the vision ended and Brutus had faithfully committed it to memory, he gave thanks to the goddess and made her a vow and a promise that if he could have the land she promised him in the dream, he would make a temple and statue for her and always pay her honour. Then he related his vision, as it was shown to him, to his men who were waiting for him and had been in the temple.

703 Then they all went back to the ships, and sailed and rowed so much, and had so much wind and good weather that in a round thirty days they came to the gates of Africa.[1] But they kept pressing on, passing the Saline Lake and the altars of the Philistines. They travelled through Rucikadam and the mountains of Azaré.[2] There they found pirates, who caused them much trouble by fighting them. But the Trojans beat them and took many goods from them, through which they became rich and powerful. They crossed the river Malvan and arrived in Mauri-

---

[1] The Straits of Gibraltar.
[2] Features of this journey were appropriated by *HRB*, probably from *HB* chap. 15, describing the journey of the Scythians to Ireland. The geographical names here were in turn borrowed from Orosius, *Historia Adversum Paganos* I, chap. 2, in his description, not of a journey, but of

North Africa. He mentions the lake of Salinae, (2.90), the Altars of the Philaeni (a frontier town in Cyrene, 2.87), the city of Rusiccada in Numidia (2.92; now Skikda), the Uzarae mountains (2.92; *Zarec* in *HRB* chap. 17; *VV*: *Azare*), and the Malva river (Muluya river, separating Algeria and Morocco).

Pur viande e pur bevre quere
Sunt de lur nés eissu a terre;
Tute la terre unt desguastee,
D'une mer a l'altre robee.
Robe e aveir unt asez pris,
Puis se sunt a la veie mis.
Siglé unt e passé mult prés
Des bornes que fist Herculés,
Unes colonnes k'il ficha,
730 Ço fu uns signes k'il mustra
Ke dessi la aveit conquis
U il aveit cez piliers mis.
Les sereines unt la trovees
Ki lur nés unt mult desturbees
Sereinnes sunt monstres de mer,
Des chiefs poënt femes sembler,
Peison sunt del nomblil aval, [1]
As mariniers unt fait maint mal.
Vers occident es granz mers hantent,
740 Duces voiz unt, dulcement chantent;
Par lur duz chant les fols atraient
E a deceivre les asaient.
Li fol home ki lur chanz oient [2]
De la dulçur del chant s'esjoient;
Lur veie oblient e guerpissent
E, se par tens ne s'avertissent,
Tant les funt par mer foleier
Ke sovent les funt periller;
U al mains lur dreit eire perdent.
750 Par mainte feiz as nés s'aerdent
E tant les tienent e demorent
Ke a roche u en peril corent. [3]
Mult funt a criendre les sereines
Kar de felonie sunt pleines;
Ne puet pas d'eles eschaper
Huem ki bien ne s'en seit guarder.
Figure portent de Diable,
La cui ovre est tant delitable
E tant est duce a maintenir
760 K'a peine s'en poet l'on partir;

E cil ki a s'ovre s'aert
Sa dreite veie e sun cors pert,
Si come cil vait malement
Ki as sereinnes trop entent.
Li Troïen les aperçurent,
Lur chanz oïrent sis conurent; [4]
Oï en aveient parler
Si nes voldrent mie escolter;
A lur nés entur s'aerdeient,
A bien pruef neier nes faiseient;   770
A grant peine s'en eschaperent
E juste Espaine trespasserent.
     La troverent a un rivage
Des Troïens de lur lignage
Quatre granz generaciuns,
Que Antenor, uns des barons,
Amena de Troie fuitis
Quant li Greu les orent conquis;
Corineüs les mainteneit, [5]
Ki lur sire e lur dux esteit.   780
Corineüs esteit mult granz,
Hardiz e forz come gaianz;
Cil ad oï e entendu
Que cele gent de Troie fu
Qui aloent tere querant
Qu'il eüssent a remanant.
De lur venue fu mult liez
Si s'est a els acompainiez;
E de sa gent bien grant partie
Se sunt mis en sa compainie. [6]   790
Brutus l'ama mult e cheri,
E mult ad en lui boen ami. [7]
     Quant il murent des porz d'Espaine
Lur eire pristrent vers Bretaine:
N'ert pas Bretaine encor nomee
Ainz ert Armoriche apelee.
A destre main Peitou laisserent;
Tant siglerent e tant nagierent
Que al rivage vindrent dreit
La u la mer Leire receit.   800

---

[1] MS P reading—*Peison*—restored.
[2] MS P reading—*chanz*—restored.
[3] MS P reading—*en*—restored.
[4] MS P reading—*chanz*—restored.
[5] MS P: *Corneus*.
[6] MS P reading—*sa*—restored.
[7] MS P reading—*ad*—restored.

The Trojans reach Spain and France

tania. They disembarked, in order to seek food and drink, and ravaged the whole land, plundering from shore to shore. They took plenty of booty and possessions, then went on their way. They passed and sailed very close to the boundaries established by Hercules,[1] a column he set up as a sign to show he had conquered up to the place he put these pillars.

733 They found the Sirens there, who greatly troubled their ships. Sirens are sea monsters, with heads seemingly of women, who are fish from the navel down. They have done much harm to sailors. They frequent the great oceans in the West, have soft voices and sing sweetly. By their sweet song they attract fools and try to deceive them. The foolish men who hear their songs take pleasure in their sweetness; they forget and abandon their way and, if they do not perceive it in time, are made to wander so much over the seas that often they perish, or at least lose their right path. Many times the Sirens cling to the ships and grasp and delay them so much that they run into rocks or danger. They are greatly to be feared, because they are so treacherous: a man unable to protect himself cannot escape them. They get their shape from the Devil, whose handiwork is so delightful and so sweet to live with that it is hard to leave, and he who holds fast to it loses his path and his right way, just as he who listens overmuch to the Sirens comes to a bad end. The Trojans noticed them, they heard their songs and recognised them; they had heard tell of them and had no wish to listen. The Sirens clung around their ships, very nearly sinking them. With great difficulty they escaped and reached Spain.

773 There they found, on the banks of a river, Trojans from their race, four whole generations descended from the fugitives whom lord Antenor had brought from Troy when the Greeks had defeated them. Corineus, their lord and duke, governed them. He was a very powerful man, bold and strong as a giant. He had heard and understood that these people, travelling in search of land which they could have in abundance, were from Troy. He was very glad of their coming and accompanied them, and a large part of his people accompanied him. Brutus greatly loved and cherished him, and found him to be a very good friend.

793 Once they had left the Spanish ports, they made their way towards Brittany. It was not yet called Brittany, but bore the name Armorica. Leaving Poitou on their right, they sailed and rowed so hard that they came straight to the shore where the sea receives the Loire. There, where the Loire joins the sea, the whole fleet

---

[1] Wace has to explain the Pillars of Hercules, whereas *HRB* (chap. 17) does not: a difference in the education of the audience?

La u Leire a la mer s'asemble[1]
Vint la navie tute ensemble.
Set jurz unt illuec atendu,
Le païs e l'estre veü.
Goffiers, ki ert reis de Peitiers,
I enveia ses messagiers
Pur enquerre quel gent esteient,
Se pais u bataille quereient;
Humbert, ki bien saveit parler,
810 Fu a cel message porter.
Corineüs ert fors eissuz,
Des nefs esteit al bois venuz
Od dous cenz homes, pur chacier
E pur la contree cerchier.
Li message l'unt encontré
Si li unt sempres demandé
Par cui los e par cui guarant
Il vait par la forest chaçant.
'Li reis, ço dient, ad fait vié
820 Qu'il n'i ait bersé ne chacié
Ne adesee veneisun
En la forest, se par lui nun.
Coment i oses bisse prendre
Puis ke li reis l'ad fait defendre?'
Corineüs ad respundu
'Se vostre reis l'ad defendu,
De sa defense ren ne sai[2]
Ne jo neient ne la tendrai.'
Humberz tint un arc sil tendi,
830 Ferir l'en volt, mais il guenchi;[3]
Corociez fu, avant sailli,
L'arc ke Humberz teneit saisi,
Parmi le chief tant l'enbati
Que la cervele en espandi.
Si compainum s'en sunt fuï
Si unt Humberz gisant guerpi;
Al rei Goffar unt descuvert
Coment l'on aveit mort Numbert.
Li reis le vult aler vengier
840 E de la terre cels chacier;

De sun servant mult li pesa.
Riches huem fu, granz genz manda.[4]
Brutus le sout par ses espies;
Totes ses nefs ad bien garnies
De bone robe e de vitaille,
Si mist enz tute la rengaille,
Si lur dist que ja n'en eississent
Pur nule noise qu'il oïssent[5]
Dessi qu'il a els reparast,[6]
U que sun estre lur mandast.   850
S'altre gent ad mis en conrei
Si est alez contre le rei.
E li reis vint si se mellerent,
D'ambedous parz granz cops dunerent;
Li Peitevin bien les requierent,
Li Troïen bien les refierent;
Lungement se sunt combatu
Que cist ne cil ne sunt vencu.
Corineüs out grant verguinne,
Ki mult ert buen en la busuine,   860
Que li Peitevin sunt si fort
Que ja ne sunt vencu ne mort.
Devers destre sa gent alie
Si lur ad fait une envaïe;
La bataille ad par mi fendue,
Destre e senestre mult en tue.
A cel enchauz perdi s'espee,
Mais une hache ad recovree,
El puin li vint par aventure.
Dunc fu la mellee plus dure;   870
Ki de la hache ert conseüz
Tut ert parmi le cors fenduz.
Li Troïen ki l'esgardouent
E li altre s'esmerveillouent[7]
Del grant hardement qu'il portout
E des granz cops que il dunout.
Trestut ad fait departir l'ost;
N'i ad nul ki atendre l'ost.
Corineüs les enchaçout
E as dos detriés lur criout: 880

---

[1] MS P reading—*s'asemble*—restored.
[2] MS P reading—*ren*—restored.
[3] MS P's reading of line restored.
[4] MS P reading—*granz genz*—restored.
[5] MS P reading—*noise*—restored.
[6] MS P reading—*reparast*—restored.
[7] MS P reading—*s'esmerveillouent*—restored.

Corineus attacks the Poitevins

arrived. For a week they stayed there, observing the country and the way of life. Goffar,[1] king of Poitiers, sent his messengers to enquire what sort of people they were and if they sought peace or war; the eloquent Humbert was about to carry this message. Corineus disembarked and went into the forest with two hundred men, to hunt and to scrutinize the countryside. The messengers came upon him and at once asked him by whose advice and whose authority he was hunting in the forest. 'The king,' they said, 'has forbidden any shooting, hunting, or even approaching game in the forest, except by himself. How dare you take a hind when the king has prohibited it?' Corineus replied: 'If your king has prohibited it, I know nothing about his prohibition, nor shall I obey it.' Humbert held a bow; he bent it, intending to hit him, but Corineus dodged. Angry, he rushed forward, seized the bow Humbert held, and beat him over the head with it so hard that his brains spilt out.

837   His companions fled, leaving Humbert lying there, and told king Goffar how he had been killed. The king wanted to go and avenge him and drive these people from his land; he was very grieved for his servant. A powerful man, he summoned a great host. Brutus discovered this through his spies. He thoroughly provisioned all his ships with excellent booty and food, and put all the army servants inside, telling them not to come out, regardless of anything they heard, until he came back to them, or let them know their situation. He arranged his other men into troops and proceeded against the king.

853   And the king came and the two sides joined battle, each striking great blows. The Poitevins attacked them hard, the Trojans fought back hard; for a long time they fought without either winning. Corineus—of great value in the situation— felt great shame that the Poitevins were so strong they were neither defeated nor dead. He rallied his men towards the right and attacked the other side, breaking through the ranks and killing many to the right and left. In the pursuit he lost his sword, but gained an axe, which by chance came to hand. Thus the fighting was even more brutal: everyone reached by the axe was split right down the body. Looking at him, the Trojans and the other side both marvelled at his great daring and his great blows. He completely routed the army; no one dared await him. Corineus pursued them and behind their backs shouted: 'Cowards, why are

---

[1] *HRB* chap. 18: king of Aquitaine. Wace habitu-
ally 'updates' and vernacularises geographical
names.

'Malvaise gent, pur quei fuiez,
Ki combatre vus deviez?
Pur quei alez vus trestornant?
Quidez me vus veintre en fuiant?
Mustrez que vus avez ci quis
Si defendez vostre païs .
Vus fuiez trop vilainnement
Ki fuiez pur mei sulement;
Ja estes vus plus d'un millier
890 Si fuiez pur un chevalier.
Ne savez cele part fuïr
Que jo ne vus face murir;
Mais riches conforz vus puet estre
Que vus murrez od ceste destre
Dunt jo ai maint bon cop duné
E maint millier d'omes tué
E maint gaiant par mi trenchié
E en enfern maint enveié.
E quatre e quatre, e treis e treis,
900 Venez ça, ferez demaneis!'
Suharz, uns des reals, oï[1]
Sun grant orguil e sun fier cri;
Od treis cenz chevaliers armez
Est vers Corineüm turnez.
De tutes parz li sunt coru;
Jal quiderent aveir vencu,
Mais Corineüs s'adreça,
A Suharz vint, tel li duna
Qu'il le fendi en dous meitiez
910 D'en sum le chief dessi as piez.[2]
Des altres fist tel tueïz
Come leüns fait de berbiz,
Nuls n'i aveit defensiun
Plus que berbiz contre leün.
Brutus od tuz ses Troïens
Li vint aider parmi lé rencs;
Dunc crut la noise e crut l'ocise,
Mainte alme i out fors de cors mise.
Briefment vus en dirrai la fin,
920 Vencu furent li Peitevin.

Gofier, ki en out grant pesance,
Pur querre aïe ala en France
As doze pers ki la esteient,
Ki la terre en doze parteient.
Chescuns des duze en chief teneit
E rei apeler se feseit.
Tuit doze unt a Gofier pramis
A vengier de ses enemis
E il les en ad mercied;
Dunc unt lur homes assembled.   930
  Brutus fu liez de la victorie
E del gaain e de la glorie;
Tutes les terres ad guastees,
Les viles arses e robees.
Mult unt robé, mult unt guasté;
A un tertre sunt aresté,
En sum unt fait un chastelet,
Unc ainz n'i out eü recet,
Ne burc, ne vile, ne maisun;
Mais, si com nus lit avum,[3]   940
Par l'ovrainne de cele gent
Out Turs primes comencement,
Turs la cité, ki encor dure,
Qui Turs out nun d'une aventure
Ki jesqu'a poi vus sera dite
Si come jo la truis escrite.
Li Troïen se sunt atrait
El chastel quant il l'orent fait;
Dous jurz i aveient esté
Puis que il l'aveient fermé;   950
Es vus Gofier od les Franceis,
Od les contes e od les reis;
Le tertre vit achastelé,
A merveille li ad pesé.
'De duel, dist il, me puis dever,
Duel me devreit del sens geter:
Les feluns vei ki m'unt chacié
E ki mun regne unt eissillied,
E desur ço, estre mun gré
Unt fait chastel en m'erité.   960

---

[1] MS P: *Huharz.*
[2] MS P reading—*D'en sum*—restored.
[3] MS P reading—*lit*—restored.

The Trojans build Tours

you fleeing him you should fight? Why are you running away? Do you think you'll defeat me by flight? Show me what you came for and defend your country. If you're just fleeing from me, your flight is most infamous. You must be more than a thousand, fleeing from one knight. You don't know where to flee without my killing you. But this will comfort you enormously: that you will die by this right hand, with which I've given many splendid blows, and killed many thousands of men, and cleft many giants in two, and sent many to hell. Three by three and four by four, come on, strike without delay!'

901 Suharz, one of the king's men, heard his proud cry and his great arrogance. With three hundred armed knights he turned towards Corineus. They ran at him from all sides, believing they had certainly defeated him. But Corineus rose, came towards Suharz, and gave him such a blow that he split him in two halves from the top of his head down to his feet. The others he slaughtered as a lion does sheep; they were as defenceless as sheep before a lion. Brutus with all his Trojans came to his aid amidst the ranks. Then the tumult and the slaughter increased, for he separated many a soul from its body. I will quickly tell you the outcome: the Poitevins were beaten. Goffar, greatly distressed, went to France to get help from the twelve peers there[1] among whom the land was divided. Each of the twelve was an independent nobleman and had himself called king. All twelve promised Goffar vengeance on his enemies, and he thanked them. Then they gathered their men together.

931 Brutus was delighted with the victory, the booty and the glory. He laid the whole land waste, burning and pillaging the cities. Great was the spoil and the plunder. They stopped at a hill and on top of it built a fort; till then, it had never borne stronghold, city, town nor house, but, according to what we have read, it was by the labour of these people that Tours first came into being, the city of Tours, which still stands and took its name from an event which in a little while will be told you, just as I found it written down.[2] When the Trojans had made the castle, they gathered together in it; they spent twelve days there after building it.

952 Then Goffar arrived, with the French counts and kings. He saw the fortified hill and it greatly grieved him. 'Sorrow will send me out of my mind,' he said, 'sorrow will make me lose my senses. I see the wretches who have driven me out and ravaged my kingdom and, on top of that, they have, against my will, made a castle in the land of my inheritance. Lords of France, let us arm at once and sharply

---

[1] *HRB* chap. 19: Goffar goes to Gaul and gets help from twelve kings. Wace shows the influence of *chansons de geste*.

[2] Wace dispenses with *HRB*'s reference to Homer testifying to the foundation of Tours (chap. 19),

but shows constant interest in why and how places get their names—see para. 1007. Tours called after Turnus goes back to *HB* chap. 10, but that is the Turnus who is killed by Aeneas.

Baron franceis, tost nus armum
E vivement les assaillum!'
Dunc s'armerent si se partirent;
Doze conreiz des Franceis firent, [1]
Puis sunt dreit al chastel venuz,
E cil dedenz sunt fors eissuz,
Li Franceis les unt bien feru
E cil les unt bien receü;
Es vus bataille bien ferue,
970 Chescuns del bien ferir s'argue. [2]
As premiers cops, en poi de tens,
En fu le mielz as Troïens:
Plus de dous mile unt morz jetez
Des Franceis, e plusurs naffrez.
Grant masse ariere les ruserent,
Mais li Franceis se recrierent,
E lur force tuz tens cresseit
Kar la lur gent tuz tens veneit;
Mis les unt par force el chastel. [3]
980 Dunc fu as Franceis le plus bel,
Le chastel unt tant assailli
Ke la nuit vint quis departi.
El chastel out bien grant trepeil;
A mie nuit unt pris conseil
Que Corineüs s'en istreit,
La sue gent od sei merreit
E en un bois s'embuchereit [4]
Ki assez pruef d'illuec esteit,
E quant Brutus se combatreit
990 Al matinet, del bois saldreit;
As Franceis survendreit as dos
Sis avreient entr'els enclos;
Issi purreient descunfire
Gofier le rei e sun empire.
Cel conseil unt tenu a buen.
Corineüs e tuit li suen
S'en eissirent al coc chantant,
El bois furent einz l'ajornant.
Brutus fist le chastel guaiter,
1000 Le plus des suens ad fait veiller,

E bien par matin s'en eissi,
As Franceis vint sis envaï.
Dunc refu fiere la bataille,
Mais sempres a la començaille,
Ainz que venist Corineüs,
Fu ocis niés Bruti Turnus.
Turnus ert de grant hardement
E fort ert merveillusement;
De force ne de vasselage
N'out sun per en tut le barnage, 1010
Ne qui ferist tant fierement
Fors Corineüm sulement;
Mult esteit hardiz e mult forz.
Des Franceis aveit sis cenz morz
Od sa main sule e od s'espee
Qui mult esteit ensanglantee.
Mais de sa gent trop s'elluinna
E les Franceis trop enchauça;
E cil l'unt aclos e nafré [5]
E entr'els l'unt mort craventé. 1020
Brutus l'en traist si l'en porta
E el chastel sus l'enterra.
Pur Turno qu'illuec fu ocis
E el chastel en terre mis
Fu puis Turs la vile apelee
E Toroinne entur la contree.
Brutus forment se combateit
E sun nevu vengier vuleit.
Corineüs l'ad secoru
Ki mult i fiert de grant vertu. 1030
As Franceis vint de l'altre part
Dunt il n'aveient nul regart;
Dunc veïssiez bataille grief,
Percié maint cors, trenchié maint chef.
Ne vus savreie mie escrire
Le tueïz ne le martire,
Le damage ne la dolur
Que des Franceis fu fait le jur.
Nes porent pas lunges suffrir,
Bien tost les en estuet fuïr. [6] 1040

---

[1] MS P reading—des—restored.
[2] MS P reading—del—restored.
[3] MS P reading—par—restored.
[4] MS P reading—s'embuchereit—restored.
[5] MS P reading—aclos—restored.
[6] MS P reading—estuet—restored.

The Trojans defeat the French

attack them!' Then they armed and set off. They divided the French into twelve troops, then came straight to the castle. And those within came out; the French struck them manfully and the others retaliated in kind. Here was a well-fought battle, everyone striving to strike their best. After the first blows, in a short time the Trojans had the best of it: they killed more than twelve thousand French, and wounded many. They drove them back a long way. But the French shouted repeatedly to each other in encouragement, and their army kept growing because their people kept arriving. They forced them back into the castle.

980 Then the French had the upper hand and attacked the castle so hard that only nightfall separated the two sides. Inside the castle there was much distress. At midnight they decided that Corineus would go out, taking his men with him, and hide in a wood close by, and when Brutus fought in the morning, Corineus would rush out. He would launch an attack behind the French and, between them, they would surround them. Thus they could destroy king Goffar and his empire. They thought this decision a good one. Corineus and all his men went out at cock-crow and were in the wood before daybreak. Brutus had the castle guarded, made most of his men keep watch, and in the morning came out, went to the French and attacked them. Then, once again, the battle was hard; but at the very start, before Corineus came, Brutus' nephew, Turnus, was killed.

1007 Turnus had great daring and amazing strength; there was no one to equal him amongst the nobles for strength or valour, nor anyone who struck so fiercely except for Corineus. He was very bold and very powerful. Six hundred French had died at his hands alone, and by his sword, which was covered with blood. But he left his men too far behind and pursued the French too closely, and they surrounded and wounded him, and between them knocked him down dead. Brutus dragged him away, carried him off, and buried him up in the castle. Because of Turnus, who was killed there and buried in the castle, the town was afterwards called Tours, and the surrounding countryside, Touraine.

1027 Brutus fought fiercely and wanted revenge for his nephew. Corineus, with incessant and powerful blows, helped him. He came upon the French from the other direction when they were unaware. Then heavy fighting could be seen, many bodies stabbed through, many heads cut off. I cannot describe to you the killing or the slaughter, the losses or the torment inflicted on the French that day. They could not endure it for long but soon had to flee. The Trojans pursued them,

1041 Li Troïen les parsoeient
Ki a la glaive les ocieient. [1]
Brutus fist ses grailles soner
Si fist ses homes returner.
Conseil pristrent qu'il s'en ireient
E cele terre guerpireient;
Pris unt lur robe e pris lur preie, [2]
As nés vindrent la dreite veie.
De lur guaain lur nés chargerent
1050 E de la terre s'esluinnerent.
Tant al soleil, tant as esteilles,
Tant as avirons, tant as veilles,
A Toteneis en Dertremue
Est tute la flote venue:
Ço est l'ille dunt la deuesse
Lur fist el sunge la premesse.
Des nés a terre fors eissirent;
Mult furent lied, grant joie firent.
De la terre qu'il unt trovee
1060 Que tant unt quise e desirree,
Unt tuz les travailz ubliez [3]
E les Deus en unt merciez.
  En cele ille gaianz aveit,
Nule gent altre n'i maneit.
Gaianz erent mult corporu,
Sur altres genz erent cremu; [4]
Ne vus sai lur nuns aconter
Ne nul n'en sai, fors un, nomer.
L'un sai nomer, cel vus puis dire,
1070 Goëmagog, qui ert lur sire. [5]
Pur sa force e pur sa grandur
L'orent li altre fait seinnur.
Cist e li altre as monz fuïrent
E la plaine terre guerpirent
Pur les Troïens qu'il haieient,
E lur saietes lur traeient.
Un jur firent Troïen feste
A la maniere de lur geste;
Caroles faiseient e geus
1080 Pur la joie des novels lieus

U il esteient assené,
Qui lur esteient destiné
E a els e a lur lignage
A tenir mais en eritage.
Es vus la vint gaianz venuz,
Des cavernes des munz eissuz;
Goëmagog devant alout,
Lur sire esteit e sis menout.
As Troïens corurent sure,
Mult en ocistrent en poi d'ure,   1090
Od pierres, od tinels, od pels,
En unt morz ne sai quanz ne quels.
Quant il s'en quiderent partir
E es montainnes revertir,
Li Troïen tant les hasterent
E tant cops e tels lur donerent
Od darz, od lances, od espees
E od saetes barbelees,
Les anmes lor firent roter.
Brutus fist le plus grant guarder,   1100
Goëmagog, pur essaier
Liquels ert plus fort a lutier,
Corineüs u li jeiant,
Kar chacuns ert merveille grant.
Corineüs i acorut
Des que il seut que lutier dut;
Prés de la mer en un champ plain,
Sur une faleise al terrain,
Ad Brutus la lute assemblee;
Volentiers l'unt tuit esguardee.   1110
Corineüs se rebraça,
Esterchi sei si se molla,
Des pans de la cote se ceinst, [6]
Parmi les flancs alques s'estreinst.
Goëmagog se racesma
E de lutier s'apareilla.
Braz a braz se sunt entrepris,
Braz unt desus e desuz mis.
Es les vus ensemble jostez,
Piz contre piz, lez contre lez;   1120

---

[1] MS P reading—*a la*—restored.
[2] MS P reading—*pris lur preie*—restored.
[3] MS P reading—*les*—restored.
[4] MS P reading—*cremu*—restored.
[5] MS P: *Gomagog* here and elsewhere.
[6] MS P reading—*la*—restored.

Corineus fights Gogmagog

putting them to death by sword. Brutus had his horns sounded and made his men withdraw. They decided they would go away and leave this land. Taking their booty and their loot, they went straight to their ships. They loaded them with their plunder and left the country far behind.

1051   Travelling partly by sunlight, partly by starlight, partly with oars, partly with sails, the whole fleet arrived at Totnes in Dartmouth.[1] This was the island the goddess had promised them in the dream. They disembarked, and were very happy and joyful. They forgot all their suffering for the land they had found, so long sought and desired, and gave thanks to the gods.

1063   There were giants in this island: no one else lived there. The giants were very large and more feared than other races. I cannot tell you their names; I know none of them except one, and that one, I can tell you, was Gogmagog, their leader. Because of his strength and size the others had made him their lord. He and the rest fled to the mountains and abandoned the plains to the Trojans whom they hated, and at whom they shot arrows. One day the Trojans made a feast, according to the custom of their people. They danced and played games for joy at the new place they had reached, which was destined for them and their race to hold henceforth as heritage. Thereupon the twenty giants appeared, out of the caves in the mountains, Gogmagog their lord in front, leading them. They ran upon the Trojans, killing many in a short time; with stones, clubs and stakes were killed I do not know who or how many. When the giants were about to leave to return to the mountains, the Trojans harassed them so fiercely and gave them so many and such hard blows with spears, lances, swords and barbed arrows that they made them belch out their souls. Brutus had the greatest, Gogmagog, placed in custody, to see who was the strongest at wrestling, Corineus or the giant, for each was a great phenomenon.

1105   Corineus ran forward as soon as he knew he was to wrestle. Near the sea on a flat field, on the firm ground of a cliff, Brutus brought them together for the wrestling, willingly watched by everyone. Corineus rolled up his sleeves, braced himself and flexed his muscles; he girded himself with the skirts of his tunic and slightly contracted his sides. Gogmagog in his turn prepared himself and made ready to wrestle. They seized each other by the arms, entwining them. There they were, one against the other, chest against chest, side against side; they squeez-

---

[1] Arnold (II, p. 794), suggests translating this as: 'at the town of Totnes in the Dart estuary'. Wace adds 'Dartmouth', as in *VV* chap. 20—in fact Totnes is nine miles up river from Dartmouth—but oddly does not name the whole island, as in *HRB*'s 'Albion'.

Par detriés les dos s'enbracerent,
Par grant aïr lur mains lacerent;
Dunc veïssez tur contre tur,
Vigur mettre contre vigur,
E pied avant e pied ariere,
E engieng de mainte maniere;
Tornent de ça, tornent de la,
Chescuns fud forz si s'aïra;
Des peitrines s'entrebutouent
1130 E des jambes luin s'aforchoent;
A la fiëde s'assembloent
Si que tut dreit a munt estoent.
Dunc les veïssez bien suffler,
E nés froncir e fronz suer,
Faces nercir, oilz roïller,
Sorcilz lever, sorcilz baissier,
Denz reschinner, colur muer,
Testes freier, testes hurter,
Buter e sacher e enpeindre,
1140 Lever, sufacher e restreindre,
Baisser e drescer e esmer
E jambet faire e tost turner.
A la hanche i out maint tor fait
E sus levé e a sei trait;
Chescuns vuleit l'altre sosprendre
E checuns s'en vuleit defendre. [1]
Goëmagog s'esvertua,
Ses braz estreinst, ses mains laça,
Corineüm vers sei sacha
1150 Si que treis costes li fruissa;
Mult le bleza, petit failli
Que desuz sei ne l'abati.
Corineüs, qui fud bleciez,
A quant qu'il pout s'est auciez, [2]
Le gaiant traist de tel aïr
Que les costes li fist fruissir; [3]
Un poi aval l'ad recovré
Si l'ad contre sun piz levé,
A un derube l'ad porté [4]
1160 Entre ses braz trestut pasmé;

Ovri ses mains, lascha ses braz,
Cil fud pesanz, si prist tel quaz
Aval la faleise el rochier,
N'i remist os a depescier;
La mer tut environ rogi
Del sanc ki del cors espandi. [5]
Li leus out puis le nun e a
Del gaiant qu'illuec trebucha. [6]
   Quant la terre fud neïee
Des gaianz e de lur lignee,   1170
Li Troïen s'aseürerent,
Maisuns firent, terres arerent,
Viles e burcs edifierent,
Blez semerent, blez guaainerent.
La terre aveit nun Albion, [7]
Mais Brutus li chanja sun nun,
De Bruto, sun nun, nun li mist,
E Bretainne apeler la fist;
Les Troïens, ses compainuns
Apela, de Bruto, Bretuns.   1180
E Corineüs ad partie
De la terre a sun hués choisie; [8]
Cele partie ad apelee,
De Corineo, Corinee;
Puis, ne sai par quel entrefaille,
Fu apelee Cornewaille;
Del nun qu'el out premierement
Tient encor le comencement.
Le language qu'il ainz parloent
Que il Troïen apeloent,   1190
Unt entr'els Bretun apelé.
Mais Engleis l'unt puis remué;
La parole e li nuns dura
Tant que Gormund i ariva;
Gormund en chaça les Bretuns
Si la livra a uns Saissuns [9]
Qui d'Angle Angleis apelé erent,
Ki Engletere l'apelerent;
Tuz les Bretuns si eissillierent
Que unches puis ne redrescerent.   1200

---

1. MS P reading—*checuns s'en vuleit*—restored.
2. MS P's reading of line restored.
3. MS P reading—*fruissir*—restored.
4. MS P reading—*derube*—restored.
5. MS P reading—*ki*—restored.
6. MS G adds twenty-two lines: Brutus admires Corineus' strength, then carefully exterminates all the remaining giants.
7. MS P: *Abilon.*
8. MS P reading—*choisie*—restored.
9. MS H adds: *Puis s'en fist roi et rois en fu/ Mais aprés en France moru/ Il mist les lages et les lois/ Qu'encor tienent li Englois.*

Brutus calls his country Britain

ed each other behind their backs, angrily locking hands. There throw pitted against throw could be seen, strength against strength, feet forward, feet behind, and all manner of tricks, movements here and movements there. Each was strong and grew angry, pushing the other with his chest and splaying out his legs. Sometimes they came together so that they were on top of each other straight away. Then you could see them breathing hard, wrinkling their noses, with sweaty foreheads, blackening faces, rolling eyes, eyebrows raised and lowered, bared teeth, changed colour, heads rubbing and bumping, pushing, pulling, prodding, raising, lifting, checking, bending, straightening, calculating, kicking and quickly turning. Many a throw was made using the hips, pulling up and dragging across. Each wanted to catch the other out and each wanted to be on his guard.

1147   Gomagog fought hard. He brought his arms close together, locked his hands, and dragged Corineus towards him, breaking three of his ribs; he hurt him badly and almost threw him down beneath him. Corineus, wounded, got to his feet again as fast as he could and pulled the giant to him with such fury that he smashed his sides. He pulled him down a little way, raised him against his chest, and carried him, quite unconscious, in his arms to a cliff. He opened his hands, and let go with his arms. The giant was heavy and crashed so hard down the cliff into the rocks that not a bone remained unbroken. All around, the sea reddened with the blood spilt from the body. The place then took the name, which it still has, of the giant who fell there.

1169   When the land was cleansed of the giants and their race, the Trojans felt secure. They built houses, ploughed lands, constructed towns and cities, sowed corn and reaped it. The country was called Albion, but Brutus changed its name, calling it after his own, and he had it called Britain. He named the Trojans, his companions, Britons after Brutus. And Corineus chose part of the land for his own use, and called this part Corinee, after Corineus. Later, I do not know by what mistake, it was called Cornwall; it still bears the beginning of the name it had at first. The language which they spoke before, which they called Trojan, they now between themselves called British. But the English have since altered it. The language and the name lasted until Gurmunt[1] arrived; he drove out the Britons and handed it over to Saxons who, from being Angles, were called English and called the land England. They drove out all the Britons, who never regained power.

---

[1] See para. 13375. Wace adds this, and a characteristic reflection on language change.

Cornoaille out Corineüs
E Bretainne out tute Brutus.
Chascuns traist a sei ses amis
E les homes de sun païs.
Bien tost fu la gent si creüe
E si par la terre espandue,
Vis vus fust que lunc tens eüst
Que Bretainne poplee fust.
Brutus esguarda les montainnes,
1210 Vit les valees, vit les plainnes,
Vit les mores, vit les boscages,
Vit les eues, vit les rivages,
Vit les champs, vit les praeries,
Vit les porz, vit les pescheries,
Vit sun pople multepleier,
Vit les terres bien guainier;[1]
Pensa sei que cité fereit
E que Troie renovelereit.[2]
Quant il out quis leu covenable
1220 E aaisiez e delitable,
Sa cité fist desur Tamise;
Mult fud bien faite e bien asise.
Pur ses anceisors remembrer
La fist Troie Nove apeller;
Puis ala li nuns corumpant,
Si l'apela l'om Trinovant;
Mais qui le nom guarde, si trove
Que Trinovant est Troie Nove,
Que bien pert par corruptiun
1230 Faite la compositiun.
[Urb est latins, citez romanz,
Cestre est engleis, kaer bretanz.][3]
Por Lud, un rei ki mult l'ama
E longement i conversa,
Fu puis numee Kaerlu.
Puis unt cest nun Lud corumpu
Si distrent pur Lud Lodoïn;
Pur Lodoïn a la parfin
Londenë en engleis dist l'um
E nus or Lundres l'apelum.[4]
Par plusurs granz destruiemenz
1240 Que unt fait alienes genz

Ki la terre unt sovent eüe,
Sovent prise, sovent perdue,
Sunt les viles, sunt les contrees[5]
Tutes or altrement nomees
Que li anceisor nes nomerent
Ki premierement les fonderent.
A cel terme que jeo vus di
Ert de Judee prestre Heli,
E Philistin en lor contree
Ourent l'arche e la lei portee.   1250
    Quant Brutus out sa cité fete
E de la gent grant masse atraite,
Citedeins i mist e burgeis
Si lur duna preceps e leis
Ke pais e concorde tenissent
Ne pur rien ne se mesfeïssent.
Bretainne tint vint e quatre anz
E d'Innorgen out treis emfanz:
Si trei filz furent Locrinus
E Kamber e Albanactus.   1260
Cil trei, qui emprés lui vesquirent,
En Trinovant l'ensevelirent,
La cité que il out fundee.
Pus unt la terre devisee
Par amur e par compainie,
Si que chescuns out sa partie.
Locrin, cil ki esteit ainz nez
E plus fort ert e plus senez,
Out a sa part la region
Ki de sun nun Logres out nun;   1270

E Kamber ad la terre prise
Ki Saverne vers north devise,[6]
E quant il out cele saisie
De sun nom l'apela Kambrie,
Granz palais i fist e granz sales.
Mais ore ad nom Kambrie Guales;
Kambrie out nom, Guales aprés,
Pur la reïne Galaeis;
U Guales out Guales cest nom
Pur memorie del duc Gualon.   1280

---

[1] MS P reading—*guainier*—restored.
[2] MS P reading—*que*—restored.
[3] MS P couplet restored.
[4] For ll. 1233–38, MSS PKN substitute ll. 3761–
74; see fn. 1 on p. 96.
[5] MS P's reading of line restored.
[6] MS P reading—*ki*—restored.

The founding of New Troy

1201 Corineus had Cornwall and Brutus had all Britain. Each gathered to him his friends
and the men of his native land. Soon the people increased so much and spread so
far through the land, you would have thought Britain had been populated for a
long time. Brutus looked at the mountains, he saw the valleys, the plains, the
marshes, the woodland, the rivers and the river banks; he saw the fields and the
meadows, the harbours and the fisheries; he saw his people multiplying and the
lands growing fertile. He thought he would found a city and rebuild Troy. When
he had chosen a suitable spot, convenient and delightful, he built his city on the
Thames; it was well sited and very well made. In memory of his ancestors he had
it called 'New Troy'. Then the name became corrupted, and men called it
'Trinovant'; but whoever looks at the name will find that 'Trinovant' is 'New
Troy', which is apparent through the corruption done to the name. The words for
city are 'urbs' in Latin, 'citez' in French', 'chester' in English and 'kaer' in British. From Lud, a king who was very fond of the city and long dwelt there, it was
then called 'Kaerlu'. Then they corrupted this name, Lud, and said 'Lodoin'
instead. Finally, people call 'Lodoin', 'Londene', in English, and we now call it
'Lundres'.[1] Through many great acts of destruction wrought by foreigners, who
have often possessed the land, often seized it, often lost it, the towns and the
regions all now have different names from those their founders gave them, who
first established them. In the era I am speaking of, Eli was priest in Judah, and
the Philistines carried off into their country the Ark and the tablets of the law.[2]

1251 When Brutus had made his city, and attracted to it very many of the people, he
installed in it citizens and burgesses and gave them mandates and laws, so that
they would maintain peace and harmony and not on any account hurt each other.
He ruled Britain for twenty-four years and had three children from Innogen. His
three sons were Locrinus, Kamber and Albanac. These three, who lived after
him, buried him in Trinovant, the city he had founded. Then they amicably and
companionably divided the land so that each had his share. Locrin, the eldest,
strongest and wisest, had as his portion the region which took its name from him,
Logres. And Kamber took the land marked off by the Severn in the north of
Logres, and when he had taken it, he called it Kambrie, after his name, and
erected a great palace and great halls there. But Kambrie is now called Wales:
once it was Kambrie, and later Wales because of queen Galaes; or else Wales has
this name in memory of duke Guales.[3] Guales was very powerful and there was

---

[1] Wace expands on *HRB*'s comments to include
the transformation of 'Kaerlu' through to
'Lundres', but omits, like the *VV*, chap. 22,
HRB's references to Lud's brothers, Nennius
and Cassibellaunus.

[2] This synchronic historical reference comes from
HB via *HRB*. See also paras. 1441, 1453, 1493
etc.

[3] See para. 14842. Galaes and Guales are not in
HRB at this juncture.

Guales fud bien de grant puissance[1]
Si fud de lui grant reparlance.
Albanac, li tierz, fu li mendre,
E a celui avint a prendre
Une terre qui ert boscainne,
Que de sun nom noma Albaine:
Albaine d'Albanac ot nom,
Ço que nus Escoce apelom.
Quant li trei frere ourent parti
1290 Come bon frere e bon ami,
Senz vice e senz iniquité
Tindrent entr'els fraterneté.
Humber, ki ert reis des Humuz,
Uns hoem forment par mer cremuz,
Ki les illes alout guastant
E les rivages tuz robant,
En Escoce a un port torna
E od Albanac se mella
Pur la terre que il robout.
1300 Cruels huem fu e granz genz out;
Albanac venqui e conquist,
Lui e le plus des suens ocist.
Li altre, ki s'en eschaperent,
En Bretaine a Locrin turnerent;
Locrin e Kamber s'assemblerent
E lur frere venger alerent.
Humber de ça Escoce Watre
Loin encontr'els s'ala combatre,
Mais vencuz fu si s'en fuï;
1310 E en une eue s'enbati
Ki de sun nom Humbre est nomee,
Pur Humbro fu Humbre apelee;
Humbre cest non l'eue reçut
Pur Humbro que dedenz morut.
Il out en Alemaine esté
E mult out la pris e guasté;
Treis meschines en out ravies
Sis aveit en sa nef guerpies:
Fille a rei ert l'une pucele,
1320 Estrild out non, qui mult fu bele;

Ne poeit hoem suz ciel trover
Plus bele de li, ne sa per.
Quant neied fu e mort Humber,
Locrin e sis frere Kamber
Sunt coru as nefs, al navie,
Pur aveir la grant manancie.
Les treis meschines unt trovees
Que Humber aveit amenees.
Locrin en ad Hestrild amee
E a guarder l'ad comandee.   1330
A muiller, ço dist, la prendra,
Ja altre feme nen avra,
Kar sa belté mult li agree;
A guarder fud Hestrild livree.
Corineüs encor viveit
Ki une sole fille aveit[2]
Que cil Locrin prendre deveit;
Mais pur Hestrild la guerpisseit.
Pur amur Hestrild la laissout
E covenant en trespassout.   1340
Corineüs s'en coruça;
Tant quist Locrin qu'il le trova.
Devant lui vint irreement
E parla mult enfleement,
Une hache grant en sun col.
'Locrin, dist il, put fel, put fol,
Nuls huem ne te puet guarantir
Que ja ne t'estuece morir.
As tu ma fille refusee
Que tu aveies afiee?   1350
Que deit ço que tu ne la prenz?
Sunt ço les grez que tu me renz
Pur tun pere ki jo servi
E pur les mals que jo soffri
Des granz plaies e des mellees
Encontre genz d'altres contrees?
Pur tun pere mettre a enor
Suffri jo mainte grant suor
E meinte tribulation,
E tu m'en renz tel gueredun[3]   1360

---

[1] MS P reading—*bien de*—restored.
[2] MS P reading—*sole*—restored.
[3] MS P reading—*m'en*—restored.

Locrin and Hestrild

great talk of him. Albanac, the third, was the youngest, and it fell to him to take a wooded land which he called, after his name, Albany. Albany, which we now call Scotland, took its name from Albanac. When the three brothers had divided the land like good brothers and friends, without cunning or injustice, they continued in brotherly love with each other.

1293   Humber, king of the Huns, a man greatly feared on the high seas, who kept laying the islands waste and plundering the shores, entered a Scottish harbour and fought with Albanac over the land he was pillaging. He was a cruel man and had many fighters; he defeated and beat Albanac, killing him and most of his people. Those who escaped went to Locrin in Britain. Locrin and Kamber met and went off to avenge their brother. Humber, on this side of the Scottish Water,[1] from a distance approached to fight them, but he was beaten and fled; and he rushed into a river, which is called Humber, after him. The river received this name because of Humber who died in it. He had been in Germany, had seized much of it and laid it waste. He had abducted three girls and left them in his ship: one of them, Hestrild, who was very beautiful, was a king's daughter. No one could find under heaven anyone more beautiful than her, or even her equal.

1323   When Humber had drowned to death, Locrin and his brother Kamber ran to the ships, to the fleet, to seize the great wealth there. They found the three girls whom Humber had brought. Locrin fell in love with Hestrild and ordered her to be protected. He said he would take her to wife and would never have any other, because her beauty greatly pleased him. So they took care of Hestrild. Corineus was still alive and had a single daughter whom Locrin was supposed to marry, but he abandoned her for Hestrild. For the love of Hestrild he left her and broke his agreement. This made Corineus angry. He looked for Locrin till he found him; he came forward angrily and spoke with much indignation, a great axe hanging from his shoulders. 'Locrin, base wretch, vile fool,' he said, 'no one can protect you from dying on the spot. Have you refused my daughter, to whom you plighted your troth? What do you mean by not taking her? Are these the thanks you give me for the service I gave your father and for the hardships I endured from the great battles and fights against people in other lands? To establish your father in his domain I suffered much sweat and tribulation, and you reward me by leaving

---

[1] The Firth of Forth (Arnold II, p. 795).

Ke ne sai pur quele aliene
Lais ma fille Guendoliene.
Pur tun pere oi jo maint peril,
E or ne sai pur quel Hestrild,
Neïs tant cum tu vif me veiz,
Lais ma fille que prendre deiz.
Ne puet mie estre senz vengance
Tant cum jo avrai tel poissance
Es braz que jo ai ci levez
1370 Dunt jo ai les gaianz tuez.
Morz iés, ja seras detrenchiez!'
A tant s'est a lui aprismez
Come s'ocire le volsist,
E se devient il l'oceïst,
Mes lur ami entr'els saillirent
E l'un de l'altre departyrent.
Corineüs unt apaied
E a Locrin unt conseilled
Que tut sun covenant le tienge;
1380 Prenge la ainz que pis l'en vienge.
Dunc ad Locrin par itel guise
Guendoliene a feme prise,
Mais il nen ad mie obliee
Hestrild, qu'il out asoinantee.
Par un suen bien familier
Fist fere a Lundres un celier
Desoz terre parfundement,
La fud Hestrild celeement.
Set anz la tint issi Locrin
1390 Celeement el sozterrin.
Quant il i voleit converser
E alques longes demorer,
A sa feme acreire faiseit
Qu'un sacrefise as Deus rendeit [1]
Qu'il ne pout rendre altrement [2]
Se issi nun occultement.
   Tant la tint, tant i conversa
Qu'Hestrild une fille enfanta,
Abren out nom, mult fu plus clere
1400 Et plus bele qu'Hestrild, sa mere,

Ki mult fu bele e avenant.
Guendolien rout un enfant, [3]
Un vallet, meïsme cel an,
Sil firent apeler Madan.
Des que cil Madan pout aler
E sout entendre e sout parler,
A sun aiol l'unt fait livrer
Pur nurrir e pur doctriner.
Li termes vint ki venir dut
Que Corineüs se morut,   1410
Et Locrin, qui mais nel duta,
Guendoliene en envea
Et Hestrild ad tant enoree
Que a reïne l'ad levee.
Guendoliene fu irree
Del rei qui l'en out enveiee;
En Cornoaille s'ala plaindre,
La u sis peres soleit maindre.
Tant ensembla de ses parens [4]
E tant requist estranges genz,   1420
Grant ost mena de Cornoaille;
Contre Locrin vint a bataille
Come feme fiere e seüre.
Sur l'eue qui out nun Esture [5]
S'entrecontrerent en Dorsete;
Mais Locrin od une saiete
Fu feruz a mort si chaï
E sa gent tute s'en fuï.
Guendoliene ki venqui
La terre prist tute e saisi;   1430
En une eue fist trebuchier
Estrild e Abren e neier;
Mais ço rova e establi
Que pur l'enor de sun mari
Ki Abren aveit engendree
Fust de sun non l'eue apelee:
Puis fu l'eue u el fu getee
Del non Abren Avre nomee;
Avre qui d'Abren sun nom prent [6]
A Cristescherche en mer descent.   1440

---

[1] MS P reading—*Qu'un*—restored.
[2] MS P reading—*pout*—restored.
[3] MS P's reading of line restored.
[4] MS P reading—*ensembla*—restored.
[5] MS P reading—*out*—restored
[6] MS P reading—*Avre*—restored in ll. 1438–39.

Guendolien defeats Locrin

my daughter Guendolien for some foreigner or other. I underwent many dangers for your father, and now, even while I'm still alive, you leave my daughter, whom you were supposed to take, for some Hestrild or other. This can't go unavenged, as long as I have that strength in these raised arms with which I killed the giants. You're dead, soon you'll be cut to pieces!'

1372 At this he came closer as if to kill him, and perhaps would have done so, but their friends rushed between them and separated one from the other. They appeased Corineus and advised Locrin to keep his promise to him and to take her before worse came of it. So in this way Locrin took Guendolien to wife, but he did not forget Hestrild, whom he had made his paramour. Through a close friend, he had a cellar constructed in London, deep underground, and there Hestrild lived in secret. Locrin kept her there in this way for seven years, secret in the underground chamber. When he wanted to stay and linger for a long time, he made his wife believe he was making a sacrifice to the gods which could not be performed in any other way but a secret one.

1397 He kept her there, and had relations with her, for so long, that Hestrild gave birth to a daughter, called Abren, even more radiant and beautiful than her mother Hestrild, who was so fair and attractive. Guendolien also had a child in the same year, a boy whom they called Madan. As soon as Madan could walk, and could talk and understand, they handed him over to his grandfather to bring up and to instruct. The time came, inevitably, when Corineus died and Locrin, fearing him no longer, sent Guendolien away and paid so much honour to Hestrild that he raised her to be queen. Guendolien was angry with the king who had sent her away; she went to Cornwall, where her father used to live, to complain. She gathered so many of her kin, and sought assistance of so many strangers, that she led a great army from Cornwall. She came to fight against Locrin, like a proud and resolute woman.

1424 They met in Dorset, on the river called Stour. However, Locrin was struck by an arrow and fell dead, and all his men fled. In victory, Guendolien seized and took the whole country. She had Hestrild and Abren thrown into a river and drowned, but she commanded and laid down that, in honour of her husband who had begotten Abren, the river should receive her name. Then the river where she was thrown was called 'Avren' after Abren. Avren, taking its name from Abren, descends to the sea at Christchurch.[1]

---

[1] In *HRB* Hestrild's daughter is *Habren* and the Severn (Sabrina) is called after her (chap. 25). Wace changes it to *Avren*, from which the river Avon takes its name. On his knowledge of Dorset and Hampshire, see Houck, *Sources*, pp. 222–3.

Guendoliene fu mult fere
E merveilluse justisiere.
Dis anz out od Locrin esté
E enprés ad quinze anz regné;
Dunc sout sis filz terre tenir
Sil fist de Bretaine saisir.
Quant ele li out tut guerpi
En Cornoaille reverti;
Tant ad de terre retenu
1450 Come sis peres out eü.
Dunc esteit Samuel prophetes
E Homer ert preisiez poëtes.
    Madan prist feme e out dous filz,
L'uns fu Malins, l'altre Menbriz.
Quarante anz fu reis, puis fina,
Sun regne a ses dous filz laissa.
Mes li frere se descorderent
E pur le regne se mellerent:
Chescuns vuleit le tut tenir,
1460 Ne s'en poeient assentir.[1]
Mes Menbriz, qui traïtre fu,
Malin sun frere ad deceü.
Trives prist e trieves rova[2]
E a parlement le manda.
La u il ert al parlement,
Q'unches n'i out desfiement,
Ocist li maire le menor,
Issi conquist Menbriz l'enor.
Dunc ert Saül de Judeus reis
1470 E Eristeüs des Grezeis.
Mambriz haï tut sun lignage
E tuz les homes de sun parage.[3]
Ja si franc home n'i eüst
Ki bone terre aveir deüst
Que il n'osceïst par poisun
U par force u par traïsun.
Il guerpi sa propre moillier
Si se mist al vilain mestier[4]
Dunt li Sodomite perirent,
1480 Quant il en lur cité fundirent

E vif chaïrent en abisme.
Vint aunz fu reis, en l'an vintisme
Ala Menbriz en bois chacier,
Ço fu contre sun desturbier.
De ses veneürs departi,[5]
Ne sai cerf u beste soï,[6]
Si entra en une valee,
Illuec trova une assemblee
De lous ki erent enragiez,
Cil l'unt devoré e mangiez.   1490
Issi fu Menbriz desmenbrez
E depescied e devorez.
    Ebrauc, uns suen fiz de sa feme,
Tint enprés sun pere le regne.
Cist fud de merveillus esforz
E mult fud gros e mult fu forz;[7]
Ses riches parenz enora
E les plus povres eshalça.
Ne fu nuls huem quil guereiast
Ne qui a lui meller s'osast.[8]   1500
Ço fu li premiers ki par mer
Mut d'Engletere aillurs rober.
Il assembla un grant navie
Si prist de ses homes une partie[9]
Si ala rober les Franceis
E les Flamans e les Tieis;
Les marines tutes prea
E granz aveirs en aporta.
Longement en fu enoree
Engletere e boneüree.   1510
Al tens que cist Ebrauc regna
David le psaltier ordina
Et sa cité fist, Bethleem,
E la tor de Jerusalem,
E Silvius Latins regnout
E Nathan dunc prophetizout.
Ebrauc, ki out aveir assez,
Ver Escoce fist dous citez:[10]
Kaer Ebrac l'une apela,
L'altre cité Aclud noma.   1520

---

[1] MS P reading—*s'en*—restored.
[2] MS P reading—*rova*—restored.
[3] MS P reading—*sun*—restored.
[4] MS P reading—*se mist*—restored.
[5] MS P reading—*departi*—restored.
[6] MS P reading—*beste*—restored.
[7] MS P reading—*gros*—restored.
[8] MS P reading—*a*—restored.
[9] MS P reading—*une*—restored.
[10] MS P reading—*ver*—restored.

Madan, Menbriz and Ebrauc

1441 Guendolien was very proud, and a great dispenser of justice. She had ten years with Locrin, and after that reigned for fifteen. Then her son was able to hold sway and she put him in possession of Britain. When she had handed it all over to him, she returned to Cornwall, keeping as much land as her father had had. At this time Samuel was a prophet and Homer a celebrated poet.

1453 Madan took a wife and had two sons; one was Malin, the other Menbriz.[1] He was king for forty years, then died, leaving his kingdom to his two sons. But the brothers quarrelled and fought for the kingdom; each wanted to have the whole of it and they could not agree. But Menbriz, who was treacherous, deceived Malin his brother. He requested and made a truce and summoned him to a conference. When he was at the conference, without issuing any challenge the older brother killed the younger; thus Menbriz acquired the land. Then Saul was king of Judaea and Eristeus[2] of the Greeks.

1469 Menbriz hated all his kin and all the men of his race. There was no honourable man entitled to good land whom he did not kill through poison, violence or treachery. He abandoned his own wife and gave himself up to that pernicious behaviour for which the Sodomites perished, when they were destroyed within their city and fell, still alive, into Hell. He was king for twenty years. In the twentieth year, to his misfortune, Menbriz went hunting. He became separated from his huntsmen—I don't know if he was following a stag or some other animal—and entered a valley. There he found a pack of furious wolves who devoured and ate him. Thus Menbriz was torn limb from limb, destroyed and devoured.

1493 Ebrauc, one of his sons by his wife, then reigned after his father. He was an extraordinarily powerful man, very large and very strong. He honoured his wealthy relations and advanced the interests of the poorest of his kin. No man would make war on him or dare to fight with him. He was the first who, crossing the sea, went off pillaging abroad, away from England. He gathered a large fleet, took some of his men and went off to plunder the French, the Flemings and the Germans. He pillaged all the coasts and carried off great wealth. England was in consequence fortunate and honoured for a long while. At the period when this Ebrauc reigned, David set out the Psalms and established his city, Bethlehem, and the tower of Jerusalem, and Silvius Latinus reigned and Nathan made his prophecies.

1517 Ebrauc, who was very wealthy, constructed two cities near Scotland. He called one of them Kaer Ebrac and the other Alclud. The one named Ebrac was later

---

[1] *HRB* chap. 26: *Menpricius*; *VV*: *Menbricius*.   [2] *HRB* chap. 26: *Eristenus*; *VV*: *Eristeus*.

Cele ki out le nun d'Ebrac
Fu puis apelee Eborac;
Franceis puis cel nun corumpirent
E d'Eborac Ebrewic firent.
L'altre cité plus vers north mist
E el mont Agned chastel fist
Qui des Pulceles ad surnun;
Mais jo ne sai par quel raisun
Li chastels out nun des Pulceles
1530 Plus que de dames ne d'anceles;
Ne me fu dit ne jo nel di
Ne jo n'ai mie tut oï
Ne jo n'ai mie tut veü
Ne jo n'ai pas mie entendu, [1]
E mult estovreit home entendre
Ki de tut vuldreit raison rendre.
Ebrauc vesqui bien longement
E terre tint mult sagement.
Seissante anz vesqui tuz entiers
1540 E vint fiz out de vint moillers,
E trente filles en roünt.
Les nons as filz oiez quel sunt: [2]
Brutus Vert-Escu, Margadud,
Sisillius, Regin, Bladud, [3]
Moruid, Lagon e Bodloan,
Kimcar, Spaden, Gaül, Dardan,
Eldad, Cangu, Kerim, Luor,
Rud, Assarac, Buël, Hector. [4]
Les nuns as filz oï avez,
1550 Des meschines oïr devez:
La premiere fu Gloïgin,
Otulas, Ourar, Innogin, [5]
Guardid, Radan, Guenlian, [6]
Angarad, Guenlode, Medlan,
Mailurë, Ecub, Tangustel,
Stadud, Kambreda, Methael,
Gad, Echeïm, Nest e Gorgon, [7]
Gladus, Ebren, Blangan, Egron, [8]
Edra, Aballac e Angues,
1560 Anor, Stadiald, Galaes. [9]

Galaes fu e bele e gente
Plus que nule des altres trente;
E Methael fu la plus laie
E Guenlode fu la plus guaie;
Ourar fu la meillor ovriere
E Innogin la plus parlere,
E Anor fu la plus corteise,
Qui mielz sout demener richeise.
Gloïgin, cele fu l'ainnee
E plus fu granz e plus senee. [10]   1570
Tutes furent bien conrees
E en Lombardie menees
Al rei Silvium lur parent
Kis maria mult richement
As ligniedes as Troïens;
Kar il aveit esté lunc tens
Que les femes de Lombardie,
Jo ne sai par quel felonie,
Ne vodrent prendre mariage
As Troïens n'a lur lignage,   1580
Pur ceo furent cestes mandees
E la as Troïens donees.
Li frere, ki furent remés
Purchacerent armes e nefs
Sin alerent en Alemainne [11]
Od la juvente de Bretainne;
Assarac, un d'els ki mielz sout,
De ses freres la maistrie out.
Chastels, viles e citez pristrent
E tute la terre conquistrent.   1590
     Ebrauc out l'ainz né retenu,
Brutum, ki out nun Vert Escu;
Cist out le regne aprés sun pere
E duze anz en fu maintenere.
Leïl, sis fiz, puis sun decés,
Vint e cinc anz fu reis emprés.
Une cité, ço dist l'estorie,
Fist pur tenir de lui memorie,
Kaerleïl out nun, vers north.
Mult fu buens hom, mais vers sa mort 1600

---

[1] MS P reading—*mie*—restored.
[2] MS F adds: *Coment les enfaunz nomout/ Diray par conte cunter/ Car rime n'i ad mester.*
[3] MS P: *Sifillius, Kegim.*
[4] MS P: *Kud, Assarac, Kuer.*
[5] MS P reading—*Otulas*—restored.
[6] MS P: *Kadan.*
[7] MS P: *Hest.*
[8] MS P: *Klangan.*
[9] MS P: *Gardiald.*
[10] MS P's reading of line restored.
[11] MS P reading—*sin*—restored.

The children of Ebrauc

called Eborac; the French then corrupted this name, from Eborac to Evrewic.[1] He sited the other city further north and put a castle on Mount Agned, which is named Maiden Castle, but I do not know why the castle is called this rather than 'Ladies' Castle' or 'Handmaidens' Castle'. I was not told, nor did I invent it, nor have I heard all about it, nor have I seen it all, nor have I understood all about it, and a man who wants to give an account of everything must have a good understanding.

1537 Ebrauc lived for a long time and ruled the land very wisely. In all he lived for sixty years and had twenty sons by twenty wives, and thirty daughters as well. Here are the names of the sons: Brutus Green-Shield, Margadud, Sisillius, Regin, Bladud, Morvid, Lagon and Bodloan, Kimcar, Spaden, Gaul, Dardan, Eldad, Cangu, Kerim, Luor,[2] Rud, Assarac, Buel and Hector.

1549 You have heard the sons' names; now you should hear the daughters'. The first was Gloigin, then Otulas,[3] Ourar, Innogin,[4] Guardid, Radan, Guenlian, Angarad, Guenlode, Medlan, Mailure, Ecub, Tangustel, Stadud, Kambreda, Methael,[5] Gad,[6] Echeim,[7] Nest and Gorgon, Gladus, Ebren, Blangan, Egron, Edra, Aballac and Angues, Anor, Stadiald and Galaes. Galaes was fairer and more beautiful than any of the rest of the thirty; and Methael was the ugliest and Guenlode the liveliest. Ourar was the best worker, Innogin the most talkative, and Anor the best-mannered, who well knew how to spend wealth. Gloigin, the eldest, was the tallest and the wisest. All of them were handsomely arrayed and taken to Lombardy, to their relation king Silvius, who made them splendid marriages with men of Trojan descent, because for a long time the women of Lombardy, for what wicked reason I know not, had not wanted to marry Trojans nor their descendants. For this reason these girls were sent for and there given to Trojans.

1583 The brothers, who had stayed behind, obtained weapons and ships and went off to Germany with young men from Britain. Assarac, one of the ablest, assumed authority over his brothers. They seized castles, towns and cities and conquered the entire country.

1591 Ebrauc kept the eldest with him, Brutus, called Green-Shield. He had the kingdom after his father and ruled for twelve years. After his death his son, Leil, was king next, for twenty-five years. According to the history he made a city, as a memorial to him, called Kaerleil, in the north. He was a very good man, but

---

[1] *Alclud* is Dumbarton, *Evrewic* is York. On both, see Allen, *Lawman: 'Brut'*, pp. 416–17.

[2] *Ivor* in MS K, as in *HRB* p. 17.

[3] *HRB* chap. 27: *Oudas*; *VV*: *Otidas*.

[4] As spelt in *VV* chap. 27; *HRB*: *Ignogin*.

[5] *HRB* chap. 27: *Alethahel*; *VV*: *Methael*.

[6] *HRB* chap. 27: *Gael*; *VV*: *Gad*. On some of the names of Ebrauc's sons and daughters, see Tatlock p. 164.

[7] *HRB* chap. 27: *Chein*.

Si commença a empeirer
Qu'il ne pout terre justisier.
Si home s'entreguerreioent
E pur lui neient ne laissouent, [1]
Ne pur lui ne pur sun destreit
Ne faiseient ne tort ne dreit.
Mult l'aveient turné el bas.
Mais un sun fiz Ruhundibras
Fu emprés reis de grant justise,
1610 Ki la terre ad tute en pais mise;
Les barons fist entr'acorder
E pais premettre e pais guarder.
Cist fist Wincestre e Cantorbire
E le chastel de Cestrebire
Ki fu el mont de Paladur.
A cel chastel clorre de mur
Uns aigles, ço dit l'on, parla,
Ne sai que dist ne que nunça.
Quarante anz, un meins, regna cil
1620 Puis la mort sun pere Leïl.
Si come nus lisant trovum
A cel tens regnout Salomun [2]
Ki funda templum Domini
Si come Deus l'out establi;
Prophetizant en Israel
Amos, Aggeüs e Iohel.
    Quant Ruhundibras finé fud,
Bretainne tint sis fiz Bladud.
Bladud fu bien de grant poissance
1630 E si sout mult de nigromance;
Cil funda Bade e fist les bainz, [3]
Unches n'i ourent esté ainz.
De Bladud fu Bade nomee,
La secunde lettre l ostee;
U Bade out por les bainz cest non
Pur la merveilluse façon.
Les bainz fist chauz e saluables
E al pople mult profitables.
Lez les bainz fist temple Minerve,
1640 E pur mustrer que l'on la serve

Fist enz un fu tut tens ardant
Qui n'i failleit ne tant ne quant. [4]
Bladud mainte merveille ovra,
En tels choses se delita:
Co fu Bladud ki volt voler
Pur faire plus de sei parler;
Ço se vanta qu'il volereit
E a Londres sun vol prendreit.
Eles fist si s'apareilla
Voler vout e voler quida.   1650
Mais il avint a male fin, [5]
Kar desur le temple Apolin
Prist un tel quaz que tut quassa,
Issi folement trespassa.
    Vint anz aveit Bladud regné
Aprés la mort Ruhundibré.
L'enor avint a maintenir
Emprés sa mort sun fiz Leïr.
Leïr en sa prosperité
Fist en sun nun une cité,   1660
Kaerleïr out nun sor Sore,
Leïcestre l'apeloms ore,
Cité Leïr chescuns nons sone.
Jadis fu la cité mult bone,
Mais par une dissensiun
I out puis grant destructiun.
Leïr tint l'enor vivement
Seissante anz continuelment;
Treis filles out, n'out nul altre eir,
Ne plus ne pout enfanz aveir.   1670
La premiere fu Gornorille,
Puis Ragaü, puis Cordeïlle.
La plus bele fu la puis nee
E li peres l'ad plus amee.
Quant Leïr alques afebli
Come li huem ki enveilli,
Comensa sei a purpenser
De ses treis filles marier;
Ce dist qu'il les mariereit.
E sun regne lur partireit,   1680

---

[1] MS P reading—*E*—restored.
[2] MS P reading—*regnout*—restored.
[3] MS P reading—*cil*—restored.
[4] MS P reading—*n'i*—restored.
[5] MS P reading—*avint*—restored.

Bladud and Leir

before his death he began to decline so that he could not govern the land. His men fought amongst themselves and would not stop on his account; they would do neither right nor wrong for his sake or for the sake of his distress. They completely ruined him. But a son of his, Ruhundibras[1] was subsequently a most righteous king who established peace throughout the land; he made the barons come to terms, promise peace, and keep it too. He constructed Winchester and Canterbury and the castle of Chesterbury[2] on Mount Paladur. While this castle was being surrounded with walls, it is said that an eagle spoke, but I do not know what it said or foretold.[3] He reigned for forty years less one after the death of his father, king Leil. According to what we read in books, Solomon reigned at that time, who founded the Temple of the Lord, just as God ordained it. Amos, Aggeus[4] and Joel were prophets in Israel.

1627   When Ruhundibras died, his son Bladud ruled Britain. Bladud was very powerful and very skilled in magic. He founded Bath and constructed the baths, which had never been there before. Bath was named after Bladud, the second letter, 'l', being removed; or else Bath received its name from the baths, because of their marvellous workmanship. The baths were hot and beneficial and very useful to the population. Next to the baths he made a temple of Minerva and, to demonstrate the service paid to her, inside he made a perpetually burning fire, which never under any circumstances went out. Bladud created many marvellous things and took delight in them. It was he who wanted to fly, in order to be more talked about. He boasted he would fly, and would begin his flight in London. He made wings and put them on, wanting and intending to fly. But he came to a bad end, because on top of the temple of Apollo he had such a fall that he broke every bone in his body and thus, in his rashness, he died.[5]

1655   Bladud's reign, after Ruhundibras' death, lasted for twenty years. After his own death, his son Leir had the government of the kingdom. Leir's prosperity led him to build a city called after him: its name was Kaerleir, on the river Soar, and now we call it Leicester. Each name means 'city of Leir'. Once the city was a very fine one, but dissension has led to great destruction.[6] Leir ruled decisively over the kingdom for sixty years without a break. He had three daughters and no other heirs: he could not have any more children. The first was Gonorille, the second Ragau and the last Cordeille. The most beautiful was the youngest and the father loved her best.

1675   When Leir became rather feeble, as a man does on growing old, he began to think of marriages for his three daughters. He said he would marry them off and

---

[1] *HRB* chap. 29: *Rudhud Hudibras*.
[2] *HRB*: Shaftesbury (*Sephtesberia*, p. 18).
[3] See para. 14801, where the eagle has become a soothsayer.
[4] Haggai.

[5] Wace adds both a speculation on the origins of Bath's name and a comment on Bladud's folly.
[6] For speculation on this 'dissension' see Arnold II, p. 797.

Mais primes vuleit essaier
Laquele d'eles l'aveit plus chier. [1]
Le plus del suen doner vuleit
A cele que plus l'amereit.
A chescune parla senglement, [2]
A l'ainz nee premierement: [3]
    'Fille, dist il, jo vuil saveir
Cumbien tu m'aimes, di mei veir.'
Gonorille li ad juré
1690 Del ciel tute la deïté,
—Mult par ert plaine de veisdie—
Qu'ele l'amout plus que sa vie.
'Fille, dist il, mult m'as amé,
Bien te sera guereduné,
Kar preisee as mielz ma vieilesce
Que ta vie ne ta giesnesce.
Tu en avras tel gueredun
Que tut le plus preised barun
Que tu en mun regne ellirras
1700 A seinnur, si jo puis, avras,
E ma terre te partirai,
La tierce part t'en liverrai.'
Dunc demanda a Ragaü:
'Fille, di, combien m'aimes tu?'
E Ragaü out entendu
Come sa serur out respundu [4]
A ki sis peres tel gré sout
De ço que si forment l'amout.
Gré revout aver ensement
1710 Si li ad dit par serrement:
'Jo t'aim sur tute creature,
Ne t'en sai dire altre mesure.'
'Mult ad ci, dist il, grant amur.
Ne te sai demander grainur.
E jo te durrai a seinnur
Od la tierce part de m'enur.'
Dunc reparla a Cordeïlle,
Ki esteit la plus juenvle fille. [5]
Pur ceo que il l'aveit plus chiere
1720 Ke Ragaü ne la premiere,

Quida il qu'ele coneüst
Que mult plus chier d'eles l'eüst.
Cordeïlle out bien escuté
E bien out en sun quer noté
Come les dous sorors parlouent, [6]
Come lur pere losengouent.
A sun pere se volt gaber
E en gabant li volt mustrer
Que ses filles le blandisseient
E de losenges le serveient.   1730
Quant Leïr a raisun la mist
Come les altres, ele dist: [7]
'U ad nule fille qui die
A sun pere par presoncie
Qu'ele l'aint plus qu'ele ne deit?
Ne sai que plus grant amur seit
Que entre enfant e entre pere, [8]
E entre enfanz e entre mere. [9]
Mes peres iés, jo aim tant tei
Come jo mun pere amer dei.   1740
E pur faire tei plus certein,
Tant as, tant vals e jo tant t'aim.'
A tant se tout, ne volt plus dire.
Li peres fu de mult grant ire;
De maltalent devint tut pers,
La parole prist de travers:
Ço quida qu'ele l'escharnist
U ne deinnast u ne vulsist
U pur vilté de lui laissast
A reconuistre qu'ele l'amast [10]   1750
Si come ses serors l'amoent
Qui de tel amur s'afichoent.
'En despit, dist il, eü m'as,
Ki ne vulsis ne ne deinnas
Respundre come tes serors.
A eles dous durrai seinnurs
E tut mun regne en mariage,
E tut l'avront en heritage;
Chescune en avra la meitied.
Mes tu n'en avras ja plein pied,   1760

---

[1] MS P reading—*Laquele*—restored.
[2] MS P reading—*A chescune parla*—restored.
[3] MS P reading—*A*—restored.
[4] MS P reading—*serur*—restored.
[5] MS P reading—*la*—restored.
[6] MS P reading—*les*—restored.
[7] MS P reading—*ele*—restored.
[8] MS P reading—*enfant*—restored.
[9] MS P reading—*E*—restored.
[10] MS P reading—*ele*—restored.

Leir and his daughters

divide the kingdom between them, but first he wanted to test which of them held him most dear. He wished to give most of his possessions to the one who loved him most. He called each to him, one by one, starting with the eldest. 'Daughter,' he said, 'I wish to know how much you love me; tell me the truth.' Gonorille swore to him by all the gods in heaven—she was very cunning[1]—that she loved him more than her life. 'Daughter,' he said, 'you have loved me greatly and shall be well rewarded for it, for you have prized my old age more than your life or your youth. You shall have this reward: if you choose the most renowned lord in my kingdom as husband, you shall, if possible, have him; and I shall share out my land to you and give you the third part of it.'

1703   Then he asked Ragau: 'Daughter, tell me, how much do you love me?' And Ragau had heard how her sister replied and how grateful her father was that she loved him so much. She wanted that gratitude too and swore to him: 'I love you above any other person: I don't know how else I can measure it.' 'This is great love,' he said, 'I can't ask for more. And I will give you a husband, together with the third part of my kingdom.' Then he spoke to Cordeille, his youngest daughter. Because he held her dearer than Ragau or the eldest, he thought she would tell him she loved him much more than they did.

1723   Cordeille had listened carefully, and carefully taken note of what her sisters said and how they deceived their father. She wanted to joke with her father and, in joking, show him how his daughters were flattering him and tricking him with deceit. When Leir spoke to her as he had the others, she said to him: 'Is there anywhere any daughter who arrogantly can tell her father that she loves him more than she should? I don't know of any love greater than that between father and child, or between mother and children. You are my father: I love you as much as I should love my father. And to leave you in no more doubt: you are worth as much as you possess and I love you accordingly.'[2] At that she fell silent, not wishing to say any more.

1743   Her father was very angry: he became quite livid with fury and took her words in the wrong sense. He thought she was mocking him, and either did not wish, or would not condescend or, out of scorn for him, neglected to admit that she loved him as her sisters did, who had asserted such devotion. 'You mock me,' he said, 'when you neither wish nor deign to reply like your sisters. I will give husbands to the two of them and all my kingdom, upon their marriage, and they will have all of it as inheritance; each will have half. But you will get not a single foot of it,

---

[1] Wace adds Gonorille's cunning.
[2] Proverbial: see Morawski, *Proverbes*, no. 2281. The formula recurs in para. 1931, and is also in

HRB chap. 30; see examples quoted by John Orr in 'On Homonymics', pp. 277–8.

Ne ja par mei n'avras seinnur
Ne de tute ma terre un dur.
Jo te cheriseie e amoue
Plus ke nule altre e si quidoue
Que tu plus des altres m'amasses,
E ço fust dreit, se tu deinnasses.
Mais tu m'as regeï a front
Que meins m'eimes qu'eles ne font.
Tant cum jo t'oi plus en chierté,
1770 Tant m'eüs tu plus en vilté.
Jamais n'avras joie del mien,
Ne ja ne m'iert bel de tun bien.'
La fille ne sout que respondre;
D'ire e de hunte quida fundre.
Ne pout vers sun pere estriver [1]
Ne il ne la volt escuter.
Com il ainz pout ne demura:
Les dous ainz nees maria,
Mariee fu bien chescune,
1780 Al duc de Cornoaille l'une,
E al rei d'Escoce l'ainz nee.
Si fu la chose purparlee
Que emprés lui le regne avreient
E entr'els dous le partireient.
Cordeïlle, ki fu la meindre, [2]
Ne pout faire el mais atendre, [3]
Ne jo ne sai qu'ele en feïst, [4]
Li reis nul bien ne li pramist,
Ne il, tant fu fel, ne suffri
1790 Qu'ele en sa terre eüst mari.
La meschine en ert mult huntuse
E en sun quer mult anguissuse,
Plus pur ço qu'a tort la haeit
Que pur le prud qu'ele en perdeit.
De l'ire al pere esteit dolente;
Mes mult esteit e bele e gente,
E mult en ert grant reparlance.
Aganippus, uns reis de France,
Oï mult Cordeïlle loer [5]
1800 E que ele ert a marier.

Briefs e messages enveia
Al rei Leïr si li manda
Que sa fille a moiller vuleit,
Enveiast li, si la prendreit.
Leïr nen out mie oblié,
Ainz out bien sovent remembré
Come sa fille l'out amé;
Al rei de Francë ad mandé
Que tut sun regne ad devisé,
A ses dous filles l'ad doné: 1810
La meitied ad la premeraine
E la meitied ad la meaine; [6]
Mes, se sa fille li plaiseit,
La fille eüst, plus nen avreit.
Cil quida qui l'aveit rovee
Que pur chierté li fust vehee;
De tant l'ad il plus desirree,
Kar merveilles li ert loee.
Al rei Leïr de richief mande
Que nul aveir ne li demande;   1820
Sa fille sule si li otreit, [7]
Cordeïlle, si li enveit.
E sis peres li otreia; [8]
Ultre la mer li enveia
La fille od ses dras sulement,
N'i out altre apareillement.
Puis fu dame de tute France,
E reïne de grant puissance.
     Cil ki ses serors ourent prises,
Cui les terres furent premises,   1830
Ne voldrent mie tant soffrir
As terres prendre e a saisir
Que li suegres les en saisist
E de sun gré s'en desmeïst;
Tant l'unt guereied e destreit
Que sun regne li unt toleit
Li ducs de Cornoaille a force
E Manglanus, li reis d'Escoce.
Tut lur ad li suegres laissied,
Mes il li unt apareilled   1840

---

[1] MS P reading—*pout*—restored.
[2] MS P reading—*meindre*—restored.
[3] MS P's order of line restored.
[4] MS P reading—*en*—restored.
[5] MS P reading—*mult*—restored.
[6] MS P reading—*ad*—restored.
[7] MS P reading—*si*—restored.
[8] MS P reading—*sis*—restored.

Aganippus marries Cordeille

nor will you ever get a husband through me, nor the smallest piece of my land. I cherished and loved you more than any other and I believed you loved me more than the others did, and, had you deigned to do so, that would have been right. But you have blatantly confessed that you love me less than they do. The more I cherished you, the more you despised me. You will never delight in what I possess, and I shall never take delight in your prosperity.'

1773 His daughter did not know what to reply; she thought she would faint with anger and shame. She could not argue with her father, nor did he want to listen to her. He waited no longer than necessary to marry off the two eldest. Each was well married, one to the duke of Cornwall, the elder to the king of Scotland. The matter was so arranged that they would have the kingdom after him and divide it between them. Cordeille, the youngest, could do nothing but wait, and I do not know what she would have done since the king would promise her no property nor, so cruel was he, would he allow her to have a husband within his kingdom. The girl was most ashamed, and very distressed at heart, more because he wrongfully hated her than for the loss of any profit. Her father's anger made her miserable. But she was both beautiful and noble, and there was much talk of her.

1798 Aganippus, a king of France, heard that Cordeille was much praised and that she was unmarried. He sent letters and messengers to king Leir and told him that he wanted his daughter for wife; if he sent her, he would take her. Leir had not forgotten, but often remembered, how his daughter had loved him. He told the king of France that he had divided up all his kingdom and given it to his two daughters: the first had half and the second had half, but, if his daughter pleased him he could have her and nothing else. He who had asked for her thought he was being denied her out of affection, and desired her all the more, for he had heard her greatly praised. He sent again to king Leir, saying he asked for nothing from him, only his daughter, Cordeille, if he would send her. And her father granted her to him; he sent her, his daughter, across the sea, just in the clothes she wore, with no other apparel. Then she became lady over all France and a queen of great power.

1829 Those who had taken her sisters, to whom the domains were promised, could not wait to take the lands and seize what their father-in-law had bestowed on them and of which he had willingly divested himself. They, Manglanus[1] the king of Scotland, and the duke of Cornwall, so fought and harried him, that by force they took his kingdom from him. Their father-in-law left it all to them, but they ar-

---

[1] *HRB* chap. 31: *Maglaurus*; *VV*: *Maglaunus*.

Que li uns d'els l'avrad od sei
Ke li trovera sun conrei,
A lui e a ses esquiers
E a quarante chivaliers,
Que il alt enoreement
Quel part que il avra talent.
Le regne unt cil issi saisi
E entr'els dous par mi parti;
E Leïr ad lur ofre pris
1850 Si s'est del regne tut demis.
Manglanus out od sei Leïr;
De primes le fist bien servir;
Mais tost fu sa cort empeiree
E sa livreisun retaillee,[1]
Primes faillirent a lur duns,
Puis perdirent lur livreisuns.
Gonorille fu mult avere,
A grant eschar tint de sun pere
Ki si grant maisnee teneit[2]
1860 E nule chose n'en faiseit.[3]
Mult li pesout del costement.
A sun seinnur ad dist suvent:
'Que deit ceste assemblee d'omes?
En meie fei, sire, fols sumes
Ki tel pople avum ci atrait;
Ne set mis peres que se fait.[4]
Entrez est en fole riote;
Vielz hom est, desormais redote.
Huniz seit ki mais l'en crerra
1870 Ne ki tel gent pur lui paistra.
Li suen sergant as noz estrivent
E li un les altres eschivent.
Ki purreit suffrir si grant presse?
Li sire est fols, sa gent purverse.
Ki plus i met e plus i pert,
Ja sul nen avra gré quis sert.[5]
Mult est fols ki tel gent conree,
Trop en i ad, tiengent lur veie.
Mis peres est sei quarantisme,
1880 D'or en avant seit sei trentisme

Ensemble od nus, u il s'en aut
Od tut sun pople, nus que chaut?'
Mult i ad poi femes senz vice
E senz racine d'avarice.
Tant ad la dame amonesté
E tant ad sun seinnur hasté
De quarante le mist a trente,
De dis li retrencha sa rente.
Li peres mult s'en desdeinna[6]
E avilance li sembla   1890
Que si l'aveit l'on fait descendre.
Alez est a sun altre gendre,
Hennim, ki Ragaü aveit,
Ki en Cornoaille maneit.
N'i aveit mie un an esté
Quant cil l'ourent mis en vilté:
Se vil fu ainz, or fu mult pis:
De trente homes l'unt mis a dis,
Pus le mistrent de dis a cinc.
'Caitif mei, dist il, mar i vinc!   1900
Si vil fui la, plus sui vil ça.'[7]
A la premiere s'en rala;
Ço quida qu'ele s'amendast
E come primes l'enorast.
Mais cele le ciel en jura
Que ja od lui ne remaindra
Ne mais od un sul chevalier.
Al pere l'estut otreier.
Dunc se prist mult a contrister
E en sun quer a recorder   1910
Des biens dunt tanz aveit eüz[8]
E or les aveit tuz perduz.
'Las mei, dist il, trop ai vescu
Quant jo cest mal tens ai veü.
Tant ai eü, or ai si poi.
U est alé quanque jo oi?
Fortune, tant par es muable,
Tu ne puez estre une ure estable;
Nuls ne se deit en tei fier,
Tant faiz ta roe tost turner.   1920

---

[1] MS P reading—*sa*—restored in ll. 1853–54.
[2] MS P reading—*ki*—restored.
[3] MS P reading—*n'en*—restored.
[4] MS P reading—*se*—restored.
[5] MS P reading—*sul…quis*—restored.
[6] MS P reading—*s'en*—restored.
[7] MS P's order of line restored.
[8] MS P reading—*Des*—restored.

Leir's daughters treat him badly

ranged with him that one of them would keep him and provide for him and his squires and forty knights, so that he could go with honour anywhere he wished. Thus they took possession of the realm and divided it amongst the two of them. And Leir accepted their offer and entirely divested himself of the realm.

1851   Manglanus had Leir with him. At first he was well served, but soon the court was reduced and the allowance was curtailed. First their gifts ceased, then their rations disappeared. Gonorille was very miserly and felt nothing but contempt for her father, who had such a large retinue and did nothing. The expense annoyed her and she often said to her husband: 'What is the point of this army of men? Upon my word, sir, we are mad to have brought such people here. My father doesn't know what's going on. He's become crazily wayward: he's an old man and now he's in his dotage. Shame on anyone who now trusts him or feeds such people on his account. His servants quarrel with ours and each side shuns the other. Who could put up with such a large crowd? My lord is mad, his people wicked. The more you give, the more you waste.[1] Nobody serving them will ever get any thanks for it. One is mad to provide for such people: there are too many, let them be off. My father has forty men; from now on let there be thirty with us, or let him leave with all his people: what does it matter to us?'

1883   There are very few women without faults and without avarice rooted in their hearts. The lady so exhorted and harassed her husband that the forty were reduced to thirty, his allocation was reduced by ten. Her father grew very angry and it seemed to him a disgrace that he had been brought so low. He went to his other son-in-law, Hennim,[2] who had Ragau and lived in Cornwall. He had hardly been there a year when they treated him shamefully. If it had been bad before, now it was much worse: from thirty men they reduced him to ten, then from ten to five. 'Wretch that I am!' he said, 'would I had never come! If I was wretched there, I am more wretched here.' He returned to his first daughter, thinking she would improve and pay him honour as at first. But she swore to heaven that he should never stay with her except with just one knight alone. Her father had to agree.

1909   Then he began to be very sad and in his heart to remember all the good things he had had which he had now quite lost. 'Alas,' he said, 'I have lived too long when I see this evil day. I have had so much, and now have so little. Where has it gone, all that I had? Fortune, you are so changeable you cannot be steadfast for even one hour. No one should trust you, so quickly do you turn your wheel. You've quickly

---

[1] Proverbial. See Morawski, *Proverbes*, no. 2079.   [2] *HRB* chap. 31: *Henwinus*; *VV*: *Henninus*.

Mult as tost ta colur muee,
Tost iés chaete e tost levee.
Ki tu vuels de bon oil veeir
Tost l'as levé en grant poeir,
E des que tu turnes tun vis
Tost l'as d'alques a neient mis.
Tost as un vilain halt levé
E tost le ras desuz buté;[1]
Contes e reis, quant tu vuels, plaisses
1930 Que tu nule rien ne lur laisses.
Tant cum jo fui alques mananz
Tant oi jo parenz e serganz;
E des que jo, las! apovri,
Amis, parenz, serganz perdi.
Jo n'ai un sul apartenant
Ki d'amur me face semblant.
Bien me dist veir ma mendre fille,
Que jo blasmoe, Cordeïlle,
Ki dist que tant cum jo avreie
1940 Tant preisiez, tant amez sereie.
N'entendi mie sa parole
Ainz la blasmai e tinc pur fole.
Tant cume jo oi, tant valui,
Tant preisez e tant amez fui,
Tant trovai jo ki me blandi
E ki volentiers me servi.
Pur mun aveir me blandisseient,
Or se trestornent, s'il me veient.
Bien me dist Cordeïlle veir,
1950 Mais ne m'en soi aparceveir;
Ne l'aparçui ne l'entendi,
Ainz la blasmai si l'en haï[2]
E de ma terre la chaçai
Que nule rien ne li donai.
Or me sunt mes filles faillies
Ke dunc esteient mes amies,
Ke m'amoent sur tute rien
Tant cum jo oi alques del mien.[3]
Or m'estuet cele aler requerre
1960 Que jo chaçai en altre terre;

Mais jo coment la requerrai
Ki de mun regne la chaçai?
E nequedent saver irrai
Si jo nul bien i troverai;
Ja mains ne pis ne me fera
Que les ainz nees m'unt fait ja.
Ele dist que tant m'amereit
Comme sun pere amer deveit;
Que li dui jo plus demander?
Deüst me ele plus amer   1970
Ki altre amur me premeteit?
Pur mei deceivre le faiseit.'
    Leïr lunges se desmenta
E lungement se purpença;
Puis vint as nés, en France ala,
En un port a Chauz arriva.[4]
La reïne ad tant demandee
Qu'assez pruef li fu enditee.
Defors la cité s'arestut,
Ke huem ne feme nel conut.   1980
Un esquier ad enveié
Ki a la reïne ad nuncié
Ke sis peres a lui veneit
E par busuin la requereit;
Tut en ordre li ad conté
Coment ses filles l'unt geté.
Cordeïlle que fille fist,
Aveir que ele aveit grant prist,
A l'esquier tut l'ad livré[5]
Si li ad en conseil rové   1990
Qu'a sun pere Leïr le port
De sue part e sil confort.
E od l'aveir, tut a celé,
Aut a bon burc u a cité,
Bien se facë appareiller,
Paistre, vestir, laver, bainner.
De reials vestemenz s'aturt
E a grant enor se sujurt;
Quarante chevaliers retienge
De maisnee qui od lui vienge;   2000

---

[1] MS C: *E tost l'averas desuz buté*; MS T: *E tost l'as desuz buté*; MS H: *E un roi em plus bas torné*; MS G: *E tot le vis desuz torné*.

[2] MS P reading—*l'en*—restored.

[3] MS P reading—*del mien*—restored.

[4] MS P's reading of line restored. MS C: *Kaleis* (*HRB*: *Karitia*).

[5] MS P's reading of line restored.

Leir remembers Cordeille

changed your complexion, quickly rising, quickly falling. Those you look favourably upon, you quickly raise to great power, and as soon as you turn away your face, you quickly reduce them from something to nothing. Quickly you raise a peasant up and quickly push him[1] down again. Whenever you wish, it pleases you to leave counts and kings with nothing.

1931 'When I had any wealth, then I had family and servants; and as soon as I was poor, alas, I lost friends, family and servants. I haven't a single relation who might pretend to love me. My youngest daughter, Cordeille, whom I reproached, told me the truth when she said that as long as I had possessions, so long I would be esteemed and loved. I did not listen to her words but reproached her and thought her mad. As long as I had anything, so long was I valued, so long was I esteemed and loved and so long I found those to flatter me and willingly serve me. They flattered me for what I owned; now, if they see me, they turn away. Cordeille told me the truth but I didn't realise it; I neither noticed nor listened to her, but rebuked and hated her for it, and sent her away from my lands without a single gift. Now my daughters, once my friends, who loved me above anything else so long as I owned anything, have failed me. Now I must go and entreat the woman I banished to another land. But how can I entreat her when I banished her from my kingdom? Nevertheless, I shall go to discover if any good can be found there. She can do no less and no worse than her elders have already done me. She said she would love me as much as she should love her father. What more should I ask of her? She who promised me a different sort of love—was she intending to love me more?[2] She did it to deceive me.'

1973 Leir spent a long time lamenting and reflecting. Then he took ship, went to France and arrived at a harbour in Chauz.[3] He asked frequently for the queen, whose whereabouts close at hand were shown him. He stopped outside the city, so that no one should know him. He sent a squire to tell the queen that her father was coming and needed to ask her assistance. He told her the whole story of how his daughters had thrown him out. Cordeille, like a true daughter, took a large portion of her wealth and gave it all to the squire, asking him secretly to carry it to her father, Leir, on her behalf, and thus to comfort him. And with it, secretly, her father should go to a good town or city, have himself well equipped, fed, dressed, washed and bathed. He should attire himself in royal garments and lodge in great honour, retaining forty knights from the retinue that came with

---

[1] MS H has *roi*, 'king', here.
[2] Here Leir refers to Gonorille or Ragau.
[3] *HRB*: *Karitia*. See Arnold II, pp. 797–8 and Tatlock, pp. 92–3.

Emprés ço face al rei saveir
Que il vient sa fille veeir.
Quant cil out l'aveir recoilli
E le comandement oï,
A sun seinnur porta noveles
Que li furent bones e beles.
A une autre cité tornerent,
Ostels pristrent, bien s'atornerent. [1]
Quant Leïr fu bien atornez,
2010 Bainnez, vestuz e sojornez, [2]
E maisnee out bele assemblee,
Bien vestue e bien atornee,
Al rei manda qu'a lui veneit
E sa fille veeir vuleit.
Li reis meïsme, par noblesce,
E la reïne, od grant leece,
Sunt bien luin contre lui alé
E volentiers l'unt enoré.
Li reis l'ad mult bien receü, [3]
2020 Qui unkes ainz ne l'out veü. [4]
Par tut sun regne fist mander
E a ses humes comander
Que sun suegre trestuit servissent
E sun comandement feïssent;
Deïst lur ço que il vuldreit
E tut fust fait ço qu'il direit
Tant que sun regne li rendist
E en s'enor le restablist.
Aganippus fist que corteis:
2030 Assembler fist tuz ses Franceis;
Par lur los e par lu aïe
Apareilla un grant navie.
Ovoec sun suegre l'enveia
En Bretainne, si li livra
Cordeïlle, que od lui fust,
Qui emprés lui sun regne eüst, [5]
S'il le poeient delivrer
E des mains des gendrez oster. [6]
Cil unt bien tost la mer passee
2040 E la terre tost delivree.

As feluns gendres la tolirent
E de tute Leïr saisirent.
Leïr ad puis treis anz vescu
E tut le regne en pais tenu,
E a ses amis ad rendu
Ço que il aveient perdu.
Emprés les treis anz se morut;
En Leïcestre, u li cors jut,
Cordeïlle l'ensepeli
En la crote el temple Jani.   2050
Puis ad cinc anz tenu l'enor,
Mais ja ert vedve senz seinnor;
Emprés cinc anz l'unt guereiee
E la terre fort chalangiee
Dui fil de ses serors ainz nees
Que Leïr aveit mariees.
Pur la terre l'ante haïrent
E mainte fiez s'en combatirent, [7]
Sovent desuz, sovent desus,
Margan e Cunedagius.   2060
Al derrain Cordeïlle pristrent
E en une chartre la mistrent.
N'en voldrent prendre raençon
Ainz la tindrent tant en prison
Qu'ele s'ocist en la gaiole
De marrement, si fist que fole.
    Quant cil la terre ourent conquise,
Chescuns d'els en ad sa part prise:
Cunedages del Humbre en west,
Margan ço que devers north est; 2070
Issi tindrent dous anz la chose.
Mais coveitise ne repose:
Margan out od sei compainons
Mult envius e mult felons,
Qui n'amoent guaires la pais.
'Mult par iés, distrent il, malvais,
Qui de ço te faiz meiteier
Que tu puez bien tut desrainer.
U tu aies tute Bretainne,
U ja plein pied ne t'en remaine. 2080

---

[1] MS P reading—*ostels*—restored.
[2] MS P reading of ll. 2009–10 restored.
[3] MS P reading—*bien*—restored.
[4] MS P reading—*ainz*—restored.
[5] MS P reading—*sun*—restored.
[6] MS P reading—*des gendrez*—restored.
[7] MS P reading—*s'en*—restored.

Death of Leir

the squire. After this he was to let the king know that he had come to see his daughter.

2003 When the squire had received the money and heard the commands, he carried good and joyful news to his lord. They went to another city, took lodgings, and attired themselves handsomely. When Leir was well equipped, bathed, clothed and comfortably lodged, and had a fine collection of retainers, well dressed and turned out, he sent word to the king that he was coming and wished to see his daughter. The king himself, out of nobility, and the queen, in great gladness, came far out to meet him and took pleasure in honouring him. The king, never having seen him before, received him most hospitably. He commanded his men and proclaimed throughout his kingdom, that everyone should serve his father-in-law and do his bidding; he was to tell them what he wished and whatever he said would be done, until his kingdom was restored and he was re-established in his domain.

2029 Aganippus behaved with courtesy. He summoned all his French and with their advice and their help equipped a large fleet. He sent it with his father-in-law to Britain, and Cordeille too, to be with him, so that she could inherit the kingdom after Leir, if they could set it free and take it out of the hands of the sons-in-law. They soon crossed the sea and quickly set the whole land free. They took it away from the wicked sons-in-law and restored it all to Leir.

2043 Then Leir lived for three more years and held the whole realm in peace, and restored to his friends what they had lost. After the three years, he died. Cordeille buried him in Leicester, where his body lay, in the crypt of the temple of Janus. Then she ruled the kingdom for five years. But now she was a widow, without a husband. After five years, two sons of her elder sisters, married off by Leir, made war on her and laid strong claim to the kingdom. They hated their aunt because she had the land, and many times Margan and Cunedag fought her, sometimes victorious, sometimes defeated. In the end they captured Cordeille and put her in a dungeon. They did not want to take any ransom, but held her so long that she killed herself in prison from sorrow, a foolish deed.

2067 When they had conquered the land, each of them took his share, Cunedag from the Humber to the West, Margan the part towards the North. Thus matters remained for two years. But greed does not sleep.[1] Margan had some very envious and wicked companions with him, who had little love for the land. 'What a coward you are,' they said, 'sharing this, when you could easily claim all of it. You should either have all Britain, or not a single foot of it. When you are the eldest,

---

[1] Probably proverbial. See Morawski, *Proverbes*, no. 704 for an analogy.

Viltance est, quant tu es ainnez,
Que le plus en ait li puis nez.
Passe le Humbre, saisis tut,
Pren les terres tutes de but!'
Margan ad lur conseil creü,
Mais malement l'unt deceü.
Le Humbre od sa force passa,
Arst e destruit, prist e preia.
Cunedages, qui grant gent out,
2090 Vint contre lui cum il ainz pout.
Mes Margan ne l'osa atendre
Ne bataille contre lui prendre;
De terre en terre ala fuiant,
Cunedages l'ala soant.
Margan en Guales s'en fuï,
E cil en Guales le soï;
En Guales fu pris e tuez
E en Guales fu enterrez.
La contree u il fu ocis
2100 E u il fu en terre mis
De Margan out Margan cest nom,
Unches n'i soi altre achaison.
Puis out Cunedages tut sous
Ço que ot esté entr'els dous.
Trente treis anz ad reis vescu
E le regne en grant pais tenu.
Al tens cestui fist Romulus
La cité de Rome, e Remus;
Freres furent, mais par envie
2110 Jeta li uns l'altre de vie.
Ezechias lores viveit,
Ki de Judee reis esteit,
Cui Deus quinze anz vie aluina
Pur ço qu'amerement plura.
Pur ço fu fait el tens Ysaïe,
Ki dist en une prophecie
Que une virgine concevreit
E de la virgene uns filz naistreit
Ki avreit nun Emmanuel,
2120 Qui deveit salver Israhel.

Emprés la mort de Cunedage
Regna un fiz qu'il out mult sage,
Rival out num, mult par fu pruz,
Et mult se fist amer a tuz.
En sun tens pluie de sanc plut
Treis jurs entiers, ne sai que dut,
E tel plenté de musches crut
Dunt mainte gent d'engrot morut;
De la pluie ki plut vermeille
E des musches fud grant merveille.   2130
La gent en fu tute en effrei
E chescuns out poür de sei.
Quant Rivail, li reis, fu feniz,
Le regne out emprés lui sis fiz
Qui aveit nun Gurgustius.
Puis refu reis Sisillius,
E puis Lago, niés Gurgusti,
E puis Kimare, fiz Sisilli. [1]
Gorbodiagnes fu emprés;
Cist out dous fiz mals e engrés,   2140
Li ainz nez d'els out num Ferreus
E li secunz out nun Porreus.
Unc ne se pourent concorder,
Ne trieve entr'els ne pais guarder.
Lur pere aveient encor vif
Quant il comencerent l'estrif
Del regne e de la seinnurie,
Par coveitise e par envie.
Li ainz nez dist que tut avra,
Li altres dit qu'il li toldra.   2150
Porreus out mult le quer felon,
Sun frere vult par traïson
U par alcun enging ocire.
Ferreus le sout, ki l'oï dire;
En France, ultre mer, s'en fuï;
Tant ad le rei Suart servi
Qu'il repaira od grant navie
E od bien grant chevalerie.
A sun frere se combati,
Mais malement l'en eschaï,   2160

---

[1] MS P reading—*E*—restored.

Margan and Cunedag

it's shameful that the youngest should have more. Cross the Humber, seize the lot, and take the lands outright!' Margan trusted their advice, but they wickedly deceived him. He crossed the Humber with his army, burnt and destroyed, robbed and plundered. Cunedag, who had many men, came to meet him as fast as possible. But Margan dared not await him or take battle against him. He fled from place to place, Cunedag pursuing him. Margan fled to Wales and Cunedag followed him to Wales; in Wales he was captured and killed and in Wales he was buried. The region where he was killed and where he was buried takes its name of Margan from Margan; I know no other reason for the name.[1]

2103 Then Cunedag had quite to himself what had previously been shared by the two of them. He lived as king for thirty-three years and kept the kingdom in great peace. In his time Romulus and Remus built the city of Rome; they were brothers, but out of envy one deprived the other of life. Hezekiah was then alive, king over Judaea, whose life God prolonged for fifteen years because of his bitter weeping. This was done in the time of Isaiah, who said in a prophecy that a virgin would conceive, and from the virgin a son would be born, called Emmanuel, who would save Israel.[2]

2121 After Cunedag's death reigned a very wise son of his, by the name of Rival.[3] He was very brave and much loved by all. In his time a bloody rain fell for three whole days—I do not know what that signified—and flies increased in such multitudes that many people died from disease. People were amazed at the crimson rain and the flies; they were terrified, and everyone was afraid for himself. When king Rival died, his son Gurgustius ruled the realm after him. Next came Sisillius, then Lago,[4] nephew of Gurgustius and then Kimare, son of Sisillius. Then came Gorbodiagnes.[5] He had two wicked and violent sons, the elder called Ferreus and the younger Porreus. They could never agree nor keep a truce or peace between them. Their father was still alive when they began, out of greed and envy, a struggle for the kingdom and for power. The elder said he would have it all, the other said he would take it from him.

2151 Porreus had a most wicked heart: he wanted to kill his brother treacherously or through some trick. Ferreus knew this as he had heard him say so. He fled overseas to France and served king Suart[6] so well that he returned with a large fleet and many knights. He fought his brother, but he was unlucky: he was killed

---

[1] According to Arnold II p. 798, this today is Morgannwg in Glamorgan; see however Tatlock p. 68.
[2] Wace adds Hezekiah and the details of Isaiah's prophecy; see Arnold II, p. 798.
[3] *HRB* chap. 33: *Rivallo*.
[4] *HRB* chap. 33: *Iago*.
[5] *HRB* chap. 33: *Gorbodugo*; *VV*: *Gorbodiago*; i.e. Gorboduc.
[6] *HRB* chap. 33: *Suhardus*; *VV*: *Suardus*.

Kar ocis fu premerement
E si chevalier ensement.
Ludon, lur mere, ki ert vive,
Se tint a morte e a chaitive
Del mal e de la cruelté
Que sis fiz out l'altre tué.
Ele aveit le mort plus amé
Sin ad cuilli le vif en hé. [1]
Une nuit que cil se giseit
2170 E tut aseür se dormeit,
Es vos la mere od ses anceles,
Cotels tranchanz suz lur aisseles,
La gargate li unt trenchiee,
Fud mes mere si enragiee!
Deus! ki vit mais si fait pecchié!
Tut l'unt par pieces detrenchié.
Lungement fud grant reparlance
De Ludon e de sa venjance,
Ki pur l'un filz l'altre murdri
2180 E pur l'un filz les dous perdi.
   Quant Ferreus fud morz e Porreus,
N'i out filz ne fille remés
Ne eir procein de lur lignage
Ki tenir peüst l'eritage.
Li riche humme se guereierent,
Li forz les fiebles eissillerent,
Chescuns sulunc ceo qu'il poeit
Ses povres veisins conquereit.
N'i aveit ki tenist dreiture
2190 Ne ki guardast dreit ne mesure.
Li un les altres traïsseient,
Nis li parent s'entr'ocieient
Pur lur aveir e pur lur terres;
Par tut aveient mortels guerres.
Quatre barons i out mult puissanz [2]
E plus richement contenanz,
Ki les altres a els suzmistrent
E lur terres tutes purpristrent. [3]
Chescuns ad purpris entur sei,
2200 E chescuns se fait clamer rei, [4]

E chescuns guereia sun per,
E chescuns vult l'altre grever.
En Escoce regnout Stater
E de Logres ert reis Pinner,
Rudac de Guales reis esteit
E Clotem Corneuaille aveit.
Cist Cloten deüst tut aveir,
Kar l'om n'i saveit plus dreit eir,
Mais cil qui esteient plus fort
N'orent cure de sun acort.   2210
Clotem out puis un filz mult gent,
Ki fud de mult grant hardement;
Bels fud e proz e halt creüz,
Si out num Dumwallo Molmuz;
Hardiz fud e bels e corteis.
Cist trespassad tretuz les reis
Ki en Bretainne ourent esté
De hardement e de bealté.
Des que il pout armes porter
Unkes ne vout plus surjurner;   2220
La terre de Logres conquist,
Pinner, qui reis en ert, ocist.
Puis volt Escocoe e Guales prendre,
Mais li rei s'en voldrent defendre; [5]
Contre lui unt fait aliance
Par serement e par fiance.
Dedenz sa terre a force entrerent,
Mult destrurent e mult roberent. [6]
Rudac i ert od les Gualeis
E Stater od les Escoteis;   2230
Mult aloent chastels pernant,
Maneirs e viles deguastant.
Dumwallo les ad encontrez,
Ki aveit trente mil armez.
Grant tumulte e grant corneïz
Out al premier encuntreïz,
Maint cop unt pris e meint doné, [7]
Maint hume mort e maint nafré,
Maint escu frait e meint percied,
Elme frait, halberc desmailled.   2240

---

[1] MS P reading—*sin*—restored.
[2] MS P reading—*quatre*—restored.
[3] MS P reading—*lur*—restored.
[4] MS P reading—*fait*—restored.

[5] MS P reading—*s'en*—restored.
[6] MS P reading—*roberent*—restored.
[7] MS P's reading of line restored.

Death of Porreus and Ferreus

straightaway and his knights likewise. Ludon, their mother, who was still alive, was mortally distraught at the evil and cruelty of one son killing the other. She had loved the dead man more and came to hate the living. One night when he was lying down and sleeping in complete confidence of safety, along came his mother and her maidservants, sharp knives under their armpits, and they cut his throat. Was there ever such a crazed mother? God! Who ever saw such a sin! They hacked him all to pieces. For a long time there was much talk of Ludon and her vengeance who, for the sake of one son, murdered the other and for one son lost both.

2181 When Ferreus and Porreus were dead, there was no son nor daughter nor close relation from their kin who could inherit. The men of power fought each other, the strong injuring the weak; everyone, as far as he could, subjugated his poorer neighbour. There was no one to uphold righteousness or maintain justice or restraint. The one betrayed the other and even relatives killed each other for their possessions and their lands. Everywhere there was war to the death. There were four lords of great power and splendid appearance who made all the others subordinate to them and seized all their lands. Each seized the lands around theirs, each had himself proclaimed king, each made war on his peer and each wanted to injure the other. Stater reigned in Scotland and Pinner was king of Logres, Rudac was king of Wales and Cloten held Cornwall.

2207 This Cloten should have had everything, for no one knew a more rightful heir than him, but those stronger than him paid no attention to what he wanted.[1] Cloten had a most noble son, who possessed great daring. He was handsome, brave and tall. He was called Dumwallo Molmuz[2] and he was bold, fair and well-mannered. He surpassed all the kings who had ever lived in Britain for daring and beauty. As soon as he could bear arms, he would no longer delay: he conquered the land of Logres and killed Pinner, its king. Then he wanted to take Scotland and Wales, but their kings wished to defend themselves. They made an alliance, through oaths and pledges, against him. They entered his land by force, with much destruction and much devastation. Rudac was there with the Welsh and Stater with the Scots; they went about taking many castles and laying dwellings and towns waste.

2233 Dumwallo met them with thirty thousand armed men. There was great uproar and much blowing of horns at the first encounter, with many a blow given and taken, many men killed and many wounded, many shields shattered and many pierced, helmets smashed and hauberks broken. The battle lasted a long time

---

[1] Wace adds Cloten's strong claim to kingship.

[2] Dumngual Moilmut appears in the early Welsh genealogies. See Tatlock p. 280.

La bataille ad longes duré
E lunges unt entr'els duté
Qui plus fort ert e qui veintreit,
Kar chescuns bien se combateit.
Dumwallo fud mult enginnus
E del veintre mult coveitus;¹
Sis cenz ad pris de ses privez,
Des plus hardiz, des plus pruvez;
Des armes a ses enemis,
2250 Qui giseient el champ ocis,
Les fist armer priveement,
E il se rarma ensement.
Puis lur ad dist: ' Od mei vendrez,
E ceo que jeo ferai ferez.'
Dunc ad guardé e aguaited
E par espies encerchied
Ou Rudac e Stater esteient
E en quel liu se combateient.
Puis lur est de travers coruz
2260 Come s'il fust od els venuz.
As dous reis ad les suens jostez,
Pus lur ad dit: ' Ferez, ferez!'²
Legierement les unt ateinz
Sis unt endous entr'els esteinz;
Puis se sunt tut serreement
Retrait ariere vers lur gent,
Les armes unt entr'els jus mises,
E les premereinnes unt prises,
Que li lor nes entrepreïssent
2270 E pur altres les oceïssent.
Quant il se refurent armé
E a lur gent furent justé,
Dunc les recuillent a ferir,
Mais cil nes pourent pas suffrir;
Pur la mort de lur chevetainnes
Se departirent les compainnes,
E Dumwallo lur corut sure,
Desconfit les ad en poi d'ure.³
Quant il out la terre conquise,
2280 Par tut le regne ad tel pais mise,

Unc puis ne ainz n'i out tel pais,
Ne n'avrad il, ceo crei, jamais.
Corone d'or se fist cist faire;
Unches n'oï de rei retraire
Qui en Bretainne anceis regnast,
Ki d'or corone en chief portast.
Il fist un establissement
E si en fist confermement,
Que tut li temple e les citez⁴
Eüssent si granz dignetez   2290
Que ja huem, tant meffait n'eüst,
Se il dedenz entrer poüst,
Ja fust puis pur home adesez,
Ainz s'en alast quites clamez.
Quites ralast a sun ostel
E quite eüst tut sun chatel.
Puis establi que pais eüssent,
Ne par nul home adesez fussent⁵
Cil ki as charues serreient
Ne cil ki as citez irreient,   2300
Ne a temple ne a marchié;
E ki nul en avreit tuchié
En la merci fust de sa vie,
Come repris de felonie.
Cist mist les lagues e les leis
Que encor tienent li Engleis.
Quarante anz fud reis, puis fina;
Sa gent a Lundres l'enterra
Lez le temple sainte Concorde,
Si come l'estorie recorde,   2310
Un temple que il fist funder
Pur concorde e pur pais guarder.
   De sa muiller aveit dous filz
De gentil lignage, gentilz,
L'ainz nez Belin, li secunz Brenne.
Entre ces dous ourent le regne.
A Brenne, qui esteit li mendre,
Avint Northumberlande a prendre
E Cateneis e quanqu'i a
Devers north des le Humbre en la; 2320

---

¹ MS P reading—*coveitus*—restored.
² MS P reading—*ad dit*—restored.
³ MS P reading—*les ad*—restored.
⁴ MS P reading—*tut*—restored.
⁵ MS P reading—*par*—restored.

Reign of Dumwallo Molmuz

and for a long time it was doubtful who was the stronger and who would win, because each fought well. Dumwallo was very wily and determined to win. He took six hundred of his friends, the boldest and the most experienced, and secretly had them put on the armour of those of his enemies who were lying dead in the field. He did the same. Then he said to them: 'Come with me, and do what I do.' Then he observed and kept watch and inquired through spies where Rudac and Stater were and in what place they were fighting. He ran up to them from the side, as if he had accompanied them, bringing his men next to the two kings. Then he shouted to them: 'Strike, strike!' They easily reached them and put an end to both. Then, in close formation, they all retreated back towards their men, stripped off the armour and resumed what they wore at first, so that their own people did not attack them as enemies and kill them. When they were armed again and next to their own men, then they resumed the attack. But the enemy could not resist them: the troops were scattering, following the death of their leaders, and Dumwallo assailed them. In a little while they were defeated.

2279　When he had conquered the land, throughout the kingdom he established such peace that there has never been anything similar before or since, nor, I think, will there ever be. He had a crown of gold made for himself; I have never heard tell of any king formerly reigning in Britain who wore a golden crown on his head. He made a statute, which he then confirmed, that all the temples and cities should have such great privileges that no man, if he could gain entry, whatever wrong he had done, could be reached, but could get off scot free. He could freely return to his house and freely have all his property. Then he laid it down that those at the plough should have peace, unmolested by anyone, and so should those entering the cities, going either to temple or market; and anyone who touched them would, being apprehended for crime, incur capital punishment. He established the laws and customs which the English still keep. He was king for forty years, then died. His people buried him in London, beside the temple of holy Concord, as the history relates, a temple which he founded to maintain peace and harmony.

2313　By his wife he had two sons, noble and of noble lineage, the elder called Belin, the younger Brenne. The kingdom was divided between these two. It fell to Brenne, the younger, to take Northumberland and Caithness and whatever was

Ne l'en volt Belin plus partir,
E cel lui fist de lui tenir,
Si que Brenne l'en servireit
E a seinnur l'en conustreit. [1]
Belin retint tut en sa baille
Logres, Guales e Cornewaille.
Issi unt cinc anz bien tenu
Que l'uns a l'altre n'ad neü;
Mais entur Brenne out paltoniers
2330 E menteürs e losengiers
Qui tant distrent e enhorterent
Que li frere s'entremeslerent.
Un en i out mult malartous,
E de parler mult enginnus;
Bien sout trobler une raison
E esmover une tençon,
Bien sout fere un encusement
E tresturner un jugement,
E si il sun prud en feïst
2340 Ne li chalut qui que perdist.
'Forment, dist il, nus merveillum,
Mais que dire nel te volum,
Que tu de si grant heritage,
De si grant terre e de si large
Come tis peres tint sa vie,
As pris issi povre partie;
E de cel tant com tu en as
—Ne sai cum tu l'en serviras—
Deiz tun frere Belin servir
2350 E de lui deiz terre tenir.
Iés tu desoignant u bastarz?
Iés tu plus vil u plus cuarz,
Que tu l'en deiz porter homage?
Dunc ne fustes vus d'un parage?
Qui porta tei, si porta lui,
E d'un pere estes vus andui. [2]
E quant vus estes amdui frere,
D'un pere né e d'une mere,
Pur quei ad Belin digneté
2360 Sur tei e sur tun herité?

Rump l'aliance e rump la fei
Que est entre Belin e tei,
Ki te tornë a deshonur;
Ja mar le tendras a seinnur.
Crei tes barons, crei lur conseil.
En meie fei, jeo m'en merveil [3]
De baron de tun vasselage
A qui l'en face tel viltage.
Belin ad parti e choisi.
De quel aconte ad il parti?   2370
Quel partie en deit estre fait,
Mais ki plus purrat plus en ait.
Jeo ne sai neient d'altre dreit,
Mais al meilllur le mielz en seit.
Plus forz e plus hardiz iés tu;
Ço ad l'om assez coneü
Des que tu Ceoflo venquis,
A qui tu Escoce tolis,
Ki reis de Moriane esteit
E Escoce guaster vuleit.   2380
Puet cel estre tu l'as suffert,
E tun corage en as covert
Pur ceo que nus n'en parliom.
Or en parlum si te loom
Que tu tut prenges e tut aies.
Que dotes tu, de quei t'esmaies?
Nus ne te faldrum pur noz vies;
E se tu en nus ne te fies
Que prod n'aies chevalerie,
Va en Norwege quere aïe.   2390
Li reis Elfinges t'aidera,
Une fille ad qu'il te dorra.
Pren sa fille si l'en ameinne,
E des Norreis aveir te peinne;
Tant des Norreis, tant des Escoz,
Tant des estranges, tant des noz,
Tel ost, se tu vuels, pués joster [4]
Dunt maint regne purras guaster;
Ja tis freres ne t'atendra,
Ne el regne ne remaindra.   2400

---

[1] MS P reading—*l'en*—restored.
[2] MS P reading—*estes vus*—restored.
[3] MS P reading—*m'en*—restored.
[4] MS P's reading of line restored.

Brenne is encouraged to rebel

north of the Humber. Belin did not want to part with more and he made him hold the land from him, so that Brenne should serve him for it and recognise him as lord. Belin kept under his control all Logres, Wales and Cornwall. Thus they ruled well for five years, neither harming the other.[1]

2329 But around Brenne there were scoundrels, liars and knaves who kept telling and exhorting the brothers to fight each other. One of them was very crafty and cunning of speech, skilful at muddying an argument and stirring up a dispute. He was expert at accusations and overturning judgements, and if he could turn it to his advantage, he did not care who was the loser. 'We're amazed,' he said, 'but don't want to tell you so, that you have taken such a poor share of such a great inheritance of large, broad lands as your father held in his lifetime; and with what you have must serve your brother Belin—I don't know how you *will* serve him— and hold your land from him. Are you baseborn, a bastard? Are you viler or more cowardly, that you must pay him homage? Are you not of the same lineage? Whoever bore you, bore him, and you both have the same father. And since you are both brothers, born of one father and one mother, why does Belin have authority over you and your heritage? Break the bond and the allegiance between Belin and you, which dishonours you, and never call him lord again. Trust your barons, trust their advice. Upon my word, I'm amazed such an outrage is done to a lord of your valour.

2369 'Belin shared out the land and made his choice. On whose account did he share it? Some division has to be made, but he who can do more, has more. I know of no other rights than that the best goes to the best man. You are stronger and bolder; that was recognised when you conquered Ceoflo,[2] from whom you took Scotland, when he was king of Moriane[3] and wanted to lay Scotland waste. Perhaps you have endured this and concealed your feelings because we did not speak of it. Now we do speak, and we advise you to take everything and have everything. What do you fear, why are you dismayed? We will not fail you, to save our lives; and if you can't rely on us, because you have no brave knights, go and seek help from Norway. King Elfinges[4] will help you; he will give you his daughter. Take his daughter and bring her back and strive to get some Norsemen. Many Norse, many Scots, many from other countries, many from ours—you can put together such an army, if you wish, that you could lay many a kingdom waste. Your brother will never expect you, nor will he ever stay in the realm. But go quickly, and

---

[1] *HRB* (chap. 35) has an initial period of fraternal wars, reduced by *VV* and omitted by Wace who, on the other hand, following the *VV*, greatly expands the following speech by the troublemaker.

[2] *HRB* chap. 35: *Cheulfus*. See Tatlock pp. 128–9.
[3] For varying identifications of Moriane, see Arnold II, pp. 798–9.
[4] *HRB* chap. 35: *Elsingius*; *VV*: *Elfingius*.

Mais va tost e plus tost revien,
E celeement te contien,
Que Belin ne s'en aparceive
E par engieng ne te deceive.'
Quant cil out cest conseil doné
E li altre l'ourent loé,
Brennes volentiers les creï,
Bien quida faire, si failli.
En Norwege ad la mer passee,
2410 La fille Elfinges ad rovee;
E Elfinges li graenta
E od grant aveir li duna,
Si li dist qu'il li aidereit
Tant que Bretainne tut avreit.
Assez fu ki a Belin dist
U Brennes alad e qu'il quist.
Bien ad quidé e suspecied,
Quant tel plai fait senz sun congied,
Que tost i avreit felonie.
2420 Veisdie fist contre veisdie;
Se Brennes le volt enginner,
Il s'en sout bien cuntreguaiter. [1]
Northumberlande ala saisir,
Les chastels prist sis fist guarnir;
N'i laissa fortelesce a prendre
Que Brennes nel peüst susprendre.
Par tuz les chastels mist guardens;
Tenir les quide mais tuz tens,
Que ja sis freres mais nes ait;
2430 Armes e blé i ad atrait.
Il meïsmes, od tut sun efforz, [2]
Fu as rivages e as porz,
Que sis freres ne s'i embate
Senz contredit e senz barate.
Brennes out la nuvele oïe
Que sa terre out Belin saisie;
Feme out prise e fait sun afaire;
Od grant gent se mist el repaire.
La dame ert assez bele e gente,
2440 Mais li plaiz li desatalente.

Ele out, lunc tens aveit passé,
Le rei de Danemarche amé,
Gudlac, qui mult l'aveit amee [3]
Si li deveit estre dunee,
Mais Brennes l'en ad desturbé;
E ele ad a Gudlac mandé
E tut le conseil descovert
Que Brennes l'ad e il la pert,
E, si forment ne se purchace,
Jamais ne girrat en sa brace.   2450
Gudlac, li reis des Daneis, sout
Que Brennes s'amie en menout.
O tant de nefs cum aver pout
Le repaire Brenne guaitout;
S'amie li vuldreit tolir
S'il en poeit en liu venir.
Il l'eüst, ceo diseit, eüe,
Se par lui ne l'eüst perdue.
Les dous flotes s'entrecontrerent,
Nefs contre nefs s'entrehurterent,   2460
Hurt contre hurt, fort contre fort,
Cop contre cop, bort contre bort.
Maint bort i ot frait e percied,
Maint home ocis e maint neied.
Fort sunt de ça, fort sunt de la,
Mais la flote Brennes pleia
Si turna en desconfiture, [4]
E cil Gudlac, par aventure,
A une de lur nefs avint
U la dame ert, si la retint.   2470
N'out que faire des altres nefs;
Cele retint si est remés.
E Brennes s'en alad fuiant,
De sa feme mult dementant.
Quant Gudlac out fait sun eschec,
A terre vulsist estre al sec, [5]
E ja esteit al repairrer,
Mais ore oyez quel desturber!
Une turmente grant leva;
Li tens mua, li venz turna,   2480

---

[1] MS P reading—s'en—restored.
[2] MS P reading—tut—restored.
[3] MS P reading—l'aveit—restored.
[4] MS P reading—en—restored.
[5] MS P reading—al—restored.

Brenne is given the Norwegian princess

return even quicker, and keep your actions secret, so that Belin doesn't notice you and craftily deceive you.'

2405 When he had given this advice and the others had praised it, Brenne willingly believed them. He thought he was acting well, but he was mistaken. He crossed the sea to Norway and asked for Elfinges' daughter; and Elfinges consented and gave her along with much wealth and said he would help him until he owned all Britain. There were plenty of people to tell Belin where Brenne went and what he sought. Since this affair had been conducted without his leave, he thought and suspected that there would soon be treachery. He countered guile with guile: if Brenne wished to trick him, he was well able to be on his guard. He went and seized Northumberland, took the castles and provisioned them; he did not omit to capture any fortress where Brenne could take him unawares. He put guards on all the castles, intending to keep them for ever, so that his brother could never have them again. Weapons and corn were brought to them. He himself, with his whole army, manned the shores and the ports so that his brother could not attack without opposition and difficulty.

2435 Brenne heard the news that Belin had seized his land. He took his wife, concluded his business and returned with many followers. The lady was very lovely and fair, but she disliked the match. A long time ago, she had loved Gudlac,[1] the king of Denmark, who returned her love, and she was to have been his, but Brenne had deprived him of her. She had sent to Gudlac and told him of the whole agreement, whereby Brenne had her and Gudlac had lost her, and, if he did not exert himself, he would never lie in her arms. Gudlac, the Danish king, knew Brenne was taking his beloved away. With as many ships as he could, he watched for Brenne to set out home; he wished to take his beloved from him, if he could manage to reach her. He would have had her, he said, if he had not, through Brenne, lost her.

2459 The two fleets met and the ships attacked each other, pitting knock against knock, strong man against strong man, blow against blow and timber against timber. Many a plank was smashed and pierced, many a man killed and many drowned. Strong men were on this side and that, but Brenne's fleet yielded and turned away in defeat, and by chance Gudlac came upon one of their ships where the lady was and captured it. He had no concern for the other ships; he detained this one and stayed behind. And Brenne fled, lamenting his wife. When Gudlac had taken his booty, he wanted to return to dry land, and he was already turning back when trouble intervened. A great storm arose: the weather altered, the

---

[1] *HRB* chap. 36: *Guithlacus*; *VV*: *Gudlacus*.

Tona e plut e esclaira;
Li ciels neirci, li airs trobla;
La mer mella, undes leverent,
Wages crurent e reverserent.
Nefs comencent a perillier,
Borz e chevilles a fruisser;
Rumpent custures e borz cruissent,
Veilles depiecent e mast fruissent;
N'i poeit hom lever la teste, [1]
2490 Tant par esteit grant la tempeste.
Les nefs furent tost departies
E en plusurs terres fuïes.
Cinc jurs unt issi enduré
A la fort mer, al gros orré;
Gudlac, od treis nefs sulement,
Ad tant coru aval le vent
Al quint jur vint en Engleterre;
Mult fud liez quant il vint a terre
Od la dame que il amout.
2500 Mais il ne conut ne ne sout
En quel terre il ert arivez,
Tant aveit esté esguarez.
Cil qui les rivages guardouent
E qui les porz eschaugaitouent,
Unt Gudlac e ses compainnuns
Pris, e s'amie e ses prisuns,
Sis unt a Belin presentez.
Cil les ad a guarder livrez,
Qui sor la marine atendeit
2510 Quant sis freres Brennes vendreit.
Cil qui od la dame pris furent
La verité al rei conurent
Come Brennes aveit ovré
E en Norwege al rei esté,
E coment Gudlac l'out trové
E coment l'out desbareté.
Brennes n'out guaires demoré;
Grant navie read assemblé
Si est arivez en Escoce
2520 Od grant navie e od grant force.

A sun frere Belin manda
E par messages li prea
Que sa feme ne retenist;
Delivrast la si li rendist,
E ses chastels li delivrast,
En sa terre si s'en alast.
E se il tost ne li rendeit
Tute sa terre guastereit.
Belin ne crienst point la manace, [2]
Ne nule rien que Brennes face;   2530
Tut plainnement l'ad escondit.
Quant Brennes entendi e vit
Que par amor rien n'i avreit
Ne preiere rien n'i valdreit,
Ses compainnuns aparailla
E ses eschieles ordena;
Juste le bois de Calatere
S'entrecuntrerent li dui frere.
Li uns ad mult l'altre haï
E li uns ad l'altre envaï;   2540
Li uns vers l'altre ad chevalché,
Li uns ad l'altre manacié.
Quant les dous oz s'entrecontrerent,
Par grant fierté s'entremellerent;
De darz i out grant lanceïz
E de pieres grant geteïz
E de lances grant boteïz
E d'espees grant chapleïz.
Gettent, lancent, fierent e botent,
Cheent, jambetent, almes rotent;   2550
Li Breton furent li meillur
E li Norreis li soldeiur;
Nes pourent pas longes suffrir,
As nefs les en estut fuïr.
Mais Belin les vait parsiuant,
Qui mult les vait acravantant;
A vinz, a cenz e a milliers
Muerent as chans e as sentiers.
Brennes, ki le mal comença,
A grant peinne s'en eschapa;   2560

---

[1] MS P reading—*N'i*—restored.   [2] MS P reading—*la*—restored.

Belin defeats Brenne

wind changed direction, there was thunder and lightning and rain. The sky darkened, the air thickened; the sea became tempestuous, waves reared up, breakers rose and fell. The ships were soon in danger: planks and pegs began to be smashed, seams were broken and boards holed, sails were rent and masts shattered. No one could raise his head, the tempest was so fierce. The ships were soon dispersed and scattered to many lands.

2493 For five days they remained in this way on the raging sea in a strong wind. Gudlac, with only three ships, ran so fast before the wind that on the fifth day he reached England. He was very glad to reach land with the lady he loved. But he neither knew nor recognized the country where he had arrived, so far was he out of his way. Those guarding the shores and keeping watch on the ports took Gudlac and his companions, his mistress and his prisoners, and presented them to Belin. He, waiting on the coast for the coming of his brother Brenne, handed them over to be guarded. Those taken with the lady revealed the truth to the king: how Brenne had acted and had gone to the king in Norway, and how Gudlac had found him and how he had routed him.

2517 Brenne did not delay; he gathered another great fleet and took it to Scotland along with a large army. He sent word to his brother Belin and requested him through messengers not to detain his wife. He should hand her over and return her, restore his castles to him and then depart into his own land. If he did not return her soon, Brenne would lay all his lands waste. Belin was not in the least frightened by the threat, or by anything Brenne could do, and flatly refused.

2532 When Brenne saw and understood that he would get nothing voluntarily and entreaty was useless, he armed his companions and arranged his troops. The two brothers met beside the wood of Calatere.[1] One strongly hated the other and that other had invaded the first's lands; the first had ridden out to fight the second, and the second had threatened the first. When the two armies met, they fiercely joined battle; there was much throwing of spears, casting of stones, thrusting of lances and slaughter with swords. They threw, struck, hit and thrust; they fell, kicked helplessly and belched out their souls. The British were better, the Norwegians mere mercenaries. They could not stand it for long and had to flee to their ships. But Belin pursued them, quite exterminating them; by twenties, hundreds and thousands they died in the fields and on the paths. Brenne, who

---

[1] In Scotland, later situated by Wace near Alclud (Dumbarton). See para. 3510.

Une nacele al port trova, [1]
Sei dozime dedenz entra,
Unches des suens plus n'en mena;
Devers France la mer passa.
Tuz ses compainnuns out perduz,
Morz e nafrez e retenuz.
Quant li mort furent enterré,
Quinze mile furent numbré,
Ne nul n'en sunt mie eschapé
2570 Qui ne seient a mort nafré.
Quant cil afaire fu feniz
E li freres s'en fu fuïz,
Belin ad tenu sun concille
A Everwic, dedenz la vile,
Si quist conseil quei il fereit
Del rei Gudlac que il teneit;
E Gudlac mandé li aveit
De la prison u il esteit
Ke de Belin s'enor tendreit,
2580 E sis huem liges devendreit,
E de Danemarche par ban
Li rendreit treü chescun an.
De ceo li fereit seürtance
Par ostages e par fiance,
Se il l'en lessout quite aler
E s'amie quite mener.
Li reis coveita mult a faire
De Danemarche sa tributaire. [2]
Par le los de sa baronie
2590 Delivra Gudlac e s'amie;
Mais de Gudlac ad pris homage
E serement e salf ostage
De tenir li sun covenant, [3]
Si l'en laissa aler a tant.
Gudlac issi s'en departi
E en sa terre reverti;
S'amie en ad od sei menee
Que par grant peinne out achatee.
    Belin tint l'enor vivement
2600 E mult se contint sagement.

Paisibles fud e pais ama,
Pais establi e pais guarda;
Tote Bretaine porala,
Les contrees avirona;
Vit les mores, vit les boschages,
Vit les eues, vit les passages,
Que l'on ne poeit prod passer
Ne de cited a l'altre aler. [4]
Par vals, par mores e par monz
Fist fire chauciees e ponz;   2610
Bons ponz fist faire e chemins hauz
De pierre, od sablun e od chauz.
Primes fist faire une chauciee,
Qui encor puet estre enseinnee,
Del lunc de la terre, mult grant:
Fos l'apelent li païsant,
Qui comença en Toteneis [5]
E si finist en Cateneis;
Vers Cornewaille comença,
E dedenz Escoce fina.   2620
Del port de Hamtone sor mer
Fist un chemin chaucied mener
Jesqu'en Guales a Saint Davit,
E la ultre en la mer fenit.
De cité en cité ala
Tant come la terre li dura. [6]
Dous chauciees refist de lé,
Ki le païs unt traversé.
Quant li reis out les chemins faiz, [7]
Ceo rova qu'il eüssent pais;   2630
Tote pais e quitance eüssent,
E si en sun demeinne fussent,
Que ki nul en violereit,
Sis demainnes forfaiz sereit.
Brennes, qui fud alez en France,
De sa terre out hunte e pesance,
E de sa feme mult grainnur
Qu'il perdi par tel deshonur.
Sei doziesme de compainuns
Servi le rei e ses barons.   2640

---

[1] MS P reading—*nacele al*—restored.
[2] MS P reading—*De*—restored.
[3] MS P reading—*sun*—restored.
[4] MS P reading—*l'altre*—restored.

[5] MS P reading—*comença*—restored.
[6] MS P reading—*li*—restored.
[7] MS P reading—*les*—restored.

Belin rules Britain while Brenne escapes to France

had begun the trouble, barely escaped. He found a small boat in a port, boarded it with a dozen, no more, from among his men, and crossed the sea to France, He had lost all his companions, who were dead, wounded or captured. When the dead were buried, they numbered fifteen thousand; not one escaped who was not mortally wounded.

2571 When the business was finished and his brother had fled, Belin held his council at York, within the town, and asked for advice on what to do with king Gudlac, whom he held captive. Gudlac sent word to him from his prison that he would hold his domain from Belin and become his liege man, and render him tribute, publically proclaimed throughout Denmark, every year. He would guarantee this through oaths and through hostages, if he would let him go free and take his mistress with him. Belin was very eager to make Denmark his tributary. By his barons' advice he freed Gudlac and his beloved; but he received homage from Gudlac and reliable hostages and an oath to keep his agreement, whereupon he let him go. So Gudlac departed and returned to his land, taking his beloved with him, whom he had acquired with much suffering.

2599 Belin ruled the realm decisively and behaved very wisely. He was peaceful and peace-loving, establishing and keeping the peace. He travelled the length and breadth of Britain, traversing the regions and seeing the marshes and the woods, the rivers and the fords and that no one could cross or go from one city to the other. Across valleys, through marshes and between mountains he had bridges and causeways made. They were good bridges and raised roads, made of stone, with sand and lime. First of all he had a highway made which can still be pointed out: it is very big, running the length of the land. The peasants call it Fosse;[1] it began in Totnes and ended in Caithness, starting near Cornwall and ending in Scotland. From the port of Hampton on sea he made a road which led all the way to St David's in Wales[2] and finished in the sea beyond. It went from city to city as long as the land lasted. He made two more roads crossing the breadth of the country. When the king had made the roads, he commanded that peace be kept upon them. There had to be peace and freedom on them, and if there were any people in his realm who committed any act of violence on them, their lands would be forfeit.

2635 Brenne, who had gone to France, felt ashamed and angry about his land and even more so about his wife, whom he had lost with such dishonour. He and his eleven companions served the king and his lords. He was a daring and brave knight and

---

[1] Wace adds this. Gaimar, *Estoire* ll. 4365–72, refers to the Fosse Way (as does Book I of *HA*) and Belin's road.

[2] The Icknield Way.

Chevalers ert hardiz e pruz,[1]
Si se faiseit amer a tuz.
Ne failleit mie as livreisuns
Ne as soldees ne as duns;
Mult ert preisez pur sa proësce
Et mult amez pur sa largesce,
Kar largement se conteneit,
Mult donout e mult despendeit.
Quant il se fu bien acointiez
2650 E par la terre fu preisiez,[2]
As reis e as altres seinnors
Demanda aïe e succurs
A conquere sun heritage
Dunt Belin li faiseit tolage.
Trespassez est a la parfin
Jesqu'en Burguine, al duc Seguin;
Cil ad Brenne mult enoré
E mult li ad del suen doné.
Brennes parlout corteisement
2660 Si ert de grant afaitement;
De bois saveit e de riviere
E deduz de mainte maniere,
Gent cors aveit e bel visage;
Bien semblout home de parage.
E li duc ert de grant poeir,
Mais il n'aveit emfant ne eir
Fors une fille solement,
E cele ert ja de tel juvent,
Tant creüe e tant amendee,
2670 Bien poeit estre mariee.
Brennes sout bien le duc servir
E bien parler a sun plaisir;
Mult plout al duc sa contenance
E mult ama sa remanance;
Sa fille a feme li duna
E de sa terre l'erita,
Se si ert que il filz n'eüst
De sa muiller ainz qu'il murust.
Cil de l'enor l'unt mult amé,
2680 E tenu l'unt en grant chierté;

E il se sout bien faire amer
Par bel parler, par bien duner.
N'ert pas enchor li anz passez
Puis que Brennes fu mariez,
Quant li ducs, sis suegres, morut;
Duc fu Brennes, l'enor reçut.
Li baron qui ainz amé l'orent
L'amerent puis plus, se plus pourent,[3]
Kar il lur donout largement
E parlout amiablement.   2690
Mult l'amouent li Burguinun,
Li chevalier e li baron;
Assez out grant terre e grant rente,
E muiller out e bele e gente,
Mais il n'ad mië oblié
Que Belin l'out desherité,
Que li out tut toleit sun fieu.[4]
Des que il vit e tens e lieu,
Genz assembla, quist chevaliers,
Preia veisins, prist soldeiers;   2700
Od grant ost vint en Normendie,
Illec apareilla navie.
Quant il fu prest e il out vent,
La mer passa tut salvement.
Belin, ki sa venue sout,
Od tant de gent cum aver pout
Vint a bataille contre lui;
Grant gent ourent e fiere andui.[5]
Ja esteient as armes prendre,
E al ferir e al defendre,   2710
Quant entr'els dous vint Toruuenne,
Mere Belin e mere Brenne.
Entre les dous oz vint tremblant,
Veille ert si alout trutenant.[6]
Tant ad quis Brenne e demandé
Que li baron li unt mustré.
Al col li ad sun braz jeté,
Mult l'a baisé e acolé;
N'aveit pieç'a a lui parlé,
Si l'aveit lunges desirré.   2720

---

[1] MS P reading—*hardiz*—restored.
[2] MS P reading—*fu*—restored.
[3] MS P reading—*plus*—restored.
[4] MS P reading—*que*—restored.
[5] MS P reading—*fiere*—restored.
[6] MS P reading—*trutenant*—restored.

Brenne marries a Burgundian princess

made everyone love him. He was not backward with rations or wages or gifts: his bravery earned him much praise, and his generosity, much love, for he acted generously, greatly giving and greatly spending. When he had got to know many and was well esteemed throughout the land, he asked the kings and other lords for help and succour to reconquer his inheritance, taken from him by Belin. Finally he travelled to Burgundy and duke Seguin,[1] who paid much honour to Brenne and gave him many of his possessions.

2659   Brenne spoke courteously and possessed many skills: he knew about hunting and water-fowling and all sorts of pastimes. He had a handsome body and a fine face and certainly seemed nobly born. And the duke was a man of great power, but he had neither child nor heir, except for a single daughter, and she was already a young girl so grown up and mature that she was certainly marriageable. Brenne was well able to serve the duke and to talk so as to give him pleasure. The duke very much liked his appearance and his presence. He gave him his daughter to wife and his land to inherit, so long as he himself had no son from his wife before he died. Those in the realm loved Brenne very much and greatly cherished him; and he knew how to make himself loved through fine words and gifts.

2683   The year following Brenne's marriage had not yet ended when the duke, his father-in-law, died. Brenne became duke and received the domain. The lords who had loved him before now loved him even more, if possible, because he made them generous gifts and spoke to them kindly. The Burgundians, knights and barons, were very fond of him; he had many broad lands and large revenues; and he had a beautiful and kind wife. But he had not forgotten that Belin, by taking the whole of his domain, had disinherited him. As soon as he saw a suitable time and opportunity, he gathered men, looked for knights, entreated his neighbours and engaged mercenaries. With a great army he entered Normandy and there prepared a fleet. When he was ready and had a favourable wind, he crossed the sea quite safely.

2705   Belin, hearing of his coming, marched against him with as many men as possible, both powerful and strong. They were on the point of taking up arms, of striking and defending themselves, when between the two came Torwenne,[2] the mother of Belin and Brenne. She was old, but she hastened[3] to come with a trembling step between the two armies. She searched and asked for Brenne so much that the barons pointed him out. Throwing her arms around his neck, she showered kisses and embraces on him; she had not spoken to him for some time and had desired it for a long while. She tore all her garments down to her belt and showed

---

[1] *HRB* chap. 40: *Seginum*, duke of the Allobroges.
[2] *HRB* chap. 41: *Conwenna*; *VV*: *Tonwenna*.
[3] Arnold substitutes MS J's *oituant* (whose mean-

ing is unknown) for MS P's *trutenant* (MS N: *trotonnant*), which would appear to mean 'hastening'.

Ses vestemenz ad tuz deroz
Jesqu'a la ceinture desuz;
Ses mameles li mustra nues,
Flaistres de vieillesce e pelues.
A sun fiz parla en plorant,
Ses paroles entrerumpant,
Kar ele sangluteit sovent
E suspirout parfundement:
'Bel filz, dist ele, entent a mei;
2730 Remembre tei, remembre tei
De cez mameles que tu veiz
Que tu alaitas mainte feiz;
Remembre tei que tu eissis
De cest ventre quant tu nasquis;
Remembre tei de la dolur
Que jeo suffri de tei maint jor;
Remembre tei, filz, de cest cors,
Dunt li Criere te mist fors
Ki te crea quant tu n'esteies;
2740 Remembre tei e si me creies:
Met jus les armes que tu tiens
Ki d'alienes terres viens
E alienes genz ameinnes
Pur destruire les tuens demeines.
Faiz tu tel joie a tes amis
Que tu pieç'a mais ne veïs
Del bien ou Deus t'at eshaucié?
Faiz nus en tu tel amistié
Que tu vienz ça tun frere ocire?
2750 Repose tei, apaie t'ire.
Ja mais n'avras sorur ne frere,
Tu n'as pere, vieille est ta mere.
Deüsses tu ça repairer
Tes povres parens eissillier?
Tu nus deüsses aporter
Tes bels aneus presenter,[1]
E mustrer nus ta grant richesce
E vanter tei de ta hautesce.
Tu deüsses en pais venir
2760 E tes bels aveirs porofrir.

E tu nus viens les noz tolir,
Ki nus deüsses maintenir.
Fai ceste folie remaindre!
Se de tun frere te vuels plaindre,
Jeo t'en ferai par jugement
Tun dreit aveir plenierement.[2]
Si tu diz ceo qu'il te chaça
E de ta terre t'essilla,
Tu as tort, ne diz pas raisun;
Nuls ne t'essilla si tu nun.   2770
Tu as del tut le tort eü
Ki tut as le mal esmeü;
Cil ad le tort, que que l'en die,
Ki comence la felonie.
Bien set l'om que tu començas,
Ki en Norwege trespassas
E feme en Norwege preïs,
Que tu congied ne l'en queïs,
E les Norreis en esmeüs
Pur lui chacier, mais ne peüs.   2780
Si ne l'aveies deffié,
Ne il ne t'aveit dreit veé.
Deserité u mort l'eüsses,
Ceo set l'on bien, se tu peüsses.
Belin ne t'at mie chacied,
Einz t'at en Burguinne enveied
Pur aveir altretant u plus
Que il nen ad, qu'i ore iés ducs.
Ne te deiz pas vers lui iraistre,
Qui de Burguinne t'at fait maistre.   2790
De petit t'at levé en grant,
E de povre t'at fait manant;
Del regne aveies ta partie,
Bien faiz que tu li as guerpie;
E encore, si tei pleüst,
Northumberlande toye fust.
Laissiede l'as pur mielz aveir;
Tun frere en deiz buen gré saver
Par qui tu eüs achaisun
D'aler en autre regiun   2800

---

[1] MS P reading—*aneus*—restored.   [2] MS P reading—*tun*—restored.

Tonwenne intervenes between the brothers

him her bare breasts, withered and hairy with age. Weeping, she spoke to her son, her words broken by frequent sobs and deep sighs.

2729   'My fine son,' she said, 'listen to me: remember, remember these breasts you see, which you sucked so many times! Remember that you left this belly when you were born. Remember the anguish I suffered many a day for you. Remember, my son, this body, from which the Creator took you, who created you when you were not. Remember, and trust me: put down the weapons you hold, you who come from a foreign land, and bring foreigners to destroy your own domains. Is this the joy you bring your friends, whom you have not seen for so long, from the good fortune to which God has raised you? Is this the friendship you bear us, that you come here to kill your brother? Rest, appease your anger. You will never have another sister or brother; you have no father and your mother is old. Did you mean to return here in order to drive your wretched family into exile? You should have brought and given us your fine rings and shown us your great wealth and boasted of your high estate. You should have come in peace, proffering your fine possessions, and instead you, who should protect us, come to take away ours.

2763   'Put an end to this folly! If you want to complain about your brother, I will have you awarded, judicially, your full rights. If you say that he pursued you and banished you from your land, you are wrong, you are not in the right. Nobody banished you except yourself. You were entirely in the wrong since you set all the trouble in motion; whatever one may say, he who starts a wicked act is in the wrong. It's well known that you began it, by going to Norway and taking a wife there; you didn't ask him for leave, and you roused the Norwegians in order to expel him, but you failed. If you had not defied him, he would not have denied you your rights. You would have disinherited or killed him, if you could, that's well known.

2785   'Belin didn't expel you, but sent you into Burgundy to acquire as much, or more there than he had, since you are now duke. You should not be angry with him who has made you master of Burgundy. He has raised you from lowly to great, has made you rich, from being poor. You had your share of the kingdom, and did well to abandon it; and if you wished, Northumberland could still be yours. You left it to acquire something better. You ought to be grateful to your brother, for giving you the opportunity to go to another land to receive the large domain of which God has made you lord.

2803   'You only have one brother: you should love him. But he has the right to hold you very much to blame, for you have done him very great wrong by bringing these people against him in order to disinherit your family and devastate our land—

Pur receivre la grant honur
Dunt Dampnedeus t'at fait seinnur.
Un sul frere as, cel deiz amer;
Mais il te devreit mult blasmer,
Kar tu li as mult grant tort fait
Ki cest pople as sur lui atrait
Pur tes parenz deseriter
E pur nostre terre guaster,
Qui altretel de tei fereient,[1]
2810 Se il le desus en aveient.
Bels filz Brennes, que penses tu?
Met jus ta lance e tun escu
Si crei le conseil de ta mere,
Si t'acorderas a tun frere.
Pardune lui tun maltalent,
Il a tei le suen ensement.'
Brennes sa mere bien oï;
Pitied en out si la creï;
L'espee desceinst, l'elme osta,
2820 E del halberc se desarma.
Devant sa gent el champ sailli,
E Belin refist altresi.
E la mere les assembla
E a baiser les comanda.
Unches conte n'i out conté,[2]
Des que ele l'out comandé;
Alés se sunt entrebaisier
E dulcement entrebracier.[3]
Issi fud la guerre achevee
2830 E l'ire des freres finee.
  D'iluec sunt a Lundres venu
Si unt lur concile tenu;
Ceo fud la fin del parlement
E ceo distrent comunement,
Que vers France mer passerunt
E tote France conquerunt.
Dunc somunt Belin ses barons,[4]
E Brennes prist ses Burguinnuns;
A un terme qu'il proposerent
2840 Al port vindrent, es nefs entrerent,

Vers Francë unt la mer passee.
La gent en fu tote effree
E grant poür aveient tuit
Qu'il ne fussent en fin destruit.
A cel tens aveit plusurs reis
En France, maistres de Franceis;
Cil se sunt par conseil comun
Tenu ensemble e pris a un.
As dous freres se combatirent,
Mais li dui frere les venquirent;   2850
Ne se pourent vers els defendre,
Ainz les esteut par force rendre.
N'i ad tant riche quis atende,
Qui recet ait, qui ne lur rende.
Les chastels e les citez pristrent,
En meins d'un an France conquistrent;
Tuz li pople devant eus tremble.
Dunc unt li frere parlé ensemble[5]
Si distrent qu'il irrunt a Rome
E jesque la ne lairrunt home   2860
Ki cité ne bon chastel tienge
Qui lur huem liges ne devienge.
Dunques unt lur genz remandees
E lur maisnees assemblees.
Tant cum il pourent gent menerent,
Mongieu e Mont Ceneis passerent,
Taurins pristrent e Ivorie
E les citez de Lombardie,
Verzels e Pavie e Cremoine,
Melan e Plesence e Buluinne,   2870
L'eue passerent de Taron
Et puis passerent Munt Bardon;
Toscane unt conquise e robee,
Une terre desaloee.
Quant plus alerent purpernant
E vers Rome plus aprismant,
E cil de Rome plus fremirent,
Ki les noveles en oïrent.
En cel an dunt jeo parol ci
Aveient Romain establi   2880

---

[1] MS P reading—*altretel*—restored.
[2] MS P's reading of line restored.
[3] MS P's rhyming order restored in ll. 2827–28.
[4] MS P reading—*barons*—restored.
[5] MS P's order of line restored.

Belin and Brenne invade France and Italy

who would do the same to you, if they had the upper hand. My fine son Brenne, what do you think? Put down your lance and your shield, trust your mother's advice and be reconciled with your brother. Give up your anger against him and he will do the same to you.'

2817   Brenne listened attentively to his mother; he pitied and trusted her. He unbuckled his sword, took off his helmet and laid aside his hauberk. He sprang into the field, in front of his men, and Belin did likewise, and their mother brought them together and ordered them to embrace. As soon as she ordered it, there was no more to be said: they advanced to kiss and sweetly embrace each other. Thus the war was finished and the brothers' anger brought to an end.

2831   From there they went to London and held their council. This was the conclusion of their conference: they both said they would cross the sea to France and conquer the whole of it. Then Belin summoned his barons and Brenne his Burgundians; at a specified time, they came to the port, embarked and crossed the sea towards France.[1] The French people were quite terrified and were all very frightened that in the long run they would be vanquished. At that time there were several kings in France, lords over the French. By common agreement they joined forces and put up resistance. They fought the two brothers, but the two brothers beat them; they could not defend themselves against them but had to submit to them by force. No matter how powerful a lord was who opposed them, if he had a stronghold he had to surrender it to them. They took the castles and the cities and in less than a year conquered France, all the people quaking before them.

2858   Then the two brothers conferred together and said they would go to Rome and would leave no one alone, as far as that city, holding a town or a good castle, who did not become their liege man. Then they again summoned their men and gathered their followers, leading as many men as they could. They crossed Montgieu and Mont Cenis, took Turin and Ivrea and the cities of Lombardy, Vercelli, Pavia and Cremona, Milan, Piacenza and Bologna, crossed the river Taro and then crossed Mont Bardon.[2] They conquered and plundered Tuscany, a land of bad repute.[3] The more they overran, the closer they came to Rome and the more the Romans shuddered on hearing the news.

---

[1] *HRB* chap. 42: Gaul; *VV*: France.
[2] Wace adds this route into Italy, which Arnold suggests is a pilgrimage one, passing along the old Via Flaminia to Bologna. See Bennett, 'Wace and Warfare', p. 39. *Montgieu* is the St Bernard Pass; *Ivrea* is Eporedia, in the province of Turin. *Mont Bardon* (Blenner-Hassett, *A Study of the Place-Names*, p. 24) is 'the crest of the Ligurian Alps'.
[3] *Terre desaloee*, literally prohibited or unsanctioned land. Wace may be punning with the

opposite of *terre aloee* or allodial land, freehold and not a fief, and referring to a contemporary situation, the conflicting claims of Church and Emperor to the 'Matildine lands'. Tuscany was the *allodium* of countess Matilda of Tuscany, who willed it to the Church; after her death in 1114/1115, it was claimed by her kinsman, the emperor Henry V. The dispute between Church and Empire continued to preoccupy the Papacy for the rest of the century. See Robinson, *The Papacy*, p. 246.

Dous contes as guerres baillir
E a lur terres maintenir:
Li uns Porsenna nom aveit,
Li autres Gabius esteit.
Cil unt as senators parlé
Si lur unt conseil demandeé
Cumfaitement se contendreient:
Se as freres se combatreient,
U lur cité lur livrereient, [1]
2890 U lur feus d'els reconustreient.
Cil furent bien espouenté
Si distrent ceo en lur sené
Que neient ne se combatrunt;
Fort sunt li frere e grant gent unt. [2]
Mais se il poent pais trover
Pur premettre ne pur doner,
Vers les dous freres pais querunt;
Or e argent tant lur durunt
Que ja plus ne demanderunt,
2900 E estre ceo lur premettrunt
Treü chescun an a doner
E sis en ferunt retorner,
Ainz ke lur vile seit guastee
Ne eissillee la contree.
Que vus fereie je lunc conte?
Par cel conseil vindrent li conte
As freres, si lur aporterent
Mult grant aveir, qu'il lur donerent;
E, pur aveir lur amistied,
2910 Lur unt promis e otreied
Chescun an de Rome treü;
Li frere unt l'aveir receü;
Del treü e des covenanz
Ourent ostages remananz
De Rome vint e quatre enfanz
Des plus forz e des plus mananz.
Issi fud l'amistied fermee
Ki mult out puis corte duree.
    Li dui frere s'en repairouent;
2920 Par Lombardie trespassoent.

Sur les Alemans en aloent
Pur treü qu'il lur demandoent,
Mais li Romain les desturberent
Ki covenant lur trespasserent
En core unt laissied lor ostages
Ki esteient de lor lignages,
E l'amistied unt corumpue,
Mult fud petit par els tenue;
Kar des que Belin s'esluinna
E Brennes de Rome turna,   2930
La poür tute entr'ublierent
E lur hardement recovrerent.
Si unt pris de lur chevaliers
Ne sai quanz cenz ne quanz millers,
Bien armez e apareillez,
Sis unt soëntr'els enveiez
Pur desconfire e pur ateindre
E as trespas des mons destreindre.
Une altre partie d'els pristrent,
En Alemainne les tramistrent,   2940
Qui as Alemans s'assemblassent
E lur force entr'els ajustassent,
E les trespas des monz guaitassent
Que senz damage n'i passassent. [3]
Ceste partie pur ceo firent
Que il quiderent, si faillirent,
Que as trespas des granz montaines,
Od la presse des granze compainnes,
Fussent li frere si enclos
Detriés de cels de Rome as dos,   2950
Et de cels d'Alemainne as vis,
Que tuit fussent illuec ocis;
Kar la veie n'ert mie dreite
Ainz ert torte, lunge e estreite;
Qui en tel veie ert encontrez
Legierement ert desturbez;
Assez i poeit desconfire
Un poi de gent un grant empire.
Quant Belin e Brennes ço sourent,
Tel conseil pristrent cum il pourent,   2960

---

[1] MS P reading—*lur cité*—restored.
[2] MS P reading—*e*—restored.

[3] MS P's reading of line restored.

Rome breaks its promise to pay tribute

2879   In the year I speak of, the Romans had appointed two counts to run wars and protect their lands. One of them was called Porsenna and the other Gabius. They spoke to the senators and asked their advice on how they should act, whether they should fight the brothers or surrender their city to them, or acknowledge their overlordship. They were terrified and said in their senate that in no way would they fight; the brothers were strong, with a large army. But if they could secure peace, through promises or gifts, they would seek a peace with the two brothers. They would give them so much gold and silver that they would never ask for any more, and in addition they would promise to give them tribute each year, and thus they would make them turn back before their town was laid waste or the country destroyed.

2905   Why should I make a long story of it? Armed with this advice the counts came to the brothers, bringing many rich possessions, which they gave them, and, in order to have their friendship, promised and agreed a tribute from Rome every year. The brothers received the possessions and, for the tribute and agreements, took as hostages twenty-four children from amongst the richest and most powerful residents of Rome. Thus the friendship was secured, which had a very short duration thereafter.

2919   The two brothers returned, passing through Lombardy. They attacked the Germans, demanding tribute from them, but the Romans thwarted them by breaking their covenant. Moreover they had abandoned their hostages, who came from their own families, and had damaged the friendship, paying little regard to it, for as soon as Belin was far away and Brenne had left Rome, they entirely forgot their fear and recovered their boldness. They took I know not how many hundreds or thousands of their knights, well armed and equipped, and sent them after Belin and Brenne, to overtake, beat and harry them while they were crossing the mountains. They selected another band and sent them to Germany, in order to join the Germans, add to their strength and watch the mountain passes so that the brothers could not cross them without losses. They sent this band because they believed, should they fail, that in the great mountain passes, in the battle with many troops, the brothers would be so surrounded, with the Romans at their back and the Germans in front, that there they would all be killed. For the path was not straight but winding, long and narrow; anyone opposed on this path would be easily thrown into confusion. A few men could entirely defeat a great empire.

2959   When Belin and Brenne knew of this, they decided as best they could that Brenne

Que Brennes s'en returnereit
E as Romains se combatreit,
E de la mentie fiance,
Se il poeit, prendre venjance;
E Belins les monz passereit,
Les Alemans desconfireit;
E li quels ainz vencu avreit
Sun autre frere succurreit.
Cels de France e cels de Burguinne
2970 Mena Brennes en sa busuinne,
E Belins out ses compainnuns,
Gualeis e Escoz e Bretuns.
Mais quant li Romain aperçurent,
Cil ki en Alemainne furent,
Que Brennes ariere turnout
E que a Rome repairout,
Conseil pristrent qu'il s'en ireient
E cels de Rome succurreient;
E par un chemin qu'il saveient
2980 Brenne e sa gent devancireient.
Belin sout bien par une espie
L'eire de cele compainnie;
Le terme sout de lur repaire
E quel part il deveient traire.
Guions ad fait des païsanz;
Par fiance en prist ne sai quanz,
Que al plus dreit que il porrunt
El repaire de cels le merrunt. [1]
Es eles de Montgieu entra,
2990 E jor e nuit tant espleita
Qu'al demain vint en une valee [2]
Que li guion li unt mustree,
U li Romain passer deveient,
Que trestorner ne se poeient.
Belin guaita si defendi
Que en l'ost n'ait noise ne cri;
Bels fud li tens cum en esté,
Clere la nuit, l'air senz oré,
La lune clere cler raia;
3000 Belin el val se reconsa; [3]

E li Romain tindrent lur rote
Tut asseür, n'aveient dute;
A la lune, ki cler luseit,
S'en aloent a grant espleit,
Quant desor l'aguait s'embatirent
E a la lune luire virent
Elmes e seles e escuz.
Es les vus trestuz esperduz
E cil kis ourent atenduz
Les unt demaintenant feruz.   3010
Des que Belin cria s'enseine,
N'i out cuarz qui puis se feinne.
De tutes pars les envaïssent;
Cil s'en fuient, le champ guerpissent.
Mais il ne poeient fuïr
Ne il n'aveient u tapir,
E li Breton les esboëlent
E esmanquent e escervelent,
E as plusurs trenchent les testes
E ocient cum altres bestes.   3020
Unches l'ocise ne fina
Des le matin qu'il ajorna
Des qu'al vespre qu'il anuita
E que la nuit les desevra.
Tant cum de vifs s'en eschaperent
Es valees se trestornerent.
    A l'altre jor, bien par matin,
Rentra Belin en sun chemin; [4]
Sun frere vers Rome soï;
Brennes le sout si l'atendi.   3030
Quant li frere se rassemblerent
Plus fier e plus seür alerent;
A Rome vindrent si l'asistrent,
De plusurz parz le siege mistrent;
Perrieres, troies e multons
E engiens de plusurs façons
Firent faire e al mur hurter
Pur le mur fraindre e enfondrer.
Cil de Rome al mur les atendent,
Ki a merveille se defendent;   3040

---

[1] MS P reading—*de*—restored.
[2] MS P reading—*qu'al demain*—restored.
[3] MS P reading—*reconsa*—restored.
[4] MS P reading—*Rentra*—restored.

Belin ambushes the Romans

would turn back and fight the Romans and, if he could, take revenge for the broken faith; and Belin would cross the mountains and conquer the Germans, and whoever succeeded first would help the other brother. Brenne took for his task those from France and Burgundy, and Belin had his followers, the Welsh, Scots and Britons. But when those Romans who were in Germany realised that Brenne had turned back and was going to Rome, they decided to leave and help those in the city; and, using a route they knew, they got in front of Brenne and his men.

2981 Through a spy Belin knew all about the route taken by this band; he knew the time of their return and where they were to gather. He made the peasants his guides, getting with promises I do not know how many to take him by the most direct way they could to where the band was positioned. He came around the spurs of Montgieu and rode so hard, day and night, that the next day he came to a valley which the guides had shown him, where the Romans should pass and not be able to turn back. Belin kept watch, and forbade any noise or cry amongst his army. The weather was fine, as if in summer, the night clear, the air was still and the radiant moon shone brightly. Belin hid in the valley. And the Romans followed their path quite confidently, in no fear. By the light of the moon, shining brightly, they were moving quickly along when they came upon the ambush and saw helmets, saddles and swords shining in the moonlight. They were quite beside themselves, and those waiting for them at once attacked them. Once Belin shouted his war-cry, not even the cowards hesitated. They attacked them from all sides, and the Romans fled, abandoning the field. But they could not flee, nor did they have anywhere to hide, and the Britons disembowelled them, maimed and brained them, cut the heads off many and slaughtered them like so many beasts. The slaughter never ceased, from morning, when the day broke, till evening, when it got dark and night separated them. Anyone who escaped alive fled into the valleys.[1]

3027 Very early the next day, Belin resumed his journey, following his brother towards Rome. Brenne learnt this and waited for him. When the brothers met, they went forward more fiercely and more confidently. They arrived at Rome and laid siege to it, attacking from several directions. They had catapults, winches, battering-rams and many kinds of siege-engine made, hurling them against the walls to shatter and destroy them. The Romans awaited them on the walls, defending themselves amazingly well. With slings and crossbows, which they had at the

---

[1] The whole episode of the Britons ambushing the Romans in the pass is far more exciting in Wace than in *HRB*, partly because Wace is good at making the topography come alive, partly because he has an eye for ironic contrast—between the fine, still night and the horrors round the corner—and partly because of the bloody savagery of the fighting.

Od fundes e od arbalastes
Que il aveient totes prestes,
Jettent pierres e quarrels traient,
De nule guise nes manaient. [1]
Lancent darz e plummees ruent,
Maint en abatent e maint en tuent; [2]
Les assalz firent tuz remaindre,
Senz mur percier e senz mur fraindre.
Longement, a tuz les assalz,
3050   En fud as freres le noauz;
Mult furent bien estulteied
E de lur homes damagied.
Mais il firent, pur els vengier,
Par ire les furches drecier.
Veant les oilz a cez dedenz,
Veant amis, veant parenz,
Unt les ostages amenez
Sis unt as furches halt levez,
Vint e quatre filz as Romains,
3060   Des plus orgoillus citedeins.
Forment en furent tuit dolent
E li ami e li parent,
N'out en nul d'els que corocier,
Mais plus fort furent e plus fier,
E ço unt dit e juré l'unt
Ke jamais pais od els n'avront.
Il esteient de grant poeir
E si aveient grant espeir
En Gabao e Porsenna,
3070   Ki esteient, piece aveit ja,
Alé quere par Lombardie
E par Puille force e aie;
Cil de Rome les atendeient.
Al jor certain que il saveient
Que li conte venir deveient
Od le secors qu'il ameneient,
Se firent mult fiers e hardiz
Si unt cels de l'host assailliz;
De lur gré s'en sunt fors eissu, [3]
3080   E forment se sunt combatu.

E li conte i sunt survenu;
Dunc oissez e cri e hu.
Li Romain sunt de l'une part,
De l'altre Puilleis e Lombart,
Des Burguinuns funt grant essart:
'Filz a putains, funt il, cuart,
Venistes vus treü receivre?
Jesqu'a grant piece en serreiz seivre.
Nus vus ferum vostre sanc beivre
Pur esparnier l'eue del Teivre.   3090
Venistes vus de ça Mongieu
Pur chalengier cest nostre fieu? [4]
Nus nel tenum neient a gieu,
Kar Rome est tote nostre en fieu.
Vilanie e pecchiez feïstes [5]
Quant vus nos ostages pendistes;
Malveis conseil e lai preïstes,
Mais, si Deu plaist, mar i venistes.'
Li Romain les contralioent
E laidement les demenoent,   3100
E granz colees lur dunoent,
Mal faiseient, pis maneçoent.
Tuz les unt fait ariere traire
E mult les funt crier e braire;
Chescuns fiert bien sun aversaire,
N'en sevent nule esparne faire.
Belin e Brennes fort s'iraissent
De ces Romains ki si les plaissent,
Lur gent craventent e abatent,
Botent, fierent, ocient, matent;   3110
N'i ad si fort ne s'i deshait.
A une part se sunt retrait,
Fait unt un poi de parlement
Si runt en els pris hardement.
Lur gent firent raseürer,
Chevals restreindre, homes armer,
Puis unt fait conreiz de lur gent
Par mil, par cinquante, par cent;
Des plus hardiz, des plus aidables
Firent maistres e conestables   3120

---

[1] MS P reading—*nes manaient*—restored.
[2] MS P reading—*e*—restored.
[3] MS P reading—*s'en*—restored.
[4] MS P reading—*fieu*—restored.
[5] MS P reading—*pecchiez*—restored.

The brothers attack Rome

ready, they threw stones and shot bolts and showed them not the slightest mercy. They launched javelins and hurled leaden balls, felling many, killing many, and preventing all the assaults from penetrating the walls or knocking them down.

3049 For a long time the brothers had the worst of it in all the attacks; they suffered considerable damage and loss of men. But in revenge, they angrily erected the gallows. Before the eyes of those within, their friends and their families, they brought out the hostages and hanged twenty-four sons of the proudest Roman citizens from the gallows. All the friends and families were in anguish and every single one of them was enraged, but they were all the more bitter and determined and said and swore they would never make peace with them. Their powers were great and they placed great hope in Gabius and Porsenna, who for a long time had been seeking for help and soldiers in Lombardy and Apulia. The Romans awaited them. On the day when they knew for sure that the counts were due to arrive, bringing help, they became very fierce and bold and attacked those in the besieging army; of their own accord they came out of the city and fought vigorously.

3081 The counts then arrived: what a hue and cry could be heard! The Romans on one side, the Apulians and Lombards on the other, slaughtered great numbers of Burgundians. 'Bastards, cowards,' the Romans said, 'so you came to get tribute? You'll be deprived of that for a long time. We will make you drink your own blood, to save the water in the Tiber. Did you come from Montgieu to lay claim to this land of ours? We don't consider that a joke, for all of Rome is our domain. To hang our hostages was shameful and sinful. You chose and decided wickedly, but, please God, you will regret your coming.' The Romans opposed the Britons, put up a horrible fight and rained great blows on them, doing them injury and threatening worse still. They made them all retreat, with many howls and cries. Each one struck his enemy hard, sparing none. Belin and Brenne were very angry with these Romans who had laid them so low, felling and knocking their men down, thrusting, striking, defeating and killing them. Even the strongest were disheartened.

3112 They retreated to a distance, conferred a little and took new heart. They reassured their men, restrained the horses and armed the soldiers, then put their men into companies of a thousand, fifty and a hundred. They made chiefs and

A chescune eschiele par sei,
Quis face tenir en conrei.
Les plus hardiz combateors
Mistrent avant as fereors;
Lez cels firent destre e senestre
Arblastiers e archiers estre. [1]
Le mielz de lur gent e le plus
Descendirent des chevals jus,
En mi le champ furent a pied
3130 Ordeneement e rengied.
Cil unt par mi trenché lur lances
E guerpies lur conuissances.
Cil en irrunt le petit pas
Ferir sur la grant presse el tas,
Ja nuls d'els ne desrengera [2]
Ne pur home ne guenchira.
Dunc unt grailles e corns soné
Si sunt al ferir aturné.
Assez tost vindrent al ferir;
3140 Dunc oïssez armes croissir
E les truncs de hanstes voler, [3]
Homes chaeir e jambeter.
Ne sai que jo vus acuntasse,
D'ambes parz en morut grant masse.
Mais li Romain furent vencu,
Griefment lur est mesavenu,
Kar Gabius i fud ocis
E Porsenna, li quens, fud pris.
Li frere en Rome a force entrerent,
3150 Mainte grant richeise i troverent;
De tut firent ço que lur plout,
Aveir trova ki aveir vout.
    Quant il ourent la cité prise
E la terre tute conquise,
Brenne remist en Lombardie
E de Rome out la seinnurie;
Puis i fist mainte cruelté
Come li hoem de grant fierté;
E Belin qui s'en retorna
3160 En Engleterre repaira.

Ses viez citez fist redrecier
E les murs chaeiz enforcier; [4]
Les vieles citez redreça ,
E les viles edifia. [5]
Une en fist en Guales funder
Si la fist Kaerusc nomer
Pur ço que sur Usche sedeit,
Une eue ki emprés coreit;
Puis l'apela l'om Karlion.
Or oëz par quel achaison: 3170
Lunc tens aprés la mort Belin,
E puis que Brennes traist a fin,
Avint issi que li Romain
Engletere ourent en lur main.
Pur tenir la en lor demainne
Suffrirent longes mainte paine
E maint fais e maint costement;
Tuz tens i aveit de lur gent
Dous legiuns, u treis, u quatre,
Pur genz averses escombatre.   3180
Dunc erent Romain en grant pris.
Sis mil sis cenz seissante e sis,
Ceo esteit une legiun,
Ceo en est l'espositiun.
Quant les legiuns sujurnoent
Que nul part ne guerreioent,
En iver erent chescun an
A Kaerusc en Glamorgan, [6]
Pur l'aise e pur la grant plenté
Ki esteit en cele cité.   3190
Pur les legiuns, que jo di,
Qui la sujornoent issi,
En costume e en us turnerent
Que Kaerlion l'apelerent:
Ceo est: cité as legiuns.
Issi change l'on plusors nuns;
Pur Kaerusc fud Karlion,
Li dreiz fust Kaerlegion,
Mais genz estranges unt le nom
Abregied par subtractiun: 3200

---

[1] MS P reading—*Arblastiers*—restored.
[2] MS P reading—*nuls*—restored.
[3] MS P reading—*les truncs*—restored.
[4] MS P's order of rhymes—*redrecier, enforcier*—
restored.
[5] MS P reading—*les viles*—restored.
[6] MSS PDLCJRMT: *Karlion*.

The brothers defeat Rome

commanders of the boldest and most able-bodied and put them into each group to keep them in order. The boldest warriors they put in front amongst the fighters, and on the right and left of those placed crossbowmen and archers. They made most of their men, and the best, dismount, and drew them up on foot in the middle of the field in ordered ranks. These men cut their lances in two and discarded their devices. They were to advance at walking pace and in a group strike at the battle throng, not one of them breaking ranks or giving way for any man. Then they sounded horns and bugles and prepared to strike.[1] They started fighting very soon; then weapons could be heard shattering, lance shafts flying and men kicking helplessly as they fell. I do not know what to tell you about it; many people died on both sides. But the Romans were beaten and it turned out very badly for them, for Gabius was killed there and the count Porsenna was captured. The brothers forcibly entered Rome and found very great riches there. They did as they pleased with everything and he who wanted wealth, found it.

3153   When they had taken the city and conquered the whole land, Brenne stayed in Lombardy and had dominion over Rome; as a very violent man, he then committed many cruelties there. And Belin, turning back, returned to England. He rebuilt his old cities and strengthened the broken-down walls; he restored the old cities and built towns. He founded one in Wales and had it named 'Kaerusc', because it was situated on the Usk, a river running nearby. Later people called it 'Karlion'. Now listen to why they did so: a long time after Belin's death, and after Brenne had died, it so happened that the Romans had possession of England. To keep it in their demesne, they endured for a long time much trouble, distress and expense. They always kept two, or three or four, legions of their soldiers here, to combat hostile peoples. At that time the Romans were highly renowned. Six thousand, six hundred and sixty-six men—that was a legion, that is its definition. When the legions were at rest and not fighting anywhere, they spent the winter of every year at Kaerusc in Glamorgan, because of the comfort and great abundance in this city.[2] As I say, because of the legions who dwelt there, they changed, through custom and habit, to calling it 'Karlion', that is, City of the Legions. Thus many names are altered: from 'Kaerusc' it became 'Karlion', and by rights should be 'Kaerlegion', but foreigners removed parts of the name and

---

[1] These military tactics are added by Wace.
[2] Wace adds these numerical details on the Roman legions, but omits *HRB*'s description of
Caerleon as capital of Demetia.

De Legion Liun unt fait
E de Kaer unt e retrait
E pur tut unt Karlion dit
Si unt fait le nun plus petit.
Quant Belin out Kaerusc faite
E de la gent grant masse atraite,
A Londres, sa cité meillur
E u il ert plus a sujur,
Fist une merveilluse porte
3210 Sur l'eue qui navie aporte.
La porte fud desur Tamise
Par merveillus engins assise; [1]
En engleis ad porte a nun gate,
E cele ad nun Belinesgate [2]
Pur ço que Belin la fist faire;
Ne sai altre achisun atraire. [3]
Sor la porte fist une tur
Mult grant de laise e de haltur;
Les leis sun pere renovela [4]
3220 E haltement les conferma,
E il fud mult bons justisiers
E leials reis e dreituriers.
En sun tens fu si grant plenté
Unches grainnur n'out ainz esté,
Ne unches puis ne fud tant grande [5]
Ne de beivre ne de viande.
Tant regna Belin e vesqui
En buen poër, qu'il enveilli;
A Lundres ert quant il fina.
3230 Deus! tant li poples le plora.
Li cors fud ars, la cendre prise,
Si fud en un baril d'or mise,
En un baril trestut fait d'or,
Que l'on out pris en sun tresor.
Puis ad l'om le baril levé,
Bien seelé e bien fermé,
Tut en som la tur par defors;
N'out altre sepulture al cors.
Pur los e pur eshalcement
3240 Fud mis li cors si haltement.

Emprés Belim la terre tint
Un suens filz ki out non Gurguint;
Gurguint Bertruc li filz out nun.
Mult fu de bone ententiun,
Saives fu e de grant mesure,
E mult ama pais e dreiture.
De pais tenir e de guarder
Pout bien sun pere resembler;
Sis peres tint bien e il bien,
N'i out qui li neüst de rien   3250
Fors les Daneis, kil refuserent
E ki le treü li veerent
Que Gudlac a Belin dona,
Quant sa fame e lui delivra. [6]
Gurguint sout bien qu'il aveit dreit
En ço que sis peres teneit;
Manda sa gent, entra es nefs,
Si fist lever veilles e trefs;
Par force entra en Danemarche,
N'i out chastel, cité ne marche [7] 3260
Que il par force ne preïst,
Si l'on en pais ne li rendist.
Mainte dure bataille i fist
E le rei meïsme en ocist;
Si fist restorer sun treü
Si com sis peres l'out eü.
De tuz les barons prist humages
E feeltez e salfs ostages. [8]
Quant Gurguint d'iluec repaira,
Par Orchanie trespassa;   3270
Illuec ad trente nefs trovees
En une compainne asemblees,
D'omes e de femmes chargiees
E asez bien apareillees.
Pentaloüs les guvernout,
Lur sire esteit e sis guiout.
Gurguint enquist quels genz esteient, [9]
U aloent e que quereient.
Pentaloüs s'umilia,
Pais e trives li demanda.   3280

---

[1] MS P reading—*engins*—restored.
[2] MS P's reading of ll. 3213–14 restored.
[3] MS P reading—*achisun, atraire*—restored.
[4] MS P reading—*renovela*—restored.
[5] MS P reading—*tant*—restored.
[6] MS P reading—*sa fame*—restored.
[7] MS P's order of line restored.
[8] MS P reading—*feeltez*—restored.
[9] MS P reading—*quels genz*—restored.

Death of Belin

curtailed it. Out of 'Legion' they made 'Lion' and they also cut back on 'Kaer', and so, making the name shorter, they said, for the whole, 'Karlion'.

3205   When Belin had built Kaerusc, and brought a great many people there, he made in London, his best city where he dwelt most, a marvellous gate, by the river carrying the ships. The gate was placed, with the use of amazing contraptions, above the Thames. In English 'porte' is called 'gate', and this one is called Belinsgate,[1] because Belin had it made; there is no other reason that I can uncover. Above the gate he made a tower, very large in height and breadth. He renewed his father's laws and amply ratified them, and he was a very good judge and a law-abiding, righteous king. In his time there was such abundance as had never been before, nor was there ever so much to eat and drink since. Belin lived and reigned with great authority for so long that he grew old. He was in London when he died. Lord, how the people wept for him! His body was burnt and the ashes taken and put in a golden barrel—a barrel made entirely of gold taken from his treasury. Then the barrel, well sealed and shut, was lifted up and placed at the very top of the tower, out in the open. The body had no other tomb: it was placed so high out of praise and esteem.

3241   After Belin, one of his sons, called Gurguint, ruled the land. The son's name was Gurguint Bertruc;[2] he was full of good intentions, wise and most moderate, and cherished peace and justice. In keeping and protecting peace he certainly resembled his father; his father ruled well and so did he, nor was there anyone to annoy him except the Danes, who refused to recognise the tribute paid by Gudlac to Belin, when he set him and his mistress free, and denied it him. Gurguint knew very well that he was in the right, as his father had exacted the tribute. He summoned his men, embarked in his ships, and raised mast and sails. He entered Denmark in strength; there was no city, castle or march which he did not take by force, if it was not peacefully surrendered. He fought many a hard battle there, and killed the king himself; then he reinstituted his tribute as his father had had it. From all the barons he took homage, oaths of fealty and reliable hostages.

3268   When Gurguint was on his way home, he passed by Orkney. There he found a company of thirty ships, full of men and women and very well equipped. Pantelous was leading them, their lord and guide. Gurguint enquired what race they were, where they were going and what they sought. Pantelous prostrated himself and asked for peace and pledges of safety. When the king had granted these and

---

[1] Billingsgate.
[2] In Wace, but not *HRB*, a Guerguint count of

Hereford reappears amongst the nobles at Arthur's coronation at Caerleon (para. 10237)

Quant li reis li out otried
E il out de parler congied:
'Jo sui, dist il, chaciez d'Espaine,
Jo é tute ceste compainne.
Par mer alom ensemble querre
A remaindre alcune terre. [1]
An e demi avum erré
A faim, a sei, a mal oré,
N'avom encor trové nul lieu
3290 Ki nus puisse remaindre en fieu
Ne u nus aiom remanance,
Si en avom mult grant pesance.
Tant avom lunges navïed
Que tuit en sumes ennuied.
Mais si te veneit a plaisir
Que nus volsisses retenir
E une partie esguardasses
De ta terre, que nus donasses,
Volentiers t'en serviriom [2]
3300 E ti home devendriom.'
Gurguint ne lur volt pas laisser
Terre en sun regne a guaanier,
Nepurec bien les conseilla;
En Irlande les enveia
Si lur rova que la alassent
E cele terre coltivassent.
N'ert pas Irlande encor poplee
Ne de nule gent abitee.
Cil unt vers Irlande siglé,
3310 E reis Gurguint lur ad livré
De ses mariniers quis menerent
E ki Irlande lur livrerent.
Tant unt siglé e tant coru
Que en Irlande sunt venu.
La terre esteit encor salvage,
N'i out maison ne herbegage
Ne nule altre guaainerie,
Mais bele esteit e bien guarnie
D'eues, de bois e de montainnes,
3320 De champs arables e de plainnes.

Dunc firent loges e fuilliees
E les terres unt guaainees.
La gent crut e multiplia
E qui plus pout plus guaaina.
Pentaloüs les maistriout,
Lur sire esteit sis justisout.
En Engletere est repairiez
Gurguint, kis out la enveiez;
Sun regne tint paisiblement
Dessi a sun definement.   3330
Quant il out sun terme acompli,
Sur Usche a Karlion feni,
E quant il fu alez a fin,
L'enor avint a Guincelin.
    Guincelins fu de bone vie,
E sa moiller out num Marcie, [3]
Lettree fu e sage dame,
De buen pris e de bone fame.
Sun enging mist tut e sa cure
A saveir lettre e escriture.   3340
Mult sout e mult estudia,
Une lei escrit e trova,
Marcïene l'apela l'on
Sulunc le language breton.
Li reis Alvret, si cum l'en dit, [4]
Translata la lei e l'escrit. [5]
Quant il l'out en engleis tornee,
Marcenelaga l'ad nomee.
La reïne qui saveit tant
De Guencelin out un enfant   3350
Ki fud apelé Sisillus,
Unches nen ourent enfant plus.
Sisillus n'esteit guaires granz,
N'aveit encor que sul set anz,
Ne poeit faire dreit ne tort,
Quant sis peres trait a sa mort.
Le regne, emprés la mort sun pere, [6]
Maintint bien pur le fiz la mere
En pais e en grant quieté;
E quant li fiz fu de l'heé   3360

---

[1] MS P reading—*remaindre*—restored.
[2] MS P reading—*t'en*—restored.
[3] MS P: *Marrie*.
[4] MS P reading—*dit*—restored.
[5] MS P reading—*l'escrit*—restored.
[6] MS P reading—*sun*—restored.

Pantelous and his people settle in Ireland

given him leave to speak, he said: 'I and all this company are banished from Spain. Together we are sailing the seas to look for an abode in some other land. We have wandered a year and a half, hungry, thirsty, and in tempests, without yet finding any place which could be given to us to possess as domain or where we could take up abode, and this has given us great distress. We have sailed for so long that we are all suffering. But if it pleased you to keep us and to select a portion of your land to give us, we will willingly serve you and become your men.'

3301   Gurguint did not want to give them land to cultivate in his kingdom, yet he gave them good advice. He directed them to Ireland and asked them to go there and cultivate that land. Ireland was not yet peopled or inhabited by any race. They sailed towards Ireland and king Gurguint gave them some of his seamen, to escort them and hand Ireland over to them. They journeyed and sailed so long that they arrived in Ireland. The country was still wild, with neither house nor lodging nor any cultivated land, but it was beautiful and well supplied with rivers, forests and mountains, arable fields and plains. So they made huts and arbours and cultivated the land. The people grew and multiplied and who could do most, acquired the most. Pantelous governed them; he was their lord and governed them.[1] Gurguint, who had sent them there, returned to England. He ruled his realm peaceably until his death. When he had run his course, he died at Karlion on the Usk, and after his death the kingdom came to Guincelin.

3335   Guincelin led a good life, and his wife was called Marcie, an educated and wise woman, much esteemed and renowned. She devoted all her intelligence and care to learning to read and write. She knew much and studied much, and invented and wrote down a law, which was called Marcien, in the British language. King Alfred, they say, translated this written law. When he had changed it into English, he called it Marcenelaga.[2] The learned queen had one child by Guincelin, who was called Sisillus; after him they had no more children. Sisillus was not very big, he was only seven, unable to do right or wrong, when his father died. His mother, after his father's death, ruled the kingdom on behalf of her son very well, in peace and great tranquillity; and when her son reached the age when he

---

[1] *Partholoim* in *HRB* chap. 46, (*VV*: *Partholoum*) where his people are called the *Basclenses*. His story comes ultimately from *HB* chap. 13, where Partholon comes with a thousand people from Spain to Ireland, but in the asking permission of a king to settle, and his advice, it resembles Bede's story of the settlement of Scotland by

the Picts (Book I, chap. 1). See also fn. 3 to p. 131.

[2] Wace virtually ignores Guincelin (*HRB* chap. 47: *Guithelinus*; *VV*: *Guizelinus*) to expand on the portrait of his wife. The *lex Merciana*, or laws of Mercia, led *HRB* to invent Marcia. See Tatlock p. 283.

Que il sout terre guverner,
Sil fist la mere coroner.
Encor ert de bone vigur[1]
Quant il vint a sun derain jur.
Puis fu reis sis filz Rummarus
E puis frere celui Damus.
Cist out un fiz en soinantage
Ki fu reis par sun vasselage,
Morpidus out nun, mult fu fiers
3370 E hardiz e fort chevaliers.
Alosez fu de grant bunté,
Mais trop ert de grant cruelté;
A demesure ert de grant ire;
Sempres voleit un home ocirre.
Des que veneit al corocier
Ne saveit nul home esparnier,
Sempres li dunout de s'espee;[2]
Ja n'i eüst amur guardee,
Demaneis sempres l'ocieit,
3380 U fust a tort u fust a dreit,
E tant cum il senz ire esteit
Si faiseit quanque l'on vuleit;
En tut le regne, ki grant fu,
N'aveit home de sa vertu.
Le vis aveit bel e cors gent,
E granz dons dunout e sovent.
Larges esteit a desmesure,
De tresor assembler n'out cure.
   Li duc de Moriane alout,
3390 El tens que Morpidus regnout,
Par mer les rivages gastant,
Homes pernant e raïmant;
Mult menout gent od sei armee[3]
Ki mult ert cremue e dutee.
En Northumberlande ariva
E a guaster la comença.
Morpidus, qui mult en pesa,
Od les Bretuns k'il assembla
Encuntre lui se combati
3400 Sil desbarata e venqui.

Si dist l'on ço en verité,
Ne sai coment ço fu prové,
Que Morpidus plus en conquist
E od sa main plus en ocist
Que ne fist tute l'assemblee
De la gent qu'il out aünee.
Quant il out tut le champ vencu,
N'en ad un sul vif retenu
Que il nen ait esboëlé
U od s'espee decolé.   3410
Des ocis assemblout grant tas,
E quant il fud d'ocire las,
Tuz vifs les faiseit escorchier,
Puis mettre es rés e graïller
Pur sa grant ire saüler
Qu'il ne poeit amesurer.
El tens de sun meillur eage,
Que il ert de plus fier corage,
Vint de la mer devers Irlande
Une beste merveilles grande,   3420
Monstre marin, orible beste,
D'orrible cors, d'orrible teste;
Ço esteit marine belue,
Unc ainz ne fu tant granz veüe.[4]
Par les viles, lez les rivages,
Feseit granz duels e granz damages,
Homes e femes devurout
E les bestes es champs mangout.
Les genz s'en aloent fuiant,
Maisuns e viles guerpissant;   3430
Es bois e es hauz munz fuieient
E encor la murir cremeient.
Morpidus la plainte en oï,
Ki mult aveit le quer hardi.
En sa vertu tant se fia
Que sul a sul encontre ala;
Sul par sun cors l'ad envaïe,
Unches n'i volt aver aïe.[5]
Trop grant hardement est folie,
Fols est qui trop en sei se fie.   3440

---

[1] MS P reading—*de*—restored.
[2] MS P reading—*s'espee*—restored.
[3] MS P's order of line restored.
[4] MS P reading—*tant*—restored.

[5] MS J adds: *La beste fu merveilles fiere/ E hideuse de grant maniere/ Morpidus son cors bien arma/ Contre la beste s'en ala.*

Morpidus

knew how to govern a land, she had him crowned. He was still full of energy when his last day came.

3365 Then his son Rummarus[1] was king, and next Damus, the latter's brother. He had a bastard son, who became king through his valour. His name was Morpidus;[2] he was very fierce and bold and a strong knight. He was praised for his great qualities, but he was much too cruel. His anger was immoderate: at once he would want to kill someone. Once he was angry he would spare no one but stab him immediately. He would pay no heed to affection but always kill him at once, whether rightly or wrongly. And as long as he was not angry, he would do whatever was wanted of him. In the whole kingdom—which was large—there was no man as able as he. He had a handsome face and noble body and gave gifts amply and often. He was exceedingly generous and had no concern for amassing treasure.

3390 During Morpidus' reign, the duke of Moriane crossed the sea and laid the coastline waste, capturing men and holding them to ransom. With him he brought many armed men who were much dreaded and feared. He arrived in Northumberland and began to devastate it. Morpidus, much disturbed by this, fought him with the Britons he had assembled, routed him and beat him. They say, indeed, (but I do not know what evidence there was for it), that Morpidus conquered more men, and with his own hand killed more, than did the whole army of men he had gathered together. When he was quite victorious in the field, there was not a single captive still alive whom he did not disembowel or behead with his sword. He piled up a great heap of dead men, and when he was sated with slaughter, he had all the rest skinned alive, then put on a pyre and roasted, to appease his great fury which he could not control.

3417 In the prime of his life, when he was at his fiercest, there came over the sea from Ireland an extraordinarily large beast, a sea monster, a horrible animal with a horrible head and horrible body. It was a savage sea beast; so large a one had never been seen before. Through the towns and along the coasts it caused great suffering and harm, devouring men and women and eating the animals in the fields. The people fled, abandoning houses and towns and escaping to the woods and high mountains, and even there they were frightened of dying. Morpidus heard of the lamentations and his heart was very confident. He trusted so much in his strength that he went quite alone to meet the beast. He alone attacked it and wanted no help. Excessive boldness is folly: he who puts too much trust in

---

[1] *HRB*, chap. 47: *Kinarius*; *VV*: *Kinewarus*.
[2] *HRB*, chap. 48: *Morvidus* (born from *Tan-* *gusteaia*); *VV*: *Morpidus* (mother an unnamed concubine).

Morpidus par sun hardement
Vint al monstre mult fierement,
Traist saietes e lança dars
Si l'a nafré de plusurs pars.
Quant il nen out mais que ruer
Ne que lancer ne que jeter,
Od sul s'espee sure li corut; [1]
Mais l'espee del grant cop frut
E la beste la gule ovri,
3450 Devora le sil trangluti, [2]
Mort fu li reis par s'estultie.
Mais la beste n'est pas guarie,
Kar li reis l'aveit tant batue,
E tant nafree e tant ferue,
Que sempres murut en la place;
N'i ad vilain, joie n'en face.
De la mort le rei les conforte
La belue ki chaï morte.
Del rei ourent grant marrement,
3460 Mais ço lur fist confortement
Que la beste si tost morut;
Dunt entr'els si grant joie crut
Que tut unt le rei oblié
E tut le duel de lui finé.
    Il aveit cinc filz engendrez,
Gorgonian fu li ainz nez,
Puis Algar, e puis Elidur,
Puis Jugenes, puis Peridur.
Gorgonian, ki fu premiers,
3470 Fu reis leials e dreiturers,
Unches nuls reis plus dulcement
Ne governa terre ne gent;
Ja a escient ne mentist
Ne a home tort ne feïst;
Unches en li n'out desmesure;
E a tuz vult faire dreiture.
Leials fu, e en leialté
Vint a la fin de sun eé.
A Lundres fu sa sepulture
3480 Apareillee par grant cure.

Algar, ki emprés lui fu nez,
Fu emprés lui a rei levez;
Mais malement se descorda
E malement lui resembla.
Les nobles homes abaisça
E les non nobles aleva;
Ki aveir out, il li toli,
Quant dut veir dire, si menti.
Tresor assembla merveillus [3]
Si fu avers e coveitus.   3490
Unches n'ama home leial,
Tuz tens se delitout en mal.
Tant demena Argal tel vie [4]
E tant dura sa felonie
Que li noble home s'assemblerent
E de la terre le jeterent.
Puis unt le tierz frere amené,
Elidur, si l'unt coroné; [5]
Cil fu de mult grant amistied,
Pleins de dulçur e de pitied.   3500
Algar, cil ki fu desposed,
Par plusurs terres est aled,
Querant secors, preant aïe
Que s'enor li fust restablie.
Unches ne sout tant purchacier,
Tant requere ne tant preier,
Qu'il unches trovast ne veïst
Ki aïe li prameïst
Ne restorement de sa perte.
Par dreit busuin e par poverte   3510
Vint aprés cinc anz a sun frere
Dedenz le bois de Calatere.
Algar Elidur encontra,
Merci quist e merci trova.
Li reis vit sun frere apovri,
Pitos fu mult sin out merci,
Par mainte fiez l'ad embracied,
Acolé estreit e baisied.
A Aclud l'ad, une cité
Ki prés esteit d'iluec, mené.   3520

Gorgonian, Argal and Elidur

himself is foolish. In his presumption, Morpidus came fiercely up to the monster, shot arrows and threw spears and wounded it in various places. When he had done no more than hurl, pelt and throw at it, he ran at it with only his sword, but the sword broke from the great blow and the beast opened her jaws, swallowed him up and gulped him down. The king had died through his arrogance. But the beast did not escape, because the king had so beaten, wounded and struck it that it at once died on the spot. There was not a peasant who did not rejoice. They found solace for the king's death in the death of the monster. They were very distressed for the king, but it comforted them that the beast had come to such a speedy end, so their joy increased so much that they quite forgot the king and stopped grieving over him.[1]

3465 He had begotten five sons. Gorgonian was the eldest, then Argal, and then Elidur, then Jugenes and lastly Peredur. Gorgonian, who came first, was a just and law-abiding king; no monarch ever ruled a land or people more gently. He never knowingly lied or harmed anyone, never acted immoderately and wished to do justice to all. He was righteous, and in righteousness he came to the end of his days. His tomb was prepared in London with great care.

3481 After him, Argal,[2] the second-born, was raised to be king, but he was very different and hardly resembled him. He suppressed the nobles and exalted the base; whoever had wealth, he stole it, and when he should have told the truth, he lied. He amassed extraordinary wealth and was mean and greedy. He had no love for any loyal man but always took pleasure in evil. Argal pursued such a life for so long and his wickedness was so continual that the nobles got together and threw him out of the country. Then they brought forward the third brother, Elidur, and crowned him. He had an affectionate nature, full of gentleness and pity. Argal, once deposed, went through many lands seeking help, asking for aid to re-establish his rights. But however hard he strove, asked and begged, he never found or saw anyone who promised him help or the restoration of his loss.

3510 After five years, from sheer need and poverty, he came to his brother, within the forest of Calatere. Argal met Elidur, asked for mercy and found it. The king saw his impoverished brother, felt great compassion and had mercy on him; he embraced him many times, hugging and kissing him. He took him to Alclud,[3] a city

---

[1] Wace extends the battle with the sea monster— a sort of external symbol of Morpidus's own bestial cruelty—and makes it more satisfactory, in that Morpidus wounds and kills it, though himself swallowed up.

[2] *HRB* chap. 50: *Arthgallo*; *VV*: *Archgallo*.

[3] On Alclud and Calatere see fns 1 to pp. 41 and 65.

En sa chambre priveement
Le fist entrer celeement. [1]
Deus! ki vit mais tel pieté,
Tel amur, tel fraterneté!
Li reis se feinst que mal aveit
E que del mal murir cremeit.
Ses barons ad fait tuz mander
Qu'il le venissent visiter;
N'aveit de vivre nul espeir,
3530 Venissent le trestuz veeir.
Quant il furent tuit assemblé
Al jur qu'il lur out terminé, [2]
E il durent a lui parler,
Si lur fist a conseil rover
Que soëf e en pais venissent
Que cri ne noise ne feïssent;
Chescuns sols en la chambre entrast
E chescuns sols a lui parlast,
Kar li chief forment li duleit
3540 E la noise mal li faiseit
Cil firent sun comandement,
N'i entrassent pas autrement.
Si come chescuns enz entrout
E il al rei parler quidout,
Li reis meïsmes le perneit
Sil teneit tant e destreineit
Par ses serganz qu'illuec esteient,
Ki espees nues teneient,
Qu'il faiseit a sun frere homage.
3550 Ja ne fust de si haut parage
Que fere ne li esteüst
U demaneis illuec morust.
Quant il les out tuz fait venir
E homes Argal devenir,
E feelted ourent fait tuit,
A Everwic l'en ad conduit;
De sun chief la corone osta,
Argal sun frere en coruna.
En sun regne le restabli
3560 E sun regne tut li rendi. [3]

Pur l'enor e pur la pitied,
Pur le bien e pur l'amistied
Qu'il fist al frere busuinus,
Out il nom puis tuz tens pitus; [4]
E Argal tant s'amesura
E ses males tecches laissa
N'i out ainz reis tant mesurable,
Tant paisible, tant enorable.
Dis anz regna en sa vigur,
Puis chaï en une langur;   3570
Morir l'estut, ne pout altre estre,
Kar issi plout al rei celestre.
Dunc refu faiz Elidur reis
Si com il out esté anceis.
Mis refu en sa digneté.
Si il out ainz buens reis esté,
Puis se fist tenir pur meillur;
Mais si dui frere juveignur
Se sunt ensemble acompained
Si l'unt ensemble guerreied,   3580
E a un jur se combatirent
Mais poi aveit gent sil venquirent.
Ne sai par quel engin le pristrent
E en salve garde le mistrent;
A Lundres en une grant tur,
Illuec fu Elidur maint jur.
Cil unt le regne entr'els parti:
Del Humbre en suth devers midi
E tut aval vers occident
Out Jugenes tut quitement;   3590
Peredur out l'altre partie,
Puis rout tute la seinurie, [5]
Kar Jugenes puis ne vesqui
Que sul set anz e dunc fini. [6]
E Peredur l'enor saisi
Mais unches guaires n'en joï, [7]
Kar mort subite la tua;
E mal vesqui e mal fina.
Dunc refu fait la tierce feiz
Elidur reis e ceo ert dreiz. [8]   3600

---

[1] MS P reading—*entrer*—restored.
[2] MS P reading—*lur out terminé*—restored.
[3] MS P's reading of line restored.
[4] MS P's reading of line restored.
[5] MS P reading—*rout*—restored.
[6] MS P reading—*dunc*—restored.
[7] MS P reading—*unches*—restored.
[8] MS P reading—*ert*—restored.

Elidur rules three times

nearby and made him enter his chamber in secret. Lord, who ever saw such pity, such love and such brotherly feeling! The king pretended he was ill and feared he would die. He had all his barons summoned to come and visit him; since he had no expectation of life, they all should come and see him. When they were all gathered, on the day he had appointed, and they were to speak with him, he had them privately asked to come softly and quietly, making neither noise nor cry. Each should enter the chamber alone and each speak to him alone, for his head ached sorely and noise was bad for him. They did what he ordered and entered in no other manner. As each one entered and thought to speak to the king, the king himself seized him and had him held and restrained by his servants, who were holding their drawn swords, until he did homage to his brother. No one was so highly born that he did not have to do it, or at once die on the spot.

3553   When he had made them all come and become Argal's men, and everyone had sworn fealty, he led him to York. He removed the crown from his head and crowned Argal his brother with it. He re-established him in his kingdom and restored the whole kingdom to him. Because of the honour and the pity, the goodness and the affection he showed to the brother in need, he was henceforth always called the Merciful. And Argal so restrained himself and abandoned his bad habits that never before had there been so moderate a king, so peaceable and so honourable. He ruled energetically for ten years, then fell into a decline: he had to die, it could not be otherwise, for it so pleased the king of heaven.

3573   Then Elidur was made king once again, as he had been before. He was restored to his dignities. If he had been a good king before, now he was considered even better. But his two younger brothers banded together and made war on him; one day they joined battle, but he had fewer men and they defeated him. They seized him, I do not know by what trick, and put him in safe keeping: Elidur was in a great tower in London for many a day. They divided the kingdom between them: south of the Humber and all down towards the west fell entirely to Jugenes[1] and Peredur had the rest. Then he acquired all the power, because Jugenes lived no more than a mere seven years and then died. And Peredur seized the land, but hardly enjoyed it for long, because sudden death killed him: he both lived and died evilly.[2] Then, for the third time, Elidur was once more made king and that

---

[1] *HRB* chap. 51: *Ingenius.*

[2] *HRB* chap. 51 has a favourable portrait of Peredur, which *VV* omits.

De la tur de Lundres fu traiz
E tierce feiz refu rei faiz,
Si rad par tut ço redrecied.
Que li frere ourent empeired. [1]
Il fu essample de justise
E de pitied e de franchise
A tuz cels ki emprés lui vindrent
Ki emprés lui la terre tindrent.
Il n'out unches blasme de rien,
3610 Il vesqui bien e fina bien.
     Uns suens niés out emprés l'enor,
Filz de sun frere le major,
Le gentil rei Gorgonian.
Puis fu reis filz Argal Margan.
Cist Margan fu mult de bon aire
E mult se pena de bien faire.
Mult se fist a sa gent amer
E tut gent vult onurer.
Sis freres, Eumannus out nom,
3620 Tint emprés lui la region;
Mult out en cestui divers eir,
Unches ne sout ami aveir;
Unches ne pout aveir ami,
Tant l'ad tut li poples haï,
E il tut le pople haeit
E feseit mal quanqu'il poeit.
Neïs si sergant le haeient
E a grant enviz le serveient,
Tant l'aveient trové cruel;
3630 Mais il nen osoent faire el.
Sis anz mena sa tirrannie,
Sa cruelté e sa folie,
Puis l'unt del realme fors mis
Comunement cil del païs;
Chaciez fu e il s'en fuï
Que unches puis ne reverti.
Rei firent par electiun
D'un filz Jugenes Iwalun.
Iwallo pout mult travailler, [2]
3640 Mult pout errer, mult pout veiller,

Bien sembla as bons ancessors
De prüesce e de bones mors,
Mais ne regna pas longement,
De ço furent li suen dolent,
Mais contre mort n'ad nul refui.
Puis fud d'Engleterre emprés lui
Runo reis, le filz Peredur,
Puis Geronces, filz Elidur,
Puis fu reis sis filz Catullus,
3650 Emprés Catullum Coïllus,
E puis Porreus e puis Cherim;
Cherim fu bevere de vin;
En buens beivres turna s'entente
E tut i usa sa juvente
En beverie e en ivresce,
Unches ne fist altre prüesce;
E Deus tel eür li dona
Que unches hom nel guereia.
Treis filz que il out de sa feme
3660 L'un emprés l'altre ourent le regne,
Cil ourent nom Fulgenius,
Eldragus e Andragius.
L'un avant l'autre ourent tut trei
Engleterre, chescun par sei,
Mais assez poi de tens durerent [3]
E en mult poi de tens finerent.
Uns filz Andragis, Urian,
Regna emprés sun pere un an;
Emprés Urian, Eliud
3670 Ad le regne en grant pais tenud;
Emprés Eliud, Cledaucus,
Puis Doten, puis Gurgustius,
Puis Merean, ki mult fu bels,
Ki de chiens sout mult e d'oiseals,
Mult sout de rivere e de bois;
Quant qu'il vuleit perneit a chois;
A altre deduit n'entendeit
E cist deduiz mult li plaiseit.
De dames ert mult desirrez
3680 E mult requis e mult amez,

---

[1] MS P reading—*li*—restored.
[2] MS P: *Wallo*.

[3] MS P reading—*durerent*—restored.

A rapid succession of kings

was right. He was taken from the tower of London and again, for the third time, made king and rectified everything his brothers had harmed. He was a model of justice, piety and nobility to all those who came after him, who held the land after him. No censure ever attached to him: he lived well and died well.

3611   One of his nephews then ruled the kingdom, son of his eldest brother, the excellent king Gorbonian. Next, Margan, the son of Argal, became king. This Margan was of a most noble disposition and made every effort to act well. He wished to do honour to everyone and he made himself much beloved by his people. His brother, called Eumannus, held the land after him; he was a very different kind of heir, who never knew how to acquire friends. He could never have a friend because all the people hated him so much, and he hated all of them and behaved wickedly whenever he could. Even his servants hated him and served him most unwillingly, so cruel had they found him to be, but they dared not do otherwise. For six years he exercised his tyranny, his cruelty and his folly; then, together, the people expelled him from the land. He was chased out and fled and never came back.[1]

3637   They chose as king a son of Jugenes, Iwallo. Iwallo worked hard, travelled widely and was most diligent, much resembling his good ancestors for bravery and good character, but he did not reign for long. All his family were saddened by that, but there is no escape from death. After him, the kings of England were Rumo, son of Peredur, then Geronces, son of Elidur, then Geronces' son Catullus. After Catullus came Coïllus, then Porreus and then Cherim.[2] Cherim was a wine-bibber: he devoted his attention to good drink and spent his whole youth in drinking and drunkenness: that was the extent of his prowess. And God gave him such good fortune that no one ever made war on him. The three sons he had by his wife held the realm one after the other; they were called Fulgenius, Eldadus and Andragius. All three held England, on their own, in succession, but they lasted a very short time and very quickly came to an end.

3667   Urian, a son of Andragius, reigned for a year after his father, and after Urian, Eliud ruled the realm in great peace. After Eliud came Cledaucus, then Doten, then Gurgustius,[3] and then Merean, who was very handsome and knowledgeable about dogs and birds. He was skilled in water-fowling and hunting and could take as he liked whatever he wished; he cared for no other sport, and this one greatly pleased him. The ladies desired him very much, falling in love and en-

---

[1] Wace expands on the wickedness of Eumannus (*HRB* chap. 52: *Enniaunus*; *VV*: *Eumanius*).

[2] *HRB* chap. 52: *Iduallo, Runo, Gerennus, Katellus, Coillus, Porrex* and *Cherin. VV*: *Idwallo, Runo, Gerontius, Catullus, Coillus, Porrex* and *Cherin*.

Wace adds Cherim's love of wine and undeserved good fortune.

[3] *HRB* chap. 52: *Cloten* and *Gurgintius*; *VV*: *Gurgueius*.

Mais il n'out de feme talent
Fors de la sue sulement.
Bledudo emprés lui regna,
Sis filz fu e bien li sembla, [1]
Mais plus larges fu de duner,
Nule rien ne saveit veer
Ne a suen ués rien retenir,
A tuz vuleit le suen largir;
Mult out en lui gentil seinur.
3690 Emprés cel noble duneür
Fu reis Cap, e puis Oënus,
Emprés celui fu Sillius,
Mais cist vesqui mult petitet. [2]
Emprés lui regna Blegabret. [3]
Cist sout de nature de chant,
Unches hom plus n'en sout, ne tant;
De tuz estrumenz sout maistrie
Si sout de tute chanterie,
Mult sout de lais, mult sout de note,
3700 De vïele sout e de rote,
De harpe sout e de chorum,
De lire e de psalterium. [4]
Pur ço qu'il out de chant tel sens,
Diseient la gent en sun tens
Ke il ert deus des jugleors
E deus de tuz les chanteors.
Li reis ert mult de grant deduit,
Pur joie le siueient tuit, [5]
E il esteit tuz tens joius,
3710 Unches ne fu fel ne irus.
Archinal, sis freres, emprés
Maintint le regne e out en pais.
Emprés fu reis sis fiz Eldol,
Ki mult se fist tenir pur fol
Pur ceo, trop fu luxurius
E de femes trop coveitus;
Ja gentil feme n'i eüst,
Que de si haut parage fust,
Fust espuse, fust damisele,
3720 Pur ceo qu'ele li semblast bele,

Que il ne vulsist purgesir.
A mainte gent se fist haïr.
Redion emprés Eldol fu,
Puis ad Rederch le regne eü,
Puis fu reis Famu Penissel,
Puis Pir que le chief ot mult bel,
De chief e de cheveleüre
L'enora mult forment Nature.
Emprés Pir regna Caporus
E puis sis filz Eliguellus;   3730
Cist se contint mult sagement
E mult amesureement.
Sis fiz qui puis regna, Heli,
Quarante anz entiers reis vesqui;
Cil Heli treis fiz engendra,
Le premerain Lud apela,
Puis fu nez Cassibellanus
E emprés celui Nennius.
    Emprés Heli out Lud la terre,
Ki mult fu pruz e duiz de guerre;   3740
Chivaliers fu mult glorius
E viandiers fu merveillus,
E mult la dunout volentiers
E mult enurout chevaliers.
Lud fist citez e fist chastels,
Les viez reclost e fist novels,
E Londres, sa cité meillor,
Fist de mur clore tut entur.
Lud fist faire la grant closture
Des viez muralz, ki encor dure.   3750
As citedeins e as baruns
I fist Lud faire granz maisuns
Pur ço que l'um dire peüst
Que pruef d'iluec cité n'eüst
Que si fust bien apareillee
Ne si richement herbergee.
Jesqu'a sun tens longes avant,
Aveit nun Lundres Trinovant,
Mais pur Lud, qui mult l'enora
E mult i fu e surjorna,   3760

---

[1] MS P reading—*e bien li sembla*—restored.
[2] MS P reading—*cist*—restored.
[3] MS P: *Blecgablet.*
[4] MS J adds: *De gighe sot de sinphonie/ Si savoit assés*

d'arnonie/ De tous giex sot a grant plenté/ Plains fu de debonnaireté.
[5] MS P reading—*siueient*—restored.

King Lud and London

treating him many times, but he cared for no woman except his own wife. Bledudo reigned after him, his son who was very like him, but gave more generously. He could not refuse anything nor keep anything for his own benefit; he wanted to increase everyone's possessions. He was a very kind lord.[1]

3690 After this noble giver, Cap was king, and then Oenus, and after him Sillius,[2] but he lived a very short time. After him reigned Blegabret. He knew about the properties of song; no one ever knew more nor so much. He was master of every instrument and knowledgeable about every sort of singing. He knew all about lays and about melodies; he knew how to play the viol and the rote, the harp and the chor-on, the lyre and the psaltery. Because he understood singing so well, the people of his time called him the god of minstrels and the god of all singers. The king was high-spirited; everyone followed him joyfully and he was always jolly, never cruel or angry.[3]

3711 His brother Archinal[4] next ruled the kingdom and kept it in peace. Then his son Eldol was king, who was considered very wanton, because he was too lecherous and insatiable for women. There was no noble lady, however high-born, whether a wife or a virgin, whom he did not want to ravish if he found her beautiful. He made himself hated by many people. Redion came after Eldol; then Rederch held the kingdom, then Famu Penissel was king, and then Pir, whose head was most handsome: Nature had honoured him greatly in his head and his hair. After Pir reigned Caporus and then his son Eliguellus; he behaved very wisely and moderately.[5] His son, Heli, who then reigned, lived forty whole years as king. He begot three sons: the first was called Lud, the second Cassibelan and the last, Nennius.

3739 After Heli, Lud, who was very brave and experienced in warfare, ruled the land. He was a most splendid knight and a marvellous host, and he willingly gave many gifts and honoured many knights. Lud built cities and castles, re-walled some old ones and constructed new ones, and he had his favourite city, London, entirely surrounded by walls. Lud had the great enclosure of old walls made, which still exists. For the citizens and the lords Lud had great houses built, so that it could be said there was no city nearby so well equipped or so splendidly provided with lodgings. Until his time, and long before, London was called Trinovant, but because of Lud, who showered it with honours and spent much time there, it

---

[1] Details on Merian and on Bledudo again supplied by Wace.

[2] *HRB* chap. 52: *Sisillius*.

[3] Wace adds considerably to the portrait of Blegabret, especially his command of instruments. The psaltery was very much like a dulcimer, plucked with the fingers. See Page, *Voices and Instruments*, pp. 112–13 and 123. For *rotes* (a triangular zither), *choruns* (or *coruns*, another

kind of zither, with struck strings), psalteries plus many more instruments, see the later passage, para. 10521.

[4] *HRB* chap. 52: *Arthmaiol*; *VV*: *Archmail*. Wace adds the lechery of Eldol.

[5] *HRB* chap. 52: *Samuil, Penissel* (two kings, not one), *Capoir, Cligueillus*; *VV*: *Samuil Penissel* (one king), *Capoir, Eligueillus*. Wace adds Pir's beautiful hair.

Fud apelee Kaerlud; [1]
Puis sunt estrange home venud,
Ki le language ne saveient,
Mais Londoïn pur Lud diseient;
Puis vindrent Engleis e Saisson
Ki recorumpurent le nun,
Londoïn Lundene nomerent
E Londene longes userent.
Norman vindrent puis e Franceis,
3770 Ki ne sourent parler Engleis,
Ne Londene nomer ne sourent
Ainz distrent si com dire pourent,
Londene unt Londres nomee
Si unt lur parole guardee.
Par remuemenz e par changes
Des languages as gens estranges,
Ki la terre unt sovent conquise,
Sovent perdue, sovent prise,
Sunt li nun des viles changied,
3780 U acreü u acurcied;
Mult en purreit l'on trover poi,
Si come jo entent e oi,
Qui ait tenu entierement
Le nun qu'ele out premierement.
Quant Lud, li bons reis, fu feniz,
A Lundres fu ensepeliz
Juste une port ki ad nun
De sun nun Porlud en Bretun;
Engleis la parole unt turnee
3790 E Luddesgate l'unt nomee.
    De Lud remistrent dui enfant,
Mais guaires n'erent encor grant;
Li ainz nez fu Androgeüs
E li puis nez Tenuancius.
Cassibellan lur uncles ere,
Uns nobles huem, frere lur pere;
Cil tint l'enor pur les nevoz
E rei s'en fist clamer sur tuz. [2]
De terre fu buens maintenere,
3800 Buens chevaliers e buens donere.

Cist sout bien terre maintenir, [3]
E bien se sout faire servir.
Quant li nevo furent tant sage
E il vindrent a tel eage
Que il pourent terre baillir,
De dous contez les fist saisir.
A Androgeüm, le grainur,
Vers ki il out grainur amur,
Dona Lundres e dona Kent
A tenir de lui franchement.   3810
A Tenuancius, ki ert mendre,
Fist les Cornealleis entendre.
Issi out chescuns sun conté
Si furent conte andui clamé;
Mais de l'uncle unt reconeü
E a seinur l'en unt tenu;
Il aveit d'els la seinnurie
E tut l'altre regne en baillie.
Tant cum il furent d'un acord
Furent il bien puissant e fort;   3820
Mais puis i sorst une discorde,
Ço testemonie e ço recorde
Ki cest romanz fist, maistre Wace,
Dunt noauz fu a tut l'estrace,
Par quei Romain treü d'els ourent
Que unques ainz aveir ne purent.
    Seissante anz ainz que Jesu Crist
De Seinte Marie nasquist,
Ert Julius Cesar meüz,
De Rome ert en France venuz   3830
Pur conquerre vers occident
Les regions lointainnement:
Julius Cesar li vaillanz,
Li forz, li pruz, li conqueranz,
Ki tant fist e tant faire pout,
Ki tut le mund conquist e out. [4]
Unches nus huem, puis ne avant,
Que nus sacom, ne conquist tant.
Cesar fu de Rome emperere,
Savies huem fu e bon donere, [5]   3840

---

[1] For ll. 3761–74, MSS PN substitute ll. 1233–38: see p. 32, fn. 4.
[2] MS P reading—*s'en*—restored.
[3] MS P reading—*cist*—restored.
[4] MS P reading—*Ki*—restored.
[5] MS P reading—*fu*—restored.

Cassibellan

was called Kaerlud. Then foreigners arrived who did not know the language but said 'Londoin' for 'Lud'. Then the Angles and Saxons arrived, who corrupted the name in turn, calling 'Londoin' 'Lundene', and for a long time 'Londene' was used. Next the Normans and the French came, who did not know how to speak English nor how to say 'Londene', but spoke it as best they could. They called 'Londene' 'Londres', thus keeping it in their language. Through alterations and changes by the languages of foreigners, who have often conquered, lost and seized the land, the names of towns have changed, or become longer or shorter. Very few can be found, as I hear and understand, which have completely kept the name they first had.

3785 When the good king Lud died, he was buried in London next to a gateway, which was called after him 'Porlud', in the British language. The English altered the word and called it Ludgate. Lud had two children, but they were as yet hardly grown. The elder was Androgeus and the younger Tenuancius. Cassibellan, a noble man, was their uncle, their father's brother. He held the kingdom on be-half of his nephews and proclaimed himself king over everyone. He was a good ruler, a good knight and a generous giver. He was well able to protect the land and to command service. When his nephews were wise enough and old enough to govern land, he put them in possession of two counties. To Androgeus, the elder, whom he loved more, he gave London and Kent, to hold from him, free of dues. He made the Cornish recognise Tenuancius, the younger. Thus each had his own county and both were proclaimed counts, but they acknowledged and held their uncle as lord: he was their overlord and controlled all the rest of the kingdom. As long as they were agreed, they were very powerful and strong; but then, as master Wace, who made this translation, testifies and reports, a disa-greement arose which disadvantaged the whole race, by which the Romans got tribute from them, which they had never been able to do before.

3827 Sixty years before Jesus Christ was born of Mary, Julius Caesar was on the move: he had come from Rome into France in order to conquer those regions far to the west—Julius Caesar the noble, the strong, the brave, the conqueror who did, and could do, so much and who conquered and possessed the whole world. Never has a man, as far as we know, conquered so much, before or since. Caesar was em-peror of Rome, a wise man and a generous giver; he was renowned for great chiv-

Pris out de grant chevalerie
E lettrez fu, de grant clergie.
Quant cil de Rome ourent conquis
Environ els tut le païs,
Cesar prist congied des Romains
D'aler conquerre les lointains.
La meillur juvente assembla,
Lombardie e Montgieu passa;
Premierement conquist Burguine,
3850 Puis France e Alferne e Guascoine,
Peitou, Normendie e Bretaine,
Puis prist sun tur vers Alemaine; [1]
Par plusurs lius faiseit chastels
E citez e recez novels.
Mult espleitout de sa busuine, [2]
En Flandres vint e en Buluine;
Utre la mer loin esguarda, [3]
Une ille vit si demanda
Quel terre esteit que il veeit,
3860 Se gent, e quel gent, i maneit.
Ço li distrent li païsant
Que une ille veeit bien grant
Que Brutus tut premiers poplea
E gent de Troie i amena; [4]
De sun nun l'apela Bretainne, [4]
Si s'en fist rei e cheventainne.
Li eir ki de lui sunt venu
Unt le regne emprés lui tenu.
E Cesar lur ad repundu: [5]
3870 'Bien sai, dist il, ki Brutus fu,
Il e nus fumes d'un lignage;
Li chiés de nostre parentage
Prist a Troie comencement.
Mais, puis le grant destruement,
Se departirent li baron
Si pristrent mainte region.
De ceste ille Bretainne furent
Belins e Brennes, ki tant crurent
Qu'il pristrent Rome la cité
3880 E destrurent nostre sené.

Bien lur devum faire saveir
Que Rome est or d'altre poeir;
Fortune ad sa roe tornee
E Rome rest esviguree.
Dreiz est des or qu'a nus entendent
E que treü a Rome rendent.
Bien nus deivent ço restorer
Qu'il en firent jadis porter;
Par bref les en ferai sumundre
Si savrai qu'il vuldrunt respondre.   3890
Ja ne querreie mer passer
S'en pais vuleient graanter
Que a Rome treü rendissent
E ke de nus lur fieus tenissent.' [6]
Dunc fist ses briefs faire e porter
A Cassibelan ultre mer,
Si manda que de lui tenist
E as Romains treü rendist.
Cassibellan, quil tint a grief,
Brief refist faire contre brief;   3900
Unches saluz n'i vult escrire,
Ainz li manda cume par ire:
'Cesar, mult par nus merveillum;
En merveillant, nus desdeinum [7]
Des Romains e de lur sorfait
Ki tant durë e tant luin vait.
Ne puet soffrir lur coveitise
Que nuls hom ait, fors els, franchise.
Tut l'or del mond e tut l'argent,
Les reis, les contes, l'altre gent,   3910
Vuelent mettre suz lur empire,
Nule rien ne lur puet sofire;
Tut l'aveir vuolent a els traire,
Que deivent il de tut ço faire?
Nus, ki el chief del mund manons,
En un ille que nus tenons,
Ne vuelent Romain trespasser
Ainz nus funt treü demander.
Sire Cesar, tu nus assaies,
Treü requers ke de nus aies,   3920

---

[1] MS J adds: *Tout le prist par sa vigour/ Li Aleman
l'on fait seignour/ Quant il ot conquise Alemaigne/ Si
s'en ala en Loheraigne/ A force la conquist et France/
Et rois en fu par sa poissance.*

[2] MS P reading—*de*—restored.

[3] MS P's reading of line restored.

[4] MS P reading—*l'apela*—restored.

[5] MS P reading—*repundu*—restored.

[6] MS P's order of line restored.

[7] MS P reading—*En*—restored.

Caesar asks Cassibellan for tribute

alry and he was educated and very learned.[1] When the Romans had conquered all the countryside around them, Caesar took leave of them to go and conquer far-off lands. He gathered together the best young men and crossed Lombardy and Montgieu. First he conquered Burgundy, then the Ile de France and the Auvergne and Gascony, Poitou, Normandy and Brittany. Then he turned towards Germany: in many places he built castles and cities and new dwellings. He succeeded very well in his task, reaching Flanders and Boulogne. Looking far across the sea, he saw an island and asked what land it was he saw and whether people, and what sort of people, lived there.

3861   The peasants told him that he was looking at a very big island, which Brutus had been the first to populate, bringing people from Troy there. He named it Britain, after himself, and made himself its king and leader. The heirs sprung from him had ruled the kingdom after him, And Caesar replied: 'I know well who Brutus was; he and we were of one race. The origin of our kin began in Troy. But, after its great destruction, its lords departed and acquired many countries. From this island, Britain, came Belin and Brenne, who grew so great that they took the city of Rome and destroyed our senate. We must certainly let them know that now Rome wields a rather different power. Fortune has turned her wheel and Rome is strengthened again. From now on, it is right that they pay attention to us and render tribute to Rome. They certainly ought to restore to us what they once took away. I shall summon them by letter and find out if they wish to respond. I've no intention of crossing the sea, if they will agree peaceably to render tribute to Rome and hold their fiefs from us.'[2]

3895   Then he had his letters written and carried overseas to Cassibellan, ordering him to hold his lands from him and to render tribute to the Romans. Cassibellan, who took offence, had an answering letter dispatched. He chose not to write any greeting but angrily informed him: 'Caesar, we are amazed, and, in our amazement, we hold in contempt the Romans and their overweening pride, which lasts so long and goes so far. Their greed will not allow liberty to anyone else except them. Under their control they want to bring all the gold and all the silver in the world, kings, counts and all other men—nothing can satisfy them. They want to grab all wealth for themselves. What do they mean to do with it all?

3915   'The Romans have no intention of overlooking us, living on the edge of the world in an island we possess, but demand tribute of us. Lord Caesar, you are testing us: you demand that we give you tribute and want to make us your tributaries.

---

[1] Wace extends the panegyric of Julius Caesar, whom he sees as an ideal ruler, though he mistakenly thinks he became emperor.

[2] Wace omits Caesar's contempt for the 'degenerate' Britons in *HRB* chap. 54, mentioning, on the contrary, the achievements of Belin and Brenne.

E faire nus vuels tributaires;
Mais tu nen espleiteras guaires.
Nus avum tuz tens franc vescu
E franchement avum tenu,
E vivre devum franchement
Com li Romain dreitement,
Kar nus sumes d'une racine
E d'une gent e d'une orine.
Cesar, se tu te purpensoues
3930 E si tu raisun esguardoues,
Merveilluse hunte feïs
Que de treü nus requeïs[1]
E mettre nus vols en servage
Ki sumes de vostre parage;
Per as Romains estre devum
Ki d'un lingnage descendom.
Si savies huem, si gentil sire
Come tu es, com osas dire
Que nus deion sers devenir
3940 Ki n'avom apris a servir
Ne ja, si Deu plaist, n'aprendrum,
Ço saces tu, que nus puissom?
Tut tens avom si franc esté,
Unc huem de nostre parenté
Ne sout encor, ne ja ne sache
Come l'on deit vivre en servage;
Ne savom, s'il ne nus est dit,
Come sers en servage vit.
Franc sumes e franc volum estre;
3950 Si meïmes li Deu celestre
Nus en vuleient abaisser,
Si nus volum nus efforcier
Que nus par hume ne perdom
Ço que nus tant tenu avom.
Or poez saver, nel celum mie,
Que, tant cum nus serom en vie,
E nus maintenir nus purrum,
Nostre franchise defendrum.
Franc volum vivre e a enor
3960 Si come firent nostre anceisor.'

Quant Cesar out le brief veü,
Bien ad apertement seü
Que passer mer li estovra,
Ja altrement rien n'i avra.
Dunc fist granz nefs faire e granz barges,
Quatre vinz en i out si larges,
Unches si granz ne furent mais
Pur porter granz genz e granz fais,
Estre les altres nefs menues
Ki de partut furent venues.   3970
Quant Cesar out tut apresté
E bel tens out e bon oré,
Crier ad fait: As nefs, as nefs!
E il entrent e lievent trefs.
Buen vent ourent e tost siglerent,
Al port vindrent si ariverent.
A peinne aveient terre prise
La u la mer receit Tamise,
Es vus par la terre espandue
La novele de lur venue   3980
Cassibellan, ki bien saveit
Ke cele gent venir deveit,
Aveit assemblé les barons,[2]
Qu'il aveit de partut sumuns.
Mult i out barons e vassals:[3]
Belins i ert, sis senescals,
Ki ert si privez conseillers
E suz lui maistre justisiers;
Juste lui out ses dous nevoz
En qui il se fiout sur tuz,   3990
De l'une part Androgeüs,
De l'altre part Tenuancius;
Androgeüs menout Lundreis,
Tenuancius Corneualeis.
E Nennius de Cantorbire,
N'i sout l'on meillor hume eslire,
Frere le rei esteit puis nez,
Est a ses dous nevoz justez.
Estre les contes i out reis
Venuz a l'ost desi qu'a treis,   4000

---

[1] MS P reading—*Que*—restored.
[2] MS P reading—*les*—restored.
[3] MS P reading—*i out*—restored.

Caesar arrives in Britain

But you will never succeed. We have always lived at liberty and freely held our land, and we should live at liberty, just like the Romans, because we are from one root, one race and one origin. If you reflect, Caesar, and if you see reason, you are committing an extraordinarily disgraceful act by demanding tribute and wanting to enslave us, we who are from your kin. Since we descend from the same lineage, we should be equal to the Romans. How dare you say, a wise man, a noble lord like you, that we should become slaves, when we have not learnt to serve, nor ever will learn, God willing. Do you think we could? We have always been so free that not one of our race has yet known, nor will know, how to live in servitude; nor do we even know, unless told, how slaves *do* live in servitude. We are free and we wish to be free. Even if the heavenly gods wanted to bring us down, we would struggle not to lose, through any man's act, what we have held for so long. Now you should know, we're not concealing it, that as long as we live and can protect ourselves, we will defend our liberty. We want to live in freedom and honour, like our ancestors.'

3961   When Caesar saw the letter, he realised quite clearly that he would have to cross the sea; he would never get anything otherwise. Then he had big ships and boats made, eighty of them,[1] so broad that never before had there been such big ones, in order to carry many men and many loads, in addition to the other smaller ships, which had come in from all directions. When Caesar had prepared everything and had fine weather and a good wind, the cry went up: To ship, to ship! and they embarked and hoisted the masts. The wind was good and they sailed quickly; they reached harbour and landed. Hardly had they landed, where the Thames flows into the sea, than the news of their arrival spread through the land.

3981   Cassibellan, who was well aware these people were coming, had gathered the barons, whom he had summoned from all directions. There were many barons and vassals there: there was Belin, his seneschal, who was his privy counsellor and lord justice under him, and beside him Cassibellan's two nephews, in whom he put complete trust:[2] Androgeus on one side, Tenuancius on the other. Androgeus led the Londoners and Tenuancius the Cornish. And Nennius of Canterbury, the king's younger brother—a better man could not be chosen—was next to his two nephews. Besides the counts, as many as three kings had joined

---

[1]   *HRB* gives no numbers but Bede (I, chap. 2) mentions eighty.

[2]   Wace adds the 'complete trust' to emphasize

sharply the poignancy of later betrayal—a recurrent theme.

E chescuns aveit grant efforz:
Eridious out les Escoz[1]
E Britael les Northualeis
E Guertaet les Suthgualeis;
Chescuns i veneit de sun gré
Pur defendre sa francheté.
Tuit unt al rei conseil doné
E tuit li unt pur bien loé
Qu'il alt les Romains assaillir,
4010 Nes laist pas del rivage eissir
Ne en la terre asseürer
Ne maisun ne recet trover.[2]
Par cest conseil sunt tuit armé.
Quant il se furent acesmé
E chescuns out fait sun conrei,
Serreement e senz desrei
Alerent les Romains ferir.
Cesar, quis out veü venir,
Cria a sa gent: 'Armez vus,
4020 Jas verrez ci venir sur nus!'
Tost fu la bataille jostee
Qui lu jor fu mult effree;
Dunc veïssez chevals bien puindre,
Hanstes brandir, chevaliers joindre,
Escuz percier, seles voider,
Homes chaeir, plaies seinner.
Chevaliers jostent, archiers traient,
Bien s'esforcent e bien s'essaient.
Saietes volent come pluie,
4030 Que plaist a cels a cez ennuie.
Mult oïssez testes croissir
E veïssez nafrez morir;
Tute ert del sanc l'erbe vermeille[3]
E ço n'esteit mie merveille,
Kar li vif sur les mors esteient
E sur les morz se combateient.
Cesar out en sa compainie
Le mielz de sa chevalerie,
Ki mult s'argue e mult se baille,
4040 Mult se combat, mult se travaille.

Il n'en vait nul aconsiuant
Ki vers lui ait de mort guarant.
Ardrogeüs, od cels de Kent,
E Nennius otot sa gent
Se sunt a une part atrait
Si unt des lur un conrei fait.
Puis unt Cesarem encontré
Si se sunt a sa gent mellé.
Nennius l'ad aparceü,
Sure li vint si l'ad feru;   4050
Liez fu de ferir si haut hume[4]
Come l'empereor de Rome.
Cesar l'escu avant tendi,
Le cop Nennie recoilli;
Bien fu maniers, l'espee ot traite
Dunt il ot mainte plaie faite,
Nennium sur l'elme feri
Qu'une grant piece en abati;
El chief l'ad d'une part nafré
E tost l'eüst par mi colpé[5]   4060
Mais Nennius le cop dota,
Baissa le chief, l'escu leva,
E l'espee en l'escu cola
E si parfund i enbevra
Que Cesar ne l'en pout sachier,
Unc ne se sout tant efforcier.
Il trait l'espee e cil l'escu,
Chescuns ad bien le suen tenu.
Nennius s'en vuleit turner,
Mais Cesar le fist arester.   4070
Bien crei que Cesar l'en traïst
E l'un od l'altre retenist,
Mais la force Nennie crut
Androgius i acorut[6]
E grant compainie de Kenteis,[7]
De tutes pars ferant maneis.[8]
Cesar nes osa mie atendre,
Ki ne s'aveit de quei defendre.
S'espee ad en l'escu guerpie,
E Nennius, ki out aïe,   4080

---

[1] MS P reading—*out*—restored.
[2] MS P reading—*trover*—restored.
[3] MS P reading—*del*—restored.
[4] MS P reading—*de ferir*—restored.
[5] MS P reading—*tost*—restored.
[6] MS P reading of whole line restored.
[7] MS P reading—*compainie de*—restored.
[8] MS P reading—*ferant*—restored.

The British attack the Romans

the army, and each one had large forces: Eridious leading the Scots, Britael the Northern Welsh and Guertaet[1] the Southern Welsh. Each came of his own accord, to defend his liberty. They all counselled the king and they all gave him advice for the best—to go and attack the Romans, not to let them leave the shore nor secure land nor find shelter or lodging. At this advice, everyone armed. When they were equipped and each one had formed his company, in serried ranks and orderly fashion they advanced to attack the Romans. Caesar, who saw them coming, shouted to his men: 'Arm: soon you'll see them upon us!'

4021   Battle was quickly joined, which that day was terrifying. There you could see horses being spurred on, spears brandished, knights clashing, shields pierced, saddles emptied, men fall and wounds bleed. Knights rushed together, archers shot, men struggled hard and were hard pressed. Arrows flew like rain, pleasing some, disturbing others. You could hear many heads being cracked and see the wounded die. The grass was quite red with blood, and it was not surprising, for the living were treading on the dead and fighting over their bodies.[2] Caesar had in his company his best knights, who made every effort and exchanged many blows, fought and suffered mightily. Nobody he struck could escape death at his hands.

4043   Androgeus, with the men of Kent, and Nennius with all his people drew to one side and grouped their soldiers into a company. Then they attacked Caesar and fought his men. Nennius spied him, came at him and struck him; he was glad to hit a man as important as the Roman emperor. Caesar thrust his shield out to parry Nennius's blow; very adroitly he drew out his sword, with which he had made many a wound, and struck Nennius on the helmet, cutting a large piece of it off. He wounded him on one side of the head, and might easily have cut it in two, but Nennius feared the blow, lowered his head, raised his shield, and the sword bit into it, penetrating it so deeply that Caesar could not pull it out, however hard he tried. He tugged his sword and the other his shield, each holding tightly to his own. Nennius wanted to leave, but Caesar made him stay. I am sure Caesar would have pulled it out and kept sword and shield together,[3] but Nennius' forces increased and Androgeus ran up to him with a great company of Kentish men, striking out at once in all directions. Caesar dared not wait for them, since he had no defence. He left his sword in the shield, and Nennius, with help,

---

[1] *HRB* chap. 56: *Cridous, Britahel, Gueithaet; VV: Eridionis, Britael, Guertaet.* Wace as usual substitutes contemporary names for Albany, Venedotia and Demetia.

[2] Wace constantly evokes the horrors of war with details like this.

[3] Wace builds up a picture of a noble Caesar; this interjection is part of it.

Torna l'escu, l'espee prist
Dunt il puis maint Romain ocist;
Il n'en poeit hume ferir
Ki de sun cop peüst guarir.
De l'espee a l'empereor,
Si fort hume, si halt seinnur,
Se fist mult cointe Nennius.
Devant lui vint Labienus,
Sire ert d'une conestablie,
4090 Ceo ert de Rome grant baillie.[1]
Nenius tel cop li duna
Que le chief del cors li sevra.
Ne vus sai les mors acunter
Ne les mielz combatanz nomer,
Mais mult i chaeient suvent
E mureient espessement,
E plus en i morust assez
Si la nuit nes eüst sevrez;
La nuit vint e le jur failli
4100 Si se sunt issi departi.
Li Romain, qui mult s'esmaierent,
A lur herberges repairerent;
Lassé furent e esmaié
E d'els maïsmes damagié.
Conseil pristrent qu'il s'en ireient
E cele terre guerpireient,
Kar le païs ne conuisseient
Ne fortelesce n'i aveient.
La nuit sunt en lur nés entré
4110 Si s'en sunt vers Flandres turné.
    Quant li Breton sourent al main
Qu'alé s'en erent li Romain,
Joie firent, mult furent lied,
Mais emprés furent corucied,
Kar Nennius, li hardiz ber,
Ne pout medicine trover
De la plaie qu'il out eüe
Quant l'espee fu retenue;
Al quinziesme jor traist a mort.
4120 A Lundres, a la porte nort,

Fu ensepeliz reialment,
Mult bel e mult corteisement,
Pur ço qu'il ert frere lu rei,
Ki l'aveit chier si come sei.[2]
Dejoste le cors fu posee
En la sepulture l'espee
Qu'il retint de l'empereür;
Od lui fu mise pur enor.
L'espee ert merveilles preisee
Si ert de letres d'or merchee;   4130
Lez le helt escrit out en sum[3]
Que Crocea Mors aveit nom;
Pur ço out nom Crocea Mors
Que ja n'en fust nafré nul cors
Ki ja medicine trovast
Ki de la mort le retornast.
    Bien tost fu as Franceis conté,
Ne lur pout mie estre celé,
Que Romain erent desconfit;
Turnez les unt en grant despit   4140
E tenu se sunt pur malveis
Que fait aveient od els pais.
Lur hardement unt recoilli
Si se sunt entr'els esbaudi,
Pur ço que il ourent oï
Que li Romain ourent fuï.
S'est ki fuie, assez est ki chace,
E tel ad poür ki manace
E tel manace ki se crient
E tel chace qui poi retient.   4150
Mult unt les Romains manaciez
E mult les unt contredeinnez,
Ço distrent que malvais sereient
Se jamais d'els terre teneient,
Volentiers tuz les ocireient
Sil aconsivre les poeient.[4]
Mult haeient lur seinurie
E cremeient lur felonie;
En ço lur cresseit hardement[5]
Que l'on lur novelout suvent   4160

---

[1] MS P reading—*de*—restored.
[2] MS P reading—*si*—restored.
[3] MS P's order of line restored.
[4] MS P reading—*sil*—restored.
[5] MS P reading—*En*—restored.

The Romans retreat

turned the shield round and seized the sword, with which he then killed many a
Roman. No one he struck could survive his blow. With the sword of the emperor—such a strong man, such a noble lord—Nennius made himself most valiant. Labienus appeared before him, leader of a troop; he was the chief governor
of Rome. Nennius gave him such a blow that he severed his head from his body.

4093   I cannot tell you the number of dead, or name the best fighters, but many men
were falling at every moment and great numbers were dying, and many more
would have died if night had not separated them. Night came, daylight failed
and thus they broke off. The Romans, in great dismay, withdrew to their tents.
They were weary and disheartened and had suffered losses. They decided to go
away and leave this land, for they neither knew the country nor had any strongholds there. That night they embarked in their ships and sailed towards Flanders.[1]

4111   When the British learnt in the morning that the Romans had gone, they rejoiced
and were very glad, but later they were angry, because Nennius, that bold man,
could find no medicine to treat the wound he received when he kept the sword.
A fortnight later he died. In London, at the north gate, he was buried royally,
handsomely and in courtly fashion, because he was the king's brother, who held
him as dear as himself. In the tomb next to the body was placed the sword which
he got from the emperor; it was put there in his honour. The sword was greatly
prized, and stamped with letters of gold. On top, next to the hilt, was written
that its name was Crocea Mors.[2] It was called this because nobody wounded by it
would ever find a medicine to rescue him from death.

4137   The French very soon heard the story—it could not be concealed—that the Romans had been routed. They held them in great contempt and considered themselves weaklings to have made peace with them. They regained their daring and
among themselves took heart because they had heard of the Romans' flight. A
man in flight is not short of pursuers, and a frightened man makes threats,[3] he
makes threats because he is frightened, and his pursuer has little to hold him
back. They uttered great threats against the Romans and poured much scorn on
them, saying they would be cowardly ever to hold land from them; they would
willingly kill them all if they could catch them. They hated their domination and
feared their cruelty; and their boldness increased on frequently hearing that the
British would cross the sea and fight the Romans.[4]

---

[1] *HRB* chap. 56 (and Bede): Gaul.

[2] *Crocea Mors* = Yellow Death. Wace adds the gold
    lettering and the sword's fame; in this it re-
    sembles the swords in *chansons de geste*, like
    Durendal, Curtein or Joyeuse, worthy of an

emperor such as Charlemagne.

[3] Both these comments are proverbial. See
    Morawski, *Proverbes*, nos. 1953 and 2363.

[4] Wace draws a sarcastic portrait of the cowardly
    French—not Gauls, as in *HRB*.

Que li Bretun mer passereient
E as Romains se combatreient.[1]
Mais l'orguil as Franceis fina
Des que Cesar od els parla.
Cesar sout bien felun danter
E orguillus amesurer,
Bien sout coveitus apaier
E sun talent faire changier,
E bien se sout humilier
4170 La u force nen out mestier.
Les Franceis vit contredeinnez
E encontre lui esforciez,
E les suens humes vit naffrez
E de combatre tuz lassez,
Mielz vult de sun aveir duner
Que en bataille en dute entrer.
As ducs e as plus hals baruns
Duna d'or e d'argent granz duns;
Tant lur ad aveir espandu
4180 Come chescuns en ad volu,
E assez plus lur ad premis
S'il aveit les Bretuns conquis.
As povres ad duné franchise
E clamé quites de servise,
A cels ki erent eissilied
E de lur heritez chacied [2]
Ad pramis tuz a eriter
E lur pertes a restorer.
Des que cil unt l'aveir veü
4190 E asquanz d'els l'ourent eü,
Tut ad sun quer chescuns mué. [3]
Aveir, mult as grant poesté!
Tost as une mellee faite
E une guerre a neient traite.
Cil ki anceis Cesar haeient
E ki ocire le vuleient,
Unt pur l'or mué lur curage
E chescuns li ad fait humage
E quant qu'il lur sout demander,
4200 Neïs en Bretaine a mener.

Quant Cesar les out apaiez
E tuz les out asuagiez,
A un mult bon enginneür
Fist sur la mer faire une tur,
En Beluine siet, Odre ad nun,
Ne sai nule de tel façun; [4]
Faite fu d'estrange compas,
Lee fu desuz el plus bas,
Puis alad tut tens estreinnant
Si cume l'en l'ala halçant;   4210
[Une pierre tant sulement
Covri le plus halt mandement] [5]
Maint estage i out e maint estre,
E en chescun mainte fenestre.
Illuec fist ses tresors guarder
E ses chiers aveirs aüner; [6]
Il meïsmes dedenz giseit
Quant de traïsun se cremeit.
Dous anz en France demura,
Odre sa tur apareilla,   4220
Si ad par les citez assis
E par les terres ses baillis,
Ki as treüz receivre seient
E ki en Odre les enveient. [7]
   En ces dous anz se renforça [8]
E set cenz granz nefs assembla, [9]
Si dist qu'encor essaiereit
Si les Bretuns veintre purreit.
Ne prise rien quanqu'il ad fait
Se il en pais issi les lait. [10]   4230
Quant sun navie out purchacied
E tut sun eire apareilled,
Ses set cenz nefs ad fait chargier
De que il aveit mestier. [11]
Tant unt nagied e tant siglé
Que en Tamise sunt entré.
Ço unt pensé e esguardé,
Mais failli unt a lur pensé,
Que amunt l'eue tant irrunt
Que a Lundres ariverunt,   4240

---

[1] MS J adds: *Si aideroient les Bretons/ E menroient les Bourgheignons/ Si cacheroient les Rommains/ De ce fu Cesar toz chertains.*
[2] MS P reading—*heritez*—restored.
[3] MS P's order of line restored.
[4] MS J adds: *Molt est espesse la masiere/ Ne sai nule de sa maniere/ Par cele tur conquist la tere/ Que nos apelons Engletere/ Et boin mur fist environ faire/ Illuec fist son avoir atraire.*

[5] MSS PDLSFGRMNT omit ll. 4211–12; the couplet is supplied by Arnold.
[6] MS P reading—*aüner*—restored.
[7] MS P reading—*ki*—restored.
[8] MS P reading—*se renforça*—restored.
[9] MS P reading—*set*—restored.
[10] MS P's order of line restored.
[11] MS P reading of line restored.

Caesar builds the tower of Ordre

4163   But the arrogance of the French died as soon as Caesar spoke with them. Caesar was good at taming malefactors and keeping the arrogant in check; he knew how to satisfy the greedy and make them change their mind and he knew how to lower his sights when force was of no avail. He observed the scornful French, up in arms against him, and he observed his own men, wounded and quite exhausted with fighting. He preferred to use his wealth rather than fight, uncertain of the battle's outcome. To the dukes and greatest lords he made large gifts of gold and silver; he spread around as much riches as anyone could want, and promised them much more if they conquered the British. To the poor he gave their freedom and release from serfdom; to the exiled, banished from their inheritance, he promised to restore their lands completely and make good their losses.

4189   Once they had seen the riches, and some of them had laid hands on it, everyone had a complete change of heart. Wealth, how powerful you are! In a minute you start a fight or extinguish a war. Those who formerly hated Caesar and wanted to kill him, changed their tune for gold,[1] and everyone submitted to him and to whatever he asked of them, even to be led to Britain. When Caesar had appeased and quite pacified them, he had an excellent craftsman build a tower by the sea. It is in Boulogne and called Ordre; I do not know another like it. It was constructed with curious contours: wide below, at the bottom, then continuously narrowing as it rose. A single stone covered the room at the top. It had many storeys and many chambers, and many windows in each. There Caesar had his treasure guarded and his valuable possessions assembled. When he feared treachery, he himself slept inside. For two years he stayed in France, equipped Ordre, his tower, and established his officials throughout the cities and the countryside, in order to receive tribute and send it all to Ordre.[2]

4225   In those two years he acquired reinforcements, assembled seven hundred large ships[3] and said he would once more try to conquer the British. He attached no value to anything else he had done if he had to thus leave them in peace. When he had procured his fleet and prepared for his whole journey, he had his seven hundred ships loaded with whatever he needed. They rowed and sailed until they entered the Thames. They intended and decided (but their intention failed) to sail so far up the river that they would come to London and only then disem-

---

[1] Wace specifically has Caesar dispense money.
[2] The tower of Ordre is missing in *HRB*, though later (chap. 60) Caesar retreats to a tower at Odnea in the territory of the Moriani. The tower of Ordre actually existed, created by Caligula

and restored by Charlemagne; it was demolished in 1644. See Arnold II, p. 800 and Houck, *Sources*, p. 216.
[3] The number is in Bede (I, chap. 2) and in *VV*, chap. 59, but not in *HRB*.

E dunc a primes fors eistrunt
E as Bretuns se combatrunt.
Bretun se sunt contregarni,
Ne sai cum il ourent oï;[1]
Par Tamise unt mis pels ferrez
E bien fichiez e bien serrez,
Que ja nule nef n'i entrast
Ki a hunte ne perillast.
Quant les nefs vindrent en Tamise
4250 E la veie ourent amunt prise,
N'erent gaires amunt corues
Quant es granz pels se sunt ferues;
Dunc veïssez nefs effundrer,
Eue receivre e afundrer,
L'une nef a l'altre hurter,
E maz chaeir e trés verser,
Custures fruisser e bors fendre,
Port ne rive ne püent prendre,
Mal unt a sigle e mal a nage.
4260 Cesar a veü cel damage,
Vit le peril e vit les pels,
Crienst que par tut ait altretels,
Ariere fist les nefs vertir
E terre prendre e fors eissir.
Dunc unt lur herberges fichiees
E lur tentes apparaillees.
Es vus Cassibellan puinnant,
Ki nes ala mie esparniant,
E si nevu e si parent
4270 E li baron communement.
Des que li reis cria s'enseigne,
N'i ad coart ki puis se faine,
As herberges les vunt ferir;
Dunc oïssez armes cruissir!
Li Romain as trés les atendent,
Ki a merveille se defendent;
Lur hardement ourent pur mur
Si lur rendent estur mult dur.
Bien se tindrent premierement
4280 Sis reçurent hardiement,

Bien luin les firent tuz ruser
Si en firent maint devier.[2]
Li Bretun emprés se retindrent
E li lur hume tuz tens vindrent.
Bien se sunt esmé a treis tanz
De chevaliers tuz combatanz[3]
Que Cesar n'i out amené,
Si lur unt un puindre duné;
Grant masse ariere les unt mis,
Dunc i rout mult Romains ocis.[4] 4290
Cesar, li pruz e li hardiz,
Ke unches ne fu esbaïz,
Vit que li Bretun tel force ourent
E que li suen suffrir nes pourent,
Kar a rage se combateient
Ne nul cop d'arme ne cremeient.
Tuz ses humes mist devant sei
E il fu detriés en conrei;
Si duna as Bretuns estal
Que li suen puis n'i ourent mal. 4300
Les nefs fist a terre acoster
Si fist les suens tuz enz entrer,[5]
E il entra derainnement.
Bel tens out, bon oré, bon vent;
A Odre sa tur ariva,
Lungement illuec conversa
Pur ses humes nafrez saner
E pur les altres reposer.
Endementers qu'il sojorna,[6]
Les baruns del païs manda.[7] 4310
　　Cassibellan fu mult joius,
Ki des Romains se fu rescus;
Sun regne ad dous feiz defendu
E Cesar ad dous feiz vencu.
Pur la leesce e pur la glorie
Qu'il out de la duble victorie,
Pramist as Deus comunement
Feste a faire mult haltement
E vouz a rendre e sacrefise,
Si noma jor de tel servise.[8] 4320

---

[1] MS P reading—*l'ourent*—restored.

[2] MS F adds: *Li reis s'enseigne escriad/ Coroça sei mult li pesa/ Le destrer point se genz apele/ Lor hardement renovele.*

[3] MS P reading—*tuz*—restored

[4] MS P reading—*rout*—restored

[5] MS P's order of line restored

[6] MS P reading—*Endementers*—restored

[7] MS J adds: *Por conseil prendre qu'il feroit/ Et comment il se maintenroit/ Il li loent qu'il atendist/ Tant que plus de gent lui venist/ Il atendi en pais se tint/ Oïés conment puis lui avint.*

[8] MS P reading—*tel*—restored

The British put stakes in the Thames

bark and fight the British. The British had in turn taken protective measures (I do not know how they had heard the news). In the Thames they placed sharpened stakes, firmly set and close together, so that any ship entering the river would be ignominiously wrecked.[1]

4249 When the ships entered the Thames and made their way up it, they had hardly begun their course when they struck the great stakes. Then ships could be seen sinking, taking in water and breaking up, one ship smashing into another, masts toppling and sails falling, seams splitting and timbers breaking. They could land neither in the harbour nor on the shore and had difficulty both rowing and sailing. Caesar saw the damage, saw the danger and the stakes, and fearing it would be the same everywhere, made the fleet turn back, land and disembark. Then they pitched camp and prepared their tents.

4267 Cassibellan came spurring towards them, with his nephews, his kin and the barons all together, intent on sparing no one. From the moment the king shouted his war-cry, there were no longer any half-hearted cowards.[2] They rushed to strike at the camps; what a clash of arms could then be heard! The Romans waited for them at the tents, putting up an extraordinary defence; walled[3] around by their courage, they gave them a very tough fight. At first they held out well and received them boldly, pushing them far back and killing many. Then the British stood firm, and their men kept coming. There were about three times as many knights, all brave, as Caesar had brought, and they attacked them; they drove them back a long way and many Romans were killed.

4291 The brave and bold Caesar, never disconcerted, observed that the British had such strength, and his men could not withstand them, because they fought furiously, undaunted by the blow of any weapon. He placed all his men in front of him and he remained behind in a troop, standing firm against the British so that his men suffered no more harm.[4] He had the ships brought in to land and made all his men embark, and he embarked last of all. He had good weather, a good breeze and a good wind. He arrived at Ordre, his tower,[5] and stayed there a long time, to treat his wounded and to rest the others. While he stayed there, he summoned the lords of the land.

4311 Cassibellan was overjoyed to be delivered from the Romans. He had twice defended his kingdom and twice beaten Caesar. Out of happiness, and the glory he had acquired from the double victory, he promised all the gods to hold a most solemn festival and to make vows and sacrifices; and he named the day for this

---

[1] The story of the stakes in the Thames first appears in Bede (I, chap. 2), where the Romans avoid them, and then in *HB* chap. 20, where the stratagem routs the Romans.

[2] Formulaic; cf. para. 2981.

[3] Wace's metaphor conveys his admiration for the Romans.

[4] Wace adds this tactic of Caesar's, along with his concern for his men.

[5] *HRB* chap. 60: a tower at Odnea.

Ses demaines e ses chasez
Ad tuz sumuns e tuz mandez
Qu'a cele feste a Lundres viengent
E cele feste od lui maintiengent;
Que nuls de cels n'i ait essoigne
Ki unt esté en sa busuine.
Tuit i vindrent joiusement,
Apparaillez festivalment,
Od lur femes, od lur enfanz,
4330 Od lur altres apartenanz.
Bel fu la feste celebree
E mult i out bele assemblee.
Chescuns, si cum lui cuveneit,
Fist sacrefise en sun endreit;
Quarante mil creües vaches
E trente mil bestes salvages, [1]
Purchaciees de mainte guise,
Mist l'on le jor al sacrefise.
Emprés i out cent mil oeilles,
4340 E de volatille merveilles.
Quant il ourent sacrefié
E a mult grant plenté mangié,
Si come li jorz requereit
En la guise ki dunc coreit [2]
A deduit unt le jur turné.
Li chevalier unt bohordé,
Li bacheler unt escermi,
Pierre jeté, lutied, sailli.
A la fin des geus, al partir,
4350 Sunt alé ensemble escermir
Hirelgas, ki ert niés le rei,
Uns damoisels de grant noblei,
E Evelin, niés Androgee,
Ki mult iert bien de la contree.
Tant ad duré lur escermie
Par orguil e par aatie
Qu'il unt turné le gieu a ire
Si se pristrent folie a dire.
Tant sunt les paroles creües
4360 Qu'il vindrent as espees nues;

Ocis i fu, eneslepas,
Par mesaventure, Hirelgas;
Tute en fu la cort estormie.
Quant li reis out la chose oïe,
De sun nevu fu anguissus
E il ert mult fel e irrus;
Nurri l'aveit si l'out mult chier,
Volentiers le vulsist vengier.
Androgee ad tost demandé [3]
E sur sun fieu li ad rové   4370
Qu'il li ameint u li anveit
Evelin sun nevu a dreit
A suffrir l'esguart de sa cort
Presentement, ainz qu'il s'en turt.
Androgeüs se purpensa,
S'il li livre, qu'il l'ocirra;
Le rei conut a mult gainart
E de la cort duta l'esgart.
Si dist que ja ne l'i merra [4]
Kar francs huem est e sa cort a,   4380
E ki de lui se clamera
Vienge en sa curt e dreit li fra. [5]
Li reis, ki out le quer enflé,
Androgeüm ad deffié;
Tuit le suen, ço dit, li toldra, [6]
E se il peut si l'ocira.
Issi sunt par mal departi
E mult se sunt entrehaï;
Li reis ad ses terres guastees,
Arses, destrutes e robees.   4390
Androgeüs vit ses granz pertes;
Sout que li reis le fist a certes.
Ses messages li ad tramis
Si l'ad preiad, si l'ad requis [7]
Que ses terres ne li guastast:
Sis niés esteit, si s'acordast.
Li reis fu fel si fu irais,
Ne volt duner trive ne pais.
Androgeüs ne pout faire el
Kar le rei sout a mult cruel; [8]   4400

---

[1] MS P reading—*bestes*—restored.
[2] MS P reading—*coreit*—restored.
[3] MS P reading of line restored.
[4] MS P reading—*ja*—restored.

[5] MS P reading of line restored.
[6] MS P reading—*Tuit*—restored.
[7] MS P reading of line restored.
[8] MS P reading—*Kar*——restored.

Death of Hirelgas

celebration. He summoned and commanded all his lords and all his vassals to come to this festival in London and undertake it with him; no one was to excuse himself who had been under his command. Everyone came rejoicing, festively dressed, with their wives, their children and the rest of their kinsmen. The festival was splendidly celebrated and there was a magnificent gathering. Each one, as befitted him and his social position, made sacrifice. That day forty thousand full-grown cows and thirty thousand wild beasts, hunted in various ways, were sacrificed. Beside these, there were a hundred thousand sheep and numerous fowl.

4341   When they had sacrificed, and eaten great quantities of food, they spent the day as required, in games, according to what was then the custom. The knights jousted, the young men fenced, threw stones, wrestled and jumped.[1] At the end of the games, just before everyone departed, Hirelgas, the king's nephew, a most arrogant young man, and Evelin, Androgeus' nephew,[2] who was on excellent terms with everyone, had a fencing match. The match lasted so long that through pride and hostility the game changed to anger and they began to talk folly. Their arguments mounted until bare swords came out; Hirelgas was by misfortune killed forthwith. The whole court was in turmoil. When the king heard, he grieved for his nephew and he was cruel and angry; he had brought him up and loved him dearly, and he was eager to avenge him. He asked for Androgeus, and demanded that, in accordance with feudal duty, he bring or send him his nephew Evelin, before he left, to await, as was proper, the court's decision.

4375   Androgeus reflected that if he gave him up, he would be the cause of his death. He knew the king to be very cruel and he feared the court's decision. So he said he would not bring him: he was a nobleman and had his own court, and whoever wished to complain about Evelin should come to his court where justice would be done. The king, his heart swollen with anger, challenged Androgeus, saying he would deprive him of all he had and kill him if he could. Thus they separated in anger and great mutual hatred. The king devastated, burnt, destroyed and plundered his lands. Androgeus saw his losses were great and knew the king inflicted them deliberately. He sent him messengers to ask and beg him not to lay his lands waste: he was his nephew, and should be reconciled with him. The king was vicious and angry, and wanted neither truce nor peace.

4399   Androgeus, knowing the king to be very cruel, had no alternative: he abandoned

---

[1] Wace adds the sporting details. On *bohorder* and *escremir* see Bennett, 'Wace and Warfare', p. 52; *bohorder* was the safer activity. Compare the entertainments at Arthur's court, para. 10521.

[2] *HRB* chap. 61: *Hirelglas* and *Cuelinus*; *VV*: *Hireglas* and *Euelinus*.

Ses plaines terres ad guerpies
E ses fortelesces guarnies.
Ne trova qui l'osast secorre
Ne quil peüst del rei rescurre.
Ne volt pas en taissant fuïr
Ne perdre ço qu'il pout tenir;
Mult avra, ço dit, grant anguisse,
Se il l'orguil le rei ne fruisse.
Mal faire pur pis remaneir,
4410 Ço tient li vilains a saveir;
E un mal deit l'on bien suffrir
Pur sun cors de peior guarir;
E pur sun enemi plaissier
Se deit l'on alques damagier.
Androgeüs se conseilla
Que mult griefment damagera
La terre le rei e la sue,
Ainz que del rei ne se rescue;
Ainz se mettra en grant barate
4420 Que il l'orguil le rei n'abate.
Priveement e a celé
Ad un brief fait e seielé;
A Cesar le fist tost trametre. [1]
La sentence fu de la lettre:
'A Cesar, le pruz e le fort, [2]
Emprés la desirree mort,
Mande saluz Androgeüs,
Ki est de Lundres sire e ducs.
Cesar, suvent ad l'um veü
4430 Que tel unt grant haenge eü
Ki puis se sunt bien entr'amé
E bon ami unt puis esté.
Emprés grant ire grant amur,
Emprés grant hunte grant enur,
Ço solt a plusurs avenir
Ki se suelent entrehaïr.
Noz dous morz nus entrequesimes
Quant jo e tu nus combatimes.
Ne sai pur quei laissasse a dire,
4440 Li un de nus volt l'altre ocire;

Mais issi nus est avenu
Que jo n'i fui ocis ne tu. [3]
Encor, ce crei, t'avrai mestier
E tu me repurras aider.
Dous feiz t'iés a nus combatuz
E dous feiz as esté vencuz,
Mais or saches certainement
E jol te di veraiement,
Ne t'esteüst guerpir noz porz
Si jo n'i fusse od mun efforz.   4450
Segurement venir peüsses,
Ja pur le rei vencu n'i fusses; [4]
Mais par mei e par m'ajutorie
Out Cassibellan la victorie. [5]
Cassibellan par mei venqui,
Par mei la terre te toli.
Nostre terre par mei perdis
E par ma force t'en fuïs.
Mais de ço sui jo repentant
Que jo t'en ai esté nuisant,   4460
E jo sui ki te ramerrai
E ki la terre te rendrai.
Ço peise moi que jo te nui
E que jo od le rei i fui,
Kar mult s'est puis desmesurez
Si est en grant orguil muntez;
Unches puis nul jor ne m'ama.
Ne estre en pais ne me laissa.
Tute ma terre ad eissilliee,
La gent robee e fors chaciee,   4470
Mei meïsme en vult il jeter
E de mun fieu deseriter;
Deu en jur e pur veir te di
Ke jo ne l'ai pas deservi,
Si l'on n'apele deservir
Mun nevu de mort a guarir,
Que il eüst a mort jugied,
Se jo li eüsse laissied.
L'achaisun de nostre mellee
E dunt ele est surse e levee   4480

---

[1] MS P reading—*tost*—restored.
[2] MS P reading—*e*—restored.
[3] MS P reading—*n'i fui*—restored.
[4] MS P reading—*n'i*—restored.
[5] MS P reading—*la*—restored.

Androgeus writes to Caesar

his open fields and fortified his strongholds. He found no one who would dare help him or to save him from the king. He did not want quietly to flee, or lose what he could hold. There would be much anguish, he said, if he did not thwart the king's anger. Doing wrong to prevent worse, that is what a peasant thinks is wise; and one certainly may well dare to endure one evil in order to protect oneself from a worse one. And to subdue an enemy, one must inflict some harm on oneself. Androgeus decided that he would have to grievously harm the king's land and his own before he escaped from Cassibellan, and he would endure many troubles before humbling the king's pride. Privately and secretly he had a letter written and sealed, and quickly sent it to Caesar.

4424 This was the sense of what was written there: 'Having desired the death of Caesar, the brave and strong, Androgeus, lord and duke of London, now sends him greetings. Caesar, it is often observed that those with a great mutual hatred subsequently like each other and become the best of friends. After great anger, great love, after great shame, great honour—that happens to many who used to hate each other. When you and I fought, we sought each other's death. I don't know why I shouldn't say so: each of us wanted to kill the other. But what actually happened to us was that neither you nor I were killed there. I believe it may yet happen that I need you, and in turn you can help me. Twice you have fought us and twice you have been beaten, but now, know for certain (and I'm telling you the truth), you wouldn't have had to flee our ports if I hadn't been there with my army. You could have arrived safely, and never been beaten by the king, but Cassibellan secured victory through me and my help. Through me Cassibellan won, through me he seized the land from you. Through me you lost our land, and you fled from my armed might.

4459 'But now I regret having been troublesome to you, and I shall be the one to bring you back and surrender you the land. I am sorry I hurt you and was on the king's side, because he has since exceeded all bounds and risen to the height of arrogance. Never since has he loved me or left me in peace: he has laid my whole land waste and plundered and expelled the people. He wanted to banish even me and deprive me of my inheritance. I swear to God and tell you truly that I didn't deserve it, unless you call 'deserving' saving my nephew from death, for he would have sentenced him to death if I had let him. I want to display before your authority the reason for our quarrel, and how it arose and developed, so that you know the truth of it.

Voil mustrer a t'autorité
Si en savras la verité.
Pur l'enor que nus receümes
De tei que nus vencu eümes,
Noz amis e noz genz mandames
E a Lundres nus assemblames;
A tuz noz Deus noz vouz rendimes
E sacrefise lur feïmes.
Quant fait eümes noz servises,
4490　Renduz nos vouz, faiz sacrefises,
A divers gieus diversement
S'assemblerent comunement
Li vallet e li bacheler;
Si avint ensemble a juer
Un mien nevu qui ert od mei
E un altre nevu le rei.
Tant unt escermi e joé
Que mis niés l'altre ad surmunté.
Li niés le rei s'en coruça [1]
4500　E a ferir le maneça.
S'espee traist sil volt ferir,
E mis niés le corut saisir;
Al poin u l'espee ert le prist,
Tenir le volt qu'il ne ferist;
Ne sai coment, cil chancela
E sur l'espee s'enbruncha.
Desur chaï si se nafra;
Mort fu, unches nen redreça. [2]
Ne fu pas d'altre arme adesez
4510　Ne altrement ne fu naffrez.
Li reis le sout si m'apela
E sur mun fieu me comanda
Que mun nevu li amenasse
E a justice li livrasse.
Jo soi bien que li reis fereit,
Que pur l'ocis l'altre ocireit;
Si li dis que ma curt aveie
E en ma curt dreit l'en fereie.
Pur ço que jo li contredis
4520　E que jo sun cumant ne fis,

Destruit ma terre e mei en chace
E a ocire me manace.
Sire Cesar, pur ço te mant
Qu'a mei vienges, par covenant
Que tu Bretainne aies par mei
E jo seie rescus par tei.
N'aies tu mie suspecion
Que jol die par traisun;
Jo nel fereie pur ma vie,
Mais tost vien, sire, si m'aïe. [3]　　　4530
Aïe moi, jo t'aiderai,
E Bretainne te liverrai.
Tel est vencuz premierement
Ki reveint puis derrainement.'
Cesar oï le mandement
Si em parla estreitement.
Quant il en out as suens parlé
Par sun message ad remandé
Que pur parole nel crerra
Ne pur parole n'i vendra,　　　　　　　4540
Mais s'ostages li enveout,
Il vendreit si cum il mandout.
Androgeüs le rei cremeit,
Ki Lundres aseger vuleit;
Sun fiz prist ki out nun Scena,
En ostage li enveia,
E trente damisels mult genz
Tuz nez de ses prochains parenz,
E Cesar les fist tuz mener
En Odre sa tur e guarder.　　　　　　　4550
Des qu'il pout, es nés est entrez;
Mer passa, si est arivez,
A Dovre vint celeement,
E tut despurveüement.
Androgeüs vint la a lui
Si unt parlé ensemble andui,
Lur covenant unt afermé
E lur afaire purparlé.
　[Cassibellan s'ost asemblout,
Siege a Lundres mettre quidout;] [4]　4560

---

[1] MS P reading—s'en—restored.
[2] MS P reading—nen—restored.
[3] MS P's order of line restored.

[4] MS PDLSFGRMNT omit ll. 4559–60; these lines are supplied by Arnold.

Androgeus joins forces with Caesar

4483 'Because of the glory we had gained through beating you, we summoned our friends and people and gathered in London. We made vows to all our gods and sacrificed to them. When we had done our offices, made our vows and our sacrifices, the boys and young men got together in various kinds of games. It happened that a nephew of mine who was with me, and another of the king's nephews, competed together. Their match and fencing went on until my nephew won. The king's nephew got angry and threatened to hit him. He drew his sword, intending to strike, and my nephew rushed to grab it; he seized him by the sword-hand, to keep him from striking. The other staggered, I don't know how, and stumbled on to the sword. He fell over it and was wounded; he was dead, he never got up again. No other weapon touched him, nor was he wounded in any other way.

4511 'The king learnt of it and summoned me, and ordered me by my feudal loyalty to bring him my nephew and deliver him to justice. I knew very well what the king would do—kill him in exchange for the one who had been killed. I told him I had my own court and in that court I would give him justice. Because I refused him and did not do as he ordered, he is ruining my land, and driving me from it and threatens to kill me. For this reason, lord Caesar, I'm calling for you to join me, on the understanding that you acquire Britain through me and I am rescued by you. Don't suspect treachery in these words: for my life, I would not commit it; but come soon, lord, and help me. Help me, and I will help you and deliver Britain up to you. The man beaten in the beginning is the victor later on.'

4535 Caesar heard the request and at once took soundings. When he had spoken to his men, through his messenger he replied that, whatever Androgeus said, he would not believe a word of it, or come; but if he sent him hostages, he would come as requested. Androgeus feared the king, who was intent on besieging London. He took his own son, called Scena,[1] and sent him as hostage, along with thirty noble young men, all from his close kin by birth. And Caesar had them all led to his tower, Ordre, and guarded. As soon as possible, he embarked, crossed the sea and landed; he came secretly and unexpectedly to Dover.[2] Androgeus came to meet him there and they both talked together; they confirmed their agreement and discussed their situation.

4559 Cassibellan assembled his army, thinking to besiege London. Rumour, which flies

---

[1] *HRB* chap. 62: *Scaeva.*

[2] *HRB* chap. 62: *Rutupi Portus* (Richborough) and from there to *Dorobernia* (Canterbury). But in the twelfth century Richborough was no longer a port. MSS K and H read: *A Romenel* [Romney] *est arrivez/A Dovre vint celeement.* Arnold points out (p. 801) that Wace twice translated *Rutupi Portus* as Dover (5109 ff.)

Renumee ki par tut vole
E ki de poi fait grant parole,
Vint al rei si li ad nuncied
Que Romain erent repairied
E a Dovre erent herbergied;
Ja l'avrunt mort e eissillied,
Si vivement ne se conseille.
Li reis ad tenu a merveille
Que returné sunt cele part;
4570 Nen quidout mais aveir regart. [1]
S'ost semunst, ses barons manda,
D'aler a Duvre se hasta.
Cesar, ki a Dovre atendeit,
Quant il sout que li reis veneit
Par le conseil Androgeï
De la vile de Dovre eissi.
Assez pruef en une valee
Ad sa gent mise tute armee;
Ses compainnes appareilla
4580 E ses eschieles ordena,
E quel fereient premerain
E ki meain e ki derain.
Quant Cesar out tut ordené,
A tuz ad dist e deveé
Que pur nule rien que il veient
Li un des altres ne desreient;
N'i ait si pruz ki se desrait;
Ne si coart ki pruz ne seit;
Serreement trestuit se tiengent
4590 Dessi que cil desor els viengent.
Mais ki a els s'apriesmera
E ki desur els s'embatra,
Receü seit as fers des lances
Es vis e es piz e es pances.
Androgeüs priveement
Se mist en un enbuschement
En un bois od cinc mil armez
Tuz del rei prendre atalentez. [2]
Quant le reis a Dovre aprisma,
4600 D'un munt el val avant guarda;

Vit les Romains, elmes laciez,
Tuz del combatre apparaillez; [3]
E il rad sa gent arengiee
E de combatre aparailliee;
Puis les est alez aprocier
E fist a els traire e lancier.
Grant pose aveient ja crié
E trait e lancié e jeté,
Quant Androgius s'escria,
Ki de l'aguait se desbuscha.   4610
Li reis oï la noise ariere
E vit lever la grant puldriere;
Les Romains ne pout parmi fendre
Ne cels detriés n'osa atendre.
De travers ad pris a guenchir,
Si vout a un tertre vertir;
Quel merveille tuit le haeient
E tuit sa mort querre vuleient.
A mort se tint e a traï,
E tuit li Bretun altresi.   4620
Chescun pensa de sei guarir
Par tost aler e par fuïr.
Mielz valt fuie que fole atente,
En tost fuïr fu lur entente;
Ne sai nule altre guarisun
A gent ki n'unt defensiun.
Illuc dejuste aveit un munt,
Desus en sum alques roünt;
Tuit ert covert de bussuneiz [4]
E de rochiers e de coldreiz; [5]   4630
Tant unt fuï e tant brochied
Que le tertre unt amunt poied.
Mais al puier e al ramper
En veïssez maint enverser,
Mais puis qu'il furent sus munté
E as coldreiz furent justé,
Altresi furent asseür
Come s'il fussent clos de mur.
N'i ourent puis Romain vertu,
Tant se sunt bien tuit defendu   4640

---

[1] MS P reading—*Nen*—restored.
[2] MS P reading—*atalentez*—restored.
[3] MS P reading—*del*—restored.

[4] MS P reading—*tuit*—restored.
[5] MS P reading—*rochiers*—restored.

The British retreat to a hill

everywhere and makes much talk from little matter, reached the king, telling him that the Romans had returned and were camped at Dover. If he did not quickly take advice, they would soon banish and kill him. The king was amazed they had returned to that quarter; he did not think he would have to do with them again. He summoned his army, sent for his barons and made haste for Dover. When Caesar, waiting at Dover, discovered the king was coming, by Androgeus' advice he came out of the town. Close by, in a valley, he placed his soldiers, all armed. He prepared his companies and arranged his troops, ordering who would strike first, who in the middle and who last.

4583   When Caesar had made all his arrangements, he spoke to everyone and forbade them to break ranks, whatever they saw. There's no man so noble who cannot run away, nor so cowardly who cannot act bravely. They were all to keep close together until attacked by the other side. But whoever approached them and rushed at them would be met with the points of lances in their faces, chests and bellies.[1] Androgeus secretly hid in a wood, with five thousand armed men in an ambush, all keen to capture the king. When the king approached Dover, he looked from a hill to the valley ahead. He saw the Romans, helmets buckled on, all ready to fight, and in turn he arranged his men and prepared them for battle. Then he advanced towards the enemy, with orders to shoot and let fly at them.

4607   They had been shouting, shooting, hurling and throwing for a long time when Androgeus, erupting from the ambush, shouted his battle-cry. The king heard the noise behind and saw clouds of dust. He could not break through the Roman ranks, nor did he dare wait for those behind. He began to withdraw sideways, intending to turn aside to a hill, amazed that everyone fiercely hated him and sought his death. He believed himself dead and betrayed, and all the British as well. Everyone thought of saving his own skin, by speedy retreat and flight. Flight is better than foolishly waiting,[2] and they meant to flee with all speed. I know of no other escape for defenceless people.

4627   There was a hill nearby, whose top was somewhat rounded; it was entirely covered with bushes, rocks and thickets. They fled and rode so fast that they climbed the hill, though in climbing and crawling many could be seen falling over. But once they had reached the top and were beside the thickets, they were as safe as if enclosed by walls. Then they all defended themselves so well that the Romans

---

[1] Wace adds both Caesar's speech and his battle tactics.

[2] Proverbial. See Morawski, *Proverbes*, no. 1245.

Cesar les vait avironant,
D'ores en altres assaillant,
E quant il veit qu'il sunt si halt
Qu'il nes puet prendre par assalt,
Assis les ad tut envirun,
N'en irrunt mais, se par lui nun.
As eissues e as sentiers
Mist granz conreiz de chevaliers
E granz truncs ad fait traverser,
4650 Que cil ne pussent trespasser;[1]
Nen a mie encor oblié,
Ainz lur ad suvent repruvé,
Que mult l'aveient laidengied
E del païs dous feiz chacied.
Vassal erent Bretun pruvé,
Hardi e fort e aduré.
Ki a celui se combatirent
E dous feiz adés le venquirent[2]
Ki conquist e out tut le mund;
4660 E encor la u assis sunt
E u il nul succurs n'atendent,
Se contretienent e defendent,
Ne laissier veintre ne se vuolent
A cels ki veintre e chacier suelent.
Mais Fortune est d'altre colur,
E sa roële ad fait sun tur,
E cil sunt el desuz turné
Ki el desus ourent esté.
Li Bretun ki furent assis,
4670 Enclos entre lur enemis,
N'unt que beivre, n'unt que mangier,[3]
N'aillurs nel püent purchacier.
Ne criement arme ne assalt
Ne nul engin, mais ço que chalt
Quant faim e sei tuz les destreint,[4]
Qui senz arme e senz fer les veint?[5]
Ja ne verrez tel fortelesce,
Tant i ait gent de grant prüesce,
Ki tant seit fort e grefs a prendre,
4680 Que famine ne face rendre;

Des que faute vient de vitaille
N'i estuet altre kis assaille.
Cassibelan fu anguissus,
Ne set cum seit d'iluec rescus;
De tutes parz veit les Romains
Ki jal quident tenir as mains,
Si n'ad par quei il se combate
E la grant faim ses homes mate;
De Cesar mult crient la manaie[6]
E la grant faim forment l'esmaie.   4690
A l'empereor pais fera
U al tertre de faim murra.
Dous jurs e des qu'al tierz sofri,
Que pais ne quist ne pais n'offri;
Dunc prist li reis un messagier,
Ne sai serjant u chevalier,
Sun message li ad chargied
E a sun nevu enveied,
Androgeüm, ki ert el siege,
La cui ire forment li griege.   4700
Mandé li ad que nel hunisse;
Se guarir le puet, sil guarisse.
N'ad mie vers lui deservi
Ne tant ne l'ad encor laidi
Que il a mort haïr le deie,
Ja seit ce que il le guereie.
Ne deit l'on pas haïr a mort
Sun parent pur un poi de tort;
Encor se püent racorder[7]
E lur mesfaiz entr'amender;[8]   4710
Mais des que l'on pert sun parent
N'i ad puis nul amendement.
Entre plusurs ad eü guerre
E pris aveir e toleit terre,
Qui pur nule rien qu'il perdissent
Li un les altres n'oceïssent.
Or seit corteis, si li aït;
Ne set nul home u tant se fit.
Sa parole a Cesarem port
E, se il puet, a lui l'acort   4720

---

[1] MS P reading—*pussent*—restored.
[2] MS P reading—*feiz adés*—restored.
[3] MS P reading—*beivre n'unt que*—restored.
[4] MS P reading—*tuz*—restored.
[5] MS P reading—*Qui*—restored.
[6] MS P reading of line restored.
[7] MS P reading—*racorder*—restored.
[8] MS P reading—*mesfaiz*—restored.

Cassibellan sends to Androgeus for help

were powerless. Caesar surrounded them, attacking from time to time, and when he saw they were so high that he could not capture them through assault, he besieged them round about, so that no one could get out except through his lines. Over escape routes and paths he laid great tree-trunks and placed large companies of knights, so that no one could pass. He often castigated the British (he had not yet forgotten it) for grossly insulting him and twice expelling him from the land.

4654 The British were experienced warriors, bold, strong and tough, who had fought, and twice in succession beaten, the man who had conquered the whole world; and still, besieged and expecting no help, they resisted and defended themselves. They had no intention of being conquered by those accustomed to conquest and pursuit. But Fortune's way is different: her wheel had turned, and those who had been on top fell to the bottom.[1] The besieged British, surrounded by their enemies, had nothing to eat or drink and nowhere to get it. They were not afraid of weapons, attacks or any stratagem, but what did that matter when hunger and thirst were tormenting them all, and vanquishing them without striking a blow? You will never see a fortress, however strong and difficult to capture, with however many valiant men inside, which is not forced by famine to surrender; once there is a shortage of food, no one else need attack it.

4683 Cassibellan was in torment: he had no idea how to escape. He saw the Romans on all sides, hoping soon to capture him, he had nothing to fight with and starvation was defeating his men. He was wary of Caesar's mercy and unmanned by hunger. He would either make peace with the emperor or die of hunger on the hill. He held out for two days, then a third, neither seeking nor offering peace. Then the king took a messenger (whether man at arms or knight I do not know), gave him his message and sent him to his nephew Androgeus, taking part in the siege, whose anger much distressed him. He told him not to humiliate him: if he could save him, let him do so. He had not yet harmed him so much, or deserved of him, that he should mortally hate him, even if he had made war on him. One should not bear a relation mortal hatred for a little wrongdoing. They could still be reconciled and make amends for their misdeeds; but once one loses a relation, there can be no amendment. Many people had made war on each other, captured goods and taken land, who, however much they lost, would never kill each other. Now he must be courteous and help him: he knew nobody he trusted more. He should carry his words to Caesar and, if possible, effect an agreement,

---

[1] Wace adds this dimension to the story.

Si qu'il ne seit deseritez
Ne de sun cors desonurez.
La nen ad li niés nule enor
U li uncles ad desonur.
Androgeüs ad respundu:
'Quei ad li reis mis sire eü?
Tost ad sun curage mué;
N'ad mie encor lunc tens passé
Que il me vuleit eissilier
4730 E de tut cest païs chacier,
E mei maneçout a ocirre;
Mult ad tost atempree s'ire.
Quant hom maine trop grant ferté,
Sil turne l'on a cruelté;
Ne fait mie sire a preiser
Ki en pais se fait bald e fier;
Quant vient en guerre e en estur
Si semble lievre de poür.
Quant li reis venqui tel seinnur
4740 Cummë un fort empereür,
Penser ne dire ne deüst
Que par sei sul vencu l'eüst;
Ja par sei ne s'i combatist.
Ne ja par sei sul nel venquist.
Par mei e par ses altres homes,
Ki mainte feiz nafré en sumes,
Out Cassibellan la victorie
Dunt il ad puis mené tel glorie.
Li baron e li chivalier
4750 Sunt de la glorie parçonier;
Come chescuns mielz i conquiert
E mielz i valt e mielz i fiert
Si deit il aveir sa partie
Del pris de la chevalerie.
Bien deit l'on faire al rei saveir
Qu'il ne puet pas victorie aveir
Par sul sa main, s'altre n'i a;
Folie fist ki ço quida.
Mais bien me sui de lui vengiez,
4760 Quant il s'est tant humiliez

Que il m'ad requis e preied
Que merci en aie e pitied. [1]
Ne rendrai mie mal pur mal,
Cum a mun enemi mortal;
Mis uncles est, ne li faldrai,
Neü li ai, or li valdrai.'
Androgeüs, issi parlant,
Ala a Cesarem errant;
As genuilz le prist humlement
Si li ad dist mult dulcement: 4770
'Cesar, vencu as e conquis
Cassibellan e sun païs.
A ta merci, sire, vendra,
E des Romains sun fieu tendra.
Pren sun treü, pren sun humage,
Si ait Bretainne en heritage.
Merci en aies, lai l'ester;
Que li deiz tu plus demander
Ne mais sul que tis huem devienge
E des Romains sa terre tienge?   4780
Mult valt a seinur pieté
Mielz que ne valt altre bunté.' [2]
Cesar avant s'en trespassa;
Surde oreille fist sil laissa.
Androgeüs vint sil reprist;
Desdein li sembla, si li dist
'Esta, Cesar, n'alez avant!
Bien t'ei rendu tun covenant;
Bretaine ai mise en ta baillie,
Aveir en puez la seinnurie.   4790
Nule altre rien ne te pramis,
N'altre covenant ne te fis
Ne mais que tant m'entremettreie
Que Bretainne te livrereie.
Aveir la puez, que vuls tu plus?
Ne plaise ja Deu de la sus
Que mis uncles par nul endreit
Seit en prisun ne en destreit.
N'est pas legiers a estre ocis
Tant cum jo seie sans e vis.   4800

---

[1] MS J adds: *Molt devroit bien li rois savoir/ Que de Bretaigne sui droit oir/ Mes peres fu rois de la tere/ Que mes oncles me tout par guerre/ Grant tort avoit et mespris a/ Quant de la mort me desfia.*
[2] MS P reading—*valt*—restored.

Androgeus helps Cassibellan

so that he would not be disinherited or physically dishonoured. His nephew could acquire no honour by dishonouring his uncle.

4725 Androgeus replied: 'What has happened to my lord the king? He's quickly changed his mind: it was not so long ago that he wanted to banish me and chase me from the land and threatened to kill me. He's very soon moderated his anger. When a man displays too much pride, he is harshly judged; no lord is esteemed who in peace-time is hard and overbearing. When he enters the fight and the fray, in his fear he resembles the hare. When the king defeated a lord such as a proud emperor, he should not have thought or said that he alone defeated him. He never fought him on his own, nor did he ever beat him on his own. Through me and through his other men—who bore the many wounds for it—Cassibellan secured the victory, which he then gloried in so much. The barons and knights are partners in that glory. Just as each one does his best to win, to strike, to be valiant, so he should have his share of esteem for knightly deeds. Someone should make the king well aware that he can't gain victory with his hands alone, unless there are others there; he would be a fool to believe that. But I am well revenged on him, since he has humbled himself so low as to ask and beg me to have mercy and pity on him. I won't return evil for evil, as if to my mortal enemy; he's my uncle and I won't fail him. I've afflicted him; now I'll help him.'

4767 So saying, Androgeus went to find Caesar. On his knees he humbly begged him, saying in a most conciliatory tone: 'Caesar, you have conquered and defeated Cassibellan and his country. By your leave, sire, he will come and hold his fief from the Romans. Accept his tribute, accept his homage: he has Britain for his inheritance. Have mercy on him and let him be. What more need you ask of him than that he become your man and hold his land from Rome? Pity is more profitable in a lord than any other virtue.' Caesar passed on, turning a deaf ear and moved away. This seemed disdainful to Androgeus who rejoined him, saying: 'Wait, Caesar, go no further! I've carried out my side of your bargain: I've put Britain in your power and you can be lord of it. I promised you nothing more, I made no other bargain except that I would take enough steps to deliver Britain to you. You can have it; what more do you want? God above forbid that my uncle should in any way be imprisoned or confined. It won't be easy to kill him as long

Mis uncles est si me nurri;
Quant il quiert que jo li aï,
Sis huem sui, ne li puis faillir;
E si tu ne me vuels oïr
Que ço faces que jo te die, [1]
De tei me part si te defie.' [2]
Cesar par itant s'apaia
E ço qu'il quist li otreia. [3]
Les ostages unt demandez
4810 Sis unt d'ambedous parz donez,
E le treü unt denomé,
E li Breton l'unt graanté,
Treis mile livres chascun an.
Dunc vint avant Cassibellan
E Cesar, si s'entr'asemblerent,
Baiserent sei si s'acorderent.
Unches ne poi lisant trover,
Ne a home n'oï conter
Qu'Engleterre treü rendist
4820 Dessi que Cesar la conquist.
Quant la parole fu finee
E la concorde graantee,
Chescuns rala en sa contree [4]
Si departi cele assemblee.
Ço dient gent e bien puet estre
Que Cesar fist faire Essecestre,
Ki Essecestre est apelé
Pur ço que sur Esse est fundee.
Cesar tuit l'iver surjorna; [5]
4830 Quant esté vint, si s'en rala; [6]
Pur amistied e pur chierté
En ad Androgeüm mené,
E d'Engletere prist ostages,
De tuz les plus gentilz lignages.
    Cassibellan set anz vesqui
Puis que Cesar d'illuec parti;
Treü rendant vesqui set anz;
Ne sai s'out feme ne enfanz.
A Everwic u il feni
4840 Ad l'on le cors enseveli.

Tenuancius de Cornoaille
Out emprés lui le regne en baille;
Sis niés esteit si l'en saisi;
Freres fu cil Androgeï.
L'enor avint emprés sa fin
A sun ainz né fiz Kimbelin,
Chevalier pruz e corteis hume;
Chevalier l'aveit fait a Rome
Augustus Cesar l'emperere.
En sun tens fu nez li Salvere,   4850
Fiz Deu Jesu, ki del ciel vint,
Deus ert, mais pur nus huem devint,
E pur nostre redemptiun
Suffri en la croiz pasiun [7].
En Bretainne aveit un devin
Que l'on apelout Teleusin; [8]
Pur buen prophete esteit tenuz
E mult esteit de tuz creüz.
A une feste qu'il faiseient,
U li Bretun ensemble esteient,   4860
Li preia li reis e requist
Qu'alcune chose li deïst
Del tens ki veneit en avant;
E cil parla si dist itant:
'Home, ne seiez en tristur;
Atendu avum nuit e jur,
En terre est del ciel descenduz
Cil ki ad esté atenduz
Ki salver nus deit, Jesu Crist.'
La prophetie que cil dist   4870
Fu entre Bretuns recordee;
De lunc tens ne fu obliee.
Il out dist veirs, pas ne menti;
A cels tens Jesu Crist nasqui.
Bretuns pur ço plus tost creïrent,
Quant de Crist prechier oïrent. [9]
Kimbelin fu mult enorez
E des Romains fu mult privez.
Lur treü retenir peüst.
Ke ja demandez ne li fust,   4880

---

[1] MS P reading—*die*—restored.
[2] MS P reading—*defie*—restored.
[3] MS J: *Puis sunt li Breton amené/ E del tertre jus devalé/ Cassibellan fist son hommage/ A Cesarem le preu le sage.*
[4] MS P reading—*rala*—restored.

[5] MS P reading—*tuit*—restored.
[6] MS P reading—*rala*—restored.
[7] MS P reading—*pasiun*—restored.
[8] MS P: *Teselin.*
[9] MS P reading—*prechier*—restored.

Kimbelin

as I am alive and well. He's my uncle and he brought me up; when he asks me to help him, I'm his man and I can't fail him. And if you don't want to listen to me or do what I tell you, I'll leave you and defy you.'

4807   At that Caesar made peace with him and granted what he asked. They asked for hostages, who were given on both sides, and fixed the amount of tribute, and the British accepted it: three thousand pounds a year. Then Cassibellan and Caesar came forward and met, exchanged kisses and were reconciled. I could never read anywhere, nor hear any tale from anyone, that said England paid any tribute, until Caesar conquered her. [1] When the talking was over and the agreement accepted, each went to his own region and the gathering broke up. People say, and it may well be, that Caesar founded Exeter, which is called Exeter because it is set on the Exe. [2] Caesar stayed all winter; when summer came, he departed again. Out of friendship and affection, he took Androgeus with him, and he took from England hostages from all the noblest families.

4835   Cassibellan lived for seven years after Caesar left, paying tribute for seven years. I do not know if he had a wife or children. The body was buried at York, where he died. Tenuancius of Cornwall governed the kingdom after him; he was his nephew, brother of Androgeus, and he took it over. After his death, the domain fell to his eldest son, Kimbelin, [3] a brave and courteous man. The emperor Augustus Caesar made him a knight in Rome. In his time the Saviour was born, Jesus the son of God, who came from heaven, and was God, but for our sake became man, and for our salvation suffered death on the cross.

4855   There was a soothsayer in Britain called Teleusin: he was considered a good prophet and everyone gave him much credence. At a festival, where the British were gathered together, the king begged and asked him to tell him something of the time to come. And he spoke as follows: 'Man, sorrow no more. We have waited night and day: from heaven to earth has descended he whom we awaited, who will save us, Jesus Christ.' [4] The British remembered the prophecy he uttered; it was not forgotten for a long while. He told the truth and did not lie: Jesus was born at that time. For this reason the British were readier to believe when they heard people preach about Christ.

4877   Kimbelin was held in great honour and was close friends with the Romans. He could have kept back their tribute and it would never have been asked of him,

---

[1] Here, as in many places, Wace substitutes 'England' for *HRB*'s 'Britain', and inserts a characteristic emphasis on his own researches.

[2] Wace adds this detail.

[3] Cymbeline.

[4] *HB* (chap. 62) mentions Taliesin as a poet in the days of '*Outigern*'. *HRB* does not mention Taliesin or his prophecy. See Houck, *Sources*, p. 250.

E nequedent tuit lur rendeit [1]
Que nule rien n'en reteneit.
Cist out dous fiz, Wider l'ains né,
E Arviragum le puis né.
Dis anz fu reis e puis fina
E Wider sun fiz erita.
Cil fu chevalier merveillus,
Mais mult fu fiers e orguillus;
De l'amur as Romains n'out cure
4890 Ne ne lur vout faire dreiture;
De Bretainne les dessaisi
E lur treü lur en toli. [2]
Ne vout de rien a els entendre
Ne lur treü ne lur vout rendre.
Claudius mult s'en desdeina,
Emperere ert, sun chief jura
Que le treü restorera
E Wider deseritera.
Par commun conseil del sené
4900 Ad tant chevalchied e erré
Od mult grant ost qu'il assembla,
Qu'en Engleterre mer passa.
Port e terre prist a Porcestre;
Puis fu tel jur n'i volsist estre.
Porcestre ert dunc cité nomee,
Mais arse fu puis e guastee.
L'emperere ad Porcestre assise,
Mais pesance out ainz qu'el fust prise.
Pierre fist e mortier atraire;
4910 Devant les portes fist mur faire,
Que huem defors n'i pout entrer
Ne huem defors n'en pout turner;
Issi les quida afamer,
Nes poeit altrement grever.
Mais Wider les ad securuz,
Ki vint od plus de mil escuz,
Ensemble od lui Arviragus;
Nes pout pas suffrir Claudius;
Od le plus des suens traist as nés,
4920 Mult en ad poi el champ remés.

E nequedent suvent poineient
E bien suvent s'entr'abateient.
Claudius out od sei Hamun,
Sun conseillier e sun baron;
En lui ert tute sa fiance,
Kar mult esteit de grant vaillance.
Cil ad veü Wider combatre,
Romains ferir, Romains abatre,
Ses conreiz tenir sagement
E mener ordoneement.   4930
Bien vit que tant cum il vivreit
Bretainne prise ne sereit.
Purpensa sei en maint endreit
Coment ocire le purreit.
Un des Bretuns ad mort trové;
Priveement l'ad desarmé.
Des armes al Bretun s'arma
E as Bretuns s'entremella.
Ensemble od les Bretuns esteit,
Ensemble od les Bretuns puineit;   4940
Ensemble od les Bretuns alout,
Ensemble od les Bretuns parlout.
Tuz les deceveit l'armeüre,
E il saveit lur parleüre,
Kar a Rome entre les ostages
Aveit apris plusurs languages.
Haym saveit bien bretun parler
E des Bretuns plusurs nomer.
Tant est alez Haym traversant,
E tant ariere e tant avant,   4950
Al rei Wider s'est acostez,
E juste lui fu lez a lez;
A un trestur que li reis fist
Traist Haym s'espee si l'ocist.
Trés un trés altre se muça
E a sa gent s'en repaira
Arviragus, ki s'aperçut [3]
Que li reis mort a terre jut,
Co fu li premiers quil trova,
Mais mult petit s'i aresta,   4960

---

[1] MS P reading—*tuit lur*—restored.   [3] MS P reading—*s'aperçut*—restored.
[2] MS P reading—*E lur*—restored.

Claudius lands at Porchester

but nevertheless he paid it all and retained nothing. He had two sons, Wider[1] the elder and Arviragus the younger. He ruled as king for ten years and then died, and his son Wider succeeded. He was an exceptional knight, but very hard and proud, who cared nothing for friendly relations with the Romans or for doing them justice. He dispossessed them of Britain and withheld the tribute from them. He had no desire to listen to them or to pay them their tribute. Claudius became very angry: he was emperor, and swore by his head to restore the tribute and disinherit Wider. With the advice of the whole senate, he rode and travelled so far, with the enormous army he had assembled, that he crossed the sea to England.

4903 He landed at the harbour of Porchester. Then there followed a day such as he would rather have escaped. The city was then called Porchester, but later it was burnt down and destroyed. The emperor besieged Porchester, but it caused him grief before it could be taken. He had stones and mortar brought, and a wall built before the gates, so that no one outside could get in and no one inside could get out. Thus he thought to starve them out; there was no other way of harming them. But Wider aided them, arriving with over a thousand armed men, and Arviragus with him. Claudius could not withstand them: with most of his men he withdrew to his ships, leaving very few in the field. Nevertheless, the two sides kept attacking and fighting each other.

4923 Claudius had Hamo with him, his adviser and knight. He trusted in him completely, because he was a man of great merit. Hamo had seen Wider fight, striking and felling Romans, wisely restraining his troops and leading them in orderly fashion. He realised that as long as he lived Britain would never be captured. He reflected on the many ways in which he might be killed. He found one of the Britons dead and secretly disarmed him, donned the Briton's armour, and mingled with the British. Together he accompanied the British, attacked with them, advanced with them and spoke with them. They were all deceived by his armour, and he knew their tongue, for amongst the hostages at Rome he had learnt several languages. Hamo could speak the British tongue fluently and call many of the Britons by name.

4949 Hamo crossed the field so many times, backwards and forwards, that he drew near to king Wider until they were side by side. As the king turned, Hamo drew his sword and killed him. He first hid behind one, then another and got back to his men. Arviragus, noticing the king lay dead on the ground, was the first to find him, but stopped for a very short space; there was no opportunity to stay or time

---

[1] *HRB* chap. 65: Guider; *VV*: Gwiderius.

N'esteit mie lieus de remaindre
Ne tens de plurer ne de plaindre,
L'armeüre e la conuissance
Ad pris del rei senz demurance.
Priveement s'en est armez
Si rest sur sun cheval muntez.
Dunc veïssez chevaliers puindre,
Suvent turner e sovent joindre,
E l'enseine reial crier
4970 E les Bretuns amonester.
Nuls huem cunustre ne peüst
Que ço Wider li reis ne fust.
Li Romain fuient a desrei;
N'osent atendre sun conrei.
En dous meitiez les fist partir,
Ne se pourent contretenir. [1]
Une partie as nés turna,
E ki ainz pout entrer, entra.
Claudius est od cels turnez
4980 E od cels est es nés entrez;
As bois turna l'altre partie [2]
Qui ne pout turner al navie.
Ensemble od cels Haim s'en fuï
E Arviragus le soï.
Dit li fu e il le quidout
Que Claudius la s'en alout.
Tant unt que bois que plain coru
Qu'a un port as nés sunt venu.
De sun cheval Haim descendeit;
4990 En une nef entrer vuleit
Que marcheant illuec aveient
Ki al marchied venu esteient.
Arviragus l'ad conseü
Ki li sevra le chief del bu.
Pur ço que Haym illuec morut,
Illuec fu ocis, illuec jut,
Fu puis e est par la contree
La ville Hamtune apelee:
Ço est a dire, ço m'est vis,
5000 La vile u Haim esteit ocis.

Issi vienent surnuns suvent
Par mult poi de comencement;
E par mult petite aventure
Vient maint surnum que lunges dure.
Arviragus out Hamun mort,
Le cors laissa gisant el port.
Endementres que ço avint
Claudius a tere revint.
Tutes ses nés ad rassemblees,
A Porcestre sunt returnees.   5010
Les murs ad fraiz e depeciez
E tuz le homes eissilliez,
Arse e destrute la cité;
Unc puis ne fu en la bunté
Ne el pris ne en la valur
Qu'ele out esté devant cel jur.
Quant il out abatu Porcestre,
Od quanqu'il pout vint a Wincestre;
Arviragum assist dedenz
Od tut le plus de ses parenz.   5020
Engienz fist faire e halt drecier
As murs quasser e depecier.
Arviragus out grant pesance.
Si li sembla grant avilance
Que si esteit enclos tenuz;
De la cité est fors eissuz.
Conreiz fist de ses chevaliers,
E de dous pars mist ses archiers;
La gelde fu ensemble ariere,
Trestute armee a lur maniere.   5030
Ja esteient a l'assembler
E al lancier e al geter,
Quant li sage hume e li veillart
Se sunt turné a une part;
La perte cremeient des lur,
Si requistrent l'empereür
Pur demander que il fereit,
Si pais u bataille voleit.
E il respondi bonement
Que de bataille n'ad talent.   5040

---

[1] MS P reading—*contretenir*—restored.   [2] MS P reading—*As*—restored.

Arviragus fights Claudius

to weep or lament. Without delay he took the king's armour and device. Secretly he put them on and once more mounted his horse. Then knights could be seen spurring forward, often wheeling and often clashing, shouting the royal war-cry and exhorting the British. No one could know this man was not king Wider. The Romans fled in disarray, not daring to await his troops. He made them split into two halves, which they were unable to resist. One group returned to the ships and whoever could enter first, did so. Claudius returned with these and entered the ships with them.

4981 The other group entered the woods, since they could not return to the fleet. Hamo fled with them and Arviragus followed him. He was told, and believed it, that Claudius had gone in that direction. They hastened through both woods and plains until they came to a harbour with ships. Hamo got down from his horse; he wanted to board a ship containing merchants, who had come to the market. Arviragus overtook him and severed his head from his body. Because Hamo died there, was slain and lay there, the town was later called Hampton and is known by that name throughout the land. That means, it seems to me, the town where Hamo was killed. That is how names frequently come about, through very small beginnings; and through a tiny incident many a long-lasting name is created.

5005 Arviragus killed Hamo and left his body lying in the harbour. Meanwhile, Claudius landed once more. He gathered all his ships together and they returned to Porchester.[1] He shattered and smashed the walls, drove out all the people and burnt and destroyed the city. It never regained the eminence, renown and worth that it possessed before that day. When he had knocked Porchester down, he went to Winchester with all the troops he could muster, and besieged Arviragus, who with most of his kin was inside the city. He had machines made and raised up high, to break and smash the walls. Arviragus' heart was heavy: he felt it a disgrace to be so confined. He came out of the city, formed his knights into a company, and set his archers on two sides. The foot-soldiers together brought up the rear, all armed in their fashion.

5031 They were just about to join battle, hurl and throw, when the old and wise men went aside in a group. They feared the loss of their men and sought the emperor to ask what he would do and whether he wanted peace or war. And he readily answered that he had no wish for battle, but wanted peace and friendly relations

---

[1] *HRB* chap. 67, adds that in those days Porchester was called '*Kaerpetis*' (*VV*: *Kaerperis*), a detail one would expect Wace to enjoy and retain if he saw it.

Ainz vult la pais e vult l'amur
Fors tant que Rome i ait enur. [1]
De nul altre gaain n'ad cure
Ne mais que Rome ait sa dreiture.
Arviragum enorera;
Une fille ad qu'il li durra
Si sul vult sis huem devenir [2]
E de Rome sun fieu tenir.
Arviragus l'ad graanté,
5050 Si se sunt entr'els acordé.
En Wincestre se herbegierent,
Amis furent si s'acointerent.
D'iluec s'unt a Rome enveied
Cil ki en sunt apareillied
Pur Genoïs faire amener
Que Claudius deveit doner.
Entretant cunquist Orchenie
Par Arvirage e par s'aïe,
E altres illes envirun
5060 Que jo ne sai coment unt nun.
Li messagier lur veie tindrent
E a l'entrant d'esté revindrent;
Sin amenerent Genuïs, [3]
Gente de cors, bele de vis.
A la meschine marier,
E a lur covenanz fermer, [4]
Furent li baron de la terre
Entre Guales e Engleterre
Sur Saverne en une valee
5070 Ki mult est riche e asazee.
Pur cel plai mettre en remembrance
Firent al lieu tel enorance
Que une cité i funderent
E Gloëcestre l'apelerent.
La ville pur ço cest nun a
Que Claudius l'edifia.
Altre dient altre achesun
Qui assez bien semble raisun;
De Claudio fu engendrez
5080 Uns filz illuec, Glois fu numez.

Gloi fu de Gloëcestre sire
E dux de Guales, ço oi dire.
Pur ço que Gloi fud illuec nez
E que sire en fu renumez, [5]
Fu Gloëcestre de lui dite,
Ceste achaisun truis jo escrite.
Gloëcestre c'est cité Gloi,
Unc plus dreite raisun ne soi.
Quant Genuïs fu mariee,
A ses noces fu coronee.   5090
Emprés les noces fu la sume
Que Claudius rala a Rome.
A cel terme, ço truis lisant,
Alout saint Pierres preechant;
A Antioche aveit esté;
Mis i aveit crestienté;
A Rome ert novelment venuz,
Faisant miracles e vertuz.
   Quant alé s'en fu Claudius
Bretainne tint Arviragus;   5100
Mais a merveille se preisa
E a merveille s'orguilla.
Le treü as Romans veia
Ne d'els tenir rien ne deinna.
Li Romain a enviz perdeient
Ço ke par dreit aveir deveient.
Tramis i unt Vespasien
Od chivaliers ne sai combien.
Vespasien se mist en mer
E a Dovre volt ariver,   5110
Mais li reis, ki sout sa venue,
Li ad la terre deffendue,
E cil ad fait ses veilles tendre
Quant a Duvre ne pout port prendre.
Le lunc de la mer ad siglé
E le pais ad acosté.
A Toteneis rivage prist,
Ne trova ki li deffendist.
A Essecestre vint puinnant,
Entrer i volt en supernant;   5120

---

[1] MS P reading—*Fors tant*—restored.
[2] MS P reading—*si sul*—restored.
[3] MS P reading—*sin*—restored.
[4] MS P reading—*covenanz*—restored.
[5] MS P reading—*renumez*—restored.

Arviragus marries Claudius' daughter

provided that Rome was held in respect. No other advantage concerned him, provided that Rome got her rights. He would honour Arviragus by giving him his daughter, if he would become his man and hold his fief from Rome. Arviragus agreed, and they were reconciled. They lodged in Winchester, became friends and got to know each other. From there, they sent to Rome people prepared to bring back Genuïs, whom Claudius was to bestow in marriage. Meanwhile he conquered Orkney through Arviragus and with his help, and other surrounding islands, whose names I do not know.

5061 The messengers went on their way, and at the beginning of summer returned, bringing Genuïs, fair of body and beautiful of face.[1] For the girl's marriage and to confirm their agreement, the lords of the land were assembled on the border of England and Wales in a valley on the Severn, very rich and fertile. To remember this agreement, they honoured the spot by founding a city there and calling it Gloucester.[2] The city bears this name because Claudius erected it. Others give another reason which makes very good sense: Claudius begot a son there, called Glois. Glois was lord of Gloucester and duke of Wales, I have heard. Because Glois was born there and was named its lord, Gloucester was called after him: I find this explanation written down. Gloucester is Glois' city; I know no better reason. When Genuïs was married, she was crowned queen at her wedding. When the wedding festivities ended, Claudius returned to Rome. I find in my reading that at that time St Peter was travelling about preaching: he had been in Antioch and established Christianity there. He had recently come to Rome, performing wonders and miracles.

5099 When Claudius had gone, Arviragus ruled Britain, but he had an exceedingly high opinion of himself and became exceedingly proud. He refused to pay tribute to the Romans and did not deign to hold any lands from them. Against their will the Romans lost everything to which they were entitled. They sent Vespasian with I know not how many soldiers. Vespasian embarked and intended to land at Dover,[3] but the king, knowing he was coming, defended the land against him, and, when Vespasian could not disembark, he spread his sails. He sailed along the sea, hugging the coast. Finding no one to stop him, he landed at Totnes. He spurred on to Exeter,[4] intending to enter it unawares, but the people were ready for him, and he attacked it for a week without ever being able to invade it.

---

[1] *HRB* chap. 68, says Arviragus adores his wife (whom he calls Genuissa); the *VV* and Wace omit this.

[2] *HRB* chap. 68: *Kaerglou, id est Gloucestria*; *VV*: *Kaerglou, id est Claudiocestria*.

[3] *HRB* chap. 69: *Rutupi Portus*.

[4] *HRB* chap. 69: *Kaerpenhuelgoit*, called Exeter. According to Bede (I, chap. 3) Vespasian, sent by Claudius, brought the Isle of Wight under Roman rule.

Mais la gent en esteit garnie,
E il l'at set jors assaillie,
Unches dedens entrer ne pout.
Arviragus, ki tost le sout,
Od ses chevaliers e od s'ost,
L'a securu, ne pout plus tost.
Des le main, al soleil levant,
Dessi al vespre, a l'anoitant,
Se sunt entr'els si combatu
5130 Que cist ne cil ne sunt vencu;
A la nuit se sunt desevré,
Mais mult furent las e nafré.
Quant al demain rarmé se furent
E il combatre se redurent,
La reïne les acorda,
Genüis, ki mult s'en pena;
Ele ert mult bien enparentee,
Kar des nobles Romains ert nee.
Pur l'enor de sun parenté
5140 Ad tant d'ambedous parz loé
Que li baron s'entr'acorderent
E pais pristrent e pais donerent.
Vespasien ad sojorné
En Bretaine des qu'a l'esté;
Puis est a Rome repairiez,
E tuz joius e tuz haitez.
Arviragus, tut sun vivant,
Tint as Romains lur covenant;
Unc puis de rien ne lur falsa,
5150 Ainz les servi e eshauça
Pur l'amistied de la reïne
Ki nee esteit de lur orine.
    Marius, sis fiz de moillier
Out puis le regne a justiser.
Cil fu de mult grant sapience
E de merveilluse eloquence.
A Rome fu el tens sun pere
Nurriz od les parenz sa mere;
Mult se fist richement servir
5160 E mult se sout bien contenir.[1]

El tens que Marius regna,
Rodric en Escoce ariva;
Reis ert des Pis, si vint de Scice,
Uns huem ert mult plein de malice,
E mult amout gent a rober.
Escoce esteit venuz guaster
E mult en aveit ja guasté,
Quant Marius, ki l'a trové
Ki n'out cure de mal veisin,
Le descunfist e traist a fin.   5170
La u il out vencuz les Pis
E Rodric mort e le chief pris,
Fist une grant pierre lever,
Encor l'i puet l'on or trover,
Pur sa prüesce demustrer
E pur la chose remembrer.
En la pierre out une escriture,
Mien escient ki encor dure,
Ki testemonie l'aventure
E conte la discunfiture,   5180
Que Marius Rodric ocist
E la pur ço la pierre mist.
Encor i est, ço oi retraire,
Si l'apele l'on Vestinaire.
Les Pis que li reis ad vencuz[2]
Ad en sa terre retenuz;
De Cateneis lur fist livrer
Une grant partie a popler
Qui encor esteit en guastine
Tuz tens laissiee a salvagine.   5190
Li Pi se sunt la herbergied
Si unt aré e guaainied;
De Bretainne femes requistrent,
Mais li Bretun les escundistrent.[3]
E cil en Irlande passerent
E de la femes amenerent.
Par la terre se herbergierent,
Tost crurent e multiplierent.
    Marius vesqui lungement,
E emprés sun definement   5200

---

[1] MS P reading—*bien*—restored.
[2] MS P reading—*ad*—restored.
[3] MS P reading—*les*—restored.

Marius defeats the king of the Picts

Arviragus, who soon knew about it, helped the town as quickly as he could, with his knights and his army. From morning, at sunrise, to evening, at nightfall, the two sides fought each other so hard that neither one nor the other was defeated. At night they separated, but they were very weary and many were wounded.

5133   The next day, when they had re-armed and were on the point of resuming fight-ing, the queen, Genuïs, who was in great distress, reconciled them. She came from very exalted stock, because by birth she was from a noble Roman family. On the strength of her family's reputation, she gave so much advice to both sides that the barons came to terms and both accepted and offered peace. Vespasian stayed in Britain until the summer; then he returned to Rome, very joyful and happy. Arviragus kept the agreement with the Romans all his life, never again untrue to them in any way; instead he served them and advanced their cause, through affection for the queen who originally belonged to them by birth.[1]

5153   Then Marius, his son by his wife, had the task of governing the kingdom. He possessed very great wisdom and extraordinary eloquence. While his father was alive, Marius was brought up in Rome by his mother's relations. He saw to it that he was sumptuously attended and knew how to behave nobly.[2] During his reign, Rodric arrived in Scotland; he was king of the Picts and came from Scythia.[3] He was a thoroughly wicked man, addicted to robbery. He had come to ravage Scot-land, and had already devastated much of it, when Marius, who did not care for bad neighbours, caught up with him, defeated and killed him. In the spot where he had conquered the Picts, killed Rodric and cut off his head, he had a great stone raised, which can still be seen there, to show his bravery and record the matter. There was an inscription on the stone, still there to my knowledge, which bore witness to the event and narrated the defeat, Marius' killing of Rodric, and the reason why he put the stone there. It is still there, I have heard tell, and people call it Vestinaire.[4]

5185   The king kept in his realm the Picts he had defeated. He gave a large part of Caithness to them to populate, which was still waste-land, abandoned as wilder-ness from time immemorial. The Picts encamped there, ploughed and tilled. They sought wives from the Britons but were refused, so they crossed into Ire-land and brought back wives from there.[5] Throughout the region they settled and soon grew and multiplied.

5199   Marius lived a long time, and after his death his son Coïl reigned. He had been

---

[1] Like the *VV*, chap. 69, Wace shortens consider-ably *HRB*'s panegyric of Arviragus.

[2] Details added by Wace.

[3] The Picts from Scythia first appear in Bede I, chap. 1, probably taken from an Irish source. See Wallace-Hadrill, *Bede's Ecclesiastical History*, pp. 8–9 and Miller 'Matriliny', pp. 106–32. They then appear in *HB* chap. 15 and *HA* I, 9. *HRB*

chap. 70, names their leader as Sodric; in *VV* he is Rodric.

[4] *HRB* chap. 70: *Wistmaria*; *VV*: *Westmaria*. West-moreland, supposedly called after Marius.

[5] See Bede I, chap. 1, for the 'Scots' wives: the Irish were called *Scotti* until the 9th century, as in the invading 'Scots' in Gildas, *De Excidio*, chap. 14.

Regna Coïl ki fu sis fiz;
Od les Romains fu cil nurriz.
E mult fu bien de lur conseil,
E il le troverent feeil;
Les leis romaines out aprises
E sens e ars de plusurs guises.
Coïl se contint noblement
E servir se fist richement.
Emprés Coïl fu sis fiz reis,
5210 Luces out nun, mult fu corteis.
Luces fu de grant onesté,
Par lui reçut crestienté
Engletere premierement,
Si vus dirrai cumfaitement:
Parler oï de Jesu Crist
E des miracles ke il fist,
E des signes que cil faiseient
Ki le pople convertisseient.
A Eleutere enveia,
5220 Ki ert pape, si li manda
Enveiast lui quil baptizast
E ki la lei li enseinnast.
Quant ço oï li apostories
A Deu rendi graces e glories;
Al rei enveia Dunian
E un suen compainun Fagan,
Amdui furent clerc merveillus
E evesque religius.
Al rei vindrent sil baptizerent
5230 E la lei Deu li enseinnerent.
Emprés le rei fu sa maisnee
E sa gent tute baptizee.
Ço que li reis faiseit, faiseient,
E l'essample le rei soeient.
Li dui evesque preechouent,
E par les contrees alouent.
Par le rei e par sun otreiz,
Si come costume est e dreiz,
Firent establir evesquiés
5240 E desur ço arcevesquiés;

As evesquiés mistrent evesques,
As arcevesquiés arcevesques.
Les evesquiés unt compassees
E les paroisses devisees.
Les temples u li Deu esteient
Que li home paien creeient
Unt santifiez e mundez,
E a Deu servir consacrez.
Les fieus, les rentes, les mansiuns, [1]
E les autres possessiuns   5250
Que cil a lur ues receveient [2]
Qui es temples servir deveient
Ad li reis trestut otreied
As evesques e al clergied.
Quant Bretainne fu convertie,
E la lei Deu out recuillie,
Li reis Luces se fist mut lied
Ki vit le pople baptizied
E aturné al Deu servise.
As iglises duna franchise   5260
E de ses terres les feufa,
E granz demainnes lur duna.
Volentiers Damnedeu servi;
En pais regna, en pais feni;
Li cors a Gloëcestre jut.
Cent cinquante anz e sis morut
Puis que Deus incarnatiun
Prist pur nostre redemptiun.
Al terme de sun muriant
N'out li reis feme ne enfant,   5270
Ne prochain de sun parenté
Ki tenir peüst s'erité.
   Quant as Romains vint a saveir
Que mort esteit li reis senz eir,
Dous legiuns appareillerent,
En Bretaine les enveierent,
E un lur senator, Sever,
Pur la terre a lur ues guarder.
Sever vint od dous legiuns,
Mais mult trova Bretuns feluns,   5280

---

[1] MS P reading—*mansiuns*—restored.   [2] MS P reading—*receveient*—restored.

Britain is converted to Christianity

brought up amongst the Romans and profited from their wise counsel, and they found him loyal. He had learnt Roman laws and many sorts of knowledge and skills. Coïl behaved nobly and had himself splendidly attended. After him, his son Luces became king, a most accomplished man.[1] Luces was very upright: through him England first received Christianity, and I will tell you how.[2] He heard tell of Jesus Christ, of the miracles he did and the wonders being performed by those who were converting the people. He sent to Eleutherus, who was pope, and asked him to send someone to baptize him and teach him the Christian faith. When the pope heard this, he glorified and thanked God. He sent Dunian and his companion, Fagan,[3] to the king; both were exceedingly learned men and pious bishops. They came to the king, baptized him and taught him God's law. Following the king, his household and his family were all baptized. What the king did, they did, and followed his example. The two bishops preached and travelled throughout the country. Through the king and with his agreement, as was right and customary, they set up dioceses and, above those, archdioceses; in the dioceses they placed bishops and in the archdioceses, archbishops. They marked out the dioceses and divided them into parishes. The temples harbouring the gods in which heathen men believed, they sanctified and cleansed and consecrated to the service of God. The domains, revenues, houses and other possessions which those who used to serve in the temples received for their own use were all granted by the king to the bishops and clergy.[4]

5255　When Britain was converted and received God's law, king Luces was very happy to see the people baptized and won over to the service of God. He granted the churches privileges, endowed them with some of his lands and gave them large domains. He willingly served God and reigned and died in peace. His body lies in Gloucester. He died 156 years after God took flesh for our redemption. At the time of his death, the king had neither wife nor child, nor any close relation who could rule his inheritance.

5273　When it came to the knowledge of the Romans that the king had died without an heir, they got two legions ready and sent them to Britain, along with Sever,[5] one of their senators, in order to keep the country for their benefit. But he found the

---

[1] *HRB* chap. 72: *Coilus* and *Lucius*.

[2] According to Gildas, *De Excidio*, chap. 8, Christianity first comes to Britain in the last years of Tiberius. The apocryphal story of Lucius first appears in Bede I, chap. 4 (and see notes at end of Bede, p. 362).

[3] *HRB*, chap. 72: *Faganus* and *Duvianus*.

[4] Wace omits *HRB*'s details on flamens and archflamens, and ecclesiastical divisions of the country, and its reference to Gildas and his book about the victory of Aurelius Ambrosius (chap. 72); Aurelius's name is also omitted in *VV*.

[5] The emperor Septimius Severus.

E nequedent tant guereia
E tant premist e tant duna
Qu'une partie a lui suzmist
Par qui plus des altres conquist.
Li altre, ki s'en desdeinerent,[1]
Oltre le Humbre s'esluinerent;
E Sever tant les enchaça[2]
Que en Escoce les chaça.
E cil unt fait lur avoé
5290 De Fulgene, un vassal pruvé.
As Pics se sunt acompainied
Si se sunt ensemble alied.
Puis firent mainte invasiun
E a veüe, e a latrun,
Vers Escoce, en une cuntree
Ki suelt Deïre estre apelee.
Quant Sever s'esteit aluinniez[3]
E vers Lundres ert repairiez,
Fulgenes, ki aveit les Pics
5300 E les Escoz e les fuitis,
Perneit granz preies e prisuns,
Dunt il aveit granz raençuns.
Quant Sever en oï parler
E il les esperout trover,
En Escoce esteient fuï
E en plusurs lius departi;
Ço faiseit Fulgenes suvent
E ço dura tant lungement
Que Sever fist faire un fossé
5310 De travers le païs, de lé,
Sur le fossé fist un paliz
Halt e espés e bien jointiz,
De l'une mer a l'altre mer,
Pur sa terre clorre e guarder.
Ses enemis ad tuz forsclos;
N'i out puis de lunc tens si os
Ki le paliz osast passer
Ne pur tolir ne pur embler.
Quant Deïre fu si bien close
5320 Que Fulgenes entrer n'i ose,

As Pics e as suens conseil prist
Qu'en Scice ireit, e il si fist.
As Pics qui la erent parla;
Tant lur premist, tant les preia[4]
Que grant navie en amena
E en Engleterre arriva.
A Everwic vint, si l'assist,
E la terre environ porprist.
Dunc manda ses apartenanz,
Qu'il out el païs bien puissanz;   5330
Cil e mult altre pur s'amur
Sunt parti de l'empereür
Si se sunt del tuit a lui pris[5]
E il lur ad assez pramis.
Sever prist les altres Bretuns
Si assembla ses legiuns,
Puis ala Everwic rescorre
E cels de la cité secore.
A cels del siege s'est mellez,
E Fulgene refu armez;   5340
Forment se sunt entr'envaï
E ki mielz pout, mielz i feri.
La bataille fu bien ferue,
Mainte aume i out del cors eissue.
Fulgenes a mort nafré fu,
N'ad mie puis lunges vescu;
Sever refu illuec ocis
E grant masse de ses amis.
Mais par la preiere as Romains
Dunt mult i out de ses prochains,   5350
Fu dedenz Everwic portez
E a grant honur enterrez.
   Dous filz aveit, l'un Bassian,
E l'altre apelouent Getan.
La mere Getan fu romaine,
As seinnurs del sené prochaine;
Bassian d'une Brette ert nez,
Mais mult ert bien enparentez.
Romain unt Getan amené
A rei l'unt eslit levé.   5360

---

[1] MS P reading—*s'en*—restored.
[2] MS P reading—*enchaça*—restored.
[3] MS P reading—*aluinniez*—restored.
[4] MS P reading—*les*—restored.
[5] MS P reading—*tuit*—restored.

Sever builds a dike acros the land

Britons very troublesome. Nevertheless, he fought so hard, and promised and gave so much, that some of them submitted to him, through whom he conquered more of the others. The remainder, very indignant, moved far away, beyond the Humber, and Sever pursued them so hard that he drove them into Scotland. They made Fulgene,[1] an experienced warrior, their leader. They joined forces with the Picts and together made an alliance. Then they made many attacks, both openly and by stealth, on a country near Scotland, which used to be called Deira.[2]

5297   Once Sever had departed and gone back to London, Fulgene, who had with him the Picts and the Scots and the fugitives, took much booty and many prisoners, for which he obtained large ransoms. When Sever heard of it, and hoped to find them, they fled into Scotland and dispersed into many places. Fulgene often did this, and it went on so long that Sever had a dike built across the width of the land.[3] On the dike a palisade of stakes was placed, high, thick and closely linked, to enclose and protect his land from one sea to the other. He shut out all his enemies: for a long time afterwards there was no one so bold as to dare pass the palisade, whether his intention was to carry off or to steal.

5319   When Deira was so well sealed off that Fulgene dared not enter, he decided, on the advice of the Picts and his own people, that he would go to Scythia, and so he did. There he talked to the Picts and promised and begged them so much that he brought back a great fleet and arrived in England. He came to York, attacked it, and overran the surrounding country. Then he summoned the very powerful kinsmen he had in the land. They, and many others, for love of him left the emperor and all joined him, and he promised them a great deal. Sever took the remaining Britons, gathered his legions, and then went to relieve York and help its citizens. He joined battle with the besiegers, and Fulgene re-armed: they engaged in a fierce struggle and each struck the hardest blows that he could. The battle was well fought; many a soul left its body. Fulgene was mortally wounded and did not long survive; Sever was also killed there, along with very many of his friends. But following the Romans' entreaties, many of whom were his kin, he was carried inside York and buried there with great honour.

5353   He had two sons, one called Bassian, the other Getan. Getan's mother was Roman, a relative of Roman senators; Bassian's was British but of very good family. The Romans took charge of Getan, chose him and raised him to the kingship.

---

[1] *HRB* chap. 74: *Sulgenius*; *VV*: *Fulgenius*.
[2] One of the two Northumbrian kingdoms, the other being Bernicia. Wace's topography is a little vague here.
[3] The 'dike' (*HRB*'s 'rampart') is actually Hadrian's Wall, from Wallsend to the Solway Firth, dating from *c*.122 AD and rebuilt by Severus in

205–8. Gildas, *De Excidio* (chap. 15), incorrectly reports it as built in the time of Maximianus, and made of turf; Bede (I, chap. 5) calls it an earthwork (*vallum*), not a wall, with a palisade. Both thought the stone wall was built later. Wace has added the fence of stakes, possibly from Bede, or from *HA* I, chap. 31.

E Bretun unt Bassian pris,
Le reialme li unt pramis.
Chescuns se tint a sun parent
E al plus prochain de sa gent;
Romain unt amé lur Romain
E Bretun lur Bretun prochain.
Issi out, pur l'eslection,
Entre les freres grant tençon,
Mais Getan fu hastivement
5370 Ocis, ne sai comfaitement.
Dunc fu achevee la guerre,
E Bassian conquist la terre.
    En Bretainne out un bacheler,
Carais l'avom oï nomer,
Mult ert hardiz e enpernanz
E de sun cors ert mult poissanz;
En meint busuin s'ert essaiez,
Mult esteit pruz e mult preisez.
Assez esteit de bas parage
5380 E mult aveit povre eritage,
Mais mult plus bel se conteneit
Que sa rente ne requereit.
Bien saveit suffrir un grant fais
E mielz amout guerre que pais.
A cel tens aloent par mer
Les unes genz altres rober;
N'osout nuls huem maindre as rivages
Pur utlages e pur evages.
Ne sai que Carais out pensé,
5390 Mais a Rome dist al sené
Que de la mer guarde prendreit,
Se lur congié aveir poeit,[1]
E lé rivages guardereit
Que ullague n'i passereit,
E lur treü restorereit
Que nule rien n'en deffaldreit.
Li Romain lur prud coveiterent,
E ço qu'il quist li otreierent;
Briefs e chartres li unt livré.
5400 Es vus d'illuec Carais turné;

Par les terres ses briés mostra
E vivement se purchaça.
Nefs assembla e mariniers,
E quist serjanz e bons archiers.
Les deseritez, les fuitis,
Les robeürs e les eschis,
E cels ki terres nen aveient,[2]
Ki de l'autrui vivre vuleient,
Les bachilers hardiz e pruz
E les ullaugues manda tuz.   5410
Mult out d'omes grant compainnie
Nez e nurriz en felonie.
Quant sa flote out Carais justee,
Mainte terre ad environee;
D'une ille en altre alout passant,
Homes pernant, terres guastant;
As chevaliers e as vilains
E as veisins e as luintains
Toleit quanque tolir poeit;
Nule mesure n'en saveit.   5420
Si li ullague orent mal fait
Carais fait pis, kar rien n'i lait.
Cil qui dut la gent guarantir
N'i lait rien qu'il puisse tolir;
Mal lur fist ki guarder les dut.
E sa maisnee tuz tens crut;
N'i ad laron ne robeür,
N'i ad felun ne traïtur,
Ki od Carais aler ne vuille;
Nuls nen i vient qu'il ne recoille.   5430
Quant plus out gent, plus s'orguilla,
E quant plus prist, plus coveita;
Chastels e viles eissillout
E tut perneit e tut robout;
Mult esteit de grant presoncie
E mult coveitout seinnurie.
En Bretainne as Bretuns parlout
U sun message i enveout;
Mult lur prameteit largement
E lur diseit priveement   5440

---

[1] MS P's order of ll. 5390–92 restored.   [2] MS P reading—*terres*—restored.

Carais

And the Britons took over Bassian, promising him the kingdom. Each associated with his parent and her closest relatives. The Romans loved their Roman, and the Britons their British relation. Thus the royal election caused a great quarrel between the brothers, but Getan was, I do not know how, soon killed. So the war ended and Bassian conquered the land.[1]

5373 In Britain there was a young man whose name, so we have heard, was Carais;[2] he was bold, enterprising and physically strong. He had been tested in many battles and was very brave and highly praised. His birth was rather humble and his inheritance scant, but he behaved far more nobly than his revenue required. He knew how to endure great suffering and he preferred war to peace. At that time, people sailed the seas plundering others; no one dared dwell along the coast for fear of pirates and buccaneers. I do not know what Carais intended, but he said to the Senate in Rome that, if he had their permission, he would protect the sea and guard the coast so no pirate invaded it, and he would restore their tribute so that nothing should be wanting. The Romans wanted their profits, and granted what he asked: they gave him writs and charters.

5400 Whereupon Carais returned. He displayed his writs throughout the land and swiftly set to work. He gathered ships and sailors and looked for soldiers and good archers. Fugitives, robbers, the disinherited and the destitute, and those who had no lands and wanted to live off others, bold and brave young men and pirates—he summoned all these. They formed a large company of men, born and brought up in wickedness. Once Carais had assembled his fleet, he wandered to many countries, passing from one island to the next, seizing men and laying lands waste. From knights and peasants, from those near at hand and those afar, he took whatever he could, knowing no moderation. If the pirates had behaved badly, Carais behaved worse, for he left nothing. He who was supposed to defend the people left nothing that he could not seize; he hurt those he should have protected. And his band kept growing: there was no thief or robber, scoundrel or traitor, who did not want to go with Carais. He welcomed anyone who came.

5431 The more people he had, the more arrogant he became, and the more he took, the more he wanted. He destroyed castles and towns, seizing everything and robbing everyone. His presumption was great and so was his desire for power. He spoke to Britons in Britain or sent his messengers there, making them large promises and telling them privately that they were badly and stupidly advised if they did not make him their king, for he would expel the Romans and take them off their hands. Secretly he also talked to the Picts, of whom there were many in the

---

[1] Bede (I, chap. 5) tells us that Bassianus became emperor with the cognomen of Antoninus, while Gratian was subsequently condemned as an enemy of the state.

[2] Carausias, who held Britain 286–93. Wace expands on his portrait, on his felonious band (para. 5400), and stresses the wickedness of gamekeeper turned poacher.

Que mal conseil e fol aveient
Quant il de lui rei ne faiseient;
Kar il chacereit les Romains
E sis ostereit de lur mains.
A conseil rad as Pis parlé, [1]
Dunt en la terre out grant plenté
Ki mult erent del rei privé;
E li Pic li unt affié
Que se il al rei prent bataille,
5450 Qu'il le ferunt veintre senz faille,
E al champ del rei partirunt
E desconfire le ferunt.
Carais Bassian desfia;
Maneça le sil guereia.
Tant se sunt entremanecied
Qu'a combatre sunt aprismied.
La u il mielz se combateient
E mielz justouent e chaeient,
Li Pic, ki furent traitur,
5460 Se partirent de lur seinnur.
Li reis en els plus se creeit
Qu'en tuz les humes qu'il aveit;
Plus se creeit, plus se fiout,
E plus largement lur dunout;
E il l'unt el busuin guerpi;
Al busuin veit l'on sun ami.
Al busuin lur seinnur guerpirent,
Traïtur furent sil traïrent,
E Carais ad le rei ocis,
5470 Puis ad tut le regne conquis.
Les Pics en Escoce enveia;
Viles e terres lur duna;
Des cel tens unt li Pic esté
Tuit as Escoz entremellé.
Des que cil de Rome unt oï
Cumme Carais aveit servi,
Tramis i unt treis legiuns
E dous de lur meillurs barons.
Allec, li uns, fu mult savanz,
5480 E mult hardiz e mult vaillanz;

Livius Gallus fu od lui,
Bon chevaler furent andui.
A Carais se sunt combatu
Si l'unt desconfit e vencu.
Ocis fu e bien grant partie
De cels ki furent en s'aïe.
Puis ad Allec cels guerreiez
E suvent les ad damagiez,
Ki as Romains ourent neü
E le conseil Carais creü.   5490
Li Bretun s'en voldrent defendre, [2]
Ki ne vuleient treü rendre;
Fait unt rei par electiun
D'Asclepiodot, un baron,
Sire esteit cil de Cornoaille,
N'i ad Bretun kil contrevaille.
Dunc se sunt Bretun assemblé
E tuit se sunt entremandé.
Tant se sunt alé assemblant,
Li un les altres semunant,   5500
A Lundres unt Allec trové,
Le jor d'une sollemnité.
En un temple esteit al servise,
Si vuleit faire sacrefise.
Quant la noise oï e le cri,
Od ses armés es champs eissi
E as Bretuns se combati;
Mais sa gent trop se departi,
E Allec s'en quida fuïr,
Mais par fuie ne pout guarrir,   5510
Kar li Bretun fuiant le pristrent,
Nen pout defendre si l'ocistrent. [3]
Altretel fin Gallus preïst
Si en Lundres ne s'embatist; [4]
Les Romains fist od sei entrer,
E les portes clore e fermer. [5]
As armez fist les murs purprendre
Pur fors geter e pur defendre.
Asclepiodoz les assist
E ses corlieus par tut tramist,   5520

---

[1] MS P reading—*rad*—restored.
[2] MS P reading—*s'en*—restored.
[3] MS P reading—*Nen*—restored.
[4] MS P reading—*Si*—restored.
[5] MS P reading—*fermer*—restored.

Allec kills Carais and is killed in turn

land for they were intimates of the king, and the Picts promised him that, if he fought the king, they would without fail make him victorious, they would desert the king on the field of battle and cause his defeat.

5453 Carais challenged Bassian, threatened and declared war on him. The exchange of threats was so great that they prepared to fight. At the moment when they were fighting hardest, in the thick of striking and falling, the treacherous Picts deserted their lord. The king trusted them more than all the other men he had: he trusted them more, had more faith in them, and rewarded them more generously. And in his hour of need they left him; it is in that hour that one sees one's friends. In his hour of need they left their lord; they were traitors and betrayed him.[1] And Carais killed the king and then conquered the whole kingdom. He sent the Picts into Scotland, giving them towns and lands. From that time on, the Picts have entirely merged with the Scots.

5475 As soon as the Romans heard of how Carais had served them, they sent three legions and two of their best commanders. One of them, Allec,[2] was very wise, bold and brave. With him was Livius Gallus; both were good knights. They fought Carais, defeated and conquered him. He was killed and so were very many of those who had helped him. Then Allec made war, and often inflicted great damage, on those who had harmed the Romans and believed in Carais's advice. The Britons wanted to defend themselves, because they had no intention of paying tribute. They chose Asclepiodotus for king,[3] a baron who was lord of Cornwall: no other Briton was his equal. Then the Britons gathered and summoned each other. They continued gathering and calling each other together until they found Allec in London at a feast-day. He was at a service in the temple, intending to make sacrifice,[4] when he heard noise and shouting. He went out with his soldiers into the fields and fought the Britons. But his men were dispersed too widely, and Allec wanted to flee, but he could not save his skin through flight, for the Britons seized him as he fled; he could not stop them killing him.

5513 Gallus would have had the same end had he not rushed back into London. He made the Romans enter with him and shut and close the gates. He had armed men capture the walls, for the purposes of defence and throwing missiles. Asclepiodotus besieged them and sent his messengers everywhere, to tell and beg the barons to come and help with the siege. If they wanted to help him, they would be rid of the constant affliction of the Romans. He wanted to cleanse the land of them so that they could never take root in it again.

---

[1] Wace emphasises the treachery of the Picts even more than *HRB* does, obviously preparing us for their behaviour towards Constant, Aurelius and Uther.

[2] Allectus. In Bede (I, chap. 6), following Orosius, Allectus is Carausius's colleague and betrays him.

[3] In Bede I, chap. 6 (followed by *HA* I, chap. 36)

Asclepiodotus is the Prefect of the Praetorian Guard who defeats Allectus and restores Britain to the Empire. *HRB* and Wace have curiously transformed him into a patriotic Briton who wins a great victory over the Romans.

[4] Though Britain is now supposedly Christian, the Roman Allectus seems to be pagan.

As baruns fist dire e preier
Qu'il li viengent al siege aider.
Delivré sunt, s'aidier li vuelent,
Des Romains qui grever les sulent. [1]
Tute en vult la terre munder,
Que mais n'i puissent raciner.
Al comant Asclepiodot
Vindrent Gualeis, vindrent Escot,
De tutes pars Bretun i vindrent,
5530 E tuit cil qui lur apartindrent.
Dunc firent arbelastiers traire,
Berfreiz lever, perrieres faire.
Le mur unt fraint e effundré
Si sunt dedenz a force entré.
Dunc veïssez Romains platir, [2]
Plaiez seinier, nafrez gesir.
Unches plus grant ociement
Ne veïstes de tant de gent.
Alquant ki virent le mur frait
5540 Es fortelesces se sunt atrait, [3]
E Bretun unt purpris les burs,
E les Romains assis es turs.
Tant unt dedenz Gallum destreit
Que il lur dist qu'il se rendreit
S'il l'en laissoent vif aler
E ses compainuns vis mener,
E d'Engleterre vis eissir
Senz membre e senz vie tolir; [4]
N'i aveit qu'une legion
5550 Ke requereient cest pardon.
Ja esteit la fin graantee
E la trive prise e donee,
E li Romain s'erent rendu
E des bretesches descendu,
Quant li Bretun vindrent d'Escoce, [5]
E li Gualeis od lur grant force.
En mi la cité les troverent,
Sis pristrent tuz e decolerent.
Sur une euue en mi la cité
5560 Unt Gallum pris e decolé;

Del bu li unt le chief sevré,
L'un e l'altre unt as funz geté.
L'eue u Gallus chaï e jut
Del nom Galli sun nun reçut,
Nongallin l'apelent Bretun,
Gualebroc Engleis e Saissun.
Li nom del son diversefient,
Mais une chose senefient.
  Fait fu reis Asclepiodoz,
Ki ne fu pas malveis ne soz.   5570
Feste tint si se coruna,
E dis anz en grant pais regna;
Larruns destruist e robeors
E mult haï tuz malfaitors.
En sun tens fu l'ocision
E la grant persecution
De cels ki Damnedeu serveient
E ki en Jesu Crist creeient.
Ço fu par Diocletian,
Qui enveia Maximian,   5580
Par cruelté e par enjurie,
Pur tuz les crestïens destruire
Ki aveient abitement
Ultre Mont Geu, vers occident.
A bien pruef par tutes les terres
Erent sur crestïens les guerres;
Mult aveit grant vertu Sathans.
Dunc fu martiriez sainz Albans
E sainz Juiles e Aaron,
Dui citaain de Karlion.   5590
Tuit li evesque e li clergié
Esteient pris e martirié ;
Ne remaneit ne clers ne prestre.
Choël, uns cuens de Gloëcestre, [6]
Ki mult esteit de grant parage,
E mult esteit de fier corage,
Asclepiodot guerreia.
Tant crut la guerre e tant munta
Qu'il ensemble se combatirent
E grant damage s'entrefirent.   5600

---

[1] MS P reading—*sulent*—restored.
[2] MS P reading—*platir*—restored.
[3] MS P reading—*atrait*—restored.
[4] MS P's order of line restored.
[5] MS P reading—*Bretun*—restored.
[6] MSS CSF: *Colecestre*.

Asclepiodotus becomes king

5527   At Asclepiodotus' command the Welsh, the Scots and Britons from all directions arrived,[1] together with all their followers. Then they set crossbowmen to shoot, raised siege-towers and made mangonels. They broke down and shattered the walls and forced their way in. Then the Romans could be seen prostrate, their gashes bleeding, the wounded lying on the ground. Such a great slaughter of so many people would never be seen again. Some, seeing the walls destroyed, retreated into fortresses, and the Britons seized the surrounding districts and attacked the Romans in the towers. Within the city Gallus was so harried that he said he would yield if they spared his life and let him remove his companions and leave England alive, with life and limb unharmed. Only one legion was left to beg for this pardon.

5551   This arrangement was already agreed, and a truce was made and granted, and the Romans had yielded and come down from the parapets, when the Britons from Scotland arrived together with the Welsh and their large army. They found the Romans in the middle of the city, seized them all and beheaded them. By a river in the heart of the city they seized and beheaded Gallus; they severed his head from his body and threw both into the middle of the stream. The river where Gallus fell and lay was called after him: the Britons call it Nongallin and the English and Saxons, Gualebroc.[2] The names sound different but mean the same thing.

5569   Asclepiodotus, who was neither wicked or stupid, was made king. He was crowned with due ceremony and reigned ten years in complete peace. He rooted out thieves and robbers and treated all malefactors with enmity. During his reign occurred the slaughter and great persecution of those who served God and believed in Jesus Christ. This was done by Diocletian, who sent Maximian cruelly and unjustly to destroy all Christians living beyond Montgieu,[3] towards the west. In nearly every country Christians were attacked: Satan's strength was great. At that time were martyred St Alban and Saints Julius and Aaron, two citizens of Caerleon.[4] All the bishops and clergy were seized and martyred: neither clerk nor priest was left.

5594   Choel, a count of Colchester,[5] who was of high birth and fierce temper, made war on Asclepiodotus. The conflict spread and grew to the point that they fought

---

[1] In *HRB* chap. 76 they are the *Demeti, Venedoti, Deiri* and *Albani*.

[2] *HRB* chap. 76: *Nantgallim*; *VV*: *Nentgallin*. *Galabroc*=the Walbrook, an old London waterway, in whose bed in the 1860s numerous skulls were discovered. For scepticism about this 'evidence' backing the story, see Tatlock pp. 31–3.

[3] On Montgieu see fn. 2 to p. 73.

[4] Gildas, *De Excidio* (chap. 10) is the first to mention Aaron and Julius, as citizens of '*Legionum urbis*', which could apply to Caerleon or Chester. Bede mentions them in I, chap. 7. Wace considerably shortens *HRB*'s account of the persecution of the Christians.

[5] *HRB* chap. 78: *Coel, dux Kaercolum*; *VV*: *Cohel dux Kaercolim*. Both add '*id est Colocestrie*'. (Colchester), which MSS CSF in Wace also have, in lieu of 'Gloucester' in all other MSS. See Arnold II, p. 803 and C. Fahlin, 'Quelques remarques', p. 88.

Choël fu plus forz si venqui
Le rei ocist, l'enor saisi,
Qui qu'en pesast ne quin fust bel, [1]
D'Engleterre fu reis Choël.
Eleine, une fille, out nurrie,
Ki mult sout d'art e de clergie;
Terre sun pere aveir deveit, [2]
Kar filz ne fille altre n'aveit.
La meschine fu bien lettree
5610 E de belté assez loee;
Mult la fist Choël bien aprendre
E mult i fist maistres entendre,
Pur ço que quant li reis morust
Le regne aprés tenir seüst.
    Quant a Rome sout li senez
Qu'Asclepiodot ert finez,
N'i out Romain ki n'en fust liez,
Kar mult les out contraliez,
E lur chevaliers e lur dreiz
5620 E lur treüz suvent toleiz.
Un senator i enveierent,
Constainz out nom, mult le preiserent;
Espaine aveit anceis conquise
E suz l'empire as Romains mise;
De sun priz ne de sa valur
Ne saveit l'on home a cel jur.
Quant Constainz entra en Bretainne,
Mult out granz genz en sa compaine; [3]
Cremuz fu e sa gent cremue.
5630 Choël, ki oï sa venue,
Contre lui meller ne s'osa;
De grant pris ert, mult le dota.
Ses messages li ad tramis
Si li ad offert e pramis
Que Bretainne de lui tendra
E le treü nomé rendra.
Ne li ad, ço dist, fait nul tort,
S'il ad Asclepiodot mort
Ki lur treü tint longement
5640 E les Romains ocist vilment,

Puis tint a guise de felun
Lur terres par invasiun.
Saveir li devreient bon gré
Qui le païs ad delivré.
Constainz sout bien qu'il dist raison
Ne qu'il ne quereit se dreit non; [4]
Le regne li ad otreied,
Si unt entr'els pris amistied.
Emprés ço fu un meis passez,
5650 E li secunz esteit entrez,
Choël out mal, si enferma,
E al chief d'uit jurs devia.
E Constainz prist sa fille Eleine
Si tint la terre en sun demeine.
De sa valur ne de sun sens
Ne saveit l'om feme en sun tens,
Ne de sun pris nule meschine;
Constainz la prist, sin fist reïne.
Un filz unt entr'els desirré,
5660 E Deus lur ad un filz duné;
Constentin out non, mult l'amerent
E del bien nurrir se penerent. [5]
Unze anz u petit plus aveit,
Mult amendout e mult cresseit,
Quant Constainz chaï en langur,
Nen pot par mirie aveir retur. [6]
Ço fu la fin, morir l'estut.
    Constentin amenda e crut;
Li baron l'unt levé a rei,
5670 Ki l'amerent par dreite fei.
E la mere le doctrina;
Qui mielz l'amout, mielz l'enseina.
Des que il fu de tel eage
Qu'il sout par sei mener barnage,
Plenté ama de chevaliers,
E mult lur duna volentiers.
Si Constainz fu de grant bunté,
Constantin ad tut surmunté
La bonté Constainz e le los.
5680 Unques ne pout aveir repos

---

[1] MS P reading—*quin*—restored.
[2] MS P's reading of line restored.
[3] MS P reading—*granz genz*—restored.

[4] MS P reading—*dreit*—restored.
[5] MS P reading—*del bien*—restored.
[6] MS P reading—*Nen*—restored.

Eleine, Constant and Constantine

each other, inflicting great injuries. Choel was the stronger and won, killed the king and seized the land; regardless of whom it grieved or pleased, Choel was king of England. He had brought up a daughter, Eleine, very skilled and learned; she was to inherit her father's kingdom, for he had no other son or daughter. The girl was well educated and celebrated for her beauty. Coel had her well taught and had tutors to pay her the greatest attention, so that when the king died she should then be able to govern the kingdom. [1]

5615   When the Senate in Rome heard that Asclepiodotus was dead, no Roman existed who was not delighted, because he had strongly opposed both their knights and their dues, and often withheld their tribute. They sent a senator, called Constant, [2] whom they greatly esteemed; he had earlier conquered Spain and made it submit to imperial rule. At that time no one knew his equal for bravery and strength. When Constant entered Britain, he brought many men with him; he and his men inspired fear. Choel, hearing of his arrival, did not dare fight him; he was frightened by Constant's great reputation. He sent him messengers, offering and promising to hold Britain under his command and to restore the appointed tribute. He had done him no wrong, he said, by killing Asclepiodotus, who had for a long while withheld their tribute, wickedly killed Romans, and then had treacherously invaded and ruled their lands. They should be grateful to him for setting the land free.

5645   Constant was well aware his words made sense and that he only asked for what was just. He granted him the kingdom and they became friends. One month later, at the start of the second one, Choel felt ill, fell sick, and died a week later. And Constant took his daughter Eleine to wife and took possession of her land. There was no woman of her time to equal her for excellence or wisdom, nor any girl for renown. Constant took her and made her queen. They hoped they would have a son and God gave them one: they called him Constantine, loved him dearly, and took pains over his upbringing. He was eleven, or a little older, growing up and maturing, when Constant fell ill and medicine could not save him. That was the end, he had to die.

5688   Constantine matured and grew up. The barons, who loyally loved him, raised him to the throne. And his mother instructed him: she who loved him most was his greatest teacher. As soon as he was old enough to lead a band of warriors, he wanted to have plenty of knights and willingly gave them many gifts. If Constant had had great valour, Constantine quite surpassed his valour and his fame. He

---

[1] Wace expands here and in para. 5645 on the education and learning of Helena, making her suitable to be the mother of Constantine. In Bede I, chap. 8 (as in Orosius), Helena is Constantius's concubine and her parentage is not mentioned, but *HA* (I, chap. 37) makes her daughter of Cole, king of Colchester. See Greenway, *Henry of Huntingdon*, p. civ.

[2] Constantius.

Dessi que il out ses veisins
A sun comand tuz faiz aclins.
Constantin fu de grant cointise,
E mult ama dreite justise;
Altretels fu en sa juenvlesce
Come altres sunt en lur homesce. [1]
Les Bretuns ama pur sa mere
E cels de Rome pur sun pere,
Kar de ces dous genz esteit nez,
5690 D'ambes parz bien enparentez;
E il amout tuz ses parenz.
A Rome ert a cel jur Maxenz
Emperere mult orguillus,
Mult fel e mult malicius;
Les enors de Rome guasta
E la noble gent abaissa.
L'ordre del sené abati
E lur digneté lur toli.
Tels i out ki mult le haïrent,
5700 Lur fieus e lur maisuns guerpirent,
Ki ne vuleient od lui remaindre. [2]
A Constantin s'alerent plaindre,
Pur ço qu'il ert de lur lignage
Li plus puissanz e li plus sage. [3]
Par lui quidoent recovrer,
Si s'en vuleit od els pener. [4]
Tant li unt cil dit e rové,
E tant li unt li suen loé,
D'aler a Rome s'apresta,
5710 Archiers e chevaliers mena.
Treis oncles que sa mere aveit,
Que il amout mult e creeit,
Mena a Rome par chierté,
Sis mist en l'ordre del sené;
Li uns aveit nun Joëlin,
Li uns Trahern, li tierz Marin.
A Maxen toli sa fierté
E osta de sa poüsté.
Dunc fu Constentin emperere;
5720 E Eleine, sa bone mere,

En Jerusalem trespassa,
Tuz les vielz Judeus assembla,
Si fu par li la croiz trovee
Ki lunges out esté celee.
A l'uncle Eleine Joëlin
Duna l'on feme de halt lin,
Une Romaine mult preisee,
Ki mult ert bien enparagee.
Un fiz orent que bien norrirent,
Maximien nomer le firent.   5730
Cels qui Bretainne guarder durent,
E ki par Constentin i furent,
Prist Octaves sis decola;
Reis se fist si se coruna;
De Guales ert e cuens esteit,
E en Bretainne clamot dreit.
Les pruvoz ocist e les contes
E les bailliz e les viscuntes.
Constentin a Rome maneit,
A grainnurs ovres entendeit.   5740
Un uncle Eleine i enveia,
Trahern out nun, mult s'i fia,
Dous legiuns li fist livrer
Pur Engleterre delivrer.
Trahern a Porcestre turna,
Dous jurs entiers i sojorna;
Puis li fu la cité rendue,
Ne li pot estre plus tenue.
A Wincestre d'illuec alout,
Par force prendre la quidout,   5750
Mais Octaves li vint devant,
Ki ne l'ala mie atraiant;
En un champ ki ot nun Maisure
Fu la bataille entr'els mult dure.
Mais li Bretun grainur force orent,
E li Romain suffrir nes porent;
As porz les estut repairier.
E Trahern fist les nés chargier;
Tant ala par la mer siglant
E tant ala avironant,   5760

---

[1] MS P reading—*homesce*—restored.
[2] MS P reading—*vuleient*—restored.
[3] MS P reading of the rhymes in ll. 5703–04 restored.
[4] MS P reading—*Si*—restored.

Eleine finds the True Cross

could not rest until he had made his neighbours entirely subject to his bidding. Constantine was a very kind man, devoted to true justice; in his youth he behaved with the wisdom others acquire in their maturity. He loved the Britons because of his mother, and the Romans because of his father, for he sprang from these two peoples, was well connected on both sides, and loved all his relatives.

5692 Maxenz was in Rome at that time, a most arrogant, treacherous and wicked emperor. He ravaged Rome's domains and brought noble men low. He put an end to the senatorial rank and removed the authority of the senate. There were those who fiercely hated him and left their lands and their houses, because they did not want to stay with him. They went to complain to Constantine, because he was the wisest and most powerful of their race. Through him, if he were willing to strive alongside them, they thought they might regain their possessions. They asked and spoke to him so frequently, and his own family advised it so much, that he prepared to go to Rome, taking archers and knights. Out of affection, he took with him to Rome three of his mother's uncles, whom he greatly loved and trusted, and gave them senatorial rank. One was called Joelin, one Trahern and the third Marin.[1] He stripped Maxenz of his eminence and removed him from power.

5719 Then Constantine was emperor. And his good mother, Eleine, travelled to Jerusalem and collected together all the old Jews; thus through her was the Cross found, which had long been hidden.[2] Eleine's uncle, Joelin, was given a wife of high rank, a celebrated Roman of excellent family. They had a son, whom they brought up carefully and called Maximien.[3]

5731 Those who had to guard Britain, and who had been placed there by Constantine, were seized by Octaves[4] and beheaded. He made himself king and was crowned. He was a count from Wales and claimed rights in Britain. He killed the town governors and the counts, the officials and the sheriffs.[5] Constantine stayed in Rome, attending to greater matters. He sent one of Eleine's uncles, Trahern, whom he greatly trusted, and gave him two legions to liberate England. Trahern went to Porchester and stayed there two whole days. Then the city surrendered to him; it could not hold out against him any longer. From there he went to Winchester, thinking to take it by force. But Octaves arrived before him and did

---

[1] *HRB* chap. 79: *Joelinus*, *Trahern* and *Marius*; *VV*: *Loelinus*.

[2] Wace adds the legend (dating from the 4th century) of Helena's discovery of the Cross. See Houck, *Sources*, pp. 246–7.

[3] Wace here anticipates *HRB*, who mentions Maximianus later (chap. 81). This is Magnus Maximus, actually a Spanish usurper, who began his career by defeating an invasion of Picts and Irish and was emperor in the West 383–88; see Gildas,

De Excidio, chap. 13, Bede I, chap. 9, and *HB* chap. 27. See Dumville, 'Sub-Roman Britain', p. 180, and 'Chronology of *De Excidio*', p. 62.

[4] Octaves appears abruptly here, and only from a generalised 'Wales'. In *HRB* chap. 80 he is Octavius duke of the Gewissei. Bede (III, chap. 7) says this is the old name for the West Saxons. See Tatlock pp. 74–75 and Stenton, *Anglo-Saxon England*, p. 21.

[5] In *HRB* those killed are proconsuls.

En Escoce vint al rivage,
Grant mal i fist e grant damage.
Tutes les viles ad robees,
Arses, destruites e guastees.
Octaves oï nuveler,
Puis roï pur veir afermer,
Que Trahern Escoce guastot,
Aveir ne robe n'i laissot.
Ses genz manda, mult li fu tart
5770 Qu'il peüst estre cele part.
Ço quidot e il le diseit
Que ja Trahern ne l'atendreit.
Mais Trahern neient ne fuï,[1]
Ainz vint contre lui sil venqui;
Cil ki venqui premierement
Refu vencuz derainement.
Octaves, ki venqui avant,
En Norwege en ala fuiant
Al rei Compert, quil securust
5780 Contre Trahern se il peüst.
Priveement aveit preiez
Tuz ses amis qu'il out laissiez
Qu'a lur poier s'entremeïssent[2]
Que Trahern pur lui oceïssent.
Tut ert Trahern aseürez,
E reis esteit par tut clamez.
Un jur ert de Lundres meüz,
Mais sis eires fu trop seüz;
Parmi un val boscus passout
5790 Tut asseür, rien ne dutout,
Quant uns cuens d'un aguait sailli,
Ki pur Octaven le haï;[3]
Chevaliers out od sei cent buens,
Trahern ocist entre les suens.
Dunc fist Octaven revenir[4]
E del regne le fist saisir.
Cil n'i ad un Romain laissied
Qu'il n'eit ocis u chacied.[5]
Lunges ad puis en pais tenu,
5800 E lunges ad en pais vescu.

Quant il out bien sun tens usé
E sun eage trespassé,
Purpensa sei que il fereit,
A ki Engleterre laireit,
Qu'enprés sa mort pais i eüst,
Si que discorde n'i creüst.
Une fille aveit si vulsist
Que le regne emprés lui tenist.
A ses amis en ad parlé
E alquant d'els li unt rové   5810
Qu'un des nobles Romains mandast,
Sa fille od l'enor li dunast.
Tels i out qui Cunan amerent,
Nevou le rei, si li loërent
Que Cunan de tut eritast
E sa fille aillurs mariast,
Si li dunast tut sun aveir
E de Cunan feïst sun eir.
Un noble cunte aveit illuec,
De Cornoaille Caraduec,   5820
E dist que ja n'otreiera[6]
Ne ja al rei ne loëra
Que sun eir face de Cunan;
Mais enveit pur Maximian,
Ki a Rome ert, filz Joëlin,
Cusins Eleine e Constentin,
Des Bretuns nez de par sun pere,
E des Romains de par sa mere;
D'ambes pars est de grant parage
Sil tient l'on a pruz e a sage;   5830
Dunt li li reis sa fille a feme
E eir le face de sun regne,
Si sera sa fille reïne
E tut a lui la terre acline.[7]
Car se il Cunan eritout
E sa fille aillurs mariout,
Sis mariz desraisnier vuldreit
Que l'erité aveir devreit.[8]
'Se tu, dist il, issi nel fais,
Ja en noz vies n'avrom pais.'   5840

---

[1] MS P reading—*neient*—restored.
[2] MS P reading—*poier*—restored.
[3] MS P reading—*Octaven le*—restored.
[4] MS P reading—*Octaven*—restored.
[5] MS P reading—*chacied*—restored.
[6] MS P reading—*E*—restored.
[7] MS P reading—*acline*—restored.
[8] MS P reading—*Que*—restored.

Octaves makes Maximien his heir

not give him a good reception. In a field called Maisure the fierce battle between them took place. But the Britons had a larger army and the Romans could not resist them; they had to return to port, and Trahern had the ships loaded. He sailed so far and passed so far up the coast that he came to the shores of Scotland; there he did great damage and much wickedness. He plundered, burnt, destroyed and laid waste all the towns.

5765 Octaves heard it said, and then heard it confirmed indeed, that Trahern had devastated Scotland, leaving neither property nor chattels. In a hurry to be there, he summoned his men. He believed, and said so, that Trahern would never wait for him. But Trahern did not flee, but advanced to meet him, and defeated him: he who was the first to conquer was in the end himself conquered. Octaves, initially the victor, fled to Norway to ask king Compert[1] to help him, if he could, against Trahern. He secretly asked all the friends he left behind to do all they could to kill Trahern for him. Trahern felt quite secure, and was everywhere proclaimed king. One day he travelled out of London, but his route was too well known; he was passing, quite confidently, through a wooded valley, suspecting nothing, when a count jumped out of ambush, who for the sake of Octaves hated him. He had a hundred good knights with him and killed Trahern in the midst of his men. Then he had Octaves return and put him in charge of the realm. Not a Roman was left whom Octaves did not kill or expel. For a long time he reigned and lived in peace.

5801 When he had spent his time wisely and entered upon old age, he considered what he should do and to whom he should leave England, so that there should be peace and no discord after his death. He had a daughter and wanted her to reign after him. He consulted his friends, and some of them advised him to send for one of the Roman noblemen and give him his daughter along with the kingdom. There were some who liked Cunan, the king's nephew,[2] and they advised him to pass the inheritance to Cunan and marry off his daughter to someone else: to him he could leave all his possessions, but make Cunan his heir. There was a noble count there, Caraduec of Cornwall, and he said he would never agree and never advise the king to make Cunan his heir, but Maximien should be sent for in Rome, son of Joelin, cousin to Eleine and Constantine, a Briton on his father's side and on his mother's, a Roman. He was nobly born on both sides and considered wise and brave. The king should give him his daughter in marriage and make him heir to his realm; thus she would become queen and the land would be entirely subject to her. For if he made Cunan his heir, and married his daughter to someone else, it would mean he was establishing her husband's right to have the inheritance for himself. 'If you don't do this,' he said, 'we'll have no peace for the rest of our lives.'

---

[1] *HRB* chap. 80: *Gubert*; *VV*: *Gumper*.

[2] *HRB* chap. 81: *Conan Meriadoc*. See Tatlock pp. 158–9.

Li reis se tint a cest conseil;
Dunc out en la cort grant trepeil,
Kar Cunan mult se coruça
Vers Caraduec, qui ço loa;
Contraire e folie li dist
E, s'il osast, plus en feïst.
Mais Caraduec preisa petit
Tut sun coruz e tut sun dit;
Par le rei e par sun congied
5850 Ad Mauric sun filz enveied
Ki a Maximian parlast,
E en Bretainne l'amenast. [1]
Mauric trova Rome turbee [2];
Creüe ert une grant mellee
A Rome, entre Maximian
E Valentin e Gratian,
Dous freres de bien grant poeir,
Ki vuleient l'empire aveir;
Si que Maximian partie
5860 N'i poeit aveir ne bailie.
Mauric Maximian trova,
Tut priveement li mustra
Ki il ert e dunt il veneit,
Com aveit nom e que quereit.
Maximien mult s'esjoï
Del mandement que il oï;
S'il out joie, ne m'en merveil
Ne fist mie lung apareil;
Al rei vint ki l'aveit mandé
5870 E li reis l'ad mult enoré.
Sa fille a feme li duna
E d'Engleterre l'erita.
Cunan s'en fu par mal turnez,
E as Escoz se fu justez;
Sun uncle e les suens deffia
E Maximien guerreia.
Maximien s'en defendi, [3]
Que li reis out del tut saisi,
E par mainte fiez le venqui
5880 E par mainte fiez i perdi; [4]

Issi avient bien de tel ovre
Que tels i pert que puis recovre.
A la parfin les assemblerent,
Li sage hume sis acorderent,
E Maximien li pramist
Riche hume a faire e il si fist.
    En treis anz tresors aüna
E granz aveirs, si se vanta
Que vers France mer passereit
E as Franceis se combatreit,   5890
E les Romains guereiereit
Pur les dous freres qu'il haeit,
Ki contre lui Rome teneient,
Ne concorde ne l'en quereient.
Maximien s'apareilla;
Grant gent out, grant aveir porta,
E mult demenout grant bobance. [5]
Vers occident, el chief de France,
Arriva en une contree
Ki ert Armoriche apelee.   5900
Humhanz, ki sire ert de cel pais, [6]
Manda sa gent e ses amis;
La terre lur vult defforcier
E de sun fieu les vult chacier.
Mais li Bretun furent plus fort,
Ki de ses homes unt maint mort;
Ne s'i porent prud fuisuner, [7]
En fuie les estuet turner. [8]
Maximien les parsiweit,
Ki merveilles en ocieit; [9]   5910
Bien en i morut quinze mile,
Nes pot guarir chastel ne vile.
Maximien s'en returna
E as herberges repaira;
Cunan prist, un ris li ad fait,
E riant l'ad a conseil trait: [10]
'Cunan, dist il, en suzriant,
Ceste contree est mult vaillant,
Mult me semble bien guaainable,
E plenteïve e delitable.   5920

---

[1] MS J adds: *Mauric i ala volenters/ Et fu mult loiax messagers/ Tant ala Mauric bors et plains/ Qu'i vint entre les Rommains/ Chil s'en est a Rome venus/ Mais mult les trova irascus.*

[2] MS P reading—*turbee*—restored.

[3] MS P reading—*s'en*—restored.

[4] MS P's order of ll. 5879–80 restored.

[5] MS P reading—*demenout*—restored.

[6] MS P reading—*de cel pais*—restored.

[7] MS P reading—*s'i*—restored.

[8] MS P reading—*estuet*—restored.

[9] MS P reading—*Ki merveilles*—restored.

[10] MS P reading—*E*—restored.

Reconciliation of Maximien and Cunan

5841   The king took this advice. Then there was great commotion at court, because Cunan was very angry with Caraduec for his counsel. He said unpleasant and foolish things to him and, had he dared, would have acted on them. But Caraduec set little store by all his words and his anger. With the king's permission, he sent his son Mauric to talk to Maximien and bring him to Britain.

5853   Mauric found Rome in turmoil. A great quarrel had arisen betwen Maximien, on the one hand, and Valentin and Gratian, two extremely powerful brothers, who wanted to control the empire[1] so that Maximien should have neither part nor power in it. Mauric found Maximien and in secret told him who he was and whence he came, what his name was and what he sought. Maximien was delighted when he heard the summons; his joy is no surprise. His preparations were not lengthy; he came to the king who had summoned him, and the king paid him great honour. He gave him his daughter in marriage and made him heir to England.[2]

5873   Cunan had left in anger and allied himself with the Scots. He defied his uncle and his men and made war on Maximien. Maximien, to whom the king had given everything, defended himself; many times he was victorious and many times he lost. That is the way in such matters—that the loser is later the gainer. In the end wise men brought them together and reconciled them, and Maximien promised to make him a powerful man, and did so.

5887   In three years Maximien assembled treasure and great possessions and he boasted he would cross the sea to France, fight the French and make war on the Romans, because of his hatred for the two brothers who held Rome against him and sought no treaty with him.[3] Maximien made his preparations; he had a large army, took many possessions and behaved with great pomp. He arrived in the North-west of France, in a region called Armorica. Humbauz,[4] lord of the land, summoned his men and his friends; he wanted to remove the Britons forcibly from the land and expel them from his fief. But the Britons, who killed many of his men, were stronger. Brave men could not hold out but had to flee. Maximien pursued them, killing an extraordinary number; a good fifteen thousand died, whom neither castle nor town could protect.

5913   Maximien withdrew and returned to camp. He took Cunan and smiled at him; laughing, he drew him aside. 'Cunan,' he said, smiling, 'this land is most valuable; it seems to me very fertile, abundant and delightful. Look at the soil, look

---

[1] Valentinian II and Gratian, co-emperors. See Bede I, chap. 9, and *HB* chap. 29.

[2] Wace, like *VV* chaps. 82 and 83, considerably shortens the account in *HRB* of Maximien's ar-

rival in Britain and his marriage.

[3] Wace adds this motivation.

[4] *HRB* chap. 84: *Imbaltus*; *VV*: *Humbaltus*.

Vez quels terres, vez quels rivieres,
Vez quels forez, cum sunt plenieres; [1]
Grant plenté i ad de peissun
E grant plenté de veneisun;
Unches plus bel païs ne vi.
Jo l'ai a tun ues encuvi.
Bretainne te fu otreiee,
Si fust en tei bien enpleiee,
Mais tu l'as perdue par mei
5930   E tu m'en sez mal gré, ço crei.
Mais or me fai de cel pardun;
Jo t'en rendrai tun gueredun.
De tut cest regne te saisis;
Tien ço que jo en ai conquis,
E le surplus te conquerrai
E rei e maistre t'en ferai.
Des païsanz la vuiderum
E des Bretuns la poplerum,
Si sera, quant ele ert poplee,
5940   La menor Bretaine nomee.
Ne vuil que altre gent i maine,
Pur noz Bretuns sera Bretaine.'
Cunan ad le dun receü
E mult l'en ad bon gré seü;
Parfundement l'en ad cliné
E humlement l'ad mercié,
Puis li ad premis feelté
A porter mais tut sun heé.
De cel tens, par ceste achaisun,
5950   Perdi Armoriche sun nun,
Si out cest nun Bretaine e ad,
Ne jamais, ço crei, nel perdrad.
D'illuec sunt a Rednes alé
Si unt assise la cité;
Rendue lur fu erraument,
N'i out nul contretenement.
Li hume s'en furent fuï,
Senz guarde aveient tut guerpi.
Assez ert ki ço lur diseit [2]
5960   Que ja uns trovez n'i sereit [3]

Ki ne fust a dolur tuez
E a grant hunte turmentez.
Pur ço s'en aloent fuiant
Ki ainz ainz tuit li païsant;
Issi fu la terre vuidiee
E as Bretuns tute laissiee.
E Maximien ad tut pris
E as chastels ses guardes mis.
[N'i out remés ki guaainast
Ne ki la terre laborast.] [4]   5970
[E Maximien, ki mult sout,
E ki la terre popler vout,] [5]
En la terre fist amener, [6]
Trestuz esliz a laborer,
Cent mil vilains; e chevaliers
En fist mener trente millers
Ki les païsanz maintenissent
E d'altres genz les defendissent.
Dunc ad fait Cunan coroner
E les fortelesces livrer;   5980
Ne volt pas surjurner a tant,
Vers France s'en passa avant.
France conquist e Lohierregne,
E Treives fist chief de sun regne.
Ne li pout encor ço suffire
S'il de Rome n'eüst l'empire;
Dunc prist vers Rome sun chemin
Sur Gracien e Valentin;
Lombardie e Rome conquist,
L'un en chaça e l'altre ocist.   5990
   A Dionot, un suen vassal,
Un gentil conte e un leal, [7]
Aveit Engleterre livree
E la justise comandee.
Freres Caraduec ert puis nez,
Mais Caraduec ert ja finez,
E sis fiz, ki fu al message,
E Dionot tint l'eritage;
Une fille aveit cil mult bele
Ki esteit apelee Urséle. [8]   6000

---

[1] MS P readings—*vez*—restored in ll. 5921–22.
[2] MS P readings—*ert ki ço*—restored.
[3] MS P readings—*n'i*—restored.
[4] MSS PDLJHKN omit ll. 5969–70; this couplet is supplied by Arnold.
[5] MSS PFJHKN omit ll. 5971–72; this couplet is

supplied by Arnold.
[6] MS P readings—*En la terre*—restored.
[7] MS P readings—*conte*—restored.
[8] MS J adds: *Et pus fu par mer envoie/ Et mainte autre desconseillie/ Qui durent estre mariees/ En Bretaigne outre mer menees.*

Cunan becomes king of Brittany

at the rivers, the forests—how copious they are! There are plenty of fish and plenty of game; I never saw a more beautiful land. For your benefit I have longed to have it. Britain was promised to you: it would have been in good hands, but through me you lost it and I believe you resent me for it. But now forgive me for it: I will give you your reward. I give you the whole of this land: take what I have won and I will conquer the rest for you and make you king and master of it. We will get rid of the inhabitants and people it with Britons and, when it is peopled, it will be called "Little Britain". I don't want any other people here; it will be Britain for our Britons.'

5943 Cunan received the gift and was most grateful to him. He bowed low and humbly thanked him; then he promised to be loyal to him for the rest of his life. At this moment and in this way Armorica lost its name and acquired this name of 'Britain', and has it still and never, I believe, will lose it.[1] From there they went to Rennes and besieged the city. It quickly surrendered to them; there was no opposition. The men had fled, leaving everything unprotected. There were plenty of people to tell them that if any one were found, he would be painfully killed and shamefully tortured. For this reason they fled and all the peasants fled likewise. Thus the land was emptied and left entirely to the Britons. And Maximien seized everything and put his guards in the castles. No one was left to cultivate or till the land. And Maximien, who was wise and wanted to people the country, brought over a hundred thousand peasants from England, all chosen to plough the soil, and thirty thousand knights to protect the peasants and defend them against other people.

5979 Then he had Cunan crowned and handed over the fortresses to him. After that, he did not want to stay but crossed into France. He conquered France and Lorraine and made Trèves his capital. Even this did not satisfy him if he could not control Rome, so he made his way towards Rome and Gratian and Valentin. He conquered Lombardy and Rome, expelled one brother and killed the other. England had been handed over to Dionot, one of his vassals, a noble and loyal count, and he had entrusted him with its rule. Dionot was Caraduec's younger brother, but Caraduec, and his son who had been on the embassy, were dead, and Dionot had inherited. He had a very beautiful daughter called Ursula.

---

[1] *HB* describes the British settlement of Brittany in chap. 27 and *HA* follows him (I, chap. 43). According to William of Malmesbury, *De Gestis* Book I, chap. 1, it is Constantine who founds a colony 'on the western coast of Gaul' for his British veterans. There is no real evidence for large-scale movements from Britain to Brittany till the 6th century: see Fahy, 'When did Britons become Bretons?', pp. 111–24.

Franceis, ki furent resbaudi,
Unt Cunan de guerre acuilli;
Mais Cunan s'est bien defenduz;
Unches par els ne fu vencuz.
Pur sa terre mielz guaanier,
Pur pupler e pur herbergier,
E pur sa gent asseürer,
Volt as humes femes duner.
Ne lur volt pas doner Franceises,
6010 Ne pur force, ne pur richeises,
Ne lur lignage entremeller
Ne lur terres acomuner.
Ainz ad fait Dionot requerre,
Ki en guarde aveit Engleterre, [1]
Que sa fille li otreiast,
Urséle, si li enveiast,
E des filles as vavasurs
Ki n'aveient encor seinnurs,
E des filles as païsanz
6020 E as povres e as mananz
Li enveiast quanqu'il purreit,
E il ben les mariereit:
Chescune avreit sun mariage
Sulunc l'ordre de sun parage.
Cil li ad sa fille otreiee
E od grant richeise enveiee.
Les meschines fist demander
Ki esteient a marier.
Unze mil en ad assemblees,
6030 Tutes de gentilz humes nees.
Des païsanz prist ensement
Seissante mil comunement,
Que petites, que parceües,
Bien conrees e bien vestues; [2]
Es nefs a Lundres mises furent
Od cels ki conduire les durent.
Aval Tamise sunt corues
E dessi en la mer venues:
Par cele mer parfund siglouent,
6040 Leesce e bien trover quidouent;

Es vus tempeste merveilluse;
E une nue vint pluiuse
Ki fist le vent devant turner,
L'air nercir, le jur oscurer.
Unc n'oï tant sudeement
Venir tempeste ne turment.
Li ciels trubla, li airs nerci,
Granz fu li venz, la mer fremi,
Wages comencent a enfler
E sur l'une l'altre munter.   6050
En mult poi d'ure nés traversent,
Neient, afundrent e enversent, [3]
Esturman n'i poënt aidier,
Ne nuls huem altre conseillier.
Ki dunc oïst crier meschines
E exhalcier voiz feminines,
Palmes batre, chevuls tirer,
Peres e meres regreter,
E geter granz criz e granz plainz
E reclamer Deu e ses sainz,   6060
Ki veïst cum eles mureient
E cum eles s'entreteneient,
Ja n'eüst le quer tant felun,
Qu'il n'en eüst compassiun.
Unches n'oï en nul peril
De femes fait si grant besil;
Mult par i ot nés perilies
E meschines a duel neiees;
Asquantes ki s'en eschaperent,
Ki entre paiens arriverent,   6070
Ocises furent u vendues
U en servage retenues.
Unze mil en furent menees
E en Cologne decolees; [4]
Urséle fu od celes prise,
E ovec eles fu ocise.
    Mainte en unt en la mer trovee
Wanis e Melga esguaree;
Wanis esteit reis de Hungrie;
Par mer alot od grant navie;   6080

---

[1] MS P's order of line restored.
[2] MS P reading—*bien vestues*—restored.
[3] MS P reading—*afundrent*—restored.
[4] MS P: *Culuine.*

Ursula and her companions are shipwrecked

6001   The spirits of the French had revived and they attacked Cunan, but he defended himself well and they never defeated him. To cultivate his land better, to occupy and people it and ensure the safety of his men, he wanted to give them wives. He did not want to give them Frenchwomen, using either gifts or force, nor to inter-mingle their races, nor to join their countries. On the contrary, he asked Dionot, who was in charge of England, to give him his daughter, Ursula, in marriage and to send her to him, and to send as many as possible of the as yet unmarried daughters of vassals, and the daughters of peasants, of the poor as well as the rich, and he would give them good marriages. Each would be married according to her rank.[1] Dionot granted him his daughter and sent her with many costly things. He asked for marriageable girls, and assembled eleven thousand of them, all nobly born. He likewise took from the peasants sixty thousand girls all to-gether, whether young or fully grown, well decked out and dressed. In London they were put on board ships, together with those who had to escort them. The ships sped down the Thames and from there to the sea. They sailed through this deep sea, expecting to find happiness and wealth. Then a huge storm arose and a cloud full of rain, which made the wind ahead change round, the air darken and the day grow dim. I never heard of storm and tempest arriving so quickly. The sky grew murky, the air darkened, the wind raged and the sea was in tumult; waves began to swell and crash over each other. In a very short time they made the ships drift, flooded them, capsized and sank them. The helmsmen were un-able to help or get advice from anyone else. Whoever could have heard the girls' cries, the women's raised voices, the wringing of hands,[2] the tearing of hair, the laments for fathers and mothers, and the loud weeping and wailing and calling upon God and His saints—whoever could have seen how they were dying as they clung to each other, he would have felt pity, no matter how wicked his heart. I have never heard of such a massacre of women in any other peril; there were many ships in danger and many girls miserably drowned. Some who escaped and landed amongst heathen were killed or sold or kept as slaves. Eleven thousand were led to Cologne and beheaded: Ursula was amongst those captured and was killed with them.[3]

6077   Wanis and Melga found many of them lost in the sea. Wanis was king of Hungary; he cruised the seas with a large fleet. Melga was lord of Scythia.[4] They had many

---

[1] Perhaps following the *VV*, Wace omits the ulte-rior motive given to Conan in *HRB* chap. 87—that he had always wanted Ursula—and makes him scrupulous about providing appropriate marriages. In *HRB*'s account, chap. 88, short-ened drastically in *VV*, many of the 11,000 vir-gins do not want to leave home.

[2] Literally, 'the striking of palms', a sign of de-spair.

[3] The fate of Ursula and her companions is de-scribed with many more details and pathos than in *HRB*. Wace is fond of portraying storms at sea and always shows sympathy for innocent. victims. He adds the name of their place of slaughter—Cologne—and that they fall into the hands of heathen; by so doing, he firmly identi-fies this story with that of St Ursula, martyred by the Huns. See Houck, *Sources*, p. 247 ff.—who points out that MS H describes them as '*martyres*' and '*saintes*'—and Tatlock pp. 237–40 on the legend before *HRB*.

[4] In *HRB* chap. 88, lord of the Picts.

Melga esteit de Scice sire.
Des meschines firent ocirre
Plusurs qu'il voldrent purgesir
Ki nel vuleient consentir;
Nes ocieient pas pur el,
Paen esteient cil cruel.
Ensemble acompainié s'esteient;
Dit lur ert e bien le saveient
Que Engelterre ert afebliee
6090 E des bons chevaliers voidee.
A Rome en fu partie alee,
Que Maximien out menee;
Cunan en rout l'altre partie,
Si ert la terre desgarnie.
E cil dui rei l'unt encuvie
Si l'unt par Escoce envaïe;
Tut destruistrent e exillierent,
Unches home n'i esparnierent.
Emprés unt le Humbre passé,
6100 Tut le plain païs unt guasté.
N'i aveit fors la vilanaille,
Ki n'aveit cure de bataille,
E li ullage les ocient,
E li chaitif braient e crient.
Cument fust terre defendue
Ki de bons chevalers ert nue!
Tant cum il i out des baruns
Tindrent les turs e les dunjuns;
Mandé unt pur Maximian,
6110 E il lur tramist Gratian,
Un chevalier mult succurable,
De dous legiuns cunestable.
Cil ad les assis succurruz
E les ullages tuz vencuz.
D'Engleterre tuz les geta
E en Irlande les chaça.
Entretant vindrent li cusin
E li bon parent Valentin.
Par Theodosion d'Orient,
6120 Un rei de grant afforcement,[1]

Maximian a force pristrent
En Aquilee, si l'ocistrent.
Des Bretuns ki l'orent soï
Sunt alquant mort, alquant fuï,
E Valentin rad ço saisi
Que Maximien li toli.
Gracien ne fist neient plus,
Ki d'Engleterre out le desus,
Chevetaine se fist e rei
Si demena mult grant noblei.   6130
Mult out en lui mortel tirant
E a povre gent mal faisant;
Les nobles homes enorout
E les païsanz exillout.
E li vilain s'acompainerent
Od granz turbes si se vengerent
Tut l'unt par peces depecié
Cume mastin lu enragié.
Si hume se sunt departi
E en lur terres reverti.   6140
    Quant Wanis e Melga oïrent
Que vilain de Gratien firent,
Assemblé unt les Gollandeis
E les Noreis e les Daneis,
E cels d'Escoce e cels d'Irlande,
Si purpristrent Northumberlande;
Le Humbre od lur grant gent passerent,
Chastels e viles deserterent.
Li Bretun virent la dolur[2]
E le desert faire des lur;   6150
As senaturs unt de richief
Mandé par humes e par brief,
Si a cest besuin lur aïent,
Come la gent u plus se fient,
Jamais de lur conseil n'istrunt
E tuz tens mais les servirunt.
Li Romain n'ublierent mie
La traïsun ne la boesdie
Que cil lur orent fait suvent.
Une legiun sulement   6160

---

[1] MS P reading—*afforcement*—restored.   [2] MS P reading—*dolur*—restored.

Britain is harried by Wanis and Melga

girls killed with whom they wanted to sleep and who would not consent. They killed them for no other reason; these cruel men were heathens. They had banded together: they had been told, and were well aware, that England was enfeebled and empty of good knights. Some of them Maximien had taken to Rome and Cunan had the rest, so the land was defenceless.[1] And these two kings wanted to take it and invaded it through Scotland. Everywhere they destroyed and ravaged, sparing no one. Next they crossed the Humber and laid all the countryside waste. There was no one there except people of no account, who had no desire for battles, and the brigands killed them. The wretches wailed and cried. How could the land be defended, when it was denuded of good knights?

6107   In as much as there were any barons, they held on to the castles and towers. They sent word to Maximien, and he sent them Gratian, a knight most willing to help, commander of two legions.[2] He helped the besieged and completely vanquished the brigands. He threw them all out of England and chased them into Ireland. Meanwhile the kinsmen and the powerful relations of Valentin arrived. With Theodosien from the East, a mighty king, they took Maximien by force to Aquilea and killed him. Of the Britons who had followed him, some were slain, some fled, and Valentin took back what Maximien had taken from him.[3] Gratian, who controlled England, had no need of further action; he made himself ruler and king and put on a display of great magnificence. He was a very cruel tyrant, who hurt the poor: he honoured the nobility but destroyed the peasantry. And the peasants banded together and in great crowds took revenge, tearing him to pieces as a maddened wolf does a dog. His men scattered and returned to their lands.

6141   When Wanis and Melga heard what the peasants had done to Gratian, they brought together those from Gotland,[4] the Norwegians and the Danes, the Scots and the Irish, and seized Northumberland. They crossed the Humber with their huge army and laid castles and towns waste. The Britons saw their property harmed and laid waste and for the second time sent men and letters to the senators to come to their aid, as the people they most trusted; they would never neglect their advice and always serve them. The Romans had not forgotten the treason and the trickery these people had often done them.[5] They sent them only one

---

[1] Gildas, *De Excidio*, chap. 14, first refers to Britain enfeebled and defenceless through Maximus's campaigns.

[2] According to Thorpe (p. 143), this Gratian is identical with the one in Bede I, chap. 11.

[3] *HRB* chaps. 88 and 89, confusingly has two Gratians, Gratian '*municeps*' and '[the friends of] Gratian', i.e the late emperor. Wace reduces confusion by changing the name of the latter to

Valentinian. Gildas, *De Excidio*, chap. 13, mentions the beheading of Maximus at Aquilea, as does *HB* chap. 29, so Wace's additions probably come from *HB*.

[4] For Gotland, see *HRB* chap. 153 and Tatlock pp. 106–7.

[5] Gildas, *De Excidio*, chap. 6, refers to a well-known proverb: 'the British are cowardly in war and faithless in peace.'

Lur enveierent de lur gent,
E cil vindrent delivrement,
Engleterre tost delivrerent
E les ullagues en geterent.
En Escoce les unt chaciez
E asquanz morz e detrenchiez.
Mortier e pierre unt aüné;
Un mur firent sur un fossé;
Unches kernel nen fu a dire
6170 Entre cels d'Escoce e Deïre;
Kar par illuec suvent veneient
Cil ki la terre destrueient.
Guardeins mistrent par plusurs lius,
Ki pur garder orent granz fius.
Quant il orent tut achevé
Le mur qu'il orent compassé,
As riches humes del païs
Unt a Lundres parlement pris.
Dunc distrent ço qu'il les laireient
6180 E en lur terres s'en ireient;
Pruz fussent e armes quesissent
E vivement se defendissent;
Ne poeient mie suffrir
Le cust d'aler ne de venir.
Un sage home i out ki parla,
Ki la parole avant mustra:
'Seinnurs, dist il,mainte grant perte,
E mainte grant peine unt sufferte
Alquant de noz bons anceisurs,
6190 E nus emprés, pur voz amurs.
Vos nus avez treü duné
E nus l'avum bien achaté;
Unches n'en amendames guaires,
Tut l'avum mis en voz afaires.
Se nus l'avum un an eü
Dous anz aprés l'avum perdu;
Kar unches, des que vus osastes,
Fei ne amur ne nus portastes.
Suvent truviez achaisun
6200 Par quei nus noz dreiz perdium.

Mainz de noz humes i ad morz,
E fait maint mal e fait mainz torz.
A voz busuinz nus requerez,
E fei e pais nus prametez.
E quant vus estes eschapé,
E li busuin sunt trespassé,
Dunc ne vus est guaires de nus,
Ainz vus trovum mult orguillus;
Nostre treü nus retolez,
U a enviz le nus rendez.   6210
Mielz nus vient le treü guerpir
Que issi lunges deservir;
Grant cust i ad si manum luin
E vus avez suvent busuin.
Ne poüm venir tantes feiz;
Faites le mielz que vus purreiz;
S'aler nus en poüm a Rome
Jamés n'i revendrum pur home;
Ainz vus mettrum al covenir;
Ne vus volum plus maintenir.   6220
Vus maimes vus maintenez;[1]
Defendez vus se vus poëz.
De voz anceisurs savum nus
Que fort furent e orguillus;
Ne remist a els a conquerre
Jesque a Rome nule terre.
Mult se contindrent fierement.
Mais de vus est tut altrement;
Ne sai que deit, ne dunt avient
Que nule gent sur vus ne vient   6230
Ki vostre terre ne destruie
E ki ne vus mettë en fuie.
Vus estes trestut forlignied,[2]
Ço m'est avis, par malveistied.
Pernez en vus alques d'aspresce,
Si vus membre de la prüesce
Que li barun aveir soleient
Ki les granz terres conquereient.
Quant vus voz fieus ne defendrez,[3]
Malement altres conquerrez.   6240

---

[1] MS P reading—*maimes*—restored.
[2] MS P reading—*trestut*—restored.
[3] MS P reading—*defendrez*—restored.

The Romans build another wall

legion of men, and these came quickly, soon freed England and expelled the brigands. They chased them into Scotland, killing and slaughtering some of them. Gathering mortar and stone, they made a wall on top of an earthwork;[1] no battlements were lacking to separate the people in Deira from those in Scotland, because those who ravaged the land often came from there. They posted guards in many places, who for their loyalty were given large domains.

6175 When they had quite finished the wall they had planned, they held a conference in London with the powerful men of the land. Then they told them they were leaving them and going to their own land. The Britons were brave and could take up arms and defend themselves in earnest. The Romans could no longer afford to come and go. A wise man spoke there, who said the following: 'My lords, some of our good ancestors have endured many great losses and much suffering, and so have we in our turn, on account of you. You have paid us tribute, and we have paid dearly for it; we have never benefited from it but spent it entirely on your affairs. If we had it one year, we lost it two years later, for as soon as you dared, you never gave us loyalty or affection. You often found a way to deprive us of our rights. Many of our men have died here and experienced great injury and wrongs. You seek us to help with your needs, promising us loyalty and peace, and once you are free and the need is past, you couldn't care less for us and we find you very arrogant. You take our tribute back from us, or pay it with resentment. Better for us to abandon the tribute than to serve here for so long. It's very expensive to live far away, when you are often in need of us. We cannot come so often. Do the best you can. If we leave for Rome, there will be no reason ever to return. On the contrary, we leave it to you; we don't wish to protect you any more. Protect yourselves: defend yourselves if you can.

6223 'We know your ancestors were strong and proud; scarcely any land except Rome was left for them to conquer. They behaved with pride, but you are quite different. I don't know what it means or how it happens that any attacking army can destroy your land and put you to flight. Wickedness, I think, has made you degenerate completely. If you recall the bravery those lords used to have who conquered many lands, be more rigorous. If you can't defend your own domains, you'll have difficulty conquering others. Defend yourselves against hostile men who so often cross this land. If you have those who will stand guard on the wall, we have protected you in one direction. Construct big towers and fortresses on

---

[1] This is the Antonine Wall, built between 140 and 142, from the Firth of Forth to the Clyde. Gildas describes its building (*De Excidio*, chap. 18); Bede says (I, chap. 12, followed by *HA* I, chap. 45) it was built of turf because the British lacked engineers. *HB* (chap. 23) compresses the two walls into one, locating it at the Ant- onine Wall but attributing its construction to Severus. *VV* chap. 89 describes the wall as '*vallum cum muro immensum*', an enormous earthen rampart with a wall, which is closer to Wace than the Vulgate *HRB*. See Wallace-Hadrill, *Bede's Ecclesiastical History*, p. 17.

Defendez vus de gent adverse
Ki tant suvent par ci traverse.
Nus vus avum clos d'une part,
Si vus avez ki le mur guart.
Faites granz turs e chastels forz
Sur les rivages e les porz [1]
Par unt li ullage s'embatent
Ki tant suvent vus escombatent.
Maintenez bien vostre franchise
6250   Si vus ostés d'altrui servise;
Vus fereiz mult bien nostre vuel.' [2]
A cele parole out grant duel
E grant marrement e grant plor,
Que de pitied, que de poür.
Dunc se sunt entresalué
E li Romain s'en sunt alé;
E bien distrent al departir
Que mais ne quident revenir. [3]
        Wanis e Melga unt oïes
6260   Les nuveles par lur espies
Que li Romain finablement
Aveient pris departement.
Od les Pis e od les Daneis,
Od les Escoz, od les Norreis,
En Northumberlande passerent;
Arstrent, destruistrent e roberent.
Dessi al mur n'unt rien laissié
Que tuit n'en aient eissillié. [4]
Li Bretun unt le mur guarni
6270   E cil defors l'unt assailli.
Dunc veïssiez de tutes parz
Enveier gavelocs e darz,
Quarrels e saietes voler
E od fundes pierres geter.
Cil ki del mur se defendeient
A grant poür se combateient;
De nuvel erent adubé
E des assauz forment hasté; [5]
N'osoent fors l'oil descovrir
6280   E cil defors les funt tapir.

Unches nule pluie aval vent
Ne vola plus espessement
Que saietes e darz voloent
Od les pierres que il getoent.
Li Bretun les kernels guerpirent
E ki ainz ainz s'en descendirent. [6]
Cil defors sunt al mur munté,
En plusurs lius l'unt enfundré.
Emprés unt tut aplanïed
E fossé e mur eguaillied.   6290
Puis passerent tut plainement,
Que n'i out nul defendement.
Chastels e viles unt purpris
E des Bretuns unt meint ocis.
Par tut alerent a bandun,
N'i troverent defensiun.
Unches ne trovai, ne ne truis,
Que a nul tens, avant ne puis,
I eüst morz ensemble tanz,
Que chevaliers, que païsanz.   6300
Deus! quel desert e quel eissil
De bone terre e de gentil.
Bretun furent jadis mult pruz,
Mais or sunt si mis el desuz,
Ja par els ne recoverrunt
Se d'altre part securs nen unt.
Pur chevaliers e pur securs
Unt enveié as senaturs,
E cil distrent que non ferunt,
Facent le mielz que il purrunt;   6310
Ne püent pur els, chescun an,
Suffrir tel peine e tel ahan;
Assez unt aillurs a entendre; [7]
Ne puent rien Bretun plus prendre. [8]
Li evesque s'entr'assemblerent;
Dolent furent, kar mult duterent
Que par cele gent alïene
Ne perist la lei cristïene;
Se cele chose alques durast,
Que Damnedeus nes visitast.   6320

---

[1] MS P reading—*les*—restored.
[2] MS P reading—*nostre*—restored.
[3] MS P reading—*revenir*—restored.
[4] MS P reading—*tuit*—restored.
[5] MS P reading—*forment*—restored.
[6] MS P reading—*s'en*—restored.
[7] MS P reading—*a*—restored.
[8] MS P reading—*Ne puent*—restored.

The Romans leave Britain

the coasts and in the ports, where the pirates sweep in who attack you so often. If you dispense with the help of others, guard your own liberty carefully: that would certainly meet our wishes.'[1] At these words there was great distress, much sorrow and many tears, whether from pity or fear. Then they made their farewells and the Romans left, saying as they did so that they never expected to return.

6259 Through their spies, Wanis and Melga heard the news that the Romans had finally departed. Along with the Picts, the Danes, the Scots and the Norsemen, they crossed into Northumberland. They burnt, destroyed and plundered, leaving nothing as far as the wall which had not been laid waste. The Britons fortified the wall and those outside attacked it. Then from all sides you could see javelins and spears thrown, bolts and arrows fly and stones hurled from slings. Those defending themselves on the wall fought in great fear. Shortly they were re-armed, and very hard pressed by attacks; if they only showed so much as their eyes, those outside would force them to hide. Never did any wind-driven rain fall more densely than the rain of arrows and spears, along with the stones.

6285 The Britons abandoned the battlements and got down as fast as they could. The attackers scaled the wall, shattering it in several places. Next they flattened everything and razed both ditch and wall. Then they could pass quite unhindered, because there were no defences left. They seized castles and towns and killed many of the Britons. Everywhere they passed without restraint and found no resistance. I never heard—and still haven't—of so many, at any time before or since, dying all together, whether knights or peasants. God! what waste and ruin of a good and noble land. The British had once been full of courage, but now they were beaten; they would never recover unless help came from elsewhere.[2] They sent to the Senators for knights and help,[3] and these refused them, saying they would have to do the best they could; they could not, every year, suffer such trouble and distress for them. They had plenty to attend to elsewhere; they could no longer undertake British affairs. The bishops met together, distressed; they were very afraid lest, through the foreign invaders, the Christian faith should

---

[1] In *HRB* chap. 90 it is Guithelinus, Archbishop of London, who makes this speech, i.e. a Briton reproaching Britons for their degeneracy. *VV* entirely omits the speech. Wace gives it to a Roman, complaining of British ingratitude, but omitting to state (as *HRB* does) the reason for British weakness: Maximianus has taken all the troops and youth away. The reception for the speech also varies: in *HRB* it is applauded as inspiring courage, but Wace sees the scene as pathetic. However, he does not moralise about it (cf. *HRB* chap. 91).

[2] Wace focuses more than *HRB* on this as the

nadir of British fortunes, celebrates the 'good and noble land' and looks beyond the immediate need for Roman help to the coming of the house of Constantine (and ultimately, Arthur).

[3] In *HRB* chap. 91, this is the specific—and historical—appeal to Aetius, in his third term as consul, made between 446 and 454 (Dumville, 'Chronology of *De Excidio*', p. 83). The words of the letter in Gildas, *De Excidio*, chap. 20—'the barbarians push us back to the sea, the sea pushes us back to the barbarians'—are quoted in Bede (I, chap. 13), in *HA* (I, chap. 46) and in both versions of *HRB*.

A Lundres esteit a cel tens,
Arcevesques mult eloquens,
Guencelins, de mult grant clergie,
E si esteit de bone vie.
Lundres out ainz e puis le sied
Lungement de l'arcevesquied,
Puis, ne sai par quel achaisun,
A Cantorbire le mist l'un.
Guencelins, cil bons arcevesques,
6330 Par le conseil de ses evesques
En Armoriche trespassa,
Que Cunan des Bretuns popla,
Que nus or Bretaine apelum,
D'Armoriche ad perdu le nun.
Aldroën, ki l'enor teneit,
Quarz reis emprés Cunan esteit.
Bien ert la gent multepleiee
E la terre bien herbergiee.
Li arcevesques tant erra
6340 Que Aldroën le rei trova.
Li reis le fist mult enorer,
Kar mult l'aveit oï loer;
Demanda li quei il quereit
Ki de si luin a lui veneit.
'Sire, dist il, bien poez noter,
Ne t'en esteut neient duter,[1]
Que d'ultre mer sui venuz ça,
Que grant besuin m'i amena.
Tu n'iés pas nez si nuvelment
6350 Ne ne mainz si luintainement
Que tu parler oï nen aies
Des granz dulurs e des granz plaies
Que Bretun unt suvent eü
Puis ke cil Maximien fu
Ki l'enor que tu tiens conquist
E qui Cunan seinnur en fist.
Pur la gent que cil en osterent
Ki ces terres de nus poplerent
Turna nostre gent en declin.
6360 Unches puis n'eümes veisin

Ki a nus guerre ne preïst
E qui veintre ne nus vulsist.
Jadis soleient li Bretun
Conquere mainte regiun;
Or ne püent il sulement
La lur defendre d'altre gent.
Cil de Rome aider nus soleient;
As granz busuinz nus succurreient;[2]
Guerpi nus unt, kar trop luin mainent,
Del cust e de l'eire se plainent.   6370
Granz genz assez e bones sumes
E granz compaines avum d'ummes,
Mais nus n'avum prince ne rei;
E une gent male, senz fei,[3]
Ad nostre terre si conquise,
E la gent tute si susprise,
Jamais, ço crei, ne resurdrum,[4]
Se d'altre gent securs n'avum.
Ne te puis mie recunter,
Kar mult m'est grief a recorder,   6380
Le duel e la mesaventure
Qu'eü avum e encor dure.
Pur ço sui, sire, a tei venuz,
Ki de bunté iés cuneüz,
E tu iés de nostre gent nez
E de nus vint tis parentez;
Bretun estes e nus Bretun,
E parenz sumes, ço savum,
E nus devum estre tuit un
E tuit devum aveir comun;[5]   6390
L'uns deit par l'altre estre rescus,
E vus par nus, e nus par vus.
Busuin avum, or nus secor,
Si t'iert turné a grant enor;
E tul deiz faire par nature
De parenté e de dreiture.'
Aldroën, ki fu mult pitus,
Devint tut tristes e plurus
De la tristur que il oï:
Tut en plorant li respundi: 6400

---

[1] MS P reading—*esteut*—restored.
[2] MS P reading—*succurreient*—restored.
[3] MS P reading—*fei*—restored.
[4] MS P reading—*crei*—restored.
[5] MS P reading—*tuit*—restored in ll. 6389–90.

Guincelin appeals to Brittany for help

perish, that God would not visit them if such a lapse lasted for any length of time.[1]

6321   In London at that time was a most eloquent and learned archbishop, Guincelin,[2] who also led a good life. First he had the diocese of London and then for a long while the see of the archbishopric; finally, I do not know on what occasion, they transferred him to Canterbury. Guencelin, this good archbishop, advised by his bishops, crossed over to Armorica, which Cunan had populated with Britons and which we now call Brittany; it has lost the name Armorica. Aldroen, who ruled the realm, was the fourth king after Cunan. The people had multiplied and the land was full of dwellings. The archbishop travelled until he found king Aldroen. The king paid him great honour, because he had heard him much praised, and asked him what he was seeking in coming to him from so far afield.

6345   'My lord,' Guincelin said, 'you certainly have reason to take note, nor should you be in any doubt, that I have come here across the sea because I am brought by great need. You have not been so recently born, nor dwell so far away, that you have not heard tell of the great sufferings and wounds which Britons have frequently experienced since the days of Maximien, who conquered the realm you rule and made Cunan lord of it. Because of the people removed from our land to populate this one, our nation is in decline. Ever since, there is not one of our neighbours which does not wage war on us and wants to conquer us. Once the British used to conquer many lands; now they cannot even defend theirs from other nations. The Romans used to help us; in times of great need they would succour us. They have abandoned us, because they live too far away; they complain of the expense and the journey.

6371   'We are a great, good and numerous nation, and we have large troops of men, but we have neither prince nor king, and a wicked, lawless race has so defeated our land and so harassed all the people that I fear we shall never regain power unless we have help from others. I cannot tell you again, because it hurts me so much to recount it, of the suffering and misfortune which we have had and which still continues. That is why, my lord, I have come to you, because you are known for your goodness, and born of our people, your lineage comes from us. You are British and we are British and we are related, we know, and should be as one and have everything in common. The one should be rescued by the other: both you by us and us by you. We are in need, now help us; it will redound to your honour. And you should do it out of natural feeling for our blood-ties, and for justice.'

6397   Aldroen, full of compassion, was sad and tearful on hearing of this misery. Weep-

---

[1] Wace adds these fears of the bishops.

[2] *HRB* chap. 92: *Guithelinus*; *VV*: *Guizelinus*. Wace adds details of his career.

'Si jo, dist il, vus puis valeir,
Jo vus valdrai a mun poeir.
Constentin, mun frere, enmerrez
E cunestable le ferez.
Il est chevaliers merveillus
E de guerre mult enginnus.
Dous mil armez li liverai
Des plus preisez ke jo avrai.'
Dunc ad Constentin demandé,
6410 A l'arcevesque l'ad livré.
Li arcevesques l'esguarda,
De sa main destre le seinna,
E cil clina, si vint avant,
E l'arcevesque dist itant:
      'Christus vincit, Christus regnat,
Christus vincit et imperat.'
Li reis manda ses chevaliers
Si li ad livré dous millers.
Od mult riche apareillement
6420 Les mist as nés des qu'il out vent.
Il meïsmes od els alast
Se il peüst e il osast,
Mais il aveit guerre as Franceis.
      Constentin vint a Toteneis;
Maint bon chevalier out od sei,
Chescuns quidot valeir un rei.
Vers Lundres lur eire turnerent,
De tutes parz Bretuns manderent.
N'en poeit anceis nuls pareir,
6430 Mais dunques pristrent a ploveir;
Des boschages e des muntaines
Vindrent avant od granz compaines.
Que vus fereie jo lunc plait?
Tant unt erré e tant unt fait,
La malvaise gent unt vencue
Ki la terre aveit confundue.
Puis tindrent cuncile a Cilcestre;
Tuit li barun i durent estre.
Constentin unt a rei eslit;
6440 Senz contredit e senz respit

L'unt a grant joie coruné
Si en unt fait lur avué.
Emprés li unt feme dunee
Ki des gentilz Romains ert nee. [1]
Treis vallez en out, le plus grant
Fist li reis apeler Constant.
A Wincestre le fist nurrir,
E lal fist muine devenir. [2]
Emprés fu nez Aurelius,
Si surnuns fu Ambrosius.   6450
Derainement Uther nasqui,
E ce fu cil que plus vesqui.
Li arcevesques Guncelins
Prist en guarde ces dous meschins.
Se Constentin lunges regnast,
Tute la terre en amendast,
Mais trop murut hastivement,
Duze anz regna tant sulement.
Un des Pis out en sa maisun,
Un traïtur, un mal felun,   6460
Ki l'aveit lungement servi,
Puis l'out, ne sai pur quei, haï.
Cil le mena en un vergier,
Come s'il vulsist conseillier;
La u il al rei conseillout,
Ki del felun ne se guardout,
Un cultel aveit, sil feri,
Le rei ocist, si s'en fuï. [3]
      Cil de la terre s'assemblerent;
Rei voldrent faire, si duterent   6470
Del quel des vallez rei fereient,
Petit erent e poi saveient;
Encore esteient a nurrice,
Ne saveient nule malice.
Constant l'ainz né, ki esteit maire,
N'osouent de l'abit retraire;
Vilté lur semblout e folie
A retraire de l'abeïe.
Un des dous aveient choisi,
Quant Vortigern avant sailli,   6480

---

[1] MS P reading—*des*—restored.
[2] MS P reading—*E lal fist*—restored.
[3] MS J adds: *Dont furent sans roi li Breton/ Car n'i* *avoit s'enfans non/ Del roi avoient grant dolour/ Tout li baron et li millour/ Quant il orent enseveli/ Ne l'ont noient mis en oubli.*

Constantine succeeds to the British throne

ing, he replied: 'If I can be of use to you, I will help as much as I can. Take Constantine, my brother, and make him commander. He is an exceptional knight and very cunning in battle. I will give him two thousand armed men from amongst the best I have.' Then he asked for Constantine and handed him over to the archbishop. The archbishop looked at him, blessed him with his right hand, and Constantine bowed and came forward. And the archbishop then said in Latin: 'Christ is victorious, Christ is king, Christ conquers and reigns.'[1] The king summoned his knights and gave him two thousand of them. As soon as there was a wind, he put them, richly dressed, into ships. He himself would have gone with them, had he been able and dared to, but he had war with the French on his hands.[2]

6424   Constantine came to Totnes. He had many good knights with him; each thought he was as good as a king. They set out for London, summoning Britons from all sides. Formerly none had appeared, but now they poured out of the woods and mountains, coming forward with large bands of men. Why should I make a long speech of it? They fared so well and did so much that they conquered the wicked people who had wrecked the land. Then at Silchester they held a council, which all the barons had to attend. They elected Constantine king, joyfully crowning him without opposition and without delay, and made him their lord. Then they gave him a wife, of noble Roman birth. He had three sons from her; the king called the eldest Constant, had him brought up at Winchester, and there made him become a monk. Next came Aurelius, known as Ambrosius. The last born was Uther,[3] and he was the one who lived the longest. Archbishop Guencelin took these two boys into his care.

6455   Had Constantine reigned for a long time, he would have set right the whole land, but he died too soon: his rule only lasted twelve years. One of the Picts in his household was a traitor, an evil wretch, who had long served him but then, I do not know why, began to hate him. He took him into an orchard, as if to confer, and there, as he was advising the king, who had no protection against him, he struck him with his knife, killed him and fled.

6469   The whole kingdom assembled. They wanted to choose a king but hesitated as to which of the boys it should be. These were young and inexperienced, in the care of a nurse and innocent of wrong. They did not dare take Constant, the eldest and first-born, out of his monk's habit; it seemed foolish and base to remove him from the abbey. They had chosen from among the other two, when

---

[1] This directly quotes *HRB*'s '*Christus vincit, Christus regnat, Christus imperat*' (chap. 92)—in the *VV* transferred to chap. 93 as the words uttered by Guizelinus at the Silchester coronation of Constantine.

[2] In *HRB* chap. 92 Aldroenus is practical but cool, less sympathetic than here.

[3] *HRB* chap. 93 adds '*Pendragon*' to Uther.

Uns forz huem, en Guales maneit,
Riches huem mult e cuens esteit;
De parenz ert bien enforciez
E mult cuintes e vezïez.
De bien luin avant purveeit
Ço que il enginnier vuleit.
'Que alez vus, dist il, dutant?
Faites vus rei del moine Costant. [1]
Dreiz eirs est, tolum li l'abit,
6490 Kar li altre sunt trop petit.
A nul altre l'enor n'otrei;
Tuz li pecchiez en seit sur mei.
De l'abeïe le trarai
E a rei le vus liverai.'
N'i ot nul barun ki vulsist
Que li moines reis devenist;
Orrible chose lur semblout.
Mais Vortigern, ki mal pensout,
A Wincestre est venuz puinant;
6500 Tant ala Constant demandant,
Que par le congié del priur
Parla a lui el parleür.
'Constanz, dist il, morz est tis peres;
Remise est l'enor a tes freres;
Mais tu deiz eritablement
Le regne aveir premierement.
Se tu me vuelz creistre mes dreiz,
E se tu bien m'aimes e creiz,
Des neirs dras te despoillerai
6510 E reals dras te vestirai,
Si t'osterai del muniage
Si te rendrai tun eritage.'
Cil coveita la seinurie,
Qui n'amot guaires l'abeïe;
Tuz ert ennuiez del mustier,
Legiers en ert a esluinier.
Tut ço jura e affia
Que Vortigern li demanda.
E Vortigern sempres l'ad pris
6520 E fors de l'abeïe mis;

N'i ot ki desdire l'osast,
Ki chaut, quant pur ço nel laissast.
Les dras de moine li toli
E de chiers dras le revesti.
A Lundres l'ad d'illuec mené;
N'i out guaires pople aüné;
Li archevesques morz esteit,
Ki enuindre le rei deveit;
N'i ot altre ki l'enuinsist
Ne ki sa main mettre i vulsist. 6530
Vortigern la corune prist,
Sur le chief en sum li assist,
Unches n'i out beneïçun
Se de la main Vortigern nun.
Constanz la corune reçut,
L'ordre guerpi que tenir dut;
L'ordre Deu guerpi malement,
Sin vint a mal definement;
Ne deit pas huem a buen chief traire
De faire ço qu'il ne deit faire. 6540
Le rei e sa seneschaucie
Out Vortigern bien en baillie;
Ço fist li reis qu'il li loa,
E ço toli que il rova.
Assez tost a plusurs afaires
Vit que li reis ne saveit guaires,
Ki esteit en cloistre nurriz;
E les dous freres vit petiz;
Vit les baruns del païs morz,
Vit que des vis ert li plus forz, 6550
Vit le pople alques descordable,
Vit lieu e tens bien cuvenable;
Le regne vult prendre a sa part.
Or oiez d'ume de mal art:
'Sire, dist il, jo sai de veir,
E jol te dei faire saveir,
Que assemblé sunt li Daneis
E de Norwege li Norreis.
Pur tei, ki n'iés chevalerus,
E pur la feblesce de nus, 6560

---

[1] MS P reading—*vus*—restored.

Vortigern makes Constant succeed his father

Vortigern[1] sprang forward, a man of power, who dwelt in Wales. He was a mighty count, clever and crafty, with influential kin. He had long since plotted what he wanted to contrive. 'Why are you hesitating?' he said. 'Make the monk Constant king. He is the rightful heir; let's remove his monk's habit, for the others are too young. Grant the domain to no other. May any sin be upon my own head: I will remove him from the abbey and deliver him to you as king.' Not a single baron wished the monk to become king; to them it seemed a terrible thing. But Vortigern, bent on evil, came spurring to Winchester. So insistent was he on seeing Constant that, with the prior's leave, he spoke to him in the monks' parlour.

6503 'Constant,' he said, 'your father is dead. The realm is passing to your brothers, but by right of inheritance you should have it first. If you will increase my possessions, and if you love and trust me, I will divest you of your black robe and dress you instead in a royal one. I will take you out of the monastery and restore your inheritance.' Constant, not enamoured of the abbey, coveted power; he was quite weary of the monastery and easy to take away. He promised and swore everything which Vortigern asked of him. And at once Vortigern took him out of the abbey. No one dared gainsay him: what was the point, if he was undeterred? He took off his monk's garb and dressed him in rich robes. From there he took him to London. Few people assembled; the archbishop, who should have anointed the king, was dead, and there was no other to anoint him or who wished to have a hand in it. Vortigern took the crown and placed it on top of his head: his only blessing came from Vortigern's hand alone. Constant received the crown and abandoned the vows he should have obeyed; he wrongly abandoned God's rule and thus came to a bad end. No one should succeed through doing what he should not do.

6541 Vortigern held the king and his officers firmly in his control: the king did what he advised and seized what he commanded. From several occasions early on, he saw that the king, educated in the cloister, knew very little. He saw the two brothers were very young, that the kingdom's barons were dead, that he was the strongest of those still alive, that the people were somewhat quarrelsome, and that time and place were just right for him to seize the realm for himself. Now listen to the wicked man. 'Sire,' he said, 'I know for sure, and ought to bring it to your knowledge, that the Danes, and the Norwegians from Norway, are gathering. Because you are no knight, and we are weak, they want to enter this land, to seize and

---

[1] *HRB* chap. 94: *Uortegirnus, 'consul'* of the Gewissei (for these people see fn. 4 on p. 145). Vortigern's name first appears in Bede's *Chronica Majora*, as *Uertigernus*, then in his *Historia Ecclesiastica* (I, chap. 14) as *Uurtigernus*, repeated in *HA* as *Wirtigernus*. The *Chronica* name is a Celtic one, possibly derived from a glossed text of Gildas' *De Excidio*; in the Mommsen text of Gildas, chap. 23, there is an unnamed '*superbus tyrannus*' [proud tyrant]. See introduction, p. xiv. In *HB* chap. 31 his name appears in the Old Welsh form of *Guorthigirn*; in the *ASC* for the year 449 as *Wyrtgeorn*. On Vor-tigern see Dumville 'Sub-Roman Britain' pp. 183–4 and Wallace-Hadrill, *Bede's Ecclesiastical History*, pp. 20 and 211–12.

Volent en cest païs entrer
E tes chastels prendre e guaster;
Si t'en estuet prendre cunrei
Pur defendre ta terre e tei;
Fai guarnir e guarder tes turs.
Grant poür ai de traïturs,
Si t'estuet tes chastels livrer
A cels quis sacent bien guarder.'
'Jo t'ai, dist li reis, tut livré,
6570 Si fai de tut ta volenté,
Ja sur tei cure nen prendrai, [1]
Kar tu sez mielz que jo ne sai.
Pren la terre tute en ta guarde
Que nuls n'en toille ne n'en arde.
Jo sui en tun conseil remis, [2]
Si fai le mielz que faire seis. [3]
Pren mes citez, pren mes maneirs,
Pren mes tresors, pren mes aveirs.'
Wortigern fu de grant feintise,
6580 Bien sout covrir sa cuveitise;
Quant saisi fu des fortelesces
E des tresors e des richesces:
'Sire, dist il, si te plaiseit,
Mis los e mis cunseil sereit
Que tu enveiz pur chevaliers
Des Pis d'Escoce soldeiers,
Ki od tei seient en ta curt,
Quel part que nostre guerre turt.
Les Pis purras bien enveier
6590 La u tu en avras mestier.
Par les Pis e par lur parenz
Savrum l'estre as estranges genz;
Entre nus e els parlerunt
E entre nus e els irunt.'
'Fai, dist li reis, a tun plaisir,
Tanz cum tu vuels en fai venir;
Dune lur tant cum tu vuldras
Si fai al mielz que tu savras.'
Quant Vortigern out tut saisi
6600 E le tresor out recuilli,

Des Pis manda tant cum li plot,
E cil vindrent si cum il volt.
Vortigern mult les enura,
Bien les pout, bien les abevra;
A grant joie les faiseit vivre,
Assez suvent esteient ivre.
Tant lur ad Vortigern duné,
E tant ad chescun enuré,
N'i out un sul ki ne deïst,
Oiant ki oïr le vulsist,   6610
Que Vortigern ert plus curteis
E mult valeit mielz que li reis.
Bien fust dignes d'aveir l'enur
Que li reis aveit u grainur.
Vortigern s'en glorifiout
E plus e plus les enorout.
Un jur les out bien enbevrez, [4]
E tuz les out bien enivrez,
Puis vint entr'els sis salua,
Semblant d'ume triste mustra: 6620
'Mult vus ai, dist il, eü chiers,
E servi vus ai volentiers
E ferai si jo ai de quei.
Mais ceste terre est tute al rei.
Nen puis rien duner ne despendre [5]
Dunt mei n'estuece cunte rendre.
Poi ai rentes en ceste terre;
Aillurs m'estuet plus aler querre.
El rei servir ai mis m'entente
Si n'ai pas de lui tant de rente   6630
Dunt jo tienge enoreement
Quarante serganz sulement.
Si jo cunquer, si repairez,
Kar or m'en vois, a voz cungiez.
Ço peise mei que jo vus lais,
Mais povres sui si n'en puis mais.
Si vus oëz que jo ament,
A mei venez seürement.'
Vortigern a tant s'en turna,
Fals fu e fausement parla;   6640

---

[1] MS P reading—*nen*—restored.
[2] MS P reading—*remis*—restored.
[3] MS P reading—*seis*—restored.
[4] MS P reading—*enbevrez*—restored.
[5] MS P reading—*Nen*—restored.

Vortigern sends for the Picts

ravage your castles, so you must take steps to defend yourself and your land. Have your towers fortified and guarded. I am in great fear of traitors, so you must hand over your castles to those who well know how to protect them.' 'I have handed everything over to you,' said the king, 'so do what you like with it all. I shall not assume charge over you, for you know better than I do. Take total control of the land, so that none of it is seized or burned. I continue to be guided by you: do the best you can. Take my cities, my manors, my wealth and my jewels.'

6579 Vortigern, full of deceit, well knew how to conceal his greed. When he had taken possession of fortresses, wealth and jewels, he said: 'Sire, if it please you, I would advise and counsel you to send for the Pictish mercenaries,[1] from Scotland, to be your knights and to be with you at court, wherever our war should turn. You can easily send for the Picts whenever you need them. Through the Picts and their kin we shall know what state the foreigners are in: they will negotiate, and travel, between us and them.' 'Do what you wish,' replied the king, 'make as many as you like come; give them as much as you like and do the best you can.'

6599 When Vortigern had taken everything into his possession and annexed the jewels too, he summoned as many Picts as he pleased and they arrived just as he wished. Vortigern did them much honour: he gave them good food and drink and a merry life, so that very often they were drunk. So much did he give them, and so much honour did he pay to each one, that there was not one of them who would not say, in the hearing of anyone who cared to hear it, that Vortigern was more courteous and much better than the king, that he deserved to rule the king's realm—or a greater one. Vortigern gloried in this and gave them more and more favours.

6617 One day he had given them plenty to drink, and made them well and truly drunk. Then he came among them and greeted them, pretending to be sad. 'I have held you very dear,' he said, 'and willingly served you, and will do so, if I have the wherewithal. But this land is all the king's, and I can neither give nor spend anything without rendering account for it. I hold little property in this land; I must go and seek more elsewhere. I have striven to serve the king, and from him I do not have enough to maintain honourably a mere forty men at arms. If I win land, you should return, for now, by your leave, I shall depart. It grieves me to leave you, but I am poor and can do nothing else. If you hear that I'm doing better, be sure to come to me!'

6639 Then Vortigern turned away, false at heart and speaking falsehood. Those who had drunk well entirely believed the villain: whatever he falsely said, they took

---

[1] Wace specifically makes the Picts mercenaries (see para. 6767 too). In *HRB* chap. 95 a hundred of them are invited; *VV* gives no number.

Cil, ki aveient bien beü,
Unt le felun del tut creü,
Tut unt tenu a verité
Quanque cil dist par falseté.
Si distrent entr'els: 'Que ferum
Se nus cest bon seinur perdum?
Cest fol rei, cest moine ocium,
E Vortigern a rei levum.
Dignes est d'enur e d'empire
6650 E lui i devum nus eslire.
Cist fols moines de quei nus sert?
Pur quei l'avum nus tant suffert?'
A tant sunt en la chambre entré,
Le rei unt pris e decolé;
Le chief li unt del bu sevré,
A Vortigern l'unt presenté.
Crié li unt: 'As tu veü
Cument nus t'avum retenu?
Morz est li reis, or nus retien,
Pren la corune, reis devien!'
6660 Cil cunut le chief sun seinnur;
Semblant ad fait de grant dolur,
En sun curage s'esjoï;
Mais cuintes fu si s'en covri.
Pur sa felunie celer
Fist cels de Lundres assembler,
Les traïturs fist decoler,
N'en laissa un vif eschaper.
Assez i out tels ki creeient,
6670 Mais priveement le diseient,
Que ja cil le rei ne tuchassent,
Ne ja par mal nel reguardassent,
Ne en pensé ne lur entrast,
Se Vortigern nel comandast.
Cil ki les dous freres nurrirent,
Quant il la mort le rei oïrent,
Creinstrent que ki le rei ocist
Altretel des freres feïst;
Pur la crieme de Vortiger
6680 Unt pris Aurele e pris Uther;

En la menur Bretaine alerent,
Al rei Budiz les comanderent.
Bel les reçut li reis Budiz,
Lur parenz ert sis ad nurriz;
A grant enur les conrea
E richement les aduba.
    Vortigern out les fermetez
E lé chastels e les citez;
Rei se fist, mult fu orguillus.
Mais de dous choses ert ainsus,   6690
De l'une part le guereioent
Li Pic, ki mult le maneçoent;
Lur parenz vuleient vengier
Cui il ot fait les chiés trenchier.
De l'altre part mult le grevout
Que tute gent li destinout
Que li dui frere armes aveient,
E a bref terme revendreient,
E li barun les recevreient
E lur feus d'els recunustreient;   6700
Constant, lur frere, vengereient,
Kar gent merveilluse amerreient;
Assez ert ki diseit nuveles.
Entretant vindrent treis naceles,
A Sanwiz un port arriverent, [1]
Ki genz estranges aporterent
Od bels viaires, od gent cors;
Lur sire fu Henguist, et Hors,
Dui frere de grant estature
E d'une estrange parleüre.   6710
A Vortigern, ki a cel jur
Ert a Cantorbire a sujur,
Fu tost la nuvele cuntee
Que d'une gent d'altre contree
Esteient illuec treis navees
Assembleement arivees.
Li reis ruva, ki que il fussent,
Que bone pais e trive eüssent,
E tut en pais a lui parlassent
E tut en pais s'en returnassent.   6720

---

[1] MS P reading of line restored.

The Picts kill Constant and make Vortigern king

as complete truth. Amongst themselves, they said: 'What shall we do if we lose this good lord? Let's kill this foolish king, this monk, and raise Vortigern to be king. He deserves the domain and its rule, and we should elect him to it. What use is this foolish monk to us? Why have we suffered him so long?' Then they entered the king's chamber, seized him and cut off his head. Having severed the head from the trunk, they presented it to Vortigern, shouting: 'Look how we have supported you! The king is dead: now keep us with you, take the crown, become king!' He recognised the head of his lord, and pretended to be overcome with grief. In his heart he rejoiced, but he was cunning and concealed it. In order to hide his wickedness, he called an assembly of Londoners and had the traitors beheaded, not leaving one of them alive. There were many who believed (but said so only in private) that these men would never have touched the king, nor taken a hostile attitude to him, nor would the thought have ever entered their heads, had Vortigern not ordered it of them.

6675   Those looking after the two brothers feared, when they heard of the king's death, that whoever killed the king would do the same to them. For fear of Vortigern they took Aurelius and Uther and went to Brittany, entrusting them to king Budiz,[1] who received them handsomely. He was their relative and looked after them: he equipped them honourably and knighted them with splendour.

6687   Vortigern possessed strongholds, castles and cities. He made himself king and was very arrogant. But two things worried him. On the one hand, the Picts made war on him, with many threats: they wished to avenge their kin, whom he had beheaded. On the other hand, he was disturbed by the news that everyone brought him, that the two brothers were armed and would soon return; the barons would receive them and do them homage for their domains. They would avenge Constant, their brother, because with them they would bring a great host. There were many who gave such news. Meanwhile, three little boats appeared, arriving at Sandwich, a port, and bringing strangers with handsome faces and fine bodies.[2] Their lords were Hengist and Horsa, two brothers of great height and foreign speech. The news was quickly brought to Vortigern, who that day was staying at Canterbury, that three ships belonging to people from another land had together arrived there. The king commanded that, whoever they were, they should receive pledges of peace and safety, and should peacefully speak to him and peacefully return. They heard his command and came without fear.

---

[1] *HRB* chap. 96: *Budicius*; *VV*: *Buditius*.
[2] Gildas, *De Excidio*, chap. 23 says the '*superbus tyrannus*', with his council, invites the Saxons as 'federates' to Britain to help fight 'the peoples of the north', and they arrive in three *cyula* or warships. Bede (I, chap. 14–15) dates this to the year 449, calling the invaders 'Angles or Saxons' and giving their landing-place as Thanet. *HB* (chap. 31) repeats Thanet ('in British, "Ruoihm"') but omits Vortigern's invitation. See Thompson, 'Gildas', pp. 217–18, and Dumville, 'Chronology of *De Excidio*' p. 83.

Cil oïrent le mandement
Sin alerent seürement.
Li reis esguarda les dous freres
As cors bien faiz, as faces cleres,
Ki plus grant erent e plus bel
Que tuit li altre juvencel;
'De quel terre, dist il, venez?
U fustes nez, e que querez?'
Henguist, ki maire e ainz né fu,
6730 Pur tuz ensemble ad respundu:
'De Saixone, dist il, venum,
La fumes nez e la manum.
Se tu vels oïr l'achaisun
Que nus par ceste mer querum,
Jo t'en dirai la verité,
Si nus avum ta seürté.'
'Di, dist li reis, ta raisun tute,
Ja mar de nus i avras dute.'
'Bons reis, dist Henguist, gentil sire,
6740 Ne sai si unches l'oïs dire,
Nostre terre est de gent naïve
Plus abundable e plenteïve
Que nule altre que vus sachiez
Ne dunt vus ja parler oiez.
Noz genz merveilles fructifient
E li enfant trop multiplient;
Trop i ad femes e trop humes,
Ço nus puet peser ki ci sumes.
Quant nostre gent est tant creüe
6750 Que la terre en est trop vestue,
Li prince ki les terres sunt
Tuz les juenvles assembler funt
Qui de quinze anz sunt u de plus,
Si come custume est e us;
Tut li meillur e li plus fort [1]
Sunt mis fors del païs par sort
Si vunt par altres regiuns
Querre terres e mansiuns,
Pur la multitudine espartir
6760 Que la terre ne puet suffrir;

Kar enfanz plus espés i naissent
Que ces bestes qui as chans paissent.
Par la sort ki sur nus chaï
Avum nostre païs guerpi;
Mercurius nus guverna,
Uns Deus ki nus ad conduit ça'.
Quant li reis li oï numer
Le Deu qu'il out a guverner,
Demanda li quel Deu aveient
E en quel Deu sa gent creeient.   6770
'Nus avum, dist il, plusurs Deus
A cui nus devum faire alteus,
Ço est, Febus e Saturnus,
Jupiter e Mercurius.
Altres Deus avum nus plusurs
Sulunc la siecte as anceisurs,
Mais sur tuz altres enorum
Maïsmement Mercurium,
Ki en nostre language ad nun
Woden, par grant religiun.   6780
Nostre anceisur tant l'enorerent
Que le quart jur li cunsacrerent;
Pur Woden, lur Deu qu'il amerent,
Wodesdai le quart jur numerent
E encore ad nun Wodesdai. [2]
Estre cest Deu que dit vus ai
Cultivum nus deuuesse Free,
Ki par tut est mult enuree.
Li ancien, pur faire enur,
Li unt sacré le siste jur   6790
Si l'unt, par grant auctorité,
De Frea Freesdai numé.'
'Malement, dist li reis, creez,
E malvais Dampnedeus avez;
Ço peise mei, e nequedent
Bel m'est de vostre avenement.
Vaillanz humes e pruz semblez,
E, si vus servir me vulez,
Tuz ensemble vus retendrai
E riches humes vus ferai.   6800

---

[1] MS P reading—*tut*—restored.

[2] MS P reading—*Wodesdai*—in ll. 6784–5 is restored.

Arrival of Hengist and Horsa

6723 The king observed the two brothers, with their shapely bodies and fine faces, who were taller and more handsome than all other young men. 'From which land do you come?' he said. 'Where were you born, and what do you seek?' Hengist, the elder and first-born, replied for them all. 'We come from Saxony,'[1] he said, 'there were we born, and dwell. If you want to hear the reason for our quest over the sea, I will tell you the truth, if we have your guarantee of safety.' 'Give us all your explanation,' said the king, 'you need not fear us.' 'Good king, noble lord,' said Hengist, 'I do not know if you ever heard tell, but our land is more plentifully and abundantly supplied with native inhabitants than any other you know or have heard about. Our people are exceedingly fertile and there are too many children: there are too many men, too many women, and this troubles those you see here. When our people grow so many that the land is too full of them, the prince owning the domain, as is the usage and custom, makes all the young men of fifteen or over assemble. All the strongest and best are sent out of the land, by lot, and go to other realms, looking for lands and houses, to disperse the great numbers which the land cannot bear, for children are born thicker and faster than the beasts at pasture in the fields. Through the lot which fell on us, we have left our country.[2] We were guided by Mercury, a god who led us here.'

6767 When the king heard him name the god who guided him, he asked him which god they had and in which god their people believed. 'We have several gods,' he said, 'to whom we should make altars: they are Phoebus, Saturn, Jupiter and Mercury. We have many other gods, following the religion of our ancestors, but above all others we principally honour Mercury, who in our language, with great piety, is called Woden. Our ancestors honoured him so much that they consecrated the fourth day to him: on account of Woden, their god whom they loved, they called the fourth day 'Wednesday',[3] and so it is still called. Besides this god I've told you of, we worship the goddess Frea, greatly honoured by all. To pay tribute to her, our forbears consecrated the sixth day to her and, with great reverence, called it Friday, after Frea.' 'You have a wicked faith and a wicked god,' said the king. 'It gives me pain; yet I am glad of your coming. You seem strong and courageous men and, if you wish to serve me, I shall retain you all and make you rich. Scottish scoundrels make war on me, burning my lands and pillaging my

---

[1] *HRB* chap. 98 adds: 'one of the provinces of Germany.'

[2] In *HRB* chap. 98 (Vulgate version only) Hengist

and Horsa give their names and lineage.

[3] *HRB* chap. 98: *Wonnesdei*; *VV*: *Wodnesdai*.

Larrun d'Escoce me guereient,
Ma terre ardent, mes viles preient,
Si vuldreie, si Deu plaiseit,
Kar a grant pru me turnereit,
Les Pis destrure e les Escoz
Par Deu aïe e par les voz;
Kar de la vienent e la fuient
Li Pic ki mes terres destruient.[1]
Par vus m'en vuldreie vengier,
6810   U tuz ocire u exillier.
Vus avrez bien voz livreisuns
E voz soldees e voz duns.'
Issi sunt li Saisne remés,
E al sec unt traites lur nés;
Sempres fu la curt replenie
De mult gente bachelerie.
      Ne demura pas lungement,
Li Pic mult efforcieement
En la terre le rei entrerent,
6820   Arstrent, destruistrent e roberent.
Quant le Humbre durent passer,
Li reis, ki en oï parler,
Ala encuntre od ses baruns,
Od les Saisnes, od les Bretuns.
Dunc veïssiez bataille dure,
Mult i out grant descunfiture.
Li Pic nes duterent nient,
Ki soleient veintre suvent;
Bien se tindrent premierement
6830   E ferirent hardiement,
A merveille se combatirent
E a merveille les suffrirent;
Pur ço que veintre les soleient
Lur custome tenir vuleient.
Mais lur usage unt dunc perdu
E li Saisne unt le champ vencu.
Par els e par lur adjutorie
En ot Wortigern la victorie.
Rendues lur ad lur soldees
6840   E lur livreisuns amendees.

A Enguist duna bons maneirs
En Lindesie, e granz aveirs.
Issi unt lungement esté
E lur amur ad bien duré.
Henguist vit qu'il ert necessaries
A furnir al rei ses afaires;
D'avancier sei s'entremeteit,
Cume chescuns fere devreit.
Bien sout al rei aler entur
A guise de losengeür.   6850
Un jur trova le rei haitied
Si l'ad a cunseil araisnied:
'Tu m'as, dist il, mult enoré
E assez m'as del tuen duné,
E je te serf e servirai;
Se bien l'ai fait, mielz le ferai.
Mais, puis que jo en ta curt fui,
E puis que jo ta gent cunui,
Ai jo assez aparceü,
Assez oï, assez veü,   6860
Que tu nen as barun ki t'aint.
Chescuns te het, chescuns se plaint;
Ne sai de quels enfanz parolent
Ki de ta gent l'amur te tolent.
Lur seinnur sunt cil natural,
Fiz a un lur seinnur leial;
Des qu'a poi d'ultre mer vendrunt
E ceste terre te toldrunt.
Tuit li hume mal te terminent,
Mal te vuelent, mal te destinent.   6870
Mult te heent, mult te manacent,
Mal te querent, mal te purchacent.
Pensé me sui de tei aider,
Si vuil en ma terre enveier
Pur ma feme e pur mes enfanz,
E pur altres apartenanz.
Plus seüs en seras de mei
E jo en servirai mielz tei.
Ne truveras mais qui par guerre
Te retoille plein pié de terre.   6880

---

[1]   MS P reading—*mes terres*—restored.

The Saxons help Vortigern against the Picts

towns. Please God, (because it would be greatly to my advantage), I would like to destroy the Picts and the Scots with God's help and yours. For the Picts who ruin my realm come from that land, and flee back to it again. Through your help I would like to take revenge, either killing or exiling them all. You will of course get your rations, wages and gifts.' So the Saxons stayed and hauled their boats to dry land; and before long the court was full of fine young men.

6817   Not long afterwards, the Picts entered the king's land in great strength, burning, robbing and destroying. When they were about to cross the Humber, the king, hearing of it, went to meet them with his barons, with Saxons and Britons. Then you might have seen a harsh battle and a great defeat. The Picts, accustomed to frequent victories, were not in the least afraid of them; at first they held their ground well and struck boldly, fighting prodigiously, and suffering prodigiously. Because they were used to defeating them, they wanted to keep to their usual habits. But then they lost what was habitual to them and the Saxons won the field. Through them and their help Vortigern was victorious. He gave them their wages and improved their rations. To Hengist he gave good manors in Lindsey and great possessions. So they remained for a long while and their friendship prospered.

6845   Hengist saw that he was needed to execute the king's affairs. He began to advance himself, as everyone should try and do. He well knew how to get round the king in a lying fashion. One day he found the king in a good mood and gave him some advice. 'You have greatly honoured me,' he said, 'and made me many gifts; and I serve you and shall continue to do so: if I have done well, I shall do better. But since I have been in your court, and got to know your people, I have often observed, often heard and often seen, that you have no baron who loves you. Everyone hates you, everyone complains. I don't know who these children are that they speak of, who steal from your people the love due to you. They are their rightful lords, sons of a lawful king of theirs. Soon they will come from overseas and take this land from you. All your men wish you harm: they wish you ill, they wish you a bad end. They greatly hate and greatly threaten you; they seek and strive for your downfall. I have thought of how to help you: I want to send to my country for my wife and children and other kin. You will be more sure of me, and I will serve you better. No longer will you find anyone to deprive you, in warfare,

Ja t'ai jo grant pose servi [1]
Si ai pur tei maint enemi;
Ne puis par nuit estre asseür
Fors de chastel ne fors de mur.
Pur ço, sire, si te plaiseit,
Tun pris e tun grant pru sereit
Que tu me dunasses cité
U chastelet u fermeté
U jo me peüsse gesir
6890 E asseür par nuit dormir.
Ti enemi m'en dutereient [2]
E a mesfaire t'en larreient.' [3]
'Pur ta gent, dist li reis, enveie;
Bel les receif, bel les conreie,
E jo te durrai bien de quei.
Mais tu n'iés pas de nostre lei,
Paiens es e nus cristïen,
Si nel tendreit l'um mie a bien
Que jo te dunasse recet;
6900 D'altre chose aveir t'entremet.'
'Sire, dist Henguist, tu me lai
A un des maneirs que jo ai
Un recest clore e enforcier [4]
En tant de terre, plus n'en quier, [5]
Cum jo purrai un quir estendre
E od le quir entur purprendre.
Un quir de tor tant sulement,
Si gerrai plus seürement.'
Wortigern li ad graanté,
6910 E Henguist l'en ad mercié;
Sun messagier apareilla
E pur ses parenz enveia.
Un quir de tor prist, sil fendi,
Une cureie en estendi
Dunt un grant tertre avirona.
Bons uvriers quist, chastel ferma;
Cest nun Wancastre li ad mis
En language de sun païs.
Wancastre sun nun del quir prent
6920 Sil puet l'um numer altrement

Chastel de cureie en rumanz,
Kaër Carreï en bretanz,
Pur ço que il fu mesurez
Od la curreie e compassez. [6]
    Quant Wancastre fu tut fermez,
De cels que Henguist ot mandez
Vindrent dis e oit nés chargiees
De chevaliers e de maisnees.
Sa fille li unt amenee
Ki n'ert pas encor mariee;   6930
Ronwen ot nun, si ert pulcele,
A grant merveille ert gente e bele.
A un jur qu'il out esguardé,
Ad Henguist le rei envié
A venir od lui herbergier,
E deduire e beivre e mangier,
E veer sa nuvele gent
E sun nuvel herbergement.
Li reis vint escharriement
Ki volt estre priveement.   6940
Le chastel vit, l'ovre esguarda,
Mult fu bien faiz, mult le loa.
Les chevaliers nuvel venuz
Ad a soldees retenuz.
Le jur mangerent, e tant burent
Tut li plusur, que ivre furent. [7]
Dunc est fors de la chambre eissue
Ronwen, mult bele, e bien vestue;
Pleine cupe de vin porta.
Devant le rei s'agenuilla,   6950
Mult humlement li enclina
E a sa lei le salua:
'Laverd King, Wesseil!' tant li dist; [8]
Li reis demanda e enquist,
Ki le language ne saveit,
Que la meschine li diseit.
Keredic respundi premiers,
Brez ert, si ert bons latimiers,
Ço fu li premiers des Bretuns
Ki sout le language as Saissuns: 6960

---

[1] MS P's order of line restored.
[2] MS P reading—*m'en*—restored.
[3] MS J adds: *Par moi avroies grant ayie/ Et par la moie compaignie/ Que jo feroie ça venir/ Se tu les voloies retenir.*
[4] MS P reading—*recest*—restored.
[5] MS P reading—*n'en*—restored.
[6] MS PHKRN have four more lines here—*Premierement ot nun Wancastre/ Or l'apelent plusurs Lancastre/ Si ne sevent pas l'achaisun/ Dunt Wancastre ot primes cest nun*—which Arnold (I, p. xliv) omitted as interpolation on the

grounds that it was very unlikely Wace would have thought Wancaster was Lancaster. At l. 13425 (fol. 153 r.) the scribe of MS P shows that he knew Wancastre was in Lindsey; it is not clear from the 'interpolated' lines here if he is reporting the belief of others rather than his own knowledge.

[7] MS P reading—*tut*—restored.
[8] MS P reading—*Wesseil*—restored here and in ll. 6965 and 6977.

Hengist sends for his kin

of a single foot of land. I've already served you a long while and incurred many enemies on your account; I can't rest secure at night without a castle, without walls. Therefore, sire, if it please you, it would bring you profit and renown to give me a city, fort or stronghold where I may lie and sleep safely at night. Your enemies would fear me and stop harming you.'

6893   'Send for your people,' said the king, 'receive and equip them handsomely, and I will give you the means. But you are not of our faith, you are pagan and we are Christian: if I gave you a stronghold, it would not find favour. Consider having something else.' 'Sire,' said Hengist, 'let me, at one of the manors I possess, enclose and fortify a stronghold in as much land (I ask no more) as I can stretch out a hide on and cover with the hide round about. Only a bull's hide—and I shall lie more securely.' Vortigern granted it him, and Hengist thanked him. He equipped his messenger and sent for his kin. He took a bull's hide and cut it so as to draw out a thong from it, which surrounded a great hill. He sought out good workmen and constructed a castle, giving it the name of Thongcaster in his land's tongue. Thongcaster takes its name from the hide, and one can otherwise call it 'chastel de cureie' in French and 'Kaër Carreï' in the British language, because it was measured and marked out with the thong.[1] It was first called Thwangcaster; now many call it Lancaster. They don't know the reason for it first acquiring this name.

6925   When Thongcaster was completed, eighteen ships arrived, full of those Hengist had summoned, of knights and followers. They brought him his unmarried daughter: she was called Ronwen,[2] a young girl extraordinarily fine and beautiful. On a day he had selected, Hengist invited the king to stay with him, to enjoy himself eating and drinking and to see his new followers and his new lodgings. The king came on his own, wishing to be private. He saw the castle and observed the building; it was very well done and he gave it much praise. He retained the newly arrived knights in his pay. That day they ate, and drank so much that most of them were drunk. Then out of the chamber came Ronwen, very beautiful and well dressed. She carried a full cup of wine, knelt down before the king, bowed very humbly to him, and according to her custom greeted him. 'Lord King, Wassail!' she said.[3] The king, not knowing the language the girl spoke to him, enquired what she meant. Keredic was the first to reply, a good linguist, the first of

---

[1] *Une cureie* = a thong. *HRB* chap. 99: *Thancastre* and *Castrum Corrigie. Thongcaster/Thwongchestre/ Thwangcestre* was the medieval name for Caistor in Lincs. See Arnold II, p. 805.

[2] *HRB* is the first to name her, as *Renwein*, chap. 100; *VV: Ronwen*.

[3] A Saxon salutation when drinking, literally meaning 'be in good health'. Wace's text keeps it in Middle English, as does *HRB*, chap. 100: '*Lauerd king, waesseil!*' See Wace, *Roman de Rou* I,

ll. 7331–34, and also Gaimar's *Estoire des Engleis*, ll. 3803–08, for other mentions of *weseil, drinkheil* and the custom of exchanging kisses. The story of Vortigern falling in love with Hengist's daughter is in *HB*, chap. 37, but *HRB* has added to it the details of *wassail* and *drinchail*; on the other hand, *HRB* has omitted the name of Vortigern's interpreter, Ceretic, in *HB*, while Wace has preserved it.

'Ronwen, dist il, t'a salué,
E seinnur rei t'ad apelé.
Custume est, sire, en lur païs,
Quant ami beivent entre amis,
Que cil dit Wesseil qui deit beivre
E Drincheheil kil deit receivre; [1]
Dunc beit cil tut u la meitied.
E pur joie e pur amistied
Al hanap receivre e baillier
6970 Est custume d'entrebaisier.'
Li reis, si cum cil li aprist,
Dist 'Drincheheil!' e si sorrist.
Ronwen but e puis li bailla,
E en baillant, le rei baisa. [2]
Par cele gent premierement
Prist l'un us e cumencement
De dire en cel païs 'Wesseil'
E de respundre 'Drincheheil',
E de beivre plein u demi
6980 E d'entrebaiser lui e li. [3]
La meschine ot le cors mult gent,
E de vis fu bele forment;
Bele fu mult e avenant,
De bele groisse e de bel grant;
Devant lu rei fu, desfublee,
Qui merveilles l'ad esgardee.
Tuz fu haitiez, bien ot beü,
Grant talent ad de li eü.
Tant l'ad Diables timoné,
6990 Ki maint home ad a mal turné,
D'amur e de rage l'esprist
De prendre la fille Henguist.
Deus, quel hunte! Deus, quel pecchié!
Tant l'ad Deiables desveied, [4]
Ne l'ad pas pur ço refusee
Que paene ert, de paiens nee.
Sempres l'ad a Henguist rovee,
E Henguist li ad graantee,
Mais sun cunseil en ot ainz pris
7000 A sun frere e a ses amis.

Cil unt cel plai bien cuveitied
Si unt loé e cunseillied
Que il li dunt delivrement
Si demant en duaire Kent.
Cil li duna, n'en volt el faire, [5]
Si demanda Kent en duaire.
Li reis cuveita la meschine,
Amee l'out sin fist reïne,
Paiene esteit sin fist s'uxor
A la custume paienor;   7010
Prestre n'i fist beneïçun,
Messe n'i ot, ne ureisun,
Le jur l'ama si l'out le seir
E a Henguist fist Kent aveir.
Cil saisi Kent sil tint e out;
Unches Gerangon mot n'en sout,
Ki tenu l'out par erité
Dessi que cil l'en ad geté.
    Li reis creï plus les paiens
E ama que les crestïens,   7020
E li crestïen haïrent
E sun cunseil e lui guerpirent;
Neïs si fil l'unt enhaï
E pur les paiens relinqui.
Feme aveit eü espusee,
Mais morte ert ja e trespassee;
Treis fiz aveit de li eü
Ki ja erent tut parcreü:
Li premiers ot nun Vortimer,
E puis Paschent e Katiger. [6]   7030
'Sire, ço dist Henguist al rei,
Tu es alques haï pur mei
E jo resui pur tei haïz.
Jo sui tis peres, tu mis fiz,
Ki ma fille preïs e as,
La tue merci ki la ruvas. [7]
Jo te dei par dreit cunseillier
E tu me deiz creire e aider.
Se tu vuels asseür regner
E cels ki te heent grever,   7040

---

[1] MS P reading—*kil*—restored.
[2] MS J adds: *Li rois but aprés la mescine/ Et puis devint dame et roine/ Par tel eur le roi baisa/ Que puis a feme l'espousa.*
[3] MS J adds: *La coustume fu commencie/ Ensi com jou vous ai noncie/ Encor le funt il ce m'est vis/ As hautes festes el païs.*
[4] MS P reading—*Deiables*—restored.
[5] MS P reading—*n'en*—restored.
[6] MS J adds: *Hai l'ont tout li baron/ De la tere tout environ/ Et li parent et li cousin/ Et pus en vint a male fin/ Il en mourut a deshonnour/ Et li paien tout li pluisour.*
[7] MS P reading—*La*—restored.

Vortigern marries Ronwen

the British to know the Saxon tongue. 'Ronwen,' he said, 'has greeted you and called you Lord King. The custom, sire, in her country, when friends drink together, is that the one who is to drink says "Wassail", and the one who is to receive it next says "Drinchail". Then he drinks it all, or half of it. And out of joy and friendship at offering and accepting the cup, it is the custom to exchange kisses.' The king, as soon as he learnt this, said 'Drinchail!' and smiled at her. Ronwen drank and then gave the cup to him, and as she gave it, kissed the king. It was through these people that the custom first began to say 'Wassail' in this land and to reply 'Drinchail', to drink the whole, or the half, and to exchange kisses.

6981 The girl had a fine body and a very beautiful face; she was fair and comely, handsome in shape and size. Uncloaked, she stood before the king, who could not keep his eyes off her. He was in good spirits, he had drunk well, and he greatly desired her. The Devil enticed him so much, who has turned so many men to evil, that he inflamed him with love and desire to take Hengist's daughter. God, what shame! God, what sin! The Devil led him so far astray, he would not refuse to marry her though she was a heathen, born of heathens. At once he asked Hengist for her, and Hengist accorded her, but first he took counsel with his brother and his friends. They keenly desired this affair and advised and counselled that he should quickly hand her over and ask for Kent as dower. He gave her to the king, not wanting to do otherwise, and asked for the dower of Kent. The king desired the girl, he loved her and made her queen. She was heathen and he made her his wife in the heathen fashion: no priest gave a blessing, there was neither mass nor prayer, he fell in love with her in the morning and had her in the evening, and made Kent over to Hengist. He seized Kent, held it and owned it: Gerangon,[1] whose inheritance it was, never knew a word about it until he was driven out.

7019 The king loved and trusted the heathen more than the Christians, and the Christians hated him for it, and forsook him and his council. Even his sons took to hating him and left him because of the heathen. He had had a wife, but she was dead and gone; he had had three sons from her, who were now all full-grown. The eldest was called Vortimer, the others Paschent and Katiger. 'Sire,' said Hengist to the king, 'you are somewhat hated on my account, and I am hated in turn because of you. I am your father, you my son, who took, and has, my daughter: I thank you for asking for her. By rights I should advise you, and you should trust and help me. If you wish to reign securely, and distress those who hate you, send for my son Octa and his cousin Ebissa, two excellent fighters and marvellous

---

[1] *HRB* chap. 100: *Gorangonus.*

Enveie pur mun fiz Octa
E pur sun cusin Ebissa,
Dous merveillus guerreeürs
E merveillus combateürs;
Vers Escoce lur dune terre
Kar de la vient tuz tens ta guerre.
D'averse gent te guarderunt
Que ja del tuen rien ne prendrunt;
Si porras tut tun eé mais
7050 De ça le Humbre vivre en pais.'
'Fai, dist li reis, que tu vuldras.
Mande tuz cels que buens savras.'
E Henguist sempres enveia,
Sun fiz e sun nevu manda;
E cil vindrent od treis cenz nés.
N'i ad buen chevalier remés
Ki pur aveir vulsist servir,
Qu'il n'aient fait od els venir.
Emprés vindrent altres suvent
7060 De jur en jur menuement
Od quatre nés, od cinc, od sies,
Od set, od uit, od nof, od dies.
Tost furent si paien munté,
As crestïens entremeslé,
Avisunques conuisseit l'un
Ki ert crestïen e ki nun.
As Bretuns ad mult ennuied
Si unt al rei dist e preied [1]
Que cele estrange gent ne creie
7070 Kar a veüe se desleie;
Trop ad de cels paiens atrait,
Vilanie est, grant hunte fait,
Departe les, cument que seit,
Ou tut u le plus en enveit.
Li reis lu dit que nu fera,
Bien li servent, mandez les a.
Dunc se sunt Bretun assemblé,
A Lundres sunt ensemble alé;
Vortimer unt a rei levé,
7080 L'un des treis fiz lu rei, l'ainz né.

Cil ad les Saisnes deffiez
E des citez les ad chaciez. [2]
Li reis, pur amur sa muillier,
Se tint a els, nes vult laissier,
E li fiz suvent les chaça
E suvent les desbareta;
Pruz fu e si out bone aïe.
Ço fu guerre bien aatie
De Vortimer e des Bretuns
Cuntre sun pere e les Saissuns.   7090
Par quatre feiz se combati
E par quatre feiz les venqui.
Dedesur l'eue de Derwent [3]
Se combati premierement;
Dejuste Epiford, a un gué,
Ad puis ensemble od els justé.
La s'entrevindrent cors a cors
Katiger fiz lu rei, e Hors;
Chescuns ad l'altre a mort nafré
Cume chescuns out desirré.   7100
En Kent sur mer, a un rivage,
Juste lur nés, a un passage,
Fu la tierce bataille grant,
Quant cil furent venu fuiant
D'ultre le Humbre jesqu'en Kent;
La ot grant desbaratement.
Puis s'en fuïrent en Thanet,
Dedenz la mer, en un illet.
Li Bretun la les assailleient
E tute jur les abateient   7110
Od saietes e od quarrels
Des naceles e des batels.
De l'une part les ocieient,
De l'altre part de faim mureient. [4]
Quant cil virent qu'il ne guarreient
Se la terre ne guerpisseient,
Tramis unt al rei Vortiger,
Qu'il preit a sun fiz Vortimer
Qu'aler les en laist quitement
Senz faire plus d'empeirement.   7120

---

[1] MS P reading—*dist*—restored.
[2] MS P reading—*chaciez*—restored.
[3] MS P reading—*Dedesur… Derwent*—restored.
[4] MS J adds: *La furent Saison enanglé/ Pur ce furent*

Englois clamé/ Issi li Breton les clamerent/ Quant en Tanet les enanglerent. This is spurious etymology, based on *enangler* = to corner.

Vortimer and the British defeat the Saxons

warriors. Give them land near Scotland,[1] for your battles always come from there. They will protect you from hostile people so that nothing of yours will ever be taken. For all the rest of your life, you can live in peace this side of the Humber.' 'Do what you like,' said the king, 'summon all those you know to be good.' And Hengist at once sent a message summoning his son and his nephew, and they arrived with three hundred ships.[2] There was not one good knight left, who wished to serve for wealth, whom they did not make accompany them. Then others often came, little by little, day by day, with four ships, with five, with six, with seven, with eight, with nine, with ten. So quickly did the heathen increase, intermingling with the Christians, that one could scarcely tell who were Christian and who were not. It greatly annoyed the Britons, and they spoke to the king, begging him not to trust these foreigners, for they were openly disloyal. He had collected too many of these heathen; it was wicked, and a great scandal. He should disband them, in whatever manner, and send all or most of them away. The king told them he would do no such thing: they served him well, and he had summoned them. Then the Britons assembled, and went to London together. They made Vortimer king, the eldest of Vortigern's three sons. He defied the Saxons and threw them out of the cities.

7083 The king, out of love for his wife, stood by the Saxons and did not want to forsake them. And his son kept harrying and routing them; he was valiant, and well supported. The war fought by Vortimer and the British against his father and the Saxons was savage. He attacked them four times, and four times defeated them. First he fought by Derwent Water, next at a ford near Epiford.[3] There Katiger, the king's son, and Horsa came to blows, and each mortally wounded the other, as each desired. The third great battle was in Kent, by the sea-shore next to their ships, at a ford, when the Saxons had fled across the Humber into Kent: a great rout took place there. Then they fled into Thanet, an island in the sea. There the British attacked them and every day felled them with arrows and bolts from boats and ships. On the one hand they killed them, on the other hand starved them to death. When they saw that they would not escape unless they left the country, they sent a message to king Vortigern, to ask his son Vortimer to let them go scot-free, without further injury. The king was continually with them

---

[1] *HRB* chap. 101 is more specific: the lands 'near to the Wall between Deira and Scotland'.

[2] *HRB* chap. 101 adds that a man called Cherdich came too.

[3] *HB* chap. 44 mentions four battles fought by Vortimer [*Guorthemir*]: the first is on the river Darenth [*Derguentid*], the second at '*Episford, in nostra autem lingua Rithergabail*', which Morris translates 'in our language Rhyd yrafael'. The *ASC* mentions a battle between Vortigern and Hengist and Horsa, in which Horsa is killed but Hengist 'succeeds to the kingdom' at Aylesford [Ægelesthrep] in 455, identified by Swanton as 'the ford on the river Medway in mid-Kent' (pp. 12–13). See also *HA* II, chap. 3.

Li reis tuz tens od eus esteit
Que nule feiz n'en departeit.
Endementres que il alout
E cele trive purchaçout,
Saisne sunt en lur nés entré,
Fort unt nagied e fort siglé,
Al plus qu'il pourent s'esluinerent,
Lur fiz e lur femes laisserent;
A grant poür s'en eschaperent,
7130 En lur cuntrees s'en ralerent.
    Quant cil s'en furent eschapé,
Bretun furent asseüré,
E Vortimer a tuz rendi
Ço que chescuns par els perdi.
Pur les iglises redrecier
E pur la lei Deu anuntier
Ki malement esteit tenue,
Pur Henguist ki l'out corumpue,
Vint en Bretaine sainz Germainz,
7140 Si l'i enveia sainz Romainz,
Ki de l'apostolieté
De Rome aveit la poësté.
Sainz Lous de Treies vint od lui,
Evesque furent buen andui,
Li uns d'Aucerre, li altre de Troies,[1]
D'aler a Deu sourent les veies.
Par els fu la lei recuvree
E la gent a fei returnee,
Par els vint maint huem a salu.
7150 Maint miracle, mainte vertu
Fist Deus pur els dous e mustra;
Tute Engleterre en amenda.
Quant la lei Deu fu restablie
E Bretaine reconvertie,
Oez cum faite deablie:
Par grant haenge e par envie
Ronwen, cume male marastre,
Fist envenimer sun fillastre
Vortimer, que ele haeit,
7160 Pur Henguist, que chacié aveit.

Quant Vortimer sout qu'il murreit,[2]
Ne que par mire ne guarreit,
Tuz ses baruns ad apelez
Si lur ad ses tresors livrez
Dunt il aveit mult aüné.
Oiez que il lur ad ruvé:
'Chevaliers, dist il, retenez,
Livreisuns e duns lur dunez,
Vostre terre e vus maintenez
E des Saisnes vus defendez   7170
Que ja sur vus nes atraiez.
Mun travail e les vos vengiez.
Faites, pur els espouenter,
Mun cors el rivage enterrer,
E tel sepulture lever
Que lungement pusse durer[3]
E ki d'alques luin seit veüe
Sur la mer, devers lur venue.
Ja la u il mun cors savrunt
Ne vif ne mort ne turnerunt.'   7180
Li gentil ber issi parla,
Issi morut, issi fina.
A Lundres fu le cors portez
E a Lundres fu enterrez;
N'unt mie le cors enterré
La u il lur out comandé.
    Dunc refu faiz Vortiger reis
Si cum il ot esté anceis.
Pur sa feme, ki l'en preia,
Pur Henguist, sun suegre, enveia;   7190
Ço li manda qu'il repairast,
Mais petit de gent amenast
Que li Bretun ne s'effreassent
Ne de richief se remedlassent.
Vortimer, sis fiz, esteit morz,
N'ert nul mestier de grant efforz.
Henguist repaira volentiers,
Mais il mena treis cens millers
D'umes armez, Bretuns cremeit,
Si fereit el que fait n'aveit.   7200

---

[1] MS P's wording of line restored.
[2] MS P reading—*murreit*—restored.

[3] MS P reading—*pusse*—restored.

Ronwen poisons Vortimer

and never left them. While he went to obtain this truce, the Saxons entered their ships and, rowing and sailing furiously, departed as fast as they could, leaving behind their sons and their wives. They escaped in great fear and returned to their own land.

7131 When they had escaped, the British were reassured, and Vortimer restored to everyone what they had lost through the Saxons. To rebuild the churches and to proclaim God's law, which was poorly observed because Hengist had corrupted it, St Germain came to Britain, sent there by St Romain, who held the apostolic power in Rome. St Lupus of Troyes came with him, both good bishops, one from Auxerre, the other from Troyes, who knew the paths to God.[1] Through them religion was restored and the people returned to the faith; through them many a man came to salvation. God made and revealed many a miracle, many a wonder, for these two; all England was the better for it.

7153 When God's law was re-established and Britain again converted, hear what devilry was perpetrated. Through great hate and envy Ronwen, like a wicked stepmother, had her stepson Vortimer, whom she hated, poisoned, because of Hengist whom he had exiled. When Vortimer knew he was dying and could not be healed by any doctor, he called all his barons together and gave them the many treasures he had collected. Listen to what he asked them. 'Retain knights,' he said, 'give them gifts and allowances, protect your land and yourselves and defend yourselves against the Saxons so that you never bring them back. Avenge your suffering and mine. To terrify them, have my body buried on the shore and such a tomb raised as may last a long while and be seen from a great distance at sea, in their direction. Neither dead nor alive will they return where they know my body rests.' The noble lord spoke thus, thus ended, thus died. The body was carried to London and buried in London: they did not bury it where he had bidden them.[2]

7187 Then Vortigern was made king once more, as he had been before. Because his wife begged him to, he sent for Hengist, his father-in-law. He summoned him to return, but to bring only a few people with him, so that the British should not take fright and once more interfere. Vortimer his son being dead, there was no need for a great company. Hengist returned willingly, but he brought three hundred thousand armed men; he feared the Britons, and would behave differently

---

[1] This passage occurs earlier in *HRB* (chap. 100). In Bede (I, chap. 17) Germanus and Lupus come to Britain to fight the Pelagian heresy; in *HB* (chap. 47) Germanus reproaches Vortigern for incest with his daughter and tries to convert him.

[2] Cf. *HB* chap. 44, where Vortimer's death is not through poison; he asks for a tomb by the coast, but is buried in Lincoln. In *HRB* chap. 102 (Vulgate) the tomb is supposed to be a bronze pyramid.

Quant li reis sout qu'il repairout
E que tanz humes amenout,
Grant poür out, ne sot que dire,
E li Bretun orent grant ire,
Si distrent qu'il se combatreient
E del païs les chacereient.
Henguist, ki out le quer felun,
Manda al rei par traïsun
Que pais e trives lur dunassent
7210 E entretant a els parlassent;
Pais amoent e pais vuleient,
Pais desirroent, pais quereient;
Ne vuelent mie guerre aveir
Ne par force illuec remaneir.
Cels retiengent qu'il eslirrunt,
E tuit li altre s'en irrunt.
Bretun unt la trive dunee
E d'ambes parz fu afiee.
Ki se creinsist de traïtur?
7220 De parlement unt assis jur.
E li reis manda a Henguist
Que eschariement venist,
E Henguist l'ad bien graanté
Si ad encontre remandé
Ke nule arme n'i ait aportee [1]
Pur poür de esmuver mellee. [2]
As granz plaines de Salesbire,
Lez l'abeïe d'Ambresbire,
Vindrent de dous pars a cel plai,
7230 Le jur des Kalendes de mai.
Henguist ot tuz ses compainuns
Bien enseinniez e bien sumuns
Qu'en lur chauces cultels portassent
Tels ki de ambes parz trenchassent.
Quant il as Bretuns parlereient
E tuit entremellé serreient,
'Nim eure sexes!'criereit, [3]
Que nuls des Bretuns n'entendreit;
Chescuns dunc sun cultel preïst
7240 E sun procain Bretun ferist.

Quant tuit furent al parlement
Entremellé comunement,
E li Bretun entr'els seeient
Ki desarmé, senz arme, esteient,
Henguist ' Nem eure sexes!' cria; [4]
Chescuns dunc sun cultel sacha
E chescuns feri emprés sei.
Henguist, ki fu juste le rei,
Le traist a sei par le mantel
Si laissa faire le maisel.   7250
E cil ki tindrent les cultels
Parmi chapes, parmi mantels,
Parmi piz e parmi buëles
Firent passer les alemeles.
Cil cheent envers e adenz;
Sempres en i ot quatre cenz
E seissante en la place morz
Des plus riches e des plus forz.
Alquant s'en alerent fuiant,
Od pieres lur cors defendant.   7260
Eldulf, uns cuens de Gloëcestre,
Tint un grant pel en sun puin destre,
A ses piez l'out gisant trové,
Ne sai ki l'i aveit porté;
Od le grant pel se defendi,
Maint en tua e abati;
Bien en ocist seissante e dis,
Pruz ert li cuens e de grant pris.
La presse fist si departir
Que nuls nel pot en char ferir.   7270
Assez li unt cultels lancied
Mais ne l'unt pas en char tuchied.
A sun cheval vint traversant,
Qu'il ot mult bon e bien curant;
A Gloëcestre s'en fuï,
Sa cité e sa tur guarni.
Saissun voldrent le rei tuer,
Mais Henguist lur prist a crier:
'Laissiez le rei, maint bien m'ad fait,
E maint travail ad pur mei trait.   7280

---

[1] MS P reading—*aportee*—restored.
[2] MS P reading—*esmuver*—restored.
[3] MS P: *Nin.*
[4] MS P's order of line restored.

Night of the Long Knives

from before. When the king knew he was back, and had brought so many men, he was so frightened, he knew not what to say, and the Britons were furious. They said they would attack and drive them from the land. Hengist, who had a wicked heart, sent a treacherous message to the king, asking for peace and a truce, and a parley: they loved and desired peace, they wished and sought it. They had no wish for war, nor to stay there by force. The Britons should keep only those they chose, and all the rest would depart. The Britons allowed the truce, and it was sworn on both sides.

7219 Who suspected treachery? They appointed a day for the parley. And the king sent word to Hengist that he should come with few retainers,[1] and Hengist agreed willingly, and suggested in return that no weapons should be carried, for fear of starting a fight. On wide Salisbury Plain, next to Amesbury Abbey, the two sides came for conference, on the first day of May. Hengist had instructed and taught all his friends to be sure to carry sharp two-edged knives in their boots. When they were mingling with the Britons and talking to them, he would call out: 'Grab your knives!', which none of the Britons would understand.[2] Each would then take his knife and strike the Briton next to him. When they were all at the parley, mingling together, and the Britons, unarmed and defenceless, were seated, Hengist cried: 'Grab your knives!' Then each drew his knife and struck the one nearest him. Hengist, next to the king, held him fast by the cloak, and let the carnage happen. And those who held the knives ran the blades through cloaks, through mantles, through chests and bowels.The Britons fell over and down. Soon there were four hundred and sixty dead there, from among the noblest and mightiest. Some fled, defending themselves with stones. Eldulf, count of Gloucester, held a great stake in his right hand: he had found it lying at his feet and not known who had brought it there. He defended himself with it, killing and cutting down many. He certainly disposed of seventy men: he was a valiant count, of great renown. He cut through the crowd so that no one could wound him. Many knives were thrown at him but none touched him. He battled through to his horse, an excellent and speedy one, and fled to Gloucester, fortifying his tower and his city.

7277 The Saxons wanted to kill the king, but Hengist shouted to them: 'Leave the king, he has done much for me and endured much hardship on my account. I

---

[1] Keller translates *eschariement* as 'alone'; I prefer the *AND*'s 'scantly accompanied', which fits the context better.

[2] *HRB* chap. 104: '*Nemet oure saxas*'; *VV*: '*Nimet eoyre seaxas*'. The great variety of spelling of these two lines (7237 and 7245) in Wace's MSS indicate scribal problems with the Anglo-Saxon

words. The story first appears in *HB* chap. 46, where the Saxon words are also used but no location is mentioned. On similar stories in Ireland and on the Continent, see Anderson, 'Dalriada', pp. 106–32. Like the *VV*, Wace omits *HRB*'s burial of the corpses near 'Kaercaraduc now called Salisbury' by the holy Eldadus (chap. 104).

Guarder le dei cume mun gendre;
Mais face nus ses citez rendre
E ses fortelesces livrer,
Se il sa vie vult aveir.'[1]
Issi remist qu'il ne l'ocistrent,
Mais en anels de fer le mistrent;
Tant l'unt lié e tant destreit
Qu'il lur jura que tut rendreit.
Lundres lur rendi e Wincestre,
7290 Nichole, Everwic e Cicestre.
Pur quitance de raençun
E pur eissir de la prisun
Lur otrea en feu Sussexe
E tut Essexe e Midelsexe,
Pur ço que prés erent de Kent
Que Henguist ot premerement;
Pur remembrer la traïsun
Des cultels, orent issi nun;
Sexes, ço dient li Engleis,
7300 Plusurs culteus sunt en Franceis,
Mais cil les nuns alques varient
Ki ne sevent que senefient.
Engleis le repruvier oïrent
De la traïsun que cil firent,
La fin de la parole osterent,
Les nuns des cultels tresturnerent,
Pur oblier la desonur
Que fait orent lur anceisur.
   Vortiger tut lur ad guerpi,
7310 Ultre Saverne s'en fuï;
Luin en Guales s'en trespassa,
Illuec fu, illuec conversa.
Venir fist ses sortisseürs
E de ses humes les meillurs;
Conseil en quist que il fereit,
En quel guise se maintendreit;
Se plus fort gent l'envaïsseit,
Cumfaitement se defendreit.
Loé li unt si cunseilier
7320 Que tel tur face edifier

Que ja par force ne seit prise
Ne par engin d'ome conquise;
Dedenz seit quant ele iert garnie
Que gent adverse ne l'ocie.
Dunc fist eslire e fist guarder
Liu convenable a tur funder.
A gré li vint e a plaisir
Qu'il la fereit el munt d'Erir.
Maçuns quist, les meillurs qu'il sout,
E fist uvrer a l'ainz qu'il pout.   7330
Cil unt comencied a ovrer,
Pierre a mortier a aloer,
Mais quanqu'il unt le jur uvré[2]
Est la nuit en terre afundré;
Quant plus ovroent haltement
E plus chaeit el fundement.
Issi firent plusurs jurnees
Ki en terre sunt affundrees.
Quant li reis sout e aparçut
Que s'uvraine altrement ne crut,   7340
A ses devins requist cunseil.
'Par fei, dist il, jo m'esmerveil
Que ceste ovre puet devenir;
Ne la puet terre sustenir.
Guardez, enquerez que ço deit
E cument terre la tendrei.'
Cil unt deviné e sorti,
Mais, puet cel estre, il unt menti,
Se un hume trover poeit
Que senz pere aveir nez sereit,   7350
Oceïst le, le sanc preïst,
E od le mortier l'espandist,
Par ço purreit s'ovre durer
Si purreit asseür ovrer.
Dunc ad fait li reis enveier
Par tute Guales e cerchier
Se ja tels huem esteit truvez
Que devant lui fust amenez.
Turné s'en sunt li quereür
Par plusurs cuntrees plusur.[3]   7360

---

[1] MS P reading—*aveir*—restored.
[2] Here MS D substitutes decasyllables for 170 lines (up to 7582). Then it adds 672 decasyllables of Merlin's prophecies, ending with: *Eus mettet Helias a bone fin/ Ki en romanz translata de Merlin/ E duinst a s'alme en pareis repos/ A qui hum fait honur e gré e los:/ Amen dium tuit ki l'avum oi/*

Que Deus de lui e de nus ait merci. AMEN. At 7583 D rejoins company with the other MSS (which specifically say the prophecies will not be translated).
[3] MS J adds: *Et vunt ensamble doi et doi/ Quierent par tout de par le roi/ Et vunt tel home demandant/ Mais n'en trouverent tant ne quant.*

Vortigern's tower

should protect him, as my son-in-law. But let us make him render up his cities, and hand over his fortresses, if he wants to have his life.' So they did not kill him, but put him in iron chains. They so bound and oppressed him that he swore he would give them everything. He gave them London and Winchester, Lincoln, York and Chichester. To release himself from ransom, and get out of prison, he gave them in fee Sussex and all Essex and Middlesex, because they adjoined Kent, which Hengist held before. They thus were called '-sex' to commemorate the Treachery of the Knives. 'Sexes' is the English word for knives; there are many kinds of knife amongst the French, but they have somewhat changed their names, so that they do not know what 'sexes' means. The English heard themselves reproached for the treachery they had done, removed the end of the word and completely changed the name for knives, to forget the dishonour committed by their ancestors.[1]

7309   Vortigern abandoned everything to them and fled over the Severn. He travelled deep into Wales and there he stayed. He sent for his soothsayers and his best men, and sought their advice as to what he should do and how protect himself, how defend himself if a stronger force attacked him. His counsellors advised him to construct such a tower that it could never be taken by force nor conquered by any stratagem of man. Once it was equipped, he should live inside so that no evil people could kill him. Then he had a search made to choose a suitable place to build the tower. It pleased and suited him to do it on mount Erir.[2] He sought out masons, the best he knew, and made them set to as fast as possible. They began to labour, and to lay out stones and mortar, but whatever they built during the day sank into the ground during the night; the higher they built it, the greater was its fall, down to its foundations. In this way many days of work sank into the ground. When the king knew and realised that his undertaking would not succeed, he asked his soothsayers for advice. 'Indeed,' he said, 'I wonder what can become of this work: earth cannot sustain it. Search and enquire as to why, and how the earth might support it.' They announced and predicted—though possibly they were lying—that if he could find a man born without a father, kill him, take his blood and sprinkle it on the mortar, then his building would endure and he could work in safety.

7355   So the king sent throughout Wales, to see that, if ever such a man were found, he should be brought before him. Many searchers left for many regions. Two of

---

[1] MS P adds Vortigern's gift of Sussex, Essex and Middlesex, and the false etymological link. This is omitted in MSS JH (and F omits the false etymology); these MSS have perhaps corrected the text to be closer to *HRB*? See Tatlock p.

386 fn. 24 on knives, *sax* and Saxons in Widiukind of Corvey.

[2] Snowdon. *HB*, from which the story of Vortigern and Merlin comes (chaps 40–42), gives both names.

Dui, ki alerent un chemin,
Vindrent ensemble a Kermerdin.
Devant la cité, a l'entree,
Aveit d'enfanz grant assemblee,
La erent venu pur juer;
Cil les pristrent a esgarder.
Entre les altres ki juerent
Out dous vallez ki se mellerent,
Ço fu Merlin e Dinabuz,
7370 Li uns vers l'altre est irascuz;
Li uns l'altre contraliout
E sun lignage reprovout:
'Tèis tei, dist Dinabuz, Merlin;
Jo sui assez de plus halt lin
Que tu nen iés si te repose.
Ne sez ki es, malvaise chose?
Ne deiz pas vers mei estriver
Ne mun lignage repruver.
Jo sui nez de reis e de cuntes,
7380 Mais si tu tes parens acuntes,
Ja tun pere ne numeras,
Kar tu nel sez, ne ne savras.
Unc tun pere ne cuneüs
Ne tu unches pere n'eüs.'
Cil ki les vallez escultouent,
Ki tel hume querant alouent,
Quant il oïrent la tençun,
As veisins vindrent d'envirun
Pur enquerre qui cil esteit
7390 Ki unches pere eü n'aveit.
E li veisin unt respundu
Que unches pere n'out eü,
Ne la mere ki l'ot porté
Ne sout ki l'aveit engendré.
De sun pere rien ne saveient,
Mais mere aveit qu'il cunusseient,
Fille ert al rei de Demecie,
Ço esteit de Guales partie.
Nunaine esteit de mult bone vie[1]
7400 En la ville en une abeïe.

Dunc sunt cil al provost alé;
De par le rei li unt rové
Que Merlin, ki unches n'out pere,
Seit menez al rei, e sa mere.
Li provoz nel volt refuser;
Andous les fist al rei mener.
Li reis les reçut bonement
Si parla amiablement:
'Dame, dist il, cunuis mei veir,
Nel puis, se par tei nun, saveir,   7410
Ki engendra tun fiz Merlin.'
La none tint le chief enclin;
Quant ele out pensé un petit:
'Se Deus, dist ele, me aït,
Unches ne cunui ne ne vi
Ki cest vallet engenuï.
Unches n'oi, unches ne soi
Si ço fu huem de ki jo l'oi.
Mais ço soi jo de ver e sai,
E pur veir le regeherai,   7420
Quant jo fui alques grant nurrie,
Ne sai se fu fantosmerie,
Une chose veneit suvent
Ki me baisout estreitement.
Cumë hume parler l'oeie,
E cumë hume le senteie,
E plusurs feiz od mei parlout
Que neient ne se demustrout.
Tant m'ala issi aprismant
E tant m'ala suvent baisant,   7430
Od mei se culcha si conçui,
Unches hume plus ne conui.
Cest vallet oi, cest vallet ai,
Plus n'en fu, ne plus n'en dirai.'
Dunc fist li reis venir Maganz,[2]
Un clerc ki mult esteit savant,[3]
Si demanda s'estre poeit
Ço que la nune li diseit.
'Trové avum, dist il, escrit,
Qu'une manere d'esperit   7440

---

[1] MS P reading—*Nunaine*—restored.
[2] MS P reading—*Maganz*—restored.
[3] MS P reading—*ki mult esteit*—restored.

Merlin

them, travelling the same road, together arrived in Kermerdin.[1] In front of the
city, at its entrance, there was a great crowd of children, gathered there to play,
and they began to observe them. Amongst those at play were two boys quarrel-
ling, Merlin and Dinabuz.[2] One was angry with the other, opposing him and insulting his family. 'Hold your tongue, Merlin,' said Dinabuz 'stop, because I am
of a much nobler lineage than you. Don't you know who you are, you wicked
thing? You shouldn't quarrel with me or insult my family. I am born of kings and
counts, but if you consider your parents, you can never name your father, for you
don't know him, nor will you. You never knew your father nor did you ever have a
father.' Those who were seeking just such a man, on hearing the boys and their
quarrel, approached the neighbours round about to enquire who he was, who had
never had a father. And the neighbours replied he had never had a father, nor did
his mother, who had borne him, know who had begotten him. They knew nothing of his father, but he had a mother known to them: she was the daughter of the
king of Demetia, part of Wales. She was a nun of exemplary life in an abbey in the
town.

7401   Then these men went to the town governor. On behalf of the king they asked
him for the fatherless Merlin, and his mother, to be taken to the king. The governor did not wish to refuse and had both of them taken to the king. He received
them well and spoke pleasantly. 'Lady,' he said, 'tell me truly, for only through
you can I know it: who begot your son Merlin?' The nun bowed her head. After
reflecting a while, she said: 'God help me, I never knew or saw who engendered
this boy. I never heard, I never knew if it was a man who gave me him. But this I
knew and know to be true, and I will admit its truth: when I was a full-grown
novice, some thing—I don't know if it was an apparition—often came to me and
kissed me intimately. I heard it speak like a man; I felt it as if it were a man, and
many times it spoke with me, without ever making itself known. So long did it
continue to approach me and to kiss me that it lay with me and I conceived. I
knew no other man. I had this boy, I have him still; there was no more to it and I
shall say no more.'[3]

7435   Then the king made Maganz come forward, a wise and learned man, and asked

---

[1] Carmarthen. On the town's onomastic link to
Merlin, see Jarman, 'The Merlin Legend', *AOW*,
pp. 131–32, 137. It is *HRB* which calls the boy
Merlin ('also called Ambrosius') and localises
him here (chap. 108, Vulgate only); in the *HB*
chap. 42, he is Ambrosius (also called *Emrys
Guletic*, Emrys the Overlord) at Glywysing in
Glamorgan, who is presumably the Ambrosius
who later drives Vortigern out and is called the
'great king of the British nation' (chap. 48)—a
reference to the historical British king
Ambrosius Aurelianus and his victories against
the Saxons, mentioned in Gildas, *De Excidio*,
chap. 25, and Bede I, chap. 16. On the conflation
of several separate figures into Merlin, see
Jarman, above.

[2] *HRB* chap. 106: *Dinabutius*; *VV*: *Dinabucius*.

[3] I have translated MS H's version of l. 7434
here—*plus n'en soi, et plus n'en dirai*—which I prefer to the reading in MS P.

Est entre la lune e la terre.
Ki vult de lur nature enquerre,
En partie unt nature humaine
E en partie suveraine.
Incubi demones unt nun;
Par tut l'eir unt lur regiun,
E en la terre unt lur repaire.
Ne püent mie grant mal faire;
Ne püent mie mult noisir
7450 Fors de gaber e d'escharnir.
Bien prenent humaine figure
E ço cunsent bien lur nature.
Mainte meschine unt deceüe
E en tel guise purgeüe;
Issi puet Merlin estre nez
E issi puet estre engendrez.'
'Rei, ço dist Merlin, mandé m'as;
Que me vuels, pur quei me mandas?'
'Merlin, dist li reis, jal savras;
7460 Oïr le vuels e tu l'orras.
Une tur ai fait comencer
E fait mettre pierre e mortier,
Mais quanque l'en ad le jur fait
Afundre en terre e dedenz vait.
Ne sai s'en as oï parler,
Ne puis le jur tant faire ovrer
Que la nuit ne seit enfundré;
Mult i ai ja del mien guasté.
Ço dient mi devineür
7470 Que ja ne cheverai ma tur[1]
Se tis sanc nen est dedenz mis
Pur ço que senz pere nasquis.'
'Ja Deu, ço dist Merlin, ne place
Que par mun sanc ta tur estace.
Pur menteürs ferai tenir,
Si tus faiz devant mei venir,[2]
Tuz cels qui de mun sanc sortirent;
Menteür furent si mentirent.'
Li reis les ad fait demander
7480 Sis fist a Merlin amener.

Quant Merlin les ot esguardez:
'Seinnurs, dist il, ki devinez,
Dites que deit e dunt avient
Que ceste ovraine ne se tient.
Se vus ne me savez respundre
Pur quei la tur en terre afundre,
Cument savez vus deviner
Que par mun sanc deivë ester?
Dites que ad el fundement
Pur quei la tur chiet tant suvent, 7490
E puis dites quei i esteuet
E par quel chose tenir puet.
Se vus ne nus faites saveir
Ke desuz fait l'ovre chaeir,[3]
Cument sera chose creable
Que par mun sanc seit mielz durable?[4]
Dites al rei le desturbier,
Puis direz quei i ad mestier.'
Tuit li devineür se tourent
A Merlin rien dire ne sourent.   7500
'Sire rei, dist Merlin, entent;
Desuz ta tur, el fundement,
Ad un estanc grant e parfunt
Par quei ta tur en terre funt.
E que tu certement me creies,
Fai fuïr la terre si veies.'
Li reis fist fuïr si trova
L'estanc que Merlin enseinna.
'Seinnur, ço dist Merlin, oiez,
Vus que querre me faisiez   7510
Pur mesler el mortier mun sanc,
Dites que ad en cest estanc.'
Cil furent tuit taisant e mu,
Ne bien ne mal n'unt respundu.
Merlin al rei se returna,
Oiant ses humes l'apela.
'Fai, dist il, cest estanc vuider
E par ruisels l'eue espuiser.
Al funz ad dous draguns dormanz
En dous pierres chieves gesanz.   7520

---

[1] MS P reading—*ne cheverai*—restored.
[2] MS P reading—*tus*—restored.
[3] MS P reading—*l'ovre*—restored.
[4] MS P reading—*durable*—restored.

Merlin explains the collapse of the tower

him if what the nun said could be true. 'We have found it written,' he said, 'that there exists a kind of spirit between moon and earth. For whoever wishes to know their nature, they are partly human and partly supernatural. They are called incubus demons; their realm is the air and they frequent the earth. They cannot do great wickedness, they cannot cause much harm except deceive and deride. They easily take human shape and it agrees well with their nature. They have deceived many girls and ravished them in this way. Thus might Merlin be born and thus might he be begotten.' 'King,' said Merlin, 'you have sent for me: why did you do so, what do you want of me?' 'Merlin,' said the king, 'you shall know; you wish to hear and you shall hear. I began making a high tower, using stone and mortar, but whatever is constructed during the day sinks into the ground. I don't know if you have heard tell of it: no matter how much is built during the day, it collapses during the night. Much of my wealth has already been wasted on it. According to my soothsayers, I shall never complete my tower unless your blood is inside it, because you were born without a father.'

7473 'God forbid,' said Merlin, 'that your tower should stand firm through my blood. If you make all those men, who prophesied about my blood, come before me, I shall have them adjudged liars: they were liars and lied.' The king had them sent for, and brought to Merlin. After he had observed them, Merlin said: 'My prophetic lords, say why this building will not stand. If you cannot answer me why the tower sinks to the ground, how can you foretell it will stand up through my blood? Say what it is in the foundations that makes the tower so often fall; then say what is needed and what will make it stand. If you cannot tell us what it is underneath that makes the work fall, how is it believable that my blood should make it last longer? Tell the king of the obstruction; then tell us what is needed.' All the soothsayers kept quiet and could answer him nothing. 'My lord king,' said Merlin, 'listen. Below your tower, in the foundations, is a great, deep pool, which makes your tower collapse. And so that you can believe me, dig up the ground and see.' The king had the ground dug up and found the pool Merlin had indicated. 'My lords,' said Merlin, 'listen: you who searched for me in order to slake the mortar with my blood—say what is in this pool.' They were all silent and mute, with never a good nor a bad word. Merlin turned back to the king and called to him in the hearing of his men. 'Have this pool drained,' he said, 'and draw off the water through trenches. At the bottom are two sleeping dragons, lying in two hollow stones. One of the dragons is all white, the other red as blood.'

Li uns des draguns est tuz blancs,
Li altre ruges cume sancs.'
Quant l'eue fu fors espandue
E par ruisels tute escurue,
Dui dragun sunt des funz sailli,
E forment se sunt envaï;
Par grant fierté s'entr'assaillirent
Si que tuit li baron les virent.
Bien les veïssiez escumer
7530 E des geules flambes jeter.
Li reis juste l'estanc s'assist;
Merlin preia qu'il li desist
Que li dragun senefioent
Ki par tel ire s'assembloent.
Dunc dist Merlin les prophecies
Que vus avez, ço crei, oïes,
Des reis ki a venir esteient,
Ki la terre tenir deveient.
Ne vuil sun livre translater
7540 Quant jo nel sai interpreter;
Nule rien dire nen vuldreie [1]
Que si ne fust cum jo dirreie. [2]
Li reis ad mult loé Merlin
E mult le tint a buen devin;
Demanda li quant il murreit
E par quel mort il finereit,
Kar de sa fin ert en effrei.
'Guarde, dist Merlin, guarde tei [3]
Del feu as enfanz Constentin,
7550 Kar par lur feu vendras a fin.
D'Armoriche sunt ja esmeu [4]
Par mer siglent a grant vertu.
De ço te puis faire certein
Qu'a Toteneis vendrunt demain.
Mal lur as fait, mal te ferunt,
De tei griefment se vengerunt.
A tun mal lur frere traïs
E a tun mal rei te feïs,
E a tun mal en cest païs
7560 Paens e Saisnes atraïs.

Dous encumbriers as de dous parz,
Ne sai del quel primes te guarz:
D'une part Saisne te guerreient
Ki volentiers te destruereient,
De l'altre part vienent li eir
Qui cest regne vuelent aveir;
Bretaine vuelent desrainer
E lur frere Constant venger.
Se tu or puez fuïr si fui,
Kar li frere vienent andui.   7570
Aureles primes rei sera
E par puisun primes murra.
Uther, sis freres, Pendragon,
Tendra emprés la regiun;
Mais trop tost serra engrotez
E par tes eirs envenimez.
Sis filz, ki iert de Cornoaille,
Cume senglers fiers en bataille,
Les traïturs devurera
E tuz tes parents destruira;   7580
Cil sera mult vaillanz e pruz,
Ses enemis conquerra tuz.'
    Merlin sa parole fina,
E Vortiger d'illuec turna.
El demain plus ne demura,
La flote as freres arriva
En Dertremue, a Toteneis,
Od chevaliers e od herneis.
Es vus Bretuns joianz e liez,
Les uns des altres enforciez.   7590
Ensemble se sunt ralïed
Ki ainz erent esparpillied;
Henguist les aveit fait tapir
E par bois e par munz fuïr, [5]
Ki out destruit la baronie
Od les cultels, en felonie.
Bretun se sunt ensemble trait,
D'Aurele unt seinur e rei fait. [6]
Vortiger, ki cel plai oï,
En Guales fu, si se guarni.   7600

---

[1] MS P reading—*nen*—restored.

[2] Here 'Wilhelme', the scribe of MS L, inserts Merlin's prophecies in twelve-syllable lines after this preface: *Mes jo Wilhelme vus dirrai/ Des altres profecies ço ke jo sai/ Si cum les ai oi ditees/ E en altre rime translatees/ En tele rime cume joes oi/ Ore vus dirrai si cum jo qui/ Quant les profecies serrunt finees/ En tele rime cume sunt ditees/ A meistre Wace repeirerai/ E sun livere avant cunterai.* The prophecies ap-pear much the same as those in a quire in MS P, in a different hand, inserted between ll. 7584–5. See the British Library's *Catalogue*, pp. 85–6.

[3] MS P's wording of line restored.

[4] MS P reading—*esmeu*—restored.

[5] MS P's order of line restored.

[6] MS P's order of line restored.

Merlin forecasts Vortigern's death

7523 When the water was drained and all carried off by trenches, two dragons rose from the depths and fiercely attacked each other. They fought with great violence so that all the barons saw them. They could be seen foaming at the mouth and spewing flame from their jaws. The king sat by the pool and begged Merlin to tell him what the dragons and their angry battle meant. Then Merlin made the prophecies which I believe you have heard, of the kings who were to come and who were to hold the land. I do not wish to translate his book, since I do not know how to interpret it; I would not like to say anything, in case what I say does not happen.[1]

7543 The king praised Merlin greatly and considered him an excellent prophet. He asked him when he would die, and by what kind of death, for he was terrified of his end. 'Beware,' said Merlin, 'beware of the fire from Constantine's children, for you will meet your end through that fire. Already they have left Armorica and are crossing the sea in strength. Of this you can be sure: tomorrow they will be at Totnes. You have done them wrong: they will do you wrong and exact grim revenge. It was your wickedness which betrayed their brother, your wickedness which made you king and your wickedness which attracted Saxons and heathen to this land. Dangers await you on both sides; I don't know which you should guard against first. On the one hand, the Saxons make war on you and would willingly destroy you; on the other, the heirs approach, wanting the realm. They want to claim Britain and avenge Constant, their brother. If then you can flee, do so, for both brothers are coming. Aurelius will be king first, and then be the first to die, by poison. Uther Pendragon, his brother, will then hold the kingdom; but too soon he will sicken and be poisoned by your heirs. His son, from Cornwall, fierce as a boar in battle, will devour the traitors and destroy all your kin. He will be valiant and brave, conquering all his enemies.'

7583 Merlin finished speaking and Vortigern went his way. The next day, without delay, the brothers' fleet arrived in Dartmouth, at Totnes,[2] with knights and equipment. The Britons, fortified by these people, were joyful and happy. Formerly dispersed, they gathered together. Hengist, having wickedly destroyed the barons with knives, had made the rest hide, and flee into the mountains and woods. The British assembled and made Aurelius their king and lord. In Wales, Vortigern heard of the matter and took steps to defend himself. With his bravest men he sought protection in a castle called Genoire by the Wye, a fast-flowing river. Those

---

[1] A reference to chaps 109–117 of *HRB* which contain the prophecies of Merlin, in the process demonstrating some scepticism. But MS L inserts Merlin's prophecies at this point, as MS D does too, for 670 lines, after l. 7582 (printed in Arnold's Appendix I, vol. II pp. 781–5).

[2] See fn. 1 to p. 29.

A un chastel, Genoire out nun,
Ala querre guarantizun, [1]
E de sa gent li plus vaillant,
Juste Waie, une ewe curant,
Waie l'apelent li veisin
E la cuntree ad nun Hergrin;
Ço fu desur Doare, un munt,
Ço dient cil ki de la sunt.
Wortiger se guarni forment
7610 D'armes, de vitaille e de gent;
Se il pur ço peüst guarir
Assez s'en out fait bien guarnir.
Lur baruns unt li frere pris,
Tant unt le rei Vortiger quis
Qu'en un chastel l'unt asseigied;
Assez i unt trait e lancied;
Volentiers prendre le vuleient
Kar a merveille le haeient.
Se li frere l'orent haï,
7620 Vortiger l'out bien deservi;
Ocis out lur frere Constant
E Constentin lur pere avant,
Senz main mettre, par traïsun,
Si que pur veir le saveit l'un.
Aldulf, li quens de Gloëcestre,
Ki des Gualeis saveit bien l'estre, [2]
Ert huem Aurele devenuz
E od lui fu en l'ost venuz.
'Eldulf, dist Aureles, pur Dé,
7630 As tu ja mun pere ublié
Ke te nurri e te feufa,
E mun frere, ki mult t'ama?
Andui volentiers t'enurerent,
Mult te creïrent, mult t'amerent;
Par l'engin a cest suduiant,
A cest parjure, a cest tirant,
Furent ocis, encor vesquissent
Se par sun engin ne perissent.
Se tu de cels eus marrement, [3]
7640 Pren de Wortiger vengement.'

Par sul cest amonestement
Se sunt armé comunement;
Atrait unt fait, bois aporté
Tut unt empli un grant fossé;
Puis unt en l'attrait le feu mis.
E li feus est el chastel pris,
Del castel se prist en la tur
E as maisuns ki sunt entur.
Dunc veïssiez chastel ardeir
Flambe voler, maisuns chaeir.   7650
Ars fu li reis, e cil od lui
Ki od li orent quis refui.
Quant li nuvels reis ot conquis
E turné a sei le païs,
Sur les paiens, ço dist, irreit
E la terre delivereit.
Henguist le sout, mult le duta;
Vers Escoce s'en trespassa.
Tute l'altre terre guerpi,
Ultre le Humbre s'en fuï,   7660
Kar securs e aïe e force
Deveit aveir de cels d'Escoce;
E si granz busuinz li cresseit
En Escoce s'en passereit.
Li reis de jurnee en jurnee
A cele part sa gent menee,
E li Bretun tuz tens cresseient
E tant espés a lui veneient,
Nes peüst pas nuls huem numbrer
Plus que l'areine de la mer.   7670
Mult truva li reis païs guast,
Vit que n'i ot quil guaainast;
Chastels vit destruiz e citez,
Villes arses, mustiers robez;
Paien orent tut eissillied,
N'i aveient rien esparnied.
A tuz pramist restorement
Se il repairot sainement.
Henguist sout que li reis veneit,
Que senz mesler n'en turnereit.   7680

---

[1] MS P reading—*guarantizun*—restored.
[2] MS P reading—*des Gualeis*—restored.
[3] MS P reading—*eus*—restored.

Vortigern is burnt in his tower

nearby call it Wye, and the region is called Hergrin,[1] on top of Doare,[2] a mountain; so say those who come from there. Vortigern equipped himself thoroughly, with weapons, provisions and men; if this aided him to escape, it would have been sufficient defence. The brothers took their barons and pursued king Vortigern so hard that they laid siege to him in a castle. There they constantly pelted and shot at him. They were eager to capture him, because they bore him enormous hatred. If the brothers hated him, Vortigern had certainly deserved it: he had killed their brother Constant, and Constantine their father before him, by treachery, if not with his own hands, so that people knew it to be true.

7625   Eldulf, the count of Gloucester, familiar with the customs of the Welsh, had become Aurelius' man and kept him company amongst the soldiers. 'For God's sake, Eldulf,' said Aurelius, 'have you already forgotten my father, who gave you nurture and fiefs, and my brother, who loved you dearly? Both of them willingly honoured you, and gave you much trust and much love. By the cunning of this traitor, this perjurer, this tyrant, they were slain; they would still be alive were it not for his cunning. If you grieved for them, take revenge on Vortigern.'[3] This exhortation alone made them all arm. They made a collection of wood, entirely filling a great ditch with it, and then fired it. The fire caught the castle and from the castle spread to the tower and to the houses round about. Then the castle could be seen burning, with flames flying and houses falling. The king was consumed, along with all those who had sought refuge with him.[4]

7653   When the new king had conquered and appropriated the land, he said he would move against the heathen and liberate the realm. Hengist heard of it, and greatly feared it.[5] He journeyed to Scotland, abandoning all the other lands, and fled over the Humber, because he expected to have help, succour and forces from the Scots, and if his plight grew worse, he could pass into Scotland. As day followed day, the king led his men there, and the numbers of British kept increasing, and flocked to him in such crowds that no one could number them any more than the sands of the sea. The king found the realm badly laid waste and saw no one was tilling it; he saw castles and cities destroyed, towns burnt, churches plundered. The heathen had laid everything waste and spared nothing. He promised everyone compensation if he returned safely from battle.

7679   Hengist knew the king was coming and would not turn back without a fight. He

---

[1] *HRB* chap. 119: *Genoreu*; *Hergign*; *Cloartius*; *VV*: *Genoreu*; *Herging*; *Cloareius*. On these locations see Arnold, vol. II, p. 805, Thorpe, p. 187 and Tatlock pp. 72–3.

[2] See Tatlock p. 72 for an identification with Little Doward in Monmouthshire.

[3] Wace, like the *VV*, cuts short a much longer speech in *HRB* chap. 119.

[4] In *HB* chap. 47, Vortigern is destroyed in his fortress, Cair Guorthigirn, by fire from heaven.

[5] Wace, like the *VV*, omits a passage in *HRB* chap. 120, praising Aurelius.

Ses compainuns volt conforter
E hardement lur volt doner.
'Barun, dist il, ne dutez mie
Cele malvaise compainie.
Assez savez ki Bretun sunt,
Ja cuntre vus ne se tendrunt. [1]
S'un poi lur poëz cuntr'ester,
Ja nes verrez puis arester.
Od mult poi de gent mainte feiz
7690 Les avez vencuz e destreiz.
Se il unt grant gent, vus que chaut?
Lur multitude rien ne valt;
Petit fait a criendre compaine
Ki ad fieble e fol chevetaine.
De malvaise gent senz seinnur
Ne deit l'um mie aveir poür;
Enfes est quis ad a guier,
Ne puet encor armes porter.
Nus sumes bon combateür
7700 E espruvé en maint estur;
Pur noz vies nus defendum,
Kar n'i ad altre raençun.' [2]
    Henguist laissa l'amonester;
Ses chevaliers fist tuz armer.
Cuntre Bretuns hastivement
Ad chevalchié celeement.
Desarmez les pensot truver
Sis quidot tuz desbarater,
Mais Bretun, qui paens cremeient,
7710 E jur e nuit armé esteient.
Quant li reis sout que il veneient
E que combatre se vuleient,
En un champ ki bel li sembla
Conduist sa gent sis ordena.
Treis mille chevaliers armez
Qu'il out d'ultre mer amenez,
Trestuz tenuz a buens vassals,
Fist d'une part estre es chevals.
Des Gualeis ad fait dous compaines;
7720 Les uns fist ester es muntaines,

Que paen munter n'i peüssent
Pur nul busuin que il eüssent;
Les altres fist el bois ester,
E l'entree del bois guarder,
Que paen ne s'i enbatissent
Que li Gualeis nes oceïssent.
Les altres fist el champ descendre,
Pur bien ester, pur bien defendre.
Quant il out tut apareillied
Si cum um li out enseinied,   7730
Od ses humes fu naturals
Que il conut as plus leials;
Juste lui fist tenir s'enseine
U sa gent se traie e estreine.
Li cuens Eldulf fu a sun lez,
E des altres baruns assez.
'Deus, dist Eldulf, tant liez sereie
Se jo l'ure veeir poeie
Qu'a Henguist peüse avenir.
Bien me devreit dunc suvenir   7740
Que il ocist lez Anbrebiere,
Tut la flur de nostre empiere,
Tut le premerain jur de mai,
Quant jo a peine en eschapai.'
As paroles qu'Eldulf diseit,
Ki de Henguist se complaineit,
Es vus el champ venu Henguist,
Ki grant masse del champ purprist.
Ne firent pas grant demurer
A la bataille comencer.   7750
Des qu'il se sunt entreveü,
Sempres se sunt entrecoru.
Dunc veïssiez vassals combatre,
Les uns les altres entr'abatre;
Cez assaillir e cels defendre,
Granz cops receivre e granz cops rendre,
Les uns les altres enverser
E sur les mors les vifs passer;
Escuz percier, hanstes cruissir,
Naffrez chaeir, chaeiz murir.   7760

---

[1] MS P reading—*vus*—restored.
[2] MS J adds: *Or soions hardi et seur/ Faisons de nous*   *casteax et mur/ Or soions tout hardi et fort/ U autrement sommes tot mort.*

Aurelius' army fights Hengist

wished to comfort his companions and put heart into them. 'My lords,' he said, 'don't be afraid of these second-rate troops. You know well enough they are British and can never hold out against you. If you put up even a little opposition against them, you'll never see them resist again. With very few men you have often conquered and demolished them. If they are many, what does it matter? Their numbers are worthless, and an army with a weak and foolish leader is little to be feared. No one should be afraid of a wretched, leaderless army. He who commands them is a child, he can't even bear arms yet. We are good fighters, tested in many a battle. Let's fight for our lives, for there's no other way of saving our skins.' His exhortation finished, Hengist had all his knights arm. He quickly and quietly rode against the Britons, thinking to find them unarmed and thus to rout them all. But the Britons, fearing the heathen, were armed both day and night. When Aurelius realised the heathen were approaching and wanted a battle, he led his men into a battlefield he thought suitable, and drew them up in order.[1] On the one side, on horseback, he arranged three thousand armed knights, all reckoned to be good warriors, whom he had brought from overseas. He divided the Welsh into two companies and placed one in the mountains, so that the heathen could in no circumstances retreat there. He put the others in the woods, guarding the entrance to the forest, so that the pagans could not rush into it without the Welsh killing them. He made the rest go down into the field, to stand fast and put up good resistance.

7729 When he had arrayed everything as he had been advised, he placed himself with those men true to him, whom he knew to be the most loyal. Next to him he had his standard planted, to which his men gathered and clung. Count Eldulf was at his side, and many of the other barons. 'God, how happy I would be,' said Eldulf, 'if I could see the moment when I reach Hengist. Then I ought to remember how, at Amesbury, he killed the whole flower of our kingdom on the very first day of May, when I barely made my escape.' As Eldulf was saying these words and indicting Hengist, Hengist himself and his army appeared in the field, occupying a large part of it. They were not slow to begin battle. As soon as they saw each other, they at once rushed together. Then you could see warriors fighting, one assaulting the other, some attacking, some defending, receiving and giving great blows, one felling the other, the living trampling the dead. Shields were pierced, lances shattered; the wounded fell, the fallen died. The heathen called on their false idols, the Christians on God; the heathen fought valiantly, the Christians

---

[1] In *HRB* chap. 121 the field is called *Maubeti*;
the *VV* has no name for it. See Tatlock p. 21.

Paien lur fals Deus apeloent
E crestïen Deu reclamoent.
Bien se combateient paien
E assez melz li crestïen. [1]
Lur conreiz firent departir
Si lur firent le champ guerpir;
Cops receveient granz e gros,
Si lur estuet turner les dos.
Quant Henguist vit les suens turner,
7770 Les dos as cops abanduner,
A Coningesburc vint puinant,
Illuec quida truver guarant.
Mais li reis l'alad parsoant,
Criant as suens: 'Avant, avant!'
    Quant Henguist vit qu'il le soeient,
E que el chastel l'asserreient,
Melz se volt combatre defors
E mettre en abandun sun cors
Que laisser dedenz assaeir,
7780 Quant de succurs n'aveit espeir.
Sa gent ratraist e recuilli, [2]
A combatre les restabli.
Es vus bataille de rechief,
Aspre mellee e estur grief.
Paien se furent reverti,
Si out li uns l'altre enhardi.
Li crestïen dunc i perdissent
E li paien mult en preïssent,
Kar trop veneient a desrei,
7790 Mais li trei mil en un conrei
Ki furent a cheval, i vindrent
Quis succururent e maintindrent.
Paien forment se combateient,
Quel merveille, ke bien saveient
Que ja vif n'en eschapereient
Se defendre ne se poeient.
Eldulf vit Henguist sil conut,
Haï l'out e haïr le dut;
Tens vit e liu presentement
7800 D'acomplir sun desirrement.

Espee traite li corut;
Henguist fu fort, le cop reçut.
Es vus les dous vassals justez,
Les branz tuz nuz, escuz levez.
Mult lur veïssiez cops dubler
E des aciers le feu voler.
Gorlois, li cuens de Cornoaile,
Vint cume pruz en la bataille;
Eldulf l'ad veü aprismer,
Plus seür se fist e plus fier;   7810
A guise de hardi vassal
Corut Henguist prendre al nasal,
A sei le traist si l'enbruncha,
Par vive force l'en mena.
'Chevaliers, dist il, Deu merci,
Mun desirrier ai acompli;
Pris avum cestui e vencu
Ki maint mal nus ad esmeü.
Ociez cest chien enragiez
Ki de nus unches n'out pitiez. [3]   7820
Cist esteit li chiés de la guerre,
Ki eissillié ad nostre terre.
La victorie en voz mains tenez
Se vus cestui ocis avez.'
Dunc fu Henguist bien justisiez;
En chaines mis e liez
Al rei Aurele fu livrez;
Bien fu destreiz e bien guardez.
Sis fiz, ki el champ fu, Octa, [4]
Sis cusins od lui, Ebissa,   7830
A peine se sunt eschapé
E en Ewerwic sunt entré;
La cité unt dedenz guarnie
Od tant cum il orent d'aïe.
Plusur altre fuï s'en sunt
Ki bois, ki plain, ki val, ki munt.
Li reis fu lied de cele glorie
Que Deus li out duné victorie;
Dedenz Coningesburc entra,
Treis jurs entiers i surjurna   7840

---

[1] MS P's order of couplets ll. 7761–62 and 7763–64 restored.

[2] MS P reading—*ratraist*—restored.

[3] MS P's readings—*enragiez*, *pitiez*—restored in ll. 7819–20; order of l. 7820 restored.

[4] MS P's order and wording of line restored.

Defeat of Hengist

even better. They made their troops scatter and abandon the field. The great and heavy blows these received forced them to turn their backs. When Hengist saw his men retreat and turn their backs to the blows, he spurred his horse towards Conisbrough,[1] thinking to find protection there. But the king kept pursuing him, crying to his men: 'Forward, forward!'

7775 When Hengist saw they were following him, and would besiege him in the castle, he wished rather to fight outside and risk his person than be inside and let himself be attacked, when he had no hope of help. He withdrew and reassembled his men, returning them to the fight. Once more there was battle, heavy fighting and a violent fray. The heathen turned back, each rallying the other. Thus the Christians suffered losses and the heathen captured many of them, because they fell into disarray. But the mounted troop of three thousand appeared to aid and support them. The heathen fought doggedly; no wonder, because they knew well they would never escape alive if they could not defend themselves. Eldulf saw Hengist and recognized him. He hated him and had reason to; now he saw the time and place to accomplish his desire. He ran at him with drawn sword. Hengist was strong and withstood the blow. The two warriors were joined in battle, with bare blades and raised shields. You could see their blows redouble and the sparks fly from the steel.

7807 Gorlois, count of Cornwall, came boldly towards the fray. Eldulf saw him approaching; it made him prouder and more resolute. Like a valiant warrior he ran and seized Hengist by the nose-guard, dragging him towards him and forcing down his head, carrying him off by brute force. 'Knights, God be thanked,' he said, 'my desire is fulfilled. We have captured and defeated the man who has caused us so much harm. Kill this mad dog, who never had pity on us. He is the source of the war which has laid our land waste. You hold victory in your hands if you kill him.' Then Hengist was properly brought to justice. He was bound and chained and handed over to king Aurelius; they guarded and confined him closely. His son Octa, who was in the field, and his cousin, Ebissa, escaped with difficulty and entered York. They equipped the city within with as many men as they had. Many others had fled, whether to the forest, the plain, the valleys or the mountains.

7837 The king was happy with the glory of the victory God had given him. He entered Conisbrough and stayed three whole days there, in order for the wounded to be cared for and the weary to rest. Meanwhile he spoke to the barons and asked

---

[1] In Yorkshire. *HRB* chap. 123: *Cununoeburg*; *VV*: *Cunungeburg*.

Pur les naffrez medeciner
E pur les lassez reposer.
Entretant as baruns parla,
Comunement lur demanda
Quei del felun Henguist fereit,
S'il le tendreit u l'ocirreit. [1]
Eldadus est en piez levez,
Frere le cunte Eldulf puis nez,
Evesques ert religius,
7850 De lettres mult escientus:
'Jo vuil, dist il, de Henguist faire,
Cest traïtur, cest adversaire,
Ço que Samuel fist jadis
Del rei Agag, quant il fu pris.
Agag esteit mult orguillus,
Reis d'Amalec mult glorius;
Les Judeus tuz tens guereiout
Mal lur faiseit, mal les menout,
Lur terres preiout e ardeit
7860 E mult suvent les ocieit.
Puis fu, a sa mesaventure,
Pris, en une disconfiture.
Devant Saül fu presentez,
Ki dunc esteit reis corunez.
Quant Saül enquist qu'il fereit
D'Agag, ki livré li esteit,
En piez se leva Samuel,
Uns sainz prophete d'Israël;
Unches de plus grant sainteé
7870 Ne sout l'un hume en sun eé.
Cil Samuel Agag saisi,
Par plusurs pieces le parti;
Tut l'ad par pieces decolpé
E par la cuntree geté.
Savez que Samuel diseit
Quant il d'Agag pieces faiseit?
Agag, maint hume as travaillié,
Maint hume ocis, maint eissillié,
Tu as mainte aume de cors traite
7880 E mainte mere triste faite,

Maint enfant as fait orphenin,
E tu es or venuz a fin.
Ta mere senz enfant ferai
E t'aume de tun cors trarai.
Ço devez faire de cestui
Que Samuel fist de celui.'
Par l'example qu'Eldadus dist
Sailli Eldulf si prist Henguist,
Fors de la vile le mena,
S'espee traist sil decola.   7890
Li reis fist le cors conreer
E sepelir e enterrer
A la guise que cil faiseient
Ki le lei paenur teneient.
Li reis se contint vivement,
Ne sojorna pas lungement;
A Everwic vint od grant ost,
Ses enemis dedenz enclost;
Octa, fiz Henguist, ert dedenz
E partie de ses parenz.   7900
Cil vit que nul succurs n'avreit
Ne defendre ne se purreit.
Purpensa sei qu'il se rendreit;
En aventure se mettreit;
Mult humlement merci quereit, [2]
S'il la truvot, bel li sereit.
Issi fist cum il out pensé
E si parent li unt loé;
De la cité a pied eissi
E trestuit si hume altresi.   7910
Octa, ki premier al rei vint,
Une chaene de fer tint.
'Sire, dist il, merci, merci!
Trestut li Deu nus unt failli [3]
U nus sulum aveir fiance.
Tis Deus est de grainur puissance;
Miracles fait e granz vertuz
Ki par tei nus ad tuz vencuz.
Vencuz sui, a ta merci vienc,
Tien la chaeine que jo tienc   7920

---

[1] MS P reading—*l'*—restored.
[2] MS P reading—*quereit*—restored.
[3] MS P reading—*Trestut*—restored.

Death of Hengist

them all together what he should do with the wicked Hengist: should he keep him or kill him? Eldadus rose to his feet, younger brother of Count Eldulf, a pious and most learned bishop. 'I want,' he said, 'to do to Hengist, this traitor and enemy, what Samuel once did to king Agag, when he was captured. Agag, the boastful king of the Amalekites, was very arrogant. He constantly made war on the Jews, did them harm and ill-treated them, pillaged and burnt their lands and frequently killed them. Then, by mishap, he was defeated and captured. He was brought before Saul, then the crowned king. When Saul enquired what he should do with Agag, who had been handed over to him, Samuel rose to his feet, a holy prophet of Israel. There was no man in his lifetime to equal him for saintliness. This Samuel seized Agag and divided him into many pieces; he cut him all up into bits and scattered him throughout the land. Do you know what Samuel said while he cut up Agag? "Agag, you have injured many men, killed many, impoverished many; you have separated many a soul from its body and grieved many a mother, orphaned many a child, and now are you come to your end. I will make your mother childless and separate the soul from your body." What Samuel did to him, you should do to this man.' Following the example Eldadus cited, Eldulf jumped up and seized Hengist, led him out of the town, drew his sword and cut off his head. The king had the body prepared, interred and buried according to the custom of those who observe the heathen law.

7895   The king acted briskly and did not delay. He came to York with a great army and hemmed his enemies in. Octa, Hengist's son, was inside with some of his kin. He saw he would get no help and could not defend himself. He resolved to surrender, take the risk, and most humbly seek mercy; if he found it, he would be content. He did as he had planned, and his relatives praised him: he left the city on foot and all his men likewise. Octa, the first to reach the king, held an iron chain. 'My lord,' he said, 'mercy, mercy! All the gods we used to trust have let us down. Your God is more powerful: he performs miracles and great wonders, so that through you he has conquered us all. I am conquered, I come seeking your mercy. Take this chain I bear and do what you like with me and with my men too.

Si feras de mei tun talent
E de mes humes ensement.
Tut avum mis a tun plaisir
De vie e de membres tolir.
Mais, si tu vis nus reteneies,
Grant servise de nus avreies;[1]
Lealment te servirium
E ti hume devendrium.'
Li reis fu de grant pieté;
7930　Envirun sei ad esguardé
Saveir que li barun dirreient
E coment l'en conseillereient.
Eldadus, li bons ordenez,
Parla avant, cume senez:
'Bien est, dist il, e fu e ert
Que merci ait ki merci quiert,
Kar ki merci nen ad d'altrui
Ne Deus merci n'avra de lui.
Cist de merci aveir t'essaient,
7940　Merci quierent e merci aient.
E Bretaine, ki est lunge e lee[2]
Par plusurs lius est desertee;
Fai lur en partie livrer
Sis fai arer e laborer,
Si vivrunt de lur guaainages.
Mais primes en pren bons ostages
Que lealment te servirunt
E lealment se contendrunt.
Cil de Gabaon merci quistrent
7950　Quant Judeu jadis les conquistrent;
Merci quistrent, merci truverent,
E Judeu quites les clamerent.
Ne devum mie estre peiur[3]
Que Juideu furent a cel jur.[4]
Merci preient, merci receivent,
D'or en avant murir ne deivent.'
Li reis terre lur otreia,
Cumë Eldadus li loa,
Dejuste Escoce a guaainer;
7960　Dunc s'alerent la herbergier,

Mais primes dunerent ostages,
Enfanz de lur meillurs lignages.
　Quinze jurs fu puis en la vile,
Ses genz manda si tint concile.
Ses baruns, ses clers, ses abbez
E ses evesques ad mandez;
Lur fius e lur dreiz lur rendi,
Puis comanda e establi
Que li mustier refait serreient
Que li paien destruit aveient.　　7970
Entretant departi ses oz
Si fist vecuntes e prevoz
Ki ses demaines restorassent
E ki ses rentes li guardassent.
Maçuns fist querre e charpentiers
Si fist refaire les mustiers;
Les eglises de par la terre
Ki destruites erent par guerre
Fist li reis tutes restorer
A Deu servir e aorer.　　　　　7980
D'illuec est a Lundres turnez,
U il esteit mult desirrez.
La cité vit mult empeiree
E de bons citedeins voidee,
Maisuns guastes, mustiers chaeiz;
Assez l'ad plainte mainte feiz.
Les mustiers fist repareillier
E clers e burgeis repairer,
As leis ki ainz soleient estre.
Emprés vint li reis a Wincestre;　7990
Iglises e maisuns e turs
Refist cum il out fait aillurs.
Puis est alé a Ambresbiere
Pur visiter le cimetire
U cil erent ensepeli
Ki as cultels furent murdri.
Maçuns e bons enginneürs
E charpentiers manda plusurs;
La place de l'occisiun
Que Henguist fist par traïsun　　8000

---

[1] MS P reading—*grant servise*—restored.
[2] MS P reading—*E*—restored.
[3] MS P reading—*mie*—restored.
[4] MS P reading—*Juideu*—restored.

Octa settles in Scotland

Everything is at your disposal—to take our lives and our limbs. But if you wish to keep us alive, you will receive great recompense: we will serve you loyally and become your men.'

7929 The king was filled with compassion. He looked round to see what the barons would say and how they would counsel him. The good priest Eldadus spoke first, like a wise man: 'It is, was, and always will be good,' he said, 'for him who seeks mercy to receive it, for God will have no mercy on him who has none on others. These men try to have mercy from you; they seek mercy and they should have it. Britain, extensive and broad, is in many places deserted. Give them a part of it and make them plough and till it: they can live off what they cultivate. But first take good hostages from them, who will serve you faithfully and fight loyally. Once upon a time, the Gibeonites asked for mercy, when the Jews conquered them. They sought mercy, they found mercy, and the Jews released them. We should not be worse than the Jews were that day. They beg for mercy: they should receive it and henceforth should not die.' The king, as Eldadus advised him, granted them land near Scotland to cultivate. So they went to dwell there, but first they gave him hostages, children from their noblest families.

7963 He then spent a fortnight in the city, summoning his people and holding council. He summoned his barons, clerks, abbots and bishops, restoring to them their lands and their rights. Then he commanded and ordained that the churches which the heathen had destroyed should be rebuilt. Meanwhile, he disbanded his army and created sheriffs and governors who would restore his domains and be in charge of his revenue. He had a search made for masons and carpenters and rebuilt the monasteries; throughout the land, the churches destroyed by war were all restored by the king, to serve and worship God. From there he returned to London, where they longed for his coming. He saw that the city was much damaged and deprived of good citizens, with houses laid waste and churches collapsed, and many times he greatly lamented it. He had the churches repaired and made the clerks and citizens return to the observances performed there before. Next the king came to Winchester and rebuilt churches, houses and towers as he had done elsewhere. Then he went to Amesbury[1] to visit the graveyard of those who had been murdered with the knives. He summoned many masons, good engineers and carpenters; he wanted to do honour to the site of the treacherous killing by Hengist with such a monument as might last for ever.

---

[1] In *HRB* chap. 127 Aurelius visits a monastery on Mount Ambrius near Salisbury. See Thorpe, *Geoffrey of Monmouth: History*, p. 195.

Vuleit de tel ovre onorer
Ki tuz tens mais peüst durer.
Tremorius, un sages huem,
Archevesques de Karliom,
Li rova que Merlin mandast
E par sun cunseil en errast; [1]
Nuls hom mielz nel conseillereit
A faire ço ke il voldreit;
Kar d'ovrer ne de deviner
8010 Ne poeit l'um trover sun per.
Li reis volt mult Merlin veer
E oïr volt de sun saveir;
A Labanes, une funtaine,
Ki en Guales ert, bien luintaine,
Ne sai u est, kar unc n'i fui,
Fist li reis enveier pur lui.
Cil vint al rei qui l'out mandé,
E li reis l'ad mult enuré.
A grant enur le recuilli,
8020 Mult le joï, mult le cheri.
Mult le preia, mult le requist
Qu'il l'enseinast, qu'il li deïst
Del tens ki esteit a venir,
Mult en voleit par lui oïr.
'Sire, dist Merlin, nu ferai,
Ja ma buche nen uverai
Se n'est par grant necesseté
E dunc par grant humilité.
Se jon parloe par vantance [2]
8030 Ne par eschar ne par bobance,
Li espirites que jo ai,
Par ki jo sai ço que jo sai,
De ma buche se retrareit
E ma science me toldreit,
Ne ma buche ne parlereit
Plus ke buche d'altre fereit.
Lai ester les devins segreiz;
Pense de ço que faire deiz.
Se tu vuels faire ovre durable,
8040 Ki mult seit bele e covenable

E dunt tuz tens seit mais parole,
Fai ci aporter la carole
Que gaiant firent en Irlande,
Une merveilluse ovre e grande
De pieres en un cerne assises,
Les unes sur les altres mises.
Les pieres sunt teles e tantes,
Tant ahuges e tant pesantes,
Que force d'ome k'ore seit
Nule d'eles ne portereit.'   8050
'Merlin, dist li reis, en riant,
Des que les pieres peisent tant
Que huem nes purreit remuer,
Ki mes purreit ci aporter;
Cume se nus en cest regné
Avium de pieres chierté?'
'Reis, dist Merlin, dunc ne sez tu
Que engin surmunte vertu.
Bone est force e engin mielz valt;
La valt engin u force falt.   8060
Engin e art funt mainte chose
Que force comencer nen ose.
Engin puet les pieres muveir
E par engin les poez aveir.
D'Aufrice furent aportees,
La furent primes compassees;
Gaiant de la les aporterent; [3]
En Irlande les aloerent.
Mult suelent estre saluables
E as malades profitables. [4]   8070
Les genz les soleient laver
E de l'eue les bainz temprer. [5]
Cil ki esteient engroté
E d'alcune enferté grevé,
Des laveüres bainz feseient,
Bainoent sei si guarisseient
Ja pur enferté qu'il sentissent
Altre mecine ne quesissent.'
    Quant li reis e li Bretun surent
Que les pieres tel valur ourent,   8080

---

[1] MS P reading—*errast*—restored.
[2] MS P reading—*jon*—restored.
[3] MS P reading—*aporterent*—restored.
[4] MS P reading—*as*—restored.
[5] MS P reading—*les*—restored.

Merlin advises Aurelius

8003 Tremorius, a wise man who was archbishop of Caerleon, asked him to send for Merlin and act according to his advice. No man would counsel him better on what he wanted to do, for neither in action nor in prophecy could one find his equal. The king greatly wished to see Merlin and hear his wisdom. He sent for him at Labanes, a far-off spring in Wales (I don't know where, because I was never there).[1] Merlin came to the king who had summoned him, and the king paid him great honour, receiving him with respect. He made much of him, treasured him, and begged and prayed him to teach and inform him of the time to come: he dearly wished to hear of it from him. 'Sire,' said Merlin, 'I will not do so; I will never open my mouth unless it is really necessary, and then only with great humility. If I spoke boastfully, in jest, or arrogantly, the spirit I possess, from whom I know what I know, would leave my mouth and take my knowledge with him, and my mouth would no longer speak differently from any other. Leave secret divination alone; think of what you must do. If you wish to create a durable monument, beautiful and fitting, and remembered forever, have the Giants' Dance brought here, made in Ireland.[2] It is a huge and marvellous work of stones set in a circle, one on top of the other. The stones are so many and of such a kind, so enormous and so heavy, that no man nowadays would be strong enough to lift them.' 'Merlin,' said the king, laughing, 'since the stones weigh so much that no man can move them, who could bring them here? As if we had a dearth of stones in this realm!' 'King,' answered Merlin, 'then you don't know that skill surpasses strength. Might is good, skill better; skill prevails where might fails.[3] Skill and art achieve many things which might doesn't dare to start. Skill can move the stones and through skill you can possess them. They were brought from Africa, where they were first constructed; giants took them from there and placed them in Ireland. They used to be most beneficial and useful to the sick. People used to wash the stones and mingle this water with their baths. Those who were ill and suffering from any disease prepared baths from these cleansing waters, bathed themselves, and were cured; they never sought any other medicine, for whatever infirmity they might suffer.'

8079 When the king and the British realised what worth the stones possessed, they all

---

[1] In *HRB* chap. 128 this spring is called *Galabes* (*Galahes* in the *VV*), in the territory of the Gewissei; see fn. 4 to p. 145.

[2] *HRB* chap. 128 says the 'Giants' Ring' is on Mount Killaraus—see *Brut*, para. 8119.

[3] Probably proverbial: see Hassell, *Middle French Proverbs*, E 36 and Le Roux de Lincy, *Livre des Proverbes*, p. 296 for similar sayings.

Mult furent tuit entalenté
E tuit orent grant volenté
D'aler aporter la carole
Dunt Merlin faiseit tel parole.
Uther unt ensemble choisi,
Il meïsmes s'en purofri,
Que en Irlande passereit
E quinze mil armez merreit
Ki as Irreis se combatreient
8090 S'il les pieres lur defendeient;
Merlin ensemble od els irreit
Ki les pieres enginnereit.
Quant Uther ot sa gent mandee,
En Irlande ad la mer passee.
Gillomanius, ki ert reis,
Manda sa gent e ses Irreis,
Les Bretuns prist a manacier
E del païs les volt chacier.
E quant il sout que il quereient,
8100 Que pur pieres venu esteient,
Assez s'est alez d'els gabant:
La folie aloent querant,
Ki aveient pur pieres querre
Trespassé mer en altre terre;
Ja une, ço dist, nen avrunt
Ne ja une n'enporterunt.
Legierement les pout despire,
Mais grief furent a desconfire.
Tant despist e tant maneça
8110 E tant les quist qu'il les trova.
Sempres se sunt entrevenu
E bien se sunt entreferu.
Ireis n'erent pas bien armé,
Ne de combatre acustumé;
Les Bretuns aveient despiz,
Mais Bretun les unt desconfiz;
Li reis s'en est alez fuiant,
De vile en vile tresturnant.
Quant Bretun furent desarmé
8120 E bien se furent reposé,

Merlin, ki ert en la compaine,
Les mena en une muntaine
U la carole esteit assise
As gaianz, qu'il aveient quise.
Killomar li munz aveit nun
U la carole esteit en sun.
Cil unt les pieres esguardees,
Assez les unt environees;
E li uns ad a l'altre dit,
Ki unches mais tel ovre vit: 8130
'Cument sunt ces pieres levees
E cument serunt remuees?'
'Seinurs, dist Merlin, assaiez
Se par vertu ke vus aiez
Purrez ces pieres remuer,
E si vus les purrez porter.'
Cil se sunt as pieres aërs
Detriés, devant e de travers;
Bien unt enpeint e bien buté;
E bien retrait e bien crollé;   8140
Unches par force a la menur
Ne porent faire prendre un tur.
'Traiez vus, dist Merlin, en sus,
Ja par force nen ferez plus.
Or verrez engin e saveir
Mielz que vertu de cors valeir.'
Dunc ala avant si s'estut,
Entur guarda, les levres mut
Comë huem ki dit oreisun;
Ne sai s'il dist preiere u nun.   8150
Dunc ad les Bretuns rapelez:
'Venez avant, dist il, venez!
Or poëz les pieres baillier,
A voz nefs porter e chargier.'
Si come Merlin enseinna,
Si cum il dist e enginna,
Unt li Bretun les pieres prises,
As nés portees e enz mises.
En Engleterre les menerent,
A Ambresbire les porterent   8160

Stonehenge is removed to England

had a great wish to go and carry off the Dance of which Merlin made such report. Together they chose Uther—and he himself came forward—to cross into Ireland, taking fifteen thousand armed men, to fight the Irish if they denied them the stones. Merlin would go with them to manœuvre the stones. When Uther had summoned his men, he crossed the sea to Ireland. Gilloman, who was king, summoned his people and his Irishmen and began to threaten the British, wanting to expel them from the land. And when he heard what they sought, that they had come for the stones, he derided them at length: those who, seeking stones, crossed the sea to another land, went in search of folly. Not a single one, he said, should they have, nor would they ever carry one off. He found it easy to despise them, but defeating them was harder. He despised and threatened them for so long, he looked for them so hard, that he found them. At once the two forces came together and exchanged blows. The Irish were not well armed, nor used to combat; they had despised the British, but the British defeated them. The king ran away, fleeing from town to town.

8119   When the British had disarmed and thoroughly rested, Merlin, who was in the company, led them to a mountain where the Giants' Dance, which they had sought, was situated. The mountain, on whose top was the Dance, was called Killomar. They completely surrounded the stones and examined them, and each said to the other that he had never seen such a work. 'How can these stones be raised and how will they be moved?' 'My lords,' said Merlin, 'try and see if you can move these stones with the strength you have, and if you can carry them.' They grasped the stones behind, in front and sideways; they pushed and thrust them hard, pulled and shook them hard, but however much force they used, they could not find a solution. 'Rise,' said Merlin, 'you will do no more by force. Now you shall see how knowledge and skill are better than bodily strength.' Then he stepped forward and stopped. He looked around, his lips moving like a man saying his prayers. I don't know if he said a prayer or not.[1] Then he called the Britons back. 'Come here,' he said, 'come! Now you can handle the stones, and carry and load them into your ships.' As Merlin instructed, as he devised and told them, the Britons took the stones, carried them to the ships and placed them inside. They brought them to England and carried them to Amesbury, into the fields nearby.[2]

---

[1] In *HRB* chap. 130 Merlin is less mysterious and uses 'machines'; the *VV* makes his methods 'those of a true magician' (Wright II, p. l).

[2] *HA* (I, chap. 7) is the first to describe Stonehenge, as one of the four wonders of England, but only uses this story of its origins in the third version of *HA*, influenced by *HRB*. See Greenway p. 23, fn. 32.

En la champaine illuec dejuste.
Li reis i vint a Pentecuste;
Ses evesques e ses abez
E ses baruns ad tuz mandez;
Altre gent mult i assembla,
Feste tint si se coruna.
Treis jurs tint grant feste e al quart
Duna croces par grant esguart
A saint Dubriz de Karlion
8170 E d'Everwic a saint Sanson.
Andui erent de grant clergie
E andui mult de sainte vie.
E Merlin les pieres dreça,
En lur ordre les raloa;
Bretun les suelent en bretanz
Apeler carole as gaianz,
Stanhenges unt nun en engleis,
Pieres pendues en franceis.
    Quant la grant feste fu finie,
8180 La curt le rei s'est departie.
Paschent, un des fiz Vortiger,
Pur poür d'Ambrosie e d'Uther,[1]
Guales e Bretaine guerpi,
Vers Alemaine s'en fuï.
Humes purchaça e navie
Mais n'out mie grant compainie;
En Bretaine north arriva,
Viles destruit, terres guasta,
Mais lunges ester n'i osa,
8190 Kar li reis vint, ki l'en chaça.
Quant Paschent refu a la mer,
N'osa la dunt il vint turner;
Tant corut a sigle e a nage,
En Irlande vint al rivage.[2]
Al rei de la terre parla,
Sun estre e sun busuin mustra.
Tant ad Paschent le rei preied,
E tant unt entr'els cunseillied,
Ço distrent que mer passereient
8200 E as Bretuns se combatreient,

Paschent pur sun pere vengier
E pur s'erité chalengier,
Li reis pur querre vengement
De cels ki orent nuvelement[3]
Lui vencu e sa gent robee
E la carole od els portee;
Pris se sunt andui par fiance
De querre a chascun d'els vengance.
Od tant d'esforz cum aver porent
Passerent mer quant bon vent orent.   8210
En Guales sunt tuit arivé
E en Meneve sunt entré.
Meneve ert lores cité bele
Que l'um or Saint David apele.
Li reis Ambrosie se giseit,[4]
A Wincestre ert si languisseit;
Engrotez ert, lungement jut
Qu'il ne guari ne ne morut.
Quant il out oï de Paschent
E del rei d'Irlande ensement,   8220
Ki en Guales venuz esteient
E sa terre guaster vuleient,
Uther sun frere i enveia;
N'i pout aler, ço li pesa.
A Uther dist qu'il les quesist
E que a els se combatist.
Uther ad mandé les barons
E tuz les chevaliers sumuns.
Tant pur la lunge veie aler
E tant pur la gent aüner,   8230
Mult demura, lunc terme mist
Ainz qu'il en Guales parvenist.
Endementres qu'il demura
Eappas a Paschent parla;
Paiens ert, de Saixonie nez,
Ki mult esteit enlochonez;
De medicine se faiseit sage[5]
Si saveit parler maint langage,
Fel esteit e de male fei.
'Paschent, dist il, en un segrei,[6]   8240

---

[1] MS P reading—d'Ambrosie—restored.
[2] MS P: Irrande here and l. 8220.
[3] MS P reading—nuvelement—restored.

[4] MS P reading—Ambrosie—restored.
[5] MS P reading—medicine—restored.
[6] MS P's wording of line restored.

Paschent plots against Aurelius

At Pentecost the king arrived, summoning all his bishops, abbots and barons. Many other people gathered there, a feast was held, and he was crowned. For three days he held a great feast and on the fourth, after great deliberation, he gave bishoprics to the saintly Dubric of Caerleon and Sanson of York. Both were men of great learning and most holy life. And Merlin erected the stones, restoring them to their proper order. In the British language the Britons usually call them the Giants' Dance; in English they are called Stonehenge, and in French, the Hanging Stones.

8179 When the great feast was finished, the king's court departed. One of Vortigern's sons, Paschent,[1] fearful of Ambrosius[2] and Uther, left Wales and Britain and fled to Germany. He acquired men and a fleet for money, but his company was not large. He arrived in northern Britain, destroying towns and laying lands waste, but he did not dare to stay there long, because the king arrived and chased him away. When Paschent was back at sea, he did not dare return whence he had come. He sailed and rowed so far that he came to the shores of Ireland. He spoke to the king of that land and revealed his identity and his plight. Paschent begged the king so urgently, and they conferred with each other so much, that they agreed to cross the sea and fight the British, Paschent in order to avenge his father and claim his inheritance, and the king in order to seek revenge on those who had recently defeated him, robbed his people and carried off the Dance. They both pledged to seek vengeance for each other. With as many troops as possible, they crossed the sea when there was a favourable wind. They all arrived in Wales and entered Menevia. This was at the time a beautiful city, nowadays called St David's.[3]

8215 Ambrosius the king lay sick: he languished in bed at Winchester, infirm, and for a long time between recovery and death. When he heard that Paschent, and the Irish king too, had come to Wales intending to ravage his realm, he sent his brother Uther there; he was distressed he could not go himself. He told Uther he was to seek them out and fight them. Uther summoned the barons and all the knights. Partly because he had to gather men together, partly because of the long journey, he was much delayed and it was a long time before he reached Wales. While he delayed, Eappas[4] spoke to Paschent. He was a heathen, born in Saxony and most learned, knowledgeable about medicines and fluent in many languages, a wicked man with an evil faith. In private, he said: 'Paschent, you have long hated the king: what will you give me if I kill him?'

---

[1] *HRB* chap. 131: *Pacentius*; *VV*: *Pascencius*.

[2] Ambrosius is the cognomen of Aurelius: see para. 6424.

[3] Wace adds this detail of the city.

[4] *HRB* chap. 132: *Eapa/Eopa*; *VV*: *Eappa*.

'Tu as piece ad le rei haï;
Que me durras se jo l'oci?'
'Mil livres, dist il, te durrai,
Ne jamais jur ne te faldrai
Si tu ta parole acomplis
Que li reis seit par tei ocis.'
'Ne jo, dist il, plus ne demant.'
Issi firent lur covenant,
Paschent de mil livres duner
8250 E cil del rei empuisuner.
Eappas fu mult enginnus
E de l'argent fu coveitus.
De dras munials se vesti,
Corune fist, halt se tundi;
Cume muines rés e tunduz,
E cume muines revestuz,
Od cuntenance munial,
Est alez a la curt real.
Trichierre fu, mire se fist,
8260 Al rei parla si li pramist
Qu'a brief terme le fereit sain
S'il se vuleit mettre en sa main.
Tasta al pulz e vit l'urine;
Bien sout, ço dist, del mal l'orine,
E bien le sout mediciner.
Ki deüst tel home duter?
Li gentilz reis guarir vuleit
Cume chescuns de nus vuldreit.
N'aveit dute de traïsun,
8270 Es mains se mist a cel felun.
E cil li ad puisun dunee
De venim tute destempree,
Puis le fist chaudement covrir
E gesir en pais e dormir.
Des que li reis fu eschaufez
E li venim al cors medlez,
Deus, quel dolur! murir l'estut;
Mais quant il sout que murir dut,
A ses homes dist kil gaitouent,
8280 Si veirement cum il l'amouent,

Qu'a Stanhanges sun cors portassent
E illuec dedenz l'enterrassent;
Issi fu morz, issi feni,
E li traïtres s'en fuï.
    Uther fu en Guales entrez,
A Meneve ot Ireis trovez.
Une esteille est dunc aparue
Ki a plusurs genz fu veüe;
Cumete ot nun sulunc clergie,
Muement de rei senefie.   8290
Clere esteit merveillusement,
Si getot un rai sulement.
Uns feus, ki de cel rai eisseit,
Figure de dragun faiseit;
De cel dragun dui rai veneient,
Ki par la gule fors eisseient,
Li uns sur France s'estendeit,
E desi a Muntgieu luiseit;
Li altres vers Irlande alout
E en set rais se devisout;   8300
Cheschuns des set rais luiseit cler
E sur la terre e sur la mer.
Del signe ki fu tel veüz
Fu li pueples tut cumeüz;
Uther forment s'en merveilla
E merveilles s'en effrea.
Merlin ad preied qu'il li die
Que si fait signe senefie,
E Merlin mult se conturba, [1]
Duel out al quer, mot ne sona.   8310
Quant sis esperiz repaira,
Mult se plainst e mult suspira:
'Hé Deus, dist il, cum granz dolurs,
Cum grant damage, cum granz plurs
Sunt avenu ui en Bretainne!
Perdu ad sun buen chevetainne;
Morz est li reis, li bons vassals
Ki des dolurs e des granz mals
A ceste terre delivree
E des mains as paiens ostee.'   8320

---

[1] MS P reading—*conturba*—restored.

Aurelius is poisoned

'I will give you a thousand pounds,' he said, 'nor will I ever fail you, if you are as good as your word, that you'll kill the king.' 'I don't ask for more,' he said. So they struck their bargain: Paschent to give him a thousand pounds, and he to poison the king. Eappas was very cunning, and keen to get the money. He dressed in monk's clothes and gave himself a tonsure, cropping his hair on top. Shorn and tonsured like a monk, and dressed like a monk, with a monk's bearing, he went to the royal court. He was a scoundrel: he made himself out to be a doctor, spoke to the king and promised him that he would restore him to health shortly, if he would put himself in his hands. He felt his pulse and inspected his urine. He said he was well aware of the source of the trouble, and was quite able to cure it. Who might suspect such a man? The noble king wished, as any of us might do, to get better. He feared no treachery and put himself in the hands of this villain. And he gave him a potion, all mixed up with poison, then had him warmly covered and made him lie in peace, to sleep. As soon as the king warmed up, the poison penetrated his body and God, what agony! He had to die. But when he knew he was to die, he told his men, who watched over him, that if they truly loved him, they should carry his body to Stonehenge and bury it within the stones. Thus he died and came to his end, and the traitor escaped.

8285 Uther entered Wales and found the Irish at Menevia. Then a star appeared, seen by many people. According to the educated, it was called a comet and signified a change of king.[1] It was extraordinarily bright and only one ray came from it. A flame issuing from this ray was shaped like a dragon, and from this dragon's mouth two beams appeared, one stretching over France and shining as far as Muntgieu,[2] the other towards Ireland and divided into seven rays. Each of the seven shone brightly over land and sea. At the sight of such a sign, the people were quite shaken. Uther marvelled greatly at it and was much dismayed. He begged Merlin to tell him what such a sign meant. And Merlin was very troubled; he was grieved at heart and spoke not a word. When breath came back to him, he lamented and sighed bitterly. 'Oh God,' he said, 'what great grief, what great loss, how many tears, have today befallen Britain! She has lost her noble leader: the king is dead, that valiant warrior who delivered this land from grief and harm and the hands of the heathen.' When Uther heard about that good lord, his brother,

---

[1] Wace adds this couplet.   [2] See fn. 2 to p. 73.

Quant Uther oï de sun frere,
Del bon seinnur, qui finez ere,
Mult fu dolenz, mult s'esmaia;
Mais Merlin issil conforta:
'Uther, dist il, ne t'esmaier.
N'i ad del mort nul recovrier.
Espleite ço que tu as quis;
Combat tei a tes enemis.
La victorie demain t'atent
8330 Del rei d'Irlande e de Paschent;
Demain te combat si veintras
E de Bretainne rei seras.
Li signes ki fu del dragun
Nus fist significatiun
De tei ki pruz iés e hardiz; [1]
Li uns des rais, ço est uns fiz
Que tu avras, de grant puissance,
Ki conquerra jesqu'ultre France;
Par l'altre rai, ki ça turna
8340 E en set rais se devisa,
T'est une fille demustree,
Ki vers Escoce ert mariee.
Plusur bon eir de li naistrunt
Qui mers e terres conquerunt.'
Quant Uther ot bien esculté
Come Merlin l'ot conforté,
La nuit fist ses genz reposer,
E par matin les fist armer.
La cité vuleit assaillir;
8350 Mais Ireis, quil virent venir,
Pristrent lur armes, conreiz firent,
E a combatre fors eissirent.
Fierement se sunt combatu
Mais assez tost furent vencu.
Kar li Bretun ocistrent Paschent [2]
E le rei d'Irlande ensement;
Cil ki remistrent el champ vif
S'en turnerent as nés fuitif.
Uther, kis ad sewiz emprés,
8360 Les fait murir tut desconfés.

Tels i out ki s'en eschaperent,
Ki en lur nés fuiant entrerent
E en mer se firent enpeindre,
Pur ço nes pout Uther ateindre.
Quant il ot feni sun afaire,
Vers Wincestre prist sun repaire,
Le mielz od lui de sun barnage.
En l'eirre encontra un message
Ki li ad dit veraiement
Que li reis ert mort e cument,   8370
E li evesque par grant cure
Aveient fait sa sepulture
Dedenz la carole as gaianz,
Si cum il dist a ses serjanz
E a ses baruns en sa vie.
Quant Uther out la chose oïe
A Wincestre est venuz puinant,
E li puples li vint devant,
Plurant e criant a un cri:
'Uther sire, pur Deu, merci!   8380
Morz est cil ki nus mainteneit
E ki les granz bienz nus faiseit;
Or nus maintien, pren la corune
Que eritez e dreiz te dune;
E nus, bel sire, t'en preium,
Ki tun prud e t'enur volum.'
Uther vit que sis pruz esteit
E que mielz faire ne poeit;
Liez fu de ço que cil li distrent [3]
E sempres fist ço qu'il requistrent;   8390
La corune prist, reis devint,
L'enur ama, la gent maintint.
Pur enur e pur remembrance
Del dragun ki fist demustrance
Que pruz esteit e reis sereit
E eirs bien conqueranz avreit,
Fist faire Uther d'or dous draguns
Par le conseil de ses baruns.
L'un en fist devant sei porter
Quant en bataille dut aler;   8400

---

[1] MS P's order of line restored.
[2] MS P reading—*li*—restored.

[3] MS P reading—*cil*—restored.

Uther defeats Paschent and becomes king

who had perished, he felt great grief and dismay. But Merlin comforted him thus. 'Uther,' he said, 'don't be dismayed; there is no remedy for death. Carry out what you intended; fight your enemies. Victory awaits you tomorrow over the Irish king and Paschent; fight tomorrow and win, and you will be king of Britain. The sign of the dragon meant you, who are brave and bold; one of its beams signified a son which you will have, of great power, who will be victorious as far as France and beyond. Through the other beam, which diverged here and split into seven rays, a daughter is signified, who will make a Scottish marriage. Many good heirs will be born of her, who will conquer land and sea.'

8345   When Uther had listened carefully to Merlin's words of comfort, he made his men rest that night, and in the morning had them armed. He wanted to attack the city, but when the Irish saw him coming, they seized their weapons, divided themselves into companies, and came out to fight. They fought fiercely but were soon defeated, for the British killed Paschent, and the king of Ireland too. Those who remained alive on the battlefield turned and fled to their ships. Uther, who followed after them, made them die quite unshriven. There were those who escaped by fleeing to their ships and rushing out to sea, so that Uther could not reach them. When his business was finished, he went back towards Winchester and the best of his barons with him. On the way he met a messenger, who told him that indeed the king was dead, and how he had died, and that the bishops had with great care put his tomb inside the Giants' Dance, as he had instructed his servants and his barons when still alive. When Uther heard this, he came spurring into Winchester, and the common people came before him, weeping and crying out: 'Lord Uther, for God's sake, mercy! He who protected us and did us great good is dead. Now protect us: take the crown, bestowed on you by right and inheritance. And we, noble lord, beg you to do so, desiring only your honour and profit.' Uther saw it was to his advantage and that he could not do better. He was glad of what they said and at once did what they asked: he took the crown, became king, loved the realm and protected the people. In honour and memory of the dragon, which had signified he was valiant and would be king, and would have victorious heirs, Uther, advised by his barons, had two golden dragons made. One of them he had carried before him when going into battle; the other he presented to Winchester, to the diocesan church. Ever after, for this reason, he

L'altre ad a Wincestre otreied,
A l'iglise de l'evesqued.
Tuz tens puis, par ceste achaisun,
Fu numez Uther Pendragon;
Pendragon cist nuns, en bretanz,
Chiés est de dragun en rumanz. [1]
    Octa, ki fiz Henguist esteit,
A qui li reis duné aveit
Granz terres e granz mansiuns,
8410 A lui e a ses compainuns,
Quant il oï que cil ert morz
Ki mainteneit les granz efforz,
Petit preisa le nuvel rei,
Serement ne li dut ne fei;
Amis e parenz assembla,
Sis cusins od lui Eosa; [2]
Cil dui furent maistre sur tuz
E cil dui erent li plus pruz.
La gent que Paschent out menee,
8420 Qui a Uther ert eschapee,
Unt retenue en lur aïe;
Assez orent grant compainie.
La terre unt cil tut purprise
Si cum li Humbres la devise
Vers Escoce, de lunc, de lé;
Puis sunt a Everwic alé
La cité entur assaillirent
E cil dedenz se defendirent
Que paien nule rien n'i pristrent; [3]
8430 Mais grant gent orent sis assistrent.
Uther vult sa cité rescure
E ses amis dedenz succure;
A Everwic vint tut errant,
De tutes parz sa gent mandant.
Del siege vult paiens partir,
Sis est alez maneis ferir.
Aspre fu e grief la medlee,
Mainte aume i ot del cors sevree.
Paien furent de grant vertu
8440 Si se sunt bien entretenu,

Nes porent pru Bretun grever
Ne dedenz els a force entrer;
En sus les estut resortir,
E quant il s'en voldrent partir
Cil del siege les parsoïrent,
Ki merveillus damage en firent;
Tant les unt alé parsoant,
D'ures en altres ateinnant,
A un munt les vindrent menant
E la nuit les parti a tant.   8450
Danien li munz aveit nun,
Alques esteit aguz en sun;
Roches i ot e granz destreiz,
E environ espés coldreiz.
Bretun se sunt al munt aërs,
Tant dreit a munt, tant de travers;
Le tertre unt tut en sun purpris
E li paien les unt assis,
Ke desuz erent en la plaine;
Entur assistrent la muntaine.   8460
Li reis fu mult en grant effrei
Que de ses humes, que de sei.
En dute fu que il fereient,
Cumfaitement guarir purreient.
Gorlois, uns cuens cornoalleis,
Mult pruz, mult saives, mult corteis,
Ert od lu rei, alques d'eage,
Il esteit mult tenuz pur sage;
A celui unt cunseil requis
E lur affaire unt sur lui mis,   8470
Kar il ne feïst cuardie
Pur menbre perdre ne pur vie.
'Conseil, dist il, me demandez;
Mis conseilz est, se vus vulez,
Que celeement nus armum
E de cest tertre devalum;
Noz enemis alum ferir,
Qui asseür quident dormir.
Nen unt poür ne n'unt dutance
Que nus vers els portum mais lance;   8480

---

[1] MS G adds: *Uther fust molt de grant poissance/ Et en ce ot molt grant fience/ Ainçois que il fust coroné/ Que par seingne fust demonstré/ Que rois seroit et heirs avroit/ Dont grant repallance seroit/ Ce li dona grant vasselage/ Et molt granment en son corage/ En sa vie vout encomplir/ Fust bien ou mal ne vot guerpi/ Quar* *bien savoit et veirs estoit/ Que de quanque il en prendroit/ A bon chief vendroit a la fin/ Si mençongier n'estoit Merlin/ Por ce ne vout onc riens doter/ Trestoz ses faicz vout achever.*

[2] MS P: *Cosa.*

[3] MS P reading—*n'i*—restored.

Octa attacks the British

was called Uther Pendragon: this British name, Pendragon, means Dragon Head in French.

8407   The king had given tracts of land and great houses to Octa, Hengist's son, and his friends. When Octa heard that he who had maintained large armies was dead, he set no store by the new king: he owed him neither oath nor loyalty. He gathered friends and family together, including his cousin Eosa[1]: these two were the boldest, and masters over the rest. They retained as allies those men led by Paschent who had escaped Uther, and had a very great company. They overran on every side all the land from the boundary of the Humber up to Scotland. Then they went to York and attacked the city, and those inside defended themselves, so that the heathen captured nothing, but there were many men besieging them. Uther wanted to rescue his city and help his friends inside. He came at once to York, summoning his men from all sides. He wished to make the heathen give up the siege, and immediately advanced to strike them. The battle was violent and arduous, and many a soul was there parted from its body. The heathen were very powerful and put up a spirited resistance; the brave British could neither do them damage nor force an entrance through them. They had to withdraw far off, and when they wanted to retreat, the besiegers chased them, inflicting great injury. They pursued them so hard, overtaking them from time to time, that they brought them to a mountain, and night then separated them. The mountain was called Danien,[2] and at its top was rather steep; there were rocks and huge defiles and dense thickets round about. The Britons made for the mountain, some ascending to the top, others going round its sides. They occupied the whole hill and the heathen, down below in the plain, attacked them, besieging the mountain round about.

8461   The king was much dismayed, both for his men and for himself. He was doubtful about what they could do and how they could escape. Gorlois, a Cornish count, very brave, sagacious and courteous, was with the king; a man of mature years, he was considered to be very wise. They asked him for advice and put the situation before him, for he would not have acted in a cowardly way to save his limbs or his life. 'You ask me for advice,' he said. 'My advice is—if you agree—to arm ourselves secretly and descend this hill: we shall strike our enemies, who imagine they sleep in safety. They have neither fear nor dread that anyone will ever bear

---

[1] Is Eosa confused with Ebissa (para. 7019)? In *HRB* there is a clear distinction: Ebissa is a younger brother of Octa and Eosa is a 'kinsman'. In the *Brut*, both Eosa and Ebissa are called 'cousins' and the wide variety of MSS variants— *Cosa, Ossa, Cossa, Eosa, Ebissa, Obissa*—suggests confusion. MS P calls Eosa *Cosa* throughout.

[2] *HRB* chap. 136: *Damen*; three of *VV*'s eight MSS have *Danien*.

Le matinet nus quident prendre
Si nus ci les vulum attendre.
Alum a els celeement
Sis ferum el tas sudement! [1]
Mar i avra ordre tenu
Ne corn suné, ne cri ne heu.
Ainz que il seient esveillé
En avrum nus tant detrenchié
Ja cil ki nus escheperunt
8490   Cuntre nus mais ne turnerunt.
Mais primes a Deu prametum
Que vers lui nus amenderum,
E des pecchiez que fait avum
Penitance e pardun querum,
E guerpissum nos felonies
Que fait avum tutes noz vies,
E depreum le Salveür
Qu'il nus maintienge e dunt vigur
Contre cels ki en lui ne creient
8500   E qui ses cristïens guereient,
Pur co iert Deus ensemble od nus
E si serum par lui rescus;
E des que Deus od nus sera,
Ki est qui nus desconfira?'
Par le conseil que cist duna, [2]
E si cum il dist e loa,
Unt pramis a Deu humlement
De lur vies amendment.
Dunc sunt armé, e a celé
8510   Sunt jus del tertre devalé.
Paiens troverent tuz gisanz,
Tuz desarmez e dormanz.
Dunc veïssiez grant tueïz
E merveillus deglageïz,
Ventres percier, piz enfundrer,
Testes e piez e puinz voler.
Si cum li liuns orguillus,
Ki de lunges est fameillus,
Ocist mutuns, ocist berbiz,
8520   Ocist ainnels granz e petiz,

Tut ensement Bretun faiseient,
Riches e povres ocieient.
Par les champs erent endormi
E puis furent si esbahi
Unches ne tindrent plai d'armer
Ne d'illuec ne porent turner;
E li Bretun les deglagoent
Ki tuz senz armes lé truvoent;
Percent ventres, percent corailles,
Traient bueles e entrailles.   8530
Li seinnur qui la guerre esmurent,
Octa e Eosa, pris furent; [3]
A Lundres furent enveied
E en chartre mis e lied.
Si alcuns del champ eschapa,
La nuit obscure le salva.
Ki fuïr s'en pout si fuï,
Unches ami n'i atendi;
Mais mult en i ot plus ocis
Que il n'en eschapa de vifs.   8540
  Quant Uther fu d'illuec turnez,
Par Northumberlande est passez,
De Northumberlande en Escoce,
Od grant maisniee e od grant force.
La terre ad tute avirunee
Tant cum ele est e lunge e lee;
La gent, ki esteit senz justise,
Ad tute atraite a sun servise.
Par tut le regne tel pais mist
Unches reis ainz si grant n'i fist. [4]   8550
Quant vers north ot fait sun afaire
A Lundres dreit prist sun repaire,
E li jurz de Pasche veneit
Que il coruner se vuleit.
Ducs e cuntes e citaains, [5]
Tuz les luintains e les procains,
Et trestut sun altre barnage
Semunst par brief e par message
Que od lur femes espusees
E od lur maisnees privees   8560

---

[1] MS P reading—*sis*—restored.
[2] MS P reading—*cist*—restored.
[3] MS P: *Cosa*.

[4] MS P reading—*n'i*—restored.
[5] MS P reading—*citaains*—restored.

Uther defeats Octa

a lance against them again. They expect to seize us in the morning—if we want
to await them here. Let's go to them by stealth and strike suddenly at the whole
pack! They will never be able to keep order, blow a horn or shout a battle-cry.
Before they are awake we will have slaughtered so many of them that none of
those escaping us will ever again resist us. But first let us promise God that we
will make amends to Him, and seek penitence and forgiveness for our sins, and
abandon our wickedness, which we have committed all our lives. And let us pray
to the Saviour to support us and strengthen us against those who don't believe in
Him and attack His Christians. In this way God will be with us and rescue us;
and once God is with us, who can possibly defeat us ?'[1]

8505   By his advice, and according to his words of counsel, they humbly promised God
to amend their lives. Then they armed and stealthily came down from the hill.
They found all the heathen lying asleep and quite unarmed. Then great killing
and amazing slaughter could be seen: speared bellies, smashed chests, heads,
feet and fists flying. Just like the proud lion, long hungry, who kills sheep, ewes
and lambs large and small, so did the British kill both rich and poor. They were
asleep among the fields, and the next minute they were so engulfed they could
pay no heed to arming, nor could they flee the spot. And the British, finding
them quite unarmed, slaughtered them: they pierced bellies and hearts, and
dragged out their bowels and entrails. The lords who had started the war, Octa
and Eosa, were captured. They were sent to London, bound and put in a dungeon. If anyone escaped from the field, they were saved by the dark night. He
who could flee, fled, not waiting for any friend; but many more were slain there
than escaped alive.

8541   When Uther left that place, he passed through Northumberland, and from Northumberland into Scotland,[2] with a great company and great army. He traversed
the length and breadth of the whole land, attracting all those people without
government to his allegiance. No previous king had ever established such great
peace throughout the kingdom as he did. When he had finished his business in
the North, he made his way straight to London, and Easter Day approached,
when he wished to be crowned. He summoned by letter and message all those
far and near—dukes, counts, citizens—and all the rest of his barons, with their

---

[1] Gorlois's speech here is close to that in *VV* chap.   [2] *HRB* chap. 17: to the town called Alclud.
136 and considerably more pious than in *HRB*
(Vulgate).

A Lundres seient a la feste,
Kar feste vult tenir honeste.
Tuit vindrent si cum il manda
E ki feme out si l'amena.
Bien fu la feste celebree,
E, quant la messe fu finee,
Al mangier est assis li reis
Al chief de la sale, a un deis.
Li barun s'assistrent entur,
8570 Chescuns en l'ordre de s'enur.
Devant lui s'est, enmi sun vis,
Li cuens de Cornoaille assis,
Lez lui sist Ygerne, sa feme,
Nen ot plus bele en tut le regne;
Curteise esteit e bele e sage
E mult esteit de grant parage.
Li reis en ot oï parler;
E mult l'aveit oï loer;
Ainz que nul semblant en feïst,
8580 Veire assez ainz qu'il la veïst,
L'out il cuveitee e amee,
Kar merveilles esteit loee.
Mult l'ad al mangier esguardee,
S'entente i ad tute turnee.
Se il mangout, se il beveit,
Se il parlout, se il taiseit,
Tutes eures de li pensot
E en travers la regardot.
En regardant, li surrieit,
8590 E d'amur signe li faiseit.
Par ses privez la saluot
E ses presens li enveot,
Mult li ad ris e mult clunied
E maint semblant fait d'amistied;
Ygerne issi se conteneit
Qu'el n'otriout ne desdiseit.
As gas, as ris, as cenemenz
E as saluz e as presenz
Le senti bien li cuens e sout
8600 Que li reis sa mulier amout,

Ne ja fei ne l'en portereit
Se il en aise la teneit.
De la table u il sist sailli,
Sa feme prist si s'en eissi;
Ses compainuns ad apelez,
As chevals vint si est muntez.
Li reis li ad emprés mandé
Qu'il li fait huntage e vilté [1]
Ki senz congié vait de sa cort;
Face li dreit, arriere turt.   8610
E se il de ço se defaut,
Deffie le, quel part qu'il aut,
Ne se puet mais en lui fier.
Cil ne volt mie returner,
De la court ala senz congié.
E li reis l'ad mult manacié,
Mais li cuens a petit le tint,
Ne sout pas dunc que puis l'en vint.
En Cornoaille reverti,
Dous chastels aveit, cez guarni.   8620
Sa feme mist en Tintajuel,
Ki fu sun frere e sun aiuel. [2]
Tintajuel ert bien defensables,
N'esteit par nul engin pernables,
De faleise est clos e de mer;
Ki sul la porte puet guarder
Mar avra dute ne reguart
Que huem i entre d'altre part.
Li cuens ad la Ygerne enclose,
En altre liu mettre ne l'ose   8630
Que toleite ne seit e prise.
Pur ço l'ad en Tintajuel mise.
E il mena ses soldeiers
E le plus de ses chevaliers
A un altre chastel qu'il out,
Ki le plus de sun feu gardot. [3]
Li reis sout qu'il se garnisseit
E ke de lui se defendreit.
Tant pur le cunte guerreier
Tant pur la cuntesse aprismer,   8640

---

[1] MS P reading—*huntage*—restored.
[2] MS P reading—*frere*—restored.

[3] MSS CGR add: *Dimilioc fu* (C: *ert*) *apelez*/ *Le chastel ou il fu* (C: *est*) *alez.*

Uther sees Ygerne

wedded wives and private retinues, to come to London for the feast, for he wanted
to hold a magnificent one. Everyone obeyed his summons, and whoever had a
wife, brought her.

8565   The feast was properly celebrated and, once mass was ended, the king sat down
to eat at the head of the hall, on a dais. The barons sat around him, each according to the importance of his fief. In front of him and opposite was seated the
count of Cornwall, and next to him sat Ygerne, his wife.[1] There was no fairer in
all the land: she was courteous, beautiful and wise, and of very high rank. The
king had heard her spoken of and much praised. Before giving any sign of it,
indeed, even before seeing her, he had loved and desired her, for she was exceedingly celebrated. During the meal he kept watching her and gave her all his attention. Whether he ate or drank, spoke or kept silent, he always thought of her,
and watched her out of the corner of his eye. As he looked at her, he would smile
and make her loving signals. He sent her greetings through his close friends, and
presents; he addressed frequent laughs and winks to her, and showed many signs
of love. Ygerne behaved in such a way as neither to consent nor refuse. From the
jests, the laughs, the signs, the greetings and the gifts, the count was well aware
and knew that the king loved his wife. and would never be loyal to him if he
could have her at his disposal. He sprang up from his seat at the table, took his
wife and went out; calling to his companions, he went to mount his horse.

8607   The king sent word after him that to leave his court without permission was a
shameful and disgraceful deed. He should do the right thing and return; and if
he failed to do this, the king repudiated him, wherever he had gone, and could
no longer trust him. Gorlois did not want to return: he left the court without
leave. And the king uttered great threats against him, but the count cared little
for that, not knowing then what was to come. He returned to Cornwall and
provisioned the two castles he possessed. His wife he placed in Tintagel,[2] which
had been his brother's and grandfather's. Tintagel was easy to defend and could
not be captured by any engine of war, being closed in by cliffs and the sea; whoever kept guard just on the door would never fear or worry about men finding
entrance elsewhere. There the count confined Ygerne: he did not dare put her
elsewhere in case she was seized or abducted. And he led his mercenaries and
most of his knights to another castle he owned, which protected the greater part
of his domains.[3] The king knew he was getting equipped and would defend him-

---

[1] *HRB* chap. 137: *Ingerna*; *VV*: *Igerna/Ygerna*. Note
that here men and women eat together, though
later (para. 10437) we are told that on feast days
British men and women eat separately.

[2] *HRB* chap. 137: *Tintagol*; *VV* MSS have this plus

a range of other spellings.

[3] MSS CGR add that this second castle was called
Dimilioc, obviously conforming to *HRB* Vulgate
chap. 137; the name is not in the *VV*.

De par tut ad sa gent mandee,
L'eue de Tambre ad trespassee. [1]
Al chastel u li cuens ert vint,
Prendre le volt, mais cil se tint.
E il i ad le siege mis,
Une semaine i aveit sis
Qu'il ne poeit le chastel prendre
Ne li cuens ne se vuleit rendre,
Kar le rei d'Irlande atendeit,
8650 Ki a securs venir deveit.
Li reis haï le demurier
Si li ad pris a ennuier,
L'amur Ygerne le hastout
Que il sur tute rien amout.
Ulfin, un suen baron privé,
Ad priveement apelé:
'Ulfin, dist il, conseille mei,
Mis conseilz est trestut en tei.
L'amur Ygerne m'ad suspris,
8660 Tus m'ad vencu, tut m'ad conquis,
[Ne puis aler, ne puis venir,
Ne puis veillier, ne puis dormir,] [2]
Ne puis lever, ne puis culchier,
Ne puis beivre, ne puis mangier,
Que d'Ygerne ne me suvienge;
Mais jo ne sai cum jo la tienge.
Morz sui se tu ne me conseilles.'
'Ore oi, ço dist Ulfin, merveilles.
Le cunte avez grevé de guerre
8670 E a eissil metez sa terre,
E lui cloëz en cel chastel.
Quidez que sa feme en seit bel?
Sa feme amez, lui guerriez,
Ne sai conseil cum vus l'aiez,
Ne vus en sai conseil duner;
Mais faites Merlin demander,
Qui de maint art est enbeüz,
E il est a cest ost venuz.
S'il ne vus en seit conseillier, [3]
8680 Nuls ne vus en puet aveier.'

Li reis, par le conseil Ulfin,
Fist mander e venir Merlin.
Tut li ad sun busuin mustré;
Preié l'ad e merci crié
Que conseil le dunt, se il puet,
Kar senz cunfort murir l'estuet
Se d'Igerne sun bon ne fait;
Quierë e face que il l'ait.
Del suen li durra se il vuelt,
Kar mult ad mal e mult se delt.   8690
'Sire, dist Merlin, tu l'avras,
Ja pur Ygerne ne murras.
Tut t'en ferai aveir tun buen,
Ja mar m'en durras rien del tuen.
Mais Ygerne est forment guardee,
En Tintajuel est enserree,
Que ja nen iert par nul efforz
Pris ne conquis, tant par est forz.
Bien sereit l'entree, e l'eissue,
Par dous bons humes defendue.   8700
Mais jo te mettrai bien dedenz
Par nuvels medecinemenz;
Figure d'ume sai muer
E l'un en l'altre tresturner,
L'un faz bien a l'altre sembler
E l'un faiz bien a l'altre per.
Le cors, le vis, la cuntenance
E la parole e la semblance
Que li cuens ad de Cornoaille
Te ferai tut aveir senz faille.   8710
Que te fereie jo lung cunte?
Tel te ferai cume le cunte,
E jo, ki ovec tei irai,
La semblance Bretel prendrai,
E Ulfin, ki od nus sera,
A Jurdan tuz resemblera.
Li cuens ad ces dous forment chiers
Cume ses privez cunseilliers.
Issi poez entrer el chastel
E acomplir tut tun avel;   8720

---

[1] MS K: *Cambre.*
[2] MS P omits ll. 8661–62; couplet supplied from
   MS D.
[3] MS P reading—*seit*—restored.

Merlin advises Uther

self against him. To attack the count, as much as to approach the countess, the king summoned his men from all directions and crossed the Tambre.[1] He came to the count's castle and wanted to capture it, but the count held out. And he besieged it: he laid siege to it for a week without being able to take it, or the count being ready to yield, for he awaited the king of Ireland who was to bring help.

8651 The king hated the delay and began to suffer. Love for Ygerne, whom he adored above all else, afflicted him. He secretly called to him Ulfin,[2] a baron who was one of his intimates. 'Ulfin,' he said, 'advise me: I depend on you entirely for help. Love for Ygerne has struck me down, completely defeating and conquering me: I can neither come nor go, wake nor sleep, arise nor rest, eat nor drink, without thinking of her. But I don't know how to possess her. Without your advice, I'm a dead man.' 'These are astonishing words,' said Ulfin. 'You have harassed the count with war, destroyed his lands and confined him to this castle. Do you think that pleases his wife? You love the wife and make war on the husband! I don't know what sort of help you need; I can't advise you. But send for Merlin: he is steeped in many an art, and he has arrived to join your company. If he can't advise you, no one can be your guide.'

8681 Counselled by Ulfin, the king summoned Merlin to come to him and revealed what he needed. He begged and prayed him to advise him, if he could, for without help he must die, unless he could have his will of Ygerne. He besought him to help him. He would reward him, if that was his wish, for he was in great distress and suffering. 'Sire,' said Merlin, 'you shall have her; you shall never die on Ygerne's account. I shall make you have all your desire and never shall you give me anything of yours. But Ygerne is strongly guarded, locked inside Tintagel, which is so strong it can never be taken or conquered by force. There will be two good men defending both entry and exit. But I will easily get you inside, using new potions: I know how to change a man's face and turn one into another; I can certainly make one resemble another and be similar to him. I will make you assume, without fail, the body, face, bearing, speech and appearance of the count of Cornwall. Why need I say more? I will make you resemble the count while I, accompanying you, will take Bretel's appearance and Ulfin, who will be with us, will exactly resemble Jordan. The count cherishes these two as his intimate counsellors. Thus you can enter the castle and carry out all you desire: you will never be noticed or suspected to be another man.' The king had complete faith in

---

[1] Other MSS have the *Cambre* or *Camble*, the river Camel as opposed to the river Tamar (which separates Cornwall from Devon). On this, a

detail introduced by Wace, see Tatlock p. 60 and Pelan, *La Partie Arthurienne*, pp. 155 and 158.
[2] In *HRB* chap. 137 he is *Ulfin Ridcaradoch*.

Ja n'i seras aperceüz
Ne pur altre hume mescreüz.'
Li reis ad bien Merlin creü
E sun conseil ad bien tenu.
A un barun priveement
Livra la cure de sa gent.
Merlin fist ses enchantemenz,
Vis lur mua e vestemenz;
En Tintajuel le seir entrerent.
8730 Cil, ki cunuistre les quiderent,
Les unt receüz e joïz
E a joie les unt serviz.
Li reis od Ygerne se jut
E Ygerne la nuit cunçut
Le bon rei, le fort, le seür,
Que vus oëz numer Artur.
    Les genz le rei sorent bien tost
Que li reis n'esteit mie en l'ost;
Ni out barun que il cremissent
8740 Ne pur ki rien faire vulsissent.
Pur le demurer qu'il duterent,
Lur armes pristrent si s'armerent;
Senz faire eschele e senz conrei
Al chastel vindrent a desrei,
De tutes pars l'unt assailli.
E li cuens fort se defendi,
Mais al defendre fu ocis
E li chastels fu sempres pris.
Alquant ki d'illuec eschaperent
8750 A Tintaguel nuncier alerent
Cument lur est mesavenu
De lur seinur, qu'il unt perdu.
As nuveles que cil diseient
Ki del cunte la mort plaineient,
Leva li reis, avant sailli:
'Taisiez, dist il, n'est mie issi.
Tuz sui vifs e sains, Deu merci,
Si cum vus poeiz veer ci.
Ceste nuvele n'est pas veire;
8760 Ne tut creire ne tut mescreire.

Mais jo vus dirrai bien pur quei
Ma gent est en dute de mei.
Del chastel senz congié turnai
Si que a hume ne parlai.
Ne dis mie que fors eississe
Ne ke jo ça a vus venisse,
Kar de traïsun me cremeie.
Mais ore criement qu'ocis seie
Pur ço que il ne m'unt veü
Puis que li reis al chastel fu.   8770
De mes humes ki ocis sunt
E del chastel que perdu unt
Nus puet turner a grant ennui.
Mais bien restait que jo vifs sui.
Cuntre le rei la fors iestrai,
Pais querrai si m'acorderai
Ainz que il cest chastel assiee
E ainz que nuals nus eschiee;
Kar se il çaenz nus susprent
Nus plaiderum puis plus vilment.' 8780
Ygerne ad cel cunseil loé,
Ki tuz tens ot le rei duté,
E li reis l'ad dunc embraciee
Si l'ad al departir baisee.
A tant est del chastel eissuz,
Ses desirriers out tuz eüz.
Quant fors furent en lur chemin
Li reis e Ulfin e Merlin,
Tels fu chescun cum estre dut
E chescuns sa furme reçut.   8790
A l'ost vindrent delivrement.
Saveir vuleit li reis cument
Li chastels fu si tost conquis
E se li cuens esteit ocis.
Assez fu ki li ad cunté
E d'un e d'el la verité.
Del cunte li pesa, ce dist,
Ki ert ocis, pas nel volsist.
Mult le plainst, mult le regreta,
A ses baruns s'en coruça;   8800

Uther disguises himself as Gorlois

Merlin and followed his advice. He secretly handed over to a baron the charge of his men. Merlin performed his enchantment and changed their faces and clothes, and in the evening they entered Tintagel. Those who thought they knew them, received and welcomed them, and joyfully served them. The king lay with Ygerne, and that night Ygerne conceived that king—the good, strong and resolute—whose name you will know as Arthur.

8737 The king's men soon realised that the king was not with the army. There was not a single baron who was not afraid and who wanted to do something. Because they feared delay, they seized their weapons and armed themselves. Without orders or battle formation, they impetuously approached the castle and attacked it from all sides. And the count strongly defended himself, but in the defence he was killed and the castle was soon taken. Some of those who escaped went to tell Tintagel what a misfortune they had had in losing their lord. Hearing their news and their laments over the count's death, the king rose and emerged: 'Silence,' he said, 'it is not so. I am quite safe and sound, thank God, as you can see. This news is not true: don't believe everything you are told.[1] However, I shall tell you the reason my men feared for my life. I left the castle without taking leave and thus speaking to no one; I revealed neither my departure, nor my arrival amongst you, for I feared treason. But now they fear I have been killed, because they have not seen me since the king gained the castle. The death of my men, and the castle they have lost, may give us grave difficulties. But the good news is that I'm alive. I will go out to meet the king, seeking peace, and I will come to terms before he besieges this castle and before worse may befall. For if he surprise us here, we shall have more ignominy in pleading our cause.'

8781 Ygerne, constantly in fear of the king, praised this decision; and he then embraced and kissed her, as he left. Thereupon he left the castle, having gained all his desires. When the king, Ulfin and Merlin were outside and on their way, each regained his own form and was as he should be. They came quickly back to the army. The king wanted to know how the castle was so speedily taken and if the count were slain. There were many who could tell him the truth on both matters. He was grieved the count was slain, he said; that had not been his wish. He was full of regrets and compunction, and angry with his barons. He seemed very

---

[1] Proverbial. See Morawski, *Proverbes*, no. 1389.

Semblant fist que mult l'en pesast,
Mais poi i out qui ço quidast.
A Tintaguel est returnez,
Cels del chastel ad apelez;
Dist lur ad: pur quei se defendent,
Morz est li cuens, le chastel rendent;
Ne püent aveir nul succurs
De la cuntree ne d'aillurs.
Cil sourent que li reis dist veir,
8810 Ne de rescusse n'unt espeir.
Les portes del chastel ovrirent,
La fortelesce li rendirent.
Li reis ot mult Ygerne amee,
Senz ensuine l'ad espusee.
La nuit ot un fiz cunceü
E al terme ad un fiz eü,
Artur ot nun; de sa bunté
Ad grant parole puis esté.
Emprés Artur fu Anna nee,
8820 Une fille, que fu dunee
A un barun pruz e curteis,
Loth aveit nun, de Loeneis. [1]
   Uther regna bien lungement,
Sains e salfs e paisiblement.
Puis empeira de sa vigur
Si chaï en une langur;
De grant enfermeté langui,
Lungement jut, mult afebli.
Sergant ki a Lundres esteient,
Ki la chartre guarder deveient,
8830 De la lunge garde ennuied
E de pramesses adulcied,
Octa fiz Henguist delivrerent
E de la chartre le jeterent,
E Eosa, sun compainun; [2]
Que par pramesses, que par dun, [3]
La garde des prisuns guerpirent
E od les prisuns s'en fuïrent.
Quant cil furent en lur cuntrees,
8840 E lur genz rourent assemblees,

Assez unt Uther manacié
E grant navie unt purchacié;
Od granz turbes de chevaliers
E od serganz e od archiers
Sunt en Escoce trespassé,
Le païs unt ars e guasté.
Uther, ki malade giseit,
E ki aider ne se poeit,
Pur sa terre e pur lui defendre
Livra sur tuz a Loth, sun gendre, 8850
La cure de ses oz guier
E des chevaliers soldeier,
A cels dist qu'a lui entendissent
E ço qu'il lur dirreit feïssent,
Pur ço que curteis ert e larges
E assez pruz e assez sages.
Octa les Bretuns guerreia,
Mult out grant gent, mult s'orguilla.
Tant pur la feblece del rei,
Tant pur venger sun pere e sei,   8860
Bretainne mist en grant effrei,
Ne volt duner trive ne fei.
E Loth l'ad suvent encuntré,
E suvent l'ad desbaraté,
Mainte fïee l'ad vencu,
Mainte fïee i rad perdu,
Kar custume est de tel ovrainne
Que tels i pert que puis guaaine.
Puet cel estre Loth le venquist
E del païs fors le meïst,   8870
Mais li Bretun s'entr'orguillierent
E ses sumunses desdeinerent,
Pur ço k'altresi franc esteient
E altretant e plus aveient.
Issi dura la guerre e crut
Tant que li reis s'en aperçut,
E cil del païs dist li unt [4]
Que si barun feinnant s'en vunt.
Oiez d'ume de grant fierté!
Ne laissa pas pur s'enferté;   8880

---

[1] MS J adds: *De li fu nés li quens Walweins/ Qui tant fu preudom de ses mains.*
[2] MS P: *Cosa.*
[3] MS P reading—*pramesses*—restored.
[4] MS P reading—*dist*—restored.

Octa and Eosa escape

distressed, but there were few who believed him. He returned to Tintagel and called to those inside the castle, asking them why they defended it: the count was dead and they should surrender it, since they would get no help from the rest of the country or elsewhere. They knew the king spoke the truth and they had no hope of rescue. They opened the gates of the castle and yielded the fortress up to him. The king, deeply in love with Ygerne, married her without delay.[1] She had conceived a son that night and in due course bore him. His name was Arthur: his greatness has been celebrated ever since. After Arthur, Anna was born, a daughter who was bestowed on a noble and courteous baron, Loth of Lothian.[2]

8823 Uther reigned peaceably a long time, safe and sound. Then his strength began to fail and he fell sick; weakened by severe illness, he lay for a long time much enfeebled. The soldiers in charge of guarding the prison in London grew bored with their long task and, sweetened with promises, set free Hengist's son Octa and released him from prison together with Eosa, his friend. Whether due to promises or gifts, the guards abandoned the prisons and fled, along with the prisoners. When these were in their own lands, and had once more gathered their men, they issued great threats against Uther and acquired a large fleet. With big crowds of knights, men-at-arms and archers, they crossed into Scotland, burning and wasting the land. Uther, lying sick, and unable to help himself, in order to defend his realm and himself, bestowed upon Loth, his son-in-law, the entire charge of commanding his army and rewarding his knights. He told them to listen to Loth and do what he told them, because he was courteous, generous and very noble and wise.

8857 Octa made war on the British. He had large numbers of men and grew very arrogant. In part owing to the king's weakness, in part to Octa's desire to avenge his father and himself, he terrified Britain, for he gave neither truce nor pledge. Loth often encountered him and often routed him; many times he beat him, many times he lost in his turn, for that is the way in such matters, that the loser one minute is the gainer the next. Perhaps Loth might have defeated him and expelled him from the land, but the British encouraged each other's arrogance and disdained Loth's commands, because they were just as noble and possessed just as much, and more. Thus the war dragged on, and grew, until the king noticed it and the people told him his barons were a half-hearted lot. Listen to what this man did in his great rage! His illness did not restrain him: he would no longer stay behind, he said, but wanted to see his barons in the army. He had

---

[1] *HRB* chap. 138 talks of mutual love uniting Uther and Ygerne, but *VV* and Wace omit this.

[2] *HRB* chap. 139: *Lodonesia.*

Ne volt mais, ço dist, remaneir,
Ses baruns vult en l'ost veeir.
Porter se fist cumë en biere
A chevals, en une litiere.
Or verra, ço dist, kil sivra
E si verra ki remaindra.
Cels fist mander e fist sumundre
Ki ne deinnoent ainz respundre
Ne Loth, ne sum comandement,
8890 E cil vindrent delivrement.
A Verolam vint li reis dreit,
Ki a cel tens cité esteit;
Saint Alban i fu martiriez,
Mais puis fu li lieus eissilliez
E la cité tute destrute.
La out Octa sa gent conduite
E dedenz la cité l'out mise;
E li reis l'ad defors assise.
Engiengs fist faire as murs fruissier,
8900 Mais fort furent, nes pout blecier.
Octa e li suen s'esbaudirent,
Ki des engienz se defendirent.
A un matin la porte ovrirent
E a combatre fors eissirent.
Desdein lur semblout e vil chose
Que porte i fust pur le rei close,
Qui en biere les guerreiout
E en bataille en biere alout,
Mais lur orguil, ço crei, lur nut,
8910 E cil venqui ki veintre dut;
Vencu fu e ocis Octa
E sis buens cusins Eosa. [1]
Plusur ki s'en sunt eschapé
Sunt vers Escoce trespassé,
Lur seinnur firent de Colgrim,
Ami Octa e sun cusin.
    Pur la victorie e pur l'enor
Que Deu duna al rei cel jur,
Est il de joie suz sailliz,
8920 Cume s'il fust sains e guariz;

Forment se prist a esforcier
Pur ses baruns esleecier.
Quant dreciez se fu en estant,
A ses humes dist en riant:
'Mielz vuil jo en biere gesir
E en lunge enferté languir,
Que estre sain e en vertu
E estre a desonur vencu.
Mult valt mielz murir a enur
Que lunges vivre a desonur.   8930
Saisne m'unt tenu en despit
Pur ço que jo gis en mun lit;
Assez se sunt de moi gabé,
E demi mort m'unt apelé;
Mais or ad, ço nus est avis,
Li demi morz vencu les vifs.
Alum soëntre cels ki fuient,
Ki mun fieu e les voz destruient.'
Quant li reis out un poi esté,
E a ses homes out parlé,   8940
Suëntre les fuitis alast,
Ja pur s'enferté nel laissast,
Mais li barun li unt ruvé
Que il sujurt en la cité
Tant que Deus del mal le reliet;
Kar mult criement qu'il li en griet.
Issi remist qu'il nes soï,
Malades jut, l'ost departi;
Sa gent en ad tute enveiee
Fors sul sa privee maisnee.   8950
    Li Saisne, qui furent chacied,
Quant il se furent ralïed,
Ço penserent, si orent tort,
Que se le rei aveient mort
N'i avreit eir ki lur nuisist
Ne ki la terre lur tolist.
Murdrir le vulent par puisun,
Par venim u par traïsun,
Kar en lur armes ne se fient
Tant, que par lur armes l'ocient.   8960

---

[1] MS P: *Cosa*.

Defeat and death of Octa and Eosa

himself carried as if on a bier by horses, in a litter. Now he would see, he said, who followed him and who stayed at home. He summoned and sent for those who formerly had deigned to respond neither to Loth nor to his command, and they speedily came.

8891   The king went straight to Verulam, a city at that period, where St Alban had been martyred; but subsequently the place was laid waste and the city quite destroyed. There Octa had led his men, and installed them within the city; without, the king laid siege. He had engines made to shatter the walls, but they were strong and he could not damage them. Octa and his people, warding off the siege-engines, rejoiced. One morning they opened the gate and came out to fight: it seemed contemptible and base to them that the gate should be shut on account of a king making war on them from a bier and going into battle on a litter. But their pride, I believe, was their downfall, and he who deserved to conquer, conquered. Octa and his good cousin Eosa were defeated and slain. Many who escaped fled towards Scotland, and took Colgrin as their leader, friend and cousin of Octa.

8917   From joy at the victory and the glory which God had given the king that day, he sprang from his bed as if healthy and well. He made strenuous efforts to encourage his barons. When he was on his feet, he said laughing to his barons: 'I'd rather lie on a bier and grow feeble through long illness than be healthy and strong and shamefully defeated. Much better to die with honour than to live long with dishonour.[1] The Saxons despised me because I lay in my bed; they made a mockery of me and called me half-dead; but now, it seems to us, the half-dead have defeated the living. Let's follow these fugitives, who destroy my lands and yours.' When the king had waited a while, and spoken to his men, he would have gone after the fugitives and not been constrained by sickness, but the barons asked him to stay in the city until God delivered him from ill health, because they feared he would suffer from it. So he stayed and did not follow them; he lay sick, and the army departed. He had sent all his people away except only for his private household.

8951   When the exiled Saxons re-assembled, they thought, wrongly, that if they had killed the king he would have no heir to harm them nor deprive them of land. They wished to murder him by means of poison, venomously and treacherously, because they did not trust so much to their weapons to kill him. They chose

---

[1] Proverbial: see Hassell, *Middle French Proverbs*, M 228.

Humes unt eslit malfaisanz,
Ne vus sai dire quels ne quanz;
Deniers e terres lur pramistrent,
A la curt le rei les tramistrent
Vestuz en povre vesteüre,
Pur espier en quel mesure
Purreient al rei avenir,
E si jal purreient murdrir.
E il se mistrent en tapinage, [1]
8970 Ki parler sorent maint langage;
A la curt le rei s'aprismerent
E de la curt l'estre espierent.
N'i porent pas tant espier [2]
Qu'al rei peüssent atochier,
Mais tant unt alé e venu
Qu'il unt oï, qu'il unt veü
Que li reis eue freide usout,
Nul altre beivre ne gustout,
Kar l'eue esteit a sun mal seine.
8980 Tuz tens beveit d'une funtaine
Ki juste la sale surdeit,
Nule altre tant ne li plaiseit.
Cil ki la mort le rei quereient
E ki ocire le vuleient,
Quant virent qu'il n'i avendreient
Ne par arme ne l'ocireient,
La funtaine unt envenimee,
Puis sunt fuï de la cuntree
Que il n'i fussent entercied.
8990 Atendu unt e oreillied
Quant e cument li reis murreit,
Kar a brief terme finereit.
Quant li reis volt beivre e il but,
Entuschiez fu, murir l'estut;
De l'eue but, emprés enfla,
Teinst e nerci, sempres fina.
E tuit cil ki de l'eue burent
Emprés la mort le rei, mururent,
Tant ke la chose fu seüe
9000 E la malice aperceüe.

Dunc fu la cumune assemblee
E la funtaine unt estupee;
Tant i unt de la terre porté, [3]
Un muncel unt desus levé.
   Quant Uther li reis fu finez,
A Estanhanges fu portez,
Illuec dedenz fu enterrez
Juste sun frere, lez a lez.
Li evesque s'entremanderent
E li barun s'entr'assemblerent;   9010
Artur, le fiz Uther, manderent,
A Cilcestre le corunerent. [4]
Juvencels esteit de quinze anz,
De sun eage fors e granz.
Les thecches Artur vus dirrai,
Neient ne vus en mentirai;
Chevaliers fu mult vertuus,
Mult fu preisanz, mult glorius;
Cuntre orguillus fu orguillus
E cuntre humles dulz e pitus;   9020
Forz e hardiz e conqueranz,
Large dunere e despendanz;
E se busuinnus le requist,
S'aidier li pout, ne l'escundist.
Mult ama preis, mult ama gloire,
Mult volt ses faiz mettre en memoire,
Servir se fist curteisement
Si se cuntint mult noblement.
Tant cum il vesqui e regna
Tuz altres princes surmunta   9030
De curteisie e de noblesce
E de vertu e de largesce.
   Quant Artur fu reis nuvelment,
De sun gré fist un serement
Que ja Saisne pais nen avrunt [5]
Tant cum el regne od li serunt;
Sun uncle e sun pere unt ocis
E trublé unt tut le païs.
Sa gent sumunt, soldeiers quist,
Mult lur duna, mult lur pramist,   9040

---

[1] MS P reading—*E il*—restored.
[2] MS P reading—*n'i*—restored.
[3] MS P reading—*la*—restored.
[4] MSS FT: *Cirecestre*; MS H: *Circestre*; MS S: *Cirencestre*.
[5] MS P reading—*nen*—restored.

Death of Uther and succession of Arthur

some wicked men, I cannot tell you whom, or when, and promised them money and lands. They sent them to the royal court poorly dressed, to spy out in what way they could reach the king and murder him. And these men, fluent in many languages, stealthily approached the court and spied on its circumstances, but however hard they spied, they could not reach the king. But they came and went so much that they saw and heard that the king used to drink cold water, and tasted no other liquid, because water was beneficial for his illness. He always drank from a spring near the hall; no other pleased him so much. When those seeking the king's death, wanting to kill him, saw that they could not reach him, nor slay him with some weapon, they poisoned the spring and then fled the country, so as not to be recognised. They waited and listened for when and how the king would die, for his end would come soon. When the king wanted to drink, and drank, he was poisoned, and had to die; he drank the water, then swelled up, changed colour, darkened, and before long died. And all those who drank the water, after the king's death, died, so that the thing was known and the wicked deed recognised. Then the community gathered and blocked up the spring; so much earth was brought that a hill was raised.

9005 After the death of Uther the king, he was carried to Stonehenge and there buried within, by the side of his brother. The bishops sent word to each other and the barons assembled; they summoned Arthur, Uther's son, and crowned him at Silchester.[1] He was a young man of fifteen, tall and strong for his age. I will tell you about Arthur's qualities and not lie to you. He was a most mighty knight, admirable and renowned, proud to the haughty and gentle and compassionate to the humble. He was strong, bold and invincible, a generous giver and spender, and if he could help someone in need, he would not refuse him. He greatly loved renown and glory, he greatly wished his deeds to be remembered. He behaved most nobly and saw to it that he was served with courtesy. For as long as he lived and reigned, he surpassed all other monarchs in courtesy and nobility, generosity and power.

9033 Arthur had not long been king when, of his own free will, he swore an oath that as long as the Saxons were in the land they would have no peace. They had slain his uncle and his father and harried the whole land. He summoned his men and sought mercenaries, making them generous gifts and promises. He summoned

---

[1] Silchester was the former Roman town of Calleva Atrebatum.

Tant manda gent e tant erra
Que Everwic ultrepassa.
Colgrim, ki, puis la mort Octa,
Maintint les Saisnes e guia,
Escoz e Pis out en s'aïe
E des Saisnes grant compainie.
Encuntre Artur s'ala combatre
E sun orguil vuleit abatre.
Dejuste l'eue de Duglas
9050 S'entrevindrent a un trespas;
Mult en i chaï d'ambes parz
Od lances, od quarrels, od darz,
Mais vencu fu a la parfin
Si s'en ala fuant Colgrim.
Artur, ki l'ala parsoant,
En Everwic le vint chaçant;
Colgrim en la cité se mist
E Artur envirum l'assist.
Baldulf freres Colgrim esteit,
9060 Ki sur la marine attendeit
Le rei d'Alemaine Cheldric;
Quant il oï qu'a Everwic
Ot Artur sun frere asegied
E que del champ l'aveit chacied,
Mult fu dolenz, mult ot grant dol,
Ovec sun frere fust, sun vuel.
L'atente de Cheldric laisça,
A cinc lieues de l'ost ala,
Si s'enbuscha en un boschage.
9070 Que des humes de sun linage,
Que d'estranges qu'il ot menez,
Out ovec lui sis mil armez.
Par nuit vuleit l'ost esturmir
E del siege faire partir,
Mais alcuns quis vit esbuschier
Le curut al rei acuintier.
Artur sot de Baldulf l'aguait;
A un cunseil ad Cador trait,
Ki esteit cuens de Cornoaille,
9080 Ki pur murir ne feïst faille.

Livra li sis cenz chevaliers
E de la gelde treis milliers
Sis enveiad celeement
Sur Baldulf en l'enbuschement.
Unches li Saisne mot n'en sorent[1]
Ne cri ne noise oï n'en orent
Dessi que Cador s'escria,
Ke de ferir ne se targa.
Plus en ocist de la meitied,
Ja n'en laissast aler un pied   9090
Se la nuit obscure ne fust
E se li bois ne li neüst.
Baldulf s'en tresturna fuiant,
De buissun en buissun muçant;
Perdu ot de sa compainie
Le mielz, e la grainur partie;
Ne se sout coment cunseillier
Qu'a sun frere peüst aider,
Mult volentiers od lui parlast
Se il peüst e il osast;   9100
Al siege ala cume juglere
Si feinst que il esteit harpere;
Il aveit apris a chanter
E lais e notes a harper.
Pur aler parler a sun frere
Se fist par mi la barbe rere
E le chief par mi ensement
E un des gernuns sulement,
Bien sembla lecheür u fol.
Une harpe prist a sun col.   9110
Pose s'est issi contenuz
Que de nul ne fu mescreüz.
Tant ala sus e jus harpant
Qu'a la cité s'aprismat tant
Que cil del mur l'unt entercied
Si l'unt a cordes sus sachied.
Ja erent al desesperer
E de fuïr e d'eschaper,
Quant la nuvele vint as trés
Que venuz ert, od sis cenz nés   9120

---

[1] MS P reading—*n'en*—restored.

Defeat of Colgrin and Baldulf

so many men, and covered so much ground, that he travelled beyond York. Colgrim, who since Octa's death had maintained and led the Saxons, had a great company of them, and also Picts and Scots to help him. He marched to meet Arthur and puncture his pride. They met in a pass near the river Douglas;[1] many were felled on both sides, by lances, javelins and bolts, but finally Colgrim was defeated and fled. Arthur, pursuing him, chased him as far as York, where Colgrim occupied the city and Arthur laid siege to it round about.

9059 Baldulf, Colgrim's brother, was waiting on the coast for Cheldric, the king of Germany. When he heard that Arthur was laying siege to his brother in York, and had chased him from the field, he was full of grief and distress, and wished he were with him. He gave up waiting for Cheldric, went five miles away from the army, and lay in ambush in a wood. What with the men of his lineage, and foreigners he had brought, he had with him six thousand armed men. He intended to overwhelm Arthur's army by night and make it give up the siege, but someone who saw them in ambush ran to tell the king. Arthur learnt of Baldulf's trap, and took the advice of Cador, count of Cornwall, who even in peril of death would not let him down. He put Cador in charge of six hundred knights and three thousand foot-soldiers and sent them secretly against Baldulf in the ambush. The Saxons never heard a word, nor cry, nor any sound until Cador, attacking without delay, shouted his battle-cry. He killed more than half of them, and would not have let a single one escape if the night had not been dark and the wood a painful impediment.

9093 Baldulf turned and fled, taking cover from bush to bush. He had lost the best, and the greater part, of his band, and was at a loss how to help his brother; he would very much have liked to speak with him, if he dared and had the chance. He went in the guise of a minstrel to the siege and pretended he was a harper; he had learned to sing and to harp lays and melodies. In order to reach his brother, he had his beard shaved off one side of his face, and the hair on his head and his moustache treated likewise, so that he looked just like a scoundrel or a fool.[2] He had a harp round his neck. For a while he behaved in such a way that no one suspected him. He went harping here and there to such an extent that he came close enough to the city for those on the walls to recognise him, and they pulled him up with ropes. They were in despair as to how to fly or escape, when news arrived by ship that Cheldric, with six hundred ships, had landed at a port in Scotland and was coming to the siege in strength. But he believed, and indeed said, that Arthur would never wait for him. Nor did he: he did not wait, for his friends advised him in no way to stay for Cheldric, nor to fight him, his men being numerous and fierce. He should retreat to London and if Cheldric were to

---

[1] See fn. 3 to p. 231 on Arthur's named battles.
[2] Cf. the hairstyle of the fool in the late 12th or early 13th century *Folie Tristan* and see Weiss, *Birth of Romance*, p. 124, note 5. *Lecheür* (scoundrel) may also mean lecher. Severe punishments often included shaving the head.

Cherdric en Escoce, a un port,
E al siege veneit a fort;
Mais il quidout, e bien diseit,
Que ja Artur ne l'atendreit
Nu fist il, pas ne l'atendi,
Kar ce li distrent si ami
Que Cheldric neient n'atendist
Ne a lui ne se combatist,
Gent aveit merveilluse e fere.
9130 A Lundres se traïst arrere,
E si Cheldic la le soeit,
Plus asseür s'i combatreit, [1]
Kar ses communes mandereit
E sa gent chescun jur crestreit.
Artur ad ses baruns creüz;
A Lundres est od els venuz.
Dunc veïssiez terre meslee,
Chastels guarnir, gent effree.
Artur de ço se conseilla
9140 Que pur Hoel enveiera,
Sun nevu, fiz de sa sorur,
Rei de Bretainne la menur;
La sunt si parent, si cusin,
E la meillur gent de sun lin.
A Hoel ad ses briefs tramis,
E par messages l'ad requis. [2]
Manda li, s'il ne li aiue,
Tute ad sa terre en fin perdue;
Mult iert grant hunte a sun linage
9150 S'il pert issi sun heritage.
Hoel oï la grant busuinne,
Ne quist achaisun ne essuinne,
E si baron e si parent
S'apareillerent ignelement; [3]
Lur nefs unt tost apareillees,
D'umes e d'armes bien chargees.
Duze mil orent chevaliers
Estre serjanz e estre archiers;
Bon oré orent, mer passerent,
9160 Al port de Hamtune ariverent.

Artur a joie les reçut
E a enur, si cum il dut.
Ne firent nul demurement
Ne plai de lunc acuintement;
Li reis ad ses geldes mandees
E ses maisnees assemblees;
Senz noise e senz lunge parole
Alerent ensemble a Nichole
Que li fel Cheldric ot assise,
Mais ne l'aveit mie encor prise.   9170
Artur fist ses humes armer;
Senz corn e sanz graille suner,
Trestut despurveüement,
Cururent sur l'adverse gent.
Unches si faite occisiun
Ne si laide destructiun
Ne tel besil ne tel dolur
Ne fu de Seisnes en un jur.
Gettent armes, laissent chevals,
Fuient par munz, fuient par vals, 9180
Par les eues vunt trebuchant
E mult espessement neiant.
Bretun, quis enchacent as dos,
Ne lur laissent aveir repos;
Des espees dunent granz cops
Es cors e es chiés e es cols.
Dessi al bois de Colidon
S'en alerent fuiant Saisson,
De tutes pars sunt al bois trait
Si unt del bois lur recet fait;   9190
E Bretun unt le bois guardé,
Tut entur l'unt aviruné.
Artur duta qu'il s'en fuïssent
E que par nuit del bois eississent;
D'une part fist le bois trenchier
E bien espessement plaissier,
Arbre sur arbre traverser,
E trunc sur trunc fist encroer.
De l'altre part se herberja,
Puis n'en eissi nuls ne entra.   9200

---

[1] MS P reading—*s'i*—restored.
[2] MS P reading—*messages*—restored.
[3] MS P reading—*ignelement*—restored.

Battle of Lincoln

follow him there, Arthur would fight more confidently, because he could summon the common people and the numbers of his men would increase every day.

9135 Arthur trusted his barons and came to London with them. Then a land in disarray could be seen: castles were being fortified, people were terrified. Arthur was advised to send for his nephew Hoel, his sister's son, king of Brittany.[1] There his kin were, his cousins and the best men of his race. Arthur sent letters to Hoel and a request by messenger, telling him that if he did not help him, he would completely lose all his realm. His lineage would be covered in shame if he thus lost his inheritance. Hoel understood the importance of the matter and looked neither for pretext nor excuse; and his relatives and barons quickly prepared themselves. They soon equipped their ships, laden with men and weapons. There were twelve thousand knights, as well as archers and men-at-arms. The wind was fair and they crossed the sea, arriving at the port of Southampton. Arthur received them with joy and honour, as was fitting. They wasted no time but greeted each in few words. The king summoned his foot-soldiers and gathered his troops, and noiselessly and without more ado they went together to Nichole,[2] which the wicked Cheldric had besieged but not yet taken.

9171 Arthur made his men arm and, sounding neither horn nor trumpet, fell quite unexpectedly upon the enemy. Such a slaughter, such violent destruction, such a massacre and such suffering was never before inflicted on the Saxons in a single day. They threw down their weapons, left their horses and fled through the mountains and valleys, reeling through the rivers and drowning in large numbers. At their backs, the British gave them no rest; they struck great blows with their swords on bodies, heads and necks. The Saxons fled as far as Celidon Wood[3] and gathered there from all sides, making it their refuge. And the British guarded the wood, entirely surrounding it. Arthur feared lest the Saxons escape and leave the wood at night. He had some of the trees in one part cut down and made into a thick barrier[4] of interwoven branches, tree crossing tree and trunk hooked to trunk. He camped on the other side, whereupon no one went in or out.

---

[1] *HRB* chap. 144: 'Hoelus, son of Budicius'. There is some domestic confusion here, copied from *HRB*. Anna, Arthur's only known sister, has already been married to Loth of Scotland.

[2] *HRB* chap. 145: *Karluideoit*; *VV*: *Kaerliudcoit* (but five MSS have variants on 'Lincoln').

[3] *HB*, chap. 56, attributes twelve victorious, named, battles to Arthur (probably derived from a Welsh battle-catalogue poem; see Dumville, 'Historical Value', p. 13). Four of them are fought on the river Douglas (cf. *Brut* l. 9049). The seventh is fought in *silva Celidonis, id est Cat Coit Celidon* (Celyddon Forest, that is, the battle of Celyddon Coed). Welsh poems (12th century and earlier) about Merlin mention him going

mad after the Battle of Arfderydd (dated 573 AD in the *Annales Cambriae*) and wandering in the Forest of Celyddon (i.e. the Caledonian forest). Geoffrey of Monmouth picks this legend up in his *Vita Merlini* (*c.*1150), but in the *HRB* chap. 145 he seems to have thought Celidon Wood was in the South. (Jarman, 'The Merlin Legend', *AOW* pp. 117–33). Arnold refers (II, p. 807) to Robert of Brunne's mention of a Colidon Wood near Lincoln. *HA* (II, chap. 18) quotes *HB*'s battle-list, adding 'none of the places can be identified now'.

[4] The earliest reference to 'plashing' woods. See Bennett, 'Wace and Warfare', p. 57.

Cil del bois forment s'esmaierent,
Ki ne burent ne ne mangerent.
N'i out tant fort, ne tant savant,
Ne tant riche, ne tant manant,
Ki la eüst od sei porté
Ne pain ne vin, ne char ne blé;
N'i eurent que treis jurs esté
Quant de faim furent tuit maté.
Quant virent que de faim mureient,
9210 E que par force n'en ireient,
Cunseil pristrent quel plai fereient:[1]
Lur robe e lur armes larreient,
Lur nés sulement retendreient
E al rei ostages durreient
Que tuz tens mais pais li tendreient,
E treü par an li soldreient,[2]
Se vis les en laissot aler
E senz armes lur nés mener.
Artur ad cel plai graanté,
9220 Cungied lur ad d'aler duné;
Ostages retint remananz
De tenir li ses cuvenanz,
Lur nés lur ad tutes rendues
E lur armes ad retenues.
E cil se sunt mis a la mer
Senz robe e senz armes porter.
Luing erent a une veüe,
La terre aveient deperdue,
Ne sai quel cunseil il truverent,
9230 Ne ki cil furent quil dunerent,
Mais returné unt lur navie
Entre Engletere e Normendie;
Tant unt nagied, tant unt siglé,
En Dertremue sunt entré;
A Toteneis vindrent a port.
Es vus puple destruit e mort!
Fors de lur nés a terre eissirent,
Par tut le païs s'espandirent,
Armes quistrent e robes pristrent,
9240 Maisuns arstrent, humes ocistrent,

Le païs unt tuit traversé,[3]
E pris tut quanqu'il unt truvé;
As vilains lur armes toleient,
De meïsmes les ocieient.
Devenesire e Sumersate
E grant partie de Dorsete
Unt eissillé e mis en guast,
N'i truverent kis destrubast;
Li barun ki alques poeient
En Escoce od le rei esteient.   9250
Tant par champaines, tant par veies,
Robes portant e menant preies,
Dessi a Bade Saissun vindrent,
Mais cil ki enz furent se tindrent.
    Artur, ki en Escoce esteit,
E cels d'Escoce destrueit
Pur ço qu'il l'orent guereied
E a Cheldric orent aidied,
Quant il sout que paien faiseient,
Ki a Bade siege teneient,   9260
Ses ostages fist sempres pendre;
Nes vout guarder, ne plus atendre.
Hoel de Bretainne guerpi,
Dunt il se tint a mal bailli,
Gesant en Aclud la cité,
Ne sai de quel enfermeté.
Od tant de gent cumë il out
Vint a Bade, cum il ainz pout,
Le siege vuleit departir
E ses humes dedenz guarir.   9270
Juste un bois, en unes granz plaines,
Fist Artur armer ses compaines.
Sa gent parti e ordena
E il meïsmes se rarma.
Ses chauces de fer out chauciees,
Beles e bien aparailliees,
Halberc out buen e bel vestu,
Tel ki de tel rei dignes fu;
Chaliburne out ceinte, l'espee,[4]
Qui bien fu lunge e bien fu lee;   9280

---

[1] MS P reading—*quel*—restored.
[2] MS P reading—*soldreient*—restored.
[3] MS P reading—*tuit*—restored.
[4] MS P reading—*l'*—restored.

The Saxons are spared, but return

9201 Those in the wood were in great dismay, since they could neither eat nor drink. There was no one, however strong, wise, rich or influential, who had taken bread, wine, meat and corn in there with him. After only three days they were quite overcome with hunger. When they saw they would die of starvation and could not get out by force, they accepted advice to plead for terms. They would leave their booty and their weapons behind, only keeping their ships, and would give the king hostages, as a sign they would perpetually keep peace with him and pay him yearly tribute, if he would let them go alive and depart unarmed in their ships. Arthur accepted this plea and gave them leave to go. He retained the rest as hostages, that the promises to him might be kept, returned all their ships to them, and kept their weapons. And they put out to sea without weapons or booty.

9227 They were far out of sight and had lost the land from view when (I do not know what advice they found, nor who gave it to them) between England and Normandy they turned their fleet around. They rowed and sailed so hard that they came to Dartmouth; they landed at Totnes. How they harried and killed the people! They swarmed off their ships onto land and spread through the region, seeking weapons, taking booty, burning houses, killing men. They covered the countryside and took everything they found; they seized the peasants' weapons and killed them likewise. They ravaged and wasted Devonshire, Somerset and a large part of Dorset and found no one to hinder them: the barons who could have done something were in Scotland with the king. Through the countryside, or along the roads, carrying booty and leading herds, the Saxons arrived at Bath, but those inside the town held out against them.

9255 When Arthur—who was in Scotland vanquishing the Scots because they had attacked him and aided Cheldric—learnt of the heathen's doings, and their siege of Bath, he summarily had his hostages hanged. He did not wish to keep them nor delay further. He left Hoel of Brittany behind, whom he thought to be in a bad way, lying sick of I know not what illness in the city of Alclud,[1] and came to Bath as soon as he could, with as many men as he could muster. He wanted to raise the siege and save his men inside. Beside a wood, in a great plain, Arthur had his troops arm.

9273 He divided and arranged his men and he himself put on his armour. He donned his greaves, well and finely made, and put on a handsome coat of mail, worthy of such a king. His sword Chaliburne was girded on, both long and broad. It was

---

[1] See fn. 1 to p. 41.

En l'isle d'Avalun fu faite, [1]
Ki la tient nue mult se haite.
Helme ot en sun chief cler luisant,
D'or fu tut li nasels devant
E d'or li cercles envirun;
Desus ot purtrait un dragun;
El helme ot mainte piere clere,
Il ot esté Uther, sun pere.
Sur un cheval munta mult bel
9290 E fort e curant e isnel,
Pridwen, sun escu, a sun col.
Ne sembla pas cuart ne fol.
Dedenz l'escu fu par maistrie
De ma dame sainte Marie
Purtraite e peinte la semblance,
Pur enur e pur remembrance.
Lance ot redde, Run aveit nun,
Acerez fu li fer en sun,
Alques fu luncs e alques leez,
9300 Mult ert en busuine dutez.
    Quant Artur ot sa gent armee
E sa bataille cunree,
Le petit pas les fist errer;
Nen volt laisser un desreer [2]
Dessi qu'il vindrent al ferir.
Mais cil nes pourent sustenir;
A un munt ki pre ert turnerent [3]
E ki ainz ainz en sum munterent;
Illuec se sunt cuntretenu
9310 E forment se sunt defendu,
Cume s'il fussent clos de mur.
Mais poi i furent asseür,
Kar Artur la les envaï,
Ki lur veisineté haï.
Cuntremunt les ala soant
E ses humes amonestant:
'Veez ci, dist il, devant vus,
Les desleiez, les orguillus
Ki vos parenz e voz cusins
9320 E voz amis e voz veisins

Unt tuz destruiz e eissilliez
E vus meïsmes damagiez.
Vengiez vos amis, vos parenz,
Vengiez les granz destruiemenz,
Vengez les pertes, les travailz,
Que cil vus unt tantes feiz faiz. [4]
Je vengerai les felunies
E vengerai les feimenties,
E vengerai mes anceisurs
E lur peines e lur dolurs,   9330
E vengerai la revenue
Que il unt fait a Dertremue.
Si entr'els nus poüm enbatre
E de cel tertre aval abatre,
Ja cuntre nus n'aresterunt
Ne defense vers nus n'avrunt.'
    A cez paroles Artur puinst,
A la peitrine l'escu juinst;
Ne sai quel des Saisnes ateinst
Jus a la terre mort l'empeinst;   9340
Avant s'en passe si s'escrie:
'Deus aïe, sainte Marie!'
'Miens est, dist il li premiers cous,
A cestui ai sun luier sous.'
Dunc veïssiez Bretuns aidier,
Saisnes abatre e derochier;
De tutes pars les avirunent,
Lancent e butent e cops dunent.
Artur fu mult de grant aspresce,
De grant vigur, de grant prüesce.   9350
L'escu levé, l'espee traite,
Ad cuntremunt sa veie faite;
La presse ad tute derumpue,
Destre e senestre mult en tue.
Quatre cenz il suls en ocist,
Plus que tute sa gent ne fist.
Faire lur faiseit male fin;
Mort fu Baldulf, morz fu Colgrin,
E Cheldric s'en ala fuiant,
Il e altre, par un pendant;   9360

---

[1] MS P: *Avarun*.
[2] MS P reading—*Nen*—restored.
[3] MS P reading—*pre*—restored.
[4] MSS PN invert ll. 9323–24 and 9325–26.

Battle of Bath

made in the isle of Avalon, and brought joy to whoever held it unsheathed.[1] The helmet on his head gleamed brightly; the nose-guard in front and the surrounding hoop were all of gold, and at the top was painted a dragon. Many precious stones were in the helmet; it had belonged to his father Uther. He mounted a fine horse, strong, speedy and fleet of foot, with Pridwen, his shield, round his neck, and resembled neither coward nor fool. Inside the shield, the image of my Lady St Mary was artfully depicted and painted, in her honour and memory.[2] Ron was the name of his straight lance: its iron was covered with steel at the tip, and it was fairly long and broad, much feared in times of need.

9301   When Arthur had armed his men and disposed his army, he made them advance slowly, not wanting anyone to break ranks until they came to strike. But the Saxons could not withstand them; they turned to a nearby hill and vied with each other to gain the summit. There they held out and defended themselves as vigorously as if they were surrounded by walls. But they were hardly secure, for Arthur attacked them there, hating their proximity. He followed them aloft, exhorting his men. 'Behold before you,' he said, 'the false and arrogant wretches who have ruined and destroyed your family and kin, your friends and neighbours, and harmed you yourselves. Avenge your friends, your kin, avenge this great destruction, avenge the losses, the suffering, which they have inflicted on you so many times. I will take vengeance on their perjury and wicked deeds, I will avenge my forefathers and their grief and misery, and I will take vengeance on the return of the Saxons to Dartmouth. If we can rush amongst them and strike them down from this hill, they will never resist us or have any defence against us.'[3]

9337   At these words Arthur spurred his horse, protecting his breast with his shield. I do not know which Saxon he reached, but he struck him dead to the ground. Sweeping onward, he shouted: 'May God help us, St Mary! Mine is the first blow,' he said, 'I've put paid to this one.' Then the British could be seen joining in, striking and smashing Saxons; they surrounded them on all sides, rushing and thrusting and delivering blows. Arthur fought with great harshness, power and valour. With raised shield and drawn sword, he made his way up, smashing through the throng, killing to right and left. He killed four hundred alone, more than were killed by his whole army, and he brought them to an evil end.[4] Baldulf died,

---

[1] Arthur's sword is variously spelt *Chaliburn*, *Calibore, Calibuerne, Caliburn* in some of the *Brut* MSS, but called *Escalibor* in three 13th and 14th century MSS (JHR). In *HRB* chap. 147 its name is *Caliburnus*. In the Welsh tale *Culhwch and Olwen*, *c*.1100, Arthur's sword is *Caletfwlch*, his lance *Rongomynyat* and his ship *Prydwen*. See Bromwich and Evans, *Culhwch and Olwen*, pp. lxxxi, 64–5, 147.

[2] In *HB* chap. 56 Arthur carries the image of the Virgin on his shield.

[3] *HRB* chap. 146 has a shorter speech of Arthur

and a longer one from archbishop Dubricius. The *VV* omits both.

[4] This is the last of *HB*'s named battles fought by Arthur (cf. fn. 3 to p. 231). It is Gildas (chap. 26) who first mentions the siege of Badon Hill ('*mons Badonicus*'), where the Saxons are routed; he does so soon after giving the name of Ambrosius Aurelianus as leader of the British, though it is unclear if Ambrosius actually fights at Badon. Bede (I, chap. 16) then mentions Ambrosius and the Badon victory together. *HRB* identifies Badon with Bath.

As nés voleient revertir
E enz entrer e els guarir.
Artur oï qu'il s'en fuieient
E que as nés turner vuleient.
Cador de Cornoaille ad pris,
Emprés les fuanz l'ad tramis,
Od lui dis mile chevaliers
Des meillurs e des plus legiers.
Artur vers Escoce turna,
9370 Kar un més vint ki li nunça
Que cil d'Escoce ourent assis
Hoel, pur poi ne l'ourent pris.
Cheldric fuieit vers la navie,
Mais Cador fu de grant veisdie
Par une veie qu'il saveit
D'aler a Toteneis plus dreit
Cheldric e sa gent devanci;
As nés vint, d'umes les guarni.
Vilains i mist e païsanz,
9380 Puis ala cuntre les fuianz;
Dui e dui, trei e trei fueient,
Si cum il mielz fuïr poeient;
Pur aler plus legierement,
E pur fuïr delivrement
Aveient lur armes getees;
Ne portouent que lur espees.
De venir as nés se hastoent,
Kar par les nés guarir quidoent.
A trespasser l'eue de Teigne,
9390 Lur vint Cador, criant s'enseinne;
Es vus Saisnes tuz esbaïz
E sus e jus tuz departiz!
Al munt poier de Teignewic
Fu ateint e ocis Cheldric;
Li altre, si cum il veneient,
A gleive e a dolur mureient.
Cil ki eschaper s'en poeient
De tutes parz as nés fueient,
E cil des nés les saietoent,
9400 E en la mer les trebuchoent.

Tels i aveit ki se rendeient,
Tels i aveit ki s'ocieient.
Par boscages e par muntaines
Se muçoent a granz compainnes;
Tant s'i mucierent, tant i furent [1]
Que de faim e de sei mururent.
    Quant Cador ot fait cele ocise,
E la terre out tute en pais mise,
Soëntre Artur s'achemina,
Des qu'en Escoce ne fina.   9410
Artur ad turné en Aclud, [2]
Sun nevu aveit succurud;
Tut l'aveit sain e salf truvé,
Guariz esteit de s'enferté.
Escot del siege se partirent
Quant la venue Artur oïrent;
En Mureïf luin s'en fuïrent,
Dedenz la cité se guarnirent;
La quiderent Artur atendre
E la se quiderent defendre.   9420
Artur sout qu'il se rasembloent
E cuntre lui se ralioent;
Jesqu'a Mureïf les soï,
Mais il s'en sunt avant fuï.
En l'estanc de Lumonoï
Sunt par les isles departi.
En l'estanc ad seissante illels
E grant repaire i ad d'oisels.
En chescun ille ad un rochier,
Illuec suelent aigle nigier,   9430
Faire lur niz e tenir aire;
E, si cume j'oï retraire,
Quant males genz venir soleient
Ki Escoce guaster deveient,
Tuit li aigle s'entr'assembloent,
Combateient sei e criouent;
Un jur u dous u tres u quatre [3]
Les veïssiez entrecombatre;
Ço ert significatiun
Encuntre grant destructiun.   9440

---

[1] MS P reading—s'i—restored.
[2] MS P reading—turné—restored.
[3] MS P reading—tres—restored.

Defeat of the Saxons

Colgrim died, and Cheldric fled, he and others beside, down a slope; they wanted to get back to the ships, enter them and protect themselves.

9365   Arthur heard they were in flight and intent on returning to the ships. He had Cador of Cornwall sent after the fugitives, and with him ten thousand of the best and swiftest knights. Arthur then turned towards Scotland, for a messenger came to tell him that the Scots had besieged Hoel and almost captured him. Cheldric was fleeing towards his ships, but Cador was very cunning: through his knowledge of a more direct path to Totnes, he got ahead of Cheldric and his men. He came to the ships and equipped them with men, installing peasants and farmers; then he chased the fugitives. Two by two and three by three they fled, as they best could. To run more freely and flee quicker they had jettisoned their arms and only carried their swords. They hastened towards the ships because they thought to escape in them. As they were fording the river Teign,[1] Cador came upon them, shouting his war-cry. The Saxons were utterly aghast, and everywhere totally scattered. Climbing the mountain of Teignwic, Cheldric was overtaken and slain. The others, as they came up, died painfully by the sword. Those who could escape, fled from all sides to the ships, and those inside the ships transfixed them with arrows and toppled them into the sea. Some surrendered, some killed themselves. They hid in woods and in the mountains, in large bands; there were so many in hiding that they died of hunger and thirst.

9407   When Cador had carried out this slaughter, and restored the land to complete peace, he rode after Arthur, not stopping till he reached Scotland. Arthur had gone to Alclud, bringing aid to his nephew; he found Hoel quite safe and sound, cured of his illness. The Scots, hearing of Arthur's arrival, abandoned the siege and fled far away, into Moray,[2] protecting themselves inside the city. There they thought to await Arthur and there to defend themselves. Arthur knew they were gathering and rallying against him, and followed them to Moray, but they had fled further still. In the lake of Lumonoi[3] they were dispersed amongst the islands. In the lake there are sixty islands, much frequented by birds. In each island is a rock and there eagles make their nest and eyrie. And, from what I have heard, when wicked people used to come to lay Scotland waste, all the eagles would gather, fighting and crying. You could see them at war for a day, or two, or three or four; it was a portent of great destruction.

---

[1] In *HRB* Vulgate chap. 148, the Saxons flee to the Isle of Thanet; *VV* leaves the locality unspecified. Wace has changed it to the West Country and introduced a river and a mountain.

[2] *HRB* chap. 149: *Mureis*; *VV* calls it '*Mireif/Murielf civitatem Albanie*' and Wace follows suit in think-ing it is a town, not a district.

[3] *Stagnum Lumonoy* is in *HB* chap. 67, as are the other two marvellous lakes; *HRB* chap. 149 took the name to refer to Loch Lomond, which is not in Moray.

Li lacs esteit granz e parfunz,
Kar, des valees e des munz,
Seissante eues dedenz chaeient
E illuec tutes remaneient,
Fors une, ki en mer descent
Par une eissue sulement.
Escot en l'eue s'enbatirent,
Par les illes se departirent.
E Artur enpruef se hasta,
9450 Batels, chalanz, nés aüna,
Tant les assailli e guarda,
Tant les destrainst e afama,
A vinz, a cenz e a milliers,
Chaeient morz par les graviers.
Gillamarus, uns reis ireis,
Ki vint aidier as Escoteis,
Assez pruef d'Artur arriva;
E Artur cuntre lui ala,
Al rei ireis se combati,
9460 Mult legerement le venqui;
Lui e sa gent en fist fuïr
E en Irlande revertir,
Puis est a l'estanc repairiez
U il out les Escoz laissiez.
    Es vus evesques e abbez,
Muines e altres ordenez,
Cors sainz e reliques portant,
Pur les Escoz merci querant.
Es vus lé dames des cuntrees, [1]
9470 Tutes nu piez, eschevelees,
Lur vesteüres decirees
E lur chieres esgratinees,
En lur braz lur enfanz petiz;
Od pluremenz e od granz criz
As piez Artur tuit s'umilient,
Plurent e braient, merci crient:
'Sire, merci! ce dient tuit;
Pur quei as cest païs destruit?
Aies merci des entrepris
9480 Que tu, sire, de faim ocis.

Se tu nen as merci des peres,
Veies ces enfanz e ces meres,
Veies lur fiz, veies lur filles,
Veies lur genz que tu eissilles!
Les peres rend as petiz fiz,
E as meres rend lur mariz; [2]
Rend a ces dames lur seinnurs
E les freres rend as sururs!
Assez avum espeneï
Que li Saissun passent par ci;   9490
N'est giens par nostre volenté
Qu'il unt par cest païs passé.
Ço peise nus que par ci passent;
Mult nus damagent, mult nus lassent.
Si nus les avum herbergiez,
Tant nus unt il plus damagiez,
Noz chatels unt pris e mangiez
E en lur terres enveiez.
N'avium ki nus defendist
Ne ki cuntr'els nus guarantist.   9500
E si nus les avum serviz,
Nus le feïmes a enviz.
La force ert lur, nus suffriun,
Ki nul succurs n'atendium.
Li Saissun esteient paien
E nus erium crestïen,
De tant nus unt il plus grevez
E plus laidement demenez.
Mal nus unt fait, tu nus faiz pis;
Ço ne t'iert mie enur ne pris,   9510
D'ocire cels ki merci querent,
Ki par ces roches de faim muerent.
Vencu nus as, mais lai nus vivre;
Quel part que seit, terre nus livre!
Fai nus, se vuels, vivre en servage,
E nus e tut nostre lignage;
Aies merci des crestïens;
Nus tenum la lei que tu tiens.
Crestïenté iert abaissiede
Se ceste terre est eisselede,   9520

---

[1] MS P reading—*Es*—restored.   [2] MS P reading—*meres*—restored.

Loch Lomond

9441 The lake was huge and deep, for it was fed by sixty streams from the valleys and mountains, and all of them remained within it except one, which found its way to the sea through one outlet alone. The Scots disappeared into the lake and scattered among the islands. And Arthur hastened after them, collecting boats, barges and ships. He watched them so carefully, attacked them so severely, harried and starved them so much, that in their twenties, their hundreds and thousands, they fell dead on the beaches. Gillomar, an Irish king coming to help the Scots, landed very close to Arthur, and Arthur moved against him; he fought the Irish king and defeated him very easily. He made him and his men flee back to Ireland; then he returned to the lake where he had left the Scots.

9465 Thereupon bishops, abbots, monks and other priests appeared, carrying the remains and relics of saints, and asking for mercy on the Scots. And on the other side appeared the women of the land, their feet and heads quite bare, their clothes torn and their faces scratched, their little children in their arms. With tears and loud cries they all fell at Arthur's feet, weeping and wailing and begging for mercy. 'Mercy, my lord!' they all said. 'Why have you destroyed this land? Have mercy on those wretches whom you, my lord, are starving to death. If you don't have mercy on the fathers, then look at these children and these mothers. Look at their sons, their daughters, their families, ruined by you! Give fathers back to their little sons, husbands back to the mothers; give lords back to their ladies and brothers back to their sisters! We paid sufficient penalty when the Saxons came this way: it was no wish of ours that they should enter this land. It grieves us they came here: they have exhausted and harmed us. If we harboured them, they harmed us even more; they seized and devoured our property and sent it home to their lands. We had no one to defend us, or protect us against them. And if we did serve them, we did it unwillingly. They had the power, we endured it, not expecting any help. The Saxons were heathen and we were Christian; they molested us all the more for it and treated us all the more wickedly. They did us wrong; you do worse still. Neither honour nor renown will come to you from killing those who ask for mercy, who die of hunger among these rocks. You have conquered us, but let us live; give us land, wherever it may be! If you wish, make us live in slavery, both us and all our family, but have mercy on Christians: we hold the faith you hold. Christianity will be brought low if this land is ravaged,

E ja en est peri le plus.'
Artur fu mult buens el desus;
De cel chaitif pople ot pitié
E des sainz cors e del clergié; [1]
Vie e membre lur parduna,
Lur humages prist sis laissa.
    Hoel ad le lac esguardé,
E a sa gent en ad parlé;
Merveilla sei de la grandur,
9530 E de laise e de la lungur; [2]
De tanz isles s'esmerveilla,
E des roches dunt tant i a,
De tanz aigles e de tanz niz
E de lur noise e de lur criz;
Tut ad a merveille tenu
Quanque il ad illuec veü.
'Hoel, ço dist Artur, bels niés,
De cest estanc merveilliez t'iés.
Assez plus te merveilleras
9540 D'un altre estanc que tu verras
Pruef de cest, en ceste cuntree.
La place dedenz est quarree,
Vint piez de lunc, vint piez de lé
E cinc piez de parfundeté.
As angles de quatre cornieres
Ad peissuns de quatre manieres;
Ja cil ki en l'un angle sunt
En l'altre angle ne passerunt,
E si n'i ad nule devise
9550 Ne defense de nule guise
Que l'on i puisse aparceveir
N'a main sentir n'od oilz veeir; [3]
Jo ne sai se huem l'enginna
U nature l'apareilla.
D'un altre estanc te redirai
Dunt jo merveiller te ferai:
Juste Saverne, en Guales, siet;
Quant li flos munte, dedenz chiet;
Mais ja mer tant ne muntera
9560 Ne floz dedenz tant ne charra

Que ja seit al flot muntant pleins.
U floz munt plus u floz munt meins,
Ja al flo ne surundera
Ne ses rives ne cuvera.
Mais, quant la mer entur retrait,
E floz ariere s'en revait,
Dunc verrïez l'eue lever,
Rives cuvrir e surunder,
Od granz turbes en halt voler
E chans muillier e aruser.   9570
Se hume i ad del païs né
Ki l'aut veeir, le vis turné,
L'eue sempres volet en halt
E sur ses dras e sur lui salt;
Ja ne serra de cel poeir
Que ne l'estuce jus chaeir; [4]
Maint en ad issi trebuchied
E maint en ad issi neied.
Si huem i vait le dos avant,
Lé taluns turnez reculant,   9580
Desur la rive puet ester
E tant cum il vult demurer,
Ja par l'eue n'iert adesez
Ne atuchiez ne arusez.'
'Grant est, dis Hoel, la merveille,
E merveillus ki l'apareille.'
    Dunc fist Artur ses cors corner,
Grailles e busines suner;
Ço fu signes de returner.
A sa gent fist cungié duner   9590
De repairer a lur maisuns
Ne mais a ses privez baruns.
Cil s'en turnerent tuit joiant,
D'Artur lur rei grant plai faisant;
Unches, ço dient en Bretaine,
N'out mais si vaillant chevetaine.
Artur a Everwic turna;
Jesqu'al Noel i sujurna.
Le jur de la Nativité
Ad illuec a la feste esté.   9600

---

1 MS P's line order—*sainz cors*—restored.
2 MS P reading—*E de*—restored.
3 MS P reading—*oilz*—restored.
4 MS P reading—*estuce*—restored.

The marvellous lakes

and already most of it is destroyed.'[1] In victory Arthur was magnanimous: he took pity on these wretched people and on the clergy with their holy relics. He spared them life and limb, received their homage and left them alone.

9527   Hoel looked at the lake, and spoke about it to his men. He was amazed by its size, both in its breadth and its length; he marvelled at its many islands and many rocks, at so many eagles and so many nests, and at their noise and cries. Whatever he saw there he considered extraordinary. 'Hoel, my fine nephew,' said Arthur, 'you are amazed at this lake. You will be even more amazed at another lake you can see, nearby in this land. The space it occupies is square, twenty feet long by twenty feet wide, and five feet deep. In the angles of the four corners are four kinds of fish; those in one corner will never cross into another, and yet there is no separation or prohibition of any sort that one can perceive, either by touch or by sight. I don't know whether man contrived it or nature created it. I will tell you of yet another lake which will amaze you: it is near the Severn, in Wales.[2] When the tide rises, it floods into it; yet no matter how high the sea rises, or how much the tide floods into it, it is never filled by the rising tide. Whether the tide rises higher or lower, the lake is never inundated by it and never overflows its banks. But, when the sea round about retreats, and the tide ebbs backwards, then you may see the water rise, cover and swamp the banks, fly up with great whirlwinds, and water and soak the fields. If a native of the country goes to see it, facing towards it, at once the water will spout up and pour over his clothes and himself, and no matter how strong he is, he will have to fall in. It has in this way made many fall in and many drown. If a man approaches with his back to it, his heels facing it, he can stand on the bank and as long as he wants to stay, he will never be reached by the water, neither touched nor soaked.' 'This is a great wonder,' said Hoel, 'and He who created it is wonderful too.'

9587   Then Arthur had his horns blown and his bugles and trumpets sounded, as the signal to return. He gave his men leave to go back to their homes, all except for the barons who were his close friends. They left joyfully, full of talk about Arthur, their king. Throughout Britain it was said that they had never had such a valiant leader. Arthur went to York and stayed there till Christmas, feasting there on Christmas Day. He saw the city was greatly impoverished, weakened and dam-

---

[1] In *HRB* chap. 149 this speech is given to the bishops.

[2] The second lake, unnamed in *HRB*, corresponds to *HB*'s *Finnaun Guur Helic*, the Fount of Gorheli (chap. 70); the third, called in *HRB_Linligua* (chap. 150), corresponds to *HB*'s *Linn Liuan* (chap. 69) (*Llyn Lliwan* in *Culhwch and Olwen*)—

here the phenomenon of the Severn Bore is described. The author of this part of the *HB* is using an old tradition of listing certain extraordinary geographical features, known as the Marvels of Britain. See Roberts, 'Culhwch and Olwen', *AOW* pp. 88–90 and Bromwich and Evans, *Culhwch and Olwen*, p. 168.

La cité vit mult apovrie,
E empeiriee e afeblie;
Mult vit iglises desertees,
Maisuns chaeites e guastees.
Piram, un sage chapelein,
Ki ne l'out pas servi en vain,
Fist de l'arcevesquied saisir
Pur les iglises maintenir
E pur les mustiers restorer
9610 Que paien orent fait guaster.
Pais fist li reis par tuit crier [1]
E les vilains fist laburer;
Les frans humes deseritez
Ad de tut sun regne mandez;
Lur eritez lur ad rendues,
Feus dunez e rentes creües.
Treis freres de mult grant parage
I aveit, de real lignage,
Loth, Agusel, e Urïen,
9620 Enparenté esteient bien.
Lur anceisurs orent tenu,
E il emprés, tant cum pais fu,
La terre des le Humbre en north
Par dreit, senz faire a hume tort.
Artur lur ad lur feus renduz
E lur eritages creüz;
A Urïen, al premier chief, [2]
Rendi Mureïf senz relief
E senz luer qu'il en eüst,
9630 Si li ruva que reis en fust;
Reis esteit clamez a cel tens
Cil ki sire ert des Mureifens. [3]
Escoce ad Angusel dunee,
E il l'aveit en feu clamee.
A Loth, ki aveit sa serur
E tenue l'aveit maint jur,
Rendi li reis tuit Loeneis
E duna autres feus en creis.
Encor esteit Walwein, sis fiz,
9640 Jofnes damoisels e petiz.

Quant Artur out sa terre assise
E par tuit out bone justise,
E tuit sun regne out restoré
En l'ancïene digneté,
Genuevre prist, sin fist reïne,
Une cuinte e noble meschine;
Bele esteit e curteise e gent,
E as nobles Romains parente;
Cador la nurri richement
En Cornoaille lungement,　　9650
Cume sa cusine prochainne;
E sa mere resteit romaine.
Mult fu de grant afaitement
E de noble cuntienement,
Mult fu large e buene parliere,
Artur l'ama mult e tint chiere;
Mais entr'els dous n'orent nul eir
Ne ne porent emfant aveir.
　　Artur, quant iver fu passez
E od le chaut revint estez,　　9660
E mer fu bele a navïer,
Fist sun navie apareiller.
En Irlande, ço dist, ireit
E tut Irlande cunquerreit.
Ne fist mie Artur lunge atente,
Mander fist sa meillur juvente
E cels ki mielz sourent de guerre,
Riches e povres de sa terre.
Quant passé furent en Irlande,
Par la terre pristrent viande;　　9670
Vaches pristrent e pristrent bués,
E ço que a mangier out ués.
Gillomur, li reis de la terre,
Sout que Artur ert alez querre;
Sout les noises, sout les nuveles,
Sout les plaintes, sout les quereles
Que faiseient la vilainaille
Ki perdue orent lur almaille.
Combatre s'ala cuntre Artur,
Mais ne fist mie a buen eür　　9680

---

[1] MS P reading—*tuit*—restored, as in ll. 9637, 9642, 9643 and 9707.

[2] MS P reading—*al*—restored.

[3] MS P reading—*des*—restored.

Arthur marries Guinevere

aged; many churches were deserted and houses fallen and ruined. He made Piram, a wise chaplain who had not served him in vain, take over the archbishopric, in order to maintain the churches and restore the monasteries which the heathen had destroyed. The king had peace proclaimed throughout and set the peasants to work. He sent throughout his realm for those nobles who had been disinherited, restored their inheritances to them, and granted them fiefs and revenues.

9617   There were three high-born brothers, of royal lineage and well-connected, Loth, Angusel and Urien.[1] Their ancestors, and they after them, had held by right, as long as peace reigned, the land north of the Humber, wronging no man. Arthur restored their fiefs to them and increased their heritage. In the first place he returned Moray to Urien without payment[2] or charge, and asked him to be once more its ruler. At that time, the lord of the people of Moray was called king. He gave Scotland to Angusel, and he claimed it as his fief. To Loth, who had been his sister's husband for a long time, he gave all Lothian, and other fiefs beside.[3] Walwein,[4] Loth's son, was as yet a young and small boy.

9641   When Arthur had established his realm, and justice throughout it, and restored his whole kingdom to its former dignity, he took Guinevere[5] as his queen, a graceful and noble girl. She was beautiful, courteous and well-born, of a noble Roman family. For a long while Cador had had her brought up in Cornwall in excellent fashion, as befitted his close kinswoman; his mother had been Roman. Her manners were perfect, her behaviour noble, and she talked freely and well. Arthur loved her deeply and held her very dear; but the two of them produced no heir nor could they have any children. [6]

9659   When winter was past, summer's warmth had returned, and it was safe sailing the seas, Arthur had his fleet prepared. He said he would go to Ireland and conquer it all. He did not delay long but summoned the flower of his young men, and those most experienced in war, rich and poor alike from his realm. When they had crossed into Ireland, they seized their food from the land, taking cows and oxen and whatever was necessary to eat. Gillomar, king of the country, heard that Arthur had gone in search of these; he heard of the tidings, the brawls, the complaints and laments made by the peasantry, who had lost their herds. He

---

[1] Urien is an historical character, ruler of the northern British kingdom of Rheged, who led Welsh resistance to the English in the second half of the sixth century. See Hunter Blair, *Anglo-Saxon England*, pp. 41–2 and Thomson, 'Owain', *AOW*, p. 160.

[2] *Relief*: the payment a feudal heir would normally have to make to his overlord when he took possession of his estate on the death of his parent.

[3] As in *HRB*, Scotland is thus divided into three parts: Scotland, Lothian and Moray, here seen as a region, not a town (see fn. 2 to p. 237).

[4] Gawain; *HRB* chap. 152: *Gwalgwanus*; *VV*: *Walwanus*. Both say Modred is Loth's other son.

[5] Wace only names Arthur's queen twice—here and at l. 11176, where MS P calls her *Ganhumare*, close to *HRB*'s *Ganhumara* in chap. 177; in chap. 152 she is called *Guenhuuara* (*VV*: *Guenhauer/ Guenwara/Gwennuara*). See Arnold's list of variants in both *HRB* and the *Brut*, II p. 808. Delbouille thought it likely that Wace did not know the exact name of the queen ('Témoignage', p. 197).

[6] Wace adds this important detail.

Kar si hume furent trop nu;
N'orent halberc, n'urent escu,
Ne saietes ne cunuisseient
Ne od arc traire ne saveient.
E li Bretun, ki arcs aveient,
Espessement a els traeient;
N'osoent les oilz descuvrir
Ne ne saveient u tapir.
9690 Mult les veïssiez guandillier
E l'un endreit l'autre mucier,
Turner as bois e as buissuns
E as villes e as maisuns, [1]
De lur vies querant respit.
Vencu furent e descunfit.
Li reis vout en un bois guenchir,
Mais atainz fu, ne pout guandir;
Artur l'en chaça tant e quist
Qu'il le cunsut e qu'il le prist;
Mais cil fist a Artur humage
9700 Si prist de lui sun heritage;
A remanant duna ostage
De rendre par an treüage.
    Quant Artur out cunquis Irlande,
Trespassez est jesqu'en Islande; [2]
La terre prist tute e cunquist
E a sei tute la sumist; [3]
Par tuit volt aver seinnurie.
Gonvais, ki ert reis d'Orchenie,
E Doldanim, reis de Godlande,
9710 E Rummaret de Wenelande
Orent tost la nuvele oïe,
E chescuns i aveit s'espie,
Que Artur sur els passereit
E tuz les isles destruereit.
N'aveit suz ciel d'armes sun per,
Ne ki tel gent peüst mener.
Pur poür que sur els n'alast
Ne que lur terres ne guastast,
Senz esforcement, de lur gré,
9720 Sunt en Islande a lui alé.

De lur aveirs tant li porterent,
Tant pramistrent e tant dunerent,
Pais firent, si hume devindrent,
Lur eritages de lui tindrent.
Treü unt pramis e numé,
Ostage en ad chescuns duné;
Par tant sunt tuit en pais remis, [4]
E Artur est venuz es nés;
En Engleterre est revenuz
E a grant joie est receuz. [5]   9730
    Duze anz puis cel repairement
Regna Artur paisiblement,
Ne nuls guerreier ne l'osa
Ne il altre ne guereia.
Par sei, senz altre enseinement,
Emprist si grant afaitement
E se cuntint tant noblement,
Tant bel e tant curteisement,
N'esteit parole de curt d'ume,
Neis de l'empereür de Rome.   9740
N'oeit parler de chevalier
Ki alques feïst a preisier,
Ki de sa maisnee ne fust,
Pur ço qu'il aveir le peüst;
Si pur aveir servir vulsist,
Ja pur aveir ne s'en partist.
Pur les nobles baruns qu'il out,
Dunt chescuns mieldre estre quidout,
Chescuns se teneit al meillur,
Ne nuls n'en saveit le peiur,   9750
Fist Artur la Runde Table [6]
Dunt Bretun dient mainte fable.
Illuec seeient li vassal
Tuit chevalment e tuit egal;
A la table egalment seeient
E egalment servi esteient;
Nul d'els ne se poeit vanter
Qu'il seïst plus halt de sun per,
Tuit esteient assis meain,
Ne n'i aveit nul de forain.   9760

---

[1] MS P readings—*as…as*—restored in ll. 9692–93.
[2] MSS DLR: *Gutlande*.
[3] MS P reading—*sumist*—restored.
[4] MS P reading—*remis*—restored.
[5] MS P reading—*est*—restored.
[6] MS P reading—*Runde*—restored.

The Round Table

went off to fight Arthur, but was unsuccessful, because his men were quite defenceless: they had neither hauberks nor shields, they knew nothing of arrows or
how to draw a bow. And the British, who had bows, shot arrows at them in great
numbers, so that they dared not expose their eyes, nor did they know where to
hide. They could be seen making their escape in large numbers, one hiding next
to another, running into woods and bushes, towns and houses, seeking for mercy
on their lives. They were defeated and beaten. Their king tried to dodge into a
wood, but was overtaken and could not escape. Arthur harried and attacked him
so much that he caught up with him and took him. But Gillomar did homage to
Arthur and received his heritage back from him. He gave hostages in perpetuity,
to ensure he paid yearly tribute.

9703 When Arthur had conquered Ireland, he travelled as far as Iceland, taking and
conquering the whole land, and submitting it entirely to him: he wanted to rule
everywhere. Gonvais, king of Orkney, Doldani, king of Gotland, and Rummaret
of Wenelande[1] all heard the news, each from their spies, that Arthur would come
their way and destroy all the islands. There was not his equal in the whole world
for military might, nor anyone who could lead such an army. Afraid he would
attack them and ravage their lands, they freely and without constraint went to
him in Iceland. They brought him so many of their possessions, promised and
gave so much, that peace was made and they became his men, holding their
heritage from him. They promised and appointed a truce, and each gave hostages. In this way everybody stayed in peace, and Arthur returned to his ships; he
came back to England and was welcomed with great joy.

9731 For twelve years after his return, Arthur reigned in peace. No one dared to make
war on him, nor did he go to war himself. On his own, with no other instruction,
he acquired such knightly skill and behaved so nobly, so finely and courteously,
that there was no court so talked about, not even that of the Roman emperor. He
never heard of a knight who was in any way considered to be praiseworthy who
would not belong to his household, provided that he could get him, and if such a
one wanted reward for his service, he would never leave deprived of it. On account of his noble barons—each of whom felt he was superior, each considered
himself the best, and no one could say who was the worst—Arthur had the Round
Table made,[2] about which the British tell many a tale. There sat the vassals, all
equal, all leaders; they were placed equally round the table and equally served.
None of them could boast he sat higher than his peer; each was seated between

---

[1] Orkney and Gotland come from *HRB* chap. 153
(with kings *Gunvasius* and *Doldavius/Doldanius*);
Wace has added the mysterious Rummaret of
Wenelande, identified by critics since Tatlock
with Wendland, of the Slavic Wends, against
whom a campaign took place in 1147, while
Wace was writing. Arnold's suggestion that it
refers to Vinland is, however, supported by York,
'Wace's *Wenelande*', pp. 112–18.

[2] This is the first appearance of the Round Table.
See Foulon, 'Wace', in *ALMA* pp. 99–100, and
Schmolke-Hasselmann, 'Round Table'. Wace
also adds a famous passage (para. 9785) on the
stories about Arthur.

N'esteit pas tenuz pur curteis
Escot ne Bretun ne Franceis,
Normant, Angevin ne Flamenc
Ne Burguinun ne Loherenc,
De ki que il tenist sun feu,
Des occident jesqu'a Muntgeu,
Ki a la curt Artur n'alout
E ki od lui ne sujurnout,
E ki n'en aveit vesteüre
9770 E cunuissance e armeüre
A la guise que cil teneient
Ki en la curt Artur serveient. [1]
De plusurs terres i veneient
Cil ki pris e enur quereient,
Tant pur oïr ses curteisies,
Tant pur veeir ses mananties,
Tant pur cunuistre ses baruns,
Tant pur aveir ses riches duns.
De povres humes ert amez
9780 E des riches mult enurez.
Li rei estrange l'envioent
Kar mult cremeient e dutoent
Que tuit le munde cunquesist [2]
E lur digneté lur tolist.
Que pur amur de sa largesce,
Que pur poür de sa prüesce,
En cele grant pais ke jo di,
Ne sai si vus l'avez oï,
Furent les merveilles pruvees
9790 E les aventures truvees
Ki d'Artur sunt tant recuntees
Ke a fable sunt aturnees:
Ne tut mençunge, ne tut veir,
Ne tut folie ne tut saveir. [3]
Tant unt li cunteür cunté
E li fableür tant flablé
Pur lur cuntes enbeleter,
Que tut unt fait fable sembler.
Par la bunté de sun curage
9800 E par le los de sun barnage

E par la grant chevalerie
Qu'il out afaitee e nurrie,
Dist Artur que mer passereit
E tute France conquerreit;
Mais primes en Norwege ireit,
Loth sun sururge rei fereit.
Sichelins, li reis, morz esteit,
Ki fiz ne fille eu n'aveit; [4]
A sun muriant out rové
E rové l'out en sa santé   9810
Que Loth de Norwege reis fust,
Sun feu e sun realme eüst;
Sis niés esteit, n'aveit altre eir,
Loth deveit par dreit tut aveir. [5]
Quant Sichelin l'out establi
E il quida que fust issi,
Li Norreis tindrent a folie
E sun comant e s'establie;
Quant il virent le rei finé,
Le regne unt tut a Loth veé;   9820
Ne voldrent estrange hume attraire
Ne d'estrange hume seinnur faire;
Ainz sereient tuit viel chanu
Qu'il l'eüssent decuneü;
A cels d'altre terre durreit
Ço qu'il a els duner devreit;
Rei ferunt d'un de lur nurriz
Ki amera els e lur fiz;
Issi unt, par ceste achaisun,
Riculf fait rei, un lur barun.   9830
Quant Loth vit que sun dreit perdreit
Se par force nel cunquereit,
Artur sun seinnur ad requis,
E Artur li ad bien pramis
Que tut le regne li rendra
E ke Riculf mal le bailla.
Grant navie e grant gent manda,
Dedenz Norwege a force entra;
Mult ad destrutes les cuntrees,
Villes arses, maisuns robees.   9840

---

[1] MS P reading—*en*—restored.
[2] MS P reading—*tuit*—restored.
[3] MS P reading—*Ne*—restored.
[4] MS P reading—*eu n'aveit*—restored.
[5] MS P's order of line restored.

Loth invades Norway

two others, none at the end of the table.[1] No one—whether Scot, Briton, French-
man, Norman, Angevin, Fleming, Burgundian or Lorrainer—whoever he held his
fief from, from the West as far as Muntgieu, was accounted courtly if he did not
go to Arthur's court and stay with him and wear the livery, device and armour in
the fashion of those who served at that court. They came from many lands, those
who sought honour and renown, partly to hear of his courtly deeds, partly to see
his rich possessions, partly to know his barons, partly to receive his splendid
gifts. He was loved by the poor and greatly honoured by the rich. Foreign kings
envied him, doubting and fearing he would conquer the whole world and take
their territories away.

9785   In this time of great peace I speak of—I do not know if you have heard of it—the
wondrous events appeared and the adventures were sought out which, whether
for love of his generosity, or for fear of his bravery, are so often told about Arthur
that they have become the stuff of fiction : not all lies, not all truth, neither total
folly nor total wisdom. The raconteurs have told so many yarns, the story-tellers
so many stories, to embellish their tales that they have made it all appear fiction.

9799   Prompted by his own noble disposition, the advice of his barons, and the large
body of knights he had equipped and nurtured, Arthur said he would cross the
sea and conquer all France. But first he would go to Norway and make his brother-
in-law Loth king there. Sichelin[2] the king had died, without son or daughter; on
his death-bed he had asked, as he had asked when in health, that Loth should be
king of Norway and hold his domain and his kingdom. He was his nephew, he
had no other heir, so Loth by right should have everything. If Sichelin had ordained this, and thought it would be so, the Norwegians considered both his
command and his decree folly. When they saw the king was dead, they utterly
refused Loth the kingdom. They had no desire to call upon a foreigner or make a
foreigner their lord; they would have to be all old greybeards before recognizing
him. He would give to others abroad what he should give to them. They would
make a trusted vassal king, who would cherish them and their sons. For this
reason they thus made Riculf, one of their barons, king.

9831   When Loth saw he would lose his rights if he did not conquer them by force, he
appealed to Arthur, his lord, and Arthur promised him that he would give him all
the kingdom and Riculf had been wrong to accept it. He summoned a large fleet
and large army, and entered Norway by force. He inflicted great damage on the
land, burning towns and plundering houses. Riculf would not flee nor leave the

---

[1] See Félix Lecoy, '*Meain* et *Forain* dans le *Roman*   [2] *HRB* chap. 154: *Sichelmus*; *VV*: *Sichelinus*.
de Brut', *Romania* 86 (1965), pp. 118–22.

Riculf ne volt mie fuïr
Ne le païs ne volt guerpir;
D'Artur defendre se quida,
La gent de Norweige aüna,
Mais poi out gent e poi amis,
Vencu fu Riculf e ocis;
Des altres i out ocis tant
Mult i out poi del remanant.
Quant Norwege fu delivree,
9850 A Loth l'ad tute Artur dunee,
Mais que Loth d'Artur la tendreit
E a seinnur le cunustreit.
De saint Soplice, l'apostoire,
La ki aume ait repos e gloire, [1]
Ert Walwen nuvelment venuz,
Chevaliers pruz e cuneüz.
[Cil li aveit armes dunees,
Mult i furent bien aluees.] [2]
Pruz fu e de mult grant mesure,
9860 D'orguil ne de surfait n'out cure;
Plus volt faire que il ne dist
E plus duner qu'il ne pramist. [3]
    Quant Artur out Norwege prise
E Loth l'ot bien en sa justise,
Les vaillanz humes les meillurs,
Les plus hardiz cumbateürs,
Fist tuz eslire e aüner
E nés e barges eschiper.
Od les altres genz qu'il menot,
9870 Quant bel tens vit e bon vent ot,
En Danemarche trespassa;
La terre a sun ués cuveita.
Aschil, ki ert reis des Daneis,
Vit les Bretuns, vit les Norreis,
Vit Artur ki tut cunquereit,
Vit que tenir ne se purreit.
Ne se volt laissier damagier
Ne sa bone terre empeirer,
Sun or ne sun argent despendre,
9880 Sa gent ocire, ses turs rendre.

Tant dist, tant fist, tant purchaça
E tant pramist e tant duna
E tant requist e tant preia,
Al rei Artur se concorda;
Feelté fist, sis huem devint,
Sun regne ot tut, d'Artur le tint.
    Artur fu liez del grant espleit
E del cunquest que il faiseit.
Ne li pout mie encor suffire;
De Danemarche fist eslire   9890
Buens chevaliers e buens archiers
Ne sai quanz cenz ne quanz milliers;
Mener les volt od sei en France
E il si fist senz demurance.
Flandres e Buluinne conquist,
Viles saisi e chastels prist.
Sagement fist sa gent cunduire,
Ne volt pas la terre destruire,
Viles ardeir ne robes prendre;
Tut fist veer e tut defendre   9900
Fors viande e beivre e provende,
E si l'um trove ki la vende,
A buens deniers seit achatee,
Ne seit toleite ne robee.
France aveit nun Galle a cel jur
Si n'i aveit rei ne seinnur;
Romain en demainne l'aveient
E en demainne la teneient.
En guarde ert a Frolle livree
E il l'aveit lunges guardee;   9910
Treüz e rentes receveit
E par termes les trameteit
A Rome a Leu, l'empereür. [4]
Frolle fu mult de grant vigur;
Des nobles humes ert de Rome,
Ne dutot par sun cors nul hume.
Frolles sot par plusurs messages
Les saisines e les damages
Que Artur e sa gent faiseient,
Ki as Romains lur dreit toleient. [5]   9920

---

1 MS P reading—*e*—restored.
2 MSS PDLJABKGRN omit ll. 9857–58; this couplet is supplied by Arnold.
3 MS J adds: *A Rome l'ot fait envoier/ Ses peres por lui enseignier/ Et com Wavains fu adoubés/ Au roi Artus s'en est alés/ Por lui servir et hounourer/ Molt se pena d'armes porter.*

4 MS J: *Ce fu del tans l'empereür/* then adds: *Cesar le fort conquereour/ Qui conquist France et Alemaigne/ Et si conquist tote Bretaigne/ C'om tenoit de l'empereour.*
5 MS P readings—*faiseient* and *toleient*—restored in ll. 9919–20.

Arthur invades France

country; he thought he could defend himself against Arthur, and gathered together the men of Norway, but he had few men and few friends. He was conquered and slain. So many of the others were killed that very few were left. When Norway surrendered, Arthur gave it all to Loth, on condition that Loth held it from him and acknowledged him as overlord. Walwein had recently returned, a renowned and valiant knight, from St Soplice,[1] the pope, may his soul have rest and glory. He had given him armour, which was well bestowed. Walwein possessed bravery and great moderation; he had no time for pride or arrogance. He would do more than he said, and give more than he promised.

9863 Once Arthur had taken Norway and Loth had it well under his control, he had the best of the brave men, the boldest warriors selected and gathered and barges and ships equipped. When he had fine weather and a good wind, he crossed into Denmark, leading his other men as well. He desired the country for himself. Aschil, king of the Danes, considered the British, the Norwegians, the all-conquering Arthur, and saw that he could not resist. He did not want himself harmed or his good land despoiled; he neither wished his gold and silver spent, nor his people killed, nor his towers surrendered. He said, did and strove so much, promised and gave so much, asked and begged so much, that he reached an agreement with king Arthur: he did homage, became his man, and held his whole kingdom in the king's name.

9887 Arthur was pleased with this great achievement and the conquests he was making. It was not yet enough for him. He had the best knights and best archers in Denmark chosen, I do not know how many hundreds or thousands of them, and wished to take them with him into France, which he did without delay. He conquered Flanders and Boulogne, seized towns and took castles. He made his men behave prudently, not wanting the land destroyed, the towns burnt or booty taken; he prohibited and forbade them anything except meat, drink and fodder, and if anyone could be found to sell it to them, it should be bought with good money, not seized or stolen. In those days, France was called Gaul and had neither king nor overlord. It belonged to Rome, who possessed it. It was in Frollo's charge and he had guarded it a long time; he received tribute and revenues and sent them, at set times, to the emperor Leo in Rome.

9914 Frollo was a man of great prowess; one of the Roman nobility, he was physically afraid of no one. He knew, from many messengers, of the seizures and the damage which Arthur and his men were carrying out, robbing the Romans of their

---

[1] *HRB* chap. 154: *Sulpicius.*

Tuz les humes armes portanz
Al feu de Rome apartenanz
Dunt il quidout aveir aïe,
E ki erent en sa baillie,
Fist tuz sumundre e tuz venir
E bien armer e bien guarnir.
A bataille ala cuntre Artur,
Mais nel fist mie a bon eür;
Descunfit fu, si s'en fuï,
9930 De ses humes maint i perdi,
Que ocis, que nafrez, que pris,
Que returnez en lur païs.
Ne ço merveille nen esteit,
Kar Artur trop grant gent aveit;
Kar es terres qu'il out conquises
Ne as cités que il out prises,
Nen out il qu'il peüst laissied,
Buen chevalier ne hume a pied,
Ki de combatre eage eüst
9940 Ne ki combatre se peüst,
Qu'il nen eüst od sei mené
U qu'il nen eüst puis mandé.
Mult out gent estrange mandée,
Estre sa maisnee privee,
Ki ert de chevaliers osez
E de combateürs pruvez.
Li Franceis a lui se turnoent,
Cil ki poeient e osoent,
Tant pur sun cuintement parler,
9950 Tant pur sun largement duner,
Tant pur la noblesce de lui,
Tant pur poür, tant pur refui;
A lui aloent, pais faiseient,
Lur feus de lui recunusseient.
    Frolle, de la descunfiture,
Vint a Paris grant aleüre,
Ne s'osa aillurs arester
Ne ne se volt aillurs fier;
Recet defensable quereit
9960 Kar Artur e sa gent cremeit.

A Paris fist la guarnisun
Porter, des viles d'envirun;
A Paris Artur atendra
E a Paris se defendra.
Tant de la gent ki vint fuitive,
Tant de la gent d'illuec naïve,
Mult fu d'umes la cité plainne.
Chescuns en sun endreit se peinne
De blé e de viande atraire
E des murs e des portes faire.   9970
Artur sout que Frolles faiseit,
Ki a Paris se guarnisseit;
Emprés lui vint si l'asega,
Es burs entur se herberga;
L'eue e la terre fist guarder
Que viande n'i pout entrer.
La ville tindrent bien Franceis,
E Artur i sist prés d'un meis;
Grant pople aveit en la cité,
De viande orent tost chierté;   9980
Tut le purchaz e tut l'atrait
Qu'en poi de tens aveient fait
Orent tost mangié e usé;
Mult veïssez pople afamé!
Poi unt vitaille, e grant gent sunt;
Enfant e femes grant duel funt;
Si la gent povre en fust creüe
La cité fust bien tost rendue.
Mult vunt criant: 'Frolle, que faiz?
Pur quei ne quers a Artur paiz?'[1]   9990
Frolles vit le pople destreit
Pur la vitaille ki failleit,
Vit lé genz, ki de faim mureient,
E vit que rendre se vuleient,
Vit la cité mise a eissil.
Mielz volt sun cors mettre en peril
E en abandun de murir
Que plainement Paris guerpir;
Bien se fiout en sa bunté.
Al rei Artur ad fors mandé   10000

---

[1] MS J adds: *Nus avuns çaiens grant famine/ N'avomes pain ne blé ne frine/ Nel poons mais plus endurer/ La cité nos estuet livrer.*

Siege of Paris

rights. He had all those men able to bear weapons and belonging to Rome's domain, whom he thought could help him and who were in his jurisdiction, summoned, armed and well equipped. He went to do battle with Arthur but was unsuccessful:[1] he was defeated and fled, losing many of his men, whether slain, wounded, captured or deserting back to their homes. Nor was this surprising, because Arthur had a very large army, for from the lands he had conquered and the cities he had taken there was not a single man left behind, good knight or foot-soldier, of fighting age or ability, whom he did not take along with him, or subsequently summon. He summoned many foreigners, in addition to his household, made up of bold knights and proven fighters. The French, those who could and who dared, went over to his side, partly because of his clever words, partly because of his generous gifts, partly because of his nobility, partly out of fear, or for refuge. They went to him, made peace and acknowledged him as their overlord.

9955 After Frollo was defeated, he came to Paris in great haste, not daring to stop anywhere or trust anyone. He was seeking a secure refuge, because he feared Arthur and his army. He had provisions brought into the city from the surrounding towns; at Paris he would await Arthur and at Paris he would defend himself. Partly from the people who had fled there, partly from its native inhabitants, the city was swollen with men. Each according to his own place in society strove to collect corn and meat and to make walls and doors. Arthur knew Frollo was equipping himself at Paris; he approached him and began a siege, lodging in the surrounding towns. He had a watch set by water and on land so that food could not get in. The French held out well and Arthur sat there nearly a month. There were many people in the city and soon they were short of food; all that they had acquired and collected in a short time was soon eaten and used up. They were starving! There was little food and many people. The women and children wept and wailed; if it had been up to the poor, the city would soon have surrendered. They kept crying: 'Frollo, what are you doing? why don't you ask Arthur for peace?'

9991 Frollo saw the people distraught for lack of food and men dying of hunger, saw they wished to surrender and saw the city made destitute. He preferred to endanger his body and risk his life rather than totally abandon Paris; he relied upon his valour. He sent word to king Arthur that the two of them should come to the island and fight in single combat, and whoever killed the other, or could take him

---

[1] Formulaic: see Gillomar in para. 9659.

Que il dui en l'isle venissent
E cors a cors se combatissent,
E li quels d'els l'autre ocirreit
U qui vif veintre le purreit
La terre tut a l'altre eüst
E tut France receüst,
Si que li poples ne perist
E que ville n'en destruisist.
Artur volt mult cel mandement
10010 E mult li vint bien a talent.
La bataille ad par els dous prise
Si cume Frolles l'out requise.
Issi firent duner lur guages
E mistrent d'ambes pars ostages,
Cil de l'ost e cil de Paris,
Des cuvenanz ki erent pris.
Es vus les dous vassals armez
E dedenz l'isle el pré entrez!
Dunc veïssiez pople fremir,
10020 Homes e femes fors eissir,
Sur murs saillir e sur maisuns
E reclamer Deu e ses nuns
Que cil venque que pais lur tienge
Si que mais guerre ne lur vienge.
La gent Artur, de l'altre part,
Sunt en escult e en esguart,
E deprient le Rei de glorie
Qu'il dunt a lur seinnur victorie.
Ki dunc veïst les dous vassals
10030 Armez seeir sur lur chevals,
Lur destriers isnels pur saillir,
Escuz lever, hanstes brandir,
Dire peüst e veir deïst
Que dous hardiz vassals veïst.
Chevals orent bons e isnels,
Escuz, halbercs e helmes bels;
N'ert mie legier a saveir
Pur esguarder ne pur veer
Ki plus forz ert ne ki veintreit,
10040 Kar chescun buen vassal pareit.

Quant il furent apareillied,
De dous parz se sunt esluinied;
Esporunant, rednes laschiees,
Escuz levez, lances baissees,
S'entr'alerent entreferir
Amdui, de merveillus aïr.
Mais Frolles al ferir failli,
Ne sai se sis chevals guenchi,
E Artur ad Frolle feru
Desus la bucle de l'escu, [1]   10050
De sun cheval l'ad luin porté
Tant cum hanste li ad duré.
Desur lui puinst, traite s'espee. [2]
Ja fust la bataille achevee
Quant Frolles sur ses piez sailli,
Cuntre Artur sa lance estendi;
Sun cheval dreit al piz feri,
Dessi al quer li enbati;
Le cheval e le chevalier
Fist tut ensemble trebuchier.   10060
Dunc veissiez gent esturmir,
Bretuns crier, armes saisir,
La trive eüssent violee
E l'eue en l'isle trespassee,
E tuit fuissent al chapleïz, [3]
Quant Artur est en piez sailliz;
Leva l'escu, le chief covri,
Frolle od s'espee recoilli.
Frolles fu mult pruz e hardiz,
Ne fu pas lenz ne esbahiz,   10070
S'espee hauça cuntremunt,
Artur feri en mi le frunt;
Frolles fu forz e li cops granz,
E li branz fu dur e tranchanz;
Le helme quassa e fendi,
Li halbercs falsa e rumpi,
En mi le frunt Artur nafra,
Li sancs el vis li devala.
Quant Artur se senti nafré
E il se vit ensanglenté,   10080

---

[1] MS P reading—*Desus*—restored.
[2] MS P reading—*s'espee*—restored in ll. 10053 and
   10068.
[3] MS J adds: *Et Frolles fust sempres occis/ Quant Artus*

*dist estes em pais/ Pur moi ne vus mouvés huimais/
Callibourc traist s'espee nue/ A Frolle sera chier ven-
due.*

Arthur fights Frollo

alive, would have all the other's land and receive all France, so that the people would not die or the city be destroyed. Arthur liked this request very much and it greatly pleased him. He agreed to this combat between the two of them, just as Frollo had requested it. Thus pledges were exchanged and hostages taken on both sides, from the army and from Paris, guaranteeing the agreement.

10015 Then the two armed warriors appeared and entered the meadow on the island. You could see the people in tumult, men and women coming out, jumping on walls and houses and calling upon God by all His names to let him who would give them peace, win, so that war never came to them again. Arthur's men, on the other hand, were listening and watching, and praying the King of glory to give their lord victory. Whoever could then have seen the two warriors, seated armed on horseback, their steeds ready to leap forward, raising their shields and brandishing their spears, could say, and say truly, that he saw two bold fighters. They had good, fast, horses, fine shields, hauberks and helmets; it was not easy to tell, seeing them, who was the strongest or who would win, for each seemed a brave fighter. When they were ready, each removed to a distance and with reins loosed, shields raised and lances lowered, they both spurred to strike each other with extraordinary violence. But Frollo missed his stroke—I do not know if his horse swerved—and Arthur struck him above the shield boss, carrying him a full lance's length from his horse. He charged at him and drew his sword; the battle would have been over, but Frollo jumped to his feet and stuck his lance out towards Arthur. He hit his horse full in the chest and pierced him to the heart, making horse and rider topple together. You could see how alarmed men were: the British were shouting and seizing their weapons. They would have broken the truce and crossed the water to the island and started a massacre. Then Arthur got to his feet, raised his shield, covered his head and gave Frollo a welcome with his sword.

10069 Frollo was very brave and bold, and neither slow nor scared. He raised his sword aloft and struck Arthur in the middle of the forehead. Frollo was strong, the blow heavy and the sword hard and keen. It broke and split the helmet, damaged and shattered the hauberk and wounded Arthur in mid-forehead, so that the blood ran down his face. When Arthur felt the wound and saw his own blood, he was so angry he went pale and livid with fury. He did not fail to rush forward, with

Mult fu iriez, nerci e teinst,
Avant passa, puint ne se feinst;
Caliburne out, s'espee, el puin,
Qu'il out eüe en maint besuin.
Frolle ad en sum le chief feru,
Des qu'es espaudes l'a fendu;
Traist e empeinst e cil chaï,
Cervele e sanc tut espandi,
Unches helmes n'i out mestier
10090 Ne li halbercs qu'il ot mult chier.
Des piez un poi eschaucirra,
Illec murut, mot ne suna.
Cil de la ville e de l'ost crient,
Li un plurent, li altre rient.
Li citaain pur Frolle plurent
E nequedent as portes curent;
Artur unt receü dedenz
E ses maisnees e ses genz.
Dunc veïssiez Franceis venir
10100 E lur humages purofrir
E Artur reçut lur humages
E de pais tenir prist ostages.
A Paris lunges sujurna,
Baillis assist, pais ordena.
    S'ost devisa en dous parties
Si establi dous compainies;
A Hoel, sun nevu, livra
L'une meitied, si li ruva
Que od cels conqueïst Angou,
10110 Gascuine, Averne e Peitou,
E il Burguinne cunquerreit
E Loherregne s'il poeit.
Hoel fist sun comandement
Sulunc sun establissement;
Berri conquist, e puis Toruigne,
Ango e Alverne e Wascuine.
Guitart, ki ert ducs de Peitiers,
Fu pruz, si out bons chevaliers.
Pur tenir sa terre e ses dreiz
10120 Se combati par plusurs feiz;

Suvent chaça, suvent fuï,
Suvent conquist, suvent perdi.
A la parfin vit, s'il perdeit,
Que a peine recovereit.
Pais fist e concorde a Hoel,
Kar, fors de tur e de chastel,
Nen out remis rien a guaster, [1]
Ne cep ne vinne a estreper.
A Artur jura feelté,
E Artur l'ad mult puis amé.   10130
Les altres parties de France
Conquist Artur par grant puissance.
    Quant il out tute en pais la terre
Que de nul lieu ne li surst guerre,
As vielz humes, as afemez,
Qu'il out lunges od sei menez,
Rendi lur duns e lur soldees
Sis renveia en lur cuntrees.
Les bachelers e la juvente
Ki de conquere orent entente,   10140
Ki n'orent femes ne emfanz,
Retint en France od sei nef anz.
Es nef anz que il France tint [2]
Mainte merveille li avint,
Maint orguillus home danta
E meint felun amesura.
A unes Pasches, a Paris,
Tint grant feste de ses amis.
A ses humes rendi lur pertes
E guereduna lur desertes;   10150
Sun servise a chescun rendi
Sulinc ço qu'il aveit servi.
A Kei, sun maistre senescal,
Un chevalier pruz e leal,
Duna tut Angou e Angiers
E cil le reçut volentiers.
A Bodoer, sun buteillier,
Un sun demaine cunseillier,
Duna tut en feu Normendie,
Ki dunc aveit nun Neüstrie.   10160

---

[1] MS P reading—*remis*—restored.

[2] MS P reading—*nef*—restored in ll. 10142–43.

Arthur conquers all France

Caliburn in his hand, his sword which he had had in many a time of need. He struck Frollo on top of his head and split it down to his shoulders. Pulling out his sword, he pushed, and Frollo fell, scattering brains and blood; he had no more need of helmet or the hauberk he cherished. For a while his feet kicked; then he died without a word. The people in the city and the army shouted, the former weeping, the latter laughing. The citizens wept for Frollo, yet ran to the gates. They received Arthur, his household and his men, inside. Then the French could be seen coming to offer their homage, and Arthur received it and took hostages as a guarantee of peace. He stayed a long while in Paris, appointing a governor and regulating the peace.

10105 He divided his army into two parts and established two companies. One half he gave to Hoel, his nephew, and asked him to conquer with it Anjou, Gascony, Auvergne and Poitou, and he should conquer Burgundy and Lorraine if he could. Hoel carried out his command as he had ordained it: he conquered Berry, then Touraine, Anjou, Auvergne and Gascony. Guitart, duke of Poitiers, was a brave and good knight. To keep his land and his rights he fought many times, often in pursuit, often in flight, often winning and often losing. Finally he saw that if he lost he would have trouble recovering. He made peace and a treaty with Hoel because, apart from towers and castles, nothing was left to destroy, neither plants nor vines to be despoiled. He swore fealty to Arthur, and the king afterwards held him very dear. Then Arthur mightily conquered the remaining parts of France.

10133 When he had brought peace to the whole land, so that no part erupted in war, he presented gifts and wages to the old men and to those enfeebled, who had long been in his army, and sent them back to their own lands. As for the young and unmarried men, with neither wives nor children, who expected more conquests, he kept them with him in France for nine years. In the nine years he held France, many marvels happened to him, he tamed many a proud man and kept many a villain in check. One Easter, he held a great feast for his friends in Paris. He compensated his men's losses and rewarded their deserts, repaying each one's service according to what he had done. To Kei, his chief seneschal, a brave and loyal knight, he gave all Anjou and Angers, which was gratefully received. To Bedoer, his cup-bearer, one of his privy counsellors, he gave all Normandy in fief, which then was called Neustria. These two were his most faithful subjects and knew all his deliberations.[1] And he gave Flanders to Holdin, Le Mans to his cousin

---

[1] *HRB* chap. 155: *Kaius*; *VV*: *Keyus/Keius*; *Bedeurus*. The seneschal and cup-bearer (*dapifer* and *pincerna*) were two of five great officers of state in the royal household (see Weiss, *Birth of Romance*, pp. 159–60). The importance of Kei and Bedoer in Arthur's household perhaps reflects the fact that they are his main companions in Welsh literature of *c.*1100 or earlier; see Sims-Williams, 'Welsh Arthurian Poems', *AOW* p. 39 and Bromwich and Evans on *Pa Gur* in *Culhwch and Olwen* pp. xxxiv–xxxvi. Cei is referred to in *Culhwch and Olwen* as *swyddwr* = *dapifer.*

Cil dui erent mult si feeil
E saveient tut sun cunseil.
E Flandres duna a Holdin, [1]
Le Mans a Borel sun cusin,
[Buluine duna a Ligier
E Puntif duna a Richier]. [2]
A mulz sulunc lur genterise,
A plusurs sulunc lur servise
Duna ses delivres enurs
10170 E les terres as vavasurs.
    Quant il out ses baruns feufez
E fait riches tuz ses privez,
En avril, quant esté entra,
En Engleterre trespassa.
Mult veïssiez a sun repaire
Humes e femes joie faire;
Baisent les dames lur mariz
E les meres baisent lur fiz;
Filz e filles baisent lur peres
10180 E de joie plurent les meres;
Cusines baisent lur cusins
E les veisines lur veisins.
Les amis lur amies baisent [3]
E, quant leus est, de plus s'aaisent;
Les antes baisent lur nevuz;
Mult aveit grant joie entre tuz.
Par rues e par quarefors
En veïssiez ester plusors
Pur demander cument lur est
10190 E que unt fait de lur cunquest,
Que unt fait e que unt trové
E pur quei unt tant demuré.
Cil recuntent lur aventures
E les batailles forz e dures
E les travailz qu'il unt eüz
E les perilz qu'il unt veüz.
    Artur enura tuz les suens,
Mult ama e duna as buens.
Pur ses richeises demustrer
10200 E pur faire de sei parler,

Prist cunseil si li fu loé
Qu'a la Pentecuste en esté
Feïst sun barnage assembler
E dunc se feïst coruner;
A Karlion en Glamorgan
Mandast tuz ses barons par ban.
La cité ert bien herbergiee
E mult esteit bien aaisee;
A cel tens, ço distrent li hume,
De riches palaiz semblot Rome. 10210
Karliun dejuste Usche siet,
Un flum ki en Saverne chiet;
Cil ki d'altre terre veneient
Par cele eue venir poeient;
De l'une part ert la riviere,
De l'altre la forest pleniere.
Plenté i aveit de peissun
E grant plenté de veneisun;
Beles erent les praeries
E riches les guaaineries.   10220
Iglises out en la cité
Dous, de bien grant autorité:
L'une ert de saint Juile, un martyr,
Nonains i out pur Deu servir,
L'altre esteit d'un suen compainun
Que l'om claimeit saint Aarun;
La fu li siez de l'evesquied,
Mult i aveit riche clergied,
E chanuines de grant clergie
Ki saveient d'astronomie;   10230
Des esteiles s'entremeteient,
Al rei Artur suvent diseient
Cumfaitement li avendreit
Des ovres que faire vuleit.
Bon ert a cel tens Karlion,
Ne fist puis se empeirer non.
    Pur les riches herbergemenz
E pur les granz aaisemenz,
Pur les bels bois, pur les bels prez,
Pur les bels lieus que vus oëz,   10240

---

[1] MSS PHABKRN erroneously have *Buluine*
(which belongs to Ligier, as MS P's scribe states
at l. 10312).

[2] MSS PSHABKGRN omit ll. 10165–66; the couplet is supplied by Arnold.

[3] MS P's order of line restored.

The court at Caerleon

Borel, Boulogne to Ligier and Puntif to Richier.[1] To many according to their nobility, to several according to their service, he gave what domains were available,[2] and to minor nobles he gave lands.

10171 When he had given his barons fiefs and made all his friends rich, he crossed to England in April, at the start of summer. Men and women could be seen celebrating his return: the ladies kissed their husbands and the mothers their sons, sons and daughters kissed their fathers and mothers wept for joy, cousins and neighbours embraced, as did sweethearts who, when opportunity allowed, indulged themselves rather more. Aunts kissed their nephews—for everyone, joy was widespread. In streets and at crossroads many people would congregate to ask the new arrivals how they were and what had they done with their conquests, how they had acted, what they had found and why they had been away so long. They in turn told of their adventures, the harsh and bitter battles, the hardships they had endured and the dangers they had seen.[3]

10197 Arthur honoured all his men, especially cherishing and rewarding the best ones. To display his wealth and spread his fame, he took counsel and was advised to assemble his barons at Pentecost, in summer, and then to be crowned.[4] He summoned all his barons by proclamation to Caerleon, in Glamorgan. The city was well situated and extremely wealthy. Men said at that time that its rich palaces made it another Rome. Caerleon lies on the Usk, a river flowing into the Severn; those coming from overseas could arrive on this river. On one side was the river, on the other the dense forest. There was plenty of fish and a wealth of game; the meadows were lovely and the fields fertile. There were two churches in the city, both prestigious: one called after St Julius, the martyr, where there were nuns to serve God, and the other after his friend, St Aaron.[5] This was the seat of the archbishop, and there were many noble priests, and most learned canons who knew about astronomy. They concerned themselves with the stars and often told king Arthur how the works he wished to perform would come to pass. Caerleon was a good place then; it has deteriorated since.

10237 Because of the handsome lodgings, the great comforts, the fine woods and beautiful meadows, because of these excellent places you have heard of, Arthur wished to hold his court there. He made all his barons come: he summoned his kings and his counts, his dukes and his viscounts, barons, vassals, bishops and abbots. And those who were summoned came, as was fitting, to the feast. From Scotland came king Angusel, dressed handsomely and well; from Moray, king Urien and

---

[1] None of these four is in *HRB* here, though Borel, Holdin and Ligier appear soon, chap. 156.

[2] *Delivrer* means 'fallen into escheat', i.e. these domains had come into Arthur's hands because their owners had died without heirs.

[3] This passage of rejoicing is entirely added by Wace.

[4] On plenary courts, where the crown could be worn in state, see Thorpe, *Geoffrey of Monmouth: History*, p. 226, fn. 2.

[5] For Julius and Aaron see fn. 4 to p. 141.

Vout Artur la sa curt tenir.
Tuz ses baruns i fist venir:
Manda ses reis, manda ses cuntes,
Manda ses ducs e ses vescuntes,
Manda baruns, manda chasez,
Manda evesques e abez. [1]
E cil vindrent ki mandé furent
Si cum a feste venir durent.
D'Escoce i vint reis Augusel,
10250 Apareillied mult bien e bel,
De Moraife Urian, li reis,
E Ewein, sis fiz, li curteis, [2]
Stater, li reis des Sutwaleis,
E Cadüal des Nortwaleis.
Cador de Cornoaille i fu,
Que li reis ad mult chier tenu,
Morud, li cuens de Gloëcestre,
E Mauron, cuens de Guirecestre,
Guerguint, li cuens de Hereford,
10260 E Bos, li quens d'Oxineford;
De Bade, Urgent, Cursal de Cestre,
E Jonathas de Dorecestre.
Anaraud vint de Salesbiere
E Kimmare de Cantorbiere.
Baluc vint, li cuens de Cilcestre,
E Jugeïn de Leïcestre,
E Argahl de Waruic, uns cuens
Ki en la curt out bien des suens.
Altres baruns i out plusurs
10270 Ki n'orent pas menurs enurs;
Li fiz Apo i fu, Donaud,
E Regeïm, le fiz Elaud;
Fiz Coïl i fu, Cheneüs,
E li fiz Catel, Cathleüs;
Fiz Cledauc i fu, Heldelin,
E li fiz Trunat, Kibelin.
Grifu i fu, fiz Nagoïd,
Run, fiz Neton, e Margoïd,
Glofaud e Kincar, fiz Aungan,
10280 E Kimmar e Gorboïan,

Kinlint, Neton e Peredur
Que l'om clamot fiz Elidur.
De cels ki en la curt serveient
Ki des privez le rei esteient,
Ki sunt de la Roünde Table,
Ne vuil jo mie faire fable;
D'altres de menur teneüre
I aveit tant, n'en sai mesure ;
Mult i out abez e evesques,
E dels païs treis arcevesques,   10290
Cel de Lundres, cel d'Everwic,
E de Karlion saint Dubric:
De Rome out la legaciun
Si fu de grant religiun;
Pur s'amur e pur s'oreisun
Vint maint enferm a guarisun.
Lundres out a cel tens le sied,
E out puis, de l'arcevesquied,
Dessi que li Angleis regnerent,
Ki les iglises deserterent.   10300
Assez out en la curt baruns [3]
Dunt jo ne sai dire les nuns:
Gillamur i fu, reis d'Irlande,
E Malvaisus, li reis d'Islande,
E Doldanïed de Gollande,
Ki n'unt pas plenté de viande.
Achil i fu, reis des Daneis,
E Loth, ki ert reis des Norreis,
E Gonvais, li reis d'Orchenie,
Ki maint utlage out en baillie.   10310
D'ultre mer li cuens Ligier vint,
Ki de Buluine l'enur tint,
De Flandres i fu cuens Holdin
E de Chartres li cuens Gerin;
Cil amena par grant noblei
Les duze pers de France od sei.
Guitart i vint, cuens de Peitiers,
E Keis, ki esteit cuens d'Angiers,
E Bedoer de Normendie,
Ki dunc aveit nun Neüstrie;   10320

---

[1] MS J adds fourteen lines on the nationalities of those summoned.

[2] MS J adds four lines: *Loth de Loenois i vint/ Qui molt grant part de la cort tint/ Avoec lui vint Gawains ses fieus/ Qui molt estoit frans et gentieus.*

[3] MS P reading—*en*—restored.

The barons attend court

Ewain the courteous, his son.[1] Stater came, king of South Wales, and Cadual of North Wales; Cador of Cornwall, whom the king held dear, was there, Morvid count of Gloucester, and Mauron count of Worcester, Guerguint, count of Hereford, and Bos, count of Oxford. From Bath came Urgent, from Chester, Cursal, and from Dorchester, Jonathas. Anaraud came from Salisbury and Kimmare from Canterbury. Baluc count of Silchester came, and Jugein from Leicester, and Argahl from Warwick, a count with many of his relations at court.

10269 There were many other barons whose lands were no less: Donaud, son of Apo and Regeim, son of Elaud; Cheneus, son of Coil, and Cathleus, son of Catel; the son of Cledauc, Edelin, and the son of Trunat, Kimbelin. Grifu was there, son of Nagoid, Run, son of Neton, and Margoid, Glofaud, and Kincar, son of Aingan, and Kimmar and Gorboian, Kinlint, Neton and Peredur, called the son of Elidur.[2] I do not want to tell stories about those serving in court who were friends of the king and belonged to the Round Table. There were so many others of lesser rank there, I could not count them all. There were many abbots and bishops, and the three archbishops in the land: from London, from York, and saintly Dubric from Caerleon. He was the papal legate and a man of great piety: through his love and prayers many a sick man was cured. At that time, and subsequently, the see of the archbishopric was in London, until the English ruled, laying the churches waste.

10301 There were many barons at court whose names I do not know. Gillomar, king of Ireland, was there, and Malvaisus, king of Iceland, and Doldani of Godland, a country rather short of food. Aschil was there, king of Denmark, and Loth, king of Norway, and Gonvais, king of Orkney, who controlled many pirates. From overseas came count Ligier, who held the fief of Boulogne, from Flanders count Holdin,

---

[1] Owan or Ywain, hero of poems by Taliesin (Roberts, 'Geoffrey of Monmouth', *AOW* p. 109), here mentioned earlier than in *HRB*.

[2] See *HRB* chap. 156. The list of men is an element imported from Welsh genealogies, which preserved ancient British traditions (Piggott, 'Sources', p. 282). In *HRB* (Vulgate) the names in the first group are: *Anguselus, Urianus, Caduan* king of North Wales, *Eddelin* king of South Wales, *Cador*, archbishop *Dubricius, Moruid* of Gloucester, *Mauron* of Worcester, *Anaraut* of Salisbury, *Arthgal* of Warwick, *Iugin* of Leicester, *Cursalem* of Caistor, *Kinmarc* of Canterbury, *Galluc* of Winchester, *Urgennius* of Bath, *Ionathal* of Dorchester and *Boso* of Oxford. The *VV* has: *Anguselus, Urianus, Caduallo Lauith, Stather* king of South Wales, *Cador, Morwid, Mauron, Anaraud, Archgal, Iugein, Cursalem, Kimmare, Galluc* of Silchester, *Urbgennius, Ionathal* and *Boso*. Wace seems closer to the names of people and cities

in the *VV* here. He has added *Guerguint* of Hereford, perhaps remembering Belin's son Gurguint Bertruc (l. 3243). *HRB*'s *Cursalem* comes from '*Kaicestria*', probably Caistor. Wace renders it here and later (l. 12358) as *Cestre*, which could be either Caistor or Chester, but at ll. 12753–4 he definitely identifies *Cestre* with Chester. The *VV* omits all those names in the second group which in the Vulgate are prefixed by the Welsh *map*, son of, such as *Donaut Mappapo* and *Cheneus Mapcoil*. Wace's *Elidur*, like *HRB*'s *Eridur* (*Map-eridur*), seems to be a distortion of *Eleuther*, Peredur's father in Welsh genealogy. Both Peredur and Elidur occur earlier in *HRB*, as sons of Morvid, and kings associated with Dumbarton (Alclud). Peredur, like Owain, Urien and Dunaut, seems to be another hero of the 6th-century British North. See fn. 1 on Urien, p. 243; see also Roberts ('Geoffrey of Monmouth') and Lovecy ('*Historia Peredur*'), *AOW* pp. 109, 175–76.

E del Mans i vint cuens Borel
E de Bretaine i vint Hoel.
Hoels e tuit cil de vers France
Furent de noble cuntenance,
De beles armes, de bels dras,
De bels lorains, de chevals gras.
N'out remis barun des Espaine [1]
Dessi al Rim vers Alemainne,
Ki a la feste ne venist
10330 Pur ço kil la sumunse oïst, [2]
Tant pur Artur, tant pur ses duns,
Tant pur cunustre ses baruns,
Tant pur veeir ses mananties,
Tant pur oïr ses curteisies,
Tant pur amur, tant pur banie,
Tant pur enur, tant pur baillie.
   Quant la curt le rei fu justee,
Mult veïssez bele assemblee,
Mult veïssez cité fremir,
10340 Servanz aler, servanz venir,
Ostels saisir, ostels purprendre,
Maisuns vuider, curtines tendre,
Les mareschals ostels livrer,
Soliers e chambres delivrer,
A cels ki n'aveient ostels
Faire loges e tendre trés.
Mult veïssiez as esquiers
Palefreiz mener e destriers,
Faire estables, paissuns fichier,
10350 Chevals mener, chevals lier,
Chevals furbir e abevrer,
Aveine, foerre, herbe porter.
Mult veïssiez en plusurs sens
Errer vaslez e chamberlens,
Mantels pendre, mantels plaier,
Mantels escurre e atachier,
Peliçuns porter vairs e gris,
Feire semblast, ço vus fust vis.
   Al matin, le jur de la feste,
10360 Ço dit l'estorie de la geste,

Vindrent tut trei li arcevesque
E li abé e li evesque;
El palais le rei corunerent
E puis al mustier le menerent.
Dui arcevesque le menoent,
Ki a ses dous costés aloent;
Chescuns l'un braz li susteneit
Dessi qu'a sun siege veneit.
Quatre espees i out a or
Que pont, que helt, que entretor; 10370
Quatre rei cez quatre portoent,
Ki dreit devant le rei aloent;
Cist mestiers lur aparteneit
Quant li reis feste e curt teneit:
Cil d'Escoce e cil de Nortguales
E li tierz esteit de Sutguales;
Cador de Cornoaille esteit
Qui la quarte espee teneit;
N'aveit pas menur digneté
Ke se il eüst realté. 10380
Dubric, ke de Rome ert legat
E de Karlion ert prelat,
Enprist a faire le mestier,
E ço esteit en sun mustier.
La reïne, de l'altre part,
Fu servie par grant esguart;
Devant la feste aveit mandees
E a cele feste assemblees
Les gentilz dames del païs;
E les femes a ses amis, 10390
Ses amies e ses parentes,
E meschines beles e gentes
Fist a la feste a li venir
Pur la feste od li maintenir.
En sa chambre fu corunee
E al temple as nonains menee.
Pur la grant presse departir
Que uns lieus ne peüst sufrir,
Quatre dames ki devant vindrent
Quatre columbes blanches tindrent; 10400

---

[1] MS P reading—*remis*—restored.   [2] MS P reading—*kil*—restored.

Coronation of Arthur

and from Chartres count Gerin, bringing with him, in great splendour, the twelve peers of France. Guitart, count of Poitiers, came, and Kei, count of Angers, and Bedoer from Normandy (then called Neustria), and from Le Mans came count Borel and from Brittany Hoel. Hoel and all those from France had noble bearing, fine weapons, handsome clothes, splendid trappings and sleek steeds. There was not a single baron, from Spain to the Rhine near Germany, who did not attend the feast, provided he heard the summons. Some came because of Arthur, some because of his gifts, some to know his barons, some to see his wealth, some to hear his courtly speech, some out of love, some because they were commanded, some for honour, some for power.

10337 When the king's court was assembled, a fine gathering could be seen, and the city was in tumult, with servants coming and going, seizing and occupying lodgings, emptying houses, hanging tapestries, giving marshals apartments, clearing upper and lower rooms, and erecting lodges and tents for those who had nowhere to stay. The squires could be seen busy leading palfreys and war-horses, arranging stabling, sinking tethering-posts, bringing and tethering horses, rubbing them down and watering them, and carrying oats, straw and grass. You could see servants and chamberlains moving in several directions, hanging up and folding away mantles, shaking their dust off and fastening them, carrying grey and white furs: you would have thought it just like a fair.[1]

10359 In the morning of the feast day (according to the story in the chronicle), all three of the archbishops, as well as the abbots and bishops, arrived. Inside the palace, they crowned the king and then led him to the church. Two archbishops, one on each side, went with him, each supporting an arm, until he came to his seat. There were four swords of gold—the pommels, the hilts, or the parts in between[2] were all gilded—borne by four kings, who walked directly in front of the king. This was their office when Arthur held court and a feast day. They were the kings of Scotland and North Wales; the third came from South Wales and Cador of Cornwall held the fourth sword. He was no less dignified than if he had been royal. Dubric, the pope's legate and the prelate of Caerleon, undertook to perform the office, as it was in his own church.

10385 The queen, for her part, was attended with great pomp. She had invited beforehand, and now gathered round her on the feast day the noble ladies of the land, and she made her friends' wives, her female friends and relations, and beautiful, noble girls, all come to her to observe the festival with her. She was crowned in her rooms and led to the nuns' church. To make a path through the great crowd,

---

[1] This whole paragraph is added by Wace.

[2] See Tobler-Lommatzsch, *Altfranzösisches Wörterbuch*, 3, 650–51, *s.v.* entrecor.

As quatre esteient mariees
Ki portoent les quatre espees.
Emprés la reïne veneient
Altres dames, ki la siueient,
Od grant joie e od grant leesce
E od merveilluse noblesce.
Mult esteient bien afublees,
Bien vestues, bien aturnees;
Maint en i peüssez veeir
10410 Ki mainte altre quidout valeir;
Mult i aveit chiers guarnemenz,
Chiers aturs e chiers vestemenz,
Riches bliauz, riches mantels
Riches nusches, riches anels,
Mainte pelice vaire e grise
E guarnemenz de mainte guise.
As processiuns out grant presse,
Chescuns d'aler avant s'engresse.
Quant la messe fu comenciee,
10420 Ke le jur fu mult exalciee,
Mult oïssiez orgues suner
E clers chanter e orgener,
Voiz abaissier e voiz lever,
Chanz avaler e chanz munter;
Mult veïssiez par les mustiers
Aler e venir chevaliers;
Tant pur oïr les clers chanter,
Tant pur les dames esgarder,
D'un mustier a l'altre cureient,
10430 Mult aloent e mult veneient;
Ne saveient certainement
Al quel fussent plus lungement;
Ne se poeient saüler
Ne de veeir ne d'esculter;
Se tuz li jurs issi durast,
Ja, ço qui, ne lur ennuiast. [1]
    Quant li servise fu finez
E Ite missa est chantez,
Li reis ad sa curune ostee
10440 Qu'il aveit el mustier portee;

Une curune menur prist,
E la reïne ensement fist;
Jus mistrent les grainnurs aturs,
Plus legiers pristrent e menurs.
Quant li reis turna del mustier,
En sun palais ala mangier.
La reïne en un altre ala
E les dames od sei mena:
Li reis manga ovec ses humes
E la reïne ovec les dames,   10450
A grant deduit e a grant joie.
Custume soleit estre a Troie
E Bretun encore la teneient,
Quant ensemble feste faiseient
Li hume od les humes manjoent,
Que nule feme n'i menoent;
Les dames manjoent aillurs,
N'i aveit ke lur serviturs.
Quant li reis fu al deis assis,
A la custume del païs   10460
Assis sunt li barun entur
Chescuns en l'ordre de s'enur.
Li seneschals, Kei aveit nun,
Vestuz d'ermine peliçun,
Servi a sun mangier le rei,
Mil gentilz homes ovec sei
Ki tuz furent vestu d'ermine;
Cil serveient de la cuisine,
Suvent aloent e espés,
Escueles portant e més.   10470
Bedoer, de l'altre partie,
Servi de la buteillerie,
Ensemble od lui mil damaisels
Vestuz d'ermine, genz e bels;
Od cupes e od nés d'or fin
E od hanaps portoent vin.
N'i aveit hume ki servist
Ki d'ermine ne se vestist.
Bedoer devant els alout
Ki la cupe le rei portout;   10480

---

[1] MS P reading of line restored.

The coronation feast

which would not allow any room, four ladies, walking in front, held four white doves. The ladies were the wives of those who carried the four swords. After the queen followed other ladies, joyfully, happily and in the noblest fashion. They were splendidly garbed, dressed and adorned. Many a one could be seen who thought she was as good as many of the others. They had the most expensive garments, costly attire and costly vestments, splendid tunics, splendid mantles, precious brooches, precious rings, many a fur of white and grey, and clothes of every fashion.

10417 At the processions there was a great crowd, with everyone pushing forward. When mass began, which that day was especially solemn, you could hear a great sound of organs and the clerics singing and playing, voices rising and falling, chants sinking and soaring.[1] Many knights could be seen coming and going through the churches. Partly to hear the clerics sing, partly to look at the ladies, they kept going to and fro from one church to the other. They did not know for sure in which they were the longest; they could not have enough of either seeing or hearing. If the whole day had passed this way I believe they would never have got bored.

10437 When the service was ended, and the last words of the mass sung[2] the king removed the crown he had worn in church, and assumed a lighter one, and the queen did the same. They took off the weightier robes and donned lesser, lighter ones. When the king returned from church, he went to his palace to eat. The queen went to another and took her ladies with her: the king ate with his men and the queen with the ladies, with great joy and pleasure. It used to be the custom in Troy, and the British still adhered to it, that when they gathered for a feast day, the men ate with the men, taking no women with them, while the ladies ate elsewhere, with no men except their servants.[3] When the king was seated on the dais, in the manner of the land the barons sat all round, each in order of his importance.[4] The seneschal, called Kei, dressed in robes of ermine, served the king at his meal, with a thousand nobles to help him, all dressed in ermine. They brought food from the kitchen and moved about frequently, carrying bowls and dishes. Bedoer, on the other side, brought drink from the buttery, and accompanying him were a thousand pages, handsome and fair and dressed in ermine. They brought wine in cups, bowls[5] of fine gold and goblets. No man

---

[1] See Page, *Voices and Instruments*, pp. 121–22, who suggests the *chanter* and *organer* performed by clerics is a reference to two kinds of vocal music: *chanter* is performing plain-chant, *organer* is singing liturgical polyphony.

[2] Literally: Go, the mass [is ended].

[3] This contradicts para. 8541.

[4] This more familiar medieval seating plan would seem to contradict the idea of the Round Table; see Schmolke-Hasselmann, 'Round Table', p. 51.

[5] The *nés* were cups shaped like ships.

Li dameisel emprés veneient,
Ki les baruns del vin serveient.
La reïne rout ses servanz,
Ne vus sai dire quels ne quanz;
Richement e bel fu servie,
Ele, e tute sa compainie.
Mult veïssiez riche vaissele,
Ki mult ert chiere e mult ert bele,
E de mangiers riche servise
10490 E de beivres de mainte guise.
Ne puis tut ne ne sai numer,
Ne les richesces acunter.
De buens homes e de richesce
E de plenté e de noblesce
E de curteisie e d'enur
Portout Engleterre la flur
Sur tuz les regnes d'envirun
E sur tuz cels que nus savum.
Plus erent curteis e vaillant
10500 Neïs li povre païsant
Que chevalier en altres regnes,
E altresi erent les femes.
Ja ne veïssiez chevalier
Ki de rien feïst a preisier
Ki armes e dras e atur
Nen eüst tut d'une culur;
D'une culur armes faiseient
E d'une culur se vesteient,
Si rerent les dames preisiees
10510 D'une culur apareillees.
Ja nul chevalier n'i eüst,
De quel parage que il fust,
Ja peüst aveir druerie
Ne curteise dame a amie,
Se il n'eüst treis feiz esté
De chevalerie pruvé.
Li chevalier mielz en valeient
E en estur mielz en faiseient,
E les dames meillur esteient
10520 E plus chastement en viveient.

Quant li reis leva del mangier,
Alez sunt tuit esbanier;
De la cité es chans eissirent,
A plusurs gieus se departirent;
Li un alerent bohorder
E lur isnels chevals mustrer,
Li altre alerent escremir
Ou pierre geter ou saillir;
Tels i aveit ki darz lançoent
E tels i aveit ki lutoent.   10530
Chescuns del gieu s'entremeteit
Dunt entremettre se saveit.
Cil ki ses compainnuns venqueit
E ki d'alcun gieu pris aveit,
Esteit sempres al rei menez
E a tuz les altres mustrez,
E li reis del suen li donout
Tant dunt cil tuz liez s'en alout.
Les dames sur les murs muntoent
Pur esgarder cels ki juoent;   10540
Ki ami aveit en la place
Tost li turnot l'oil e la face.
[Mult out a la curt jugleürs,
Chanteürs, estrumenteürs;
Mult peüssiez oïr chançuns,
Rotruenges e novels suns,
Vïeleüres, lais de notes,
Lais de vïeles, lais de rotes,
Lais de harpes, lais de frestels,
Lires, tympes e chalemels,   10550
Symphonies, psalteriuns,
Monacordes, timbes, coruns.
Assez i out tresgeteürs;
Joeresses e jugleürs;
Li un dient contes e fables,
Alquant demandent dez e tables.
Tels i ad juent al hasart,
Ço est un gieu de male part;
As eschecs juent li plusur
U a la mine u al grainnur.   10560

Court entertainments

serving was not clad in ermine. Bedoer went before them carrying the king's cup; the pages came close behind, to serve the barons with wine.

10483 The queen also had her servants; I cannot tell you how many or who they were. She and her whole company were served nobly and well. Many splendid dishes could be seen, expensive and beautiful, lavish helpings of food and drinks of many kinds. I neither can nor know how to describe everything, nor enumerate the objects of luxury. Beyond all the surrounding realms, and beyond all those we now know, England was unparalleled for fine men, wealth, plenty, nobility, courtesy and honour. Even the poor peasants were more courtly and brave than knights in other realms, and so were the women too. You would never see a knight worth his salt who did not have his armour, clothing and equipment all of the same colour. They made their armour all of one colour and their dress to match, and ladies of high repute were likewise clothed in one colour. There was no knight, however nobly born, who could expect affection or have a courtly lady as his love, if he had not proved himself three times in knightly combat. The knights were the more worthy for it, and performed better in the fray; the ladies, too, were the better and lived a chaster life.

10521 When the king rose from his meal, everyone went in search of amusement. They went out of the city into the fields and dispersed for various games. Some went off to joust and show off their fast horses, others to fence or throw the stone or jump. There were some who threw javelins and some who wrestled. Each one took part in the game he knew most about. The man who defeated his friends and who was prized for any game was at once taken to the king and exhibited to all the others, and the king gave him a gift of his own so large that he went away delighted. The ladies mounted the walls to look at those who were playing and whoever had a friend quickly bent her eyes and face towards him. There were many minstrels at court, singers and instrumentalists: many songs could be heard, melodies sung to the rote and new tunes, fiddle music, lays with melodies, lays on fiddles, lays on rotes, lays on harps, lays on flutes, lyres, drums and shawms, bagpipes, psalteries, monochords, tambourines and choruns.[1] There were plenty of conjurors, dancers and jugglers. Some told stories and tales, others asked for dice and backgammon. There were some who played games of chance—that's a cruel game—but most played chess or at dice or at something better.[2] Two by

---

[1] For *rotes, choruns* and psalteries see fn. 3 to p. 95. This description of music at court is added by the *Brut*, but not by all its MSS: see fn. 1 to French text, p. 266.

[2] MS K has: *Au geu del mat ou au mellor*; MS G has:

U a la mine au gieu majors. One line seems to apply to chess, the other to a game with raised stakes. See Arnold and Pelan, *Partie Arthurienne*, fn. to p. 93.

Dui e dui al gieu s'acompainnent,
Li un perdent, li un guaainnent,
Cil envient qui le plus getent,
As altres dient qu'il i metent;
Sur guages empruntent deniers,
Unze pur duze volentiers;
Guages dunent, guages saisissent,
Guages prenent, guages plevissent,
Suvent jurent, suvent s'afichent,
10570 Suvent boisent e suvent trichent;
Mult estrivent, mult se curucent,
Suvent mescuntent, suvent grucent;
Dous e dous getent e puis quernes,
Ambesas e le tiers e ternes,
A la fïee getent quines,
A la fïee getent sines;
Sis, cinc, quatre, trei, dous e as
Unt a plusurs toleit lur dras.
Buen espeir ad ki les dez tient;
10580 Quant sis compainz les ad si crient.
Assez suvent noisent e crient;
Li un as altres suvent dient:
'Vus me boisiez, defors getez,
Crollez la main, hochez les dez!
Jo l'envi avant vostre get!
Querez deniers, mettez, jo met!'
Tels i puet aseeir vestuz
Ki al partir s'en lieve nuz.] ¹
    Treis jurs dura la feste issi.
10590 Quant vint al quart, al mecresdi,
Li reis ses bachelers feufa,
Enurs delivres devisa;
Lur servises a cels rendi
Ki pur terres l'ourent servi;
Burcs duna e chasteleries
E evesquiez e abeïes.
A cels ki d'altre terre esteient,
Ki pur amur al rei veneient,
Duna cupes, duna destriers,
10600 Duna de ses aveirs plus chiers.

[Duna deduiz, duna joiels,
Duna levriers, duna oisels,
Duna peliçuns, duna dras,
Duna cupes, duna hanas,
Duna palies, duna anels,
Duna blialz, duna mantels,
Duna lances, duna espees,
Duna saietes barbelees.
Duna cuivres, duna escuz,
Ars e espiez bien esmoluz,   10610
Duna lieparz e duna urs,
Seles, lorains e chaceürs.
Duna haubercs, duna destriers,
Duna helmes, duna deniers,
Duna argent e duna or,
Duna le mielz de sun tresor.
N'i out hume qui rien valsist
Qui d'altre terre a lui venist
Cui li reis ne dunast tel dun
Qui enur fust a tel barun.] ²   10620
    Artur fu assis a un deis,
Envirun lui cuntes e reis.
Es vus duze humes blancs, chanuz,
Bien afublez e bien vestuz;
Dui e dui en la sale vindrent
E dui e dui as mains se tindrent;
Duze esteient, e duze rains
D'olive tindrent en lur mains.
Petit pas, ordeneement,
Mult bel e mult avenantment   10630
Par mi la sale trespasserent,
Al rei vindrent sil saluerent;
De Rome, ço distrent, veneient
E messagier de Rome esteient.
Une chartre unt desvolepee,
A Artur l'ad un d'els livree
De part l'empereür de Rome.
Oëz de la chartre la sume:
'Luces, ki Rome ad en baillie
E des Romains la seinurie,   10640

---

¹ MSS PDLFHABNT omit ll. 10543–88; some
or all of these lines occur in MSS Vatican (see
Arnold II, p. 790), Hague (10567–88, with
10575–76 omitted), K, C, E, J (up to 10562),
OS and GR (though displaced to occur after l.
10492, and R omits ll. 10553–54).

² MSS PDLCFHABNT omit ll. 10601–20; some
or all of these occur in MSS KEGJ (though displaced), ORS and Hague (10589–601 omitted;
10602–03 are replaced with two very similar
lines).

Arrival of the Roman ambassadors

two they joined in the game, some losing, some winning; some envied those who made the most throws, or they told others how to move. They borrowed money in exchange for pledges, quite willing only to get eleven to the dozen on the loan; they gave pledges, they seized pledges, they took them, they promised them, often swearing, often protesting their good intentions, often cheating and often tricking. They got argumentative and angry, often miscounting and grousing. They threw twos, and then fours, two aces, a third one, and threes, sometimes fives, sometimes sixes. Six, five, four, three, two and ace—these stripped many of their clothes. Those holding the dice were in high hopes; when their friends had them, they made a racket. Very often they shouted and cried out, one saying to the other: 'You're cheating me, throw them out, shake your hand, scatter the dice! I'm raising the bid before your throw! If you're looking for money, put some down, like me!' The man who sat down to play clothed might rise naked at close of play.[1]

10589 In this way, the feast lasted three days. When it came to the fourth, a Wednesday, the king gave his young men fiefs and shared out available[2] domains. He repaid the service of everyone who had served him for land: he distributed towns and castles, bishoprics and abbeys. To those who came from another land, for love of the king, he gave cups and war-horses and some of his finest possessions. He gave playthings, he gave jewels, he gave greyhounds, birds, furs, cloth, cups, goblets, brocades, rings, tunics, cloaks, lances, swords and barbed arrows. He gave quivers and shields, bows and keen swords, leopards and bears, saddles, trappings and chargers. He gave hauberks and war-horses, helmets and money, silver and gold, the best in his treasury. Any man worth anything, who had come to visit him from other lands, was given such a gift from the king that it did him honour.

10621 Arthur was seated on a dais, with counts and kings around him. Twelve white-haired men now appeared, well dressed and equipped. Two by two they entered the hall, each pair linking hands. They were twelve and they carried twelve olive branches in their hands. In a slow, suitable and measured fashion, they impressively crossed the hall, came to the king and greeted him. They came from Rome, they said, and were Rome's envoys. They unfolded a charter and one of them delivered it to Arthur, on behalf of the Roman emperor. This was the burden of the charter.

10639 'Luces, the ruler of Rome and lord of the Romans,[3] sends king Arthur, his enemy,

---

[1] See Jean Bodel's *Jeu de Saint Nicolas, c.*1200, for extended representations of similar dice games where 'he who throws most takes the lot' (l. 870 and notes pp. 82–88). This description of dice-playing, like that of Arthur's gifts (ll. 10601–20), is added by the *Brut* but not in all the MSS: on the other hand Wace omits a passage in *HRB* chap. 157 on the gifts of bishoprics and archbishoprics.

[2] 'Escheated': see fn. 2 to p. 257 above.

[3] In *HRB* there is a difference between the emperor Leo (chap. 155) and Lucius Hiberius, described, somewhat inconsistently, as procurator of the Republic (chap. 158). Wace appears to confound the two, making Lucius (whose second name, denoting his Spanish origin, he keeps as *Hiber*, ll. 11085, 12451) Emperor here, whereas Leo was called Emperor at l. 9913.

Mande ço qu'il ad deservi
Al rei Artur, sun enemi.
Mult me desdein, en merveillant,
E me merveil, en desdeinant,
Que par surfait e par orguil
Oses vers Rome ovrir tun oil.
Mult me desdein, mult me merveil
A cui e ou tu prenz conseil
De prendre cuntre Rome estrif
10650 Tant cum tu sez un Romain vif.
Mult par as fait grant estultie
Ki ver nus as pris envaïe[1]
Ki tut le mund jugier devum
E ki le chief del mund tenum.
Ne sez encor, mais tul savras,
Ne l'as veü, mais tul verras
Cum grant chose est a corucier
Rome, ki tut deit justiser.
Tu iés eissuz de ta nature
10660 E trespassé as ta mesure.
Sez tu ki es e dunt tu viens
Ki noz treüs prenz e retiens?
Noz terres e noz treüz prenz;
Pur quei les as, pur quei nes renz?
Pur quei les tiens, quel dreit i as?
Se mais les tiens, que fols feras.
Si tu lunges les puez tenir
Que nus nes te façum guerpir,
Dire purras, si ert merveille,
10670 Que li leons fuit pur l'oëille
E ke li lous fuit pur la chievre
E li levriers fuit pur le lievre.
Ne puet mie issi avenir
Ne nature nel puet sufrir.
Julius Cesar, nostre ancestre,
Mais poi le preises, puet cel estre,
Prist Bretaine, sin out treü
E nostre gent l'ad puis eü.
Des altres illes envirun
10680 Treü lunges eü avum.

L'un e l'altre, par presuntrie,
Nus as toleit, si faiz folie.
Encor as fait grainur huntage
Dunt plus nus est que del damage;
Frolle, nostre barun, as mort,
E France e Flandres tiens a tort.
Pur ço ke tu nen as duté
Rome, ne sa grant digneté,
Te sumunt li senez e mande
E en sumonant, te comande   10690
Que tu seies en mi agust
A Rome a lui, que qu'il te cust,
Apareillez de faire dreit
De ço ke tu li as toleit,
Si feras satisfaction
De ço que nus t'acuseron.
E si tu vas rien purluinnant
Que si nel faces cum jo mant,
Muntgeu a force passerai,
Bretaine e France te toldrai.   10700
Ne qui pas que tu m'i atendes
Ne que de mei France defendes;
Ja de ça mer, al mien espeir,
Ne t'oseras faire veeir.
E si tu ultre mer esteies
Ja ma venue n'atendreies.
Ne savras en nul liu tapir
Dunt jo ne te face saillir;
Lïed a Rome te merrai
E al sené te liverrai.'   10710
   A ceste parole out grant bruit
E mult se corucierent tuit.
Mult oïssiez Bretuns crier,
Deu arramir e Deu jurer
Que cil serrunt desenuré
Ki cel message unt aporté.
Mult eüssent as messagiers
Dit laienges e repruviers,
Mais li reis se leva en piez
Ki lur cria: 'Taisiez, taisiez!   10720

---

[1] MS P reading—*ver*—restored.

Lucius' message

what he has deserved. In my amazement, I am also angry, and in the midst of my anger I am amazed, that in insolence and pride you have dared cast a greedy eye on Rome. I am angry and amazed as to where and from whom you were advised to contend with Rome, so long as you know a single Roman alive. You have been very stupid to attack us, who are entitled to sit in judgement on the whole world and who are the leaders of the world's capital. You don't know yet, but you will, you haven't seen, but you will, how grave it is to anger Rome, who has the right to rule over all. You have done what you had no right to do and exceeded your permitted bounds. Do you know who you are and whence you come, that you seize and hold our tributes? You take our lands and our tributes: why do you have them, why are they not restored? Why do you hold them, what right do you have? You will be a fool to keep them. If you manage to hold them for long, without our forcing you to surrender them, you can say (and it will be amazing) that the lion flees the lamb, the wolf flees the kid and the greyhound flees the hare. It cannot happen thus, nor will nature suffer it. Julius Caesar, our ancestor (but perhaps you respect him little), captured Britain, took tribute from it, and our people have always received it since. We have long taken tribute from the other islands round about. In your presumption you have taken both from us: you are mad. You have also done us a greater injury, which matters more to us than any loss: you have slain Frollo, our baron, and wrongfully hold France and Flanders. Because you have feared neither Rome nor her great authority, the Senate summons and orders you, commands you through its summons, to appear before it in Rome, in mid-August, no matter what it costs you, ready to do reparation for what you have taken and make amends for the charge against you. And if you reject any of my commands and do not do them, I will cross Muntgieu in strength and deprive you of Britain and France. I do not believe you will wait for me, nor defend France against me; it is my conviction you will never dare to show your face beyond the channel. And if you were overseas, you would never await my arrival. There is no place you'll be able to take cover out of which I won't rout you. I'll bring you in chains to Rome and hand you over to the Senate.'

10711 At these words there was tremendous uproar and everybody was furious. The British could be heard shouting, swearing by God and taking Him for witness that those who had brought this message would be dishonoured. The messengers would have been received with many reproaches and much abuse, but the king got up and shouted: 'Silence, silence! They are messengers, they shall not be harmed; they are only bearing their lord's message. They can say what they like, but no one shall hurt them.'[1]

---

[1] Wace lengthens the Roman ambassadors' speech and adds the resulting uproar and Arthur's respect for their rights.

N'i avrunt mal, messagier sunt,
Seinnur unt, sun message funt;
Dire purrunt quant qu'il vuldrunt,
Ja par hume mal n'i avrunt.'
Quant la noise fu trespassee
E la curt fu raseüree,
Ses dux, ses cuntes, ses privez
Ad tuz li reis od sei menez
En une sue tur perrine
10730 Que l'un clamot Tur gigantine.
Cunseil illuec prendre vuleit
Qu'a cez messagiers respundreit.
Ja esteient sur les degrez
Barun e cunte, lez a lez,
Quant Cador dist en suzriant,
Oiant le rei, ki ert avant:
'En grant crieme ai, dist il, esté,
E mainte feiz en ai pensé,
Que par oisdives e par pais
10740 Devenissent Bretun malveis.
Kar oisdive atrait malvaistied
E maint hume ad aperecied.
Uisdive met hume en peresce,
Uisdive amenuse prüesce,
Uisdive esmuet les lecheries,
Uisdive esprent lé drueries.
Par lunc repos e par uisdive
Est juvente tost ententive
A gas, a deduit e a tables,
10750 E a altres geus deportables.
Par lunc sujur e par repos
Poüm nus perdre nostre los.
Pose avum esté endormi,
Mais Damnedeu, sue merci,
Nus ad un petit reveilliez, [1]
Ki Romains ad encuragiez
De chalengier nostre païs
E les altres qu'avum cunquis.
Si Romains en els tant se fient
10760 Que ço facent que par brief dient,

Encor avrunt Bretun enur
De hardement e de vigur.
Ja lunge pais nen amerai
Ne unques lunge pais n'amai.'
'Sire cuens, dist Walwein, par fei,
De neient estes en effrei.
Bone est la pais emprés la guerre,
Plus bele e mieldre en est la terre;
Mult sunt bones les gaberies
E bones sunt les drueries.   10770
Pur amistié e pur amies
Funt chevaliers chevaleries.'
A cez paroles que cil distrent
En la tur vindrent si s'asistrent.
    Quant Artur les vit tuz seanz,
Tuz ententis e tuz taisanz,
Un poi se tut e si pensa;
Puis leva sun chief si parla:
'Barun, dist il, ki estes ci,
Mi compainun e mi ami,   10780
Compainun de prosperité
E compainun d'adversité,
Se grant guerre m'est avenue,
Vus l'avez od mei sustenue.
Si jo ai perdu ou cunquis,
L'un e l'altre avez od mei pris.
De ma perte estes parçunier
E del guaain quant jo cunquier.
Par vus e par vostre adjutorie
Ai jo eü mainte victorie.   10790
Menez vus ai en maint besuin
Par mer, par terre, e pruef e luin; [2]
Tuz tens vus ai truvez fedeilz
En afaires e en cunseilz;
Mainte feiz vus ai espruvez
E tuz tens vus ai buens truvez.
Les terres de ci envirun
Ai par vus en subjectiun. [3]
Oï avez le mandement
E des lettres l'entendement   10800

---

[1] MS P reading—*reveilliez*—restored.
[2] MS P reading—*e pruef*—restored.
[3] MS J substitutes four lines for ll. 10791–98: *Par*
vostre aiue ai France prise/ Et autres jusqu'en Frise/
France m'a hon hui calengié/ Et por ma tere manecié.

Reactions of Cador and Walwein

10725 When the noise had died down and the court was reassured, the king took all his dukes, counts and friends with him into a stone tower of his, called the Giants' Tower. There he wanted to take counsel on what he would reply to these messengers. The barons and counts were already on the stairs, side by side, when Cador said, smiling, in the king's hearing, who was ahead: 'I've often thought and been very afraid that the British would become weaklings through peace and idleness. For idleness attracts weakness and makes many a man lazy. Idleness brings indolence, idleness lessens prowess, idleness inflames lechery and idleness kindles love affairs. Much rest and idleness makes youth give all its attention to jokes, pleasure, board games and other amusing sports. Through long rests and inactivity we could lose our renown. For a while we have been asleep, but thanks be to God, He has awoken us a little, by encouraging the Romans to lay claim to our country and to the others we have won. If the Romans have so much confidence in themselves as to do what their letter says, the British will recover their reputation for boldness and strength. I never loved a long peace, nor shall I ever do so.' Indeed, my lord count,' said Walwein, 'you are upset about nothing. Peace is good after war and the land is the better and lovelier for it. Jokes are excellent and so are love affairs. It's for love and their beloved that knights do knightly deeds.'[1] As they were saying these words, they entered the tower and sat down.

10775 When Arthur saw them all seated, all attentive and quiet, he was silent a while, thinking. Then he raised his head and spoke: 'Barons here assembled,' he said, 'my friends and companions, companions in prosperity and in adversity, if any great battle has come my way, you have endured it with me. In victory or defeat, the renown has been yours as much as mine. You share in my loss, and also in my success when I am victorious. Through you and your help I have had many a victory. I have led you in many a battle over sea, over land, far and near, and always I have found you loyal in conduct and counsel. I have tested you many times and always found you true. With your help the neighbouring lands are subject to me.

10799 'You have heard the demand and the purpose in those letters and the arrogance

---

[1] Wace adds this reply of Walwein to Cador.

E le surfait e la fierté
Que li Romain nus unt mandé.
Assez nus unt cuntraliez
E assez nus unt manaciez;
Mais, si Deus guarist mei e vus,
Bien serum des Romains rescus.
Riches sunt e de grant poeir
Si nus estuvreit purveeir
Que purrum dire e que ferun,
10810 Avenantment e par raisun.
Quant chose est avant purveüe
Mielz est el besuin maintenue;
Ki veit la saiete venir
Tresturner se deit ou covrir;
Tut ensement devum nus faire.
Li Romain vuelent a nus traire
E nus devum apareillier
Qu'il ne nus puissent damagier.
De Bretaine treü demandent,
10820 Aveir le deivent, ço nus mandent;
Des altres isles ensement
E de France demainement.
E de Bretaine premierement[1]
Respundrai jo avenantment:
Cesar, ço dient, la cunquist;
Forz huem esteit, sa force fist;
Ne se pourent Bretun defendre,
Treü lur fist a force rendre.
Mais force n'est mie dreiture
10830 Ainz est orguil e desmesure.
L'um ne tient mie ço par dreit[2]
Que l'um ad a force toleit.
Bien nus leist par dreit ço tenir
Qu'il solent a force tolir.
Repruvé nus unt les damages
E les pertes e les huntages
E les travailz e les poürs
Qu'il firent a noz anceisurs;
Vanté se sunt qu'il les venquirent,
10840 Treüz e rentes lur tolirent.

Tant les devum nus plus grever
E plus nus unt a restorer;
Haïr devum ki cels haïrent
E cels laidir ki cels laidirent.
Mal lur firent, ço nus reprovent,
Treü en orent e treu ruevent.[3]
Tenir vuelent en eritage
La hunte as noz e le tolage.
Treü de Bretaine aveir suelent,
Pur ço de nus aveir le vuelent.   10850
Par meïsme ceste raisun
E par altretel achaisun
Poüm nus Rome chalengier
E bien la poüm desrainier;
Belin, ki fu reis des Bretuns,
E Brennes, duc des Burguinuns,
Dui frere, de Bretainne né,
Chevalier vaillant e sené,
A Rome vindrent si l'assistrent,[4]
Assaillirent la si la pristrent;   10860
Vint e quatre ostages pendirent
Si que tuit lur parent les virent;[5]
Quant Belin d'illuec repaira,
Rome a sun frere comanda.
Larrai ester Brenne e Belin
Si parlerai de Costentin:
De Bretaine fu, fiz Eleine;
Cil tint e out Rome en demeine.
Maximian, reis de Bretaine,
France conquist e Alemaine,   10870
Muntgeu passa e Lumbardie
E de Rome out la seinurie.
Cil furent mi parent procain;
E chescuns out Rome en sa main!
Or poëz oïr e saveir
Qu'altresi dei jo Rome aveir
Cum il Bretaine, par raisun,
Se nus as anceisurs guardum.
Romain de nos orent treü
E mi parent l'unt d'els eü.   10880

---

[1] MS P reading—*E*—restored.
[2] MS P reading—*par*—restored.
[3] MS P reading—*e*—restored.
[4] MS P reading—*vindrent*—restored.

[5] MS P reading—*les*—restored. MS J adds four lines: *Qui lor donerent en ostage/ Qui lor donroient treuage/ Lor convenances lor rompirent/ Por ce lour ostages pendirent.*

Arthur's reaction

and pride of the Romans' orders. They've insulted and threatened us enough but, if God preserves you and me, we shall be delivered from them. They are wealthy and powerful and we shall have to ponder what it is suitable and right to say and do. When something is planned in advance, it's easier to sustain it in an emergency. Whoever sees the arrow coming should flee or hide; just so should we do. The Romans intend to advance towards us and we should make ready, so that they can't harm us. They demand tribute of Britain and tell us they should have it, tribute from other islands too and from France in particular. And first of all I shall make fitting reply about Britain. They say Caesar conquered it: he was a powerful man and took it by force. The British could not defend themselves; he constrained them to render tribute. But force is not justice,[1] but overweening pride. What is taken by force is not justly held. We are certainly allowed to hold by right what they used to take from us by force. They have shamed us with the harm and losses, the disgrace, suffering and fear they inflicted on our ancestors; they have boasted that they defeated them and took tribute and money from them. We have all the more reason to injure them and they have the more to restore to us. We should hate those who hated our ancestors and hurt those who hurt them. They did them wrong and that shames us; they took tribute and demand it again. They would like to inherit those exactions and our shame. They were accustomed to tribute from Britain, so they want it from us.

10851 'For exactly the same reason and the same cause we may lay claim to Rome, and easily justify it. Belin, king of Britain, and Brenne, duke of Burgundy, were two brothers, born in Britain, brave and wise knights who came to Rome and besieged it. They attacked it and took it, hanging twenty-four hostages in the sight of all their kin. When Belin came away, he entrusted Rome to his brother. Let us leave Brenne and Belin and speak of Constantine, who came from Britain and was Helena's son. He held Rome and had it in his power. Maximien, king of Britain, conquered France and Germany, crossed Muntgieu and Lombardy and ruled over Rome. These were my close kin, and each had Rome in his hands! Now you can hear and know that I have as much reasonable right to Rome as Rome to Britain, if we look at our ancestors. Rome got tribute from us and my kin got it from them. They lay claim to Britain, I to Rome! This is the gist of my

---

[1] Proverbial: see Morawski, *Proverbes*, no. 758.

Il cleiment Bretaine, e jo Rome!
De mun cunseil est ço la sume
Que cil ait la rente e la terre
Ki purra sur l'altre conquerre.
De France e des altres cuntrees
Que de lur mains avum ostees
Ne deivent il nul plai tenir
Quant il nes voldrent guarantir,
Ou il ne voldrent ou il ne porent, [1]
10890 U, puet cel estre, dreit n'i orent,
Kar a force, par cuveitise,
Les teneient en lur servise.
Or ait tut ki aver le puet;
Altre dreiture n'i estuet.
Li emperere nus manace,
Ne vuille Deus que mal nus face!
Noz terres, ço dit, nus toldra
E pris a Rome me merra;
Petit nus prise, poi me crient,
10900 Mais, se Deu plaist, si il ça vient,
Ainz qu'il se puisse repairier
N'avra talent de manacier.
Quant jo chalenz e il chalenge,
Ki tut purra prendre, si prenge!'
    Quant Artur li reis out parlé
E as Bretuns out ço mustré, [2]
Tels i out ki emprés parlerent
E tels i out ki esculterent.
Hoel parla emprés lu rei:
10910 'Sire, dist il, en meie fei,
Mult paroles raisnablement,
Nuls n'i puet mettre amendement.
Mande ta gent, semunt tes humes
E nus ki ci a ta curt sumes.
Trespasse mer senz demurance,
Passe Burguine, passe France,
Passe Muntgeu, pren Lumbardie!
L'empereür, ki te deffie,
Met en errur e en effrei
10920 Qu'il n'ait leisir de grever tei.

Tel plai unt Romain esmeü
Dunt il serunt tut cunfundu.
Damnedeus te vuelt exalcier;
Ne demurer ne te targier;
Met l'empiere en ta poësté
Ki mettre s'i vuelt de sun gré.
Membre tei que Sibille dist
Es prophecies qu'ele escrist:
Trei Bretun de Bretaine eistreient
Ki Rome a force conquereient. [3]   10930
Dui de cels sunt ja trespassé
Ki de Rome unt seinur esté:
Li premiers de cels fu Belin
E li secunz fu Costentin;
Tu iés li tiers ki Rome avras
E Rome a force conquerras;
En tei sera la prophecie
Que Sibille dist acomplie.
Pur quei demures a saisir
Ço que Deus te vuelt eslargir?   10940
Exalce tei, exalce nus,
Ki de ço sumes curius.
Veraiement dire poüm
Que cop ne plaie ne cremum
Ne mort, ne travail, ne prisun
Tant cume nus t'enur querun.
E jo merrai en ta compaine
Ainz que ta busuine remaine
Dis mile chevaliers armez,
E si tu n'as aveir assez,   10950
Tute ma terre enguagerai,
L'or e l'argent t'en liverrai,
Ja mar m'en lairas un denier
Tant cum tu en avras mestier.'
Emprés la parole Hoel
Dist li reis d'Escoce, Angusel,
Freres fu Loth e Urïen:
'Sire, dist il, Hoel dit bien.
E, quant tu ceste chose enprenz,
Parole a cels ki sunt çaenz,   10960

---

[1] MS P reading—*il ne porent*—restored.

[2] MS P reading—*as Bretuns*—restored.

[3] MS P reading—*conquereient*—restored.

Hoel's speech

advice: he who can defeat the other should get the money and the land. They should stop talking about France and the other lands, which we have taken off their hands, if they don't want to protect them. Either they don't want to, or can't, or, perhaps, they have no right to, because through greed they keep them in fief by force. Now may he who can get it, have it all: there's no need for any other right! The emperor threatens us; God forbid he does us any harm. He says he will take our lands and bring me bound to Rome; he values us little, he has small fear of me, but, God willing, if he comes here, before he returns he won't feel like making threats. If I and he both lay claim, then may he who can take it all, seize it!'

10905 When Arthur the king had spoken and revealed this to the barons, there were some who spoke next and others who listened. Hoel spoke after the king. 'Sire,' he said, 'upon my word, you speak most reasonably, no one could better it. Command your people, summon your men and us who are here at your court. Cross the sea without delay; cross Burgundy, France and Muntgieu, and take Lombardy! Disturb and frighten the emperor who defies you, so he has no chance of hurting you. The Romans have set in motion a business that will quite destroy them. The Lord God wants to raise you up; don't hesitate or delay. He is putting the empire in your power of his own accord. Remember what the Sibyl said, in her written prophecies: three Britons would arise from Britain to conquer Rome by force. Two of those, who were lords of Rome, have already passed away: the first of them was Belin and the second Constantine. You will be the third to have Rome and conquer it by force. In you the Sibyl's prophecy will be fulfilled. Why wait to seize what God wishes to grant you? Exalt yourself, exalt us, who desire it. Indeed we can say we fear neither blow nor wound, neither death, hardship nor prison, as long as we seek your honour. And, so that your affair be not neglected, I shall give you for companions ten thousand armed knights; and if you don't have enough wealth, I shall pledge all my land and give you its silver and gold. You must never leave me a penny as long as you have need of it.'

10955 After Hoel's words, the king of Scotland, Angusel, brother of Loth and Urien, spoke. 'Sire,' he said, 'Hoel has spoken well. And, if you undertake this thing,

U li mielz est de tun barnage
Ki de Rome oënt le message.
Saches que chescuns te fera
E cumbien chescuns t'aidera;
Orë est ués de purveeir
D'aïe e de cunseil aveir.
Tuit cil ki de ta terre sunt
Ke de tei terres e feus unt [1]
Te deivent aidier e valeir;
10970 Si ferunt il, a lur poeir.
Jo n'oï unques mais nuvele
Ki tant me semblast bone e bele
Cume des Romains guerreier;
Unc nes poi amer ne preiser.
Des que jo unc rien entendi
Romains e lur orguil haï.
Quel hunte de malvaise gent
Ki a nul altre enur n'entent
Ne mais a aveir amasser
10980 Ke bone gent deit deffier.
L'emperere folie fist
E en grant barate se mist
Ki deffiance te manda;
Encor, ço crei, tel jur sera,
Ne la vuldreit aveir mandee
Pur ceste tur d'argent rasee.
Tel plai unt Romain cumencied
Dunt il serunt tuit corucied.
E se il ja nel cumençassent
10990 E se ja primes n'en parlassent,
Sil deüssum nus comencier
E de nostre gré guerreier
Pur nostre parenté vengier
E pur lur orguil abaissier
Ki ço vulent dire e pruver
Que nus devum treü duner.
Ce dient que nostre anceisur
Treü solent duner as lur;
Ne qui pas que treü dunassent
11000 Ne que treü lur enveiassent;

Nel dunerent pas ne rendirent,
Mais cil a force lur tolirent.
E nus a force lur tolum!
Nus e noz anceisurs vengum.
Vencu avum mainte medlee
E mainte grant guerre achevee;
Que valt quant que vencu avum
Se nus les Romains ne vencum?
Unches nen oi tel desirrier
Ne de beivre ne de mangier   11010
Cume jo ai de veer l'ure
Que nus nus entrecurum sure
Sur les chevals, pris les espiez,
Escuz a cols, helmes laciez.
Deus! quels avers, Deus! quels tresors,
Se Deus guarist de mal noz cors,
Avrunt cil ki aveir vuldrunt,
Jamais jur povre ne serunt.
La verrum nus les bels aveirs,
La verrum nus les bels maneirs, 11020
La verrum nus les bels chastels
E les chevals forz e isnels;
Ço m'est vis que jo ja i seie
E que jo ja vencuz les veie.
Alum, alum Rome conquerre,
Si tolum as Romains la terre! [2]
Quant nus avrum Rome conquise,
Les humes morz, la cité prise,
En Lohierrenne trespassum
E Lohierrenne conquerum,   11030
E Lohierregne e Alemainne,
Que nule terre ne remainne
De ça les munz ki ne seit tue.
N'i ad ki de nus se rescue,
Tut prendrum a dreit e a tort.
E que m'uevre a mun dit s'acort,
Jo meïsmes od tei irrai
E dous mil chevaliers menrai,
E de gent a pied tel plenté,
Ja par hume n'ierent numbré.'   11040

---

[1] MS P's order of line restored.   [2] MS P reading—*la*—restored.

Angusel's speech

speak to those who are here, the best of your barons, who heard the message from Rome. Know what each will do for you and how each will help you. Now we need to plan how to get help and advice. All those from your kingdom, who hold fiefs and land from you, should help and assist you, and so they shall, as best they can. I never before heard news which seemed so good and fair to me as this, of fighting the Romans. I can never like or esteem them. Ever since I learned of them, I hated the Romans and their pride. How shameful of a wicked race, who are intent on nothing else honourable, only on amassing wealth, and must defy virtuous people. The emperor acts stupidly and lays up great trouble for himself by sending you a challenge. I believe the day will come when he will wish he had not done so, even for this tower filled with silver.

10987 'The Romans have begun such a business as will punish them all. And even if they had never begun it, even if they had not spoken of it first, we would have had to begin it and of our own accord make war, to avenge our kin and abate their pride, who think fit to say and assert that we should render tribute. They say our ancestors used to give tribute to theirs; I don't believe they gave or sent tribute. They neither gave it nor rendered it, but it was taken from them by force. And we will wrest it by force from them! We will avenge ourselves and our ancestors. We have won many a battle and carried out many a great war; but what good are any of our conquests if we do not defeat the Romans? Never did I have such a desire for food and drink as I have to see the moment when we attack each other on horseback, spears gripped, shields round our necks, helmets laced. Lord, what wealth! Lord, what treasure (if God protect us), will those who want wealth have; they'll never be poor again. There we shall see fine possessions, handsome dwellings, splendid castles and strong, speedy horses. I feel I'm already there and already see them defeated. On, then, to conquer Rome! Let us take the Romans' lands! When we have conquered Rome, slain the men, taken the city, we'll cross into Lorraine and conquer it, both Lorraine and Germany, so that no country remains on this side of the mountains which is not yours. No one shall escape us: we shall seize everything, rightly or wrongly.[1] And so that my deeds match my words, I myself will go with you and bring two thousand knights and so many foot-soldiers, no one will ever be able to count them.'

---

[1] Wace adds Angusel's exhortations to conquer more than Rome and the 'rightly or wrongly'— an important issue in later Arthurian literature like the alliterative *Morte Arthure*.

Quant li reis d'Escoce out parlé,
Tuit ensemble unt dit e crié:
'Huniz seit en ki remaindra
E ki sun poeir nen fera!'
Quant chescuns out dit sun pensé
E Artur out tuit esculté, [1]
Ses briefs fist faire e seeler;
As messages les fist livrer
E mult les fist tuz enurer
11050 E mult lur fist del suen duner.
'A Rome, dist il, poëz dire
Que jo sui de Bretainne sire.
France tienc e France tendrai
E des Romains la defendrai.
E ço sachiez veraiement
Qu'a Rome irrai prochainement,
Nun mie pur treü porter
Mais pur treü d'els demander.'
    Li message d'Artur turnerent, [2]
11060 A Rome vindrent si cunterent
Cumfaitement Artur truverent,
U e cument a lui parlerent.
Mult esteit, ço diseient, larges,
Mult esteit pruz, mult esteit sages,
Mult ert de bon afaitement
E de riche cuntienement.
Nuls, ço diseient, ne purreit
Suffrir le cust que il sufreit;
Mult esteit riche sa maisnee
11070 E mult ert bien apareillee.
Treü pur neient li quereient
Kar il diseit qu'il le durreient.
Quant li barun de Rome oïrent
Que li message respundirent,
E les chartres qu'il aportoent,
E lur paroles s'acordoent [3]
Que Artur pas nes servireit [4]
E que treü d'els requerreit,
A l'empereür unt loé,
11080 E cil los li vint bien a gré,

Que tut sun empire mandast,
Muntgieu e Burguine passast,
Al rei Artur se combatist,
Regne e curune li tolist.
Lucius Hiber ne targa,
Reis e cuntes e dux manda
Que en juignet, al diesme jur, [5]
Si cum chescuns aimes s'enur
Seient a Rome a lui, tuit prest
De querre Artur la u il est.   11090
Cil vindrent tuit delivrement
Ki oïrent le mandement.
Epistrod vint, le rei de Grece,
E Echion, dus de Boëce;
Hirtac i vint, li reis des Turs,
Chevaliers out forz e segurs;
Pandras i vint, li reis d'Egypte,
E de Crete reis Ypolite;
Cist aveit bien grant seinurie,
Ki cent citez out en baillie.   11100
De Sire i vint reis Evander
E de Frige dus Teücer,
De Babiloine Micipsa
E d'Espaine Alimphatima.
De Mede i vint li reis Boccus
E de Libe Sertorius,
De Bithine Polidetes
E d'Iture li rei Xerses.
Mustenfar, ki Alfrike tint,
Qui luin maneit e de luin vint,   11110
Affricans amena e Mors
E porter fist ses granz tresors.
De cels de l'ordre del sené,
Qui en Rome orent digneté,
Vint Marcel e Luces Catel,
Cocta e Gaïus Metel.
Altres baruns i out assez
Dunt jo n'ai pas les nuns trovez.
Quant il furent tuit assemblé,
Quatre cent mil furent numbré   11120

---

[1] MS P reading—*tuit*—restored, as in l. 11091.
[2] MS J adds four lines: *A la mer vinrent si passerent/ Pus cevaucierent lor cevaus/ Tant errerent et puis et vaus.*
[3] MS P reading—*E*—restored.
[4] MS P reading—*nes*—restored.
[5] MS P reading—*en juignet*—restored.

Lucius assembles his army

11041   When the king of Scotland had finished, everyone said and shouted all together:
'Shame on whoever stays behind and doesn't do his best!' When each one had
spoken his mind and Arthur had heard them all out, he had his letters composed
and sealed. He had them delivered to the messengers and saw to it they were
greatly honoured and given large gifts from his possessions. 'In Rome,' he said,
'you can say I am lord of Britain. I hold France and will hold it and defend it
against Romans. And know indeed that I shall shortly go to Rome, not to bring
tribute but to demand it.'[1]

11059   The messengers left Arthur, came back to Rome and reported exactly how they
found Arthur and where and how they had spoken to him. They said he was very
generous, brave and wise, had excellent manners and noble behaviour. Nobody,
they said, could support the expenditure he allowed; his retinue was magnificent and very well dressed. It was no use asking him for tribute, for he said *they*
would give it to *him*. When the Roman lords heard the messengers' replies and
heard the charters they brought, they recalled their words that Arthur had no
intention of paying and would demand tribute from them; and they advised the
emperor, and this advice was to his taste, that he should summon his whole empire, cross Muntgieu and Burgundy, and fight king Arthur, depriving him of kingdom and crown.

11085   Lucius Hiber did not delay; he summoned kings, counts and dukes to be in
Rome with him on the tenth day of July, if they loved honour, all ready to seek
out Arthur wherever he might be. Those hearing the summons came very quickly.
Epistrod came, king of Greece, and Echion, duke of Boetia; Hirtac came, king of
the Turks, with strong and resolute knights; Pandras came, king of Egypt, and
king Ypolite from Crete—he had very great power, with a hundred cities at his
command. From Syria came king Evander and from Phrygia duke Teucer, from
Babylon Micipsa and from Spain Aliphatima. From Media came king Boccus and
from Libya Sertorius, from Bithynia Polidetes and king Xerses from the Iturei.[2]
Mustensar, who controlled Africa, dwelt afar off, and came from afar, brought
Africans and Moors, and also his great treasure. From the numbers of the Senate,
who had high office in Rome, came Marcel and Luces Catel, Cocta and Gaius
Metel.[3] There were many other barons whose names I have not found. When
they were all assembled, they were four hundred thousand in number, and a total

[1] Wace invents Arthur's generosity, his words to
the ambassadors and also their subsequent report to Rome; all enhance the king.

[2] Arnold and Pelan, *Partie Arthurienne* p. 160, interpret these as a people in Palestine.

[3] *HRB* chap. 163: *Epistrophus, Mustensar, Aliphatima, Hirtacius* king of the Parthians, *Bolcus*
(*VV: Boccus*), *Sertorius, Serses* (*VV: Xerses* of the

Mirci), *Pandrasus, Misipsa* (*VV: Micipsa*), *Politetes,
Tencer* (*VV: Teucer*), *Euander, Echion, Ypolitus, Lucius
Catellus, Marius Lepidus, Gaius Metellus Cocta,
Quintius Miluius Catulus* and *Quintus Carucius* (*VV:
Caritius*). See Tatlock pp. 122–4 who draws at-
tention to two Arabic names (*Mustensar* and *Ali-
phatima*).

E cent e quatre vint muntanz
Estre gelde e estre servanz.
Quant prest e apareillied furent,
Entrant august de Rome murent.
   Artur out sa curt departie,
As baruns tuz out quis aïe.
Tuz les out numé par lur nuns
E chescun out par nun sumuns
Qu'il li aït a sun poeir
11130 Si cum il vuelt s'amur aveir;
Died quanz chevalers merra
Chescuns sulunc le feu qu'il a.
Ireis, Gollandeis, Islandeis,
Daneis, Norreis e Orcheneis
Sis vinz mil armez unt pramis
A la guise de lur païs;
N'esteient mie chevalier
Ne ne saveient chevalchier;
Tuit a pied portoent lur armes,
11140 Haches, darz, gavelocs, gisarmes.
Cil de Normendie e d'Angou, [1]
Cil del Maine, cil de Peitou,
Cil de Flandres, cil de Buluine,
Od tutes armes, senz ensuinne,
Quatre vinz mil armez pramistrent;
De tant deivent servir, ço distrent.
Duze cunte d'altre puissance,
Que l'on clamot les pers de France,
Qui od Gerin de Chartres furent,
11150 De duze cenz le numbre acrurent;
Chescuns cent chevaliers pramist,
De tant deveit servir, ço dist.
Dis millers en pramist Hoel
Dous milliers d'Escoce Agusel.
De Bretaine, sa propre terre,
Que l'um or claimed Engleterre,
Fist Artur numbrer chevaliers
Od halbercs seissante milliers.
La gelde e les arbalastiers
11160 Ne les servanz ne les archiers

Ne sai numbrer, ne cil ne firent
Qui la grant ost ensemble virent.
   Quant Artur sout quel gent avreit
E quanz armez chescuns merreit,
A chescun rova e bani
Que al terme qu'il establi
Venist chescun od sun navie
A Barbeflued en Normendie.
Quant li Bretun orent cungied, [2]
En lur terres sunt repairied;   11170
Lur humes firent aprester,
Cels qu'il durent od els mener.
A Modret, un de ses nevuz,
Chevalier merveillus e pruz,
Livra en guarde Artur sun regne
E a Ganhumare, sa feme.
Modret esteit de grant noblei
Mais n'esteit pas de bone fei.
Il aveit la reïne amee,
Mais ço esteit chose celee;   11180
Mult s'en celout; e ki quidast
Que il feme sun uncle amast,
Maïsmement de tel seinnur
Dunt tuit li suen orent enur;
Feme sun uncle par putage
Amat Modret si fist huntage.
A Modret e a la reïne,
Deus! tant mal fist cele saisine,
Comanda tut fors la corune.
Puis vint passer a Suthamtune;   11190
La furent les nefs amenees
E les maisnees assemblees.
Mult veïssiez nés aturner,
Nés atachier, nés aancrer,
Nés assechier e nés floter,
Nés cheviller e nés cloer,
Funains estendre, maz drecier,
Punz mettre fors e nés chargier,
Helmes, escuz, halbercs porter,
Lances drecier, chevals tirer,   11200

---

[1] MS P: *Ongou*.

[2] MS P reading—*li Bretun*—restored.

Arthur assembles his army

of one hundred and eighty thousand, except for foot-soldiers and servants.[1] When they were equipped and ready, they left Rome at the beginning of August.

11125   Arthur concluded his court and asked for help from all the barons. He named them all by their names and summoned each by name to help him as best he could, if he wished to keep his love, and to say how many knights he would bring, each according to the size of his domain. The Irish, those from Gotland, the Icelanders, the Danes, the Norwegians and those from Orkney promised one hundred and twenty thousand men armed in the fashion of their lands: they were not knights nor knew how to ride. They went on foot, bearing their weapons: axes, javelins, throwing-spears and broadswords. Those from Normandy and Anjou, Maine and Poitou, Flanders and Boulogne, promised without delay eighty thousand men in full armour; so many should be useful, they said. Twelve counts from other sovereign states, who accompanied Gerin de Chartres and were called the peers of France, swelled the numbers by twelve hundred: each promised a hundred knights, saying they should be useful. Hoel promised ten thousand and Angusel, two thousand Scots. From Britain, his own land (now called England), Arthur reckoned he had sixty thousand knights with hauberks. I cannot count the number of foot-soldiers, crossbowmen, servants or archers, nor could those who saw the great army assembled. When Arthur knew what people he would have and how many armed men each would lead, he commanded and summoned everyone to come at the appointed time, each with his fleet, to Barfleur in Normandy. When the Britons had taken leave, they went home to their lands and made ready the men they would take with them.

11173   To Modret, one of his nephews, a great and valiant knight, and to Guinevere, his wife, Arthur committed the charge of his kingdom. Modret was of noble birth, but disloyal. He was in love with the queen, but this was not suspected. He kept it very quiet; and who would have believed he could love his uncle's wife, especially the wife of such a lord, whose kin all held him in honour? Modret loved his uncle's wife shamefully and was dishonourable. To Modret and to the queen— alas! how unfortunate that he gave them possession!—Arthur entrusted everything but the crown.[2] Then he came to Southampton, for the sea crossing. There the ships were gathered and the troops assembled. There you could see many a ship being prepared, moored, anchored, dried out and floated, pegged and nailed, its cordage stretched, its masts raised and its gangplank lowered, loaded with helmets, shields and hauberks, with lances aloft, horses dragged along, knights

---

[1] This confusing statement on the numbers in Lucius' army is taken from equally confusing figures in *HRB* (chap. 163): 400,000 'in total' but 160,000 'when all counted'. (The *VV* has 180,000). Wace follows *HRB*'s figures for Ar-

thur's army too, but wisely does not try to add them up. See Thorpe's note, *Geoffrey of Monmouth: History*, p. 235.

[2] Wace adds Modret's love for the queen, and an intimation of disaster.

Chevaliers e servanz entrer,
E l'un ami l'altre apeler.
Mult se vunt entresaluant
Li remanant e li errant.
Quant as nés furent tuit entré
E tide orent e bon oré,
Dunc veïssiez ancres lever,
Estrens traire, hobens fermer,
Mariniers saillir par cez nés,
11210 Deshenechier veilles e trés;
Li un s'esforcent al windas,
Li altre al lof e al betas; [1]
Detriés sunt li guverneür,
Li maistre esturman li meillur.
Chescuns de guverner se peinne
Al guvernal, ki la nef meine:
Aval le hel si curt senestre [2]
E sus le hel pur cure a destre.
Pur le vent es trés acuillir
11220 Funt les lispriez avant tenir [3]
E bien fermer es raelinges.
Tels i ad traient les gurdinges,
E alquant abaissent le tref
Pur la nef curre plus süef.
Estuïns ferment e escotes
E funt tendre les cordes tutes,
Uitages laschent, trés avalent,
Boëlines sachent e halent,
Al vent guardent e as esteilles,
11230 Sulunc l'uré portent lur veilles;
Les braiols funt lacier al mast
Que li venz par desuz ne past.
A dous ris curent u a treis.
Mult fu hardiz, mult fu curteis
Cil ki fist nef premierement
E en mer se mist aval vent,
Terre querant qu'il ne veeit
E rivage qu'il ne saveit.
     Les genz Artur a joie aloent,
11240 Buen vent aveient, bel sigloent:

A mie nuit par mer cureient,
Vers Barbeflete lur curs teneient, [4]
Quant Artur prist a semuillier,
Endormi sei, ne pout veillier.
Vis li fu, la ou il dormeit,
Que haut en l'air un urs veeit
De vers orient avalant, [5]
Mult lai, mult fort, mult gros, mult grant;
Mult esteit d'orrible façun.
D'altre part veeit un dragun   11250
Qui de vers occident volout
E de ses oilz flambe getout;
De lui e de sa resplendur
Reluseit terre e mer entur.
Li draguns l'urs envaïsseit
E cil forment se defendeit,
A mervaille s'envaïsseient
E a merveille se fereient,
Mais li draguns l'urs enbraçout
E a terre l'acraventout. [6]   11260
Quant Artur out un poi dormi,
Del sunge qu'il vit s'esperi;
Eveilla sei si se dreça, [7]
As clers e as baruns cunta
Tut en ordre la visiun
Qu'il vit de l'urs e del dragun.
Alquant d'els li unt respundu
Que li draguns qu'il out veü
Esteit de lui senefiance,
E li granz urs ert demustrance   11270
D'alcun gaiant qu'il ocirreit,
Ki d'estrange terre vendreit;
Li altre d'altre guise espunent,
Nequedent tuit a bien le turnent;
'Ainz est, dist il, ço m'est viaire,
La guerre que nus devum faire
Entre mei e l'empereür;
Mais del tut seit el Creatur.'
     A ces paroles ajurna,
Bel tens fist, li soleilz leva;   11280

---

[1] MS J adds four lines: *Les sigles vindent sus amont/ Pus vunt corant en mer parfunt/ Les cordes sunt en lor lieu mises/ Et fremees et bien asises.*
[2] MS P reading—*aval*—restored.
[3] MS P reading—*lispriez*—restored.
[4] MS P reading—*Barbeflete*—restored.
[5] MS P reading—*avalant*—restored.
[6] MS P reading—*l'acraventout*—restored.
[7] MS P reading—*Eveilla*—restored.

Arthur's dream

and servants embarking, and friends calling to each other. Those staying behind and those departing kept exchanging greetings.[1]

11205 When they had all embarked and the tide and the wind were in their favour, then you could see anchors raised, stays pulled, guy-ropes secured and sailors bounding through the ships unfurling sails and canvas. Some strove with the windlass, others with tacking and with yard-ropes; behind them were the pilots, the best master helmsmen. Each one applied himself to manœuvring the rudder, which steers the ship: below the tiller-bar to go left and above it to go right. To capture the wind in the sails, they brought forward the fore-leeches[2] and drew hard on the bolt-ropes. These weigh on the bunt-lines and somewhat lower the sails, so the ship runs more sweetly. They secured the studding-sails and sheets and tautened all the ropes; they slackened the running-ropes, brought down the sails, hauled and tugged the bowlines and observed the wind and the stars, setting their sails according to the breeze. They strapped the brails[3] to the mast so that the wind did not tug at them from underneath. They took two or three reefs in the sails. How bold and skilled was the man who first made a ship and put to sea before the wind, seeking a land he could not see and a shore he could not know.

11239 Arthur's men went on their way joyfully, sailing fast with a good wind. At midnight they were crossing the sea, with their course set for Barfleur, when Arthur began to nod; he fell asleep and could not stay awake. As he was sleeping, it seemed to him that he saw a bear, high in the sky, come flying down from the East; it was very ugly, strong, mighty and large, most horrible in appearance. From the other direction he saw a dragon, flying from the West, his eyes shooting flame. The land and sea round about glistened from his radiance. The dragon attacked the bear, who strongly defended himself; their onslaughts and blows were amazing, but the dragon gripped the bear and threw him to the ground. When Arthur had slept a little longer, the dream he had seen roused him; he woke, sat up and told the clerics and the barons the dream, in its proper order, which he had had of the dragon and the bear. Some of them answered him that the dragon he had seen signified himself and the great bear meant some giant he would kill, who would come from a foreign land. The others expounded it in a different way, but nevertheless they all interpreted it favourably. 'It seems to me,' he said, 'that it is, on the contrary, the war we must start between the emperor and myself. But may it be all in the Creator's hands.'

11279 Dawn broke at these words; the sun rose and it was fine weather. They arrived in harbour very early, at Barfleur in the Cotentin, and disembarked as soon as they

---

[1] Wace adds this picture of embarkation and the following detailed account of navigation. On this whole passage see Arnold II, p. 810.

[2] *Lispriéz* or leech-prows: the leech was the per-pendicular or sloping side of a sail (*OED*).

[3] The brails are small ropes on the sail-edges for trussing, or clewing up, the sails before furling (*Concise Oxford Dictionary*).

Al port vindrent assez matin
A Barbeflued en Costentin.
Cum ainz porent des nés eissirent,
Par la cuntree s'espandirent;
Ses genz ad Artur atendues
Qui n'erent mie encor venues.
N'aveit mie mult atendu
Quant il oï e dit li fu
Que uns gaianz mult corporuz
11290 Ert de vers Espaine venuz,
Niece Hoel Eleine out prise,
Ravie l'out, el munt l'out mise
Que l'um or saint Michiel apele.
N'i aveit altel ne chapele,
De flo de mer muntant ert clos.
N'aveit hume el païs si os,
Ne bacheler, ne païsant,
Tant orguillus ne tant vaillant
Qui s'osast al gaiant combatre
11300 Ne la ou il esteit enbatre.
Quant cil del païs s'assembloent
E pur combatre el munt aloent
Suvent par mer, suvent par terre,
Ne li ert guaires de lur guerre;
Lur nés as roches depeçout,
Maint en tuout, maint en neiout,
Tut l'aveient laissié ester, [1]
Ne l'osouent mais adeser.
Mult veïssiez les païsanz
11310 Maisuns vuider, porter enfanz,
Femes mener, bestes chacier,
Es munz munter, es bois mucier.
Par bois e par deserz fueient
E encor la murir cremeient.
Tute esteit la terre guerpie,
Tute s'en ert la gent fuïe.
[Li gaianz out nun Dinabuc,
Que puisse prendre mal trebuc!] [2]
    Quant Artur en oï parler,
11320 Kei apela e Bedoer,

Sis senescals fu li premiers
E li altre sis buteilliers;
N'en volt parler a nul altre hume. [3]
Cele nuit sempres de prin sume
Fist cez dous e lur esquiers
Lur armes prendre e lur destriers.
Ne volt mie ost od sei mener
Ne cest afaire a tuz mustrer;
Ço cremeit se il le seüssent
Que del gaiant poür eüssent,   11330
E il ert tels e tant valeit
Qu'a lui destruire sufiseit.
Tute nuit unt tant chevalchied,
Tant unt erré, tant unt brochied,
Par matin vindrent al rivage
La ou il surent le passage.
Sur le munt virent feu ardeir,
De luin le poeit l'um veeir.
Un altre munt i out menur
Ki n'ert mie luin del grainur;   11340
Sur chescun aveit feu ardant.
Pur ço alad Artur dutant
El quel munt li gaianz esteit
E el quel munt le truvereit;
N'i out ki dire li seüst
Ne ki le jur veü l'eüst.
A Bedoer dist qu'il alast,
E l'un e l'altre munt cerchast;
Tant le queïst qu'il le truvast,
Puis revenist si li nunciast.   11350
Cil est en un batel entrez,
Al plus procain munt est passez;
N'i poeit altrement entrer,
Kar pleins esteit li floz de mer.
Quant venuz fu al munt prochain
E il muntout sus al terrain,
El munt oï grant plureïz,
Granz plainz, granz suspirs e granz criz.
Poür out si prist a fremir,
Kar le gaiant quida oïr.   11360

---

[1] MS P reading—*tut*—restored.
[2] MSS PABKN omit ll. 11317–18.
[3] MS P reading—*N'en*—restored.

Arthur travels to Mont St Michel

could, scattering through the countryside. Arthur waited for those of his men who had not yet arrived. He had not waited for long when he heard, and was told, of a hulking giant who had come from Spain, seized Hoel's niece Eleine, raped her and set her on the mountain now called after St Michael. There was neither altar nor chapel there; it was surrounded by the sea's tidal waters. There was no man in the land so bold, no young man, whether noble or peasant, however proud or brave, who dared to fight the giant or venture into his neighbourhood. When the people round about assembled and approached the mountain to fight him, sometimes coming from the sea, sometimes from the land, he cared nothing for their efforts: he smashed their ships with rocks, killing and drowning many. They had all let him alone and not dared approach him. You could see peasants all leaving their houses, carrying children, leading women, hustling animals and climbing mountains or hiding in woods. They fled into forests and wilderness, still fearing to die even there. The whole land was abandoned, all its people fled. The giant was called Dinabuc: bad luck to him!

11319   When Arthur heard of this, he called Kei and Bedoer; the first was his seneschal, the second his cup-bearer. He wished to talk to no one else. At once, as night fell, these two and their squires had their arms and horses made ready. Arthur did not want to take an army with him or reveal this business to everyone; he feared that, if they knew, they would be afraid of the giant and he thought his own person and worth were quite sufficient to destroy him. All night they rode so fast, they spurred so hard, they travelled so far, that by morning they came to the shore where they knew there to be a crossing. They saw a fire burning on the mountain, visible far and wide. There was also a fire burning on another, lesser, peak, not far from the larger one. This made Arthur hesitate over which mountain the giant was on, and on which mountain he would find him. There was no one who could tell him or who had seen the giant that day. He told Bedoer to go and search both mountains, and to seek until he found him, then to return with the news.

11351   Bedoer got into a boat and crossed to the nearest mountain; there was no other way of approaching it, because the tide was at the full. When he came to the nearest mountain and was climbing it, he heard a great weeping and wailing, great laments and cries. He was afraid and began to tremble, for he thought he heard the giant. But soon he took courage; he drew his sword and went on. He recovered his daring, and thought and wished he could fight the giant and put

Mais sempres se raseüra;
S'espee trait avant ala.
Recovré out sun hardement;
En pensé out e en talent
Que al gaiant se combatreit,
En aventure se metreit;
Pur poür de perdre la vie
Ne vuldreit faire cuardie.
Mais cest pensé out il en vain,
11370 Kar, quant il fu desus el plain,
Un fu ardant vit sulement
E un tumblel fait nuvelment.
La tumbe esteit nuvelment faite;
Li cuens vint la, s'espee treite.
Une vielle feme ad truvee,
Ses dras deruz, eschevelee;
Dejuste le tumblel giseit,
Mult suspirot, mult se plaineit,
Eleine suvent regretout,
11380 Grant duel faiseit, granz criz getout.
Quant ele out Bedoer veü,
'Chaitif, dist ele, ki es tu?
Quel mesaventure te meine?
A duel, a dulur e a peinne
T'esteut hui ta vie finer
Se li gaianz te puet trover.
Maleüré, fui, tien ta veie,
Ainz que li adversiers te veie!'
'Bone feme, dist Bedoer,
11390 Parole a mei, lai le plurer.
Di mei ki es, e pur quei plures,
En cest ille pur quei demures,
Ki giest en ceste sepulture?
Cunte mei tute t'aventure.'
'Jo sui, dist ele, une esguaree,
Une lasse maleüree;
Ci plur pur une dameisele
Que jo nurri a ma mamele;
Eleine out nun, niece Hoel,
11400 Ci gist li cors en cest tumblel.

A nurrir m'esteit comandee;
Lasse, pur quei me fu livree?
Lasse, pur quei l'ai tant nurrie
Quant uns diables l'ad ravie;
Uns gaianz mei e li ravi
E mei e li aporta ci.
La pucele volt purgesir,
Mais tendre fu, nel pout suffrir;
Trop fu ahueges, trop fu granz,
Trop laiz, trop gros e trop pesanz;   11410
L'aume li fist del cors partir,
Nel pout Eleine sustenir.
Lasse dolente, ma dulçur,
Ma joie, mun deduit, m'amur
Ad li gaianz a hunte ocise
E jo l'ai ci en terre mise.'
'Pur quei, dist li cuens, ne t'en vas,
Quant tu Eleine perdue as?'
'Vels tu oïr, dist ele, pur quei?[1]
Gentil hume e curteis te vei,   11420
N'i ad ver tei nule celee.[2]
Quant Eleine fu deviee,
Dunt jo quidai del sens eissir,
Kar a hunte la vi murir,
Li gaianz me fist ci remaindre
Pur sa luxurie en mei refraindre;
Par force m'ad ci retenue
E par force m'ad purgeüe.
Sa force m'estuet otreier,
Ne li puis mie defforcier.   11430
Jo nel faiz mie de mun gré,
A guarant en trai Dampnedé.
Ne faut guaires qu'il ne m'ad morte,
Mais plus fui vielle e plus fui forte
E plus fui granz e plus fui dure[3]
E plus hardie e plus seüre
Que ne fu damisele Eleine.
E nequedent sin ai grant peinne,
Trestuz li cors de mei s'en duelt,
E s'il vient ça, si cum il suelt,   11440

---

[1] MS P's order of line restored.
[2] MS P reading—*ver*—restored.
[3] MS P readings—*fui*—restored in ll. 11434–35.

The old woman tells Bedoer her story

himself in jeopardy. He would not be a coward, on pain of losing his life. But this thought was in vain for, when he was up on the plateau, he saw only a burning fire and a new-made tombstone. The tomb was recently made; the count approached it with drawn sword. He found an old woman, bare-headed, her clothes torn, lying beside the tombstone. She kept sighing and sobbing and lamenting Eleine, grieving bitterly and uttering loud cries. When she saw Bedoer, she said: 'Wretch, who are you? What misfortune brings you here? If the giant finds you, your life must end today in grief, pain and anguish. Poor unfortunate, fly, be off before the devil sees you!' 'Good woman,' said Bedoer, 'speak to me, stop crying. Tell me who you are and why you weep, why you stay on this island and who lies in this tomb. Tell me everything that has happened to you.'

11395 'I am a lost creature,' she said, 'a miserable wretch, weeping here for a girl I suckled at my breast, Hoel's niece Eleine, whose body lies here under the stone. She was given me to suckle: alas! why was she given me? Alas! for what purpose did I feed her so, when a devil raped her? A giant raped her and me and brought us both here. He wanted to ravish her, but she was delicate and could not stand it; he was too huge, too large, too ugly, too gross and too heavy. He made her soul leave her body; Eleine could not endure it. Alas, wretch that I am! the giant shamefully slew my gentle one, my joy, my treasure, my love, and here have I buried her.' 'Why do you not go,' said the count, 'since you have lost Eleine?' 'Do you wish to hear why?' she said. 'I see you are a noble and courteous man: nothing shall be hidden from you. When Eleine expired—which made me nearly lose my mind, for I saw her die in shame—the giant made me stay here, to assuage his lechery. By force he kept me here and by force he raped me. I have to yield to his strength, I cannot prevent him. I do not consent to it—I call God to witness! He came near to killing me, but I was older and stronger, bigger and tougher, more hardened and more resolute than lady Eleine. But all the same I'm in great pain, all my body is in agony. And if he comes here, as he usually does, to satisfy his lechery, you will be killed, you can't escape. He's over there, on that smoking

Pur sa luxurie refrener,
Ocis iés, n'en poez eschaper.
La sus est, en cel munt ki fume,
Sempres vendra, ço est sa custume.
Fui tost, amis, qu'as tu ci quis?
Que ci ne seies entrepris.
Lai mei plaindre e faire mun duel,
Morte fusse piece ad, mun vuel;
Mar vi d'Eleine l'amistied.'
11450 Dunc en out Bedoer pitied;
Mult dulcement la conforta,
Puis la guerpi si s'en ala. [1]
Al rei vint si li ad cunté
Ço qu'il out oï e truvé;
De la vieille, qui duel faiseit,
E d'Eleine, ki morte esteit,
E del gaiant, ki conversout
En cel grainur munt ki fumout.
    D'Eleine fu Artur dolenz,
11460 Mais ne fu pas cuarz ne lenz;
Al flo retraiant de la mer
Ad fait ses compainuns munter.
Al grainur munt vindrent tant tost
Cume la mer le munt desclost.
Lur palefreiz e lur destriers
Cumanderent as esquiers;
Cuntremunt sunt alé tut trei [2]
Artur e Bedoer e Kei.
'Jo irrai, dist Artur, avant,
11470 Jo me combatrai al gaiant. [3]
Vus vendrez enprés mei arriere
E bien guardez que nuls nel fiere [4]
Tant cum jo me purrai aider,
Ne ja si jo n'en ai mestier.
Cuardie resemblereit
Se nuls fors mei s'i combatreit.
E nequedent, si vus veez
Mun busuin, si me sucurez.'
Cil unt ço qu'il quist otreied,
11480 Puis unt tuit trei le munt poied.

Li gaianz al feu se seeit,
Char de porc al feu rostisseit;
En espeiz en out quit partie
E partie es charbuns rostie;
La barbe aveit e les gernuns
Suilliez de char quite es charbuns.
Artur le quida ainz susprendre
Qu'il peüst sa maçue prendre;
Mais li gaianz Artur choisi,
Merveilla sei, en piez sailli,   11490
Sa maçue ad el col levee
Ki mult esteit grosse e quarree,
Dui païsant ne la portassent
Ne de terre ne la levassent.
Artur le vit en piez ester
E de ferir bien acesmer;
S'espee traist, l'escu leva,
Sun chief covri, le cop duta,
E li gaianz tel li duna
Que tut li munz en resuna   11500
E Artur tut en estuna,
Mais forz fu, puint ne chancela.
Artur senti le cop pesant,
S'espee tint, leva le brant,
Le braz hauça e estendi,
Le gaiant sus el frunt feri;
Les dous surcilz li entama,
Li sans es oilz li devala.
Escervelé e mort l'eüst,
Ja recovrer n'i esteüst,   11510
Mais li gaianz ad la maçue
Cuntre le cop en haut tenue;
Guenchi le chief, en haut s'estut,
E nequedent tel cop reçut
Que tut le vis ensanglenta
E la veüe li trubla.
Quant il senti ses oilz trubler,
Dunc veïssiez geiant dever!
Cume sengler parmi l'espied,
Quant li chien l'unt lunges chacied,   11520

---

[1] MS P reading—*s'en ala*—restored.
[2] MS P reading—*tut*—restored.
[3] MS P reading—*Jo*—restored.
[4] MS P reading—*nel*—restored.

Arthur fights the giant

mountain, and soon he will come, that's his habit. Be quick, flee, my friend; what did you seek here? Do not be captured; leave me alone to weep and wail. If I had my way, I would have died long ago; alas for Eleine's love!'

11450 Then Bedoer had pity and gently comforted her, before leaving her and returning. He came to the king and told him of what he had heard and found: of the old woman and her lamentation, of Eleine and her death, and of the giant, who dwelt in the larger, smoking, mountain. Arthur grieved for Eleine, but he was neither cowardly nor slow and at ebb tide he made his companions mount their horses. They came in a short while to the larger mountain, as the sea uncovered it. They entrusted their palfreys and steeds to the squires and all three, Arthur, Bedoer and Kei, began to climb. 'I will go ahead,' said Arthur, 'and fight the giant. You will follow me closely afterwards. Take care that no one strikes a blow, so long as I am able to help myself and so long as I don't need it. It would look like cowardice if anyone except me were to fight. Nevertheless, if you see I'm in need, help me.' They agreed to what he asked; then all three climbed the mountain.

11481 The giant was sitting by the fire, roasting pork. He had cooked some of it on a spit and roasted part in the coals. His beard and whiskers were filthy with the meat cooked on charcoal. Arthur hoped to surprise him before he could seize his club, but the giant saw him. He was amazed, jumped to his feet and shouldered his club, which was so large and square that two peasants could neither carry it nor lift it from the ground. Arthur saw him standing all ready to strike; he drew his sword, raised his shield and covered his head, fearful of the blow. And the giant gave him one, such that the whole mountain echoed and Arthur was quite stunned by it, but he was strong and did not stagger. He suffered the heavy blow, gripped his sword, raised the blade, with his arm aloft and outstretched, and struck the giant high in the forehead, mangling his two eyebrows, so that the blood ran down into his eyes. He might have brained and killed him, he would never have recovered, had the giant not held up his club high to withstand the blow; he turned his head and kept steady on his feet. Nevertheless, he received such a blow that bloodied his whole face and blurred his vision.

11517 When he realised his eyes were blurred, the giant went mad. Just as a boar, impaled on the spear, long harried by the dogs, rushes at the huntsman, so he furiously dashed at the king and grasped him, not releasing him despite the sword.

S'embat cuntre le veneür,
Tut ensement, par grant irur,
Curut al rei si l'enbraça,
Unc pur s'espee nel laisça. [1]
Granz fu e forz, par mi le prist,
A genuilluns venir le fist,
Mais cil sempres s'esvertua,
En piez revint si se dreça.
Artur fu forment aïrus
11530 E merveilles fu engiegnus;
Corucied fu e poür out.
Efforça sei tant cum il pout;
A sei trait e de sei empeinst,
Grant vertu out, pas ne se feinst;
En saillant guenchi de travers,
De l'enemi s'est desaers.
Des qu'il se fu de lui estors
E delivré senti sun cors,
Mult fu isnels, entur ala,
11540 Ore ert de ça, or ert de la,
Od l'espee suvent ferant;
E cil alout as mains tastant;
Les oilz aveit tuz plainz de sanc,
Ne connuisseit ne neir ne blanc.
Tant ala Artur guandissant,
Suvent detriés, suvent devant,
Que de Caliburne l'alemele [2]
Li enbati en la cervele.
Traist e enpeinst e cil chaï,
11550 Eschaucirra si fist un cri;
Tel escruis fist al chaement
Cum chaenes ki chiet par vent.
Dunc cumença Artur a rire,
Kar dunc fu trespassee s'ire.
De luin s'estut si l'esgarda,
A sun buteillier comanda
Que al gaiant le chief trenchast,
A sun esquier le livrast; [3]
A l'ost le volt faire porter
11560 Pur faire a merveille mustrer.

'Eü ai, dist Artur, poür.
N'en oi mais de gaiant grainur
Fors de Rithon tant sulement
Ki aveit fait maint rei dolent.'
Rithon aveit tanz reis cunquis
E tanz vencuz, e tanz ocis, [4]
Des barbes des reis, escorchiees,
Out unes pels apareilliees,
Pels en out fait a afubler,
Bien deüst l'om Rithon tuer.   11570
Par grant orguil e par fierté
Aveit al rei Artur mandé
Que la sue barbe escorchast
E bonement li enveiast,
E, si cum il plus forz esteit,
E plus des altres reis valeit,
La sue barbe enurereit
E a ses pels urle en fereit.
E si Artur cuntrediseit
Ço que Rithon li requereit,   11580
Cors a cors ensemble venissent
E cors a cors se combatissent
E li quel d'els l'altre ocirreit,
U que vif veintre le purreit,
La barbe eüst, preïst les pels,
Si feïst faire urle ou tassels.
Artur a lui se combait,
El munt d'Arave le venqui;
Les pels out, la barbe escorca;
Unches puis Artur ne truva   11590
Gaiant ki fust de tel vigur
Ne dunt il eüst tel poür. [5]
Quant Artur out le munstre ocis
E Bedoer out le chief pris,
Joius e lied del munt turnerent,
A l'ost revindrent si cunterent
Ou e pur quei orent esté,
Puis unt le chief a tuz mustré. [6]
Hoel fu dolenz de sa niece,
Grant marrement en out grant piece, 11600

---

[1] MS P reading—*s'espee*—restored.
[2] MSS JHR: *Escalibourc/Escalibor.*
[3] MS P reading—*sun*—restored.
[4] MS P reading—*e tanz ocis*—restored.
[5] MS G adds: *Mais icist molt plus fort estoit/ Et molt graingnor vigor avoit/ Que onques Rithon n'en ost jor/*

Quant il fust de graingnor vigor/ Et plus oribles et plus laiz/ Plus hisdos et plus contrefaiz/ Au jor que Artur le conquist/ El mont S. Michiel ou l'ocist.
[6] MS J adds: *Cil furent lié de la nouvele/ Fist faire al mont une capele/ Mais a Hoel n'estoit pas bele.*

Arthur fights the giant

Huge and strong, he seized him in the middle and forced him to his knees, but the king at once struggled hard, got back on his feet and stood up. Arthur's blood was roused and he was also amazingly wily. Both angry and afraid, he made every effort: he pulled the giant to him and pushed him violently. As he was very strong, he did not hesitate, but with a jump dodged sideways and so got out of the enemy's clutches. As soon as he had escaped from him and felt his body free, he swiftly dashed around the giant, now here, now there, repeatedly striking him with his sword. And the giant groped about with his hands, his eyes full of blood, unable to tell black from white. Arthur kept weaving and dodging so much, sometimes behind, sometimes in front, that he drove Caliburn's blade into the giant's brain. He pushed and pulled and the giant fell, kicking, with a cry; in his fall he crashed like an oak felled by the wind.

11553 Then Arthur began to laugh, for now his anger was past. He stood at a distance and looked at him, and told his cup-bearer to cut off the giant's head and give it to his squire; he wanted it carried to the army and exhibited as a marvel. 'I was afraid,' said Arthur, 'more than of any other giant, except only Rithon, who mortified so many kings.' Rithon had conquered and defeated so many kings, and killed so many, that he had had a skin cloak made of their beards which he had stripped off, a cloak for him to wear. Rithon certainly had to be killed. In great pride and arrogance he had ordered Arthur to strip off his own beard and kindly send it to him and, as he was stronger and worth more than other kings, Rithon would honour his beard and use it for the cloak's border. And if Arthur refused Rithon's request, they would come together face to face and fight each other, and whoever killed the other, or took him alive, would get the beard and add it to the cloak as border or fringe. Arthur fought him and defeated him on mount Arave; he flayed him and stripped off his beard. Never since had he found a giant of such strength or who frightened him so much.[1]

11593 When Arthur had killed the monster and Bedoer taken his head, they left the mountain joyful and happy and returned to the army, to tell them where they had been and why. Then they showed the head to them all. Hoel grieved for his niece and suffered great distress for a long while, ashamed she should have died in that way. He had a chapel of Our Lady St Mary, now called Eleine's Tomb, built on

---

[1] *HRB* chap. 165: *Ritho* and *Mt Aravius*. On the affinity of this story with those in *Culhwch and* *Olwen*, see Roberts, 'Geoffrey of Monmouth', *AOW* p. 108 and Tatlock pp. 388–9.

Hunte out que si esteit perie.
De ma dame seinte Marie
Fist faire el munt une chapele
Que l'un or Tumbe Eleine apele;
Del tumblel ou Eleine jut
Tumbe Eleine cest nun reçut,
De la tumbe ou li cors fu mis
Ad Tumbe Eleine cest nun pris.
   Quant cil d'Irlande venu furent
11610 E li altre ki venir durent,
Artur, de jurnee en jurnee,
Ad Normendie trespassee;
Chastels e viles trespasça,
E sa gent crut e espeisça;
Tuit aloent en sa busuine.
France passa, vint en Burguine,
A Ostum vuleit dreit aler,
Kar oï aveit nuveler
Que cil de Rome la veneient
11620 E la cuntree purperneient;
Luces Hiber les cundueit
Ki de Rome l'enur teneit.
Quant Artur dut l'eue passer
Que vus oëz Albe numer,
Li païsant li acuintierent
E ses espies li nuncierent
Que pruef d'illuec, se il vuleit,
L'empereür truver purreit;
Ses herberges e ses fuillees
11630 Aveit bien pruef d'iluec fichiees.
Tant aveit gent, tant reis menot,
Od tels maisnees chevachot,
Que fols sereit s'il l'atendeit;[1]
Ja sa gent n'i fuisunereit.
Cuntre un hume aveit cil quatre;
Feïst pais, laissast le cumbatre.
Artur neient ne s'esmaia;
Hardiz fu, en Deu se fia;
Oï aveit mainte manace.
11640 Sur Albe, en une forte place,

Ad un chastelet cumpassé,
Grant gent aveit, tost l'out fermé;
Le chastelet pur ço ferma
Que ses herneis illuec laira,
E si grant cuite li cresseit
Al chastelet recuvrereit.
Dunc ad dous cuntes apelez
Bien sages, bien enloquinez,
De grant parage esteit chescuns:
Gerin de Chartres fu li uns,   11650
Li altres Bos d'Oxenefort,
Ki bien conuit e dreit e tort.
A cez dous ad Walwein justé
Qui a Rome out lunges esté.
Pur ço qu'il erent bien preisied,
Bien cuneü, bien enseinnied,
Ad li reis cels ensemble pris
E a l'empereür tramis;
Manda li qu'il s'en returnast,
France esteit sue, n'i entrast.   11660
S'il ne s'en vuleit returner,
Par bataille venist pruver
Al premerain jur qu'il vuldreit[2]
Li quels i avreit grainur dreit,
Kar Artur, tant cum il vivreit,
Des Romains France defendreit;
Par bataille l'aveit cunquise
E par bataille l'aveit prise,
E Romain ancïenement
L'orent par bataille ensement;   11670
Or reseit bataille pruvance
Li quels d'els dous deit aveir France.
   Li messagier d'Artur turnerent,
Sur lur meillurs chevals munterent,
Halbercs vestuz, helmes laciez,
Escuz as cols, pris les espiez.
Dunc veïssiez cez chevaliers,
Ces bachelers, cez plus legiers,
Ki a Walwein vunt cunseillant
E a cunseil li vunt preiant   11680

---

[1] MS P reading—*sereit*—restored.   [2] MS P reading—*vuldreit*—restored.

Arthur arrives in Burgundy

the mountain; the name comes from the tombstone where Eleine lay, from the tomb where the body was buried.

11609 When the Irish had arrived, and those others who were due to come, Arthur progressed through Normandy, day after day. He passed by castles and towns, and his army grew and increased, everyone helping him in his task. He crossed France and came to Burgundy. He wanted to go straight to Autun,[1] because he had news that the Romans were on their way there and overrunning the country; they were led by Lucius Hiber, who held the domain of Rome. When Arthur was about to cross the river you know as the Aube, he was told by the peasants and informed by his spies that nearby he could find the emperor, if he wished. The emperor had pitched his tents and his arbours very close by. He had so many men, he led so many kings and rode with such retinues that Arthur would be mad to wait for him: his men could never resist theirs, it was four against one. He should make peace and abandon the fight. Arthur was not dismayed: he was confident and put his trust in God. He had heard plenty of threats. In a secure place on the Aube he built a fort, put there a large number of men, and soon fortified it. He did this so that he might leave his equipment there and, if he were in great danger, return to the fort.

11647 Then he called for two counts, most wise and eloquent and each of high birth. Gerin of Chartres was one, the other Bos of Oxford,[2] who well knew what was right and what wrong. To these he added Walwein, who had spent a long time at Rome. Because they were much esteemed, well known and well educated, the king sent them in a group to the emperor. He commanded him to turn back and not to enter France, which was Arthur's. If he would not turn back, he should come on the first day he wished to prove in battle which of them had the greater right, for Arthur, so long as he lived, would defend France from the Romans. He had won it and captured it in battle, and long ago the Romans had done likewise. Now battle could once again prove which of them should have France.

11673 The messengers took leave of Arthur and mounted their best horses, wearing their hauberks, their helmets laced up, their shields round their necks and their swords in their hands. Then certain young knights could be seen, the most irresponsible ones, going to Walwein, advising him and secretly begging him that, in the court where he was going, he should do something, before he left, to precipitate the war which for so long had been impending. It would turn out badly,

---

[1] *HRB* chap. 166: *Augustudunum.*

[2] *HRB* chap. 166: *Boso de Uado Boum* (a joking rendition of 'Ox-ford', as opposed to *Boso Ridocesis*, '*id est Oxenfordie*' in chap. 156) and *Gerin Carnotensem.*

Que la ou il vait, en la curt,
Face tel chose, ainz qu'il s'en turt,
Que la guerre seit comenciee
Ki tant ad esté manaciee;
Turné sereit a malvestied,
Quant tant se sunt entr'aprismed,
Qu'alcune juste n'i feïssent
E que si tost se departissent.
Cil passerent une muntaine
11690   E puis un bois, puis une plaine;
Les herberges virent de l'ost
E il i vindrent assez tost.
Dunc veïssiez Romains venir
E chevaliers des trés eissir
Pur les treis messages veeir
E pur les nuveles saveir.
Demandant vunt que il quereient
E se pur pais faire veneient;
Mais cil estal ne plai ne tindrent
11700   Dessi qu'al empereür vindrent.
Devant sa tente descendirent;
Lur chevals defors tenir firent;
Devant l'empereür alerent,
Le mandement Artur cunterent.
Cheschuns ad dit ço que li plout
E ço que buen a dire sout;
Li emperere tut oï,
E quant li plot si respundi.
'D'Artur, ço dist Walwein, venum,
11710   E le message Artur portum.
Si hume sumes, il est sire;
Tut devum sun message dire.
Par nus te mandë e defent,
Quel sachent tuit comunement, [1]
Que en France tun pied ne mettes
Ne de France ne t'entremettes.
France tient e France tendra,
Cume sue la defendra.
Ço te mande que rien n'i prenges
11720   E si tu sur lui la chalenges,

Par bataille seit chalengee
E par bataille deraisnee.
Romain par bataille la pristrent
E par bataille la cunquistrent,
E il l'a par bataille eüe
E par bataille l'ad tenue;
Par bataille reseit pruvé
Kin deit aver la poësté.
Demain, seinz altre demurance,
Vien, si tu vuels desrainer France;   11730
Ou tu t'en va, si t'en repaire,
Returne t'en, n'as ci que faire!
Nus avum pris, tu as perdu.'
Li emperere ad respundu
Que returner ne s'en deveit,
France esteit sue, avant irreit;
Ço li pesout se il perdeit,
Il cunquerreit quant il purreit;
Mais il quidout al suen espeir
France cunquerre e France aveir.   11740
    Quintilien emprés lui sist
Ki la parole emprés lui prist;
Sis niés esteit, mult orguillus,
Chevaliers mult contralius.
'Bretun, dist il, sunt vanteür
E mult sunt bon manaceür.
Vantances e manaces unt,
Assez manacent e poi funt.'
Encor, ço crei, avant parlast
E les messages rampodnast,   11750
Mais Walwein, ki s'en coruça,
S'espee traist, avant passa,
Le chief li fist del bu voler;
As cuntes dist: ' Alez munter!'
E li cunte muntent amdui,
Walwein od els e cil od lui.
Chescun a sun cheval se prent
Si s'en turnent delivrement,
Escuz es cols, lances es mains;
Cungied n'i pristrent des Romains. [2] 11760

---

[1] MS P reading—*quel*—restored.   [2] MS P reading—*n'i*—restored.

Walwein carries a message to Lucius

when each side had got so close to the other, if they never had the chance of a joust and separated so soon. The messengers crossed a mountain, then a wood, then a plain. They saw the enemy's tents and arrived there very soon. Then the Romans could be seen coming and knights leaving their tents, to see the three messengers and to discover the news. They kept asking what they sought and if they came to make peace, but the messengers neither stopped nor took heed until they came to the emperor. They dismounted before his tent and had their horses held outside; they went before the emperor and told him of Arthur's command. Each of them said what he pleased and what he knew was right to say. The emperor heard it all and replied at his leisure.

11709   'We come from Arthur,' said Walwein, 'and we bear Arthur's message. We are his men, he is our lord; we must all deliver his message. Through us he orders and forbids you (let it be known to all) to set foot in France or concern yourself with it. He holds France and shall hold it, defending it as his own. He orders you to take nothing from it, and if you lay claim to it from him, it must be disputed through battle and through battle justified. The Romans took it through battle and won it through battle, and he has got it through battle and held it through battle. Through battle it can once more be proved who should control it. Tomorrow, without more ado, come, if you wish to lay claim to France; or go, turn back, be off, there's nothing for you here! We have won, you have lost.'

11734   The emperor replied he had no reason to return: France was his and he would advance. It would grieve him if he lost, he would win if he could; but in his opinion he believed he could conquer and hold France. Quintilien[1] sat by him and spoke next; he was his nephew and very proud, a most refractory knight. 'Britons,' he said, 'are boasters and make some very fine threats. They're all boasts and threats, they menace in plenty and do little.' He would, I think, have spoken further and insulted the messengers, but Walwein, who was furious, drew his sword, rushed forward and made his head fly from his body. 'To horse!' he said to the counts, and they both mounted, Walwein with them, they with him. Each seized his horse and quickly left, shields on necks, lances in hand: they took no leave of the Romans.

11761   The court was all in uproar! The emperor shouted loudly: 'What are you doing?

---

[1] *HRB* chap. 166: *Gaius Quintillianus.*

Es vus la curt tute esturmie!
Li emperere forment crie:
'Que faites vus? Huniz nus unt,
Pernez les mei, mar en irrunt!'
Dunc oïssiez crier vassals
'Armes, armes, chevals, chevals!
Or tost, or tost, muntez, muntez,
Puinez, puinez, curez, curez!'
Mult veïssiez cel ost fremir,
11770 Seles mettre, chevals saisir,
Prendre lances, espees ceindre,
Esperuner pur tost ateindre.
E li cunte s'en vunt fuiant,
D'ures en altres regardant.
Romain les siwent a desrei,
Ke par chemin, ke par chaumei,
Ci dui, ci trei, ci cinc, ci sis,
Ci set, ci oit, ci noef, ci dis.
Un en i out ki puint avant,
11780 Cheval out buen e tost curant,
Ses compainuns vint trespassant
E mult suvent alout criant: [1]
'Estez ça, chevalier, estez!
Vilanie est que ne turnez.'
Gerin de Chartres tresturna,
L'escu prist, la lance esluinna,
Del buen cheval luin le porta
Tant cum la lance li dura.
Puis li ad dit: 'Or est noauz;
11790 Vostre cheval fait trop granz salz;
[Vus nus avez sewiz trop tost
Encor fuissez vus mielz en l'ost,] [2]
Vus fuissiez mielz ariere es trés
Que vus fuissiez ici remés.'
Bos esguarda que Gerin fist
E la cuntraire oï qu'il dist;
Envie out de faire altretal;
Vira le chief de sun cheval,
Cuntre un chevalier s'eslaissa
E cil a lui, qui nel duta.
Bos le feri parmi la gule
11800 Dessi al col en la meoule,

E cil chaï, gule baee,
Ki la lance aveit engulee.
E li cuens li cria: ' Dan maistre,
D' itels morsels vus sai jo paistre. [3]
En pais seiez, ci vus gisez,
Cels ki vus siuent atendez.
Dites a cels qui ci vendrunt
Que li message par ci vunt.'
Un en i out, de Rome né,
De Romains bien enparenté,   11810
Romain l'apeloent Marcel;
Cheval aveit forment isnel;
Muntez esteit as deraains,
Puis passa tuz les premerains;
N'aveit mie lance portee,
Pur tost aler l'out ubliee.
Cil alout ateinnant Walwein,
Esporunant, laschied le frein.
Ja l'aveit pris a costeier,
Ne li poeit mie esluinnier;   11820
Sa main tendeit a Walwein prendre,
Pramis l'aveit tut vif a rendre.
Walwein vit que si tost veneit
E que si tost curre poeit;
Ses resnes tint, si s'arestut,
E cil fu prés sil trescurut. [4]
Al trespas traist Walwein s'espee,
El chief li ad tute enbevree,
Jesqu'es espaules le fendi,
Unques li helmes nel guari;   11830

Cil chaï si fina sa vie
E Walwein dist par curteisie:
'Marcel, en enfern ou tu vas
A Quintilien nunceras,
Par tei li mand e tu li di
Que Bretun sunt assez hardi;
Lur dreit vuelent bien desrainer
E plus faire que manacier.'
Dunc rad Walwein ses compainuns,
Gerin e Bos, par nun semuns   11840

---

[1] MS P's order of line restored.
[2] Couplet from MS P restored.
[3] MS P reading—*d'itels*—restored.
[4] MS P reading—*sil*—restored.

The Romans pursue the messengers

They have shamed us! Capture them for me; they'll never get away!' Then knights could be heard shouting: 'To arms, to arms, to horse, to horse! Quickly, quickly, mount, mount, spur, spur, run, run!' The army could be seen in tumult, saddling, seizing horses, gripping lances, girding on swords and spurring to catch up. And the counts were in full flight, looking behind them from time to time. The Romans followed them in disorder, whether along the roads or across the fields, here in twos, there in threes, here in fives, there in sixes, here in sevens, there in eights, here in nines, there in tens. One of them spurred ahead, passing his companions with his good and speedy horse, and he kept shouting: 'Wait, knights, wait! If you don't turn back, you're craven!' Gerin of Chartres turned round, took his shield, drew back his lance and with its whole length knocked him off his good horse. Then he said to him: 'Now you are worse off: your horse leapt ahead far too fast. You've followed us too quickly; you'd be better off with the army. You would do much better to be back in the tents than stay here.'

11793 Bos watched what Gerin did and heard his unpleasant remarks. He wanted to do something similar. He turned his horse's head and rushed towards a knight, who met him unfraid. Bos struck him through the throat as far as the marrow of his neck-bone, and he fell, mouth agape, having swallowed the lance. And the count shouted at him: 'My lord and master,[1] I can feed you on such choice morsels. Be at peace, lie here and wait for those who follow you. Tell those who are to come that the messengers went this way.' One man, born in Rome and of noble Roman kin, was called Marcel[2] and had a very fast horse. He was among the last to mount and then overtook all those in front. He did not carry a lance: he had forgotten it in the haste of departure. Spurring, he caught up with Walwein and slackened his bridle; already he had begun to jostle him so that Walwein could not move away. He stretched out his hand to grab Walwein, having promised to hand him over alive.Walwein saw he came so quickly and could travel so fast; he drew rein and stopped, and the other man was so close that he overran. As he passed by, Walwein drew his sword and plunged it entirely into his head, splitting it down to the shoulders. The helmet gave him no protection; he fell and his life ended. And Walwein said courteously: 'Marcel, carry a message to Quintilien in hell, where you are going. Through you I inform him, and you must tell him, that the British are pretty confident; they certainly intend to claim their rights and do more than just threaten.'

11839 Then, calling his companions Gerin and Bos by name, Walwein summoned each of them to turn round and fight one of the pursuers. Walwein told them and they

---

[1] Literally, 'sir master'. *Dan* often prefixes a title, sometimes abusively and ironically, as here.

[2] *HRB* chap. 166: *Marcellus Mutius*.

Que chescuns arriere turnast,
A un des enchauçanz justast.
Walwein lur dist e il le firent,
Treis Romains sempres abatirent.
Li message bien s'en aloent
E li destrier tost les portoent
E li Romain les enchaçoent
Ki de nient nes esparnioent.
Mult les aloent ateinant
11850 E des lances suvent butant,
Mult lur dunoent granz colees,
Or des lances, or des espees;
Mais unc nes pourent tant ferir [1]
Qu'un en peüssent retenir
Ne nafrer ne deschevalchier
Ne de nule rien damagier.
Un en i out, cusin Marcel,
Sur un cheval forment isnel;
Dolenz fu mult de sun cusin
11860 Qu'il vit gesir lez le chemin.
Travers les chanz esporunout,
Les treis messages costeiout,
A traverse ferir vuleit,
Mais Walwein bien l'aparceveit,
Sur lui puinst si l'ala ferir,
Unc cil n'out de turner laisir.
Sa lance laissa jus chaeir
Ki ne li pout mestier aveir, [2]
S'espee traist, ferir quida,
11870 Leva le braz, le puin halça,
E Walweint li ad tut trenchied
Le braz que cil aveit hauchied, [3]
L'espee e le braz e le puin
Li fist voler el champ bien luin.
Altre cop li eüst duné,
Mais cil de Rome l'unt hasté.
Issi alerent enchauçant
Tant qu'a un bois vindrent fuiant
Ki ert entr'els e le chastel
11880 Que Artur aveit fait nuvel.

Artur out sis mil chevaliers
Tramis emprés les messagiers
Pur les bois e les vals cerchier
E pur la cuntree espier.
Encuntre les messages fussent,
Si mestier ert sis securussent.
Un bois aveient trespassé
E dejuste erent aresté,
Sur lur chevals armé seeient,
Des messages guarde perneient, 11890
D'umes armez od granz compaines
Virent covrir tutes les plaines.
Lur messages unt cuneüz
E les enchauceürs veüz.
Enmi les vis lur sunt sailli [4]
A une voiz e a un cri.
Romain sempres se resortirent,
Par les champaines s'espandirent;
Tels i out ki furent irried
Que tant aveient enchaucied, 11900
Kar Bretun bien les envaïrent,
Qui al turner maint en ferirent,
Maint en unt ataint e maint pris,
Maint trebuchied e maint ocis.
Petreïus, uns riches ber,
N'out en Rome d'armes sun per,
Dis mil armez out en baillie,
Tant out en sa cunestablie.
Cil oï parler de l'aguait
Que li Bretun aveient fait. 11910
Isnelment od dis mil escuz
Ad celz de Rome securus.
Par dreite force e par destreit,
Od les armez qu'il cundueit,
Fist les Bretuns el bois rentrer,
Ne porent mie cuntr'ester.
Dessi al bois dura la chace
Que ne li porent tenir place.
Al bois se sunt cuntretenu.
E al bois se sunt defendu. 11920

---

[1] MS P reading—*nes*—restored.
[2] MS P reading—*Ki*—restored.
[3] MS P reading—*cil*—restored.
[4] MS P reading—*les*—restored.

Petreïus atacks the Britons

did so, at once laying three Romans low. The messengers galloped off, the horses carrying them swiftly, and the Romans pursued them, showing them no mercy. They kept reaching them and striking them with lances; they gave them great blows, now with lances, now with swords, but they could never strike them enough to catch one of them, nor wound, unhorse nor harm them in any way. There was a cousin of Marcel, on a very swift horse, who was most distressed about his kinsman, whom he saw lying by the road-side. He spurred over the fields and drew level with the three messengers, intending to strike them sideways, but Walwein noticed him, spurred at him and went to strike. He never had an opportunity to turn, but let his lance fall, which he did not need, drew his sword, thinking to strike, raised his arm and his fist, and Walwein completely cut off the arm he had raised, making sword, arm and fist fly far over the field. He would have given him another blow, but the Romans were pressing him hard. Thus they were pursued until they came fleeing to a wood, which was between them and the castle which Arthur had newly made.

11881 Arthur had sent six thousand knights after the messengers, to scour the woods and valleys and spy out the land. They would be in the messengers' direction and if need be, they could help them. They had traversed a wood and stopped beside it, sitting on horseback in their armour, when they noticed the messengers and saw the plains quite covered with large bands of armed men. They recognized their messengers and saw the pursuers. With one shout and unanimously they jumped out at them. The Romans at once withdrew, scattering throughout the fields. There were some who were angry they had pursued so far, because the Britons made a determined attack on them, striking many as they withdrew, reaching and taking many, overthrowing and killing many. There was a noble lord, Petreïus,[1] unequalled in Rome for feats of arms, who had ten thousand armed men under his control: so many were at his command. He heard tell of the ambush which the Britons had made and speedily helped the Romans with ten thousand men. By pure force and compulsion, with the troops he led, he made the Britons retreat to the wood; they could not resist. The pursuit lasted right up to the wood, because they could not stand their ground. In the wood, they fought back and in the wood they defended themselves. Petreïus attacked them, but lost many of his men, because the Britons cut them down and dragged

---

[1] *HRB* chap. 166 (Vulgate only) calls him *Petreïus Cocta.*

Petreïus les assailli,
Mais de sa gent mult i perdi
Kar li Bretun les abateient
E dedenz le bois les traeient;
Mult ert espés le chapleïz
Entre le bois e le larriz.
   Quant Artur vit le demurier
Que faiseient li messagier,
Ne que cil pas ne reveneient
11930 Ki emprés cels alé esteient,
Ider, le fiz Nu, apela,
Cinc mil chevaliers li livra;
Emprés les altres les tramist
Si li ruva qu'il les quesist.
Walwein e Bos se combateient
E li altre bien i fereient,
Grant noise i aveit e grant hu,
A tant vint Ider, le fiz Nu:
Dunc sunt Bretun esvigoré,
11940 Le champ avant unt recovré.
Ider poinst, s'enseine escria,
E cil od lui qu'il amena.
Bien fu la puingte parfurgniee
E mainte sele i out vuidiee,
Maint cheval pris e guaainied
E maint chevalier trebuchied.
Petreïus l'estor maintint,
Sa gent restreinst, ariere vint,
Bien sout fuïr, bien sout turner,
11950 Bien sout chacier, bien sout ester.
Suvent veïssiez beles chaces
E turneier par plusurs places.
Ki hardiz fu, hardi truva,
Ki juster volt, sempres justa,
Ki ferir volt sempres feri,
Ki ne se pout tenir chaï.
Bretun puineient a desrei,
Ne vuleient estre en cunrei,
Desirrus erent de juster
11960 E desirrus d'armes porter;

Chevalerie desirroent,
Pur ço suvent se desreoent;
Ne lur chaleit cument qu'alast
Mais que la guerre cumençast.
Petreïus fu mult engrés,
Ses bons humes tint de sei prés,
Bien sout d'estur, bien sout de guerre,
Bien sout atendre e bien requerre;
Suvent turnout, suvent puineit,
Cels ki chaeient rescueit.   11970
Bos d'Oxinefort aperçut,
Ki de l'estur l'estre cunut,
Que senz perte n'en turnereient
Se Petreïum n'ocieient,
U ocieient u perneient,
Kar Romain par lui se teneient
E li Bretun trop folement
S'embateient entre lur gent.
Des plus hardiz e des meillurs
Traist a cunseil od lui plusurs.   11980
'Barun, dist il, parlez od mei,
Vus ki Artur amez de fei.
Cumenciez avum cest estur
Senz le seü nostre seinur;
Si bien nus eschiet, bien sera, [1]
Si malement, il nus harra.
Si nus sumes li surdeior
Que de cest champ n'aion enor,
Hunte e damage recevrum
E le haenge Artur avrum.   11990
Pur ço nus estuvreit pener
De Petreïum encumbrer,
Que vif ou mort le puissum prendre
E vif ou mort a Artur rendre.
Altrement partir n'en poüm
Que nus grant perte n'i aium.
Faites tuit ço que jo ferai
E la puiniez ou jo puindrai.'
Cil distrent que bien le ferunt;
Quel part que Bos irra irrunt. [2]   12000

---

[1] MS P reading—*eschiet*—restored.

[2] Following Arnold's edition, from l. 12000 MS D is used as base text.

Ider brings reinforcements

them inside the wood. The fighting was very heavy between wood and hillside.

11927　When Arthur saw the messengers were delayed, and those who had gone after them had not returned, he called Ider son of Nu[1] and entrusted him with five thousand knights. He sent them after the others, asking him to look for them. Walwein and Bos were both fighting and the others were dealing hard blows, there was a great din and clamour, when Ider son of Nu arrived. Then the Britons took new heart and recovered the ground in front. Ider spurred forward, shouting his war-cry, and so did those with him. The charge was well carried out and there were many saddles emptied, many horses captured and won and many knights overthrown. Petreïus kept up the fight but checked his men and retreated; he well knew when and how to flee, to turn back, to pursue and to stand fast. There splendid pursuits could be seen and combats in many places. Whoever was bold, found his match in boldness, whoever wanted a single combat, soon found it, whoever wanted to strike, soon struck, and whoever could not hold out, fell. The Britons drove forward impetuously, not caring to be organized into troops: they wanted to prove themselves in single combat and to bear weapons, they wanted knightly deeds, and so they often broke ranks. They did not care how the battle went, as long as it started.

11965　Petreïus fought fiercely, keeping his best men close to him; he was experienced in fighting and war, knowing when to wait and when to attack. Sometimes he wheeled, sometimes he rushed forward, rescuing those who fell. Bos of Oxford, who knew the way the fight was going, realized they would not escape without losses unless they slew Petreïus, slew him or captured him, for it was because of him that the Romans held out, and the Britons foolishly rushed around among their men. He secretly called aside to him several of the boldest and best. 'My lords,' he said, 'you who loyally love Arthur, speak with me. We have started this battle without the knowledge of our lord. If all goes well with us, it will be well with him; if it goes badly, he will hate us. If we are the losers, and get no honour on this field, we shall be humiliated and harmed and the recipients of Arthur's hate. For this reason we must make an effort to trap Petreïus, so as to take him alive or dead and, alive or dead, hand him over to Arthur. Otherwise, we cannot get away without great losses. Do everything I do and where I spur ahead, follow me.' They said they would certainly do so[2] and would go wherever Bos went.

12001　When Bos had those he wanted with him and had discovered and seen which

---

[1]　*HRB* chap. 166: *Hiderus filius Nucii; VV: Hiderius/ Hidorius/Biderius, filius Nu/Nuth*. Ider or Yder (Welsh *Edern*) joins Arthurian legend at an early stage: he is depicted (as *Isdernus*) on the Modena archivolt (between 1099 and 1120), and is in *Culhwch and Olwen*. See Loomis, 'Oral Diffusion',

ALMA pp. 60–61 and Bromwich and Evans, *Culhwch and Olwen* l. 182 and pp. 70–71.
[2]　The translation from this point is of MS D. For consistency I have retained in translation MS P's spelling of names e.g. *Bedoer*, not *Beduer*.

Quant Bos ot od sei ces qu'il volt,
E espié e veü ot
Li quels Petreïus esteit
Ki tuz les altres mainteneit,
Cele part puinst mult fierement
E li altre comunement.
Unkes n'i pristrent fin ne cesse [1]
Dissi qu'il vindrent en la presse
U Petreïus chevalchot
12010 Ki les meisnies guvernot.
Bos le cunut, juste lui puinst,
Lur dous chevals ensemble joinst,
Les braz geta si l'enbraça;
En sa cumpaigne se fia,
De sun gré se laissa chaeir;
Merveilles peüssiez veeir!
En la grant presse chaï jus,
Entre ses braz Petreïus.
Bos tint e Petreïus traist;
12020 Mult s'esforça qu'aler l'en laist.
Romein curent a la rescusse,
Ki lance porte tost l'estrusse;
Quant les lances lur sunt faillies,
As espees caplent furbies;
Petreïum volent rescurre
E Bretun volent Bos securre.
Mult veïssiez fiere asemblee,
Estur espés, dure medlee,
Healmes pleier, escuz percier,
12030 Halbercs falser, hanstes brisier,
Seles voidier, seles turner,
Humes chaeir, humes nafrer;
Bretun l'enseigne lur seignur,
E cil de Rome crient la lur. [2]
Li un s'esforcent que il l'aient
E li altre tut tens l'en traient,
Avisunkes cuniseit l'un
Ki ert Romein, ki ert Bretun,
Fors as paroles e as criz,
12040 Tant iert espés li capleïz.

Walwein par la grant presse vait,
Od s'espee la veie fait,
Fiert e enpeint, caplë e bute,
Maint en abat, meint en desrute,
N'i ad Romein ki ses cops veie
Ki ne li face, s'il puet, veie.
Yder turna de l'altre part, [3]
Ki des Romeins fait grant essart;
Gerin de Chartres li adiue.
Li un pur l'autre s'esvertue;   12050
Petreïum unt trespassé
E Bos od lui unt adossé,
E Bretun unt Bos relevé,
Sur un cheval l'unt remunté.
Petreïum unt retenu,
Ki maint cop aveit receü;
Parmi la presse l'unt mené
Dedenz lur force a salveté.
A bones gardes l'unt laissié,
Puis unt l'estur recumencié.   12060
Cil furent senz meinteneür
Cume nef senz guverneür
Que venz quel part que volt enpeint,
Quant il n'i ad ki dreit la meint;
Altresi fud de la cumpaigne
Ki ot perdu sun chevetaine;
Ne fud mie puis defensable
Qu'el ot perdu sun cunestable.
Bretun les vunt mult demenant
E a granz turbes abatant;   12070
Les abatuz vunt trespassant
E les fuianz vunt ateignant;
Les uns pernent, les uns ocient,
Les uns despuillent, les uns lient;
Puis runt retrait lur cumpaignuns,
El bois vindrent a lur prisuns.
Petreïum en unt porté,
A lur seignur l'unt presenté,
Altres prisuns od lui asez;
Arthur les en ad merciez.   12080

---

[1] MS D reading—*n'i*—restored.
[2] MS D reading—*e*—restored.
[3] MS D reading—*turna*—restored.

Petreïus is captured

man Petreïus was, who was upholding all the rest, he spurred most fiercely in that direction and the others with him. They neither stopped nor stayed till they reached the melée where Petreïus was riding, controlling the troops. Bos recognized him, spurred up to him and forced the two horses into close proximity. He threw out his arms and gripped him and, trusting to his companions, of his own accord let himself fall. This was an amazing thing to see! He fell to the ground, in that great throng, with Petreïus clutched in his arms. Bos tugged and Petreïus pulled, struggling hard to escape. The Romans ran to the rescue and those carrying lances soon broke them; when lances failed them, they fought with their polished swords. They wanted to rescue Petreïus and the Britons wanted to help Bos. A fierce clash could be seen, a mighty struggle, a hard melée, with helmets bent, shields pierced, hauberks broken, lances shattered, saddles emptied, men wounded and falling. The Britons shouted their lord's war-cry, the Romans shouted theirs. One side strove to get Petreïus, the other side was continually pulling him back and scarcely could Roman be told from Briton, except by words and cries, so thick was the fray.

12041 Walwein pushed through the great press, making his way with his sword; he struck and smote, fought and thrust, felling many, crushing more. No Roman seeing his blows did not make way for him, if he could. On the other side moved Ider, making great slaughter amongst the Romans, helped by Gerin of Chartres, each fighting hard for the other. They overtook Petreïus and knocked him and Bos over, and the Britons raised Bos to his feet and remounted him. They kept a grip on Petreïus, who had received many blows, and led him through the fray to within the safety of their forces. They left him carefully guarded and then began the battle all over again. The Romans were without someone to control them, like a ship without a pilot, driven by the wind whichever way it wishes, when there is no one to steer her aright. So it was with the troops who had lost their leader; because their commander was missing, they could no longer defend themselves. The Britons kept driving them about and knocking great crowds of them down. They overran the fallen and reached those in flight; they captured some, they killed some, they stripped some and they bound some. Then they pulled their companions back and returned to their prisoners in the wood. They brought Petreïus with them and presented him to their lord, and many other prisoners with him. Arthur thanked them and told them he would increase the domains of each if he were victorious.

12083 Arthur had the prisoners guarded and handed them over to jailers. He discussed

Puis lur ad dit, se il venqueit,
Que a chascun sun fieu creistreit.
   Arthur fist les prisuns guarder
E as guardes les fist livrer;
Purparlé ad e cunseil pris
Qu'il les tramettra a Paris;
En chartre les fera tenir
Tant qu'il en face sun plaisir,
Kar se il en l'ost les retient,
12090 Cument que seit perdre les crient.
Dunc aparailla quis merra
E establi quis cunduira:
Chador e Borel e Richier
E Beduer le buteillier,
Quatre cuntes de bien halt lin,
Rova li reis lever matin,
Ki od les prisuns tant alassent
E tant lunges les cunveassent
Que li meneür seür feussent
12100 E la dute passé eüssent.
L'emperere par ses espies
Ot tost les noveles oïes
Que cil par matin muvereient
Ki les prisuns mener deveient.
Dis mil chevaliers fist munter,
Tute noit les rova errer
Tant que les prisuns devancissent,
S'il poeient sis rescusissent.
Sextorius, de Libe sire,
12110 E Evander, li reis de Sire,
E de Rome Caricius
E Catellus Walerteius,
Chascun de ces quatre ot grant terre
E chascun fud bien duit de guerre,
Cil furent eslit e sumuns
D'aler rescurre les presuns,
Chevetaine des altres furent.
Dis mil armez, le seir, s'esmurent;
Cil del païs les cundueient,
12120 Qui les dreites veies saveient.

Tute nuit unt tant chevalchié
E chevalchant tant espleitié,
El chemin de Paris entrerent,
Un lieu cuvenable troverent
A faire lur enbuschement;
Iloc s'esturent quietement. [1]
Es vus el mein la gent Arthur
Chevalchant alques aseür,
E nequedent agueit dutoent;
En dous cumpaignes chevalchoent.   12130
Chador e Borel od lur gent
Chevalchoent premierement,
Li quens Richier e Beduer,
Ki les prisuns durent garder,
Od cinc cenz armez les sieweient
E les prisuns mener feseient,
Les puinz detriés les dos lïez
E desuz les chevals les piez.
Es vus cels devant sur l'agueit
Que cil de Rome aveient fait,   12140
E Romein saillent tuz ensemble,
Tute la terre crolle e tremble!
Hardiement les envaïrent
E cil forment se defendirent.
Beduer e Richier oïrent
La grant tumulte, les cops virent;
Les prisuns firent arester
E en un lieu seür turner;
A lur escuiers les livrerent
E a garder lur cumanderent.   12150
Puis laissierent chevals aler,
E ne cesserent d'espuruner [2]
Des qu'il furent justé as lur;
Dunc se tindrent a grant vigur.
Romein ça e la vunt puignant,
Ne voldrent mie entendre tant
A descunfire les Bretuns
Cum a rescurre les prisuns.
E Bretun ensemble puineient
E ensemble se reteneient,   12160

---

[1] MS D reading—*quietement*—restored.   [2] MS D reading—*E*—restored.

The Romans ambush the Britons

it and took the advice to send them to Paris; they would be kept in prison until he could do what they wished with them, for if he kept them amongst his men, he feared he would lose them, come what may. So he equipped those who would take them and decided on those who would lead them. Cador, Borel, Richier and Bedoer the cupbearer, four counts of exalted lineage, were asked by the king to rise early and go with the prisoners, escorting them until those conducting them were safe and had crossed through the danger zone. Through his spies, the emperor soon heard the news that those due to escort the prisoners would leave early. He had ten thousand knights mount and asked them to journey all night, in order to get ahead of the prisoners and, if possible, rescue them. Sertorius, lord of Libya, Evander, king of Syria, and Caricius and Catellus Vulteïus from Rome— each of these four had large lands and was experienced in warfare. They were chosen and summoned to go and rescue the prisoners and to lead the rest. That evening ten thousand armed men set out. They were guided by the country folk, who knew the right paths. They rode so hard that night, and advanced so far in their ride, that they met the road to Paris and found a suitable spot to make their ambush. There they quietly remained.

12127   In the morning, there were Arthur's men, riding fairly confidently, and yet they feared a trap. They travelled in two bands. Cador and Borel, with their men, rode first and the counts Richier and Bedoer, who were in charge of the prisoners, followed them with five hundred men, escorting the prisoners, with their hands tied behind their backs and their feet tied under the horses. Then those in front came upon the ambush which the Romans had made, and all the Romans rushed out at once; the ground quite shook and shuddered! Boldly they attacked them, and the Britons strongly defended themselves. Bedoer and Richier heard the loud clamour and saw the blows. They had the prisoners seized and removed to a secure place; they handed them over to their squires and ordered them to guard them. Then they gave free rein to their horses, not sparing the spur until they reached their people, when they fought vigorously. Everywhere the Romans were rushing about, intent not so much on defeating the Britons as on rescuing the prisoners. And the Britons together spurred forward and together held back, advanced and retreated together and defended themselves together. And the Romans rushed up and down, seeking the prisoners here and there; they were so

Ensemble aloent e veneient
E ensemble se defendeient;
E Romein sus e jus cureient,
Ça e la les prisuns quereient;
As prisuns tant querre entendirent
Que de lur gent mult i perdirent.
Bretun par cunreiz se partirent
E quatre eschieles establirent:
Chador od les Cornualeis[1]
12170 E Beduer les Herupeis,
Richier ot des suens un conrei,
Borel rot ces del Maine od sei.[2]
Li reis Evander aparçut
Que lur force e lur gent descrut,
Ensemble les fist tuz restraindre,
Quant as prisuns ne pot ateindre,
Puis les fist ensemble tenir
E ordeneement ferir.
Dunc en orent Romeins le pris
12180 E as Bretuns en fu le pis;
Mult les greverent, mult en pristrent
E quatre des meillors ocistrent:
Er, le fiz Yder, i fud morz,
Uns chevaliers vaillanz e forz,
E Hyrelgas de Periron,
N'i aveit plus hardi nisun,
E Aliduc de Tyntaiol,
Dunt si parent orent grant dol,
E Mauric Chadorkeneneis,
12190 Ne sai s'esteit Bret u Gualeis.
Borel des Mans, uns gentilz cuens,[3]
Ki grant mestier aveit as suens,
Se cunteneit hardiement
E mult amonestot sa gent.
Mes desur lui puinst Evander,
De la lance li fist lu fer[4]
Parmi la gule trespasser,
Borel chaï, ne pot ester.
Bretun s'aloent esmaiant
12200 Que de lur gent perdeient tant;

Cuntre un d'els i ot set Romeins.
Jas voleient saisir as meins,
Mort u pris u descunfit fussent
E lur prisuns perdu eüssent,
Mes Guitard, li cuens de Peitiers,
Ki guardot cel jor les forriers,
Ot sempres la novele oïe
Que des Romeins une partie
Esteient as prisuns rescurre.
Cele part laissa chevals curre,   12210
Ovoc li trei mil chevaliers[5]
E li forier e li archiers.[6]
Romein a ferir entendeient,
Ki les Bretuns descunfiseient,
Quant Guitart vint od ses meisnees
Espurunant, lances beissees;
Plus de cent en deschevalchierent
Ki unques puis ne redrescierent.
Es vus Romeins tuz esbaïz
E tuz se tindrent pur huniz;   12220
Quidoent que Artur venist
E sa gent tute le siewist.
Quant tant virent des lur chaeir,
De guarisun n'orent espeir.
Cil de Peitou bien les asaillent
E li Bretun pas ne lur faillent;
Li un pur les altres s'avivent
E des Romeins abatre estrivent,
E Romein turnerent lur dos,[7]
Tuz descuverz e tut desclos;   12230
As herberges voldrent vertir,
Ne saveient aillors guarir.
Bretun les unt lunges chacié
E lur ocis unt bien vengié,
Bien les chacierent e ateinstrent,
Ki d'els abatre ne se feinstrent.
Reis Evander e Catellus
E des altres cinc cenz u plus
Furent ateint e abatu,
Esquanz morz, esquanz retenu;   12240

---

[1] MS D reading—*od*—restored.
[2] MS D reading—*rot*—restored; MS J adds four lines: *Pus vunt les Romains envair/ Hardiement les vunt ferir/ La veissiés Bretons combatre/ E les Romains a tere batre.*
[3] MS D reading—*des*—restored.
[4] MS D reading—*la*—restored.
[5] MS D reading—*chevaliers*—restored.
[6] MS D reading—*archiers*—restored.
[7] MS D reading—*lur*—restored.

The ambush is foiled by Guitart

intent on finding the prisoners that they lost many of their men. The British divided themselves into companies and established four sections: Cador had the Cornish and Bedoer the Herupeis,[1] Richier had a troop of his own men and Borel had with him the men from Maine.

12173 King Evander noticed that their own might and men were diminishing and, since they could not reach the prisoners, he made them all hold back; then he made them keep together and strike in military formation. Then the Romans came off best and it was the worse for the Britons: they were harried, many of them were captured and four of the best were slain. Er, Ider's son, died there, a strong and brave knight, Hyrelgas of Periron (no one was bolder than him), Aliduc of Tintagel (whose kin were much grieved) and Mauric from Cahors[2]—I do not know if he was Breton or Welsh. Borel of Le Mans, a noble count very useful to his men, acted boldly and greatly exhorted his troops. But towards him spurred Evander; he forced the iron of his lance through Borel's throat and he fell, not able to stand. Britons left the field in dismay at losing so many of their men; there were seven Romans for every one of theirs. Soon they would have been captured, killed, taken or destroyed, and would have lost their prisoners, but Guitart, count of Poitiers, who was that day in charge of the foragers, before long heard the news that a party of the Romans was about to rescue the prisoners. He charged in that direction, and with him three thousand knights, as well as the foragers and archers. The Romans were busy striking and discomfiting the Britons, when Guitart arrived, spurring, with his troops, their lances lowered. They unhorsed more than a hundred, who never got up again.

12219 The Romans were quite aghast and all thought they were done for. They thought Arthur had arrived, followed by his whole army. When they saw so many of theirs fall, they lost hope in escape. The Poitevins attacked them hard and the Britons were not far behind; both made every effort for each other and struggled to cut the Romans down. And the Romans turned to flee, exposing their uncovered, defenceless backs. They wanted to get back to camp, they knew no other place where they could escape. The Britons pursued them a long while and took ample vengeance for their dead; they chased and overtook them, not failing to cut them down. King Evander and Catellus, and five hundred or more of the rest, were hit and struck down, some killed, some captured. The Britons seized as many as they could and as many as they could take away; then they returned to the road where the battle had occurred. They looked for Borel, the good count of Le Mans, and their dead, among the fields. They found the count lying in a pool of

---

[1] This is the earliest mention of the Herupeis, (or Hurepoix), the inhabitants of La Hérupe, an ancient term designating Neustria (the land between the Seine, Marne and Loire). See Houck, *Sources,* pp. 197–200.

[2] See Tatlock pp. 105–6

Tant en pristrent cum prendre voldrent
E tant cum amener en porent,
Puis sunt el chemin returné
U la bataille aveit esté;
Borel, le bon cunte des Mans,[1]
E lur morz quistrent par les champs.
Le cunte troverent gisant
Ensanglanté, l'alme espirant.
Porter en firent les nafrez
12250 E les ocis unt enterrez.
A cels qui Arthur ot rové,
E si cum il ot cumandé,
Les premerains prisuns chargierent
E a Paris les enveerent.
Les altres pris novelement
Firent lier estreitement;
Al chastel od els les menerent,
A lur seignur les presenterent;
L'aventure e l'agueit li distrent
12260 E tuit ensemble li pramistrent,
S'il as Romeins se cumbateit,
Que senz dutance les veintreit.
     L'emperere sot l'aventure
E sot la grant descunfiture,
Sot d'Evander, ki ert ocis,
Sot des altres ki erent pris,
Vit sa gent forment esmaïe
E vit la guerre cumencie,
Vit que suvent li meschaeit
12270 E vit que rien ne cunquerreit;[2]
Mult fud hainus, mult s'esmaia,[3]
Pensa e pensa e duta;
En dutance fud qu'il fereit,
Si a Arthur se cumbatreit
U sun riere ban atendreit
Ki enprés lui venir deveit.
La bataille forment dutot
Pur ço que rien n'i guaainot.
Cunseil prist qu'a Hostum irra
12280 E par Lengres trespassera;

Sa gent fist sumundre e muveir;
A Lengres vindrent de halt seir,
En la cité se herbergierent
E es valees s' alogierent.[4]
Lengres seeit al chief d'un munt
E les valees entur sunt.
     Arthur sot tost qu'il voldrent faire
E quel part il deveient traire;[5]
Bien sot que pas ne cumbatreit
Dessi que greinur gent avreit;   12290
Nes volt pas laissier sujorner
Ne prés de lui aseürer;
A quanqu'il pot, celeement,
Fist sumundre e mander sa gent.
Lengres ad laissié a senestre,
E ultre s'en passa a destre;[6]
L'empereür volt devancir
E la veie d'Hostum tolir.
Tute noit ad, dissi el mein,
Erré od s'ost que bois, que plein,   12300
Tant qu'il vint en une valee
Que Soeïse ert apelee;[7]
Par icele valee passot[8]
Ki d'Ostum a Lengres alot.
Ses humes fist Arthur armer
E ses cumpaignes ordener,
Quel ure que Romein venissent
Que prestement les recuilissent.
Herneis e tute la frapaille
Que nul ués n'orent en bataille   12310
Fist dejuste un munt arester
E cumpaigne d'armez sembler,
Que cil de Rome, s'il les veient,
De la multitudine s'esfreient.
Sis mil, sis cenz, seisante e sis
En une eschiele, tuz de pris,
Mist en un bois, desus un tertre,
Ne sai a destre u a senestre.
Moruid, li cuens de Gloëcestre,
Dut chevetaine de cele estre.   12320

---

[1] MS D reading—*des*—restored.
[2] MS D reading—*cunquerreit*—restored.
[3] MS D reading—*mult fud hainus*—restored.
[4] MS D reading—*s'alogierent*—restored.
[5] MS D reading—*deveient*—restored.
[6] MS D reading—*E ultre s'en passa*—restored.
[7] MS K: *Suïson*.
[8] MS D reading—*icele*—restored.

Lucius moves to Langres

blood, breathing his last. They had the wounded borne away and buried the slain. To those of whom Arthur had requested it, and as he had ordered, they entrusted the first lot of prisoners and sent them to Paris. The rest, recently taken, they had tightly bound. They led them to the castle with them and presented them to their lord, telling him of the events and the ambush, and they all together promised him that if he fought the Romans, he would, without doubt, defeat them.

12263   The emperor learnt what had happened and learnt of the great defeat, learnt that Evander had been killed and the others had been taken. He saw that his men were in great dismay and battle had started; he saw that matters kept going wrong for him and he saw he would acquire nothing. He was filled with hatred and dismay, he thought and thought and was full of doubts. He was in doubt as to what he should do, whether to fight Arthur or await the rest of his vassals, who were to follow after him. The battle gave him much cause for fear because it would profit him nothing. He decided to go to Autun by way of Langres. He summoned his men and set them on the move; they arrived in Langres late in the evening, encamped in the city and lodged in the valleys. Langres lies on top of a hill and valleys surround it.[1]

12287   Arthur soon learnt what they wanted to do and which way they were to take. He knew very well the emperor would not fight until he had more men, and he did not want to let them rest or get close enough to protect him. As far as he could, he secretly had his men summoned and sent for. He by-passed Langres, on his left, and went beyond it, bearing right: he wanted to get ahead of the emperor and block the road to Autun. All night until morning came, he travelled with his army, through wood or plain, until he came to a valley called Soeïse.[2] Everyone going from Autun to Langres had to pass through this valley.

12305   Arthur had his men armed and his troops drawn up, so that, whatever time the Romans came, they could readily receive them. He had the equipment and the camp-followers, who were no use in a battle, stationed beside a hill, in the guise of an armed band, so that if the Romans saw them, they would be terrified of the great numbers. He put six thousand, six hundred and sixty-six men,[3] all excellent, in a troop in a wood above a hill, whether on the right or the left I do not know. Morvid,[4] count of Gloucester, was to be leader of this group. To them, the

---

[1]   Wace adds this correct description of Langres.

[2]   *HRB* chap. 168: *Sessia*; *VV*: *Siesia*. Different localities have been proposed: see Arnold and Pelan, *Partie Arthurienne*, p. 118, for the valley of the Suize, a tributary of the Marne, Tatlock pp. 102–3, and Thorpe, *Geoffrey of Monmouth: History*, p. 247, fn. 1, for Saussy. On Val-Suzon as a likely candidate, see Matthews, 'Where was Siesia-Sessoyne?' and Keller, 'Two Toponymical

Problems'.

[3]   Numbers vary. In *HRB* chap. 168 there are 5,555; in MSS CSB 10,700; in MS G 10,656. But see l. 12349.

[4]   In *VV* chap. 168: *Hoel*; no name given in *HRB*'s Berne MS (the Vulgate) but '*Morvid*' supplied by Wright. On the inconsistency of the *VV* modification, see Wright II, p. lxxii.

A cels dist li reis: ' Ci estez!
Pur nule rien ne vus movez.
Si mestiers est, ça turnerai
E les altres par vus tendrai,
E si Romein, par aventure,
Turneient a descunfiture,
Puigniez aprés sis ateigniez,
Ociez les, nes esparniez!'
E cil distrent: ' Bien le ferum.'
12330   Dunc prist une altre legiun
Des nobles humes, des vassals,
Healmes laciez, sur lur chevals,
Cels mist en un lieu veable, [1]
N'i ot fors lui nul cunestable.
La fud sa meisnie privee
Qu'il ot nurrie e alevee.
En mi fist tenir sun dragun
Que il portot pur gumfanun;
[Des altres tuz fist uit cumpaignes,
12340   En chascune ot dous chevetaines;] [2]
A cheval fud l'une meitié
E li altre furent a pié.
A ces ensemble cumanda
E ço lur dist e lur pria
Que cil qui a cheval serreient,
Quant cil a pié se cumbatreient,
De travers les Romeins ferissent
E de travers les envaïssent.
Cinc mil, cinc cenz, cinquante cinc
12350   Chevaliers tuz pris en esling [3]
Ot chascune eschiele numbrez,
De tutes armes tuz armez.
En quatre furent establies,
Les cumpaignes en oit parties,
Quatre deriere, quatre devant; [4]
En mi fud l'autre gent mult grant,
Chascun armé en sa maniere.
Le frunt de l'eschiele premiere
Ot Auguissel d'Escoce en baille,
12360   L'autre Chador de Cornuaille;

L'autre cumpaigne ot Bos en mein
E li cuens Gerin de Chartein;
La tierce eschiele fud livree,
Bien cunree e bien armee,
A Aschil, lu rei des Daneys,
E a Loth, lu rei des Noreis; [5]
La quarte prist Hoel en guarde,
Walwein od lui, ki ne cuarde.
Emprés ces quatre ot altres quatre
Raparaillies a cumbatre: 12370
De l'une fud Key justisiers
E Beduer li buteilliers;
Beduer ot les Estrueis,
Key Angevins e Chinoneis.
Al cunte de Flandres Holdin
E a Guitard le Peitevin
Fud l'autre eschiele cumandee,
E il l'unt volentiers guiee.
Quens Yugeïn de Leïrcestre
E Jonathas de Dorecestre   12380
La setme eschiele reçurent, [6]
Seignur e cunestable furent. [7]
Li cuens de Cestre Corsalen
E de Bade li cuens Urgen
Orent l'uitme eschiele en baillie
E Arthur en els mult se fie.
Les bons servanz, les bons archiers
E les vaillanz arbelastiers
Mist de dous parz defors la presse
Pur traire bien a la traverse;   12390
Tuit cil furent devant lu rei,
Il fud detriés od sun cunrei.
Quant Arthur ot fait ses parties
E ses eschieles establies,
Oiez qu'il dist a ses nurriz,
A ses baruns e a lur fiz:
'Barun, dist il, mult me cunfort
Quant jo voz granz buntez recort,
Voz granz vertuz, voz granz cunquez;
Tut tens vus trois hardiz e prez.   12400

---

[1] MS D reading—*lieu veable*—restored.
[2] MSS DL omit ll. 12339–40; this couplet is supplied by Arnold.
[3] MS J: *a eslis*. See Arnold and Pelan, *Partie Arthurienne*, fn. to p. 135.
[4] MS D reading—*deriere*—restored.
[5] MS J: *d'Arcanois*; MS R: *Orcaneis*.
[6] MS D reading—*eschiele*—restored.
[7] MS D reading of line restored.

Arthur arranges his troops

king said: 'Stay here! Whatever happens, don't move. If need be, I shall move here and direct the others your way, and if the Romans by any chance withdraw in defeat, spur after them and catch them up. Kill them, don't spare them!' And they replied: 'We'll do it.'

12330 Then he took another legion of noble men, vassals, mounted and with helmets laced on, and put them in a more visible spot. They had no commander but him: this was his own retinue, whom he had raised and nurtured. In the midst he had his dragon held aloft, his own personal banner. From all the others he made eight companies, with two commanders in each; half the companies were on horseback, half on foot. He gave commands to all these together, praying and asking that when the infantry was fighting, the mounted men should strike and attack the Romans from the side. Each division numbered five thousand, five hundred and fifty-five knights, all chosen from the best[1] and all armed from top to toe. The eight companies were drawn up in groups of four, four in front and four at the rear, and in the middle were great numbers of other men, each armed in his fashion.

12358 Angusel of Scotland was in charge of the front of the first division and Cador of Cornwall of the rest. The second company was controlled by Bos and count Gerin of Chartres; the third, well armed and equipped, was given to Aschil, the Danish king, and Loth, the Norwegian one. Hoel took command of the fourth and Walwein (no coward he) with him. After these four were four more, ready for combat. Kei and Bedoer the cup-bearer controlled one; Bedoer had the Herupeis and Kei the Angevins and those from Chinon. Another division was commanded by Holdin, count of Flanders and Guitart the Poitevin, who willingly led it. Count Jugein of Leicester and Jonathas of Dorchester received the seventh company and were its lords and commanders. Cursal, the count of Chester, and count Urgen of Bath had charge of the eighth division and Arthur had great trust in them. He put good servants, fine archers and brave crossbowmen outside the throng, on either side, to be able to shoot well from the flank. All these were in front of the king and he was behind with his own company.

12393 When Arthur had divided them and drawn up his companies, hear what he said to his retainers, his barons and their sons. 'My lords,' he said, 'I am much cheered when I remember your many virtues, your great might, your many conquests. I've always found you ready and bold. Your prowess keeps increasing, keeps grow-

---

[1] For this obscure phrase—l. 12350—I have adopted Arnold and Pelan's interpretation *(Partie Arthurienne,* p. 135).

Vostre prueise tut tens creist,
Tut tens avive, ki k'en peist.
Quant jo record e jo purpens
Que Bretaigne est en vostre tens
Par vus e par voz cumpaignuns
Dame de trente regiuns,
Mult sui liez, mult me glorifi,
E en Deu e en vus me fi
Que vus encor plus cunquerez [1]
12410 E plus prendrez e plus avrez.
Voz prüesces, voz bones meins
Ont dous feiz vencu les Romeins;
Saciez que mis cuers me devine
E tute rien le me destine
Que vus encor hui les ventreiz,
Sis avrez dunc vencu treis feiz.
Vus avez vencu les Norreis,
Vus avez vencu les Daneys,
Vus avez vencu les Franceis
12420 E France tenez en lur peis. [2]
Bien devez veintre les peiurs
Quant vencu avez les meillors.
Tributaires vus voldrunt faire [3]
E treü voldrent de nus traire
E France voldrent recuvrer; [4]
Tel gent quiderent ici trover [5]
Cum il ameinent d'orient;
Mais un de nus valt de ces cent.
Nes alez vus neent dutant,
12430 Kar femmes valent altretant.
Bien nus devum en Deu fier;
Ne devum pas desesperer,
Od un petit de hardement,
Que nus veintrum legierement.
Ja pur hume ne me faldrez
Ne ja pur hume ne fuierez; [6]
Bien savrai que chascun fera
E bien verrai ki mielz ferra;
Par tut irrai e tut verrai
12440 E a chascun busuin serrai.'

Quant la parole fud finee
Que li reis out dite e mustree,
A une voiz li respundirent
Tuit ensemble cil ki l'oïrent
Que mielz vuelent iloc murir
Que del champ senz victorie issir.
Mult les oïssiez aramir,
Serremenz faire e feiz plevir
Que pur murir ne li faldrunt,
Tel fin cum il fera ferunt.   12450
    Lucius fud d'Espaine nez,
Des Romeins bien enparentez;
Anz aveit de bone juvente
Meins de quarante e plus de trente;
Hardiz ert e de grant curage,
Fait aveit ja maint vasselage;
Pur sa force e pur sa valur
L'aveit l'um fait empereür.
De Lemgres par matin turna,
A Hostum dreit aler quida;   12460
Meüe esteit sa grant gent tute,
Mult esteit large e grant la rute.
Quant il oï e sot l'agueit
Que Arthur ot devant lui fait,
Vit que cumbatre li estuveit [7]
U ariere returnereit;
Returner ne deignot il mie,
Kar ço semblereit cuardie
E si enemi l'ateindreient
E grant damage li fereient,   12470
Kar cumbatre ensemble e fuïr
Ne puet l'um mie bien furnir.
Ses reis, ses princes e ses ducs,
Dunt bien i ot dous cenz u plus,
E cels qui erent del sené,
Manda, si ad a els parlé.
'Pere, dist il, gentil seignur,
Bon vassal, bon cunquereür,
Fiz fustes as bons anceisurs
Ki cunquistrent les granz enurs. 12480

---

[1] MS D reading—*cunquerez*—restored.
[2] MS D reading of line restored.
[3] MS D reading—*voldrunt*—restored.
[4] MS D readings—*voldrent*—restored in ll.
   12424–25.
[5] MS D reading—*quiderent*—restored.
[6] MS D reading—*fuierez*—restored.
[7] MS D reading—*li*—restored.

Arthur and Lucius address their troops

ing, regardless of whom it offends. When I remember and reflect that Britain is, in your time and through you and your companions, mistress of thirty realms, I am overjoyed, I glory in it, and I trust in God and in you to conquer yet more, seize and have yet more. Your exploits, your own mighty hands, have twice defeated the Romans. You must know that my heart tells me, and everything ordains it, that today you will defeat them again, and then you will have beaten them thrice. You have beaten the Norwegians, the Danes and the French and you hold France against their will. You should certainly be able to defeat the worst when you have defeated the best. They will want to make you tributaries and extract tribute from us, and they will want to recover France. They will expect to find here the sort of men they are bringing from the East, but one of us is worth a hundred of theirs. Don't be afraid of them, for women are worth as much. We must trust in God and not lose the hope that, with a little daring, we shall easily defeat them. Never fail me for anyone and never flee for anyone: I shall certainly know what everyone is doing and certainly see who does best. I shall go everywhere and see everything and be at every fight.' When the words which the king had said and expounded were finished, all those who heard him replied together with one accord that they would rather die there than leave the field without victory. You could hear them mustering, swearing oaths and making pledges that on pain of death they would not fail him, but make the same end as he did.

12451 Lucius was born in Spain, of good Roman stock. He was still youthful, less than forty but more than thirty, bold and courageous. He had already done many brave deeds : on account of his strength and valour he had been made emperor. In the morning he left Langres, thinking to go straight to Autun. The whole of his great army was on the move; the road was large and wide. When he heard and learnt of the trap which Arthur had set in front of him, he saw he would either have to fight or retreat. He did not deign to retreat, because it seemed cowardly and his enemies would overtake him and do him great harm, for to fight and fly at the same time is hard to accomplish. He summoned his kings, his princes, his dukes (of whom there were two hundred or more) and senators, and spoke to them.

12477 'Peers, noble lords,' he said, 'good and victorious vassals, you are the descendants of worthy ancestors who conquered large domains. It is through them that Rome

Par els est Rome chief del mund
E ert, tant cum Romein vivrunt.
Cil cunquistrent le grant empire;
Hunte est s'en nostre tens empire.
Gentil furent e vus gentil,
De vaillant peres vaillant fil. [1]
Chascun de vus ot vaillant pere,
E lur valur oi en vus pere.
Chascun s'en deit forment pener [2]
12490 De sun bon pere resembler;
Hunte puet aveir kil desert [3]
Ki l'erité sun pere pert [4]
E ki par malveistié guerpist
Ço que sis peres li cunquist.
Jo ne di mie, ço saciez,
Que jo vus tienge a empeiriez;
Pruz furent, e vus estez pruz,
E jo vus tieng a vaillanz tuz.
Seignurs, jo vei e vus veez,
12500 Jol sai e vus bien le savez [5]
Que la veie nus est toleite
Ki a Hostum alot plus dreite.
Aler ne passer n'i poüm
Si par bataille n'i passum.
Ne sai quel robeür novel,
U robeür u laruncel,
Nus unt devant close la veie
Par unt jo mener vus deveie.
Il quidoent que jo fuïsse
12510 E que la terre lur guerpisse,
Mes jo m'aloe tresturnant
Pur els faire venir avant.
Or se sunt enbatu sur nus.
Prenez voz armes, armez vus!
S'il nus atendent sis ferrum
E sil s'en fuient sis siewum.
Metum frein a lur engresté
Si destruium lur poësté!'
    Dunc saillirent as armes prendre,
12520 Ne voldrent mie plus atendre.

Lur bataille unt aparaillie,
Lur cunreiz faiz, lur genz rengie; [6]
Mult i ot reis e ducs paiens
Entremedlé as cristïens,
Ki de Rome lur fieus teneient
E pur lur fieus Romeins serveient.
Par trenteines, par quarenteines,
Par seisanteines, par centeines,
Par legiuns e par milliers
Departirent lur chevaliers,   12530
Maint a pié e maint a cheval,
Les uns el munt, les uns el val;
Puis sunt, tuit rengié e serré,
Cuntre la gent Arthur alé;
De l'une part de la valee
Entre la gent romeine armee, [7]
De l'altre part, enmi lur vis,
Orent Bretun lu champ purpris.
Dunc oïssiez grant corneïz
E de greilles grant suneïz;   12540
Serreement, süef passant,
S'entrevindrent entr'aprismant;
Mult veïssiez, a l'aprismier,
Saetes traire e darz lancier;
N'i poeit hum sun oil ovrir
Ne sun viaire descuvrir.
Saetes volent cume gresle,
Trestut en trubble l'air e medle.
Dunc vindrent as lances briser.
E as escuz fraindre e percier;   12550
Les hanstes dunoent grant cruis,
Bien halt en voloent li truis.
Enprés vindrent al capleïz
E as granz cops des branz furbiz.
Dunc i ot estur merveillus,
Unques ne vi plus perillus
Ne plus medlé ne plus espés;
Ki ferir volt, tost en ot mes.
Fols n'ebaïs n'i ot mestier, [8]
Cuard ne s'i sot cunseillier.   12560

---

[1] MS D reading—*peres*—restored.
[2] MS D reading—*s'en*—restored.
[3] MS D reading—*kil*—restored.
[4] MS D reading—*ki*—restored.

[5] MS D reading—*Jol*—restored.
[6] MS D reading—*genz*—restored.
[7] MS D reading—*entre*—restored.
[8] MS D reading—*ebais*—restored.

The armies meet

leads the world and shall do, as long as Romans are alive. They conquered our great empire; it's shameful if, in our lifetime, it declines. They were noble, and so are you, valiant sons of valiant fathers. Each of you had a valiant father, and their valour appears in you today. Each of you must strive to resemble his excellent father; shame on him who deserts, who loses his father's inheritance and who abandons through wickedness what his father conquered for him. I am not saying, you know, that I consider you've gone downhill: you were brave, and you are brave, and I consider you all valiant. My lords, I see and you see, I know and you certainly know, that our way, which ran straight to Autun, is blocked. We cannot travel along it unless we fight our way through. I don't know which recent robber, which robber or bandit, has closed to us the way ahead by which I was to take you. They thought I would flee and leave the land to them, but I have turned around to lure them out in front. Now they have attacked us. To arms, seize your weapons! If they await us, we will strike them and if they flee, we will pursue them. Let us curb their violence and destroy their power!'

12519 Then they leapt to take up their weapons, unwilling to wait any longer. They prepared their army, took their measures and set their men in ranks. There were many pagan kings and dukes mingled with the Christians, who held their fiefs from Rome and for those fiefs were subject to the Romans. By thirties and forties, by sixties and hundreds, by legions and thousands they divided up their knights, many on foot, many on horseback, some on the hill, others in the valley. Then, all in serried ranks, they advanced against Arthur's men.[1] The Roman army entered the valley at one end; at the other end, in front of them, the Britons had taken possession of the field. Then a great blowing of horns and bugles could be heard. With resolution and calmness they approached and came together, and at this approach many arrows were shot and spears thrown; no one could open his eyes or uncover his face. Arrows flew like hail; the air grew quite dark and murky with them. Then they set to breaking lances and shattering and piercing shields; there was great cracking of lances and their stumps flew high in the sky. Next they came to sword-play and huge strokes with shining blades. Then the fray was extraordinary, you never saw a more dangerous one, nor more thick and confused. Anyone keen to strike there had ample opportunity. Those who were stupid or aghast served no purpose; cowards were at a loss. The great crowd and press prevented one man from hitting another. The battlefield could

---

[1] *HRB* chap. 170 has a detailed account of the arrangement of the Roman forces under various named commanders; the *VV* omits it all, as does Wace, though he takes care to mention Lucius' pagan allies.

L'un a ferir l'autre desturbe
La grant espesse e la grant turbe.
Mult veïssiez le champ fremir,
L'une eschiele l'autre envaïr,
L'un cunrei a l'altre hurter,
Les uns ferir, les uns buter,
Les uns venir, les uns turner,
Les uns chaeir, les uns ester,
Hanstes brisier, retrois voler,
12570 Traire espees, escuz lever,
Les forz les fiebles craventer,
Les vifs les muranz defuler;
Rumpre cengles, rumpre peitrels, [1]
Seles voidier, fuïr chevals.
Lungement s'entrecumbatirent
E lungement s'entreferirent
Que cil de Rome ne ruserent
Ne sur Bretuns ne recuvrerent.
N'iert mie legier a saveir
12580 Ki deveit la victorie aveir,
Dessi que l'eschiele aprisma
Que Beduer od Key mena.
Cil virent que poi cunquereient
E que Romein bien se teneient;
Par ire e par dreit maltalent,
Od lur cumpaigne estreitement,
Entre les Romeins s'enbatirent
La u la greinur presse virent.
Bien fiert Beduer, bien fiert Key:
12590 Deus! quels baruns en curt a rei,
Quel seneschal, quel buteillier!
Tant servent bien des branz d'acier.
Quels dous vassals, s'alques vesquissent!
Mult orent fait e plus feïssent.
Mult vunt la presse derumpant
E mult en vunt agraventant.
Lur grant cumpaigne vient aprés,
Ki mult s'argue, e fiert adés;
Maint cop i ot pris e duné,
12600 Maint hume ocis e maint nafré.

Beduer s'enbat en la presse,
Ki ne repose ne ne cesse.
De l'altre part Key ne refine;
Maint en abat, maint en suvine.
Si alques tost se retenissent
E a lur gent se restreinsissent
Tant que Bretun les parsiewissent
E li altre cunrei venissent,
Grant pris e grant pru i eüssent
E de murir guaris se fussent;   12610
Mes il furent trop talentif
E de ferir avant braidif;
En lur granz buntez se fioent
E es granz genz que il menoent;
Ne se sorent mie esparnier,
La bataille voldrent percier. [2]
Mes une eschiele unt encuntree
Que li reis de Mede ot menee;
Boccus ot nun, paens esteit,
Mult esteit pruz, grant gent aveit.   12620
Li cunte sunt a cels medlé,
N'unt mie lur grant gent duté.
Ço fud bataille bien ferue
E medlee bien maintenue
Entre paens e Sarazins
E Estrueis e Angevins.
Li reis Boccus un glayve tint;
Mal ait sis cors quant il i vint!
Les dous cuntes ad descunfiz:
Beduer halt feri el piz; [3]   12630
De la lance parmi le cors
Li fist passer le fer tut fors.
Beduer chiet, li cuers li part,
L'alme s'en vait, Jesus la guart.
Key ad trové Beduer mort;
En talent ad que il l'en port,
Mult l'aveit chier e mult l'amot.
Od tant de gent cum il menot [4]
Fist ces de Mede departir
E la place lur fist guerpir.   12640

---

[1] MS D reading—*peitrels*—restored.
[2] MS D's order of ll. 12613–16 restored.
[3] MS D reading—*Beduer halt*—restored.
[4] MS D reading—*cum il menot*—restored.

Boccus kills Bedoer

be seen in tumult, one division attacking another, one company colliding with another, some striking, some shoving, some advancing, some withdrawing, some falling, some standing, with lances broken, splinters flying, swords drawn, shields raised, with the strong overthrowing the weak and the living trampling on the dying, with saddle-girths broken, breastplates smashed, saddles emptied and horses in flight.

12575   For a long time they fought, for a long time they struggled, because the Romans did not withdraw nor did they gain ground over the Britons. It was not easy to know who should have the victory, until the division approached which was led by Bedoer and Kei. They saw they were gaining little and the Romans were holding fast. In anger and pure fury they straightaway rushed with their company upon the Romans, into where they saw the fray was thickest. Bedoer struck hard, Kei struck hard: Lord! what fighters the king had at court! what a seneschal, what a cup-bearer! They performed such service with their steel blades. What a pair of fighters, had they lived a while! They had done much and would have done more. They went smashing through the press, laying many men low. Their large band followed them, pressing forward and knocking down; they took and gave many a blow, slew and wounded many a man. Bedoer rushed into the fray, without respite or rest. Kei, for his part, never stopped; he knocked down many, he laid many flat. If they had beaten a retreat somewhat, and given ground, with their men, until the British could follow them up and the other troops come, they would have gained great renown and great advantage and they would have been protected from death. But they were too hot-headed and eager to keep striking forward; they trusted in their great valour and in the numerous men they led, and they had no thought of sparing themselves but wished to penetrate the fray.

12617   But they encountered a division led by the king of Media; he was called Boccus and was a pagan, a very brave man, with many troops. The counts joined battle with them, not in the least afraid of their great numbers. It was a well-fought battle and well-sustained conflict, between heathens and Saracens and Herupeis and Angevins. King Boccus held a sword—a curse on his coming! He slashed at the two counts and struck Bedoer high in the chest. With his lance he pierced him right through the body. Bedoer fell, his heart broke asunder and his soul left him: Christ protect him! Kei found Bedoer dead. He wanted to bear him away: he had greatly loved and cherished him. With as many men as he had, he made those from Media withdraw and abandon the spot. But, during the wait and de-

Mes, al targier e a l'atendre
Qu'il fist al cors Beduer prendre,
S'est li reis de Libie apresmez,
Sertor ot nun, mult fud preisiez,
Grant turbe aveit de gent paene
Qu'il aveit de sa gent demeine. [1]
Cil unt Key nafré mortelment
E mult unt ocis de sa gent, [2]
Mult l'unt nafré, mult l'unt feru,
12650 Mes il ad bien lu cors tenu.
De ses humes le remanant
L'aloent entur defendant;
Porté l'unt a l'orin dragun
Volsissent cil de Rome u nun.
   Hyerelgas fud niés Beduer,
Ki mult soleit sun uncle amer;
De ses amis, de ses parenz,
Prist cil tant qu'il en ot treis cenz
Od healmes, od halbercs, od branz,
12660 Sur bons chevals forz e curanz.
Cels asembla en un cunrei,
Puis lur ad dit: ' Venez od mei,
La mort mun uncle voil vengier.'
Dunc prist Romeins a aprismier;
Le rei de Mede ad espié,
Al gumfanun l'ad entercié.
Sur cel cunrei ala ferant,
L'enseigne Arthur suvent criant
Cum hume ki est forsenez,
12670 Ki ne puet estre amesurez;
Ne crient huem ne rien qu'il troisse [3]
Mes que sun uncle vengier puisse.
Si cumpaignun od lui s'esleissent,
Les escuz pris, les lances beissent;
Mult en ocïent, mult enversent, [4]
Par desus les chaeiz traversent;
En l'eschiele al rei se sunt mis
Qui Beduer aveit ocis.
Od la vertu des bons chevals
12680 E od l'aïr des bons vassals,

Destre e senestre vunt turnant
E Hyrelgas les vait menant.
Des qu'al gumfanun ne cesserent
U il lu rei Boccus troverent.
Hyrelgas l'ot bien avisé,
Sun cheval ad vers lui turné,
Parmi la presse avant s'enpeinst,
En sum lu chief Boccus ateinst;
Forz fud li bers, li cops fud granz
E li branz fud durs e trenchanz.   12690
Li healmes fendi e quaissa, [5]
La coiffe del halberc falsa;
Gesqu'as espalles le trencha,
Li cuers creva, l'alme en ala
E Hyrelgas les braz tendi, [6]
Lu cors retint qu'il ne chaï,
[Devant sei le traist en travers,
Sur sun cheval le tint envers,] [7]
Devant sei en travers lu traist,
Unc cil ne cria ne se braist.   12700
Li chevaliers fud aïrus
E li chevals fud vigurus;
Entre sa gent se traist ariere
Que paien ne Romein nel fiere.
La presse depart e derumpt,
Si cumpaignun veie li funt.
Juste sun uncle l'ad porté,
Tut l'ad par pieces decolpé
Puis ad dit a ses cumpaignuns:
'Venez, dist il, fiz a baruns!   12710
Alum ocire ces Romeins,
Ces palteniers, fiz a puteins;
La gent ki en Deu n'ad creance
Ne ki en Deu nen ad fiance
Unt amené en cest païs
Pur nus ocire noz amis; [8]
Alum ocire les paens [9]
E ensement les cristïens
Ki as paens se sunt justé
Pur destruire cristïenté.   12720

---

[1] MS D reading—*aveit de sa gent*—restored.
[2] MS D's order of line restored.
[3] MS D reading—*huem*—restored.
[4] MS D reading—*mult enversent*—restored.
[5] MS D reading—*quaissa*—restored.

[6] MS D reading—*les*—restored.
[7] MSS DLSRPN omit ll. 12697–98; this couplet is supplied by Arnold.
[8] MS D reading—*e* omitted—restored.
[9] MS D reading—*ocire*—restored.

Hyrelgas avenges Bedoer

lay it took to rescue Bedoer's body, the king of Libya approached. He was called Sertorius and was much renowned; he had a great crowd of heathen men from amongst his own people. These mortally wounded Kei and killed many of his men. They gave him many wounds, they struck him many blows, but he held on to the body. The rest of his men rallied round to defend it and carried it to the golden dragon, whether the Romans wished it or not.

12655 Bedoer's nephew was Hyrelgas,[1] who had greatly loved his uncle. He took so many of his friends and relations that he had three hundred, with helmets, hauberks and swords, mounted on good, strong and swift horses. He gathered them into a troop and then said to them: 'Come with me: I'm going to avenge my uncle's death.' Then he began to draw near the Romans. He saw the king of Media and recognized him from his banner. At this company he launched himself, continually shouting Arthur's war-cry, like a madman who cannot be restrained. He did not fear anyone or anything which he found, provided that he could avenge his uncle. His companions rushed forward with him, grabbing their shields and lowering their lances. They killed and laid low many and pressed forward over the fallen, reaching the division of the king who had slain Bedoer. Combining the power of good horses with the impetuosity of good vassals, they wheeled right and left, led by Hyrelgas. They never stopped till they reached the banner and king Boccus. Hyrelgas took a good look at him and turned his horse in his direction, rushing ahead out of the throng, and he hit Boccus on top of his head. The knight was strong, his blow was mighty and the blade hard and sharp. It split and broke the helmet and rent the hauberk coif asunder, cleaving him down to the shoulders. His heart burst, his soul fled, and Hyrelgas stretched out his arm to grasp the body before it fell. He pulled it in front of him, across his horse, and held it face up; he pulled it across and before him, and it uttered never a cry or a howl.

12701 The knight was impetuous and the horse powerful; he made his way back to his men unhurt by pagan or Roman. He broke and smashed through the fray and his companions made way for him. He set Boccus' body down next to his uncle and hewed it all into pieces. Then he said to his friends: 'Come on, you barons' sons! Let's go and kill these Romans, these bastards and sons of whores. They have brought into this land people with no faith or trust in God, to kill us and our friends. Let's go and kill the heathen, and the Christians likewise, who have united with the heathen to destroy Christianity. Come and test your strength!'

---

[1] As distinct from Hyrelgas of Peiron, para. 12173.

Venez asaier voz vertuz!'
   Es les vus el champ revenuz;
Dunc oïssiez noises e criz
E veïssiez grant capleïz
Healmes e branz estenceler
E des aciers le fu voler.
[Li bons ducs de Peitiers Guitart
N'alot mie cume cuart;
Endreit sei bien le champ maintint.
12730 Cuntre lu rei d'Alfrike vint;
Li uns l'altre forment feri,
Mes li reis d'Alfrike chaï
E li cuens s'en passa avant,
Alfricans e Mors ociant.] [1]
Holdin, qui ert duc des Flamens,
Ki teneit Bruges e teneit Lens, [2]
Turna encuntre la cumpaigne
Alifatin, un rei d'Espaine.
Tant se sunt entrecumbatu
12740 E tant se sunt entreferu
Que ocis fud Alifatin
E ocis fud li cuens Holdin.
Lygier, ki ert cuens de Buluine,
Justa al rei de Babiloine;
Ne sai dire ki mielz feri,
Mes chascun d'els l'autre abati,
Morz fud li cuens, morz fu li reis.
Altres cuntes i ot morz treis,
Balluc e Cursal e Urgent;
12750 Chascun des treis meneit grant gent.
Urgent esteit de Bade sire
E Balluc cuens de Wiltesire;
Cursal de Cestre cuens esteit,
A ces de Guales marchiseit.
Cist furent ocis en poi d'ure,
D'ambes parz se cureient surre. [3]
Les genz que cil mener deveient
E ki lur gumfanuns sieweient,
Vindrent a l'eschiele ruisant [4]
12760 Que Walwein alot cunduiant

E Hoel od lui, sis cumpainz,
Tel dui vassal ne furent ainz.
Unkes el siecle trespassé
N'orent tels dous baruns esté
De bunté ne de curteisie.
Ne de pris de chevalerie.
Cil de Bretaine la menur
Siewent Hoel lur seignur [5]
La lur cumpaigne esteit tant fiere
E hardie de tel maniere 12770
Presse ne turbe ne dutoent;
Par tut aloent, par tut perçoent, [6]
Cels ki ainz lur humes chaçoent
E a turbes les graventoent
Firent sempres les dos turner
E maint enfirent devïer. [7]
Od les granz cops que il dunoent
E od la gent que il menoent
Vindrent dissi al gumfanun
Ki portot l'egle d'or en sum. 12780
La troverent l'empereür
E de sun barnage la flur,
Od lui erent li gentil hume
E li bon chevalier de Rome.
La veïssiez estur mortel;
Unc ne veïstes, ço quit, tel.
Kymar, ki ert cuens de Triguel,
Ert en la cumpaigne Hoel;
Mult esteit de grant vasselage,
Des Romeins feseit grant damage. 12790
Mes un Romein ki ert a pié
Le rua mort od un espié. [8]
Od lui ot mort dous mil Bretuns,
Estre treis nobles cumpaignuns:
L'un de ces treis ot nun Jaguez,
De Bodloan esteit venuz,
Li secunz fud Richomarus
E li tierz fud Boclovius.
N'en ot mie en l'eschiele sis
De lur valur ne de lur pris. 12800

---

[1] MSS DLSHBPNT omit ll. 12727–34; present
  in MSS CJKGR and Hague.
[2] MS D reading—*Bruges*—restored.
[3] MS D reading—*cureient*—restored.
[4] MS D reading—*ruisant*—restored.

[5] MS D reading—*siewent*—restored.
[6] MS D reading—*par tut perçoent*—restored.
[7] MS D reading—*devier*—restored.
[8] MS D reading—*un*—restored.

The Britons reach the Roman standard

12722 Whereupon they returned to the field. Then you might have heard brawls and shouts, and seen heavy fighting, helmets and swords glittering, and sparks flying from the steel. Guitart, the good duke of Poitiers, did not behave like a coward, but kept up the fight around him. He came up to the king of Africa; each gave the other hard blows, but the king of Africa fell, and the count pressed forward, killing Africans and Moors.[1] Holdin, the Flemings' duke, who held Bruges and Lens, wheeled to attack the division of Aliphatima, a Spanish king. They attacked and hit each other so much that Aliphatima was killed and so was count Holdin. Ligier, count of Boulogne, fought the king of Babylon; I do not know who struck the best, but each brought the other down and the count and the king both died.

12748 Three other counts died, Baluc and Cursal and Urgent. Each of the three headed many men: Urgent was lord of Bath and Baluc count of Wiltshire. Cursal was count of Chester, which borders on Wales. These were killed very quickly, attacked from both sides. The men they had to lead, and who followed their banners, withdrew to the division commanded by Walwein and Hoel, his friend, with him; there never were two such vassals. In ages past there have never been two such lords for goodness, courtesy, excellence and chivalry. Those from Brittany followed Hoel, their lord. Their company was fierce and bold in such a way that they feared neither press nor throng but reached and thrust everywhere. Those who had just been pursuing them and laying them low in heaps, they soon made turn tail, and left many in the throes of death. Through the great blows they dealt and the men they led, they came right up to the banner with the golden eagle on top. There the emperor was, with the flower of his knights, and with him were the noble men and valiant knights of Rome.

12785 There a deadly battle could be seen; its like could never, I think, have been seen before. Kimar, count of Triguel, was in Hoel's company. His valour was great and he did much damage to the Romans. But a Roman foot-soldier struck him dead with a sword. With him died two thousand Bretons, including three noble friends: one of the three was called Jaguz, from Bodloan, the second was Richomarcus and the third, Boclovius.[2] There were not six men in the division with their

---

[1] These deeds of Guitart are absent in eight MSS, including P and D, and also absent in *HRB*.

[2] *HRB* chap. 173: *Chinmarhogus 'consul Trigerie'*, *Richomarcus, Bloccouius* and *Iagwiuius de Bodloano*; all absent from *VV*.

Si cunte fussent cil u rei,
A tut dis mes, si cum jo crei, [1]
Fust parole de lur pruesce;
Mult esteient de grant aspresce.
Essart feseient des Romeins;
Nuls ne veneit entre lur meins
Ki n'eüst la vie finee,
Fust od lance, fust od espee.
En l'eschiele a l'empereür
12810 S'embateient devant les lur, [2]
E cil de Rome les suppristrent,
Tuz treis ensemble les ocistrent.
    D'ire e de rage furent plein
Hoel e sun cusin Walwein,
Quant il la grant ocise virent
Que cil de Rome des lur firent.
Pur les enemis damagier [3]
E pur lur cumpaignuns vengier
Se sunt entr'els cume leün
12820 Entré, bestes mis a bandun;
Romeins destruient e essartent,
Cops e colees lur departent.
Cil de Rome fort se defendent,
Maint cop receivent, maint cop rendent,
Bien tienent e bien sunt tenu,
Bien fierent e bien sunt feru,
Bien butent e bien sunt buté,
Bien hurtent e bien sunt hurté.
Walwein fud de mult grant aïr,
12830 Unques ne fud las de ferir;
Tut tens fud fresche sa vertu, [4]
Unques sa mein lasse ne fu.
Forment alot Romeins chaçant [5]
E forment s'alot esforçant
Qu'a l'empereür avenist
E que od lui se cumbatist.
Tant ad alé e tant ad fait
E tant enpeint e tant retrait,
L'empereür ad encuntré,
12840 Chascun ad altre bien avisé. [6]

L'emperere ad Walwein veü,
E Walwein ad lui cuneü.
De grant vertu s'entreferirent,
Mult furent fort, pas ne chaïrent.
L'emperere fud granz e forz,
Juefnes, hardiz, de grant esforz,
Engignus e de grant prüesce;
Mult ot grant joie e grant leesce
Que a Walwein se cumbateit
Dunt si grant renomee esteit;   12850
S'il en poeit vif eschaper,
A Rome s'en quidot vanter.
Halcent les braz, les escuz lievent,
De merveillus cops s'entregrievent.
Mult se anguissent, mult s'en hastent, [7]
De mainte guise s'entretastent;
Chascun l'autre forment requiert
E chascun l'autre forment fiert;
Des escuz volent les asteles
E des aciers les estenceles;   12860
Fierent desus, fierent desuz,
Mult par esteient andui pruz;
S'il eüssent le champ commun
Tost fust la fin faite de l'un.
Mes cil de Rome recovrerent;
A l'egle d'or se rasemblerent,
L'empereür unt securu,
Pur poi ne l'orent ja perdu.
Les Bretuns unt ariere mis
E lu champ unt sur els purpris.   12870
Arthur vis sa gent resortir
E cels de Rome resbaldir
E lu champ cuntre lui purprendre;
Ne pot ne ne volt plus atendre.
Od sa cumpaigne vint criant:
'Que faites vus? Alez avant!
Veez mei ci, vostre guarant;
N'en laissiez un aler vivant.
Jo sui Arthur ki vus cundui,
Ki pur hume de champ ne fui.   12880

---

[1] MS D reading—*dis*—restored.
[2] MS D reading—*s'embateient*—restored.
[3] MS D reading—*les*—restored.
[4] MS D reading—*fud*—restored.
[5] MS D reading—*chaçant*—restored.
[6] MS D's order of line restored.
[7] MS D reading—*s'en*—restored.

Walwein fights Lucius

valour and renown. Had they been counts or kings, I think there would have been talk ever after of their prowess. They were quite ruthless, and slaughtered the Romans: no one who fell into their hands was not finished off, whether by lance or by sword. They rushed ahead of their troops on to the emperor's company, and the Romans captured them and slew all three together.

12813   Hoel and his cousin Walwein were full of anger and fury when they saw the great slaughter the Romans were making of their men. To destroy their enemies and avenge their friends, they came upon them like lions, like beasts let out of their cage. They demolished and slaughtered Romans, dealing them out hits and blows. The Romans strongly defended themselves, receiving and giving many a blow. They attacked well, and were well attacked, they struck well, and were well struck, they pushed well and were well pushed, did great harm and were in turn much harmed. Walwein's violence was ferocious; he never wearied of striking, his strength was always fresh and his hand never tired. He vigorously pursued Romans and vigorously pressed forward in order to get to the emperor and fight with him. He advanced so far and performed so much, rushed forward and backward so often, that he encountered the emperor, and each carefully scrutinized the other. The emperor saw Walwein and Walwein knew who he was. With great force they hurtled together; both were strong and neither fell. The emperor was tall and strong, young, bold and with great vigour, intelligent and of great prowess; he was joyful and delighted to be fighting Walwein, whose fame was so great. If he could escape it alive, he intended to boast of it in Rome.

12853   They raised their arms, held their shields up and attacked each other with extraordinary blows. They hurt and harassed and hit each other in many ways. Each strongly attacked the other and vigorously struck him. Splinters flew from the shields and sparks from the steel. They fought up and down, both being exceptionally brave. Had they had the field to themselves, an end would soon have been made of one of them. But the Romans recovered; they rallied to the golden eagle and helped the emperor, having nearly lost him. They repulsed the Britons and took possession of the field. Arthur saw his men retreating, the Romans taking heart and ocupying the battlefield against him. He could and would not wait any more. With his company he advanced, shouting: 'What are you doing? Forward! See, I'm here to protect you; don't leave a single man alive. It's Arthur leading you, who never flees the field. Follow me, I'll lead the way, and take care

Siewez mei, jo ferai la veie,
Guardez que nuls ne s'i recreie. [1]
Remenbrez vus de vos buntez,
Ki tanz regnes cunquis avez. [2]
Ja d'icest champ vif ne fuirai; [3]
U ci veintrai u ci murrai!'
    Dunc veïssiez Arthur cumbatre,
Humes ocire, humes abatre,
Halbercs rumpre, healmes quasser,
12890 Testes e braz e puinz colper.
Calibuerne tient, mult l'ensanglante; [4]
Cui il ateint, mort l'agravente. [5]
Ne puis ses cops mettre en escrit;
A chescun cop un hume ocit.
Cume leon, ki faim destreint,
Ocist quel beste qu'il ateint,
Tut ensement li bons reis fait,
Cheval ne hume vif ne lait.
Cui il puet ferir ne plaier;
12900 Mires n'i puet aver mestier;
Ja de sun cop hume ne guarra, [6]
Ja si petit nel plaiera.
De la veie Arthur fuient tuit
Cume berbiz ki pur lu fuit.
Lu rei de Libe ad cunseü,
Sertor ot nun, riches huem fu;
Lu chief li ad sevré del bu,
Puis li ad dit: 'Mal aies tu
Ki ci venis armes porter
12910 Pur Calibuerne ensanglanter.'
Cil ne dit mot, ki mort se jut.
Polidetes lez lui s'estut,
Riches reis ert, de Bithynie,
Une terre de paenie.
Arthur l'ad devant lui trové,
Merveillus cop li ad duné;
Des espalles lu chief li rest,
Li chiefs chaï, li bucs remest. [7]
As cops Arthur e a ses diz
12920 Unt Bretun Romeins envaïz

E Romein encuntre s'anguissent,
Espees traient, lances fruissent;
Des Bretuns grant damage funt,
Cuntre lur force a force estunt.
Arthur les vit, mult li en creist,
De Calibuerne granz cops meist.
L'emperere pas ne sujorne,
La gent Arthur ocit a urne;
Ne se poënt entr'encuntrer
Ne l'uns ne puet l'autre adeser, 12930
Tant par est granz entr'els la presse
E la bataille si engresse.
Bien fierent cist, bien fierent cil,
Tost en veïssiez murir mil.
Fierement s'entrecumbateient
E fierement s'entr'ocieient.
N'iert mie aparant ki veintreit
Ne ki vencuz ne mort serreit,
Quant Moruid vint od sa cumpaine,
Ki ert el bois, en la muntaine, 12940
U Arthur recuvrer deveit
Si de sa gent li meschaeit;
Sis mil e sis cenz chevaliers
E seisante sis, od destriers,
Od clers healmes, od blancs halbers,
Lances dreites, amunt les fers,
De la muntaine descendirent,
Que cil de Rome nul n'en virent.
Detriés lur vindrent sis ferirent,
Lur bataille par mi fendirent, 12950
Les uns des altres departirent,
E tels i ot qu'il abatirent.
As chevals les vunt defulant
E as espees ociant.
N'i porent puis Romein ester
Ne ne porent puis recuvrer;
A granz turbes s'en vunt fuiant.,
Les uns les altres abatant.
L'emperere fud abatuz,
El cors d'une lance feruz; 12960

---

[1] MS D reading—*s'i*—restored.
[2] MS D reading—*cunquis*—restored.
[3] MS D reading—*d'icest*—restored.
[4] MS D's reading of line restored.
[5] MS D reading—*l'agravente*—restored.
[6] MS D reading—*hume*—restored.
[7] MS J adds: *De l'ame fu li cors tuit vuit/ Et li cevaus par tout s'en fuit/ Dont oissiés crier Artur/ Romain s'en vunt a mal eur.*

Morvid's troops help the Britons to win

no one gives up. Remember your own greatness, you who have conquered so many realms. I shall never leave this field alive: here I either conquer or die!'

12887 Then Arthur could be seen in the fray, killing men and laying them low, breaking hauberks, splitting helmets, cutting off heads and arms and fists. He brandished Caliburn, covered in blood; whoever he reached, he knocked him down dead. I cannot write down all his blows: with each one, he killed a man. As a lion, driven by hunger, kills whatever animal it can reach, just so did the good king, leaving neither horse nor man alive. Whoever he struck or wounded had no use for a doctor; no one ever survived his blow, however slight the wound. All fled from Arthur's path, like sheep before the wolf. He pursued the Libyan king, called Sertorius, a man of power, and severed his head from his body. Then he said to him: 'Curse you for bearing arms here, to make Caliburn bloody.' But the dead man said not a word. Polidetes was next to him, a wealthy king from Bithynia, a heathen land. Arthur saw him in front of him and gave him an amazing blow: he cut off his head at shoulder-level. The head fell, the trunk remained. At Arthur's blows and words, the Britons attacked the Romans and the Romans eagerly set at them, drawing their swords and shattering their lances. They inflicted great damage on the Britons, opposing force with force. Arthur saw them: it increased his efforts and he struck huge blows with Caliburn. The emperor did not hang back but likewise killed Arthur's men one after the other. They could not meet or touch each other, so thick was the press between them and so savage the fray.

12933 On both sides men fought well, and soon you could see a thousand die. They fiercely attacked and fiercely slew each other. It was not clear who would win nor who would be defeated and slain, when Morvid arrived with his company, who had been in the forest on the mountain, where Arthur was to muster his forces if misfortune overtook his army. Six thousand, six hundred and sixty-six knights, on horseback, with bright helmets and white hauberks, straight lances and raised swords, swept down from the mountain, unseen by the Romans. They came up behind and struck them, splitting their army in two, separating one from the other and laying all and sundry low. They trampled them with their horses and slew them with their swords. After that, the Romans could not stand their ground nor recover, but fled in great crowds, knocking each other down. The emperor was knocked over and pierced through the body with a lance. I cannot say who laid him low, nor can I say who struck him; he was attacked in the press and in

Ne sai dire ki l'abati
Ne ne sai dire kil feri;
En la presse fud entrepris
E en la presse fud ocis;
Entre les morz fud mort trovez,
El cors d'une lance nafrez.
Cil de Rome e cil d'orient
E li altre comunement
A quanqu'il poënt del champ fuient;
12970 Bretun les chacent e destruient;
Tant en ocient, tuit s'en lassent,
Par desus les ocis trespassent;
Sanc veïssiez curre a ruissels
E ocis gisir a muncels,
Bels palefreiz e buens destriers
Par les champs aler estraiers.
    Arthur se fist joius e lié,
Que l'orguil de Rome ot pleissié,
Graces rendi al Rei de glorie,
12980 Par qui il ot eü victorie.
Cerchier ad fait tuz les ocis,
Ses humes prendre e ses amis;
Les uns fist iloc enterrer,
Les uns en lur terre porter. [1]
Par la cuntree, as abeïes,
En fist enterrer granz parties.
Le cors fist de l'empereür
Prendre e guarder a grant enur;
A Rome en biere l'enveia
12990 E a cels de Rome manda
Que de Bretaine qu'il teneit
Altre treü ne lur deveit,
E qui treü li requerreit
Altretel li enveereit.
Key fud, ki ert a mort nafrez,
A Chynon, sun chastel, portez;
Key cumpassa e fist Chynon
E de Key ot Kynon cest nun.
Ne vesqui mie lungement,
13000 Asez murut hastivement;

Enterrez fud en un boscage
Lez Kynon, en un hermitage.
A Bayues en Normendie,
Dunt il aveit la seignurie,
Unt Beduer enseveli
Devers la porte, vers midi. [2]
En Flandres fud Holdin portez
E en Terrüene enterrez;
Lygiers fud portez en Buluine.
    Arthur, ki remist en Burguine, [3]   13010
Tut l'ivern iloc sujorna;
Les citez prist e apaia.
En esté volt Mungyeu passer
E a Rome voleit aler,
Mes Modred l'en ad returné.
Deus, quel hunte, Deus, quel vilté!
Sis niez, fiz sa sorur, esteit,
E en guarde sun regne aveit;
Tut sun regne li ot livré
E en guarde tut cumandé.   13020
E Modred li volt tut tolir
E a sun ués tut retenir;
De tuz les baruns prist humages,
De tuz les chastels prist hostages. [4]
Emprés ceste grant felunie
Fist Modred altre vilainie,
Kar cuntre cristïene lei
Prist a sun lit femme lu rei,
Femme sun uncle e sun seignur
Prist a guise de traïtur.   13030
Arthur oï e de veir sot
Que Modred fei ne li portot;
Sa terre tint, sa femme ot prise.
Ne li sot gré d'icel servise; [5]
Sa gent tute a Hoel parti,
France e Burguine li guerpi
Si li rova que tut guardast
E que par tut pais afermast;
En Bretaine returnereit,
Cels des idles od sei merreit   13040

---

[1] MS D reading—*terre*—restored.
[2] MS D reading—*Devers*—restored.
[3] MS D reading—*remist*—restored.
[4] MS D's reading of line restored.
[5] MS D reading—*d'icel*—restored.

Modret usurps Britain

the press was slain. He was found dead amongst the dead, wounded through the body by a lance. Those from Rome and from the East, and the rest too, fled the field as fast as they could. The Britons harried and demolished them; quite weary of killing so many, they trampled the slain underfoot. You could see blood running in streams, corpses lying in heaps, and fine palfreys and war-horses roaming loose over the fields.

12977 Arthur was joyful and delighted that he had tamed the pride of Rome. He gave thanks to the King of glory, through whom he had gained victory. He had all the slain searched and his men and friends removed; some he had buried there, others carried back to their lands. Many of them he had buried throughout the country, in abbeys. He had the body of the emperor removed and kept with great honour. He sent it on a bier to Rome and informed the Romans he owed them no other tribute from Britain, which he governed, and whoever required tribute from him would be sent back in the same way. Kei, mortally wounded, was carried to his castle of Chinon; Kei planned and built Chinon, and Chinon takes its name from him. He did not live for long but soon died. He was buried in a wood near Chinon, in a hermitage. At Bayeux in Normandy, where he was lord, they buried Bedoer, beside the gate, towards noon.[1] Holdin was taken to Flanders and buried in Terrüene[2] and Ligier was carried to Boulogne.

13010 Arthur, who stayed in Burgundy, spent all winter there, capturing cities and appeasing them. In summer he wanted to cross Montgieu and go to Rome, but Modret made him turn back. God, what shame! God, what disgrace! He was his nephew, his sister's son, and had the care of his kingdom; Arthur had entrusted the whole realm to him and put it all in his charge. And Modret wanted to take it all away from him and keep it all for his own use. He took homage from all the barons and hostages from all the castles. After this act of great wickedness, Modret did another evil deed, because, against Christian law, he took to his bed the king's wife; he treacherously took the wife of his uncle and lord.[3] Arthur heard and certainly realised that Modret bore him no loyalty: he held his land and had taken his wife. He was not grateful to him for such service. He handed over all his men to Hoel and left him France and Burgundy, asking him to look after it all and to make peace throughout. He would return to Britain, taking the islanders with him, and have his revenge on Modret, who held his wife and his land. All his conquests would be of little value to him if he lost Britain, his own domain. He would rather leave Rome to be conquered than lose his own land. In a little while he would return and would, he said, go to Rome. So Arthur arrived at Wissant,

---

[1] *HRB* chap. 176: *Baioce*; *VV*: *Baiocas*. Wace adds the fake origin of Chinon (*HRB*'s *Camum*).

[2] Thérouanne, in the Pas de Calais (Arnold and Pelan, *Partie Arthurienne*, p. 162)

[3] At this point in *HRB* chap. 177 there is a re-

mark to a 'most noble lord' [*consul auguste*], i.e. Robert duke of Gloucester, and a reference to the British treatise provided by Walter of Oxford. The *VV* omits both.

E de Modred se vengereit,
Ki sa femme e s'onur teneit.
Tut sun conquest poi preisereit
Si Bretaine, sun fieu, perdeit;
Mielz volt laissier Rome a cunquerre
Que perdre sa demeine terre;
A brief terme returnereit[1]
E a Rome, ço dist, irreit.
Issi vint Arthur a Witsant,
13050 Del parjurie Modred pleinant,
Ki turné l'ot de grant cunquest;
Sun navie ot a Witsand prest.
    Modred sot d'Arthur le repaire;
Ne volt ne ne deigna pais faire;
Cheldric de Seisuine ot mandé,
Un duc, qui li ot amené
Oit cent nefs bien aparaillies,
Tutes de chevaliers chargies.
E Modred lur ot graanté
13060 E en eritage duné
Pur lur aïe e pur lur force
Del Humbre tut des qu'en Escoce,
E ço que ot en Kent Henguist,
Quant Vortiger sa fille prist.
Quant Modred ot sa gent justee,
Grand fud e bele l'asemblee.
Entre la gent ki fud paene
E la gent ki fud cristïene
Ot od halbers e od destriers
13070 Seisante mile chevaliers.
Aseür quide Arthur atendre,
Les porz li quide tuz defendre;
Ne li volt pas sun dreit guerpir
Ne querre peis, ne repentir,
E il se set tant a culpable
Que de pais querre serreit fable.
Arthur fist ses nefs eschiper;
Tant mena genz, nes sai numbrer.[2]
A Sandwiz dreit volt ariver[3]
13080 E la rova ses nefs turner,

Mais ainz qu'il fust a terre issuz
Fud Modred encuntre venuz
Od ses humes delivrement,
Ki od lui sunt par serrement.
Cil des nefs d'ariver s'esforcent,
Cil de la terre lur deforcent.
Mult s'aïrent d'ambesdous parz,[4]
Traient saetes e lancent darz,[5]
Pances e piz e testes percent
E crievent oilz s'il i adercent.   13090
Cels des nefs estuet tant entendre
As nefs cunduire, a terre prendre,
Ferir ne cuvrir ne lur list,
Par la mer mult de morz en gist;
Suvent cheent, suvent chancelent,
Traïturs ces defors apelent;
As nefs deschargier del rivage[6]
Ot Arthur d'umes grant damage;
Mult i ot bucs colpez e chiés.
La fud ocis Walwein sis niés;   13100
Arthur ot de lui duel mult grant
Kar il n'amot nul hume tant.
Anguissel fud od lui ocis
Ki d'Escocë ert poëstis;
Des altres i ot ocis maint
Que li reis mult regrette e plaint.
Tant cum il furent el sablun
N'i fist Arthur si perdre nun,[7]
Mes puis qu'il furent al terrein
E par egal furent el plein,   13110
N'i pot Modred aver duree
Ne la grant gent qu'il ot menee.
Modred ot humes concultis,
En pais e en repos nurriz;
Ne se sorent pas si cuvrir
Ne si turner ne si ferir
Cume la gent Arthur saveit,
Ki en guerre nurrie esteit.
Arthur e li suen i fereient
E des espees les serveient;   13120

---

[1] MS D reading—*returnereit*—restored.
[2] MS D reading—*genz*—restored.
[3] MS D's reading of line restored.
[4] MS D's reading of line restored.
[5] MS D reading—*e*—restored.
[6] MS D reading—*del*—restored.
[7] MS D reading—*n'i*—restored.

Arthur returns to Britain

lamenting the perjury of Modret, who had made him abandon a great conquest, and prepared his fleet there.

13053 Modret knew of Arthur's return; he neither wished nor deigned to make peace. He sent for Cheldric of Saxony,[1] a duke, who brought him eight hundred well-equipped ships, all laden with knights. And Modret, for their help and their forces, granted and gave them as a heritage all the land from the Humber to Scotland, and Hengist's land in Kent at the time Vortigern married his daughter. When Modret had gathered his men together, the army was large and splendid. What with the pagan troops and the Christian ones there were, with hauberks and horses, sixty thousand knights. He thought he could await Arthur with confidence, believing he could defend all the ports against him. He did not want to hand over his rights to him, nor seek peace, nor repent, and he knew himself to be so guilty that to seek peace would be ridiculous.

13077 Arthur manned his ships; so many were embarked, I cannot count them. He wanted to land directly at Sandwich, and commanded his ships to travel there, but before he had disembarked, Modret with his men, bound to him by oath, quickly advanced against him. Those in the ships struggled to land, those on land prevented them. Many on both sides furiously shot arrows and threw javelins, piercing bellies, chests and heads and putting eyes out if they reached them. Those in the ships had to pay so much attention to steering the boats and trying to land that they were not allowed to strike or to protect themselves; many of them lay dead in the sea. Sometimes falling, sometimes staggering, they called those on shore traitors. Unloading the ships ashore, Arthur lost many men; there many bodies and heads were severed. There Walwein, his nephew, was slain: Arthur's grief for him was very great, for he never loved any man so much. Angusel, who had dominion over Scotland, was killed with him. There were many others slain, whom the king lamented and mourned.

13107 As long as they were on the beach, Arthur could only lose, but once they were on firm ground and both forces equally on the level, neither Modret, nor the great army he had brought, could hold out. Modret had assembled men brought up to peace and quiet; they did not know how to protect themselves, to wheel and to strike, as Arthur's men did, who had been brought up to war. Arthur and his soldiers struck them and entertained them with their swords; they killed them by scores and by hundreds, slaying many, taking many captive. The slaughter was huge, and would have been greater had the evening not thwarted them. The light failed and darkness came; Arthur stopped and withheld his men. Modret's men fled. Did you think some of them helped to guide others? No one cared about anyone else, but each thought only of his own skin.

---

[1] *HRB* chap. 177 tries to distinguish this leader from Saxony from the Cheldric of Arthur's early career by calling him '*Chelric*'. The First Variant version, however, restores the '*d*'.

A vint e a cent les ocistrent,
Mult en tuerent, mult en pristrent.
Grant fud l'ocise, e plus grant fust
Se li vespres ne lur neüst;
Li jorz failli e la nuit vint;
Arthur s'estut, sa gent retint.
La gent Modred s'est mise en fuie.
Quidez que l'uns l'autre cunduie?
Nuls n'i perneit d'altre cunrei,
13130 Chascun pensot de guarir sei.
Modred s'en fuï tute nuit
Querant recet u il s'apuit;
A Lundres quida remaneir,
Mes cil ne voldrent receveir;
Tamise e Lundres trespassa,
Jesqu'a Wincestre ne fina.
En la cité se herberja,
Ses genz e ses amis manda;
Des citheeins prist feelté
13140 E humages, estre lur gré,
Qu'a lur poeir les meintendrunt
E pais e fei lur porterunt. ¹
Arthur n'ot cure de sujor,
Ki vers Modred ot grant haür.
D'Auguissel ot grant doel eü
E de Walwein qu'il ot perdu;
Grant fud li dols de sun nevou,
Le cors fist mettre ne sai u.
Sun maltalent turna e s'ire
13150 A Modred, sil poeit ocire;
A Wincestre le vint siewant,
De tutes parz gent sumunant;
La cité volt faire asiegier
E sa gent entur alogier.
Quant Modred vit Arthur e l'ost
Ki la cité envirun clost,
Semblant fist qu'il se cumbatreit
E que cumbatre se voleit,
Kar, se il lunges ert asis,
13160 N'en turnereit qu'il n'en fust pris, ²

E, se il pris estre poeit,
Ja d'Arthur vif n'eschapereit.
Tuz ses humes fist asembler,
Prendre lur armes e armer,
Par cunreiz les fist establir
E a cumbatre fors issir.
Des que cil furent fors issu,
Tuit cil de l'ost unt la curu; ³
Sempres i ot maint cop duné,
Maint hume ocis e maint nafré;   13170
A Modred prist a meschaeir,
N'i pot sa gent mestier aveir. ⁴
Mes il pensa de guarir sei;
Mesfait ot mult si crienst lu rei.
Tuz ses privez e ses nurriz
E cels qu'Arthur ot plus haïz
Asembla tut priveement,
Cumbatre laissa l'autre gent;
Vers Hamtune prist un sentier,
Unc ne prist fin des qu'al gravier.   13180
Estiermans prist e mariniers
Par pramesses e par luiers;
En mer se fist od els enpeindre
Que nel peüst Arthur ateindre.
En Cornuaille l'unt cunduit;
Arthur crient, volentiers se fuit. ⁵
Li reis Arthur Wincestre asist,
La gent venqui, la cité prist.
A Ewein, le fiz Urien;
Ki de la curt esteit mult bien,   13190
Duna Escoce en eritage
E Ewein l'en ad fait humage;
Niés Auguissel aveit esté
Si clamot dreit en l'erité,
Ne cil n'aveit ne fiz ne femme
Ki sur Ewein preïst lu regne.
Ewein fud mult de grant valur,
Mult ot grant pris e grant enur
De la medlee e de la guerre
Que Modred mist en Engleterre.   13200

---

¹ MS D readings—*les, lur*—restored in ll. 13141–42.
² MS D reading—*n'en fust*—restored.
³ MS D reading—*unt*—restored.
⁴ MS D's reading of line restored.
⁵ MS D reading—*se*—restored.

Modret flees to Cornwall

13131   Modret fled all night, in search of refuge on which he could rely. He thought he
        could stay in London, but the Londoners would not receive him. He crossed
        London and the Thames and did not stop till Winchester. He took up quarters in
        the city and summoned his men and his friends. From the citizens he took oaths
        of fealty and homage, against their will, so that they would, as far as possible,
        support them and show them loyalty and peace. Arthur, full of hatred for Modret,
        had no wish to delay. He grieved bitterly for Angusel and for Walwein whom he
        had lost. His anguish for his nephew was great, but I do not know where he put
        his body. He turned his anger and fury on Modret, if he could just kill him. He
        followed him to Winchester, summoning men from all directions; he wished to
        besiege the city and encamp his men round about.

13155   When Modret saw Arthur and the army encompassing the city, he made it appear
        he would fight, and that he wished to fight for, if he were besieged for long, he
        would not escape being captured, and if he were captured, he would never es-
        cape Arthur alive. He gathered all his men and made them take their weapons
        and arm themselves. He had them arranged into companies and made them go
        out and fight. As soon as they ventured out, the whole army fell upon them, and
        at once there were many blows dealt, and many men killed and wounded. It
        turned out badly for Modret, because his men proved useless. But he gave thought
        to saving his own skin: his misdeeds were many and he feared the king. He
        gathered in great secrecy all his intimates and dependants and those whom Arthur
        most hated, and left the other men to fight. Taking a path leading to Southamp-
        ton, he never stopped till he was on the beach. With promises and bribes he got
        helmsmen and sailors, and rushed out to sea with them so that Arthur could not
        reach him. They took him to Cornwall; he willingly fled, because he feared Arthur.

13187   King Arthur besieged Winchester, defeated the people and took the city. To Ewain,
        son of Urien, who was on good terms with the court, he gave Scotland as heritage
        and Ewain did him homage for it. He had been Angusel's nephew and claimed it
        by right of inheritance, for Angusel had neither son nor wife to take the kingdom
        ahead of Ewain.[1] He was a man of great valour, having won much renown and
        honour in the conflict and fighting which Modret had started in England.

13201   The queen knew and heard that Modret had so many times been put to flight;
        he could neither defend himself against Arthur nor dared await him in the field.
        She was staying in York, melancholy and distressed. She remembered the wick-
        edness she had done in tarnishing her honour for Modret's sake, shaming the
        good king and desiring his nephew. He had married her illicitly and she was

---

[1] *HRB* chap. 177: *Hiwenus*. This passage about
Ewain is placed earlier in the Vulgate version,
after Gawain's death and before the siege of
Winchester. The *VV* has a different ordering,
which Wace uses. This order is important, because Guinevere reacts not, as in *HRB*, to
Modret's advance on Winchester (i.e. she fears
the usurper) but to his defeat and flight (i.e. she
guiltily fears Arthur).

La reïne sot e oï
Que Modred tantes feiz fuï;
Ne se poeit d'Arthur defendre
Ne ne l'osot en champ atendre.
A Everwic iert a sujor,
En pensé fud e en tristur;
[Membra lui de la vilainie
Que pur Modred s'esteit hunie,] [1]
Lu bon rei aveit vergundé
13210 E sun nevou Modred amé;
Cuntre lei l'aveit espusee
Si en esteit mult avilee;
Mielz volsist morte estre que vive.
Mult fud triste, mult fud pensive;
A Karliun s'en est fuïe,
La entra en une abeïe,
Nune devint iloc velee,
En l'abbeïe fud celee.
Ne fud oïe, ne fud veüe, [2]
13220 N'i fud trovee ne seüe,
Pur la verguine del mesfait
E del pechié qu'ele aveit fait.
   Cornewaille ad Modred tenue,
L'autre terre ad tute perdue.
Par mer e par terre envea,
Paens e cristïens manda;
Manda Yreis, manda Norreis,
Manda Seissuns, manda Daneys,
Manda ces que Arthur haeient,
13230 Manda ces qui terre n'aveient, [3]
Manda ces qui Arthur cremeient,
E ki pur terres servir voleient; [4]
Duna e pramist e preia
Cumë huem fait ki busuin a.
Arthur fud dolenz e iriez
Que de Modred ne fud vengiez;
Mult li peise del traïtur
Que de sa terre ad nisun dur;
A Cornuaille ad gent ja trait
13240 E se peine que plus en ait;

Tenir cele e plus prendre enteise.
Arthur le set, forment li peise; [5]
Tute s'ost manda des qu'al Humbre,
Grand fut li puebles, ne sai le numbre; [6]
Grant fud la gent que li reis ot,
La quist Modred u il le sot;
Ocirre le voleit e destruire [7]
Sun traïtur e sun parjuire.
Modred nen ot de fuïr cure,
Mielz se volt mettre en aventure   13250
E en abandun de murir,
Que tantes feiz de champ fuïr.
Juste Camble fud la bataille
En la terre de Cornuaille.
Par grant ire fud asemblee
E par grant ire fud justee;
Par grant ire fud l'ovre enprise,
Grant fut la gent, grant fu l'ocise;
Ne sai dire ki mielz le fist
Ne qui perdi ne qui cunquist   13260
Ne qui chaï ne qui estut
Ne qui ocist ne qui murut.
Grant fud de ambes parz la perte,
La plaine fud des morz cuverte
E del sanc des muranz sanglente.
Dunc peri la bele juvente
Que Arthur aveit grant nurrie
E de plusurs terres cuillie,
E cil de la Table Roünde
Dunt tel los ert par tut le munde;   13270
Ocis fud Modred en l'estur
E de sa gent tut li plusur,
E de la gent Arthur la flur
E li plus fort e li meillur.
   Arthur, si la geste ne ment,
Fud el cors nafrez mortelment;
En Avalon se fist porter
Pur ses plaies mediciner.
Encore i est, Bretun l'atendent,
Si cum il dient e entendent;   13280

---

[1] MSS DLCPNT omit ll. 13207–08.
[2] MS D reading—*ne fud veüe*—restored.
[3] MS D's wording and order of lines restored in
   ll. 13230–31.
[4] MS D reading—*E ki pur terres*—restored.
[5] MS D reading—*li*—restored.
[6] MS D reading—*ne sai le*—restored.
[7] MS D reading—*le*—restored.

Arthur's last battle

badly degraded by it. She wished she were dead rather than alive. Filled with misery and dejection, she fled to Caerleon and there entered an abbey. There she took the veil and was concealed; she was neither heard nor seen, neither known nor found, because of the shame of her misdeed and the sin she had committed.

13223   Modret held Cornwall, having lost all the rest of the land. He sent over land and sea, summoning pagans and Christians: he summoned Irish, Norwegians, Saxons and Danes, he summoned those landless men who hated Arthur, who feared the king and who would serve in order to get land.[1] He gave and promised and begged, as a man does in need. Arthur was mortified and angry that he had taken no vengeance on Modret; it grieved him greatly that the traitor had even a fistful of his land. Modret had already brought men into Cornwall and was trying to get more; he aimed to hold that territory and grab others. Arthur knew this and it disturbed him. He summoned his whole army from as far as the Humber; I do not know their number but there were many people. The king's army was large and he sought Modret where he knew him to be, intent on killing him and destroying his treachery and his broken faith. Modret had no wish to flee; he preferred to stake his life and risk death rather than so often deserting the field.

13253   The battle was beside Camble[2] in the land of Cornwall. They gathered and joined battle in great anger; in great anger was the work begun, great were the numbers of men and great was the slaughter. I cannot say who did best, nor who lost or won, nor who fell or stood firm, nor who died and who lived. The losses were great on both sides, the plain was strewn with dead and bloody with the blood of the dying. Then perished the flower of youth, tended and gathered by Arthur from many lands, and those of the Round Table, famous throughout the world. Modret was slain in the fray, and the vast majority of his men, and the flower of Arthur's people, both the strongest and the best.[3]

13275   Arthur, if the chronicle is true, received a mortal wound to his body. He had himself carried to Avalon, for the treatment of his wounds. He is still there, awaited by the Britons, as they say and believe, and will return and may live again. Master Wace, who made this book, will say no more of his end than the prophet Merlin did. Merlin said of Arthur, rightly, that his death would be doubtful. The prophet spoke truly: ever since, people have always doubted it and always will, I think, doubt whether he is dead or alive. It is true that he had himself borne away to Avalon, five hundred and forty-two years after the Incarnation. It

---

[1] Wace adds the details of Modret's allies.
[2] In other MSS *Cambre* (CP) or *Tanbre* (AKR). In the *Annales Cambriae*, AD 539, Arthur and Medraut fall at the battle of Camlann. In *HRB* chap. 178 this has become the river of *Camblan*, which Thorpe identifies as the Camel. See Thorpe, *Geoffrey of Monmouth: History*, p. 259, for local legend, and Tatlock p. 60.
[3] *HRB* chap. 178 has a list of which allies fall on either side in the battle.

De la vendra, encor puet vivre.
Maistre Wace, ki fist cest livre,
Ne volt plus dire de sa fin
Qu'en dist li prophetes Merlin;
Merlin dist d'Arthur, si ot dreit,
Que sa mort dutuse serreit.
Li prophetes dist verité;
Tut tens en ad l'um puis duté,
E dutera, ço crei, tut dis,
13290　Se il est morz u il est vis.
Porter se fist en Avalun,
Pur veir, puis l'Incarnatiun
Cinc cenz e quarante dous anz.
Damage fud qu'il n'ot enfanz.
Al fiz Cador, a Costentin,
De Cornuaille, sun cusin,
Livra sun regne si li dist
Qu'il fust reis tant qu'il revenist.
　　Modred aveit dous fiz bien granz,
13300　Bien orguillus e bien preisanz;
Cil virent tuz les baruns morz,
Virent peri lé granz esforz,
Virent d'Arthur l'esluinement,
Virent lu rei fait novelment;
Les Saisnes ki od Modred erent,
Ki de la bataille eschaperent,
Unt ensemble od els alïé;
Tant les unt blandiz e preié, [1]
Retenu les unt a soldeies [2]
13310　Si lur unt granz terres dunees.
Le mielz del païs unt saisi.
L'uns d'els en Lundres s'enbati,
Li altres volt tenir Wincestre;
Issi quiderent seignur estre;
Mes Costentin les vint siewant,
Ki d'els veintre se mist en grant.
L'un frere en Wincestre trova,
En un mustier le decola
Devant l'autiel saint Amphibal;
13320　Gardez s'il fist pechié e mal.

Puis ad l'autre frere siewi;
Cil sot sa venue e oï,
En un mustier s'ala mucier,
Mes ne li pot aver mestier;
La le fist li reis decoler,
Le chief li fist del buc voler.
Treis anz regna, puis fud ocis,
Ço fud grant doel a ses amis.
A Estanhenges fud portez
E a grant enur enterrez.　　　　13330
　　Cunan, sis niés, enprés regna;
Orguillus fud, mult se preisa,
Pais ne sot faire ne garder,
Ses genz laissot entremedler.
Par les citez s'entremedloent.
E li barun se guerrioent;
Entre lui meïsme e sa gent
Aveit grant discorde suvent.
Sun uncle guereia e prist
E les dous fiz sun uncle ocist　　13340
Pur ço qu'il esteient dreit eir
E si deüssent lu regne aveir. [3]
Quatre anz fud reis e petit plus,
Enprés regna Vortyporus.
En sun tens Saidne revelerent,
La terre tute aver quiderent;
As genz firent mainte moleste,
Deus confunde tute lur geste!
Bien lur estut al cumençail,
Al rei firent maint grant travail;　13350
A la parfin s'esvertua,
Soldeiers prist, genz aüna,
Ne laissa a nul d'els manage
Dunt il n'en eüst bon hostage.
Puis tint pais jesqu'a sun decés.
Malgo, sis niés, fud reis aprés,
Ki ama mult chevalerie
E mult l'usa tute sa vie.
Les idles envirun conquist
E les humages des reis prist;　　13360

---

[1] MS D reading—*alïé, preié*—restored in ll. 13307–08.

[2] MS D reading—*soldeies*—restored.

[3] MS D reading—*E*—restored.

Constantine, Cunan, Vortipore and Malgo

was a great loss that he had no children. To Cador's son, Constantine[1] of Cornwall, his cousin, he surrendered his kingdom, and told him to be king until he returned.

13299 Modret had two sons who were very powerful, very proud and highly esteemed. They saw all the barons were dead and the large armies destroyed; they saw Arthur was gone and the king newly appointed. They got together with the Saxons who had been with Modret who had escaped the battle, and they so cajoled and entreated them that they managed to retain them with wages and gave them large tracts of land. They seized the best part of the country. One of them attacked London, the other sought to hold Winchester; thus they thought to be rulers.[2] But Constantine, extremely anxious to defeat them, pursued them. He found one brother in Winchester and beheaded him in a church, in front of the altar of St Amphibalus; consider if what he did was sinful and evil. Then he pursued the other brother; he heard and knew of his coming and went and hid in a monastery, but it was no use. The king had him beheaded there, making his head fly from his trunk. Constantine reigned for three[3] years and was then slain, which caused his friends much grief. He was carried to Stonehenge and buried with great honour.

13331 Next his nephew, Cunan,[4] reigned. He was arrogant, with a high opinion of himself; he could neither make nor keep peace and let his people fight each other. Quarrels were picked in city streets and the barons were at war; even between himself and his men there was often much strife. He made war on his uncle and seized him and killed his two sons, because they were the rightful heirs and should have had the throne. He was king for four years and a bit more. After him Vortipor[5] ruled; during his reign the Saxons rebelled, thinking to acquire the whole land. They caused people much hardship: may God destroy their whole race! At the start they had the best of it and gave the king great trouble. Finally he made a great effort, collected soldiers, gathered men together and did not overlook a single Saxon dwelling from which he could take a useful hostage. Then he kept the peace until his death.

13356 Malgo, his nephew, was king next, who was very fond of knightly deeds and performed them throughout his life. He conquered the surrounding islands and took homage from their kings. In beauty and good manners he surpassed all his ancestors. He was very handsome, very noble and very affectionate to all his kin; he

---

[1] As Arnold remarks (II, p. 813) Geoffrey of Monmouth had to fill the gap of some fifty years between the death of Arthur in 542 and the mission of St Augustine (596) reported by Bede (I, chap. 23). He drew on Gildas, *De Excidio*, chaps. 28–33, who names five 'tyrants' of 6th century Welsh kingdoms, and selected four of them: Constantine, Aurelius Caninus (= *Conan*), Vortipor and Maglocunus (= *Maelgwyn*). For

Cuneglasus he substituted Kareticus (Wace's *Cariz*).

[2] *HRB* chap. 179 here has details of deaths and successions of bishops and archbishops.

[3] *HRB* chap. 180: four; *VV*: three.

[4] *HRB* chap. 181: *Aurelius Conanus*; *VV*: just *Conanus*, with a shorter and less approbatory description.

[5] *HRB* chap. 182: *Wortiporius*.

De bealté e de bones murs
Surmunta tuz ses anceisurs.
Forment fud bels, forment fud genz,
Forment ama tuz ses parenz,
Larges fud mult a desmesure,
Unques d'aveir tenir n'ot cure.
Malgo se tint a escharni,
A deshonuré, a huni,
Que il le jor n'ot tant duné
13370 Dunt qui que seit li seüst gré.
Une sule teche aveit male
Dunt li Sodomite sunt pale;
Ne sout l'em en lui altre vice
Ne ne feseit altre malice.[1]
Cariz fud puis reis de la terre,
Mes tute la perdi par guerre;
Dolenz fud e maleürus
E a tute gent haïnus.
En sun tens vint la grant surverse
13380 De paens e de gent adverse
Que Gurmunt amena par mer,
Bien en avez oï parler,
Ki firent la destructiun
Dunt Bretaine perdi sun nun.
Gurmunz fud riches e puissanz
E de sun cors forment vaillanz;
Hardiz fud, de noble curage,
E mult esteit de grant parage;
D'Alfrike fud, fiz a un rei
13390 Ki esteit de paeine lei.
Le regne emprés sun pere eüst
E reis en fust se li pleüst,
Mes il ne volt ne ne deigna,
A un sun frere la duna,
A un suen frere juvenur
Otria sa terre e s'onur,
Si dist que ja reis ne serreit
Si realme ne cunquereit.
Par mer, ço dist, irreit conquerre
13400 Que reis serreit en altre terre.

De lui prophetiza Merlins
Que ço serreit uns lus marrins.
Mariniers prist e estiermans [2]
E nefs e barges e calans;
Cent e seisante mil armez
Tuz cuneüz e tuz numez,
Estre estiermans e mariniers,
Estre servanz e estre archiers,
Mena Gurmunt en sun navire.
Ne sai des barges numbre dire,   13410
Mult ot nefs e grant gent mena,
Mainte grant mer aviruna,
Maint idle prist, maint rei venqui,
Mainte terre prist e vei saisi.[3]
Tant ala par mer naviant,
Reis venquant, terres cunquerant,
En Yrlande vint salvement,
La terre prist delivrement.
D'Yrlande se fist rei clamer,
Puis volt en Engleterre aler.   13420
Seidnes aveit en Engleterre,
Ki as Bretuns feseient guerre;
Suvent aveient chalengié
E pur cunquerre guerrié
Twancastre en Lyndesie e Kent
Que Henguist ot premierement,
E ço que tint sis fiz Octa,
Ki vers Escoce cunversa.
Suvent aveient tut eü,
Suvent aveient tut perdu,   13430
Suvent orent duné hostages
E suvent orent fait humages
Que des Bretuns recunuistreient
E pais e triewes lur tendreient.[4]
Quant il aveient tut pramis,
Humages faiz, hostages mis,
Tant par esteit lur fei malveise,
Des que il veient lieu e aise
E des que alcuns reis mureit
U de sun cors afiebliseit,   13440

---

[1] MS J adds: *E cele fu assés vilaine/ Honis est qui tel vie maine/ Quant cil fu mors et enfuis/ Si fu aprés lui rois Caris.*
[2] MS D reading—*prist*—restored.

[3] MS D reading—*vei*—restored.
[4] MS C adds: *Mes li Saison furent traitor/ E lur traison uncore dure/ Sovent freindrent lor homages/ E si funt plusors de lor lignages.*

Gurmunt seizes Ireland

was immoderately generous and never cared about keeping his possessions. Malgo considered himself derided, dishonoured and shamed if on any day he did not give so much that anyone whatever was grateful to him. He had only one bad flaw, that which distinguishes the Sodomites; no other vice was known of him, nor did he commit any other wickedness.

13375 Then Cariz[1] was king of the land, but lost it all through war; he was wretched and unhappy and full of hatred to everyone. It was in his time that the great invasion occurred, of pagans and enemies whom Gurmunt brought across the sea—you have certainly heard tell of them—who caused the destruction through which Britain lost its name.[2]

13385 Gurmunt was rich and powerful and physically very brave. He was bold, noble of disposition and of very great lineage: he came from Africa, son of a heathen king. He inherited the realm after his father and could have been its king had he wanted, but he neither wished nor deigned to and gave it to one of his brothers. To one of his younger brothers he gave his land and his domain, and said he would never be a king unless he conquered a kingdom; he would cross the sea to conquer another land and be king there. Merlin prophesied of him that he would be a pirate.[3] He picked sailors and helmsmen, ships, barges and boats. In his fleet Gurmunt put one hundred and sixty thousand armed men, all known and famous, in addition to helmsmen and sailors, servants and archers. I cannot tell the number of boats. He had many ships and commanded many men; he crossed many great seas and seized many islands, defeating many kings and seizing many lands and roads. He sailed through the seas so long, defeating kings and conquering lands, that he arrived safely in Ireland and quickly seized the country. He had himself proclaimed king of Ireland and then wanted to move into England.

13421 There were Saxons in England, waging war on the British. They were fighting to conquer what they had often laid claim to: Thongcaster in Lindsey, and Kent, which Hengist had initially possessed and which his son Octa, who lived in the direction of Scotland, had held.[4] They had often had everything and often lost everything, they had often given hostages and often paid homage, so that the British would accept their homage and extend them peace and a truce. Once they had made all sorts of promises—paid homage, appointed hostages—they were of such bad faith that as soon as they saw place and opportunity, and as soon

---

[1] *HRB* chap. 184: *Kareticus*; *VV*: *Carecius*.

[2] Wace adds this detail on the loss of Britain's name.

[3] In *HRB* chap. 184 the African king is *Gotmundus* (*VV*: *Godmundus*). Wace adds this account of his early career. He appears here to have been transplanted from the 9th to the 6th century and is known to us from three sources: from the 12th-century *chanson de geste* (surviving in an Anglo-

Norman MS) *Gormont et Isembard*, where he is the leader of an historical invasion by Northmen of France in 881, defeated at Saucourt by Louis III; from Hariulf's late 11th or early 12th-century *Chronicon Centulense* and from Gaimar's *Estoire des Engleis* (*c.*1138: ll. 3236–76). See Arnold II, p. 813 and Houck, *Sources*, pp. 288–97.

[4] See fn. 1 to p. 175. Wace adds these details of Saxon claims.

Sempres erent a reveler
E a tolir e a rober.
En Northumberlande maneient;
La repeiroent, de la veneient. [1]
De Gurmund oïrent parler,
Ki tant esteit puissant e ber;
As Bretuns pais e triewes pristrent,
Entretant a Gurmund tramistrent;
Mult li dunerent e plus pramistrent, [2]
13450 Puis li preierent e requistrent
Que en Bretaine a els passast
E la terre lur delivrast;
Volentiers de lui la tendreient
E volentiers l'en servireient
Treü chascun an l'en durreient
E a seignur l'en cunuistreient;
Paens esteit, e il paen,
E Bretun erent cristïen;
Bien se deveient entr'aidier
13460 E cristïenté abaissier;
Si cum il erent d'une lei
Si deveient aver un rei.
    Quant Gurmund oï la requeste, [3]
Od la flote qu'il aveit preste [4]
En Northumberlande passa,
A ces de Saisuine parla;
Afermé unt lur cuvenance
Par hostages e par fiance,
Gurmund, del païs delivrer
13470 E as Seidnes en fieu livrer,
E li Seidne, de fei porter
E del treü par an duner. [5]
Dunc pristrent la terre a destruire;
Deus, quel dolur e quel injure
De bone terre, de gentil, [6]
Que turné est a tel issil!
Saisne les Alfricans cunduient,
Maisuns ardent, viles destruient;
Les chevaliers e les vileins,
13480 Les clers, les muines, les nuneins,

Batent e chacent e ocient;
La lei Damnedeu cuntralient.
Mult veïssiez terres eissillier, [7]
Femmes hunir, humes percier,
Enfanz en berz esbüeler,
Aver saisir, preies mener, [8]
Turs abatre, viles ardeir.
Li reis n'ert mie del poeir,
Ne ne poeit tant gent aver,
Que il osast Gurmund veer;   13490
Ne l'osot mie es pleins atendre,
Kar pru ne se poeit defendre.
Li paen vunt tut purpernant,
Clerc ne prestre n'i ad guarant;
Li bon esvesque e li bon moine,
Li bon abé, li bon chanuine [9]
N'unt pas seürté de lur vies;
Celles laissent e abeies,
Cors sainz e reliques en portent,
Li un les altres descunfortent.   13500
En crieme e en dolur sunt tuit;
Ki plus tost puet fuïr se fuit.
Fuient povre, fuient manant,
Fuient burgeis e païsant,
Fuient vilain e vavassur
E des baruns tuit li plusur.
Petit se fient es granz turs,
Quant il espeir n'unt de sucurs.
Chambres voident, guerpissent sales.
Li un s'en sunt fuï en Guales;   13510
Cil ki püent e ki nés unt
En Bretaine la menur vunt.
En Cornuaille sunt remés
Cil ki ne porent aver nés.
    Gurmunt ala Kariz querant,
E Kariz ala tant fuiant
Qu'en Cirecestre fud suppris,
E Gurmund l'ad iloc asis;
Ysembard vint al siege a lui,
Ne pot trover aillurs refui.   13520

---

[1] MS D reading—*de*—restored.
[2] MS D reading—*e*—restored.
[3] MS D reading—*la*—restored.
[4] MS D reading—*la*—restored.
[5] MS D reading—*del*—restored.
[6] MS D's reading of line restored.
[7] MS D reading—*terres*—restored.
[8] MS D reading—*aver*—restored.
[9] MS D's order of ll. 13495–96 restored.

Gurmunt invades Britain

as any king died or grew enfeebled, at once they reverted to rebellion, to theft and robbery. They lived in Northumberland: that was whence they came and where they returned. They heard tell of Gurmunt, who was so powerful and brave. They made peace and a truce with the British and meanwhile sent word to Gurmunt; they gave him much and promised more, then asked and begged him to cross over to them in Britain and hand the land over to them. They would willingly hold the land under him and willingly serve him; they would pay him tribute every year and recognize him as lord. He was heathen, so were they, and the British were Christian; they should certainly help each other and bring Christianity down. As they were of one faith, so they should have one king.[1]

13463   When Gurmunt heard their request, he crossed, along with his fleet which was ready to hand, into Northumberland and spoke to the Saxons. They consolidated their agreement—Gurmunt to liberate the land and hand it over as fief to the Saxons, and they in return to be loyal to him and give him tribute each year— with hostages and oaths. Then they began to ravage the land. God, what suffering and harm for a good and noble land, brought to such ruin! The Saxons showed the Africans the way, burning houses and destroying towns. They beat and hunted and killed knights and peasants, clerics, monks and nuns; they flouted the law of God. There you could see in plenty lands laid waste, women dishonoured, men impaled, children disembowelled in their cradles, possessions seized, booty taken, towers demolished and towns burnt.

13488   The king did not have enough power or enough men to dare to prevent Gurmunt, nor did he dare to oppose him in force, because he could not defend himself advantageously. The pagans continued to overrun everything. Neither scholar nor priest had any protection: the lives of the good bishops and canons, abbots and monks were not safe. They left their cells and abbeys, disheartened one and all, carrying with them the bodies of saints and holy relics. All were in fear and misery; whoever could do so, fled as soon as possible. The poor and the rich fled, the townfolk and the countrymen, the peasants and the petty nobility and the vast majority of the barons. They put little faith in high towers, since they had no hope of aid. They left their chambers, they abandoned their halls. Some fled to Wales; those who could, and who had ships, went to Brittany. Those who could get no ships stayed in Cornwall.

13515   Gurmunt went looking for Cariz, and Cariz fled until Gurmunt caught up with him in Cirencester and besieged him there. Ysembard[2] accompanied him to the

---

[1] Wace invents these messages and emphasizes the paganism in the alliance.

[2] *HRB* chap. 184: *Isembardus*; *VV*: *Ysembertus*. Gaimar's *Estoire* gives us three sieges of Cirencester: the first in ll. 853–70, by Cerdic (where the sparrow trick is used), the second in ll. 987–996, by Ceawlin and the third in ll. 3235–44 by Gurmund (Guthrum), who was a

Danish king whose army threatened the city in 878 but, following his defeat by Alfred, was baptized and moved on to occupy East Anglia; the *ASC* says he died in 890. The siege of Cirencester in *HRB* and Wace is thus a conflation. See Stenton, *Anglo-Saxon England*, pp. 253–5 and Houck, *Sources*, p. 344.

Niés lu rei Lowis esteit,
Ki de France chacié l'aveit;
De France l'aveit fors jeté
E de sun fieu deserité.
Ysembard a Gurmunt parla;
Sis hum devint, Deu renea,
Deu renea e sa creance
Pur vengier sei del rei de France.
Tant fud li chaitis deceüz,
13530 Tant fud desvez e mescreüz,
L'amur guerpi del Criatur
Si reçut la lei paenur. [1]
Paens asistrent Cirecestre;
Tels fud dedenz n'i volsist estre.
Lur paveilluns entur tendirent,
Tentes leverent, loges firent.
Tute unt guastee la cuntree,
La viande prise e portee;
La cité unt entur si close
13540 Que nul de cels issir n'en ose.
Perieres firent e berfreiz
Si l'asaillirent plusurs feiz. [2]
Lur enginz firent as murs traire,
Mes ne poeient engin faire
Que cil dedenz ne cuntrefacent.
Mairiens e cleies entrelacent,
Kernels refunt, portes afaitent,
Le jor ovrent, la nuit se guaitent;
Bretesches e murs apareillent.
13550 Quant li un dorment, li un veilent.
As defenses pieres atraient,
E nequedent forment s'esmaient,
Kar il ne sevent ne ne veient
Engin par quei defendu seient.
Cil defors suvent les asaillent
E pur els prendre se travaillent,
Mes cil se peinent del defendre;
Nes pot Gurmund par force prendre.
    Quant il veit que prendre nes puet,
13560 E que demurer li estuet,

Entur la cité fist chastels
A bretesches e a kernels;
L'un en livra a Ysembard,
Que devers lui la cité guard;
Altre livra a ses baruns
E altre as princes des Seissuns.
A sun ués fist faire une tur
U il esteit tut a sujur;
Iloc esteit, iloc giseit,
Iloc jueit, iloc dormeit.   13570
La gent dedenz n'est pas malveise:
Suvent, quant il virent alques lur aise, [3]
Funt as foreins granz asaillies, [4]
En abandun mettent lur vies.
Suvent i ot grant podneïz
E suvent grant palateïz.
Suvent en i aveit de pris,
Suvent de nafrez e d'ocis.
Mes cil defors, ki plusur sunt,
En la cité platir les funt;   13580
Illoc les chacent e enteitent,
Mes des murs prendre poi espleitent.
Lungement se sunt defendu
E lungement se sunt tenu,
E plus lungement se tenissent
Que cil par force nes preïssent,
Si feus la vile n'espreïst;
Grant mal e grant damage fist.
Cil defors, par grant tricherie
Que puis ne ainz ne fud oïe,   13590
Unt la cité tute enflambee.
Oëz cum il l'unt alumee:
Muissuns od reiz e od glu pristrent
E en croisés de noiz fu mistrent;
Od le fu firent enz repundre
Esprises de lin e de tundre;
As piez de muissuns les pendirent,
Merveilluse veisdie firent.
Al seir, quant vint a l'avesprer,
Laissierent les mussuns aler;   13600

---

[1] MS J adds: *Ysenbars a G. promist/ Que s'il en France od lui venist/ La tere lui aquiteroit/ Et roi de France le feroit.*

[2] MS D reading—*si l'*—restored.
[3] MS D reading—*virent alques*—restored.
[4] MS D reading—*as foreins granz*—restored.

Siege of Cirencester

siege; he could find refuge nowhere else. He was the nephew of king Louis, who had expelled him from France; he had driven him from France and disinherited him of his domain. Ysembard spoke to Gurmunt, became his man and renounced God; he abjured God and his faith to take revenge on the king of France. The wretch was so deluded, so astray and impious that he abandoned the Creator's love and received the heathen faith. The pagans attacked Cirencester; those within wished they were not. All around pavilions were raised, tents pitched and huts constructed. The pagans had devastated the entire country, seizing and removing any food. They surrounded the city so tightly that no one dared come out. They constructed catapults and siege-towers and made several assaults. They dragged their engines up to the walls, but they could make none which were not destroyed by those inside the city. These twined together timberwork and wattle-fencing, repaired the battlements, constructed the gates, worked by day and kept guard by night, arming parapets and walls. When some slept, the others kept watch. They gathered stones to defend themselves; nevertheless, they were very frightened, for they neither knew nor saw any engine to protect them. Those on the outside often attacked them and laboured to capture them, but the besieged took pains to defend themselves and Gurmunt could not take them by force.

13558   When he saw he could not take them and had to stay put, he constructed castles around the city, with parapets and battlements. One of these he gave to Ysembard, to watch the city in front of him. Another he gave to his barons and another to the Saxon princes. For his own use he had a tower made to rest in; he stayed there, lay there, played games and slept there. The defenders of the city were no cowards: when they saw their opportunity, they would often attack the besiegers, putting their lives at risk. There were often great displays of strength and great skirmishes; men were often captured, often wounded and killed. But those outside, who were numerous, made them retreat into the city; they chased and pushed them inside, but had little success in taking the walls.[1]

13583   For a long time the besieged defended themselves and for a long time they held out, and would have held out for longer, unable to be taken by force, had fire not engulfed the town, doing it great harm and damage. Those outside, through foul play never known before nor since, set the city entirely alight. This is how they did it. They caught sparrows with snares and bird-lime and set fire to nutshells; inside those they placed, next to the flames, inflammable matter of flax and tinder. They attached them to the sparrows' feet and performed an amazing trick. In the evening, when it came to nightfall, they released the sparrows; these

---

[1] Cirencester, along with Gloucester and Bath, was captured in 577 by Cuthwine and Ceawlin: see Swanton, *ASC* pp. 18–19 and *HA* II, chap. 25. Wace adds all the details of the siege. This was an important battle, opening the valley of the lower Severn to Saxon colonists and separating the Britons of the South-West from those living north of the Bristol Channel. See Stenton, *Anglo-Saxon England*, p. 29.

Cil s'alerent la noit logier
La u il soleient nier,
Es tas des blez e es muidluns
E es severundes des maisuns. ¹
Li feus nurri e eschalfa,
La vile esprist e aluma.
Bretun virent la vile ardeir,
Flambe voler, maisuns chaeir;
A cumbatre se cunreerent,
13610 Mes vencu furent, kar poi erent.
Li reis Kariz se tresturna;
Triés un triés altre s'en ala;
En Guales dreit la veie tint; ²
Ne sai dire que puis avint. ³
Issi fud la cité preisie
Tute destruite e eissillie.
Pur ço que par muissuns fud prise
E par muissuns issi cunquise,
La soleient jadis alquant
13620 E funt encor li païsant
La cité as muissuns nomer,
Pur la merveille recorder
Que par ces oisels fud perdue
La cité que tant ert tenue. ⁴
     Gurmund destruist meinte cité
E maint chastel d'antiquité,
Mainte yglise, mainte clergie,
Maint evesquié, mainte abeye
Ki ne furent puis restorees
13630 Ne puis ne furent abitees.
Encor i perent les ruines
E les deserz e les guastines
Que Gurmund fist en plusurs lieus
Pur tolir as Bretuns lur fieus.
Quant il ot guasté lu païs,
Les viles arses, l'aveir pris,
Lu regne ad as Sednes duné;
E il lur aveit afié
A duner s'il le cunquereit
13640 E il si fist, bien lur fist dreit.

Cil unt la terre recuillie,
Ki mult l'aveient encovie.
Pur un lignage dunt cil furent
Ki la terre primes reçurent ⁵
S'i firent Engleis apeler ⁶
Pur lur orine remenbrer,
E Englelande unt apelee
La terre ki lur ert dunee.
Tant dit Engleterre en franceis
Cum dit Englelande en engleis;   13650
Terre a Engleis, ço dit li nuns,
Ço en est l'espositiuns.
Des que Brutus de Troie vint
Tut tens Bretaine sun nun tint
Jesqu'al terme que jo vus di
Que par Gurmund sun nun perdi
Si ot novels abiteürs,
Novels reis e novels seignurs.
Cil voldrent tenir lur usage;
Ne voldrent prendre altre language.   13660
Les nuns des viles tresturnerent,
En lur language les nomerent.
     Engleis voldrent rei establir,
Mes ne se porent assentir
Que un rei sulement eüssent
E a un rei tuit suget fussent.
Ne s'acorderent mie a un,
Ainz firent, par cunseil commun,
Plusurs reis en plusurs cuntrees
Si unt les terres devisees.   13670
Plusurs feiz s'entreguerrierent
E plususrs feiz se rapaierent.
Si cum chascun plus fort esteit
Sur le plus fieble cunquereit. ⁷
Issi unt lungement esté
Que il n'orent rei curuné
Ne mustier n'i ot estoré ⁸
Ne tenue cristïenté;
[Altel sacré ne dedié,
Enfant levé ne baptizié.   13680

---

¹ MS D reading—*severundes*—restored.
² MS D reading—*la*—restored.
³ MS D reading—*avint*—restored.
⁴ MS D reading—*ert*—restored.
⁵ MS J adds: *E puis estoient enanglé/ Dont il furent anglois clamé/ Quant Vortimers les encauça/ Et en Tanet les enangla/ A force del pais les mist/ Et eus et lour*

seignor Hengist. [*enanglé* = cornered, brought to heel].
⁶ MS D reading—*s'i*—restored.
⁷ MS J here adds thirty lines on the rest of the story of Gurmund and Ysembard, with their defeat in France by king Louis.
⁸ MS D reading—*estoré*—restored.

Gurmunt gives Britain to the Saxons

flew off to spend the night where they were accustomed to nest, in heaps of corn and in haystacks and in the eaves of houses. The fires spread and, becoming very hot, set the town alight and aflame.

13607   The Britons saw the town burning, flames leaping and houses falling; they pre-pared to fight but, because they were few, were defeated. One after the other, people left; King Cariz fled. He made his way straight to Wales; I can't say what next ensued.[1] Thus the famous city was totally wrecked and destroyed. Because it was taken through sparrows and conquered by sparrows, some people formerly used to call it—and the peasants still do—'the Sparrow City', to remember the extraordinary event, that the city which had held out so long was lost through birds.[2]

13625   Gurmunt destroyed many cities and many old castles, many churches, many groups of clergy, many a bishopric and abbey which were not restored or inhabited there-after. The ruins, waste land and wilderness can still be seen which Gurmunt made in many places, in order to rob the British of their domains. When he had ravaged the country, burnt the towns and seized all possessions, he gave the kingdom to the Saxons. He had promised them he would hand it over if he con-quered it, and he did so, doing them justice. They acquired the land which they had so ardently desired. After the name of the race who first received the land, they called themselves 'English', in order to recall their origins, and called the land given to them 'England'. What in French is called 'Engleterre' is in English called 'England'; the name means 'land of the English', that is its explanation. From the time Brutus arrived from Troy, Britain always retained its name until the moment of which I'm telling you—when through Gurmunt it lost its name and acquired new inhabitants, new kings and new lords. These wished to keep their customs: they had no wish to use another language. They altered the names of the towns and renamed them in their own language.[3]

13663   The English wanted to appoint a king, but could not agree on whether to have a single monarch and all to be subject to one king. They could not agree on one, so by common consent they created several kings in several regions and so shared out the lands. Many times they fought each other and many times they restored the peace. As each grew stronger, so he defeated the weaker ones.[4] For a long time matters remained this way: they had no crowned king, and they neither restored the churches nor upheld Christianity. They consecrated no holy altars,

---

[1] *HRB* chap. 185 has a long apostrophe to the fool-ish and squabbling Britons, which is not in *VV*.

[2] Gaimar is the only other writer besides Wace (and before Laȝamon) to employ this story of the sparrows used to take Cirencester, though attributing the device to Cerdic, Ceawlin's great-grandfather. Houck, *Sources*, pp. 300–10 gives examples of stories of other cities suppos-edly captured this way.

[3] Added by Wace, aware of changes of name as turning-points in the identity of a country.

[4] *HRB* chap. 186 has a long and contemptuous account (much reduced in *VV*) of the defeated British, fighting among themselves and not at-tempting to recover their former greatness.

Cent anz e plus i ont esté
Senz lei e senz crestienté.] [1]
Parler en oï sant Gregoire
Ki a cel tens ert apostoire:
Saint Augustin i enveia,
Clers esteit bons e mult l'ama.
A lui se sunt acumpaignié
Quarante clerc forment preisié.
En Tanet vint premierement
13690 E de Tanet passa en Kent;
A Kantuorbire s'aprisma
E li puepes mult l'ennura.
Reis Aldebert, ki Kent teneit,
Del lignage Henguist esteit;
Cil ad saint Augustin oï,
Haitiez en fu, en Deu creï; [2]
Emprés lu rei fud sa meisnie
Regeneree e baptizie.
Saint Augustin mult s'esjoï
13700 Del puepe ki s'i cunverti.
El nun de sainte Trinité
Fist un mustier en la cité;
Par la terre ala sermunant,
Mustiers feisant, clers ordenant.
Par lieus trova genz de put aire
Ki a enviz voldrent bien faire;
Saint Augustin mult s' pena [3]
E lungement i travailla
Ainz qu'il les peüst aturner
13710 A Deu servir n'a Deu amer.
Quant lu païs ot puralé
E mult en ot avironé,
A Dorecestre vint errant,
La lei Damnedeu anunciant.
Lez Dorecestre ot une gent, [4]
Devers suth est prueceinement,
Saint Augustin lur sermuna
E la lei Deu lur anuncia.
Cil furent de male nature,
13720 De sun sermun ne orent cure;

La u li Sainz lur sermunot
E de lur pru a els parlot,
A ses dras detriés li pendeient
Cues de raies qu'il aveient;
Od les cues l'en enveierent [5]
E asez lunges le chacierent.
E il pria nostre Seignur
Que de cele grant desenur
E de cele orrible avilance
Ait en els signe e remembrance; 13730
E il si orent veirement
E avrunt perpetuelment,
Kar trestuit cil ki l'escharnirent
E ki les cues li pendirent
Furent cué e cues orent
E unkes puis perdre nes porent;
Tuit cil unt puis esté cué
Ki vindrent d'icel parenté, [6]
Cué furent e cué sunt,
Cues orent e cues unt,   13740
Cues unt detriés en la char
En remembrance de l'eschar
Que il firent al Deu ami
Ki des cues l'orent laidi.
E quant il fud d'els eschapé,
En une valee est entré
De Dorecestre a cinc luees
Vers north west entre dous valees;
S'est al pié del munt arestez
Od ses cumpaignuns, tut lassez. 13750
Pur reposer s'i aresturent,
Chalt e sei orent e las furent.
Saint Augustin prist a penser
Cument purreit mais endurer
La hunte que l'um li feseit;
Purpensot sei qu'il s'en irreit.
Deu li est aparu a tant,
Apertement od lui parlant:
'Tien, dist il, tun purposement
Si te cuntien seürement.   13760

---

[1] MSS DLCKR omit ll. 13679–82; these lines are supplied by Arnold.
[2] MS D reading—*Haitiez en*—restored.
[3] MS D reading—*i*—restored.
[4] MS C: *Roucestre*; MS A: *Excestre*; MS L: *A*

Mugelingtune puis voleit estre. See Allen, *Lawman: Brut*, pp. 463–64.
[5] MSS DL: *l'encuerent.*
[6] MS D reading—*d'icel*—restored.

Augustine punishes the people of Dorchester with tails

brought no children to the font nor baptized them. For over a hundred years they were without creed and without Christianity.

13683 St Gregory, pope at that time, heard tell of this. He sent St Augustine there, a good cleric whom he much loved. Forty clerics of high repute accompanied him. He first arrived in Thanet[1] and from Thanet went to Kent; he approached Canterbury and the people paid him much respect. King Aldebert,[2] who ruled Kent, was of Hengist's lineage. He heard St Augustine, was cheered by his message, and believed in God; following the king, his household was converted and baptized. St Augustine rejoiced greatly at the conversion of the people. In the name of the holy Trinity, he had a church built in the city.[3] Throughout the land he went, preaching sermons, establishing churches and ordaining priests. In some places he found base folk who were unwilling to do good; St Augustine took great pains and laboured a long while before he could convert them to the service or love of God.

13711 When he had traversed the land and passed through many places, he came to Dorchester, proclaiming God's law. Near Dorchester, to the south-east, were a people to whom St Augustine preached and proclaimed God's word. They were of an evil disposition and cared nothing for his sermon: when the saint preached and spoke to them for their own good, they hung skate-tails on his garments behind, drove him away with these tails and pursued him for a great distance. And he begged our Lord that for this great dishonour and dreadful disgrace they should receive a sign and reminder, and indeed they had one, and will have one for ever, for all those who mocked him and hung tails on him got tails and were tailed and could never lose them thereafter. Everyone from this family has been tailed ever since; they were and are tailed, they had and have tails, tails are behind them as a reminder of the way they mocked God's friend by humiliating him with tails.[4]

13745 And when he had escaped from them, he entered a glen five leagues from Dorchester, between two valleys to the north-west. At the foot of the mountain he stopped, together with his companions, all weary. They stopped to rest: they were hot, thirsty and tired. St Augustine began to wonder whether he could endure humiliation any longer. He thought he would leave. Thereupon God appeared to him, speaking quite clearly. 'Hold fast to your resolve,' He said, 'and

---

[1] Arrival in Thanet is not in *HRB* but occurs in Bede I, chap. 25 and *HA* III, chap. 3.

[2] Ethelbert. Wace adds his lineage, possibly from Bede II, chap. 5 or *HA* II, chap. 40.

[3] Added by Wace; see Houck, *Sources*, pp. 263–4. On the differences in emphasis and content between Wace and *HRB* here, see Arnold II, p. 814.

[4] Not in *HRB*. See William of Malmesbury, *De Gestis*, Bk II, chap. 84, pp. 184–85 and Goscelin, *Historia translationis*, Bk VI, pp. 408–39. It is Wace who makes the punishment fit the crime. The story of the English having tails appears to date from the 12th century. Houck, *Sources*, pp. 269–75, suggests the fish-tail story is a local one.

Tu iés mis serfs e tu me pleis
E bien me plaist ço que tu fais.
M'aïe avras, jo sui od tei,
Ço que tu requiers, ço t'otrei. [1]
Overte t'est del ciel l'entree
E a entrer t'est graantee.
Tu troveras lu ciel overt
U cil entre ki bien me sert.'
Saint Augustin ot Deu veü
13770 E sun cunfort ot entendu.
Tant l'esguarda cume il pot,
E ço fu tant cume Deu plot.
Al lieu vint u Deu ot esté,
En plurant ad iloc uré.
Jus se mist, la terre beisa
E meinte feiz s'agenuilla;
Puis ad un bastun fichié dreit
Illoc u Deu veü aveit;
Une veine d'ewe en sailli
13780 Ki tute la place cuvri,
L'ewe surt e li ruissels crut,
Sun canol fist, aval curut. [2]
N'esteit mie anceis la cuntree
Herbergie ne cultivee
Pur ço que ewe n'i cureit
Ne que funteine n'i surdeit.
Saint Augustins Deu mercia
E ses cumpaignuns cunforta;
Le lieu ad Cernel apelé
13790 U il aveit Deu esgardé;
Cernel cest nun que jo ai dit
En romanz est: Deu veit u vit.
Li clerc le poënt bien saveir,
Cerno, cernis, ço est veeir
E Deu ad nun en ebreu El;
De ces dous moz est fait Cernel.
Cerno e El sunt ajusté,
Li uns dit Vei, l'autre dit Dé;
Mais une lettre en est sevree,
13800 De la fin de Cerno ostee,

Si est par une abscisiun
Faite la compositiun;
L'un est ebreu, l'autre est latins. [3]
Ço vit e volt saint Augustins
Quant il a Cernel cest nun mist
Que remenbrance a nus feïst [4]
Que Damnedeu en cel lieu fu
E en cel lieu l'aveit veü;
Quant nus Cernel cest nun avum [5]
Saver e remenbrer devum   13810
Que Damnedeu se demustra [6]
E estre e parler i deigna. [7]
   Quant li Engleis e li Saissun,
Primes li reis, puis li barun,
Orent tut receü baptesme, [8]
De funz levé, enoint de cresme,
Saint Augustin joius en fu,
Ki mult desira lur salu.
Es terres que Bretun teneient
Ki des Engleis se defendeient,   13820
Trova moines, trova abez,
Trova set evesques sacrez,
E trova un arcevesquié
Dunt Karliun aveit le sié.
A Bangor ot une abeÿe
Ancïenement establie;
Dionot abbes en esteit.
Prés de dous mil moines aveit
Departiz en set cumpaignies;
En chascune des set parties   13830
Aveit moines prés de treis cenz;
Issi erent en set cuvenz.
Del labur de lur mains viveient,
De lur labur se susteneient.
Saint Augustins demander fist
Les set evesques, si lur dist
Que il ert de Rome legat
E d'Engleterre esteit primat,
Si deveient beneïçun
De lui receivre par raisun   13840

---

[1] MS D reading—*ço*—restored.
[2] MS D reading—*canol*—restored.
[3] MS D reading—*l'autre est*—restored.
[4] MS D reading—*a*—restored.
[5] MS D's reading of line restored.
[6] MS D reading—*se*—restored.
[7] MS J adds: *Dont s'en torna liés et joiant/ S. Augustin Dieu gratiant/ Puis converti tote la gent/ D'Engletere molt doucement.*
[8] MS D reading—*tut*—restored.

Augustine baptizes the English

act with confidence. You are my servant and pleasing to me, and what you are doing pleases me. You will have my help, I am with you, and what you ask I will grant. The doors of Heaven are open to you and you are permitted to enter; you will find Heaven open to him who serves me well.'

13769   St Augustine saw God and heard his words of comfort. He looked at him as long as he could, and as long as it pleased God. He came to the place where God had appeared and prayed there, weeping. He bent down, kissed the earth and many times fell to his knees. Then he sank a rod just in the spot where he had seen God. A spring of water spurted out, covering the whole place; the water bubbled out and the stream grew, formed a channel and ran down. The countryside had not previously been inhabited or tilled, because there was no water or spring there. St Augustine thanked God and comforted his companions. He called the place where he had looked at God 'Cernel'. This name 'Cernel' means in the vernacular 'he sees, or saw, God'. Scholars are well aware of it: *cerno, cernis* means 'to see', and God's name in Hebrew is *El*. From these two words 'Cernel' is made. *Cerno* and *El* have been put together, the one meaning 'see', the other 'God'; but one letter has been removed, taken from the end of *cerno*, so that the combination—of one Hebrew and one Latin element—is made through an excision. This was St Augustine's vision and desire, when he called Cernel by this name, that it should remind us God was in this place and he had seen him there. When we hear this name 'Cernel', we should know and remember that God made himself known and deigned both to remain and to talk there.[1]

13812   When the English and the Saxons—first the king, and next the barons—had all been baptized, sponsored at the font, and anointed with holy oil, St Augustine, who was eager for their salvation, rejoiced. In the lands held by the British, defending themselves against the English, he found monks, abbeys, seven consecrated bishops and an archbishopric whose seat was at Caerleon. There was a long-established abbey at Bangor; Dionot was abbot there.[2] There were nearly two thousand monks, divided into seven sections; in each of the seven divisions there were nearly three hundred monks, so they were in seven monasteries. They lived by the toil of their hands and supported themselves through this labour.

13835   St Augustine sent for the seven bishops and told them he was a legate from Rome and primate of England, thus by rights they ought to receive his blessing

---

[1] See William of Malmesbury, *De Gestis*, p. 185 where the spring appears after Augustine has seen God in his mind's eye and the malefactors have been pardoned and converted, and Goscelin, *Historia translationis*, which Houck thinks are Wace's main sources for the stories about Augustine. Wace follows William's etymo-

logical explanation for '*Cernel*', but his topographical precision on the region (near today's Cerne Abbas) is all his own.

[2] *HRB* chap. 188: *Dinoot*. For him and his monastery at Bangor-is-y-Coed in Clwyd, see Bede II, chap. 2.

E estre en sa subjectiun.
Cil respundirent: ' nu devum,
Kar nus nostre arcevesque avum,
Ki ad sun sié a Karliun
Par le cunfermement de Rome;
Ja nen iert tresturné par hume.
Ensurquetut nel devum faire,
Kar Engleis sunt nostre adversaire;
De noz terres nus unt geté
13850 E de noz fieus desherité.
Nus sumes e avum esté
Cristïens de cristïens né
E cil sunt de paene gent
E cunverti sunt novelment.
Desdeing nus semblë e trop vil chose [1]
Ne nuls de nus loer ne l'ose
Que seium a celui suget [2]
Ki de cels salver s'entremet
Ki de noz fieus chacié nus unt
13860 E en noz fieus remanant sunt;
E tuit cil sunt nostre enemi
Par ki Engleis sunt cunverti
E ki od els unt cumpaignie
E commune e parçonerie.'
Saint Augustin n'i pot plus prendre
Ne ne lur pot faire el entendre;
Al rei Aldebert le mustra
E cil forment s'en desdeigna.
Aldebert esteit reis de Kent;
13870 Elfrid manda, un sun parent,
Ki de Northumberlande ert reis;
Cil asemblerent les Engleis,
Lur humes e lur amis tuz, [3]
Ki plus fort erent e plus pruz.
Bangor e Dyonot l'abbé
E les moines de la cité
E l'autre clergié ensement
Volent destruire mortelment
Ki ne lur portent reverence,
13880 Ne ne lur vuelent obedience [4]

Faire lur ne professiun
Fors al prelat de Karliun;
Saint Augustin unt refusé
Par hunte d'els e pur vilté;
Chevaliers e geldes manderent,
A Leïrcestre s'asemblerent;
Par la voleient trespasser
E en Guales par la entrer. [5]
Brochinal la cité teneit,
Quens ert e des Bretuns esteit.   13890
Mandé ot quanque mander pot
E as Engleis cuntr'ester volt.
Mais Engleis se tindrent forment;
Descunfit fud, kar poi ot gent; [6]
De humes i ot grant damage [7]
E cil s'en fuï en un boscage. [8]
Li bon hermite e li bon moine
E li religius chanuine,
Cil de Bangor meïsmement,
Erent venu communement   13900
Preier Alfrid a Leïrcestre
E cels ki meistre durent estre
Que de cel pueple e del clergié
Eüssent menaie e pitié.
Li hume de religiun,
Ki ne voleient si bien nun,
Hermite, moine, clerc, vilain
E povre gent e citheein,
Ki s'aloent atapissant,
De plusurs lieus vindrent avant,   13910
Plusurs nus piez, plusurs en langes,
Querre merci as genz estranges.
Cil furent cruel e felun
E orguillus plus que leün; [9]
De ço dunt il le desus eurent
Le noalz firent que il peurent.
Deus, quel dolur! Deus, quel pechié!
N'en eurent pas greinur pitié
Que lus fameillus de berbiz;
Mult en firent grant tueïz.   13920

---

[1] MS D reading—*trop*—restored.
[2] MS D's reading of line restored.
[3] MS D's reading of line restored.
[4] MS D reading—*lur*—restored.
[5] MS D's reading of line restored.

[6] MS D reading—*descunfit*—restored.
[7] MS D reading—*de humes i*—restored.
[8] MS D reading—*E cil s'en*—restored.
[9] MS D reading—*plus que*—restored.

Massacre of the Bangor monks

and be subject to him. They replied: 'We have no need, for we have our own archbishop, with his seat at Carleon, ratified by Rome; no one will ever alter this. Besides, we should not do it because the English are our enemies: they threw us off our lands and deprived us of our domains. We are, and we have been, Christians born of Christians, and these people are heathens, and only recently converted. It seems to us contemptible and shameful—and none of us would dare to advise it—that we should be subject to the man busy with saving those who hunted us out of our lands and who have remained there. And all those through whom the English have been converted, who are friendly to them, associate with them and keep them company, are our enemies.'

13865 St Augustine could get no more from them, nor could he make them think differently. He spoke of it to king Aldebert, who became very angry. Aldebert was king of Kent; he sent for Elfrid,[1] one of his kin and king of Northumberland, who gathered the English together, their friends and all their men who were the strongest and bravest. They were intent on killing and destroying Bangor, the abbot Dionot, the city's monks and the other clergy too, who had no respect for them and would not be obedient nor publicly profess their opinions except to the prelate at Carleon. They had shamefully and basely rejected St Augustine.

13886 The English assembled knights and footsoldiers at Leicester;[2] they wanted to move from there to Wales. Brochinal,[3] a British count, held the city. He summoned whoever he could and meant to oppose the English. But the English put up a strong resistance, and he was defeated because he had few men. There were great losses to his army, and he fled to a wood. The good hermits and monks, the pious canons and also the people of Bangor together came to Leicester to beg Elfrid and those who were to be their rulers to have mercy and pity on people and clergy. Men from religious orders, devoted to good alone, hermits, monks, clerics, and peasants, poor folk and citizens who had been in hiding, appeared from many places, some barefoot, some in rags, to ask mercy from the foreigners. But these were cruel and wicked and prouder than lions; holding the whip hand, they did the worst they could to those under them. God, what misery, how heart-rending! They showed no more pity than starving men would to sheep; they

---

[1] *HRB* chap. 189: *Edelfridus*; *VV*: *Edelfridus/ Ethelfridus*. See Bede I, chap. 34 and II, chap. 2.

[2] *HRB* chap. 189: *Legecestria* i.e. Leicester, misunderstanding Bede's 'Lega-caestir, which the Britons more correctly named Carlegion', i.e. Chester. (*HA* repeats Bede. See Greenway, *Henry of Huntingdon*, pp. 162–3, fn. 29). Leicester makes no sense in this context, though nei-

ther *HRB*, Gaimar's *Estoire* (l. 1081), nor Wace seem aware of it.

[3] *HRB* chap. 189: *Brochmail*; *VV*: *Brochinail*. In Bede (II, chap. 2) and *HA* III, chap. 16, Brocmail is merely the protector of the monks, but he may have been of the Meirionydd royal line: see Davies, *Wales*, pp. 94, 98 and 102.

Dous milliers e dous cent en pristrent
Sis decolerent e ocistrent;
N'en est moine ne clerc estuers,
Martirs firent des cumfessors.
Puis voldrent a Bangor aler
Cité destruire e gent tuer.
Bretun e Gualeis ki l'oïrent
Grant asemblee encontr'els firent.
En la terre aveit treis baruns
13930 Ki erent seignur des Bretuns;
Des altres esteient seignur
Kar plus fort erent e meillor.
Bledric de Cornuaille ert sire
E si teneit Devenesire;
Issi cum l'ewe d'Esse curt [1]
De la funteine u ele surt
Des qu'en la mer u el descent
Ço tindrent Bretun lungement;
Mes Adelstan quant il regna
13940 Ultre Tambre les esluina.
Chatwan esteit reis de Northwales
E Margadud reis de Suthwales;
Tut esteit lur jesqu'en Saverne
Ki lez le munt curt de Malverne;
Mais Aedelstan tant les destreinst
Que ultre Waie les enpeinst.
Chevaliers e geldes menerent
Cil ki des altres seignur erent;
Bledric, Chatwan e Margadud,
13950 Par grant ire e par grant vertud,
Engleis e Seisnes asaillirent
E cil forment les recuillirent.
Mes Elfrid fud sempres nafrez
E fuiant est del champ turnez,
Mes merveilles i ot ocis
De sa gent e de ses amis.
Ocis fud en cele bataille
Bledric li cuens de Cornuaille.
Dunc se sunt Bretun asemblé,
13960 A Leïrcestre sunt alé;

Cadwain, ki savant ert e pruz,
Firent rei par le los de tuz.
Cil ad tuz mandez e sumuns
Serjanz, chevaliers e baruns.
Engleis, ki les cuntez teneient
E reis apeler se feseient,
Sunt tuit a sa merci venu
E si hume sunt devenu.
Puis dist qu'il passereit le Humbre [2]
Se gent plus fiere ne l'encumbre,   13970
Northumberlande destruira
E la gent tute en chacera;
Lu rei Elfrid, se il l'atent,
Si par force ne s'en defent, [3]
Prendre en champ u ocira
U vif le deseritera.
Elfrid oï que il veneit
E les manaces qu'il feseit.
Manda amis, manda parenz,
Manda ses humes, manda ses genz, [4] 13980
Manda Engleis, manda Seissuns,
Ki guerre aveient as Bretuns;
Grant fud li puoples d'ambes parz,
Que de hardiz, que de cuarz.
Li gentil hume del païs,
Ki d'ambes parz orent amis,
Virent le mal kin avendreit
E la perte ki grant serreit
Se li dui rei se cumbateient
Ki si griefment s'entrehaeient.   13990
Tant unt d'un rei a l'altre alé,
Tant unt cunseillié a parlé,
Les reis firent entr'acorder
E par ostages pais afermer. [5]
Des terres unt fait tel esguart
Que chascuns d'els en ai sa part;
E chascuns fei a l'altre port;
Elfrid ait des le Humbre en nort
E Chatwan ait del Humbre en su;
Issi unt pais entr'els tenu   14000

---

[1] MSS DLFPNT: *Osse.*
[2] MS D reading—*passereit*—restored.
[3] MS D reading—*s'en*—restored.
[4] MS D reading—*manda ses genz*—restored.
[5] MS D reading—*afermer*—restored.

Cadwan and Elfrid share the kingdom

slaughtered masses of them. They seized two thousand two hundred[1] and killed and beheaded them, nor were monks or clerics spared; they martyred those who confessed their faith.

13925 Then they wanted to go to Bangor, to destroy the city and kill the people. Hearing of this, the British and Welsh gathered a great army against them. There were three barons in the land, who were lords of the Britons; they were lords because they were strongest and best. Bledric was lord of Cornwall and held Devonshire; the Britons held for a long time the area around the course of the Exe, from the spring where it rises to its issue into the sea. But when Athelstan reigned, he expelled them across the Tamar. Cadwan was king of North Wales and Margadud king of South Wales: to them belonged everything as far as the Severn, which flows from Malvern beside the mountain. But Athelstan harried them so much that he pushed them beyond the Wye.[2]

13947 These lords—Bledric, Cadwan[3] and Margadud—led knights and foot-soldiers, and with great anger and violence attacked the English and Saxons, who vigorously repelled them. But before long Elfrid was wounded and left the field in flight; however, huge numbers of his people and his friends were killed there. In this battle Bledric count of Cornwall was slain. Then the Britons came together and went to Leicester; with the agreement of everyone they made Cadwan, who was wise and brave, king. He called and summoned everyone, knights, lords and men-at-arms. The English who were holding the earldoms, and calling themselves kings, all threw themselves on his mercy and became his men. Then he said he would cross the Humber, if a fiercer race did not trouble him, and would ravage Northumberland and expel all the people; if he overtook king Elfrid, unless he strongly defended himself, he would take him in the field or kill him or dispossess him if still alive.

13977 Elfrid heard of his coming and of his threats. He summoned friends and relations, his vassals and his people, English and Saxons, who were at war with the Britons. On both sides there were large numbers of people, whether brave or cowardly. The noblemen of the land, who had friends on both sides, saw the evil which would follow, and the great losses, if the two kings, who so bitterly hated each other, were to fight. They went so often from one king to another, and talked and advised so much, that they made the kings come to terms and make peace, using hostages. They made this decision about lands: that each of them should have his share and each make a port for the other. Elfrid was to have the land north of the Humber and Cadwan the land south of the Humber.

---

[1] *HRB* chap. 189: 1,200 (as in Bede); *VV*: 2,200. The battle of Chester is mentioned in the *Annales Cambriae* for 613; Brochmail's grandson Selyf is said to have died there.

[2] Arnold (II, p. 815) thinks the information about

Athelstan, absent in *HRB*, comes either from oral tradition or William of Malmesbury, *De Gestis*, Bk II, chap. 134, p. 148.

[3] *HRB* chap. 189: *Bledericus, Caduanus*; *VV*: *Bledricus, Cadwanus*.

E entr'els puis ot tel amur [1]
Unques n'i pot aver greinur;
Lur aveirs mistrent en commun,
Tut iert as dous, tut ert a l'un,
Greinur amur aver ne porent.
Femmes pristrent e enfanz orent,
Dous fiz orent a un termine:
Le fiz Elfrid ot nun Edwine
E Chadwallein le fiz Cadwan;
14010 Andui furent nez en un an.
Pur l'amur des peres garder
E pur les fiz faire entr'amer
Furent li fiz ensemble mis,
Ensemble nurri e apris;
D'une guise furent chalcié
E d'une guise apparaillié.
Quant il porent bien chevalchier,
Escuz porter, lances baillier,
Chevals bien puindre e bien tenir,
14020 Espees traire e cops ferir,
Chevalier furent fait ensemble
En Armoriche, ço me semble.
La les ot fait Chadwan mener
E la lur fist armes duner,
Kar si parent ki la maneient
Bretun nez de Bretun esteient.
Quant li pere furent finé
E d'icest siecle trespassé, [2]
Chascun des fiz tint s'erité;
14030 Dous anz unt puis amis esté
E dous anz unt l'amur tenue
Que lur dui pere orent eüe.
Edwine tint del Humbre en la
E Chadwalein del Humbre en ça.
Mes Chadwalein ot plus asez
Chastels e viles e citez
Que li reis Edwine n'en ot;
Curuner se fist quant il volt.
Granz festes e granz curz teneit
14040 E noblement se cunteneit.

Edwine li preia e requist [3]
Qu'il otreiast e cunsentist
Que il peüst estre sacrez
E beneïz e curunez
De la le Humbre u il maneit
Cum cil de ça le Humbre esteit.
Cil dist qu'il s'en cunseillereit
E a sa gent en parlereit, [4]
E ço que l'um l'en loereit
A brief terme li respundreit.   14050
Dejuste l'ewe de Duglas
S'entrevindrent a un trespas
Pur cele chose purveeir
Cum ele peüst plus bel seeir. [5]
As dous rives de l'ewe furent
E par messages parler durent;
Endementiers que li message,
Li plus viel hume e li plus sage,
De l'un rei a l'altre passoent
Ki les cunseilz entr'els portoent,   14060
Li reis Chadwalein descendi,
Sumeil ot grant si s'endormi.
Sun chief li tint sis niés Brienz
Ki mult ert iriez e dolenz
Que Aedwine ço requereit
Que unques mais esté n'aveit.
De curuz e de marrement
Suspira mult parfundement;
Mult suspira e mult emfla,
Espessement des oilz lerma;   14070
Lu chief lu rei en fud muidliez
Si que li reis est esveilliez;
Sa mein ad a sun chief levee,
Sa face trova arusee.
Dunc prist Brien a regarder
E Brien escrieve a plurer.
'Brien, dist li reis, que as tu?
Pur quei plures, qu'as tu veü?' [6]
'Sire, dist il, jol vus dirrai:
Curusciez sui e grant doel ai   14080

---

[1] MS D's reading of line restored.
[2] MS D reading—*d'icest*—restored.
[3] MS D reading—*request*—restored.
[4] MS C omits the episode with Brien and adds: *Ses sages homes fist mander/ Kar par conseil voleit* *ovrer/ E cil li unt tuz conseillé/ Ke le corunement seit desturbé/ Kar a mal chef purreit traire/ Si dous portent corune en une terre.*
[5] MS D reading—*ele*—restored.
[6] MS D reading—*veu*—restored.

Meeting of Edwin and Chadwalein

14000 Thus they kept the peace between them, and later there was such affection between them it could hardly be greater. They held all their possessions in common: everything both had, one had; it was impossible to have greater love. They took wives and had children, and had sons at the same time.[1] Elfrid's son was called Edwin and Cadwan's was called Chadwalein;[2] they were both born in the same year. To keep their fathers' love alive and to make the sons fond of each other, the boys were brought together and together nurtured and educated. They were given similar boots and clothes. When they could ride well, carry shields, handle lances, spur horses and stay in the saddle, draw swords and strike blows, they were knighted together in Brittany, I believe. Cadwan had them taken there and there given arms, because his kin who lived there were Britons born of Britons.[3]

14027 When the fathers died and passed from this world, each son ruled what he inherited. For two more years they were friends and for two years continued the affection their two fathers had felt. Edwin ruled on that side of the Humber and Chadwalein on this.[4] But Chadwalein had many more castles, towns and cities than king Edwin. He had himself crowned at will; he held great feasts and great courts and behaved nobly. Edwin asked and begged him to agree and consent that he could be consecrated, blessed and crowned on that side of the Humber, where he dwelt, just as Chadwalein was on this side. Chadwalein said he would take counsel and speak to his people, and what they advised he would shortly tell him.

14051 They met at a ford near the River Douglas in order to examine how this matter might be better established. They were on either side of the water and had to talk through messengers. While the messengers—the oldest and wisest men— crossed from one king to the other bearing advice, king Chadwalein dismounted; he felt very sleepy and went to sleep. His head was held by his nephew Brien, who was very miserable and angry that Edwin was asking to be what he never had been. Through anger and distress he fetched a deep sigh; he sighed and swelled with anger and his tears fell thick and fast. They wet the king's head so that he woke up; he raised his hand to his head and found his face was moist. Then he started to look at Brien and Brien burst out weeping.

14077 'Brien, what is the matter?' said the king. 'Why do you weep, what have you

---

[1] In *HRB* chap. 190, Ethelfrid repudiates his wife, pregnant with Edwin, who then gives birth to her son in Caduan's household; the *VV* omits this passage. Edwin was actually the son of Aelle, king of Deira, and brother-in-law of Ethelfrith of Northumbria.

[2] *HRB* chap. 190: *Edwinus* and *Caduallo*; *VV*: *Cadwallo*.

[3] In *HRB* chap. 190 the two boys learn chivalry and courtesy in the household of Salomon king

of Brittany; this is omitted in *VV*.

[4] On Edwin of Northumbria and Cadwallon king of Gwynedd (Bede's Caedwalla), see Stenton, *Anglo-Saxon England*, pp. 80–81; a later tradition alleged that Edwin had been fostered by Cadwallon's father, Cadfan. See Rachel Bromwich, *The Welsh Triads*, triad 26 and introduction p. xcviii, and Chadwick, 'The Conversion of Northumbria', pp. 147–55.

Que en nostre tens e par nus,
Dunt sui dolenz e curusçus,
Ad ceste terre honur perdue.
Grant hunte nus est avenue:
Dous reis curunez volez faire,
A mal chief en puissiez vus traire,
De ço que uns reis sot tenir
E dunt l'um deit un rei servir.'
Li reis pur ço que Briens dist
14090 L'otrei qu'il aveit fait desfist;
Al rei Edwine fierement
Manda qu'il nel fereit neient,
Kar li Bretun le cuntralient: [1]
Cuntre raisun serreit, ço dient,
E cuntre dreit e cuntre lei,
Que ço que deit estre a un rei
Seit parti e a dous donez
Si que chascuns seit curunez;
Ne volt lu regne retaillier
14100 Ne sa dignité abeissier.
Edwine, ki orguillus fu,
Irïement ad respundu
Que jamés cungié n'en querra,
Senz cungié se curunera
E altretel franchise avra
En sun regne cum il de ça.
Chadwalein dist s'il le feseit
Que la curune li toldreit,
Le chief ovoc li abatreit;
14110 E cil dist ço qu'il nel cremeit.
Issi sunt par mal departi
E chascuns ad l'autre haï;
Chascuns sot a l'altre mal gré
Chascun ad l'autre desfié.
Edwine fud fel e irus,
Mult fu emflez e orguillus;
De ço qu'il prie ore, ço dit,
Serra preiez jesqu'a petit.
Es vus esmeüe la guerre
14120 E a eissil mise la terre;

Tuit li plusur s'entreguereient,
Terres saisissent, viles preient.
Chadwalein grant ost asembla,
Al Humbre vint, l'ewe passa,
Northumberlande volt guaster
E Edwine tut deseriter. [2]
Edwine fud de grant curage,
Ne volt fuïr pur nul damage;
Sei e sa terre volt defendre,
Ne deigna pais ne triewe prendre. [3] 14130
Cuntre Cadwalein chevalcha
Sil venqui e desbareta;
E Chatwalein s'en volt aler
E en sa terre returner,
Mes Edwine devant lui vint
Ki la veie li clost e tint
E Chadwalein fuï aillurs.
Par boscages e par tresturs
Alad vers Escoce fuiant,
Edwine emprés l'alad querant;   14140
Grant peine e grant travail li crut;
En Irlande passer l'estut.
Li reis d'Yrlande le reçut
E henura si cum il dut
E Edwine, ki fu remés,
Quant il ne pot ateindre as nés,
Lu regne Chadwalein saisi,
Chastels destruist, turs abati,
Terres purprist, citez guasta,
Humes raïnst, viles preia.   14150
Suer Brien li fud enditee,
A Virecestre l'ad trovee, [4]
A Everwic la fist mener
E en sa chambre bien guarder. [5]
Ne sai ki li ot amené
Pelliz, un clerc d'Espaine né,
Ki mult esteit de grant clergie
E mult saveit d'astronomie.
Al curs des esteiles luisanz
E al vol des oisels volanz   14160

---

[1] MS D reading—*Bretun*—restored.
[2] MS D reading—*tut*—restored.
[3] MS D reading—*triewe*—restored.
[4] MSS DLSFJAPNT: *Wincestre*.
[5] MS D reading—*bien*—restored.

Chadwalein flees to Ireland

seen?' 'My lord,' he said, 'I will tell you. I am angry and most distressed that in our time and through us this land has lost its honour—that is why I feel grief and anger. Great humiliation has befallen us. You wish to make two crowned kings: you may come to a bad end, because one king alone is accustomed to rule and as a result a man should serve one king.'[1] As a result of what Brien said, the king repudiated what he had agreed. He proudly announced to king Edwin that he would not do it, because the Britons opposed it: they said it would be unreasonable, against justice and against law that what should belong to one king should be split and given to two, so that each was crowned. He did not wish to cut up his realm or diminish its dignity.

14101   Edwin, who was proud, replied angrily he would never ask for permission; he would be crowned without permission and have as much freedom in his kingdom as Chadwalein had in his. Chadwalein said that if he did so, he would remove his crown and his head with it, and Edwin said that did not frighten him. Thus they parted in anger, each hating the other; each bore the other ill will and each declared the other his enemy. Edwin was angry and furious, quite swollen with arrogance; because he had to ask now, he said, soon they would have to ask him. This was how war broke out and the land was laid waste. The vast majority fought each other, seized domains and pillaged towns.

14123   Chadwalein collected a large army, arrived at the Humber and crossed the river; he wished to ravage Northumberland and completely dispossess Edwin. Edwin was a most courageous man. No losses would make him flee; he was out to defend himself and his land and would not deign to arrange peace or a truce. He rode against Chadwalein, defeated and routed him. And Chadwalein wanted to leave and return to his land, but Edwin appeared before him, occupying and barring the road, and Chadwalein fled by another route. Through woods and byways he fled towards Scotland, Edwin in pursuit behind him; he endured increasing pain and sufferings and had to cross to Ireland. The Irish king received him and paid him appropriate honour, and Edwin, remaining behind, when he could not catch up with the ships, seized Chadwalein's kingdom, destroying castles, razing towers, seizing lands, spoiling cities, holding men to ransom and pillaging towns. They pointed Brien's sister out to him; he found her in Worcester and had her taken to York and carefully guarded in her room.[2] I do not know who brought him Pellit, a scholar born in Spain, who possessed very great learning and was most knowledgeable in astronomy. From the course of the shining stars and the flight of birds on the wing he knew the doings of what concerned him.

---

[1] *HRB* chap. 191: *Brianus*; he is given a much longer speech accusing the treacherous Saxons. This is omitted in *VV*.

[2] Wace here anticipates *HRB* chap. 196. Chad-walein's abduction of Brien's sister may not necessarily imply that he rapes her (Allen, *Lawman: Brut*, p. 465); it depends on the interpretation of *sa chambre* (l. 14154)—her room or his?

Les aventures cunisseit
D'iço dunt il s'entremeteit. [1]
Ne poeit rien Cadwalein faire,
Nés asembler ne genz atraire
Que li devins n'aparceüst
E que Edwine nel seüst.
Suvent appareilla navie
E suvent ot grant compainie;
Suvent se mist siglant en mer,
14170 Suvent as porz volt ariver;
Mes Edwine devant veneit
Ki la terre li defendeit;
Kar li devins tut devinot
U e quant ariver quidot.
Chadwalein ot grant marrement
Que returné fud tant suvent;
De sa terre l'orent siewi
Serjant e parent e ami;
Guerpies orent li plusur
14180 Lur erité tut pur s'amur. [2]
A cels dist qu'en Bretaine irreit,
Al rei Salomun parlereit;
Andui erent d'un parenté
E cil l'aveit suvent mandé,
Ki bien esteit de grant poeir.
Que noit que jor, que mein que seir
Unt tant curu e tant siglé
A Gernemue sunt arivé, [3]
Un isle vers soleil culchant;
14190 Ço qui que d'iloc en avant
N'ad altre terrë u gent maine
Entre Cornuaille e Bretaine.
N'orent guaires en l'idle esté
Li reis chaï en enferté;
Malade fud de fievre ague
Dunt cil returne ki bien sue;
De veneisun ot desirier,
Nul altre char ne pot mangier.
Li reis ad Brien apelé,
14200 Preié li ad e cumandé

Que char de veneisun li quiere,
Ne li chaille de quel maniere;
Ja ne vendra a guarisun
Si il n'ad char de veneisun.
Brien fud del rei anguissus,
De lui guarir fud curius; [4]
Garçons apela e vadlez,
Levriers apela e brachez, [5]
Quistrent valees, quistrent plaines,
Quistrent faleises e muntaines,   14210
Tute la terre avirunerent,
Unc cerf ne bisse ne troverent
Ne daim ne lievre ne chevrol;
Lores ot Brien mult grant dol.
Quant vit que sis uncles murreit [6]
Pur veneisun qu'il n'en aveit, [7]
Ne il ne set u il la troisse,
Un braün trencha de sa quisse,
Larder le fist e bien rostir,
Puis le fist a sun uncle offrir;   14220
Ne sai se li reis en gusta,
Mes il guari e trespassa,
E des que il pot sus lever,
Ses nefs fist mettrë a la mer,
A Kidalet ariva dreit,
Ki a cel tens cité esteit
Entre Dinan e la marine,
Encore i pert bien la ruine.
Li uns reis l'autre rei reçut
E enura que plus n'estut; [8]   14230
Sun herberjage e sun sujor
Li fist aver a grant enur,
E a sa terre recuvrer
Se sur Edwine volt aler
L'avancera mult haltement
De sun aver e de sa gent.
Tut l'ivern unt ensemble esté
E tut l'ivern unt sujorné;
Entretant unt nés purchacees,
Aïe quise, pris mainees.   14240

---

[1] MS D reading—*d'iço*—restored.
[2] MS D's reading of line restored.
[3] Arnold replaced *Gernemue* (none of whose variants were satisfactory, except perhaps MS L's *Geresye*) with *Gernerui*, from the *Roman de Rou*. See Arnold II, p. 815.
[4] MS D reading—*curius*—restored.
[5] MS D reading—*apela*—restored.
[6] MS D reading—*murreit*—restored.
[7] MS D reading—*qu'il n'en aveit*—restored.
[8] Emended by Arnold from *enura plus que ne put*. Other MSS variants show divergent views on whether Chadwalein deserves honour or not.

Brien feeds Chadwalein on his own flesh

Chadwalein could do nothing, neither collect ships nor gather men, without the soothsayer's awareness and Edwin's knowledge. Often he would equip a fleet and often have a great company; often he would begin sailing in the sea and often intended to arrive in the ports, but Edwin would get there first, to defend the land against him, because the soothsayer divined everything, where and when he thought to arrive.

14175   Chadwalein was most distressed at his frequent retreats. Soldiers, kinsmen and friends had followed him from his land; most had, for love of him, abandoned their heritage. He told them he would go to Brittany and talk to king Salomun; they were both from the same kin and Salomun, a man of great wealth, had often sent for him. Throughout night and day, morning and evening, they voyaged and sailed so hard that they arrived in Guernsey,[1] an island in the West. I believe that from there onwards there is no other inhabited land between Cornwall and Brittany. They had hardly landed on the island before the king fell ill: he was sick with acute fever, from which one can recover by profuse sweating. Unable to eat other meat, he longed for venison. The king called Brien and begged and ordered him to seek venison flesh for him, no matter how he did it; he would never be cured unless he had it.

14205   Brien was troubled about the king and anxious to cure him. He called for grooms and servants, greyhounds and hunting-dogs, and searched valleys, plains, cliffs and mountains. They covered the whole land but found neither stag nor hind, nor deer nor hare nor roebuck. Then Brien felt great misery. When he realised his uncle would die for lack of venison, and he did not know where to find it, he cut a slice from his thigh, larded and thoroughly roasted it and then had it offered to his uncle. I do not know if the king tasted any, but he recovered and survived.[2] And as soon as he could get up, he had his ships put to sea and sailed straight to Kidalet, which at that time was a city between Dinan and the coast; its ruins can still be seen.[3]

14229   The one king received the other and paid him more respect than was necessary: he gave him lodging and abode with great honour and said he would most amply assist him with his wealth and his men to recover his land, if he wished to move against Edwin.[4] They were together all winter and all winter they stayed put; meanwhile they acquired ships, sought aid and took on followers. They sent

---

[1] See Arnold II, p. 815 on the numerous MSS variants here; *HRB* chap. 193: *Garnareia*, absent from *VV*, as is the preceding description of the storm.

[2] Wace's doubts reduce the impact of this distasteful incident (*HRB* chap. 193).

[3] According to Tatlock (p. 86) and Arnold (II, p.

816), the Breton town of Aleta, north of St Servan, was destroyed by the Normans in the 11th century.

[4] In *HRB* chap. 194 both Salomon and Cadwallo make long speeches, absent in *VV*, on the enfeeblement and degeneration of the Britons.

En Engleterre unt enveé
En tapinage aparaillé
Brien, pur le devin ocire,
Ki tut saveit lur estre dire.
Purparlé unt e cunseil pris
Que, tant cum li devins est vifs, [1]
En Engleterre n'enterunt
Ne el païs n'ariverunt.
Bien set dire a quel port e quant
14250 Turnent cil qui vunt naviant.
S'il en volt prendre guarde e cure.
Brien se mist en aventure;
A Barbeflué en mer entra
E a Suthamtune ariva.
Ses dras pur plus malveis chanja
E de malveis s'aparailla;
Un bastun fist faire ferrin
Cume burdun a pelerin,
Li fers fud bien lungs e aguz,
14260 Bien fud trenchanz e esmuluz.
Brien se mist en tapinage,
Cum huem de luin pelerinage;
Veiant gent s'alot desguisant,
Bien semblot povre peneant;
Al bastun s'alot apuiant,
D'ures en altres clopignant;
Tant quist la curt e demanda
Qu'a Everwic lu rei trova.
Entre les povres s'enbati,
14270 Entre les povres s'atapi, [2]
Entre les fardus fud fardus
Cume mendis e busuinus.
Sa suer est d'une chambre issue
E Brien l'ad bien cuneüe;
En ses meins un bacin teneit,
A la reïne ewe quereit.
Brien s'enbati en sa veie
Qu'ele le cunuisse e qu'ele le veie; [3]
La suer ad le frere entercié,
14280 Mes il li ad dit e cluignié

Qu'ele ne face nul semblant
Qu'il li partienge poi ne grant. [4]
Il la baisa e ele lui,
Asez plurerent ambedui.
Defors la presse se sunt trait
Que hum ne femme nes agueit;
Ele li ad tut l'estre dit
E si li ad mustré Pellit,
Le devin, qui esteit venuz;
Par aventure ert fors issuz.   14290
Suvent veneit, suvent alot,
Entre les povres trespassot.
Brien parti de sa sorur,
Ki de lui ert en grant freür;
En la veie al devin s'est mis,
Ki passot entre les mendis;
Tant atendi e tant guaita [5]
Que li devins lez lui passa.
Del bastun de fer qu'il tint grant
Li duna tel cop en butant   14300
Par mi le cors li enbati,
Forment l'enpeinst e cil chaï,
Unques ne dist oï ne nun.
Briens i laissa lu bastun,
Senz le bastun tut cuintement
Se traist entre la povre gent
Si qu'il ne fud aparceüz.
Ne enterciez ne mescreüz.
Le jor s'est alé demuçant,
Entre les povres tresturnant,   14310
La nuit issi de la cité
Tut suavet e a celé,
De la cuntree s'esluina.
Que nuit que jor tant espleita,
A Essecestre vint sur Esse;
Es vus envirun lui grant presse
De Bretuns, de Cornualeis,
De chevaliers e de burgeis;
Demandant vunt dunt vient, u vait,
Que volt, que quiert, que dit, que fait. 14320

---

[1] MS D reading—*est*—restored.
[2] MS D reading—*s'atapi*—restored.
[3] MS D reading—*qu'ele le veie*—restored.
[4] MS D reading—*poi ne grant*—restored.
[5] MS D reading—*tant guaita*—restored.

Brien kills the soothsayer Pellit

Brien to England, in disguise, to kill the soothsayer who could tell all about their situation. They agreed and decided not to enter England nor arrive in the land so long as the soothsayer was alive. If he wished to pay heed and attention, he was quite able to say at what port and when the fleet would arrive.

14252   Brien put his life in danger: he embarked at Barfleur and arrived at Southampton. He changed his clothes for poorer ones and dressed in those; he had a stick made of iron, like a pilgrim's staff, very long and sharp, piercing and keen. Brien disguised himself as a man on a long pilgrimage; under people's eyes he went around disguised, looking just like a poor penitent. He leant on the staff and had a perpetual limp. He kept looking and asking for the court until he found the king at York. He hastened into the ranks of the poor, he hid himself amongst them; he was a wretch amongst the wretched, like a beggar and an indigent.

14273   His sister came out of a chamber and Brien recognized her; she was holding a basin in her hands, fetching water for the queen. Brien planted himself in her way so that she should see and know him. His sister recognized her brother, but he winked at her and said she should show no sign that he belonged to her in any way. He kissed her and she him and both wept.[1] They withdrew from the throng, so that they should not be spied upon by men or women. She described all the circumstances to him and pointed out Pellit, the soothsayer, who had arrived and by chance had come outside. He was constantly coming and going, moving amongst the poor. Brien left his sister, who was very frightened for him, and put himself in the path of the soothsayer, who was passing between the beggars. He kept waiting and watching until the soothsayer passed next to him. Holding his great iron staff, he gave him such a push with his blow that he thrust him through the body; he struck him vigorously and Pellit fell, never uttering a yes or a no.

14304   Brien left the staff there and without it slyly slipped amongst the poor people, so that he was not noticed or recognized or suspected. During the day, he kept hidden, back amongst the poor; at night, he left the city quietly and secretly and travelled far from the region. By night and by day he advanced so far that he came to Exeter on the Exe; here there was a great crowd around him, of Britons, of Cornish, of knights and citizens, who kept asking where he came from, where he was going, what he wanted, what he sought, what he had to say, and what he was doing. They kept asking about Chadwalein—where was he, why did he stay away so long? Brien had to tell them truly whether he would return and if he would ever rule again.

14325   'Yes,' said Brien, 'very soon you'll see him coming with such an army that Edwin will never reach him, nor be able to stay in the realm. He has many times hurt

---

[1] The disguised palmer or pilgrim hiding amongst the poor in a king's household and recognized by a woman closely connected to him is a favour- ite 12th century story motif; see the stories of Tristan, Horn, Hereward and Boeve de Haumtone.

De Chadwalein vunt demandant
U est, pur quei demure tant;
Die lur veir s'il revendra
E si jamés terre tendra.
'Oïl, dist Brien, asez tost
Le verrez venir a tel ost,
Ja Edwine ne l'atendra
Ne el regne ne remaindra.
Pur amur lu rei mainte feiz
14330 Nus ad damagé e destreiz;
Faites chastels, guarnissiez turs,
Kar jesqu'a poi avrez sucurs.'
Brien ad as Bretuns parlé,
De plusurs set la volenté;
Essecestre prist e saisi,
Tenir le volt si l'ad guarni; [1]
A sun uncle ad par brief mandé
Quei e cument il ot ovré;
Tutes li manda les noveles,
14340 E li reis quist nefs e naceles.
Li reis Salomuns, sis cusins,
Que des suens, que de ses veisins,
Li livra dous mil chevaliers
Estre estiermans e mariniers;
A Toteneis vindrent siglant,
Liez en furent li païsant.
Li reis Edwine dolent fu
Del bon devin qu'il ot perdu
E d'Essecestre que Brienz
14350 Aveit prise si ert dedenz.
Peanda, lu rei de Mercie,
Ço ert d'Engleterre partie,
Ad enveé od grant esforz
Pur guarder la terre e les porz
E pur Essecestre aseeir
S'altrement ne la puet aveir.
Peanda Essecestre asist,
Entrer volt dedenz mes nel fist;
Brien fud dedenz ki la tint
14360 Tant que li reis Chadwalein vint.

A Toteneis esteit venuz
E des nefs a terrë issuz;
Des noveles ad demandees
E noveles li sunt cuntees
Que Brien, sis niés, est asis,
Pendu serra se il est pris.
Li reis, de Brien anguissus,
E de succurre mult curius, [2]
Tant chevalcha od ses vassals
Que bois, que plains, que munz, que vals,   14370
Al siege vint cum il ainz pot.
Deus, quel joie Brienz en ot!
Chadwalein ot riches meinies [3]
E richement apareillies;
Quatre cunreiz ad establiz,
Puis ad cels del siege asailliz.
Mult en i ot que pris que morz
Des plus riches e des plus forz.
Peanda meïsmes i fud pris, [4]
N'en fud nafré, n'en fud ocis. [5]   14380
Bien fud tenu, bien fud gardez,
Ne pot mie estre delivrez
Dissi qu'il fist al rei humage
E prist de lui sun eritage.
De sun fieu li ad fait ligance,
E pur faire ferme aliance
E pur faire entr'els ferme amur
Prist Chadwalein une sorur
Que Peanda aveit, mult bele,
Gente e curteise damisele.   14390
Chadwalein les Bretuns manda,
Mult les blandi e mercia
Del travail e de la haür
Que suffert orent pur s'amur.
Tut ala gastant lu païs,
La u il sot ses enemis;
L'ewe del Humbre trespassa,
Chastels destruist, viles preia.
Edwine manda tuz les reis
Ki Seidnes furent e Engleis   14400

---

[1] MS D reading—*l'ad*—restored.
[2] MS D reading—*mult*—restored.
[3] MS D reading—*meinies*—restored.
[4] MS D reading—*i*—restored.
[5] MS D reading—*n'en...n'en*—restored.

Chadwalein and Penda become allies

and harried us for our love of the king. Construct castles, fortify towers, because soon you will get help.' Brien spoke to the British; he knew what many of them wanted. He took and seized Exeter; intending to hold it, he fortified it. By letter he told his uncle what and how he had done; he gave him all the news, and the king requested ships and boats. His kinsman, king Salomun, gave him—what with his own and those of his neighbours—two thousand knights, in addition to sailors and helmsmen. They came sailing to Totnes; the peasants were delighted.

14347 King Edwin was distressed at losing the good soothsayer and at Brien's taking and occupying Exeter. He sent Penda, king of Mercia[1]—which was part of England—to guard the land and the ports with a large army, and to besiege Exeter, if he could get it no other way. Penda laid siege to Exeter; he wanted to enter it but could not. Brien was within and held it until king Chadwalein came. The king arrived at Totnes and disembarked; he asked for news and was given them—that his nephew Brien was under siege and, if he were caught, would be hanged. Anxious for Brien and keen to help, the king rode with his vassals so hard, whether through woods, plains, mountains or valleys, that he came to the siege as soon as possible. Lord, what joy Brien felt!

14373 Chadwalein had powerful followers, splendidly equipped. He formed four companies and then attacked the besiegers; many of the mightiest and strongest, were either captured or killed. Penda himself was taken but was neither wounded nor killed. He was carefully kept and guarded; he could not be released until he did homage to the king and held his hereditary lands from him. He swore allegiance to him for his fief and, in order to make a strong alliance and establish firm affection between them, Chadwalein took one of Penda's sisters in marriage, a most beautiful, noble and courteous girl.[2]

14391 Chadwalein sent for the Britons and gave them much praise and many thanks for the suffering and hatred they had endured for love of him. He went to lay all the country waste in the region where he knew his enemies were. He crossed the River Humber, destroyed castles and sacked towns. Edwin summoned all the kings who were Saxon and English (some who were called kings in fact only governed counties) and got them all to be with him, whether from having done him homage, or out of loyalty. He rode against Chadwalein, who had no fear of him. The battle and strife between Chadwalein and Edwin took place in a field

---

[1] See Bede II, chap. 20 and Stenton, *Anglo-Saxon England*, p. 80. Penda, though of royal blood, was not yet king of Mercia but he soon became 'the central figure in English history' from 632–54. A siege of Exeter is not attributed to him.

[2] Wace adds this detail.

(Plusurs ki reis clamé esteient
Pur realtez cuntez teneient).
Edwine les out tuz od sei
Que par humages, que par fei.
Cuntre Chadwalein chevalcha
E Chadwalein nel reduta.
En un champ ki Helfelde ad nun
Fud la bataille e la tençun
Entre Chadwalein e Edwine;
14410 Mult ot entr'els mortel haïne. [1]
Edwine fud morz e sis fiz,
Ki esteit apelé Osfriz,
E mort fud li reis d'Orkenie,
Ki venuz ert en lur aïe;
Des altres i ot pris asez,
Plusurs ocis, plusurs nafrez.
Grant fud l'ocise e grant la prise
Dunt Chadwalein fist grant justise;
Cels destruist e lur parenté
14420 Ki cuntre lui orent esté;
Femmes fist ocire e enfanz,
Neïs les petiz alaitanz;
Unques n'i pot valeir eage
Ne pris ne bealté ne parage.
    D'Edwine fud remés uns eirs
Ki tint lu regne e les maneirs:
Osriz ot nun en baptistire.
Mes Cadwalein, od sun empire, [2]
Guerre e estrif cuntre lui prist,
14430 Lui e dous ses nevuz ocist
Pur ço que part del regne aveient
E eir emprés estre deveient;
Ne laissa qu'il peüst trover
Ki deüst eritage aver. [3]
Oswald aprés, un gentil ber
Pur cristïene lei guarder,
Uns nobles huem de franc curage,
Ot lu regne par eritage;
Mes Chadwalein l'en guerria
14440 Envers Escoce lu chaça.

Quant il vit que tant luin fuieit
E que ateindre nel poeit,
Nel volt mie plus luin chacier
Ne tuz ses humes travaillier;
Partie de sa gent livra
A Peanda, si li rova
Qu'Oswald chaçast tant e siewist
Qu'il le preïst e oceïst. [4]
Quant Oswald sot cel apareil,   14450
Forment li plot icel cunseil [5]
Que pur Peanda ne fuereit
Ainz l'atendreit s'il le sieweit;
[En mi un champ s'est arestez
Ki Hevenfeld est apelez.] [6]
Hevenfeld, cist nuns est engleis,
Celestiel champ en franceis.
El champ fist une croiz lever,
E a sa gent la fist aurer;
'Sainte croiz, dist il, aürez,
Merci criez, cupes batez. [7]   14460
De vos pechiez vus repentez
E des mesfaiz pardun querez.
Faites vus humblement cunfés
Que que aviengë en aprés;
[Plus aseür estre purrunt
Cil qui vivrunt u qui murrunt.]' [8]
Cil firent sun cumandement;
A genuilluns mult humblement
[Aürerent Deu e la croiz
Od humble cuer, od simple voiz;] [9]   14470
A Damnedeu merci requistrent,
Disciplines e venies pristrent.
Puis sunt apresté de cumbatre,
Si nuls sur els se vueille enbatre. [10]
Peanda vint kis asailli,
Mes malement l'en eschaï,
Kar de sa gent le mielz perdi
E il meïsmes s'en fuï;
Lu cuer ot gros e d'ire plein.
Plaindre s'ala a Chadwalein;   14480

---

[1] MS J adds: *E la bataille dura tant/ Qu'ocis furent li aucant/ Et li autre qui s'en fuirent/ Saciés que molt grant dolor fisent.*

[2] MS D reading—*od*—restored.

[3] MS D reading—*eritage aver*—restored. MS J adds: *En trestoute la tere Edwine/ Ne cose c'a lui fust acline/ Toz les ocist et detrenca/ .i. seus des parens n'i laissa.*

[4] MS D reading—*e*—restored, as in l. 14458.

[5] MS D reading—*icel*—restored.

[6] This couplet is supplied by Arnold; it is missing in MSS DLCSFAPNT.

[7] MS D's reading of line restored.

[8] This couplet is supplied by Arnold; it is missing in MSS DLCSFHAPNT.

[9] This couplet is supplied by Arnold; it is missing in MSS DLCSFA.

[10] MS D reading—*Si nuls*—restored.

Battles of Hatfield and Hevenfeld

called Hatfield.[1] Between them was mortal hatred. Edwin died and so did his son, who was called Osfrith, and the king of Orkney died, who had come to help them.[2] There were many others captured, many killed and many wounded. The slaughter was huge and so was the number of captives, to whom Chadwalein gave severe justice: he destroyed those who had opposed him and their kin too, killing women and children, even those still at the breast. Neither age nor bravery counted, neither beauty nor rank.

14425   One heir survived Edwin, who ruled his kingdom and his manors: his baptismal name was Osric.[3] But Chadwalein, from a position of power, waged war and strife against him and killed him, and two of his nephews, because they owned part of the kingdom and were due to be the next heirs. He left no one he could find who could possess the inheritance. Next Oswald inherited the kingdom—a noble lord, fit to defend the Christian faith, a great man with an honourable heart.[4] But Chadwalein made war on him, chasing him towards Scotland. When he saw he had fled so far he could not reach him, he did not want to pursue him any further nor inconvenience all his men. He gave some of his men to Penda and asked him to pursue and follow Oswald until he captured and killed him.

14449   When Oswald learnt of these preparations, the following advice gave him great pleasure: that he should not flee Penda but wait for him, should he follow him. He stopped in the middle of a field which is called Hevenfeld. This name Hevenfeld[5] is English; in French it means heavenly field. He had a cross raised in the field and made his men pray to it. 'Pray to the holy cross,' he said, 'beat your breasts and cry for mercy. Repent your sins and ask forgiveness for your misdeeds. Make a humble confession, no matter what happens next; those who are to live or to die will be in greater safety.' They did as he ordered; most humbly, on their knees, they prayed to God and the cross with a meek heart and honest voice, and they chastened themselves and made acts of contrition. Then they prepared to fight, if there was anyone who wished to attack them.

---

[1] *HRB* chap. 197: *Hedfield*. For the battle of Hatfield Chase in Yorkshire in 633, see Swanton, *Anglo-Saxon Chronicle*, p. 25 and Bede II, chap. 20. *HB* chap. 61 calls it the battle of Meicen (*Annales Cambriae*: Meigen, 630). Stenton, (*Anglo-Saxon England*, p. 81) remarks that Cadwallon 'was the only British king of historic times who overthrew an English dynasty and the British peoples never found an equal leader'. In Bede he is obviously a villain, while Edwin is virtuous; *HRB* and Wace are more neutral.

[2] *HRB* chap. 19: *Offridus* and *Gadboldo*, king of the Orkneys; *VV*: *Osfridus* and *Golboldo*.

[3] *HRB* chap. 198: *Offricus*; *VV*: *Osricus*. Osric king of Deira was, according to Swanton, *Anglo-Saxon*

Chronicle, p. 27 and Bede III, chap. 1, Edwin's cousin.

[4] Wace adds this praise of Oswald, possibly influenced by Bede.

[5] *HRB* chap. 199: *Heuenfeld*. Not in *ASC* but see '*Hefenfelth*' in Bede III, chap. 2, who reports in his previous chapter the historical defeat and death of Cadwallon by Oswald at 'Deniseburn' (Rowley Burn, south of Hexham) in 634; *HB* chap. 64 and *Annales Cambriae* call it '*Cantscaul*'. *HA* (III, chap. 34) follows Bede on Deniseburn, but in the Letter to Warinus, influenced by *HRB*, calls the battlefield '*Heuenfeld*' (*HA*, IX, chap. 8). See Stenton, *Anglo-Saxon England*, p. 81.

Jamés, ço dist, ne l'amera
Ne de lui terre ne tendra
Si d'Oswald ne li fait venjance,
Ki li ad fait si grant pesance.
Quant lur plot, lur otz asemblerent,
En Northumberlande passerent;
E cuntre Oswalt se cumbatirent, [1]
D'ambesdous parz mult i perdirent.
E Peanda Oswalt trova,
14490 Mult le haï sil decola.
Grant fud li dols e grant la perte,
Humes ocis, terre deserte,
Femmes vedves, viles guastees,
Maisuns voides, preies menees.
    Un des freres Oswald, Oswi,
Lu regne sun frere saisi;
E li barun l'unt receü,
Ki lur seignur orent perdu.
Cil vit la gent mult afieblie
14500 E la terre mult apovrie;
Vit la force Chadwalein grant,
Vit Chadwalein fort e puissant,
Vit que tenir ne se purreit
Si Chadwalein l'envaïsseit.
Mielz volt laissier sa dignité
E humilier de sun gré
Que vers tel hume guerre prendre
Dunt il ne se puisse defendre.
A Chadwalein prist parlement;
14510 Mult li duna or e argent;
En sa baillie se submist,
Sis huem devint, feelté fist,
Sun regne de li recunut,
E Chadwalein sun fieu li crut;
Issi fud la pais graantee
E issi fud lunges guardee.
    Oswi ot parenz e nevuz
Asez preisanz e asez pruz,
Ki, pur aveir part de la terre,
14520 Pristrent estrif entr'els e guerre.

Mes Oswi bien se defendi
Que nuls terre ne li toli;
De ça le Humbre les chaça.
E cil vindrent a Peanda,
Que forz hum esteit, sil requistrent,
Avers e terres li pramistrent
Sis maintenist e cunseillast
E Oswi pur els guereiast.
Peanda dist qu'il n'en osot
Si Chadwalein nel graantot;   14530
N'osereit guerre cumencier
Ne la pais enfraindre premier,
Mes il querreit, se il poeit,
Que Chadwalein l'otriereit.
A une Pentecuste avint
Que Chadwalein feste e curt tint.
[A Londres se fist curuner
E ses baruns fist tuz mander.] [2]
Oswi n'i fud mie veüz,
Ne il n'i esteit pas venuz;   14540
Ne sai s'il ne volt u ne pot,
U Chadwalein mandé ne l'ot .
Peanda en piez se dresça,
Al rei Chadwalein demanda
Que poeit estre e que deveit
Que Oswi en curt ne veneit. [3]
Tuit i esteient li barun
E li Engleis e li Bretun,
Oswi sul ne deignot servir
N'a sa curt ne deignot venir.   14550
'Essoine, dist li reis, le tient;
En enferté gist, si devient.'
Dist Peanda: ' N'est mie issi;
Vus ne cunuissiez mie Oswi.
Il ad en Seissuine enveié
Pur gent a cheval e a pié.
Gent purchace, soldeiers quiert;
Des qu'il purra e lieus en iert,
Guerre quide grant esmoveir,
Ne puet ne ne volt pais aveir.   14560

---

[1] MS D reading—*E cuntre*—restored.
[2] This couplet is supplied by Arnold; it is missing in MSS DLCSFAPNT.
[3] MS D reading—*en*—restored.

Penda plots against Oswi

14475 Penda approached to assault them, but it turned out badly for him, for he lost the best of his men and he himself fled. His heart was full and swollen with anger. Aggrieved, he went to Chadwalein: he would never love him or hold land from him, he said, if he did not take revenge on Oswald for causing him such heavy affliction. When it suited them, they gathered their armies and crossed into Northumberland; they fought against Oswald and there were many losses on both sides. And Penda found Oswald and, full of hate, cut off his head.[1] The misery and bereavement were huge: men slain, land laid waste, women widowed, towns sacked, houses abandoned and herds seized.

14495 Oswi, one of Oswald's brothers, seized his brother's kingdom, and the barons, having lost their lord, accepted him. He saw his people greatly weakened and the land much impoverished, he saw Chadwalein's great might, his strength and power, and he saw that he could not hold out if Chadwalein attacked him. He preferred to lose his high office, and of his own accord humble himself, to waging war on such a man, against whom he could not defend himself. He arranged to meet Chadwalein and gave him much silver and gold; he submitted to his power, became his man, did him fealty and homage for his kingdom, and was entrusted by Chadwalein with his fief. Thus peace was agreed and for a long time maintained.

14517 Oswi had nephews and kinsmen, valiant and of high repute, who, to get part of the land, started wars and strife.[2] But Oswi defended himself well, so that they deprived him of no land, and chased them to this side of the Humber. And these people came to Penda and, promising him wealth and lands, asked him, as a powerful man, to protect and advise them and make war on Oswi on their account. Penda said he dared not, unless Chadwalein agreed; he would not dare to start a war or be the first to break the peace, but, if possible, he would ask Chadwalein to allow him to do so.

14535 It happened one Pentecost that Chadwalein held court and a feast. He had himself crowned in London[3] and summoned all his barons. Oswi did not appear nor did he come; I do not know whether it was against his will or out of his power, or whether Chadwalein had not summoned him. Penda got to his feet and asked king Chadwalein how could it be and what did it mean that Oswi was not at court. All the barons were there, both English and British; Oswi alone had not

[1] *HRB* chap. 199 correctly states that Oswald is killed by Penda (see *ASC* 641/2: the place was 'Maserfelth', possibly Oswestry), but calls the site of the battle 'Burne', thus confusing it with the battle of Deniseburn, actually a victory for Oswald. Wace, no doubt following Bede, avoids this confusion and adds Bede's detail (III, chap. 12) that Oswald was decapitated. *HB* chap. 64 reports that Oswald kills Penda.

[2] In *HRB* chap. 200, following Bede (III, chap. 14), Oswi's troublesome kin are named as Alfridus and Orwald (*VV*: *Oiwald*; Bede: *Alchfrid* and *Ethelwald*). Historically, Cadwallon was dead by now (see previous fn. 5 to p. 363 on Heuenfeld and Deniseburn).

[3] See fn. 4 to p. 257 on plenary courts and crownwearing; the latter is omitted by MSS D, P, and LCSFANT.

Mes s'il ne vos pesot, jo voil
Aler abatre sun orguil.
Si jo vostre cungié en ai,
U vif u mort le vus rendrai;
De la terre l'en chacerai.'
Dist Chadwalein: ' Jon parlerai.'
Dunc fist Peanda fors issir
E les Engleis fors departir; [1]
Des Bretuns retint les ainz nez,
14570 Les plus riches, les plus senez;
La requeste lur ad mustree
Que Peanda ot demandee.
Lez Chadwalein sist Margadud,
Ki de Suthwales sire fud.
'Pose a, dist il, que cumença,
E pose, ço m'est vis, dura
L'ire mortel e la haenge,
Cument qu'a la parfin en prenge,
Entre nus Bretuns e Engleis.
14580 De nus grever sunt tut tens freis;
Ja nul jor ne nus amerunt
Ne fei ne pais ne nus tendrunt.
Membre vus de lur felunies,
Membre vus de lur tricheries,
Membre vus de lur cruelté,
Membre vus qu'il vus unt grevé.
Suvent avez dit e juré,
Mes vus l'avez tut trespassé,
Que ja s'oster les poïez
14590 En cest regne nes larrïez.
Quant vus destruire nes osez
U ne volez u ne poëz,
Laissiez l'un a l'autre hunir
E sis metez al cuvenir.
Peanda est des Engleis nez,
Engleis est tut sis parentez;
Oswi est engleis ensement.
N'aiez vus ja nul marrement
Se l'uns mastins l'autre pelice,
14600 L'un fel vers l'autre ust sa malice;

Laissiez l'un l'autrë estrangler
E l'un a l'autre defoler.'
A la parole Margadud
Se sunt tuit li Bretun tenud.
[Dunc fud Peanda rapelez,
Tuz pleins cungiez li fud dunez] [2]
D'Oswi mal faire s'il poeit;
Ja Cadwalein n'en grucereit.
Peanda est de curt turnez,
Mult orguillus e surquidez,   14610
E griefment Oswi guereia
E mult suvent le damaga.
E Oswi li manda suvent
E preia mult escordement
Que pais e triewes li tenist
Ne damage ne li feïst;
Or e argent, se li plaiseit,
E altres aveirs li durreit.
Peanda dist que nel fereit,
Ne jamés pais a lui n'avreit.   14620
Oswi ne fud mie malveis;
Quant il vit que ne purreit peis
Ne cuncorde ne triewe prendre,
Mult se pena de sei defendre.
L'ire munta e engroissa,
La guerre crut e espeissa.
Un jor se sunt entr'encuntré
E par ire se sunt medlé.
Oswi ot en Deu grant fiance,
Mult ot en lui ferme creance,   14630
E Peanda mult s'orguilla
Es granz meinees se fia; [3]
Mes descunfit fud e ocis,
Od lui plusurs de ses amis.
Osriz, ki fud sis ainz nez fiz,
En la curt Chadwalein nurriz,
Requist e ot sun eritage
Sin fist a Chadwalein humage.
Chadwalein fud bon justisiers,
Leal rei fud e dreituriers;   14640

---

[1] MS D reading—*fors*—restored.
[2] This couplet is supplied by Arnold; it is missing in MSS DLCSFJAPNT.
[3] MS D reading—*meinees*—restored.

Penda is killed

deigned to attend or to come to his court. 'Some reason detains him,' said the king, 'perhaps he is ill.' Penda said: 'That's not so; you do not know Oswi. He has sent to Saxony for horsemen and foot-soldiers. He is procuring men and looking for mercenaries; as soon as he has the opportunity and place, he will try to start a big war. He neither can nor will have peace. But provided it does not disturb you, I would like to go and cut his pride down to size. With your leave, I will bring him back to you dead or alive; I will hound him from the land.'

14566   Chadwalein said: 'I will discuss it.' Then he made Penda go out and the English leave. He kept back the oldest, wisest and most powerful of the Britons, and told them of the request Penda had made. Next to Chadwalein sat Margadud, lord of South Wales. 'A long time ago,' he said, 'the deadly anger and hatred began—and will last, I think, a long while, whatever happens in the end—between us British and the English. They are always eager to harm us; the day will never come when they love us or keep faith and peace with us. Remember their wicked deeds, remember their treachery, remember their cruelty, remember how they've injured you. You've often said and sworn—but you've quite overlooked it—that if only you could get rid of them, you would not allow them in the kingdom. If you don't dare to destroy them, or won't or can't, let some of them wipe out the others and thus leave them to deal with it. Penda is of English blood, all his kin are English; Oswi is English too. Don't feel any distress if one cur skins the other, one villain vents his wickedness on the other; let them mutually choke and squash each other.'

14603   All the Britons agreed with Margadud's words. Then Penda was recalled and given full permission to damage Oswi if he could; Chadwalein would certainly not complain. Penda left court full of arrogance and pride, fiercely attacked Oswi and often did him great harm. And Oswi sent him frequent messages, fervently begging him to make peace and a truce with him and not to harm him; he would give him gold and silver, if he liked, and other possessions. Penda refused to do so or ever to make peace. Oswi was no coward: when he saw he could get neither peace, agreement nor truce, he took pains to defend himself. Fury mounted and grew, the conflict spread and raged. One day they encountered each other and angrily came to blows. Oswi had great trust in God, believing firmly in Him, and Penda, filled with pride, put his trust in his powerful followers; but he was defeated and killed, and many of his friends with him.[1] Osriz, his eldest son, brought up in Chadwalein's court, asked for and received his inheritance, and did homage for it to the king.[2]

14639   Chadwalein was a good ruler, a righteous and just king. He ruled the land for

---

[1] *HRB* chap. 200 says this battle is by the river *Uunued* (*VV*: *Winied/Wumed*), following Bede III, chap. 24 and *ASC* (the unidentified *Winwidfeld*, perhaps near Leeds); see also *HA* II, chap. 34. The year was 654 and the victory meant Oswi

became overlord of the Mercians and all the southern English (Stenton, *Anglo-Saxon England*, p. 84).

[2] In *HRB* chap. 200, Penda's son is *Wlfert* (*VV*: *Wilfridus*).

Quarantë e oit anz tint terre,　　　　　Muerent pere, muerent emfant,
Suvent ot pais, suvent ot guerre;　　　Muerent seignur, muerent serjant;
A Lundres maladi e jut;[1]　　　　　　　Muert li sires, muert la muillier,
Illoc fina, iloc murut.　　　　　　　　Muerent vilain e chevalier;
Bretun orent grant doel de lui,　　　　N'estuet al fiz le pere plaindre.[3]
Mes cuntre mort n'ad nul refui.　　　Mult veïssiez poi gent remeindre
Pur lui lungement remenbrer　　　　Es veies sultives e guastes;
Firent de quivre tresjeter　　　　　　Unques tel doel nen esgardastes.
Un chevalier sur un cheval　　　　　Ne poeient pas fuisuner
14650 En apareillement real;　　　　　Tuit li vif as morz enterrer;　　14690
Dedenz fud lu cors le rei mis,　　　Cil que le mort enterrer dut
Puis fud sur une porte asis　　　　　Od le mort enterrer estut.
A Lundres, dreit vers occident,[2]　　Cil ki porent fuïr fuïrent,
Illoc estut mult lungement;　　　　Lur fieus e lur meisuns guerpirent,
Dejuste ot faite une chapele　　　　Tant pur la grant chierté de blé,
De saint Martin, mult riche e bele.　Tant pur la grant mortalité.
　Chadwaladres emprés regna,　　En sa meisun ad mal espeir
Fiz Chadwalein, niés Peanda,　　Ki la suen veisin veit ardeir.
Niés Peanda, fiz sa sorur,　　　　Chalewadres, ki reis esteit,
14660 Ço fud uns reis de grant amur.　Ki la terre guarder deveit,　　14700
En sun tens fud falte de blé,　　En Bretaine a Regnes passa
E de la falte vint chierté,　　　Al rei Alain, ki mult l'ama;
E de la chierté vint famine,　　Niés Salemun aveit esté,
Chier fud en burc, chier fu en vile;　Ki sun pere aveit mult amé.
Bien peüssiez treis jorz errer　　Il le reçut mult lïement
Ne trovissiez a achater　　　　　E cunrea mult richement.[4]
Ne pain ne blé n'altre vitaille,　　Engleterre fud apovrie,
Tant par ert grant partut la faille.　Failliz li blez, la gent perie,
De peissuns e de salvagines,　　E le plus de la terre guast,[5]
14670 De veneisuns e de racines,　　Qu'il n'i aveit qui laborast.　　14710
De fuilles e d'erbes viveient,　　Unze anz e plus fud eissillie
Altre viande nen aveient.　　　E de laboreurs voidie.
Ovoc cele mesaventure　　　　Tant cum des Bretuns i aveit
Revint une altre altresi dure;　　Es munz e es forez maneit.
Mortalité fud grant de gent　　E li Engleis ki remis erent[6]
Par air corrumpu e par vent;　　E de la famine eschaperent,
Es meisuns, es champs e es rues　　E plusur ki aprés nasquirent,
E as marchiez e as charues,　　Si cum il porent mielz vesquirent.
Manjant, alant, parlant chaeient,　Que pur les viles restorer,
14680 Sudement senz langur mureient.　Que pur les terres laborer,　　14720

---

[1] MS D reading—*maladi*—restored.
[2] MS D reading—*dreit vers*—restored.
[3] MS D reading—*le*—restored.
[4] MS J adds: *Ensi remest li rois vivant/ Mais molt avoit*

le cuer dolant/ De sa gent qui ensi morut/ E de ce que fuir l'estut.
[5] MS D's reading of line restored.
[6] MS D reading—*remis*—restored.

Famine

forty-eight years, often at peace, often at war. He fell sick and took to his bed in London, and there he came to his end and died. The Britons greatly mourned him, but there is no escape from death.[1] To prolong his memory, they cast in copper a knight on horseback in royal clothing. Inside, they put the king's body, then placed the statue on top of a gate in London, to the west, where it remained a very long time. Alongside, they constructed a very fine and splendid chapel to St Martin.

14657 Chadwalader reigned next, son of Chadwalein, nephew of Penda; he was Penda's nephew, son of his sister, and a much beloved king.[2] In his time there was a shortage of corn, and from the shortage came scarcity, and from the scarcity came famine.[3] It was scarce in the borough and scarce in town; you could easily go three days without finding bread or corn or other food to buy, so great was the dearth everywhere. People lived on fish and wild animals, venison and roots, leaves and grass; they had no other food. With this calamity came another just as harsh: the people died in great numbers, from pestilential air and wind. In houses, fields and streets, in market-places and at the plough, while eating, walking, or talking they fell, dying suddenly, without prior feebleness. Fathers and children died, lords and servants died, husbands and wives died, peasants and knights died; there was no need for a son to mourn his father. You could see very few people left in desolate and deserted streets; you never set eyes on such misery before. There were not enough living to bury the dead; those supposed to inter the dead had instead to be buried with them. Those who could flee, fled, leaving their lands and their houses, as much for the great scarcity of corn as for the plague. Seeing one's neighbour's house burn down gives the man next door little hope.[4] Chadwalader, the king, who was supposed to guard the land, crossed to Rennes in Brittany, to king Alain who was a good friend: he was the nephew of Salomun who had shown much affection to Chadwalader's father. He received him most gladly and treated him nobly.[5]

14707 England was impoverished: the corn had failed, the people had perished, and most of the land was deserted because there was no one to till it. For eleven years and more it lay waste and empty of peasantry. Such Britons as there were dwelt in the mountains and forests, and the remaining English who had escaped the famine, and others born subsequently, lived as best they could. Both to restore

---

[1] Proverbial: see Morawski, *Proverbes*, no. 417.

[2] *HRB* chap. 202: *Cadualdrus*; *VV*: *Cadwalladrus*. This is Caedwalla king of Wessex (685–88), not British but English. A sister of Penda does marry Cenwalh of Wessex (641–72) but Caedwalla is only distantly related to him.

[3] *Annales Cambriae* records a great plague in 682 and says Catgualart (= Chadwalader) dies in it. In *HRB* chaps. 202–3 the famine is preceded

by civil war amongst the Britons and the illness of Chadwalader. Wace expands on the results of the plague.

[4] Proverbial: see Morawski, *Proverbes*, nos. 823 and 1367.

[5] In *HRB* chap. 203 Chadwalader utters a long lament and reproach, seeing Britain's troubles as punishment from God for sin. On the *VV*'s changes to this, see Wright II, p. xxxii.

Unt en Sessuine la mandé
U lur anceisur furent né
Que od femmes, que od enfanz,[1]
Od meinies e od serjanz[2]
Viengent tuit esforceement,
Terres avrunt a lur talent.
Terre avrunt bone a guaainier;
N'unt de rien fors d'umes mestier.
Cil vindrent mult espessement,
14730 Od granz cumpaignes e suvent.
Par les terres se herbergierent,
Mult crurent e multiplierent;
Ne troverent kis desturbast
Ne ki les terres lur veast;
Espessement e suvent vindrent;
Les custumes e les leis tindrent
Que lur anceisur ainz teneient
En la terre dunt cil veneient.[3]
Les nuns, les lages, le language
14740 Voldrent tenir de lur lignage;
Pur Kaer firent Cestre dire,
E pur Suiz firent nomer Sire,[4]
E Tref firent apeler Tune;[5]
Map est gualeis, engleis est Sune,
En gualeis est Kaer cité,
Map fiz, Tref vile, Suiz cunté,
E alquant dient que cuntree
Swiz est en gualeis apelee
E ço que dit Sire en engleis
14750 Ço puet estre Suiz en gualeis.
[Entre Gualeis uncore dure
De dreit bretanz la parleüre.][6]
Les cuntez e les barunies,
Les cuntrees, les seignuries
Tindrent issi e deviserent
Cume Bretun les cumpasserent.
A cel tens ert Adelstan reis;
Ço fud li premiers des Engleis
Ki ot tute Engleterre en baille
14760 Fors sul Guales e Cornuaille;

Premier fud enoinz e sacrez
E premierement curunez.
Plusur dient qu'il fud bastard.
Sis peres fud li reis Edward,
Ki pur urer a Rome ala
E a saint Piere graanta
E sur l'autel en fist present
Chascun an un denier d'argent
De chascun hume hostel tenant
Dedenz sa baillie manant.   14770
Premierement ot fait cest dun
Un sun ancestre, Yne ot nun;
Li eir emprés l'unt bien rendu,
Le dun al pere unt bien tenu.[7]
   Kalewadres volt revertir
E sa terre volt maintenir;
Quant il sot qu'ele fud poplee[8]
E la mortalité passee,
En sa terre volt repairier.
Sun eire fist aparaillier,   14780
Puis pria Deu escordement
Qu'il li feïst demustrement
Se sis repaires li pleiseit,
Kar sun plaisir faire voleit.
Une voiz divine lui dist
Laissast cel eire, altre preïst;[9]
L'eire d'Engleterre laissast,
A l'apostoile a Rome alast;
[Ses pechiez iluec pardonez,
Ireit od les beneürez.][10]   14790
Engleis Bretaine aver deveient;
Ja Bretun n'i recuvereient
Jesqu'al tens que la prophecie
Que Merlin dist seit acumplie;
Ne ja ço estre ne purreit
Desi la que li tens vendreit
Que les reliques de sun cors,
De sepulture traites fors,
Serreient de Rome aportees
E en Bretaine presentees.   14800

---

[1] MS D reading—*que od enfanz*—restored.
[2] MS D reading—*meinies*—restored.
[3] MS D reading—*cil*—restored.
[4] MS D: *Siwis*.
[5] *Bries* here in MSS DLP and in l. 14746 in MSS DL; Arnold supplies *tref*, 'the only good reading', from MS S.
[6] This couplet is supplied by Arnold; it is missing in MSS DCSFJAPNT.

[7] MS D reading—*rendu* and *tenu* in their original place—restored. MS J omits ll. 14763–74 and substitutes 4000 lines about St Edward, before returning to Chadwalader.
[8] MS D reading—*fud*—restored.
[9] MS D's reading of line—with *en* omitted—restored.
[10] This couplet is supplied by Arnold; it is missing in MSS DLCSFJAPNT.

Chadwalader is told to go to Rome

the towns and till the land, they sent word to Saxony, where their ancestors were born, that they should all come in strength, with women and children, followers and servants: they could have lands as they pleased. They would find good land to cultivate: only men were lacking.

14729 These people came over in swarms, and frequently, with large bands. They camped throughout the land, growing and multiplying; they found no one to trouble them or refuse them domains. In great numbers, and often, they arrived; they adhered to the customs and laws which their ancestors had once held in the land from which they came. They wanted to keep the names, laws and language of their race: for 'kaer' they said 'chester', and for 'suiz', 'shire', and they called 'tref' 'tun'. 'Map' is Welsh, the English for it is 'son'; in Welsh 'kaer' means 'city', 'map', 'son', 'tref', 'town' and 'suiz', county, and some say a district is called 'suiz' in Welsh and what 'shire' means in English may be what 'suiz' means in Welsh. Among the Welsh the correct way of speaking the British language is still preserved.[1] Thus they ruled and distributed the counties and baronies, lands and lordships as the British had first laid them out.

14757 At that time Athelstan was king;[2] he was the first Englishman to control all England except only Wales and Cornwall. He was the first to be anointed and consecrated and the first to be crowned. Many say he was a bastard.[3] His father was the king Edward who went to worship in Rome and, as a gift on the altar, gave St Peter a silver penny every year from each man owning a dwelling and living under the king's rule. One of his ancestors, called Yne, was the first to make this gift; his heirs subsequently faithfully renewed it and continued the gift to the pope.[4]

14775 Chadwalader wanted to return and rule his land. When he discovered it was inhabited and the plague was over, he wished to go back home. He prepared his journey, then asked God from the bottom of his heart to make him some sign if his return pleased Him, because he wished to do His will. A divine voice told him to abandon this journey and take another; he was to give up travelling to England and must go to the pope in Rome. There, his sins forgiven, he would join the blessed. The English were to have Britain; the British would never recover it until the time when Merlin's prophecy was fulfilled.[5] Nor could this ever

---

[1] These characterisic comments on equivalent words in Welsh and English are supplied by Wace alone. *Suiz* is the Welsh *swydd*, county; *tref* is correctly spelt.

[2] Athelstan (king 924–40) is absent from *HRB* Vulgate here but appears in *VV* chap. 204, praised for establishing peace and security. See Wright II, p. lxi.

[3] See Arnold II, p. 816 and Houck, *Sources*, p. 251.

[4] Edward's gift of the silver penny is added by Wace. See Houck, *Sources*, pp. 252–3 and Sten-

ton, *Anglo-Saxon England*, p. 460 and fn. 1, p. 215. Wace is the only writer to make Yne the original institutor of Peter's Pence, a tax which seems to have started in the reign of Alfred; other chroniclers attribute it to Offa of Mercia.

[5] *HRB* chap. 205: 'until the moment should come which Merlin had prophesied to Arthur'; as Thorpe, *Geoffrey of Monmouth: History*, says (p. 282), this never happened. *VV* omits 'Arthur' from some of its MSS.

Kalewadres s'esmerveilla, [1]
En merveillant se conturba [2]
De cel devin anuncement
Qu'il oï si apertement;
Al rei Alein sun bon ami
Recunta ço qu'il ot oï.
Alein fist ovrir les almaires
E fist venir les bons gramaires; [3]
Les hystoires fist aporter
14810   E fist cerchier e fist pruver
Que ço que Kalewadres dit
De la visiun que il vit
Se cuncordot as diz Merlin
E Aquile le bon devin
E a ço que Sibille escrist.
Ne Kalewadres el ne fist,
Sun navie e sa gent guerpi;
Yvor apela e Yni:
Yvor fud sis fiz de s'uxor,
14820   Yni sis niez, fiz sa sorur.
'En Guales, dist il, passerez
E des Bretuns seignurs serrez,
Que pur defalte de seignur [4]
N'algent Bretun a desenur.'
Cil firent ço qu'il cumanda
E il sun eire aparailla,
A saint Serge le pape ala,
Quil cheri mult e honura;
De ses pechiez se fist cumfés
14830   E prist sa penitence aprés.
N'aveit guaires a Rome esté
Quant il chaï en enferté;
Grant fud sis mals, murir l'estut; [5]
Unze jorz devant mai murut,
Al dis e setme jor d'avril [6]
Issi del terrïen issil,
Set cenz anz e un puis que Crist [7]
De sainte Marie char prist. [8]
Le cors fud mult bel cunreez
14840   En terre le cors saint posez; [9]

L'alme munta en paraïs,
U nus seium od lui asis.
    Yvor e Yni mer passerent,
Grant navie e grant gent menerent;
Les remasilles des Bretuns,
Que nus Gualeis ore apelums,
Ki sunt devers septentrion,
Orent en lur subjection.
Unc puis ne furent del poeir
Qu'il peüssent Logres aveir;   14850
Tuit sunt mué e tuit changié,
Tuit sunt divers e forslignié
De noblesce, d'onur, de murs
E de la vie as anceisurs.
Guales cest nun a Guales vint
Del duc Gualun, ki Guales tint,
U de Galaes, la reïne,
A ki la terre fud acline.

    Ci falt la geste des Bretuns
E la lignee des baruns   14860
Ki del lignage Bruti vindrent,
Ki Engleterre lunges tindrent.
Puis que Deus incarnatiun
Prist pur nostre redemptiun
Mil e cent e cinquante cinc anz, [10]
Fist mestre Wace cest romanz. [11]

---

[1] MS D reading—*s'esmerveilla*—restored.
[2] MS D reading—*conturba*—restored.
[3] MS D reading—*les*—restored.
[4] MS D reading—*pur*—restored.
[5] MS D reading—*sis*—restored.
[6] MS D reading—*setme*—restored.
[7] MS D reading—*e un*—restored.

[8] MS D reading—*De*—restored.
[9] MS D's reading of line restored.
[10] MS D's reading of line restored.
[11] MS J continues the history of England for almost two more folios: see Le Roux de Lincy, *Brut*, p. cxv ff.

Death of Chadwalader

happen until the time came when his remains, taken from his tomb, would be brought back from Rome and presented to Britain.[1]

14801 Chadwalader was amazed and, while he marvelled, he was disturbed by this divine proclamation which he heard so clearly. He related what he had heard to his good friend king Alain. Alain had the storehouses opened and summoned good, learned scholars; he had the history-books brought, and it was investigated and proved that what Chadwalader said of his vision agreed with the sayings of Merlin and Aquila the good soothsayer[2] and with what the Sibyl wrote. Chadwalader's acts did not contradict them: he abandoned his fleet and his army, and called for Yvor and Yni. Yvor was his son by his wife, and Yni was his nephew, his sister's son. 'Cross into Wales,' he said, 'and be lords of the British, so that they do not descend into dishonour through lack of a ruler.'

14825 They did as he commanded, and he prepared his journey; he went to the pope, St Sergius, who received him with much affection and honour. He confessed his sins and then did penance. He had hardly been long at Rome before he fell ill; he was very sick and death was inevitable. Eleven days before May he died, on the seventeenth day of April, he left his earthly exile, seven hundred and one years after Christ's incarnation in holy Mary.[3] His body was handsomely adorned and the holy corpse was placed in the ground. His soul ascended to Paradise: may we sit with him there.

14843 Yvor and Yni crossed the sea, taking a large fleet and large army, and made the rest of the Britons—whom we now call Welsh and who dwell in the North—their subjects. They never again acquired sufficient power to get Logres. The Welsh have quite altered and quite changed, they are quite different and have quite degenerated from the nobility, the honour, the customs and the life of their ancestors. Wales takes its name from duke Gualo, who ruled Wales, or from queen Galaes, to whom the land was subject.[4]

14859 Here ends the story of the British and the race of lords from Brutus's lineage, who ruled England for so long. One thousand, one hundred and fifty-five years after God became man for our salvation, Master Wace made this narrative.

---

[1] It is unclear whose remains these are: Merlin's? Chadwalader's? *HRB* chap. 205 refers to saints' relics.

[2] See para. 1591 and fn. 3 to p. 43 (Aquila=eagle).

[3] See Bede V, chap. 7 who dates Caedwalla's baptism in Rome to the Kalends of May, 689, as in *HRB* chap. 206; one of *VV*'s MSS has 699. Bede names Caedwalla's successor as Ine; he was son of Cenred, only distantly related to Caedwalla, and, of course, Saxon, not British.

[4] *HRB* chap. 208 has an author's epilogue, leaving the task of describing Welsh kings to Caradoc of Llancarfan (the author of the *Vita Gildae*) and recommending William of Malmesbury and Henry of Huntingdon to stick to describing the Saxon kings, since they do not possess Geoffrey's 'book in the British language'. This is absent from the *VV* which instead names Geoffrey as *Galdfridus Arthurus Monemutensis* (see Wright II, pp. lii–liii).

BIBLIOGRAPHY

Editions, Selections and Translations of Wace's Works

Wace, *La Vie de Sainte Marguerite*, ed. E.A. Francis (Paris: CFMA, Edouard Champion, 1932) and H.-E. Keller (Tübingen: M. Niemeyer, 1990)

Wace, *La Conception de Notre Dame*, ed. W.R. Ashford (Menasha, Wisconsin: George Banta; private edition distributed by the University of Chicago, 1933)

Wace, *La Vie de Saint Nicolas*, ed. E. Ronsjö (Lund: C.W.K. Gleerup, 1942)

Wace, *Le Roman de Rou*, ed. A.J. Holden, 3 vols (Paris: SATF, Editions Picard, 1973). [Wace, *Rou*]

Wace, *Le Roman de Brut*, ed. Le Roux de Lincy, 2 vols (Rouen: Edouard Frère, 1836–8)

Wace, *Le Roman de Brut*, ed. Ivor Arnold, 2 vols (Paris: SATF, 1938, 1940). [Arnold]

La Partie Arthurienne du Roman de Brut, ed. I.D.O. Arnold and M. Pelan (Paris: Librairie Klincksieck, 1962). [Arnold and Pelan, *Partie Arthurienne*]

La Geste du Roi Arthur, ed. and trans. E. Baumgartner and I. Short (Paris: Union générale d'Editions, 1993). [Baumgartner and Short, *Geste*]

De Wace à Lawamon, ed. Marie-Françoise Alamichel, 2 vols (Paris: Publications de l'Association des Médiévistes de l'Enseignement Supérieur, 1995)

Wace and Layamon, *Arthurian Chronicles*, trans. Eugene Mason, (London: Everyman's Library, J.M. Dent, 1912, repr. 1962)

Wace and Lawman, *The Life of King Arthur*, trans. Judith Weiss and Rosamund Allen (London: Everyman's Library, J.M. Dent, 1997)

Other works cited

Anderson, Marjorie O., 'Dalriada and the creation of the kingdom of the Scots', *Ireland in early medieval Europe*, eds D. Whitelock, R. McKitterick and D. Dumville (Cambridge: Cambridge University Press, 1982), pp. 106–32. [Anderson, 'Dalriada']

The Anglo-Saxon Chronicle, ed. and trans. M.J. Swanton (London: J.M. Dent, 1996). [Swanton, *Anglo-Saxon Chronicle*]

Barron, W.R.J. and Le Saux, Françoise, 'Two aspects of Laȝamon's narrative art', *Arthurian Literature*, 9 (1989), pp. 25–56. [Barron and Le Saux, 'Two Aspects']

Bennett, Matthew, 'Wace and Warfare', *Anglo-Norman Studies*, 11 (1988), pp. 37–57. [Bennett, 'Wace and Warfare']

Blacker, Jean, '*Ne Vuil Sun Livre Translater*': Wace's omission of Merlin's Prophecies from the *Roman de Brut*', *Anglo-Norman Anniversary Essays*, ed. Ian Short (Anglo-Norman Text Society, Birkbeck College, London, 1993), pp. 49–59.

Blacker, Jean, *The Faces of Time*, (Austin: University of Texas Press, 1994).

Blacker, Jean, 'Will the real Wace please stand up? Wace's *Roman de Brut* in Anglo-Norman and Continental Manuscripts', *Text*, 9, ed. D.C. Greetham and W. Speed Hill (Ann Arbor: University of Michigan Press, 1996), pp. 175–86.

Blair, Hunter P., *An Introduction to Anglo-Saxon England*, (Cambridge: Cambridge University Press, 1974). [Hunter Blair, *Anglo-Saxon England*]

Blenner-Hassett, R., *A Study of the Place-Names in Lawman's 'Brut'*, (Stanford, California: Stanford University Publications: Language and Literature 9:1, 1950). [Blenner-Hassett, *A Study of the Place-Names*]

Bodel, Jean, *Le Jeu de Saint Nicolas*, ed. F.J. Warne (Oxford: Basil Blackwell, 1972). [Jean Bodel, *Le Jeu de Saint Nicolas*]

The British Museum Catalogue of Additions to the Manuscripts, 1936–45, Part I (London: Trustees of the British Museum, 1970). [British Museum, *Catalogue*]

Brosnahan, Leger, 'Wace's Use of Proverbs', *Speculum*, 39 (1964), pp. 444–73. [Brosnahan, 'Proverbs']

Casey, P.J., 'Magnus Maximus in Britain', *The End of Roman Britain*, ed. P.J. Casey (BAR British Series 71, 1979), pp. 66–79.

Chadwick, Nora K., 'The Conversion of Northumbria', *Celt and Saxon: Studies in the Early British Border*, ed. Nora K. Chadwick (Cambridge: Cambridge University Press, 1963). [Chadwick, 'Conversion of Northumbria']

Culhwch and Olwen, eds Rachel Bromwich and D. Simon Evans (Cardiff: University of Wales Press, 1992). [Bromwich and Evans, *Culhwch and Olwen*]

Damian-Grint, Peter, 'Truth, Trust, and Evidence in the Anglo-Norman *Estoire*', *Anglo-Norman Studies*, 18 (1996), pp. 68–72. [Damian-Grint, 'Truth, Trust, and Evidence']

Damian-Grint, Peter, '*Estoire* as Word and Genre', *Medium Aevum*, 66 (1997), pp. 189–99. [Damian-Grint, '*Estoire* as Word and Genre']

Damian-Grint, Peter, *The New Historians of the Twelfth-Century Renaissance*, (Woodbridge: Boydell Press, 1999).

Davies, Wendy, *Wales in the Early Middle Ages*, (Leicester: Leicester University Press, 1982). [Davies, *Wales*]

Delbouille, Maurice, 'Le témoignage de Wace sur la légende arthurienne', *Romania*, 74 (1953), pp. 172–99. [Delbouille, 'Témoignage']

Draak, Maartje, 'The Hague Manuscript of Wace's *Brut*', *Amor Librorum: Bibliographic and other Essays, a tribute to Abraham Horodisch*, (Amsterdam: Erasmus Antiquariaat, 1958), pp. 23–7.

Dumville, David N., 'Sub-Roman Britain: History and legend', *History*, 62 (1977), pp. 173–92. [Dumville, 'Sub-Roman Britain']

Dumville, David N., 'The Chronology of the *De Excidio Britanniae*, Book I', *Gildas: New*

Approaches, (Woodbridge: Boydell Press, 1984), pp. 61–84. [Dumville, 'Chronology of *De Excidio'*]

Dumville, D.N., 'The Historical Value of the *Historia Brittonum'*, *Arthurian Literature* , 6 (1986), pp. 1–26. [Dumville, 'Historical Value']

Fahlin, Ceri, 'Quelques remarques sur l'édition du *Roman de Brut* de Wace publiée par Ivor Arnold', *Studia Neophilologica*, 11 (1938–9), pp. 85–100.

Fahy, Dermot, 'When did Britons become Bretons? A note on the foundation of Brittany', *Welsh History Review,* 2 (1964), pp. 111–24. [Fahy, 'When did Britons become Bretons?']

Foulon, C., 'Wace', *ALMA*, pp. 94–103.

Gaimar, Geffrei, *Estoire des Engleis*, ed. A. Bell, Anglo-Norman Texts (Oxford: Basil Blackwell, 1960). [Gaimar, *Estoire*]

Geoffrey of Monmouth, *The Historia Regum Britanniae I: Bern, Bürgerbibliothek MS 568 (the 'Vulgate' Version*), ed. Neil Wright (Cambridge: D.S. Brewer, 1984). [Wright I]

Geoffrey of Monmouth, *The Historia Regum Britanniae II: the First Variant Version,* ed. Neil Wright (Woodbridge: D.S. Brewer, 1988). [Wright II]

Geoffrey of Monmouth, *The History of the Kings of Britain*, trans. Lewis Thorpe (Harmondsworth: Penguin Books, 1966). [Thorpe, *Geoffrey of Monmouth: History*]

Gildas, *De Excidio Britonum*, ed. and trans. Michael Winterbottom (London and Chichester: Phillimore, 1978). [Gildas, *De Excidio*]

Gillingham, John, 'The context and purposes of Geoffrey of Monmouth's *History of the Kings of Britain'*, *Anglo-Norman Studies*, 13 (1990), pp. 99–118. [Gillingham, 'Context and purposes']

Goscelin, *Historia translationis S. Augustini et aliorum Sanctorum,* ed. in *Acta Sanctorum*, Maii, VI, pp. 408–39.

Gouttebroze, Jean-Guy, 'Pourquoi congédier un historiographe: Henri II et Wace (1155–1174)', *Romania,* 112 (1991), pp. 289–310. [Gouttebroze, 'Pourquoi congédier']

Greenway, Diana, ed. and trans. *Henry, Archdeacon of Huntingdon, 'Historia Anglorum'*, (Oxford: Clarendon Press, 1996). [Greenway]

Hassell, James Woodrow, *Middle French Proverbs, Sentences and Proverbial Phrases,* (Toronto: Pontifical Institute of Medieval Studies, 1982). [Hassell, *Middle French Proverbs*]

The Historia Brittonum 3: The 'Vatican Recension', ed. D.N. Dumville (Cambridge: D.S. Brewer, 1985).

Houck, Margaret, *Sources of the 'Roman de Brut' of Wace*, (Berkeley: University of California Press, 1941). [Houck, *Sources*]

Jarman, A.O.H., 'The Merlin legend and the Welsh tradition of Prophecy', *AOW*, pp. 117–45. [Jarman, 'The Merlin legend']

Keller, Hans-Erich, *Etude Descriptive sur le vocabulaire de Wace,* (Berlin: Akademie-Verlag, 1953). [Keller, *Etude Descriptive*]

Keller, Hans-Erich, 'Two Toponymical Problems in Geoffrey of Monmouth and Wace: *Estrusia* and *Siesia'*, *Speculum,* 49 (1974), pp. 687–98. [Keller, 'Two Toponymical Problems']

Keller, Hans-Erich, 'Les fragments oxoniens du *Roman de Brut* de Wace', *Mélanges offerts à Carl Theodor Gossen* (Bern: Francke Verlag, 1976), pp. 453–67. [Keller, 'Fragments oxoniens']

Keller, Hans-Erich, 'Wace et Geoffrey de Monmouth: problème de la chronologie des sources', *Romania*, 98 (1977), pp. 1–14. [Keller, 'Wace et Geoffrey']

Laʒamon, *Brut*, eds G.L. Brook and R.F. Leslie, 2 vols (London: EETS OS 250, 277, 1963, 1978).

Lawman, *Brut*, trans. Rosamund Allen (London: J.M. Dent and Sons, 1992). [Allen, *Lawman: 'Brut'*]

Lapidge, M. and Dumville, D., eds *Gildas: New Approaches*, (Woodbridge: Boydell Press, 1984).

Le Roux de Lincy, *Livre des Proverbes Français*, (Paris: Adolphe Delahays, 1859). [Le Roux de Lincy, *Proverbes*]

Leckie, William, *The Passage of Dominion: Geoffrey of Monmouth and the Periodization of Insular History in the Twelfth Century*, (Toronto: University of Toronto Press, 1981).

Lecoy, Félix, '*Meain* et *Forain* dans le *Roman de Brut*', *Romania*, 86 (1965), pp. 118–22.

Lefèvre, Sylvie, 'Le Fragment Bekker et les Anciennes Versions Françaises de l'*Historia Regum Britanniae*', *Romania*, 109 (1988), pp. 225–46.

Loomis, Roger Sherman, 'The oral diffusion of the Arthurian legend', *ALMA*, pp. 52–63. [Loomis, 'Oral difusion']

Lovecy, Ian, '*Historia Peredur*', *AOW*, pp. 171–82. [Lovecy, '*Historia Peredur*']

Matthews, William, 'Where was Siesia-Sessoyne?', *Speculum*, 49 (1974), pp. 680–6. [Matthews, 'Where was Siesia-Sessoyne?']

Miller, Molly, 'Matriliny by treaty: the Pictish foundation-legend', *Ireland in early medieval Europe*, eds D. Whitelock, R. McKitterick and D. Dumville (Cambridge: Cambridge University Press, 1982), pp. 133–61. [Miller, 'Matriliny']

Morris, Rosemary, 'The *Gesta Regum Britanniae* of William of Rennes: an Arthurian Epic?', *Arthurian Literature*, 6 (1986), pp. 60–125. [Morris, 'The *Gesta Regum Britanniae*']

Nennius, *British History and the Welsh Annals*, ed. and trans. John Morris (London: Phillimore with Rowan and Littlefield, 1980). [*HB*]

Orosius, *Historia Adversum Paganos*, ed. and trans. Marie-Pierre Arnaud-Lindet, 3 vols (Paris: Les Belles Lettres, 1990). [Orosius, *Historia Adversum Paganos*]

Orr, John, 'On Homonymics', *Studies in French Language and Medieval Literature presented to M.K. Pope*, (Manchester: Manchester University Press, 1939), pp. 253–97. [Orr, 'On Homonymics']

Page, Christopher, *Voices and Instruments of the Middle Ages*, (London: J.M. Dent and Sons, 1987). [Page, *Voices and Instruments*]

Pelan, M.M., *L'Influence du 'Brut' de Wace sur les romanciers français de son temps* , (Paris: E. Droz, 1931). [Pelan, *L'Influence du 'Brut'*]

Piggott, Stuart, 'The Sources of Geoffrey of Monmouth', *Antiquity*, 15 (1941), pp. 269–86. [Piggott, 'Sources']

Proverbes Français Antérieurs au Xve siècle, ed. Joseph Morawski (Paris: CFMA, Champion, 1925). [Morawski, *Proverbes*]

Roberts, Brynley F., '*Culhwch and Olwen*, the Triads, saints' lives', *AOW*, pp. 73–95. [Roberts, '*Culhwch and Olwen*']

Roberts, Brynley F., 'Geoffrey of Monmouth, *Historia Regum Britanniae* and *Brut y Brenhinedd*', *AOW*, pp. 97–116. [Roberts, 'Geoffrey of Monmouth']

Robinson, I.S., *The Papacy, 1073–1198*, (Cambridge: Cambridge University Press, 1990). [Robinson, *The Papacy*]

Rollo, David, *Glamorous Sorcery: Magic and Literacy in the High Middle Ages*, (Minneapolis: University of Minnesota Press, 2000).

Rychner, Jean, *La Chanson de Geste*, (Geneva: Librairie E. Droz, 1955). [Rychner, *La Chanson de Geste*]

Schmolke-Hasselmann, Beate, 'The Round Table: ideal, fiction, reality', *Arthurian Literature*, 2 (1982), pp. 41–75. [Schmolke-Hasselmann, 'Round Table']

Sims-Williams, Patrick, 'The early Welsh Arthurian poems', *AOW*, pp. 33–71. [Sims–Williams, 'Welsh Arthurian Poems']

Southern, Richard, 'Aspects of the European Tradition of Historical Writing, I: from Einhard to Geoffrey of Monmouth', *Transactions of the Royal Historical Society* , vol. 20, 5th series, (1970), pp. 173–96. [Southern, 'Aspects']

Stenton, F.M., *Anglo-Saxon England*, (Oxford: Clarendon Press, 1943, repr. 1965). [Stenton, *Anglo-Saxon England*]

Thomson, R.L., '*Owain*', *AOW*, pp. 159–69. [Thomson, '*Owain*']

Thompson, E.A., 'Gildas and the History of Britain', *Britannia*, 10 (1979), pp. 203–26. [Thompson, 'Gildas']

Trioedd Ynys Prydein, The Welsh Triads, ed. Rachel Bromwich (Cardiff: University of Wales Press, 1978). [Bromwich, *Welsh Triads*]

Van Houts, Elisabeth M.C., 'The adaptation of the *Gesta Normannorum Ducum* by Wace and Benoît', *Non Nova, Sed Nove. Mélanges de civilisation médiévale dédiés à Willem Noomen*, eds Martin Gosman and Jaap van Os (Groningen: Bouma's Boekhuis, 1984), pp. 115–24. [Van Houts, 'Adaptation']

Wallace-Hadrill, J.M., *Bede's 'Ecclesiastical History of the English People'. A Historical Commentary*, (Oxford: Clarendon Press, 1988). [Wallace-Hadrill, *Bede's Ecclesiastical History*)

Weiss, Judith, *The Birth of Romance*, (London: Everyman's Library, 1992). [Weiss, *Birth of Romance*]

William of Malmesbury, *De Gestis Regum Anglorum*, trans. Joseph Stephenson (Llanerch Enterprises, 1989). [William of Malmesbury, *De Gestis*]

William of Malmesbury, *De Gestis Pontificum Anglorum*, ed. N.E.S.A. Hamilton, Rolls Series (London: Longman and Co., 1870). [William of Malmesbury, *De Gestis Pontificum]*

Wright, Neil, 'Geoffrey of Monmouth and Gildas', *Arthurian Literature*, 2 (1982), pp. 1–33. [Wright, 'Geoffrey of Monmouth']

York, Ernest C., 'Wace's Wenelande: Identification and Speculation', *Romance Notes*, 22 (1981), pp. 112–18. (York, 'Wace's Wenelande']

INDEX OF PERSONAL NAMES

The numbers given below refer to pages, not lines, in the French text. Names are given initially in the form in which they first appear; if they occur in both nominative and oblique cases, they are usually cited in the oblique form.